The *Pricke of C*

The *Pricke of Conscience*
An Annotated Edition of the Southern Recension

Edited by Jean E. Jost

with a Glossary by Hoyt Greeson

McFarland & Company, Inc., Publishers
Jefferson, North Carolina

LIBRARY OF CONGRESS CATALOGUING-IN-PUBLICATION DATA

Names: Jost, Jean E., editor. | Greeson, Hoyt, 1933– contributor. | Henry E. Huntington Library and Art Gallery. Manuscript. HM 128.
Title: The pricke of conscience : an annotated edition of the Southern Recension / edited by Jean E. Jost ; with a glossary by Hoyt Greeson.
Description: Jefferson, North Carolina : McFarland & Company, Inc., 2020 | Includes bibliographical references and index.
Identifiers: LCCN 2018050913 | ISBN 9781476671192 (softcover : acid free paper) ∞
Subjects: LCSH: Prick of conscience. | Didactic poetry, English (Middle)
Classification: LCC PR2114.P73 P75 2020 | DDC 821/.1—dc23
LC record available at https://lccn.loc.gov/2018050913

BRITISH LIBRARY CATALOGUING DATA ARE AVAILABLE

ISBN (print) 978-1-4766-7119-2

© 2020 Jean E. Jost. All rights reserved

*No part of this book may be reproduced or transmitted in any form
or by any means, electronic or mechanical, including photocopying
or recording, or by any information storage and retrieval system,
without permission in writing from the publisher.*

Front cover illustration: "The Monk's Vision," 14th century (iStock)

Printed in the United States of America

*McFarland & Company, Inc., Publishers
Box 611, Jefferson, North Carolina 28640
www.mcfarlandpub.com*

In memory of Martin Stevens,
who sent me on this journey

Table of Contents

Acknowledgments   ix
General Introduction   1

I. INTRODUCTION TO THE POEM AND MANUSCRIPT   7
   Description of HM 128, Huntington Library, San Marino, California   7
      Contents of HM 128   7
      Date, Collation, and Hands   7
      Foliation   8
      Physical Description and Page Arrangement   8
      Decoration and Textual Presentation in the Pricke of Conscience, *HM 128*   8
   Versions of the *Pricke of Conscience*   8
      Manuscript Editions   8
      Modern and Medieval Editions   9
   Provenance of the *Pricke of Conscience*, HM 128   10
      Authorship   10
      Dating   10
      Language (by Hoyt Greeson)   10
   Manuscript Choice   12
      Criteria for "Best Text" of Pricke of Conscience *Manuscript*   12
      Rationale   15
   Editorial Policy   16
      Purpose   16
      Spelling, Punctuation, Capitalization, Abbreviations and Division Markers   16
      Latin Quotations   16
      Critical Apparatus   16
      Bibliographies   17
   Notes   17

II. ***Pricke of Conscience***
Facsimile of Huntington Manuscript 128	Folio 1 recto	21
Prologue: God's Power	Folio 1r	23
Part I. Man's Wretchedness	Folio 4v	30
Part II. The Instability of the World	Folio 10v	42
Part III. Death	Folio 18v	58
Part IV. Purgatory	Folio 28v	78
Part V. Ten Signs of Doomsday	Folio 42v	106
Part VI. The Pains of Hell	Folio 69v	160
Part VII. The Joys of Heaven	Folio 77v	176

Select Glossary (by Hoyt Greeson)	211
Select Bibliography: Content of HM 128	238
Select Bibliography: Dialect, Sources, and Definitions (by Hoyt Greeson)	240
Index	241

Acknowledgments

I wish to thank the Huntington Library for its generous fellowships and permission to publish page one as a facsimile. Additionally, the Huntington Library, Bodleian Library, and British Library have offered generous hospitality and access to their valuable resources. The University of Illinois and Bradley University Library have provided background resources for this edition. I appreciate the generous sharing of microfilm readers and other amenities at California Technological Institute in San Marino where I was granted special evening privileges to work on my project.

I would like to thank both the National Endowment for the Humanities, for its 1989 "Ellesmere and Medieval Drama" Summer Seminar fellowship at UCLA and the Huntington Library, and especially its Director, the late Martin Stevens, who strongly encouraged this project which emerged from this seminar. To the members of that seminar I also offer thanks for help, good fellowship and support. To the late Larry Clopper, a previous NEH seminar Director, I owe much gratitude for generous encouragement and faith in my project.

I am most grateful to Dr. Stacy A. Waters for generously allowing me the use of his unpublished Ph.D. dissertation from Edinburgh University (1976), a transcription and edition of Book V of the *Pricke of Conscience* from Huntington Manuscript 125. His text has been the basis of comparison for Book V of HM 128, which comparison is found in the footnotes to this edition.

I am extremely grateful to Sarah Wood, co-editor of the excellent Early English Text Society edition, *Richard Morris's Prick of Conscience* with Ralph Hanna, for making a copy of their volume available to me.

I wish to thank Bradley University Offices of Teaching Excellence and Research Excellence for travel assistance to the Bodleian, British Museum, and Huntington Libraries, with special gratitude to Marjorie Robertson at the Huntington. I am also grateful to Bradley University for sabbatical time to pursue this project, and the University of Illinois for computer assistance during my sabbatical. The Department of English at the U of I has kindly shared its facilities, microfilm reader, computer, and office space. John Friedman's Paleography graduate students there have welcomed me to their class and offered useful comments, support, and camaraderie. I especially thank John Friedman for sponsoring my visit, Charles Wright for providing office space, and these and other medievalists at the U of I for their encouragement. I am grateful to Ron Szoke for lending U of I hardware, and for the knowledge and expertise to use it productively for my purposes. My thanks to Bradley University staff, especially Charles Frey and Denise Johnson who have been most helpful in facilitating this project.

Additionally, my Graduate Research Fellow Bradley Henz has worked tirelessly and efficiently with the technological and computing side of this project; I thank him for his unfailing attention to detail. Hoyt S. Greeson of Laurentian University, Sudbury, Canada, has been an invaluable expert assisting in untold ways. I thank him for his generous linguistic contributions: his fine linguistic analysis, careful glossary, introductory material on provenance, and source notes. Without his careful glossary and source information, this edition would be a much poorer product indeed. Bradley University Department of English secretaries Willie Eberer, Carolyn Rosser, Shelly Walker, Tracy Anderson, and Judy Keyster have been of great assistance. Personal and professional help is greatly appreciated from a host of facilitators, especially

David Langendorf, Mike McCauley, and Nial Johnson. After computer scrambling, my former student Cecilia Martin has intelligently recovered my text, reformatted pagination and textual jumbling, and helped correct errors which have crept into the text. Without her assistance, this project would never have come to fruition, for her expertise resolved many a computer crux.

In preparing this edition, I have been greatly assisted by the work of other scholars. Numerous experts have offered generously of their time, expertise, and support, particularly Derek Brewer for bibliographic assistance, Hoyt S. Greeson for all things linguistic, Howell Chickering, James Dean, Tony Edwards, Peter Beidler, Paul Thomas, Michael Everson, and my careful and helpful readers Robert E. Lewis, Michael Calabrese, and James Morey. Without their suggestions and advice, this edition could not have found its way to success. Finally, I thank my patient and dedicated publishers at McFarland, especially Lisa Camp, Gary Mitchem, Dré Person, Charles Perdue, and Lori Tedder, for all their assistance in so many ways. I thank them all for their scholarly expertise and encouragement. Of course, all errors are mine.

General Introduction

Historical Context

An ebullient fourteenth-century England embroiled in turmoil—social, political, and religious—stretched its battered wings toward the modern world. Johan Huizinga well captures its violent tenor, noting that at the end of the Middle Ages:

> the political stage of the kingdoms of Europe was so crowded with such fierce and tragic conflicts that the peoples could not help seeing all that regards royalty as a succession of sanguinary and romantic events: in England, King Richard II dethroned and next secretly murdered, while nearly at the same time the highest monarch in Christendom, his brother-in-law Wenzel, king of the Romans, is deposed by the elders; in France a mad king and soon afterwards fierce party strife, openly breaking out with the appalling murder of Louis of Orleans in 1407, and indefinitely prolonged by the retaliation of 1219 when Jean sans Peur is murdered.[1]

Such destabilized hierarchies contribute to the confusing turmoil of the times manifested in other equally turbulent events. In response to such chaos, the culminating years of the Middle Ages germinated radical revolution and innovation, spearheaded by the Hundred Years' War, the Revolution of 1381, the papal schism, and the radical growth of middle class literacy. R.J. Rydall points to yet another revolution, claiming:

> The revolution which affected the production of books in later medieval Europe came in two stages.... In many respects, the actual process of making-up and writing manuscripts remained unchanged even though the social and economic realities of the book trade were fundamentally transformed through the progressive displacement of parchment by paper in the course of the fifteenth century.... [I]n subtle and important ways the book trade was radically changed by the economic revolution which paper certainly represented, and by the end of the fifteenth century its impact was felt throughout Britain.[2]

While more passive and gradual than the others, this revolution was nonetheless powerful in changing the face of the medieval world. A.S.G. Edwards and Derek Pearsall make the point with numbers: "Even the most cursory comparison of the seventy-five year periods on either side of 1400 reveals a spectacular transformation: in broad figures, one is speaking of the difference between a rate of production that leaves extant about thirty manuscripts and one that leaves extant about six hundred."[3] The cliché of chaos bridging the Middle Ages and the newly born modern era has been rehearsed in virtually all domains; the following are a minuscule sampling. David Aers, in noting widespread economic disparity and resentment between aristocrats and peasantry, suggests:

> resistance ... ranged from symbolic [forms] to actions such as the evasion of taxes and the non-performance of services, to poaching, to defiance of labor legislation, to, in the last resort, violence, whether hidden or in open riot. The English rising of 1381 was part of long-term struggles between classes ... contests over moral, social, and political values.[4]

Further, the startling ramifications of the plague irrevocably shook the era, and transformed the society. Norman Cantor points out the scholarly consensus in seeing "the era from the mid–fourteenth to the mid–fifteenth century as a time of catastrophe in the form of disease, war, climate deterioration, and political decline as well as of descent into long economic depression in several parts of Europe."[5] Even the nature of warfare and its conduct underwent significant changes. As Franco Cardini points out, "A substantial transformation in military technology underlay the 'decadence' of the knighthood and its partial demilitarization between the thirteenth and the sixteenth centuries.... With the fourteenth century, firearms gave the death-blow to the military usefulness and the moral prestige of horse combatants."[6] Larry Scanlon finds that "Secular authority, political or literary was an extremely fluid category at this time, dependent on the very ecclesiastical traditions from which both secular rulers and secular writers were attempting to wrest it."[7] W.M. Ormond concurs, reporting that

> The 1370s proved to be one of the most dismal decades in the political history of later medieval England, as military reversals abroad combined with financial ineptitude, political faction and court scandals at home to generate antagonism among both the governing classes and the wider population.... Henry V himself had to face armed uprisings and threats of deposition not only from a group of religious extremists known as Lollards in 1413 but also, more seriously, from within the ranks of the royal family and high aristocracy on the very eve of the great invasion of France in 1415.[8]

Lee Patterson points to the rural world as "the most socially combative and historically progressive element of late medieval English society ... [and] the radical political program that informed late medieval peasant belligerence."[9] Clearly this was a time of great upheaval in many respects as social and political conditions were shaken to their foundations.

The most significant revolution, however, occurred in Church orthodoxy. Never quite the "Age of Faith" some modern critics have simplistically purported the Middle Ages to be, in the wake of political upheaval, this explosive era embraced religious dissent with the same fervor and passion of its more physical and even violent political counterpart. Rebellion was in the air. As Helen Barr suggests, "There was powerful support for Wycliffite ideas from members of the gentry and aristocracy but also from those excluded from institutionalized position of power."[10] The line between the two was a fine one. Janet Coleman notes that:

> It has become customary to treat social unrest and religious unrest separately and each category has become the preserve of specialists with interests either in political history or in ecclesiastical history.... But the poetry of the second half of the fourteenth century does not depict so clear a separation ... the boundary between political, religious, historical and didactic verse is necessarily vague.[11]

And in all these domains, as Huizinga indicates, "new things are being born. The tide is turning, the tone of life is about to change."[12] The directions of that change are varied, but in the religious arena, they have startling, permanent effects on society. The plague continuously ravaging the entire continent of Europe wiped out perhaps half its population; as people saw their loved ones torn away by a rapid but devastating death, their obsession with the afterlife, with rewards and punishment, and with behavior warranting each intensified.[13] Artists' subjects were often gruesome depictions of pain and suffering, *dans macabre* themes, fearful woodcuts warning mankind of its potential demise and future anguish. Literary texts likewise reflected this new concern with physical well-being, with the grotesqueries daily witnessed, and particularly with heaven and hell.

Doctrinal dispute is inevitably a political issue of power and coercion. Rampant dissent was so feared that legislation was enacted to control its incendiary contagion and virulent effects. According to Barr, "In 1402 and 1406, laws were passed to prevent the dissemination of old prophecies. Because of their code writing, such prophecies were regarded as a highly effective means of fostering dissent because a forecast of the future could reflect dissatisfaction with the present."[14] But no law could obliterate that dissatisfaction, or its written manifestation, as voluminous treatises, tracts, and poetry so well attest. Increasing discomfort with Churchmen's irregularities and power led people to question the Church's hold over their lives. Greater sophistication, with a peasant population immigrating to towns, encouraged a stronger focus on the individual and personal rather than communal. The private world of the mystics, officially accepted by the Church in many instances, endorsed the emphasis on personal. As literacy slowly became more widespread, the laity began thinking for themselves and religious dissent grew. Hierarchical thinking imposed from above was no longer easily accepted. This phenomenon of revolution affords an opportunity to study evolving religious didacticism, specifically within the *Pricke of Conscience* manuscripts, for all they have to offer. Rich in its imagery, detailed in its content, and emotional in its tone, this poem offers a splendid panorama of late medieval life to be mined for its politics, its doctrine, its social and political history, and its didactic intent. Variegated in tone, content, and attitude, it entertains as well as instructs. Furthermore, Coleman rightly insists that

> There is a long historical tradition which calls the Middle Ages the "Age of Faith," implying a single orthodoxy. Such a classification does not appear to take into account the numerous heresies, the outspoken skepticism, and the secular doubt with which the period from the downfall of Rome to the Protestant Reformation was rife.[15]

Acknowledging the fluidity of the entire age, however, does not diminish the particular volatility of its climax. The revolutionary explosion touched the physical and psychological lives of men and women of all social classes. Both who was reading at the end of the fourteenth century, and what they read underwent monumental change. A commensurate repression of dissenting belief and free expression in the face of this turnover suggests the defensive, fearful posture of churchmen. As Anne Hudson notes, "Ownership of suspicious books, a category which could cover any vernacular scriptures and extend as far as *The Pricke of Conscience* or *The Canterbury Tales*, was sufficient to bring a man or woman to trial."[16]

Unlike the preceding French-based entertainment literature, edifying literature "frequently set up contemporary spiritual and social ideals and compared these with current spirituality to find the present state of affairs wanting,"[17] according to Coleman. However, she continues, "Both categories reflected a piety and concern for social order that was characteristic of the interests of a rising urban 'middle class' and rural gentry."[18] The *Pricke of Conscience* is exemplary proof of what Coleman signals as

> the growth in lay literacy and social mobility as it was expressed in fourteenth-century literature, a literature that did not merely passively reflect its time and context but was written as an encouragement to criticize and change. There were political and socio-economic implications in its message ...[19]

An Examination of the Poem

Janet Coleman describes the *Pricke of Conscience* as a didactic verse treatise in Middle English, an exemplar of the continued production throughout the century of a large number of didactic and homiletic works in verse which indicated a shift towards an increase in private lay devotional reading in the vernacular and continued the tradition of using poetry as a medium of religious instruction.

This poem in rhymed couplets, while undoubtedly didactic, offers surprising imagery, creative juxtapositions, and unusual analogies in its seven-part depiction of the history of the world:

Prologue: God's Power
Man's Wretchedness
The Instability of the World
Death
Purgatory
Ten Signs of Doomsday
The Pains of Hell
The Joys of Heaven

Its colloquial but delightful style, charming if sometimes graphic descriptions, traditional but fresh conceptions of mankind and the afterlife remain ever-intriguing. Clearly the author envisioned a history of the world from pre-creation through the final resolution of mankind's fate. His precise, logical order and effective rhetorical and theological strategies maintain his audience's interest. His headings, either original with him or imposed at a later transmission, guide his readers, perhaps those in religious houses, and more easily facilitate location of particular passages, many of them memorable for their creative presentation.

Other sermons in this genre include instructional manuals such as *Handlynge Synne, Ancrene Wisse, Ayenbite of Inwyt, Jacob's Well, Book of Vices and Virtues, A Myrour to Lewd Men and Women, The Clensyng of Mannes Soule, The Ways to Paradys, A Lytyl Treatis, The Book Royal, Cursor Mundi*, and the *Lay Folks' Catechism*. Although each of these has its specific goals and audiences, the general goal of guiding men and women to salvation—albeit in their various ways— encompasses them all, including the *Pricke of Conscience*. This last chooses to present a history of creation with fascinating details, religious dramatizations, and folklore elements to appeal to a wide audience, both lettered and unlettered. John Friedman has kindly pointed out that the conception of man as an upside down tree, for example, seems to derive from Aristotle's *De Anima* II, 4.416a and *Poetics* REF where the tree's roots are perceived as a human mouth (see footnote 2f. 8r for further information).

What a scribe, the first reader-critic of a work, chooses to rubricate may well hold the key to its significance as the scribe perceives it. In an unpublished Leicester Ph.D. dissertation, Marie-Louise Uhart suggests the following topics the *Piers Plowman* rubricators highlighted in their work, namely moral virtues, various personae used within the poem, its sermon structure, focus on certain key elements, Piers Plowman himself, and prophetic word of the text."[20] G.H. Russell divides rubrication into types based on function: "the identification of names, personae and auctores, historical exempla and biblical texts; structural devices such as legal documents, preaching and prophecy, the sins, the appearance of Piers and the various other key episodes and structural elements of the poem."[21] Huntington 128 rubricates *only* the sins, highlighting their importance, and emphasizing the didactic intent of the work.

Vincent Gillespie comments on another aspect of the *ordinatio*, namely its column arrangement:

> Of the 115 manuscripts that may reasonably be presumed to have been originally complete, only fifteen are in a form other than a single column. The octosyllabic metre of the long work would lead one to think that a double column arrangement would have been more suitable, producing an economic use of a leaf of regular shape; the result is that most of the manuscripts are of comparatively tall, narrow format. Yet this uniformity cannot be the outcome of a centrally imposed decision: the linguistic evidence reveals that copying was geographically widely dispersed.[22]

Reasons for the shape of the text remain unclear, but perhaps this format was comparatively easier to read than the more economic double-column format, suggesting a more public use of the material, such as for reading aloud in monasteries and convents.

Significance of the Pricke of Conscience

The enormous popularity of the *Pricke of Conscience* in the century after its putative authorship of 1350 is testified by its 115 surviving manuscripts, exceeding even the *Canterbury Tales'* 84, *Piers Plowman's* 54, and *Confessio Amantis'* 51. Their sheer volume is significant, indicating the widespread currency it must have enjoyed as a guidebook to Christian living for all social classes. Most surprising, however, is that a work so obviously influential in the Middle Ages has been so neglected in recent times. To date, the work has been edited three times: by Richard Morris (Oxford, 1863), and reprinted without changes in 1973; by Ralph Hanna and Anne Wood with significant changes to Morris's edition (Oxford University Press, 2013); and by James H. Morey from the Beinecke Library's Osborn a.13 for TEAMS (Western Michigan University, 2012). These three present the Northern Version only. Since the Southern Recension is significantly different in its directness and conciseness, clearly scholars should have access to a representative version of a Southern Recension such as Huntington Library 128. In addition, critical discussion has been minimal, necessarily because other versions of the work have not been easily accessible to scholars. As McIntosh and Lewis point out:

> Unfortunately ... scholars have been hampered in their study of these important issues [of ownership, provenances, nature of contents, sources, poetic shaping]—not to mention such larger matters as the relationship of poems in the same genre, its importance in the literary and intellectual environment of the fourteenth century, the reasons for its popularity, and its influence on later literature—for lack of basic information about the manuscripts, versions, and texts of the poem.[23]

The content of the *Pricke of Conscience* reveals what its medieval audience found compelling, religiously or artistically valuable, socially confirming, personally entertaining, threatening or reassuring. It might well reveal what charmed the mind and hearts of many late fourteenth- and early fifteenth-century advocates, or what preachers felt to be enlightening and inspiring.

Texts written in the Northern dialect are most prolific, and pre-date the Southern Recensions by nearly a century. Their density in certain regions of the North coincides with the location of monasteries where they might have been produced, and certainly housed or read, although there is no specific evidence of a monastic provenance.

Their length is about 2000 lines longer than Southern Recensions, and generally elaborate a bit more than their counterparts, which express the same content in a more concise fashion.

Southern Recensions can be found at Beaumont College, Old Warren, Berkshire; in Cambridge at Pembroke College, St. John's College, and University College; in Dublin, at Trinity College, in Lichfield, two at the Cathedral (#16 and 50); in London, four at the British Library (Bodley 423, Laud Misc. 601, Royal 18 A.v., and Additional 11305); in Pendleton, New Jersey (Garrett 138); and in San Marino, three at the Huntington Library (HM 125, 128, and 130).

Doctrine of the Pricke of Conscience

To what tradition is the allegiance of this poem? First of all, the surface content of the *Pricke of Conscience* reads much like a traditional treatise, espousing standard orthodoxy in a somewhat unique fashion. Its eternal scope and grandiose vision, juxtaposed with the elaboration of detailed theological precepts, adds interest and variety in a substantially long text. Trinitarian, sacramental, penitential and apocalyptic views appear quite orthodox.

On the other hand, partisan religious encoding might well be located within this text; no doubt such subtle encoding differs from manuscript to manuscript, given the wide variations of texts recording the *Pricke of Conscience*. Before Luther's dramatic nailing of the 95 edicts on the baptistery door of Wittenberg Cathedral, the most widely considered heterodoxy within the Christian Church was Lollardy. Its tenets display a distinct divergence from accepted doctrine and attitude, and while not the exclusive voice of dissension, certainly it was the most significant.

Although basically a traditional poem, some of this heterodoxy might well be seen within the *Pricke of Conscience* manuscripts. Certain scribal deletions, such as the word "pope" in several instances may or may not indicate early anti–Catholic sentiment, for it is likely that seventeenth-century scribes inserted their objections in just such a fashion.

However, an investigation of possible counter-traditional dimension may suggest the current of change and religious exploration as well as answer related questions: Why was this text so popular, why was its dissemination so widespread, and what impact did it have on the social and religious climate of the late medieval revolution blazing in all corners?

Anne Hudson, the expert in all things Lollard, is the source for much of the following summary of the characteristics of Lollard doctrine[24] which:

- encourages literacy and schooling
- values works of scripture
- emphasizes a readily identifiable hierarchy of authority
- accepts vernacular writings
- expresses anti-clerical assumptions about hypocrisy of churchmen
- strives for precise scriptural words, as opposed to words of lesser men and subordinate authority
- values the written word

Much exploration remains to be done in comparing the *Pricke of Conscience* with Lollard tenets, but the heavy scriptural emphasis, both in quotations and as an authority, is immediately apparent.

Furthermore, the characteristics of Lollard scriptural books and anthologies include the following:

- handsome, scrupulously made documents
- professional presentation, layout, and decoration
- running titles of chapter titles and psalm numbers
- clear rubrication of texts
- most written in rather old-fashioned book hand with few cursive elements
- most sermons in anglicana formata script of great regularity and legibility
- concern for accuracy and clarity
- no figural ornamentation
- ubiquitous flourished capitals with gold leaf
- marginal decoration in leaf-and-spoon style are common
- splendid appearance for edifying material
- uniformity of text and presentation in the 31 manuscripts of the cycle
- used precise glossing and scriptural references in margins
- scrupulously differentiated between text and commentary
- patristic or medieval sources carefully and persistently rubricated, annotated, or both

Some *Pricke of Conscience* manuscripts conform to these preferences, and others do not, so perhaps further investigation

will enlighten the text in this regard. Finally, characteristics of Lollard reading practices are as follows:
- patrons pooled resources to purchase or commission books
- owned books in common
- established book-loaning system in Coventry and Leicestershire between 1511–12
- although not wealthy, often spent money for fine quality texts
- owners did not sign books and scribes did not mention themselves in colophons for fear of persecution

One example of a Lollard text is the "Glossed Gospels," a verse-by-verse and often word-by-word commentary on gospels using a revised text of the Early Version of the Lollard translation. Obviously, not every document containing certain of these features is thereby automatically to be relegated to the category of "Lollard," but these facts about the Lollard movement may help establish what texts may or may not fall into that group. Undeniably, the time *Pricke of Conscience* manuscripts were being scribed is precisely the time of greatest Lollard growth and proliferation of texts, as the following three dates suggest:

1382 John Wyclif withdrew from Oxford University and retired to Lutterworth;

1407 Archbishop Arundel forbade production of biblical transmission and ownership of translations unless they predated Wyclif and were approved by the diocesans (see Anne Hudson,[25] "Lollard Book Production" 131);

1419 Bonfire to burn Wyclif writings at Oxford (although later ownership can be established).

Whether or not these *Pricke of Conscience* texts were based on Lollard premises, the manuscripts are themselves fascinating documents that warrant further investigation.

PROVENANCE OF MANUSCRIPTS

Lewis and McIntosh claim the presumed original ur-manuscript has a *terminus ad quem* of 1325, but was most likely composed around 1350 in the North. Southern Recension scribes wrote about a century later, but given the large number of manuscripts, copying must have been an ongoing practice. Distribution of the Southern Manuscripts appears connected to monasteries such as Benedictine Abbeys spread across Southern England. By and large, these Southern versions appear to be a bit more concise, with less repetition and somewhat more structure imposed upon them.

Notes

1. Johan Huizinga, *Waning of the Middle Ages* (London: Edward Arnold and Co., 1924, rpt.1950), 9.
2. R.J. Rydall, "Materials: The Paper Revolution," in *Book Production and Publishing in Britain: 1375–1475*, Jeremy Griffiths and Derek Pearsall, eds., Cambridge UP, 1989, 11–29, here 11.
3. A.S.G. Edwards and Derek Pearsall, "The Manuscripts of the Major English Poetic Texts," in *Book Production and Publishing in Britain, 1375–1475*, Jeremy Griffiths and Derek Pearsall, eds. (Cambridge: Cambridge University Press, 1989), 257–78, here 257.
4. David Aers, "Class, Gender, Medieval Criticism, and *Piers Plowman*" in *Class and Gender in Early English Literature*, ed. Britton J. Harwood and Gillian R. Overing. (Bloomington: Indiana University Press, 1994), 60.
5. Norman F. Cantor, *Inventing the Middle Ages* (New York: William Morrow and Company, Inc.), 1991, 28.
6. Franco Cardini, "The Warrior and the Knight," in *The Medieval World*, ed. Jacques LeGoff (London: Parkgate Books, 1997), 107, 109.
7. Larry Scanlon, "The King's Two Voices: Narrative and Power in Hoccleve's *Regiment of Princes*," in *Literary Practice and Social Change in Britain, 1380–1530*, ed. Lee Patterson (Berkeley: University of California Press, 1990), 217.
8. W. M. Ormond, *Political Life in Medieval England, 1300–1450* (New York: St. Martin's Press, 1995), 10–11, 12–13.
9. Lee Patterson, "'No Man His Reson Herde': Peasant Consciousness, Chaucer's Miller, and the Structure of the *Canterbury Tales*," in *Literary Practice and Social Change in Britain, 1380–1530*, ed. Lee Patterson (Berkeley: University of California Press, 1990, 115, 153). See also Charles W. Oman, *The Great Revolt of 1381* (Oxford: Clarendon Press, 1906), Rodney Hilton, ed. *Class Conflict and the Crisis of Feudalism* (London: Verso, 1985), and *Bondmen Made Free: Medieval Peasant Movements and the English Rising of 1381* (London: Temple Smith, 1973; rpt. 1977).
10. Helen Barr, *The Piers Plowman Tradition: A Critical Edition of Pierce the Ploughman's Crede, Richard the Redeless, Mum and the Sothesegger, and The Crowned King* (London: J.M. Dent. Everyman's Library, 1993), 3.
11. Janet Coleman, *Medieval Readers and Writers: 1350–1400* (New York: Columbia University Press, 1981), 60.
12. Huizinga, 308.
13. After detailing potent examples, Huizinga concludes: "All this facility for emotions, of tears and spiritual upheavals, must be borne in mind in order to conceive fully how violent and high-strung was life at that period," 6.
14. Barr, 25.
15. Coleman, 14.
16. Anne Hudson, "Lollard Book Production" in *Book Production in Britain: 1375–1475*, Jeremy Griffiths and Derek Pearsall, eds. (Cambridge: Cambridge University Press, 1989), 125.
17. Coleman, 43.
18. Coleman, 17.
19. Coleman, 23.
20. Mary-Louise Uhart, "The Early Reception of 'Piers Plowman,'" unpublished, Ph.D. Dissertation, 1986, U of Leicester, 48..
21. G.H. Russell, "Some Early Responses to the C Version of Piers Plowman," *Viator* 15 (1984), 276–91.
22. Vincent Gillespie, "Vernacular Books of Religion," *Book Production and Publishing in England: 1375–1475* (Cambridge: Cambridge University Press, 1989), 317–44, here 332.
23. Robert E. Lewis and Angus McIntosh, *A Descriptive Guide to the Manuscripts of the Prick of Conscience* (Oxford: The Society for the Study of Mediaeval Languages and Literature, 1982).
24. Hudson, 134.
25. Hudson, 131.

Introduction to the Poem and Manuscript

Description of HM 128, Huntington Library, San Marino, California

This manuscript has received much attention from Ralph Hanna, John Fisher, Hoyt Duggan and associates, Howell Chickering and others. I am indebted to Robert Lewis and Angus McIntosh's *A Descriptive Guide to the Manuscripts of the Prick of Conscience*, which should be used as a supplement to this edition, Consuelo Dutchke's work, and the *Piers Plowman Electronic Edition* of HM 128 (eds. Hoyt Duggan, Michael Calabrese, et al.) from which much of the following information has been distilled. James H. Morey's edition of Osborn a. 13 and Ralph Hanna and Sarah Wood's *Richard Morris's Prick of Conscience* have also been very useful.

CONTENTS OF HM 128

Six articles of 219 folios done on parchment, with two contemporary parchment (at beginning and end):

1. *Pricke of Conscience*, ff. 1–16v, 25–32v; 17–24v (these two quires reversed); 33–94. Quires 1–12 in Hand A.
2. Fragment of *Piers Plowman*, B-text, ff. 95–96v (reversed order). Quire 12 in Hands A and B.
3. Commentaries on Sundays and feast days according to sarum usage, ff. 97–112v. Quires 13–14 in Hand C.
4. *Piers Plowman*, B-text, ff. 113–205, Quires 15–26 in Hands A and D.
5. *Sege of Jerusalem*, ff. 205–216. Quires 26–28 in Hand E.
6. *How the Good Wiif Tau3te Hir Dou3tir*, ff. 216–219. Quire 28 in Hand F.

DATE, COLLATION, AND HANDS

Date: Dutschke: first quarter s. xv; Lewis and McIntosh s. xv in (p. 146). Both Dutschke and Lewis and McIntosh attribute this manuscript to a Southwest Warwickshire provenance (163), scribed by six MS. Hands in anglicana. Former Huntington Curator Jean Preston believes they are "mixed secretary and anglicana scripts." Paleography suggests a common, contemporaneous origin for Articles 1, 2, and 4.

Collation: 1–27/8 (quires 3 and 4 reversed), 28; catchwords and quire signatures have been trimmed off and are no longer visible.

Designation of Hands to texts is as follows:

Hand A: Article 1, part of articles 2 and 4. Folios 1–94r, 96r (22 lines of upper half), 113r–120v. Also rubricated *Pricke of Conscience* (article 1).

Hand B: 95r, 96r (17 lines lower half), 96v—a shaky novice scribing 81 lines. According to Duggan, Calabrese, et al., "He uses a single compartment lower case "a," a "g" with a descender scooping to the left, an often ornate descender on "y" sweeping first to the left then the right, and a "d" that sometimes appears to have no complete loop but rather an incomplete triangle top. Both Hands A and D are highly skilled, clear and very easy to read, while Hand B, in contrast, is messy and unclear."

Hand C: Article 3, "Expositio sequentarium," ff.97–112v.

Hand D: Article 4, ff.121r–205r, completing scribe A's work on *Piers*.

Hand E: Article 5, ff. 205r–216r.

Hand F: Article 6, ff. 216v–219a.

Rubricator of *Piers* and the Emender of the *Pricke of Conscience*

Editors of the digital *Piers Plowman* edition speculate that "Hand A began his work with *Piers Plowman*, copying the first quire (ff. 113–20) and making a start on the second (96r), before abruptly handing [it] over to Hand B (ff. 96r-v, 95r) while he himself copied the *Prick of Conscience* (ff. 1–94).… While Hand A copied the *Prick of Conscience*, Hand D completed *Piers Plowman* (ff. 121r–205r). Hand A rubricated *Prick of Conscience* himself, but another hand is employed to rubricate *Piers Plowman*." This *Piers* rubricator is responsible for most emendations in the *Pricke of Conscience*. After

7

discussing Hands in the rest of the manuscript, the *Piers* editors conclude "Potentially, then, some sort of collaborative effort informed the production of this MS. in whatever, probably religious, community it was created." Thus the primary hand of the *Pricke of Conscience* has also scribed the first quire of *Piers*. Besides the obvious auto-corrections, many other *Pricke of Conscience* corrections have been made by the same scribe who emended and rubricated all of *Piers* (designated Scribe 3 by its most recent editors M. Calabrese, H. Duggan, et al.). I am grateful to Michael Calabrese for this information.

Foliation

The following note of 12/4/75 by Jean Preston on foliation is the current scholarly consensus:

> Kane and Donaldson state that this MS has 3 foliations, of which the first one is "right head recto, including the front flyleaf, 1–220." This is the foliation existing in the 1930s and used by Captain Haselten and H.C. Schultz in their published and unpublished notes on the MS, and also by DiRicci. Sometime after the 1930s the foliation was apparently changed to 1–219 excluding the front flyleaf—i.e., Folio 1 is now the first leaf of text instead of the front flyleaf (which is now f. i). To locate references by DiRicci or Capt. Haselten, subtract one from the folio number (e.g. his f.114 is present f.113). Kane and Donaldson references are to the present foliation, but their description of the "right" head foliation is no longer correct [source: Huntington Information File].

Physical Description and Page Arrangement

Page height varies from 242 to 248 mm, and width is consistently 168 mm, making the overall size 240 × 168 mm. The text frame is 205 × 135 (140 in article 3). Articles 1 and 2 are ruled for 40 lines per page, article 3 contains 61 lines in double columns, article 5 contains between 53 and 65 lines per page, article 6 contains only 28 to 30 lines per page, and article 7 generally has 40 lines per page, with 113r, 114v, 115r, 187r having 41, and 186v having 42.

Decoration and Textual Presentation in the *Pricke of Conscience*, HM 128

Like that of article 4, *Piers Plowman*, the text of the *Pricke of Conscience* begins with an unusually large illuminated capital *T* as the facsimile preceding folio 1 reveals, measuring 50 mm × 40 mm. Initials of *incipits* for the seven primary divisions or "parties" measure about 25 mm × 30 mm and those of subsections are about 10 to 20 mm × 10 mm marked by an initial capital, often rubricated in red and blue ink, embellished by trails of tendril flourishes highlighting those pages. The size of capitals varies throughout the document, possibly indicating the relative significance of the immediate content.

Three glossarial phrases are provided in the margins to organize the Prologus. Thirty-three paraphs mark divisions throughout the entire text (but are concentrated in Book V and beyond), written in blue ink on the rectos and red ink on the versos.

Rubrication may also indicate what a scribe perceives as significant, as noted above, in an unpublished Leicester Ph.D. dissertation, Marie-Louise Uhart finds six centers of interest among *Piers Plowman* rubricators: "The noting of moral qualities and their personifications; general and individual personae of the poem; attention to structural elements of the poem associated with sermon literature; noting of key incidents; Piers the Plowman and prophecy."[1] G.H. Russell divides rubrication into types based on function: "the identification of names, personae and auctores, historical exempla and biblical texts; structural devices such as legal documents, preaching and prophecy, the sins, the appearance of *Piers* and the various other key episodes and structural elements of the poem."[2] Huntington 128 rubricates ONLY sins, against which it is warning, highlighting their importance, and emphasizing the didactic intent of the work.

Vincent Gillespie comments on column arrangement, another aspect of *ordinatio*, or page arrangement:

> Of the 115 manuscripts that may reasonably be presumed to have been originally complete, only fifteen are in a form other than a single column. The octosyllabic meter of the long work would lead one to think that a double column arrangement would have been more suitable, producing an economic use of a leaf of regular shape; the result is that most of the manuscripts are of comparatively tall, narrow format. Yet this uniformity cannot be the outcome of a centrally imposed decision: the linguistic evidence reveals that copying was geographically widely dispersed [332].[3]

Reasons for the shape of the text remain unclear, but perhaps this column format was comparatively easier to read than the more economic double-column format; this would suggest a more public use of the material, such as for reading aloud in monasteries and convents. HM 128 does not use a double-column format, providing more space for the scribe to write and gloss.

Latin quotations are generally written in a larger hand, in a more formal textura script, and are boxed, or under- and over-lined with red ink.

Versions of the Pricke of Conscience

Manuscript Editions

The text of the *Pricke of Conscience* is preserved in approximately 115 complete or fragmentary manuscripts. Lewis and McIntosh designate ninety-seven as Main or Northern versions (MV) (ten of these being of mixed composition), dating from about 1350 through the fifteenth century; they have designated eighteen as Southern Recensions (SR). SR 1–5 and 10–12 are designated Group A, closest to the MVs; SR 6 and 15 are mixed or conflated; SR 7–9, 13–14, and 16–18 are designated Group B, further from the MVs, and scribed somewhat later.

In addition, eight extracts, two *Speculum Huius Vite*, and six Latin translations have come down to us. The major categories, Main Version and Southern Recension, represent two traditions, in two dialects, and differ in length (about 9624 lines and 7416 lines respectively) as well as language.

Manuscripts written in the Northern dialect are most prolific, and somewhat pre-date those of the Southern Recension. Their density in certain regions of the North coincides with the location of monasteries where they might have been produced, and certainly housed or read. (See Distribution Maps, Lewis and McIntosh, Appendix, pp. 171 and 173.)

Manuscripts of the Southern Recension can be found in Cambridge at Pembroke College (SR 2), St. John's College (SR 3), and University College (SR 4); in Dublin, at Trinity College (SR 5); in Lichfield, two at the Cathedral (SR 6 and 7); in London, four at the British Library: Harley 1731 (SR 8), Harley 2281 (SR 9), Royal 18 A.v. (SR 10), and Additional 11305 (SR 11); in Oxford at the Bodleian Library, Bodley 423 (SR 12), Laud Misc. 601 (SR 13), and Lyell empt 6 (SR 14); in Princeton New Jersey, Garrett 138 (SR 15); and in San Marino, three at the Huntington Library (HM 125, 128, and 130—SR 16, 17, and 18). The version formerly at Beaumont College, Old Windsor, Berkshire (SR 1) was sold at Christie's on June 28, 1973 (lot 48) and is now in Sweden (see *MAE* 64 [1995], 178).

Modern and Medieval Editions

Richard Morris edited the Northern version in 1863 (Oxford) from MV 27, British Library Cotton Galba E. IX (patched with MV 34, British Library, Harley 4196; both are dated s. xiv ex). In 1973, the text was reprinted with no alterations and no additional apparatus.

Fortunately, the newest addition to the *Prick of Conscience* production, the extensively revised version *Richard Morris's Prick of Conscience*, was published in 2013. This valuable addition in the EETS series edited by Ralph Hanna and Sarah Wood offers full annotation of this Northern text, including extensive discussion of the poem's sources. Sections on textual and literary matters explore and open the poem in new ways.

In 1976 Stacey A. Waters produced an edition of Part V, HM 125 as a Ph.D. dissertation at the University of Edinburgh. For his generous sharing of this unpublished material I am grateful. I have used variants from this Southern Recension as a point of comparison for this edition of HM 128.

As this edition of HM 128 was going through its final stages, I was delighted to hear of a new Northern Version called *Prik of Conscience*, edited by James H. Morey and released by TEAMS (Middle English Text Series), Medieval Institute Publications of Western Michigan University, in the summer of 2012. Although my work was essentially complete by its release, I have tried to include some textual comparisons of this Osborn a. 13 manuscript (Beinecke Library, New Haven) to clarify HM 128 readings. Morey's TEAMS edition will be very useful for students of all ages, and offers a modern complement to the Southern Recension edition here provided. His introductory material, as well as textual and explanatory notes, contains much valuable information about the history of this large body of texts. We are fortunate to have a convenient, early, accessible edition of the Northern Recension; I hope the Northern edition, in addition to this first-available Southern Recension (from HM 128) will enrich future opportunities to explore a truly remarkable work.

With two Northern and one Southern edition of the *Prick of Conscience* now available to the scholarly community, the opportunity to move forward in investigating this treasure has significantly advanced.

Lewis and McIntosh have summarized the following significant information for each manuscript in their *Descriptive Guide to the Manuscripts of the Prick of Conscience* (*Medium Aevum Monographs*, New Series XII, Society for the Study of Mediaeval Languages and Literature, Oxford: 1982):

1. Codicological description (material, leaves, size, number of scribes, nature of handwriting, columns and lines per page, catchwords/signatures, binding if medieval;
2. Contents of each manuscript;
3. Notes on the state of the text: title, colophon, incipit and explicit, number of lines, nature of the text, omissions, titles, capitals, page numbers where PC begins;
4. Notes on ownership and provenances;
5. Dialect discussions;
6. Bibliography: IMEV (*Index of Middle English Verse*) number, previous owners or titles, authoritative published description(s), references to *PC* in scholarship; a 2005 edition of *A New Index of Middle English Verse* has been produced by Julia Boffey and Anthony S. Edwards, London, British Library;
7. notes on textual relationship.

Lewis and McIntosh's thorough scholarship will be summarized on pp. 12–15 below.

Provenance of the Pricke of Conscience, *HM 128*

Authorship

Despite various efforts to locate a candidate, authorship remains anonymous. Attribution has been made to Bishop Grosseteste of Lincoln (1170–1253) and to Richard Rolle of Hampole (1300–49), the latter in five manuscripts. Stylistic analysis by Hope Emily Allen in 1910 (Allen, "Authorship") has disproved this authorship, but no replacement has been posited. See Lewis and McIntosh, 2–3 and Morey, 1–2.

Dating

Lewis and McIntosh claim the presumed original ur-manuscript has a *terminus a quo* of 1325, but was most likely composed around 1350 in the North; other Northern manuscripts continued to be written throughout the century and beyond. Southern Recension scribes wrote simultaneously and somewhat after the ur-manuscript, but given the large numbers of manuscripts, copying in both areas must have been an ongoing practice. The discussion of language that follows, by Hoyt Greeson, considers the linguistic dimension of HM 128 in great detail.

Distribution of the Southern Manuscripts appears connected to monasteries such as Benedictine Abbeys spread across southern England. As noted above, by and large, these Southern versions are more concise (about 75 percent of the length of Northern versions), somewhat more structured, and appear to be revisions of one or more Northern versions. Group B manuscripts of the Southern Recension category, which includes HM 128, have been well described by McIntosh and Lewis, and will not be recounted here again.

Language (by Hoyt Greeson)

The following data, based on this edition of the *Pricke of Conscience*, Huntington MS. 128, places the language of the manuscript in the West Midlands, where the dialect(s) developed from Anglian Old English. The evidence to substantiate this conclusion is based on certain phonological and morphological features generally held to be associated with the West Midlands.[4] First, the phonological evidence:

1. W.Gmc ā became æ in West Saxon but was raised in Anglian to ē when followed by a back vowel. Examples of this in LP 8040 are bere (36), dede(s) (76), clene (50).[5] The reflex of Anglian OE ă + nasal is normally o in the West Midlands, but HM 128 has both o and a. These forms and their numbers show a scribal ambivalence: name (10), nome (9); fram (19), from (96); an (90), on (52); but, man (496), mon (1). Christensson's reassessment of More, Meech and Whitehall's isogloss delimiting the boundaries of the West Midlands dialect demonstrates that there is a man area in Gl, which carries on past the southwestern corner and eastern border of Wrk, leaving a mon area in its central section. *LALME* fixes the provenance of HM 128 near this southwestern corner of Wrk.[6]

2. Prehistoric OE æ, developed from W.Gmc umlauted ai, appears as ea in WS areas, subject to breaking when followed by _lC or _ll. In Mercia and Northumbria it became a, which, when lengthened by following _lC, represented /ɔː/ and was written <o>.

3. The reflex of Anglian haldan appears in LP 8040 as holde (30), bolde (4), cold(e) (19), old(e) (32), and elde (10). When i-mutation affected Anglian a_lC, as in the case of ald + i the result was e in the non–Mercian areas of Anglia. This accounts for the form elde LP 8040.[7]

4. i-mutation similarly affects Anglian a_rC, with similar results appearing in LP 8040: scharp(e) (7), smart(e) (4); harde (20), werche (4), werk- (24).

5. OE y̆/ŷ derived from W.Gmc ŭ/û + i/j appears as u in the W.Mdls. The reflex of OE fȳr in LC 8040 is fuyr (89). Before _l both i and u occur in the W.Mdls. The reflex of OE hyll is hull throughout this area; in LC 8040 the forms hille (3), hul (1) and hull (4) appear. Before other Cc except ȝ, u normally appears. In Worc, however, forms such as lutl- and lyttel- occur, but LC 8040 contains these: litel, litil, lityl, lytel, lytil, lytle, lytul, lytyll. In most counties of the W.Mdls, OE y̆/ŷ remained unchanged, but scribes adopted the French orthographic practice of writing u in place of y, both of which represented high front rounded vowel sounds.[8] This group of forms for little in 8040 is not entirely out of line. The Item Maps for little in *LALME* II, p. 301, reveal that forms in lu- and li- or ly- appear together in many LPs of the W.Mdls area, although the lu- forms predominate in Gl and Ox. This evidence rather stands against Kristensson's findings, p. 92 and Map 8.

6. Early OE æ/ea were affected when following the initial palatals č-, š-, or ȝ-: OE ea appears as ea in WS, but remained æ in the Anglian dialect, becoming ME a in W.Mdls forms such as LP 8040 ȝate- (2), gate (10).

7. Unstressed vowels are normally written <e>, but in the W.Midls -us occurs. LP 8040 has these forms: appul (1), fadur (10), wyntur (1), and a few instances of 3sg.pres. verb suffixes in -u: -uth (4), -uþ (2). The morphological forms used in determining dialect include the 3rd.pr.pl. pronoun, the 3rd.pr.pres.indic and the 3rd.pr.pl.verb suffixes, and the pres.ppl. suffix.

8. The oblique case of the 3rd.pers.pl pronoun appears in LP 8040 as hem (482); neither them nor þem appears in any alternate form. *LALME*, II, p. 31 offers evidence, however, that forms in th- and þ- occurred further south than Moore, Meech and Whitehall claim. Their isogloss runs from north-western La almost directly down to Ru and out to The Wash, south of which these forms were not thought to appear. The orthographic practice of the HM 128 copyist was evidently not influenced by the th- forms migrating from the north.

9. These 3sg.pr.ind. suffixes occur in PL. 8-40: -eth (137), -uth (2), -yth (2), -eþ (546), -uþ (6), -yþ (6), -þe (1), -þ (1), -es (26), -ys (4), -is (2). Moore, Meech, and Whitehall's isogloss for the southern extent of the northern 3sg.pr. suffix -es extends from the southern third of Chs, southeast through the middle of Stf, northeast along the southern border of Dby, then almost directly to The Wash. Actually, an isogloss for this suffix can proceed from the southwestern corner of Sal at 4037, then on to 4239, make a loop up to 223 and back south to Stf 260, 238, and down to LP 8040 before eventually cutting through the southern part of Cam, directly across the northwestern corner of Sfx, entering Nfk to include 4656, 4663, 645 and 4564. This suggested isogloss places Wrk at the southern boundary of the 3sg.pr. suffix -es but also helps "fit" HM 128 in an area where its variety of -th/-þ suffixes can be accommodated. It fits into a small area where forms in -u cluster: -uþ occurs at 4686 and 65, -uth at 1308 and 325. 8040 fits into a cluster of spots where -eth and eþ occur. The diagnostic form, with a grapheme that distinguishes 8040 is -yþ. The same holds true for -is, a graphic variation of -es and -ys.

10. LP 8040 has the following pres.pl. suffixes: -eth (108), -yth (1), -th (39), -eþ (270), -iþ (2), -yþ (6), -þ (309), -es (8), -ys (1), -en (445). The co-occurrence of forms in -eth/-eþ and -en runs along an isogloss that starts slightly south of that suggested by Moore, Meech and Whitehall. *LALME*'s materials suggest an isogloss starting at LP 704 in Sal, carrying on through 4218, then curving to the southeast and passing through LPs 8040 and 4679 in Wrk, then carrying on to 705 and 4707 in southern Nht, and on to 4708 in Bd, and points east.[9] The co-occurrence of these pr.pl. suffixes does suggest that LP 8040 lies quite near the isogloss.

Furthermore, the orthographic traditions represented in the immediate vicinity of LP 8040 support *LALME*'s fit of this HM 128. -eth occurs at 4684, immediately north of 8040, and at 534, 677 and 517 in northern Wrk. -yþ is found at 4683, just to the northeast; -es, at 534, to the northeast; and -iþ at 4679, 4683, 65, 4675. -yþ seems to be diagnostic, occurring in close proximity in 8040 and 4683, and setting up a contrast between the three suffixes -iþ, -eþ, and -yþ, which are similar but differ by one vowel grapheme.

11. The distinctive forms of the pres.ppl. and vbl.n/adj in HM 128 are -enge (1, 5) and -yngge (2, 2), since the suffixes -ynge (29) and -yng (8) are widespread, both as prcs.ppls and vbls. The remaining vbl suffixes in HM 128 are -eng (2), -enge (4), -ing (8), -inge (10), and -ynge (4). The distribution of -yngge suggests the possibility it may have migrated from the East Midlands. Seven Mss with Nfk associations contain this form of the pr.ppl suffix: LPs 150, 4648, 4629, 4647, 4663, 4066, and 4622. It also occurs in southern Ex, Kt and Sx, in the W.Midls at Hrf 7310, close to Gl 7212, and in Wor at 7670 and 7731. In Wrk, -yngge occurs as a pr.ppl. suffix only at 6910, and just north, at 8040, where it also indicates a vbl. The data provided by *LALME* leads to the conclusion that -enge is diagnostic, distinguishing pr.ppl forms in HM 128 from that of MSS located in its immediate surroundings.

One further observation may serve to put the capstone on the data presented here, suggesting that the provenance of HM 128 is not only generally speaking in the W. Mdls, but more than likely precisely where the editorial staff of *LALME* have fitted it.

Kristensson reviews the development of OE i-mutated a/_lC groups, which Ekwall believes sets off the West Midlands dialect(s) from the East Midlands, because the language of this area is a continuation of OE West Mercian. The mutated a becomes Mercian æ, W.Midl a; in the non–Mercian Anglian area a mutated to e and East Midlands e, which, however, migrated westward. Making a strong case that a/_nasal C has wider distribution, Kristensson does conclude that mutated a does distinguish western W.Mdl dialect(s) from those of the easternmost counties included in the West Midlands: most of Dby and Gl, Nht, Lei, Ox, Wor, and Wrk. These eastern counties have e, not a, as a result of i-mutation of Anglian a. The form walle distinguishes the west, and welle, the east. HM 128 contains two instances of welle, none of walle. Kristensson's Map 10 shows ten pockets where the form welle occurs. Three of these groups are in the immediate area where *LALME* locates HM 128 and its specific provenance. The available date, then, tends to confirm the *LALME* decision to fit HM 128 near Stratford-on-Avon. Indeed, the placename Stratford, developed from I-mutation of Anglian a itself, reflects the western W.Mdl development, whereas Stretton, close to Shipston, perhaps where *LALME*'s 6910 is located, exhibits the eastern development of a. HM 128, LP 8040, apparently lies in the middle of this small area of fluctuating phonological and orthographic loyalties.

Manuscript Choice

Criteria for "Best Text" of Pricke of Conscience Manuscript

I have chosen to edit a manuscript from the group of Southern Recensions to offer the scholarly community a basis for comparison to two main versions: the one out-of-print-edition by Morris (1863) but recently re-edited by Hanna and Wood, and the newly edited manuscript by Morey (2012).

The choice of this manuscript is based on the following criteria:

- Superior text
- Textual precision—providing the best textual readings;
- High "authorial" weight (probably what the author wrote);
- Internal consistency with little textual or linguistic confusion;
- Reasonable, sound readings;
- Careful, complete execution;
- No missing or illegible folios.

Of the 18 versions of the manuscripts of the Southern Recension, six are complete; twelve are missing an initial, final or one or more medial folios; and two are conflated, using both Northern and Southern editions as sources. SR 15 Garrett 138 (Princeton Library) is a heavily scrambled and conflated manuscript. SR 1, Beaumont College, Old Windsor, Berkshire, 9, once privately owned by H.P. Kraus of New York, now MS Schøyen 689, has been purchased by Martin Schøyen of Norway (Administrative Address of the Schøyen Collection is Aasured Gard, Kjosmyrveien, N-3430 Spikkestad, Norway) and is not readily available. See Irma Taavitsainen in the General Bibliography. Also complete are SR 5, Dublin, Trinity College 69; SR 10, London, British Library, Harley 2281; SR 11, London British Library Additional 11305; and SR 17 San Marino, California, Huntington Library, HM 128. This last manuscript is a fine specimen in very good condition, clearly scribed and well rubricated, with useful *ordinatio* and few illegible lines. It is also from Group B, providing further textual and linguistic changes to examine. A brief description of each derived from Lewis and McIntosh's *A Descriptive Guide to the Manuscripts of the Prick of Conscience* will summarize their characteristics:

SR 1 Beaumont College, Old Windsor, Berkshire, 9, s. xiv: ff. 3–158 in anglicana formata hand (single columns–26 lines per page)
- Originally the *P of C* was the only text in the MS but a prayer from 15th to 16th century now is included.
- Prior Owner: "Elyzbeth Strangburn" (in 16th c. hand on f. 63)
- Place of Origin: South east Gloucestershire. Linguistically similar to SR 13
- Group A, related to SR 10 and 11
- Initially at Beaumont College, then owned by H.P. Kraus of New York, and currently owned by Martin Schøyen of Norway and not readily available.

SR 2 Cambridge, Pembroke College, 272, s. xv med.: ff. 1–143 in secretary book hand with some anglicana features (single columns—22–28 lines per page)
- Several omissions; ends imperfectly at l. 9552
- No Latin quotations or subtitles in text after f. 11
- It begins imperfectly at l. 458
- Place of Origin: South east Suffolk
- Group A, related to SR 4 and 5
- At Cambridge, Pembroke College
- Table of Contents at the beginning of each book beginning at Book II.

SR 3 Cambridge, St. John's College, 29, s. xv med.: ff. 3–119v in anglicana with Latin quotations in bastard anglicana (single columns—38–39 lines per page)
- PC preceded by *Ipotis* in the MS
- Titled "Stimulus Conscience"
- Perhaps three leaves missing between ff. 5 and 6 (corresponding to MV 77–316)
- Latin titles in margin to Books II–V
- Prior Owner: "Margaret Carew;" some names of "Chaloners" on f. 57 (in 16th century hand?)
- Place of Origin: Surrey or Sussex
- Group A—closely related to SR 12 in Book V.

SR 4 Cambridge, University Library, Ee.44.35.2, s. xiv^2: ff. 1–96v in anglicana formata (single columns—34–47 lines per page)
- Three omissions: ff. 24–25 corresponding to MV ll. 2064–2245; f. 33 corresponding to MV ll. 2821–2901; ff. 41–44 corresponding to MV ll. 3467–3809
- Table of Contents to the whole poem and each book in double columns
- English titles in text to all books; some English subtitles in text
- Place of Origin: South east Gloucestershire, not far from SR 1 and SR 13
- Group A related to SR 2 and 5 in Book V.

SR 5 Dublin, Trinity College, 69 (A.4.4), s. xiv/xv: ff. 65a–72vb, 83va–123va in textura (double columns—53–55 lines per column on ff. 83v–88v)
- Six items in this MS, with *PC* being sixth

The part of the manuscript containing the *PC* is bound incorrectly: ff. 65–72v corresponding to MV ll. 4071–5525 is displaced from between ff. 104 and 105

General Table of contents and one for each book

MS is probably of ecclesiastical origin, but belonged to a layman in the 15th century

Prior Owner: "John Hyde," noted at the end of the Psalter in the MS

Place of Origin: South Sussex

Group A, related to SR 2 and 4 in Book V; also SR 15.

SR 6 Lichfield, Cathedral, 16, s. xv: ff. 35–189v, two textura hands in *PC*: ff. 35–82v and 92–189v; ff. 83–91v. 2 quires missing (single columns–22 lines per page)

MS contains *PC* and two other texts in five versions

One quire of 8 pp. corresponding to MV ll. 7123–7856 omitted between ff. 163 and 164

Prior Owner: "William Seymore, Duke of Summerset" (1588–1660)

Place of Origin: probably Somersetshire, South Gloucestershire, or Wiltshire

Hand 2 has a strong East Anglian ingredient linking it to SR 7

Conflated MS: MV text to l. 463; a SR text thereafter where it is Group B

Related to SR 8, 13, and 16 in Book V.

SR 7 Lichfield, Cathedral, 50, s. xiv[2]: (single columns 28 ff. 1–190v, Bastard anglicana perhaps in two hands, with the change at f. 59)

Omission of last leaf; Book VII considerably rearranged

English titles in text to all books except V where it is in the margin

Frequent English subtitles; Capitals for subdivisions. Most Latin quotations are omitted

Corrections in the text: in Prologue, I; I.6 6v; II: 14v; III; 24v: IV:37; V:37: V:54; VI:84: VII 92v; Epilogue:109v

Prior Owner: "Galfridus Glasier, Chapter Clerk"

Place of Origin: Norfolk

Group B. Related to SR 15 and 17 in Book V.

SR 8 London, British Library, Harley 1731, s. xv[2]: (single columns ff. 1–149, anglicana with titles and Latin quotations in anglicana formata, 28–29 ll. per page; paper)

Followed by the *Speculum Gy de Warewyke*

Begins imperfectly at l. 59

Two omissions: 1 leaf corresponding to MV ll. 1–58; 1 corresponding to MV ll.715–82

Many interlinear corrections

Prior Owner: "Richard Reder of Petersfield, Hampshire" (who surrendered MS to Commissary General of Diocese of Winchester on July 5, 1473; perhaps suspected of heresy)

Place of Origin: North east Wiltshire

Group B, related to SR 6, 13, and 16 in Book V; ll. 5060–5441 come from a MV text.

SR 9 London, British Library, Harley 2281, s. xv in: (single columns ff. 1–64, anglicana formata 32–38 lines per page)

Ends imperfectly corresponding to MV ll. 5764–65

One other omission between ff. 24 and 25 corresponding to MV ll. 1931–2658

Capitals or spaces for capitals for subdivisions up to f. 43v

Place of Origin: South west Herefordshire

Group B, related to SR 14 and 18 in Book V.

SR 10 London British Library, Royal 18 A. V, s. xv: (single columns ff. 2–126, anglicana, 30–35 lines per page)

Many English subtitles in text and space for capital at beginning of Book I

No title or colophon

Prior Owner: "Elyot" family (in late 15th or early 16th century); note of ownership is on f. 130 and a number of "Elyot" names are on ff. 127v–128v and 129v

Place of Origin: South east Midlands

Group A, related to SR 1 and SR 11 in Book V.

SR 11 London, British Library, Additional 11305 s. xv[2]: (single columns anglicana formata, 31 lines per page on ff. 11–50v. 32 lines per page elsewhere)

Many English subtitles; Latin running titles throughout

Latin subtitles and topical notes in margins, especially in Book VII

Occasional corrections in text

Scribe: Stephen Doddensham, monk of the Charterhouse of Sheen

Prior Owner: "John Sharrock"—owned MS in 1651, lent it to "Robert Hesketh"; another possible owner is "John Semmerton" from Rustorbe (Rufford?) in Lancashire (see ff. 12, 19v)

Place of Origin: Middlesex

Group A, related to SR 1 and 10; appears to shift SR exemplars in Book V; related to SR 14; uses alternate title "The floure of conscience" at l. 9551.

SR 12 Oxford, Bodleian Library, Bodley 423, s. xv: (single columns, anglicana, Latin quotations and titles in a highly calligraphelic anglicana formata, 36–45 lines per page)

Five texts bound together by Sir Thomas Bodley; *PC* is number four, on ff. 244–354v

Incorrectly bound between ff. 262 and 267: should be 262, 264, 263, 266, 265, 267

Begins imperfectly at ll. 311–312; two omissions: four leaves before l. 244 corresponding to MV ll. 1–310; one leaf between ff. 350 and 351 corresponding to MV ll. 9465–9608

English titles to all books except III, running titles irregularly, frequent subtitles, capitals for subdivisions

Colophon containing the name "Appliton" at l. 351 with "Iste liber Constat Domino Johanni B […] Canonico ecclesie beate marie de Suthwerke" below [Southwerk, Augustinian Priory of St. Mary Overy]

Place of Origin: Perhaps Surrey or Sussex; very similar in language to SR 3

Group A, related to SR 3 in Book 5.

SR 13 Oxford, Bodleian Library, Laud Miscellaneous 601, s. xiv ex (single columns anglicana formata, 31 lines per page)

Medieval binding of only the *PC;* a late 15th-century hand has added a Litany by the Cross and Blood on f. 115v

English titles for all but Book V, which begins imperfectly

One omission: six leaves between ff. 49 and 50 corresponding to MV ll. 3677–4083

Prior Owner: "John Morgan" (written in hand of 15th or early 16th century scribe)

Place of Origin: South east Gloucestershire, similar in language to SR 1

Group B Related to SR 6, 8, and 16 in Book V.

SR 14 Oxford, Bodleian, Lyell empt. 6, s. xv in. (single columns, two anglicana hands with Latin quotations some in anglicana formata: ff. 1–99, 110–15v [north west Gloucestershire] and 99v–109v [probably south central Midlands]; 33 ll. per page)

Contents are *PC* and an eight-line Latin charm against the fever

Omission between ff. 5 and 6 corresponding to MV ll. 386 and 463

Former Owners: "Johanni Crosby," "Johannes Graunge"

Group B, related to SR 9 and 18 in Book V; related to SR 11 because of the alternate title of "flour of consciens" at 9551.

SR 15 Princeton, New Jersey, Princeton University Library, Garrett 138, now Schøyen MS 689, s. xv in: (single columns, anglicana formata, ff. 1–130, 30 lines per page)

English titles to all books, frequent English subtitles in text, capitals for subdivision

Occasional marginal notes in Latin and English especially in the first half of MS

Some corrections, folios out of order: text on f. 63 jumps from l. 3921 to l. 4047, continues from there to l. 4046 on f. 73v, and jumps ahead to l. 4616 where it continues on.

Place of Origin: Herefordshire

Conflated MS, a MV text to c. l. 715 and a SR thereafter where it is Group B, related to SR 7 and 17 in Book V. May be related to a subgroup of A (SR 2, 4, and 5).

SR 16 San Marino, California, Huntington Library, HM 125 s. xiv/xv: (single columns, anglicana formata, ff. 1–100, 37 lines per page)

One omission: 2 leaves between ff. 97 and 98 corresponding to MV ll. 8964–9125

English titles in text to all but Book II, occasional running English titles and subtitles

Capitals for subdivisions

Prior Owners: possibly "Chrystefer Byrkheade" (f. 95v), "Thomas Jhone" (f. 73v) and "Rycharde mynstrelley" (f. 98v)

Place of Origin: Gloucestershire-Worcestershire border

Group B, related to SR 6, 8, 13 in Book V. Base MS for Waters' edition of Book V.

SR 17 San Marino, California, Huntington MS 128, s. xv in. Single columns, anglicana with Latin quotations in anglicana formata, ff. 1–94, 40 lines per page

Five items with *PC* first. English titles to text in all books, many subtitles in text in all books. Running titles in Latin throughout. Capitals for subdivisions.

Marginal rubrics in Prologue. Occasional corrections in text.

No omissions. One quire out of order.

Prior Owners: possibly "betoun brygges" (f. 149), "Maude" (f. 153) [both in the same 15th-century hand]. "Aleksander London" (f. 101, 15th or 16th-century hand), and "Richard Rychard" (beginning flyleaf, 16th century)

Place of Origin: South west Warwickshire

Group B, related to SR 7 and 15 in Book V. Base MS for this edition of *PC*.

SR 18 San Marino, California, Huntington Library, HM 130, s. xiv–xv: (single columns, anglicana formata., ff. 1–120, 28–35 lines per page)

MS paginated at the bottom of every recto, foliated irregularly

Begins imperfectly at l. 77 (one leaf missing)

English titles in text, brief Latin titles in margins to all books. Capitals for subdivisions

Occasional source and topical notes in margins; some correction in text (new readings written over scrapings)

16th-century printers' marks in margins

Prior Owner: "Willelmo Smart" (on last folio); surname appears three more times on that page in the same hand, once as "W. Smart groser."

Place of Origin: Monmouthshire

Group B. Related to SR 9 and 14 in book but corrected from MS of a different tradition.

Rationale

Editing a Southern Recension manuscript of the *Pricke of Conscience* for the first time allows textual and contextual comparison, now with three other printed texts: Morris's Northern edition (MV 27 of Lewis and McIntosh's *Descriptive Guide to the Manuscripts of the Prick of Conscience*), based on British Library Cotton Galba E. IX (patched with MV 34, British Library, Harley 4196); Hanna and Wood's recent re-editing of Morris's edition; and James H. Morey's *Prik of Conscience*, TEAMS Middle English Texts Series, Kalamazoo, MI: Medieval Institute Publications, 2012 (from Osborn a. 13—Beinecke Library, New Haven). Various patterns and conclusions may be discovered by other critics who now may compare the three varied editions—representatives from both the Main Version and the Southern Recension. They may unearth what preachers and readers found important in each, what doctrines were thought significant through the transmission of the text, what changes were necessitated by its shift in dialect from a Northern original to a Southern version, and how Lollard influences can be discerned in the Southern Recension. (Thanks to Robert Lewis, private consultation.)

As noted above, eighteen manuscripts of the Southern Recension (SR) survive; I have chosen from those eight which are fully "Group B"—the furthest removed textually from the Northern Version; I am discounting the two mixed texts (SR 6 and 15) containing both Northern and Southern elements. Besides presenting a complete available text of this document in a revised form as a basis for comparison to the Northern text, with updated critical apparatus, a secondary goal is to provide a means to examine social and cultural changes, evidenced in a repeatedly, perhaps continuously produced Northern text and a Southern Recension. Further, comparisons might reveal topics readers felt important in the *Pricke of Conscience* as it developed in its transmission, as would the length or brevity of issues discussed. Also exposed are changes in the text necessitated by its shift in dialect from a Northern original to a Southern version. Lewis and McIntosh date the two Northern texts used by Morris as s. xiv ex, and HM 128 as s. xv in, thus also providing a short chronological spread for examination of these issues. Additionally, doctrinal modifications in Southern texts, particularly Group B, scribed during an era of religious change, no doubt signify evolving religious attitudes moving toward Lollard and Reformation politics.

Lewis and McIntosh note the following ten Group B or conflated manuscripts and their characteristics from which I have derived the relevant information about the condition/completeness of manuscripts:

1. Lichfield, Cathedral, 16 (SR 6)
   Conflated manuscript: MV text to l. 463: SR Group B thereafter
   Text ending at the bottom of f. 109v.
   Book VII considerably rearranged
2. Lichfield, Cathedral, 50 (SR 7)
   Text ending imperfectly at the bottom of f. 109v.
   Book VII considerably rearranged
   Most Latin quotations omitted
3. London, British Library Harley 1731 (SR 8)
   Text beginning imperfectly at l. 59; two omissions
   Latin colophons in Bk. VII
   Many interlinear corrections
4. London, British Library, Harley 2281 (SR 9)
   Text ending imperfectly with a subtitle corresponding to MV ll. 5764–65
   One other omission B1 quire of 8 leaves
5. Oxford, Bodleian Library, Laud Miscellaneous 601
   One omission: six leaves between ff. 49 and 50 (MV ll. 3677–4083
   Book V begins imperfectly
6. Oxford, Bodleian Library Lyell empt. 6 (SR 14)
   One leaf missing between ff. 5 and 6 (MV ll. 386–463)
   One folio is mutilated: folio 100
7. Princeton, New Jersey, Princeton University Library, Garrett (SR15)
   Conflated manuscript: MV text to *c*. l. 715; SR, Group B thereafter
   Text on f.63 jumps from l. 3921 to l. 4074
8. San Marino, California, Huntington Library, HM 125 (SR 16)
   One omission, probably 2 leaves corresponding to MV ll. 8964–9125 (between ff. 97 and 98)
9. San Marino, California, Huntington Library, HM 128 (SR 17)
   Complete Text
10. San Marino, California, Huntington Library, HM 130 (SR 18)
    Text begins imperfectly at l. 77 (1 Leaf missing)

Of the eight "Group B" manuscripts, Huntington Manuscript 128 stands out as the most legitimate choice for a "best text." It is textually accurate, logical, and internally consistent; the text is copied with precision and exactitude, introducing no errors, and leaving no dubious readings; it is the only complete version of Group B. The manuscript is textually clear, and does not lack a first page (as do Huntington 130, Harley 1731), have omissions or a defective last page (as does Huntington 125), or contain omissions (as do Harley 1731, Harley 2288, Lyell empt. 6, Laud Misc. 601). It has been well preserved, and is in every way a superior document from which to derive a critical edition. Since it is not a deluxe edition, and its embellishments are minimal, the focus of the scribes and their patrons was clearly the text, the most significant editorial feature.

Editorial Policy

Purpose

This edition strives to produce a text both faithful to the intent of the original poet and comprehensible to a modern scholar with general knowledge of the Middle English language. The recent edition of *The Canterbury Tales: Geoffrey Chaucer,* ed. Robert Boenig and Andrew Taylor (Ontario, Canada; Buffalo, N.Y.: Broadview Editions, 2008) provides a reasonable model: while perceiving its audience as Chaucer scholars, it nevertheless sufficiently glosses its text for comfortable reading by ambitious students. This edition also provides ample glosses for such students.

Generally, Huntington Manuscript 128 needs few emendations or clarifications since the text is in very good condition; minor irregularities (of spelling or word choice) are retained and discussed in the textual notes, as are occasional scribal errors (none of which are sufficiently serious to distort meaning).

This edition conforms as precisely as possible to the written manuscript of the base text, or when warranted, its variants. Thus, in the absence of more compelling manuscript witnesses, readings of the base text, or when necessary its variants (so noted in the textual notes), have been retained. For example, since proper nouns are generally not capitalized, they are not capitalized in the text. Editorial policy has thus been conservative. Since the base text, Huntington Manuscript 128, is such a fine, carefully scribed and preserved manuscript, few emendations have been required.

Spelling, Punctuation, Capitalization, Abbreviations and Division Markers

Middle English letters *thorn* and *yogh* have been retained to provide the greatest measure of authenticity and correspondence to the original. I have also retained the letter *i* (as in *ioye* and *iustice*) since it presents no confusion. Similarly, I have generally used *u* as written in the text rather than *v* as in modern English except for an initial *v*. Dr. Greeson's glossary does not always follow this policy.

Also for greater comprehension or clarity, I have sparingly added periods to demarcate unclear sentence units only. Since any interpolation of punctuation whatsoever is interpretive or intrusive, I have done so minimally, without sacrificing sense. The alternative, adding no punctuation whatsoever, would be an abdication of editorial responsibility. The scribe uses only (1) occasional definitive periods at the end of thoughts; (2) lightly-placed "dots" for pauses or caesuras; (3) elevated *puncti* as commas (the latter two of which I have represented by spaces and periods); and (4) abbreviation marks. On occasion, I have reduced the number of dots and *puncti* when they seem to be intrusive or distracting to the sense of the text.

Similarly, as noted above, I have followed the lower case usage of the scribe for names, cities, mountains, and places, except for capitalizing first letters of lines when he has not done so, thus closely conforming to manuscript usage. The only exception is if lower case words are confusing or unintelligible without a capital letter; in those rare cases I have capitalized them.

Abbreviations within the text have been expanded within parentheses and canceled material has been bracketed. Modern citations of abbreviations, such as in citing journals, follow the MLA bibliography format. Division markers preceding large elaborated capitals are highlighted in bold in the transcription.

In an attempt to recreate the manuscript *ordinatio* in printed form, I have reproduced the same number of textual lines on each folio as the HM 128-scribes have produced, thus creating the same number of folios. Drop capitals have been inserted where the scribes have produced decorated capitals, and represent the approximate size of the scribal capital (based on number of lines it occupies). Other scribal glossarial notes are reproduced in printed form as close to the manuscript spacing as practicable.

Latin Quotations

Most Latin quotations in the manuscript are written in a larger, more formally scripted hand, and boxed to highlight their presence. The poet has incorporated his Latin quotations into the text, often glossing them before and/or after their appearance. This edition translates them in the footnotes (a combination of Hoyt Greeson's and my translations) to indicate modifications to the original Latin. In this transcription, I have italicized them. Generally the biblical source is provided by the author in the text, although it may not always be accurate. The Latin is presented in the same hand as the Middle English but has faded to some degree. Each Latin quotation is designed as one line of text regardless of length.

Critical Apparatus

Variants: Significant variants from the base text are provided in the footnotes on each page. Obvious errors are noted in the footnotes and generally corrected; readings from Stacy Waters' HM 125, Book V, occasionally Ralph Hanna and Sarah Wood's recent edition of Morris's Northern Version of the *Prick of Conscience,* and James Morey's edition from Manuscript Osborn a.13 are so indicated in footnotes.

Glossarial Assistance: In addition to a full glossary at the end of the volume provided by Hoyt Greeson, unusual, perplexing, confusing words or changed meanings are glossed at the end of each line for ease of reading. Middle English variant-spelling modern words are not always noted unless they indicate the scribe understood the Middle English word in a different sense from that of the modern cognate.

Abbreviations: Abbreviations in both Middle English and Latin texts have been expanded, and printed in parentheses. When two possible abbreviations of a word are feasible, I have chosen the one most logical or most commonly used by this scribe.

Physical Layout: As noted above, this edition reproduces the physical layout of HM 128. Marginal demarcations or explanations by the original scribe are printed in the approximate space, approximately where they are located in the manuscript text. Folio breaks in this edition are placed as they occur in the manuscript text. Dropped and enlarged capitals are reproduced as they occur in the text, and are printed in approximately the same size as those in the manuscript (i.e., three, four, five, etc. lines high). Foliation conforms to that of the manuscript, so transcribed page breaks correspond to folio page breaks. The use of a single * indicates a flourish which completes a heading of a line, and fills the remaining space. They might be considered scribal paraphs marking new textual divisions.

Comparison of Book V in HM 125 and HM 128: Book V of HM 128 has been compared to the edition of HM 125 produced by Stacy A. Waters. I am grateful for his gracious sharing of his manuscript work. Major differences between manuscripts have been noted in the footnotes, and some lines often found in other versions which were included in brackets in HM 125 have been inserted in the notes to HM 128. I believe this supplementary comparison has added to the value of this edition, and for his contribution I am grateful to Dr. Waters. Although Professor James H. Morey's edition of Osborn a.13 was being published as this edition was being completed, I am happy to include a couple of his readings for comparison as well.

BIBLIOGRAPHIES

All books and articles mentioned by short title in the introduction or commentary are included in the general bibliography, as are selected works on the historical, political, or religious background of the *Pricke of Conscience*.

A second bibliography of linguistic references and ecclesiastical, classical and other sources is provided by Hoyt Greeson; it contains certain entries duplicated from the general bibliography because they are also specifically pertinent to lexicography. The large volume of related works, reference materials, and catalogues preclude a comprehensive listing, but those most significant to this study have been included in these two bibliographies.

Notes

1. Helen Barr, *Signes and Sothe: Language in the Piers Plowman Tradition*, Cambridge: D.S Brewer.1994, quoting Marie-Louise Uhart, "The Early Reception of 'Piers Plowman,'" unpublished. Ph.D. Dissertation, University of Leicester, 1986, 48.
2. G. H. Russell, "Some Early Responses to the C Version of Piers Plowman," *Viator* 15 (1984), 6–91, 9.
3. Vincent Gillespie. "Vernacular Books of Religion." *Book Production in England: 1375–1475* (Cambridge University Press, 1989), 317–44.
4. In the discussion to follow, the following abbreviations are used: *LALME* refers to *A Linguistic Atlas of Late Mediaeval English*; SMED to *A Survey of Middle English Dialects, 1290–1350: The West Midland Counties.* The conventional abbreviations of English county names follows the practice of *LALME*: Chs, Cheshire; Dby, Derbyshire; Nt, Nottinghamshire; La, Lancashire; Lei, Leicestershire; Nfk, Norfolk; Ox, Oxfordshire; Gl, Gloucestershire; Wrk, Warwickshire; Stf, Staffordshire; Sal, Shropshire; Wor, Worcestershire; Hrf, Herefordshire; Ru, Rutland. LP is the abbreviation for Linguistic Profile, used by the editors of *LALME* when referring to the language characteristic of a given manuscript. LP 8040 is their designation for Huntington MS 128.
5. See Gillis Kristensson, A *Survey of Middle English Dialects, 1290–1350: The West Midland Counties* (Lund: Lund University Press, 1987), pp. 10–12 and Maps 4 and 5. The earlier work is in Samuel Moore, Sanford B. Meech and Harold Whitehall, *Middle English Dialect Characteristics and Dialect Boundaries* (Ann Arbor, 1935), pp. 10–11 and isogloss D on Map I. The L(inguistic) P(rofile) of the Huntington MS. is in *A Linguistic Atlas of Late Mediaeval English*, ed. Angus McIntosh, M.L. Samuels, Michael Benson (Aberdeen: Aberdeen University Press, 1986), III, pp. 534–535.
6. See Kristensson's discussion, pp. 118-121.
7. Kristensson and *LALME* are apparently at odds on the appearance of hull(e) in most of the W.Midl counties. Maps 8 and 9 in *SMED* posit that only in Lei, Nt and Dby do forms without u prevail. *LALME*, IV, p. 198, however, cites several instances of hil and hill in Wrk LP 8040, as already noted above, has hille (3), hul (1) and hull (4).
8. Unfortunately, *LALME* does not provide data for Wor, Bck, Mx and Ex, through whose southern borders the Moor, Meech, Whitehall isogloss passes and out the Thames valley to the east coast. The data *LALME* does provide shows a tentative isogloss that actually runs from 4708 in Bd and northeast to the northern half of Cam, and thence to the northwestern corner of Sx and on to the southern part of Nfk and out to 4670, south of Norwich.
9. Kristensson's survey of the question and argument are at pp. 211–215 of *SMED 1290–1350: The West Midland Counties*.

II
PRICKE OF CONSCIENCE
SOUTHERN RECENSION

[ANONYMOUS]

Prologus.

Here bygynneþ þe ploge on þe prikke of conshceuae þe ferst teller

The myght of the fadur of heuene of goddes power
the wyt of the sone wyth hys gyftes seuene
and the goodnesse of the holy gost
god and lord of alle myghtes most
he be our helpe and oure speed
nowe and euer in al oure need
and specyally at this bygynnyng
and bryng vs alle to a good endyng amen.
Byfore as any thyng was wrought
and at bygynnyng was of ought
And at alle tymes as we schul mene þe same god was in oneheede clere
he vs ene ful in hys godhede
In thre psones and in on onhede
for cryst was eue wyth the fadur and wyth the sone
and the holy goste in onhede eue by wone
and vs as lord in substaunce and beyyng
and euer was wyth outen any bygynnyng
Bygynnyng of hym myght neuere none be
for eue he was ful god in tuyte
And he ys euer wys and ful of wyt
and as lord almyghty in his trone sytt
thulke myght was euer wyth hym in his trone
for neuere was god but he alone
Holy god ys þe bygynnynge and þe endyng of alle þyng

The same god sothely was the begynnyng
and the ferst maker of alle thyng
wyth oute bygynnynge the schulep hym callen
and endeles lord of creaturs alle
And ende of alle thyng wyth oute ende ys he
for so men may in holy bokes fynde and y se
And as he was the ferste maker of alle thyng
so schall he at the laste make the endyng
of alle thyng bothe in heuene and in helle
of men and feude and angelys to dwelle
The whyche aftyr this lyfe schuley eue loue
and alle other creatures to beth be y dyue
he but god that man made and the warld bygan
vs nowe and eue schal be bothe god and man
Alle thyng wyth his myght made he

Prologue: God's Power

Here bygynneþ þe p(ro)loge on the prikke of conscientie . þ(a)t ferst telleþ he myght of the fadur of heuene.   of goddess power.

                                              power

     The wyt of the sone wyth hys ȝyftes seuene   wisdom, gifts

     And the goodnesse of the holy gost

5   God and lord of alle myȝtes most

     He be our helpe and owre speed   helper

     Nowe and euere in al owre need

     And specyally at the bygynnyng

     And bryng us alle to a good endyng. Amen

10   Byfore ar any thing was wrought   created

     And ar bygynnyng was of ought   anything

     And ar alle tymes as we schul mene. Þe same god was in onhede clene.[1]   indicate, unity

     He ys eu(er)e ful in hys godhede.

     In thre p(er)sones and in on onhede   one, unity

15   For cryst was eu(er)e wyth the fadur and wyth the sone

     And the holy goste in onhede eu(er)e by wone   in one

     And ys as lord in substaunce and beyȝyng   essence, being

     And euer was withouten any bygynnyng

     Bygynnyng of hym myght neuere none be

20   For eu(er)e he was ful god in t(ri)nite

     And he ys euere wys and full of wytt   intelligence

     And as lord almyghty in his trone sytt   throne

     Thulke myght was euere wyth hym in his trone

     For neuere was God but he alone.

25   **How god is þe bigynnynge and þe endyng of alle þyng.**

     The same god suche was the bygynnyng

     And the ferst makere of alle thyng   creator

     Wyth out bygyninge we schulleþ hym calle

     And endeles lord of creatures alle

30   And ende of alle thyng wyth oute ende ys he

     For so me(n) may in holy bokes fynde and yse

     And as he was the ferste maker of alle thyng

     So shall he at the laste make the endyng

     Of all thyng bothe in heuene and in helle

35   Of man and fende and angelys to dwelle

     The wyche aftyr this lyf schulleþ eu(er)e lyue

     And alle othir creaturys to deth be ydryue

     Ac but god that man made and the world bygan

     Ys nowe and eu(er)e schall be both god and man.

40   Alle thyng wyth his myght made he

---

[1] The scribe has run two lines together on one line; the space under l. 12 appears to have been erased, as has the word "euere" on line seven.

23

	For wyth owte hym may no thyng be	f. 1v	
	Alle thyng he ordeyned aftyr his wylle[1]		
	In here kyndes for to stonde stylle		natures
	Wherfore creaturs that dombe beth		dumb
45	Ne conneth no wyt[2] ac bux(ou)n[3] hem me(n) seth		obedient
	To loue[4] hym as the boke wytnesseth ywys		
	In here manere and as here kynde ys		
	For all thyng that he hath wrought		
	That foloweþ his kynde and passeþ it nought		
50	Loueþ here makere and hono(ur)eth in his kynde		
	And so in that man(er)e thei haueþ hym in mynde.		
	Setthe the creat(ur)es that haueþ reso(u)n non		Since
	Loueth hym in the kynde that they beþ on		
	Than owte man that hath skyle and fey		ought, reason, faith
55	His creat(ur)e to hon(ou)r by all maner wey		
	And nat to be of wurce condycyon		
	þanne the creatures that beth wyth owte reso(u)n		
	Ffor of all thyng that god made more and lasse		
	Man ys most p(ri)ncipal and schall all othir passe		surpass
60	As ȝe schall here her aftyrward sone		
	All thyng that god made was for man alone.		
	¶ God to mannyskynde hadde grete delit	**How god made al þis**	
	Whanne þ(a)t he ordeyned for mannys p(ro)fit	**world for mannys**	
	Heuene and erthe and all the world brod	**sake.** [5]	
65	And all oþ(ir) thyng ac man to the laste ende abod		awaited
	And þo he hym made to his lyknesse in semely stat(ur)e		fitting
	And as hym that wast most wurthi creat(ur)e		
	Of alle othir bestes the whiche haue kynde		
	And ȝaf hym all so wyt, reson, and mynde		gave
70	Eu(er)e for to knowe bothe good and ylle		
	And ther to god ȝaf hym wytt at wylle		
	Bothe for to chese and for to holde		choose. maintain
	Good othir euel and whethir that he wolde		
	And all so god ordeynyd man for to dwelle		
75	And for to lyue on erthe in flesch and in felle		skin
	And to knowe his werkes and hym to hono(ur)e		
	And his hestes for to kepe in euery houre		commandments
	And ȝif he to god be bux(ou)n bycome		
	To the endeles blys he schall be y nome		taken
80	And ȝif he leue goddes hestys and to synne wende		go

---

[1] Five couplets beginning here–ll. 41-51–have each been bracketed by the scribe ln the right margin.

[2] ... lack reason or have no reason."

[3] Probably is *bux(ou)m*, which may be interchangeable with *bux(ou)n*.

[4] Possible erasure of the letter *s* after *love* here; extra space strengthens the likelihood of erasure. Other corrections by the *Piers* rubricator occur at lines 63, 65, 66, 69, and 80 on this folio.

[5] These marginal glosses in red ink are limited to the Prologue. The first use of the dotted *y* (in *mannys*) recurs throughout the *Pricke of Conscience* but especially in erasures. Charles Moorman (*How to Edit a Medieval Manuscript*, p. 20) associates a dotted *y* with a 1437–50 date, but they are found in earlier, i.e. Anglo-Saxon, texts as well. Derived from Latin the dotted *y* became much more prevalent in vernacular languages about the fifteenth century. The dotted *y* began to replace the thorn (þ) but was still pronounced as *th* as in "ye olde," *the old* .... The three marginal glosses are slightly larger in size than the text.

	The harde peynes of helle schullen be his ende	f. 2r	
	Wherfore he¹ may be y holde as a man wood		considered, mad
	Þat cheseth the euyl and leueth the good.		
	Sutthe that god made man of most dignyte		Since
85	And of alle creat(ur)es euere ys most fre		generous / noble
	Ffor aftyr his lyknesse he made hym ywys		surely
	As he that schulde haue part of hys blys		
	And most good to hym eu(er)y god ȝyueth		gives
	Þenne to any othir thyng that on erthe lyueth		
90	For whan that adam hadde don amys		wrong
	And for synne was brought into gret anguys²		
	God wolde take mankynde for his sake		lives
	And for his loue deth ther aftyr take		
	And wyth his blood hym aȝen bought		
95	And to his endeles blys hym aȝen brought		again
	Thus gret loue god tho ȝau to man		
	And many othir benefices to hym wan.		bestowed
	Wherfore uche man bothe lered and lewyd		each
	Schulde thenk on that loue þ(a)t god to hym schewyd		
100	And alle his benefices haue in his mynde		
	That he hath euere y do to al mankynde		
	And therto hym serue bothe day and nyȝt		
	For so may he do goddys wylle aryȝt		
	And hys wyttes spenden in his seruise		
105	And hem well by sett in eche man(er) wyse		fashion
	Ffor bote a man knowe kyndely what god ys		unless, by nature
	And hym self al so that he be on of his		one
	And howe a man greuyth god that doth nouȝt wel		
	And maketh hym for synne bothe fers and fel		fierce, dreadful
110	And all so howe m(er)ciful god ys at al assay		under any circumstances
	And therto g(ra)cyous ynow to alle mennys pay		enough, satisfaction
	And how ryȝtful he ys and how soþfast		truthful
	And eu(er) more hath ybe bothe ferst and last		
	And what he doth uche day to al mankynde		
115	Þis schulde eu(er)y man knowe and haue in his mynde.		
	Ffor the ryȝt wey that ledeth man to heuene blys		
	And that bryngeth man out of all anguys		
	Pryncypally ys the wey of all mekenesse		
	Drede in the loue of god in all sympulnesse		fear, simplicity
120	Þa(n) may þe way of wysdam be nome . in to which way no ma(n) may come.³		taken

---

¹Huntington Manuscript 125 reads ȝe here.
²Scribal corrections occur here at l. 92 and at ll. 97 and 100. The original text is undecipherable.
³The scribe has again run two rhymed lines together as if they were one and places a caesura or pause between them.

	Wyth oute full knowyng of god heere	f. 2v	here
	And of his myȝhtes and werkes so dere		
	Ac er that he may thilke knowyng wynne	**How a man schal knowe**	
	Him be houeth to knowe hym self wyth ynne	**hym self wiþynne.**	benefits
125	Elles he ne may no knowyng haue		
	Of þ(e) forsayd way of wysdam no it craue		previous, desire
	But sum(m)e men haue good undyrstondynge		
	Ac ȝut they beþ in many thyngys unknowynge		
	And of sum(m)e thynges haue thyng ryȝt none		
130	Þe wyche myȝt him stere goddys wylle to done.		Stir / steer
	Suche men hadde nede to lerne euery day		
	How thei schulde here lyf lede in godes lay		law
	And to knowe what myȝt hem stere and lede		guide
	To mekenesse and to loue and god forto drede		
135	The wyche ys the way as y seye y wys		surely
	That ledeth a man to heuene where ys eu(er)e blys		
	In grete p(er)ell of soule ys thulke man		
	Þat hath wytt and mynde and no good ne kan		knowing
	Ne wyl nat lerne to knowe be no sawe[1]		saying / teaching
140	The werkes of god and of his holy lawe		
	And knoweth nat what hym self ys at no reste		
	But euere lyueth forth as an unskylfull beste		irrational beast
	That hath nothir wyt, skyle, no mynde		
	Ac euere lyueth aȝens his owne kynde		against, own nature
145	Ffor he excuseth nouȝt his unkonynge		ignorance
	That useth not his wyt in lernynge		mind
	And namely of thyng that he schulde knowe		
	The whiche his herte schulde make lowe		
	And he that lytul kan schulde lerne more		knows
150	To knowe what hym nedeth in godes lore		precepts
	Ffor an unkonnyng man thorowh lernynge		
	May be brought to good undyrstondynge		
	Of many thynges to knowe and to see		
	What haueth y be and ȝut schulleth be		has been
155	That to mekenesse myȝt stere ys wylle		guide his
	God to loue and to drede and to fle all ylle.		
	Many man hath likyng tryfles to here		
	And to ydelnesse setteþ all his chere		heart
	And eu(er)e ys[2] besy in wylle and in thought		
160	To lerne thyng þ(a)t þe soule helpeȝ nought		

---

[1] The entire line has been erased, as have been parts of lines 138, 143. 144, 146, 161 and 162. I offer a representative sample of corrections throughout the manuscript rather than an exhaustive list. The corrector may be the *Piers* rubricator who corrected most non-auto-corrections of *Piers*.

[2] This is another instance of the dotted *y* used throughout, but in higher proportion by the emender in his corrections. See folio 1v, footnote 5.

	And thyng that nedful were for to knowe	f. 3r	
	To lestne or to lerne many beth wol slowe.		listen, excessively slow
	Ther fore¹ no wondyr it ys thow thei gon amys		though, wrong
	For euere in derknesse here goyng ys		
165	All oute of the ly3te of undyrstondyng		
	Of thyng that byfalleþ to ry3t knowyng		
	Ther fore euery c(ri)stene man and womma(n)		Christian
	That has wit and mynde and reso(u)n kan		
	Schulde eu(er)e be besy by alle wey		
170	To lerne all thyng that bylongeth to the fey		faith
	And so undyrstonde bothe lowde and stylle		
	Whiche ys the good wey and whiche ys the ylle		bad
	And he that the ry3t way of knowyng wol loke		
	Schulde bygynne thus as it is wryte in boke		
175	To knowe ferst hym self in all clannesse		
	For so may he come to all mekenesse		
	Ffor that ys the grond of alle vertues to laste		ground
	In the whiche alle vertues may be set faste		
	Ffor he that wel knoweth and ther to kan se		
180	What hym selfe was and ys and aftyr schall be		
	The more wysur man he may be told		wiser
	Whethir that he be 3ong othir old		
	Therfore eche wys man moste ferst lere		
	To knowen hym self p(ro)purlyche here		
185	And 3if knowe hym self wyth ynne kyndely		by nature
	Þanne schalt he knowe god the more veryly		truly
	And on hys endynge the more hys thowth caste		thought
	And on the dredful day that schal come laste.		
	He schulde also knowe þe betre what this world ys		
190	The which ys full of pompe and pryde y wys		I believe
	And lete awey folye and fowle lustes alle		give up
	And thenk what schall aftyr this lyfe falle		befall
	Ffor knowyng of alle thys schulde hym lede		
	To haue mynde of mekenesse and of dred		fear
195	Ffor so may a man come to good leuynge		
	And at the laste to good endyng hym brynge		
	And whan he schall out of this world wende		go
	He schall come to the lyf that ys wyth outen ende.		
	The bygynnyng of this p(ro)cesse y wys		
200	Ryght knowyng of a man hym self it ys		

---

[1] Several corrections beginning here on this page seem to be made by *Piers* rubricator and corrector.

	Ac sum(m)e men haueth meche lettynge	f. 3v	hindrance
	þat thei mowe nat haue full knowyng	**What þyng letteþ**	
	Of hem self that thei schulde ferst knowe	**a man to knowe**	
	And euere with mekenesse make hem lowe	**himself**	lowly
205	Ac of this mater foure thynges y¹ fynde		
	That maketh mennynes² wyttes blynde		
	And the unknowynge of hem self letteth		hinders
	Þorowh the whiche ofte hym self they forsetteth		impede themselves
	Wherfore seynt bernard bereth wytnesse to us		
210	And makeþ hys wrytyng that sayþ thus		
	Forma . favor populi sensus iuvenilis opesque		
	*Surripuere tibi noscere³ quid sit homo.*⁴		
	That is favor of folk and myche fayrnesse		
	And the wytt of ȝowthe and grete rycchesse		youth
	By reueth a man ryȝt reso(u)n and mynde		deprive ... of
215	For to knowe what he ys of kynde.		
	Thus these foure lettyth his ynsyght		obstruct / hinder
	That he forȝeteth hym self out ryȝt		
	And maketh his herte proud and hautayn		haughty
	And swythe f(ra)ward fro god ys⁵ sou(er)ayn		very disobedient
220	Ffor thes foure norscheþ bothe pomp and p(ri)de		nurse
	And makeþ othir synnes on hem to abyde		
	Ffor in what man on of thes foure ys		
	Selde ys seye any mekenesse y wis.		
	Also thei letteth a man that he may nat se		
225	The maneres of thys world so full of vanyte		
	Ne the tyme of deth whan that it schal come		
	Ne whan that he schal to the dome be nome		judgment, taken
	Ne he kan undyrstonde nothur yse		nor
	The perels that aftyr his lyfe schulleþ be		dangers
230	To eche synfull man that loueth folye		
	Ne blys that goode schull haue so hie		
	Ac in delytes setteþ her herte faste		
	And fareth as her lif schulde ay laste		acts, always
	And ȝyueth hem to all manere of ydelnesse		
235	And to all thyng that towcheþ wrecchidnesse		
	Ac suche men beth nat wyth reso(u)n ladd		lead
	But beþ in her folyes euere y lyche sadd		alike
	And what they schulde drede þey knowe ryȝt nought.		
	Therfore thei haueth no drede in her thought		

---

¹ This is yet another instance of the use of the dotted *y* used in higher proportion by the emender in corrections. See folio 1v, footnote 5.
² Likely a scribal error for *menyes*.
³ Stacy A. Waters' transcription of HM 125 has *nascere* here.
⁴ "Beauty, good will of the people, the passion and strength of youth keep you from knowing what man is" [Pseudo-Bernard, *PL* 184, col. 490]. This and other Latin quotations are under- and overlined in red ink (e.g. two red lines around a one-line quotation, three red lines around a two-line quotation, four red lines around a three-line quotation, etc.).
⁵ Probably meant to be *hys*.

240	And that ys for defaute of unknowyng	f. 4r	
	Of thynk that myght hem to drede brynge		thing
	Ʒut sum(m)e men woll nat undyrstonde		
	Suche thyng that mygth hem bryng to schonde		destruction
	Ffor thei woll nowht here but thyng that hem payeþ.		satisfies
245	Therfor david in the sawt(er) book sayth		Psalter
	Noluit intelligere ut bene ageret.[1]		
	He sayth he hath no wyl to be snel		quick
	Ne to undyrstonde owt for to do wel.		anything
	Thes wordes beth sayd by hem here		
250	Þat wyl nothur undyrstonde no lere		
	Ffor to drede god and to don his wylle		
	Ac foloweþ her lykynges and leueþ ylle		
	And for defaute of trewe fey that may be		
	For they beleueth no thyng but ʒif thei it se		
255	Ac gruccheþ whan they schulle eny good lere.		murmur
	Therfore sayth the p(ro)fit on this manere:		
	Non crediderunt sed[2] *murmuraverunt.*[3]		
	The prophete sayth thei beleuyd nought		
	Ac grucchede and were agreuyd in her thought.		grumbled
260	Thus fareth many men that byleueþ no thynge		
	That men hem telleth aʒen her lykynge		
	But gruccheþ gretly and wexeþ all froward		
	Whan me(n) telleþ hem eny thyng þat thynkeþ hem hard		
	Summe conneþ se in boke and suche thing rede		can
265	Ac lyghtnesse of herte byreueþ hem that drede		deprives
	So þat it ne may nought wyth hem dwelle		
	As our lord thus sayth in the gospelle:		
	Qui ad tempus credunt et in te(m)pore		
	temptac(i)onis recedunt.[4]		
	He sayth tyl a tyme some by leuen a thyng		
270	And passeþ ther fro in tyme of fondyng		temptation
	Also sayþ ther to the good p(ro)phete davyd		
	In a psalme of the saut(er) that accordeþ þ(ere) wyth:		psalm, Psalter
	Et crediderunt[5] *verbis eius et laudaverunt laudem eius.*		
	Cito fecerunt obliti sunt operum eius et non		
	sustinuerunt consiliu(m) ei(us):[6]		
	He sayth in his wurdes they be leued[7] wel		
275	And preysed his dedes as they couþe some del.		
	Ac sone they hadden done and his werkes for ʒete		forgotten
	And thought of his conseil no more to undyrʒete.		perceive
	Suche men beþ euere wel unstedefaste		inconstant / wavering

---

[1] "To do good they have no knowledge" [Jer. 4:22; this and all future references to biblical works derive from the Douay-Rheims translation].

[2] Waters' transcription of HM 125 reads *et* rather than *sed*.

[3] "They believed not his word, and they murmured" [Psalm 105: 24 f.].

[4] "For they believe for a while, and in time of temptation, they fall way" [Luke 8:13].

[5] HM125 inserts an *in* here.

[6] 'And they believed his words and they sang his praises. Quickly they had done [with him], forgot his works; and they waited not for his counsel' [Psalm 105: 12-13].This quotation is not included in HM 125 as transcribed by Waters.

[7] Although the text reads "be leued" the sense appears to be "beleued" *(believed)*. Some scribes treat words auch as "be leued" as one word with a prefix sometimes separated, and sometimes joined to the main word. Since both readings are legitimate, this explanation will not be repeated.

Part I. Man's Wretchedness

	That nothur loue no drede may w(i)t(h) ynne hem laste	**Prima Pars**[1] f. 4v	
280	Ac who so kan nat drede he may sone lere		knows, fears
	That wele here this tretys wyth a god ere		treatise, ear
	Thorow which he may loue god and drede sekurly[2]		surely
	And goode dedes do and fle all foly.		flee, folly
	Therfore this boke is yn Englyssh drawe		composed
285	Of dyuerse matere that beth of goddes lawe		
	To the lewyd man that beth not undyrstonynge		ignorant
	And of latyn speche beth nauȝt wel connynge		
	To make hem self wel ferst to knowe		first
	And synnes and vanytes a way for to thorowe		
290	And for to clepe hem to the ryght drede		name
	Whan thei this tretys wele heere or rede		well hear
	The whiche schal sture here conscience w(i)t(h)ynne		stir
	And thorowh thilk drede may alone bygynne		such
	Wyth the confort of the ioyes of heuene clere		
295	As men may fynde aftyrward and here.		
	This boke as it self bereth wytnesse.[3]		
	In seuene paraties[4] ys dyvyded by euenenesse.		evenly
	¶ The ferst partye to knowe and to haue in mynde[5]		part
	Ys of the wrecchidnesse of mannys kynde		nature
300	The secunde ys of the condycyon and the manere		
	Of the unstabulnesse of the world here.		Mutability / transcience
	The thrydde partye ys in this book to rede		
	Of the byt(ter) deth and whi it ys to drede.		
	The feorthe partye y wys ys of purgatorye		fourth, surely
305	Where that soules beth clansed of her folye.		sin
	The vifte partye ys of the day of dome		judgment
	And of the tokenes that byfore schull come		
	The syxte partye is of the harde peynes of helle		
	Where that dampned men schulleþ eu(er)e dwelle.		damned
310	The seueth partye is of the ioyes of heuene.		seventh
	And thus ys this book maked in partyes seuene		
	And in eu(er)y partye eche man fynde may		
	Dyuerse materys who wele assay.		test
	Here bigynneþ þe ferste part of þis book þ(a)t telleþ of mannys wrecchidnesse.[6]		
315	The ferste part of þis book in soþnesse		truthfulness
	Ys ymad of mannys wrecchidnesse		
	Ffor whan god al þyng had mad of nought		
	Than of þe foulest mattere man was wrought		

---

[1] Previous headings of "Prologus" are now replaced by "Prima pars;" the First Part begins five lines from bottom of folio. A blue paraph marks the rectos and a red paraph marks the versos throughout.

[2] The last seven words are written over an erasure here as are the last four words of line 284.

[3] The conclusion of the Prologus thus sums up the treatise's purpose of educating---man should know himself and God; written in the vernacular for easier comprehension, it lays out its logical seven-part organization. See Howell Chickering's "Rhetorical Stimulus in the *Prick of Conscience," Medieval Paradigms: Essays in Honor of Jeremy du Quesnay Adams,* ed Stephanie Hayes-Healy. 2 vols. New York, 2005, vol 1, 191-230, for an excellent survey of the poet's rhetorical devices.

[4] MED attests to no such form. This is probably a scribal error for *parties*.

[5] Interestingly, the dotted *y* is used here but not in the next two lines, containing several *y*'s. See folio 1v, footnote 5.

[6] Written in red ink; the same red and blue flower design as in the initial "T" of line 2 is repeated in small in this "T" but without faces in the outer frame.

	That was of erthe two skyles forto holde:¹	f. 5r	reasons
320	That on ys for our lord it wolde		one, because
	Of fowle mat(er) make man as in despyt		scorn
	Of lucifer hym ther wyth forto edwyt		reproach
	Whan he fel fram heuene to helle for hys p(ri)de		
	And of alle hem that fellen wyth hi(m) in that tyde		time
325	Ffor thei schulden haue the more schendschipe		shame
	And the more sorowe whan thei ther of tok kepe		
	That the man of so fowle mater schulde dwelle		
	In that place so fair² fro whennys they felle.		fair
	That othur skyle ys this who so kan it se		
330	For a man schulde the more meke be		
	Euer whan he seþ and thenkeþ in his thought		
	Of how fowl mater he ys ferst wrought		created
	Ffor god thorowh his goodnesse and his owne myght		
	Wolde saue that place in heuene so bryght		
335	That whas³ made voyde thorowh the synne of p(ri)de		empty
	And was defowled by eueryche syde.		polluted
	Ac thorowh vertu of holy mekenesse		
	That is ay contr(ar)y to all prowdnesse		
	He thought it amende in som wyse		to remedy
340	Wher by a man schuld lucyfer despyse		renounce / spite
	Ffor ther may no man into heuene come		
	But he be meke and in drede buxome		obedient
	And that proueth the gospel as it telluth us		
	Howe god saide to al his discyples rych⁴ thus		thus so
345	*Nisi efficiamini sicut parvuli: non intrabitis*		
	*in regnu(m) celoru(m)*⁵ .		
	But ȝif ȝe be god sayth as a lytyl childe		
	That ys to sey bothe meke and mylde		
	Ȝe schulleþ nat entre by no man(er) wey		type of
	In to the kyngdom of heuene þe sothe to sey		truth
350	Ac no thyng may make more meke a man		
	Þan thenke in his herte as ofte as he can		
	How that he ys mad of fowl matere		
	&⁶ ys no thyng elles bot erthe here		
	Ffor thus sayth a clerke as y yow say		
355	What is a man but fowle erthe and clay		
	And poudre that sone wiþ þe wynd breketh		powder
	And ther fore seint iob thus to god speketh:⁷		
	Memento queso q(uod) sicut lutu(m) feceris		
	*me et in pulvere(m) deduces me.*⁸		

---

1 The pace picks up here as the author begins a narrative rather than discursive discussion; the style seems a bit more emphatic and forceful than that of the Prologus.
2 The writer demonstrates that both Lucifer and humans are made of *fowle mater*, the more to spite Lucifer because humans have the chance to dwell "in that place so *fair* from whence they, i.e., Lucifer and his angels, fell."
3 A dialectical spelling of *was* used in certain shires such as Warwickshire where H.M. 128 is written here.
4 Although the scribe has not written a final *t*, he has crossed the *h*: the poet probably intended *rycht*.
5 "Unless you become as little children, you shall not enter into the kingdom of heaven" [Matt. 18: 3].
6 The ampersand beginning this line appears to be scribed over an erasure.
7 Making Old Testament figures into New Testament saints is not a unique anachronism; nor is the device of dialogue uncommon, as seen in *The Pylgrymage of the Lyf of Man* in which the Pilgrim Soul speaks to Archangel Michael and others. See also Paul's treatment of OT figures in *Hebrews* 11:1-40 where he establishes christian Figuralism or Typology.
8 "Remember, I beseech thee, that thou hast made me as the clay, and thou wilt bring me into dust again" [Job 10:9]. Job here reads *reduces* rather than *deduces*.

	He sayth þenk lord how thow madest me f. 5v	
360	Of fowle erthe and clay here for to be	
	Ryght so schal y aȝen turne at my laste ende	return
	To erthe and poudur and al to nawht wende.	powder, nothing
	Than sayth our lord of all myghtes moste	power
	To eche man that haþ on hym his holy goste	
365	*Memento homo quod cinis es et cinerem reverteris.*[1]	
	He sayth thenk man that askys thu art now	ashes
	And at the laste to ashes torne aȝen schalt thow	ashes return
	Than this scholde eche man haue in mynde	
	And knowe þe wrecchidnesse of his owne kynde	misery
370	Ffor al mannes lyf may icast be	conceived
	P(ri)ncypaly in þese partyes thre	parts
	The whiche beth þese to our und(ur)stondynge	
	Bygynnyng mydward and endynge	
	Thes thre parties beth spaces y tolde	
375	Of the lif of eche man ȝong and olde.	young
	Of þe[2] bigynnynge of mannes lif.	
	The bygynnyng of man(n)es lif that ferst ys	
	Conteyneth many wrecchidnessys ywis	
	Terfore[3] y wol or y forther passe	before, further
380	Schewe what eche a man in his bygynnyng wasse.	was
	Man was byȝete as it is well knowe	begotten
	Of foul sede al wyth synne sowe	sown
	And he wel synfully conceyvyd was	
	Wyth ynne his modur wombe in a p(ri)ue plas[4]	private
385	And thus his herburgh[5] was there y dyght	lodging
	As david wetnessyt it ^[i(n)][6] hys book aryth[7]	rightly
	Ecce eni(m) iniq(ui)tatibus concept(us) su(m) et	
	in pec(ca)tis concepit me mat(er) mea.[8]	
	Lo david sayth what a mannys kynde ys	
	In wrecchidnesse y am conceyvyd y wys[9]	misery, conceived
390	And my modur haþ conceyued me	
	In many synnes and meche caytyfte	captivity
	Ffor there dwelleþ a man in a derk dungeon	
	And in a foul stede full of corypcyon	place, corruption
	Wherynne he hadde non oþur fode	
395	But wlatsu(m) glet and fulthede of blode.	disgusting gore / slime
	Aftirward whan he was owt y brought al bare	out, brought
	Fram that dongeon his modur wombe wyth care	dungeon, womb
	And was y bore into this worlde lyght	

---

[1] [Remember, man that] dust thou art, and into dust thou shalt return" [Gen. 3:19].

[2] These first two words *Of þe*, and the capital below are smeared or worn away, the red ink barely visible.

[3] No doubt the author intended *Therfore*; however, MED indicates *terfore* is a recognized variant spelling.

[4] i.e... in the genitalia.

[5] The scribe has not indicated a medial caesura as he does elsewhere, but left a space where one would naturally fall.

[6] A carat leads the reader to an inserted "i" and abbreviation sign above the line in the same hand.

[7] This appears to be a scribal error for *aright*.

[8] "For behold I was conceived in iniquities; and in sins did my mother conceive me" [Psalm 50: 7 in *Innocent III, De Miseria Conditionis Humanae*, ed. & tr. Robert E. Lewis, Athens, GA: University of Georgia Press, 1978].

[9] This dramatic, vivid description of man's loathfulness and powerless dependence begins here with the image of an infant-as-man, in a uterus dark as a dungeon, eating disgusting gore as food.

	He hadde on hym nothur strenkþe no myght	f. 6r	
400	Neythur for to go nothur for to stonde		
	Neþur to crepe on fote no on honde.¹		nor
	Than hath a man lasse myght than a beste		
	Whan þat he is bore and semeþ leste		least
	Ffor whan a best ys y bore it may go		
405	And doþ his kynde for euer mo		
	Ac man haþ no myght in hys ȝonghede		youth
	He not whedur to go but as me(n) doþ him lede		knows not, where
	Ffor thanne he ne may noþur go ne crepe		
	But lygge and sprawle and crye and wepe		lie
410	Ffor unneþe ys a child fullyche y bore		scarcely
	That it ne cryeþ as it were forlore		lost
	And by that ylke cry sum(m)e man knowe can		
	Whethur it be a man or a womman		
	Ffor whan it ys ybore it cryeþ wa		
415	And so ȝif it be a man it seyth . A .		
	That is the ferst lett(er) of the name		
	Of our fadur adam that putte us in blame		
	And ȝif it of wom(m)anes kynde be		female gender
	Whan it is ybore it² sayþ E . E .		
420	E ys the ferst lett(er) who so takeþ hede		
	Of the name of eue þat brought us alle in drede.		terror
	Therfore a clerk made in his man(er)e		style
	A vers that is wryte of that mat(er)e		
	*Dicentes E. vel .A. quot quot nascuntur ab eva.*³		
425	He seyþ alle thei that comeþ owt of eue		
	Ne may be no way thes lette(r)s leue		
	Whan þei beþ y bore what so thei be		
	They sey ferst . A . oþur for sothe E .		or, indeed / truly
	This ys in this lyf all our bygynnyng		
430	After our burþ sorowe and wepyng		
	To the whiche our wrecchidnesse steryþ us		moves
	And þerfore innocent [ ]⁴ seyþ thus:		
	*Omnes nascimur eiulantes . ut nat(ur)e n(os)tre miseria(m) exprimamus*⁵.		
	He sayþ we be ferst y bore eu(er)ychone		everyone
435	Makyng sorowe and meche rewlyche mone		pitiful
	Ffor to schewe thulke grete wrecchidnesse		
	Of our kynde that ys full of febulnesse.		
	Naked we come hid(er) and all bare		

---

¹ The author uses this humbling picture of humanity as foil to and warning against Lucifer's pride, reiterating l. 324.
² The excessive ink used for this word does not obliterate the letters.
³ "All as are born of Eve, saying E or A" [*Innocent III, De Miseria*, ed. Robert E. Lewis, p.102. *PL* 217, col 705].
⁴ The words *the pope* have been unevenly excised and left blank, but the date of excision is uncertain. Several such deletions of *the pope* occur later in the text, probably post-Reformation excisions.
⁵ "All wailing, in order to express the misery of our nature" [Job 1:21, in *Innocent III*, ed. Lewis, p. 102].

	And ryght so we schulle hennys fare	f. 6v	
440	On thes tymes þenketh who any good kan		knows
	For thus sayth iob the wyse man		
	Nudus egressus su(m) ex utero mat(ri)s mee et		
	nudus rev(er)tar illuc.[1]		
	Naked he sayth in to this world y cam		
	And so of her wombe my modur me nam		mother, took
445	And naked y schall hennys tornen away		return
	And so schull we alle at the laste day.		
	Thus is a man at hys ferst comynge		
	Al naked and bryngeþ wyth him no thynge		
	Bote a reyme that ys fowle and all wlatsom[2]		placenta, disgusting
450	That ys his garnament whan he schal forthe com		garment / clothing
	And that nys but a blody skyn swyþe þynne		extremely
	Where wyþ he is ybore and y wrappyd ynne		
	Whan he in his modur wombe lay		
	Me thinkeþ he was tho of cold[3] aray.		then, in baleful condition
455	Thus ys a man made as ȝe mowe se		
	In mychel wrecchednesse and caytyfite.[4]		
	And ther to he schal leue but a fewe dayes		
	And seint iob to us thus opynly sayes:		
	Homo natus de muliere brevi vivens temp(or)e.[5]		
460	Seint iob sayth the man that ys bore of wom(m)a(n)		
	Leueþ but a schort tyme and sone bycomeþ wan		lives, pale
	Also eche man ys y bore to no thyng ellys		
	But to t(r)yvaile and tere as thes clerkes tellys:		tears
	Homo nascit(ur) ad laborem sicut avis ad volatum.[6]		
465	He saith man is maad to t(ra)vayle aryght		work
	As eu(er)y fowle ys y made by kynde to his flyght		bird
	Lytyl reste he haþ in his lif y wys		
	But in hys t(ra)vail euere besy he ys.		
	Ȝut is a man whan he is ybore		
470	Þe fendys childe and fram god y lore		
	Euere forto he.[7] be thorowe g(ra)ce ynome		
	And to holy baptysme þerafter come		
	Therfore it ys good that eche man undyrstonde		
	That all his bygynnyng ys full of sorowe and schonde.		shame
475	**Here bigynneþ þe mydward of mannes lif.**		middle
	That othur partye of the lif that men calleþ		
	Ys the mydward that aftur ȝowþe sone falleþ		youth
	The whiche ys fram the ferste bygynnyng		

---

[1] "Naked came I out from my mother's womb, and naked shall I return thither" [Job 1:21; also in *Innocent III*, ed. Lewis. p. 104]. The first use of mother refers to "birth mother," the second metaphorically to Mother Earth.
[2] This unpleasant, even gruesome, description of childbirth further diminishes man's status and nature.
[3] The space under "c" of cold has been erased, as has been "hys" (447), "ellys" (462) and "it ys good" (473).
[4] The "y"s in this word are dotted. See folio 1v, footnote 5.
[5] "Man born of woman, living a short time …" [Job 14:1, Douay-Rheims translation: in *Innocent III*, ed., Lewis, p 107].
[6] "Man is born to labor just as the bird to fly."
[7] This is an unusal place for a *punctus*. Neither EETS nor TEAMS uses a *punctus*. The EETS edition reads "Ay, til he thurgh grace may com" (548); the TEAMS edition reads "Ay tyl he by grace may come" (548)

	Of mannys lif in to the laste endyng	f. 7r
480	For how a man ys aftyrward fowl bycome	
	Bernard telluth in a reso(u)n that he haþ ynome	stated
	*Homo nichil aliud est qu(am) sperma . saccus stercor(um) et esca vermiu(m)*¹.	
	Seint bernard seyth as the boke us tellys	
	That a man in hys lyf ys no thing ellys	
485	Bot fowl skyn wlatsom to alle men	disgusting
	And a foul sak full of stynkyng fen²	mud
	And wormes fode that thei schullen haue	
	Whan he ys dede and y leid in g(ra)ue	
	Ac som men and wem(m)en fayre thei semeth	
490	To syght wyth oute as many man demeþ	think
	And thei scheweth nought but the white skyn	
	Ac ho so myght openly hem se whith yn³	whoever
	Ffowler careyne myght neuer non be	carrion
	For sothe than me(n)⁴ scholde sone on hem see.	
495	Therfore he that had a scharp insyght	
	And all so clere eyen and all so bryght	
	As a best that me(n) linx calles	beast
	That may se thorowh nyne stone walles	
	Whan lytyl lykyng schuld a man haue	desire
500	To be holde a woma(n) othur after her craue.	or
	Then myght he se wyth oute eny dowte	
	As wel wyth ynne as he may wyth oute	
	And ȝif a man sye hure wyth ynne aryght	see
	Sche were wlatsom for sothe to his syght.	disgusting
505	Thus fowl ys eche man wythynne ywys	
	Thow he holde him selue of any grete p(ri)s	
	Ffor he may eche day here and se	
	What he was and is nowe and aftyr schall be.	
	Ac a prowd man of this takeþ none hede	
510	Ffor him wanteþ reso(u)n that ryght schulde hym lede	he lacks
	Whan he is ȝong and loueth pleyȝynge⁵	
	Or haþ ese and welth at his lykynge	pleasure
	Or ȝif he be brouwȝt in grete wurschipe eke	honor
	What hym self ys than taketh he no kepe	care
515	Ffor hym self than(n)e he knoweþ leste	least
	And fareth as doþ an onresonable beste	

---

¹ "Man is nothing other than sperm, a sack of dung, and food for the worms" [Adapted from Pseudo-Bernard, *PL* 184: col. 490. Also Petrus Cantor, *PL* 198, col. 1757].

² Again, this graphic depiction of man's lowliness---disgusting skin, like a stinking fen, and as worms' food further deprecates him, now from the perspective of tactile and olfactory senses of touch and smell. The revolting sight of a woman's innards follows.

³ The final word of the line, "yn," is written over an erasure as is "may" (498), "wyth ynne" (502), "thow he holde" (506), and "Ffor" (507).

⁴ The abbreviation "me" of "men" is not absolutely clear but the sense calls for it; it may be an abbreviation for the final word position.

⁵ A dialectical spelling of the word "pleyȝynge" here, as is "brouwȝt" (513); neither is listed in the Middle English Dictionary. All such variants will not be noted throughout this edition.

Part I. Man's Wretchedness (517–550)

	That his owne wylle foloweþ and nat ellys	f. 7v	nothing
	As david ther of in the saut(er) bok tellys		Psalter
	Homo cu(m) in honore esset non intellexit.		
	Comparatus est iumentis insipientibus.[1]		
520	He sayth whan man is in wurschipe ybrou3t		honor
	Right good undyrstondyng haþ he nou3t		
	Therfore he may be lykned in flesch and bon		compared
	To bestes that reson ne wyt konneth non		know not
	Therfore eche man that hath wyt and mynde		
525	Schulde thenken y wys on his wrecchid kynde		
	And that he is wyth wrecchidnesse y nome		named
	As al day he may se from his body come		
	Bothe from aboue and from byneþe also		
	Al manere of felthede[2] rennynge euer mo		filth running, more
530	And how fowl he is to mannes syght		
	Seint bernard telleþ to us owtryght		straight out
	Si diligent(er) consideres quid per os quid per		
	nares cet(er)os que meatus corporis tui		
	egredit(ur): vilius sterquiliniu(m) nu(m)quam videres.[3]		
	He saith 3if thow man wylt bysyliche yse		attentively
	And biholde wyturly what thing comeþ of the		plainly
535	What þorow mowþe and nose contynuelly		mouth
	And þorow othur yssues of thi body		orifices
	A fowler matere sye thu neuer non		see
	Than ys man that ys made of flesch and bon		
	Ffor in all the tyme that a man here lyueth		
540	His kynde neuere good fruyt 3eueth		gives
	Wheþur that he lyue schort wyle or long		
	But thing that ys fowl and of stynche strong		stench
	And al ys wlatsomnesse and no thing elles		repulsiveness
	As innocent the pope in a boke telles		
545	*Herbas iniquit et arbores diligent(er) investiga . Ille*		
	de se producu(n)t fructu(m), flores, et frondes . et		
	tu de te lentes et pediculos. Ille de se effundu(n)t		
	oleu(m) vinu(m) et balsamu(m) . et tu de tu sputu(m)		
	urinam et stercus. Ille de se spira(n)t suavitatem		
	odoris . Et tu de te abhominac(i)onem fetoris[4].		
	This grete clerk telluth in his boke		
	Man he saith behold and loke		
	Herbes and tres that doth sprynge		
	And the 3eme what thei forþ brynge		take heed
550	Herbes forth bryngeþ floures and maketh hem sede		

---

[1] "Man with honour, did not understand: he has been compared to senseless beasts" [Douay-Rheims, Psalm 48:21; in *Innocent III*, ed. Lewis, p. 189].

[2] Sensory details, particularly visial, continue to mark the poem with bodily excretions running "ever mo." Smell is noted in l. 543.

[3] "If you carefully consider what passes out through the mouth and nostrils and passageways of your body, you will never behold a more vile dung pit" [Pseudo-Bernard, *PL* 184, col. 489].

[4] "Closely investigate the trees. They produce fruit, flowers, and foliage from themselves, but you, from yourself, nits and scabies. They pour forth oil, wine and balsam from themselves, but you, from yourself spit, urine, and excrement. They exude from themselves a pleasant odor. But you, from yourself an abomination of stench" [adapted from *Innocent III*, ed. Lewis, p. 104].

	And trees bryngeth fruit and maketh hem sprede	f. 8r
	And thu bryngest of thi self here	
	Nytes and luys and other vermyn eu(er)ywhere	Nits, lice
	Of herbes and trees spryngeth bawm good	
555	And oyle and wyn in help of man(nes) food.	
	Ac of the man thyng that fowl doþ stynke	
	As fen and uryn and fowle spattyng of drynke	mud, urine
	Of herbes and trees comeþ swete souour	savor
	Ac of the man cometh stynkyng breþ and sour.	
560	Such as the tres beþ wyth the bowes	boughs
	Suche is the fruit that þ(er)on growes¹	
	Ffor a man ys as a tree that stondeþ somdel hard²	
	Of wham the crop is turnyd al downward	
	And the rote is tu(rn)yd to the firmament	sky
565	As saiþe in hys boke the grete clerk innocent	

Quid est homo s(e)c(un)d(u)m forma(m): nisi queda(m) arbor
  ev(er)sa . cui(us) ra[-]dices sunt crines . trunc(us) est caput cu(m) collo .
  Stipes est p(ec)tus cu(m) alvo rami sunt ulne cum tibiis . frondes
  su(n)t digiti cu(m) ar[-]ticulis . hoc e(st) foliu(m) quod a ve(n)to
  *rapi(tur) et stip(u)la q(u)e a sole siccat(ur).*³

	He saiþ what is a man in schap but as a tre	
	Torned up that schuld be down as men may se	
	Of the whiche the rote is þat þ(er)to bylongeþ	
570	As thilk here that on the hed hongeþ.	that, head hangs
	Than is the stok next the rote growynge	
	Whyche is the heued wyth the nekke folowynge.	head
	The body of thilk tre that is yset ther to	such
	Ys the brest with the wombe also	
575	The bowes beþ the armes wyth the hondes	
	And the legges wyth þe feet þ(a)t þu⁴ upon stondes	stand
	The branches men may by reson calle	
	The toes of the feet and the fingres alle	
	That is the lef that hangeʒ nat faste	leaf
580	For hem wene awey may a wyndes blaste	go
	Ffor a man that ys bothe ʒong and lyght	
	Ne be he neu(er) so stalwurthe in fyght	strong
	And comely of schap and louely of chere	
	ʒit angres and euels mowe hi(m) sore a fere	grief, may terrify
585	And his fairnesse and his strenkþ abate	
	And than hym brynge into a feble state	
	And sone change his fayr colour	

---

[1] A brown spot, perhaps of ink, partially obliterates the "s" of "growes."
[2] John Friedman has kindly noted that the idea of man as an inverted tree probably derives from Aristotle, *De Anima* II, 4.416a and *Poetics*. See Innocent III, *De Miseria Conditionis Humanae*, ed. R. E. Lewis, p. 106.
[3] "What is man as to his shape but a kind of tree turned upside down, whose roots are his hair, the bole is his head with the neck. The trunk is his chest with the belly, the branches are his arms with the legs, the leaves are his fingers with their joints. This is the leaf that is caught by the wind and the straw dried by the sun" [adapted from *Innocent III*, ed. Lewis, p. 106; *PL* 217 cols. 705-706].
[4] These two words are written using superscript letters after the thorns.

38 Part I. Man's Wretchedness (588–625)

	And make hym fade ryght as doth the flour	f. 8v	
	Ffor a flour that is fayr to a mannys sygth		flower
590	Thorw stormes fadyn and leseth here mygth .		through, lose
	Many angres and euelys and myschefes bothe		ailments
	Ofte cometh to a man that beþ to hi(m) ful lothe		
	As feuers and droposy and the iawndyse also		jauntice
	The tisik and the goute and othur maladyes mo .		consumption
595	That makeþ his fayrnesse al away wende		go
	As stormes doth the fayr flour schende.		kill
	This scholde euere be in ensample to us		
	For why seynt iob . in his booke sayth thus		
	Homo quasi flos egredit(ur) et cont(er)itur et		
	fug(i)t velut umbra[1] .		
600	Man he saith that as flour ys bryght		
	Ferst forthe cometh to our erþlyche sytht		
	And his[2] sone y broke and passeþ away		broken
	Ryght as the schawdewe on the some(r)s day		shadow
	And neuer more in the same stat dwelleth		
605	But euer is passyng as iob us telleth.		
	Of all þis the prophet is wytnesse ywys		
	In a psalme of the sawt(er) there he sayth this:		Psalter
	Mane sicut herba transeat mane floreat et transeat vespere		
	Decidat indurat et arescat. Et c(etera).[3]		
	The p(ro)phet seith [seith][4] in thulke cas		that
610	Man passeþ away as doþ the g(ra)s		
	Erlyche at the bygynnyng of the day		
	He flo(ur)eþ and sone passeþ away		blooms
	And at eue it is a down ybrought		
	And so faduth and welkes al to nought.		withers
615	In the gynnyng of man to him was ȝeue		beginning, given
	Nyne hondred ȝere on erthe for to leue		years, live
	As clerkes in bokes ther of bereþ wytnesse		
	That now man(n)es lif is drawe into schortnesse		
	Ffor so wolde God that it scholde be		desires
620	And so he saide him selue once to ise:		
	Non p(er)manebit sp(iri)t(us) meus in ho(m)i(n)e		
	in et(er)nu(m) quia caro est eru(n)t e(ter)na dies		
	illoru(m) centum viginti anni.[5]		
	My gost he saith [ ] schall neu(er) [ ][6] dwelle		
	In man that is mad of flesch and felle		skin
	His daies schull ben to lyuen here		
625	On hundred and ther to twenty ȝere.		

---

[1] "Man [who] cometh forth like a flower, and never continueth in the same state and fleeth like a shadow" [Job 14:2; the Vulgate version appears in Innocent III, ed. Lewis. p. 161].

[2] *His* is a Warwickshire form of *is*.

[3] "In the morning man shall grow up like grass; in the morning he shall flourish and pass away; in the evening he shall fall, grow dry, and wither" [Psalm 89:6].

[4] The redundant *seith* has been lightly crossed out by a scribe.

[5] "My spirit shall not remain in man forever, because he is flesh, and his days shall be one hundred twenty years" [not Isaias, as the scribe suggests, but Gen. 6:3; Lewis attibutes it correctly to *Innocent III*, p. 107].

[6] The erased word of about four letters here and an erased letter between "saith" and "schall" (perhaps an ampersand) are indecipherable. A space remains at both erasures.

	Ac so grete age may no man now bere	f. 9r	
	For deth wol hym in schort tyme dere		harm
	Ffor the complexion of euery man		
	Ys now feblere than it was than.		weaker
630	Therfore man(n)es lyf mot the schort(er) be		must
	Ffor now it ys al þer schortest for to se[1]		
	Ffor eu(er)e the leng(er) that man schal now lyue		
	To the more greua(u)nce he schal al day ben dryue		
	And the lasse thenke that this lyf ys swete		
635	As in the sawt(er) book sayth the holy p(ro)phete		Psalter
	Si autem in potentatib(us) octoginta anni et ampli(us) eor(um) labor et dolor.[2]		
	ʒif in myghtynesse foure score ʒer men beth yfalle		years
	More is here t(ra)vayle and here sorowe w(i)t(h) alle		work
	Ac nowe wel schort(er) beth mennes dayes		
640	As iob the gentyll openly sayes		
	Nunc paucitas dieru(m) meor(um) finiet(ur) brevi.[3]		
	Nowe he saith my schort dayes that fewe were		
	Schulleþ be endyd wyth lytyl tyme here		
	And al so sone as man wexeth olde		grows
645	Þan(n)e bycometh his kynde feble and colde		
	And than(n)e anon chawngeth his complexio(u)n		temperament / humour
	And his maneres torneth in to anothur condycio(u)n		change into
	Ffor than(n)e wexeth his herte heuy and hard		
	And his heued feble and euere adonward		head
650	Than(n)e ryncleþ his face eu(er) more and more[4]		wrinkles
	And wexeth more fowler than it was byfore[5]		becomes
	Hys mynde ys schort whan he outh thenketh		anything
	His nose droppeth and bloweth . his breth stynketh .[6]		
	His sith[7] wexeth dym and loketh undyr his browe		sight, under
655	His bak croketh and gothe stowpyng lowe		bends / curves
	His eren wexeth deue and hard for to here		ears, deaf
	And his tonge in his speche may nat longe duere.		endure
	He is lyghtly wroth and wexeth al framward		angry, stubborn
	And hym torne fram wraþe it ys swithe hard.		so
660	He is coueytous and wel hard holdynge		avaricious
	His chere ys heuy and fowl and lourynge		severe, louring
	He prayseth olde men and holdeth hem wyse		
	And ʒong men hym lyketh to despyse		despise
	He is ofte syk and bygynneth for to grone		
665	And ofte angry and ther of playneth sone .		complains

---

[1] "For now it is the shortest of all."

[2] "If, however, [they live], in power eighty years, greater is their labor and sorrow" [Psalm 89-90; in *Innocent III*, ed, Lewis, p. 107]. Lewis provides a context for this quotation: "The days of our years in themselves are threescore and ten years – if, however, in the strong, fourscore years, most of them are labor and sorrow" [Lewis 106].

[3] "Now [shall] the fewness of my days be ended shortly" [Job 10:20, in *Innocent III*, ed. Lewis, p. 107].

[4] The explicit striking images for which this author is noted are evidenced here in depicting the ravages of old age.

[5] The quality of ink changes here from dark and clear to light and faded.

[6] This line is written over an erasure or faded ink which marks about five lines in this section.

[7] Again, the senses—smell, sight, hearing, taste / speech—are foremost in the author's mind and underlie his imagery.

Part I. Man's Wretchedness (666–705)

    Alle thes thyngs to an olde man falleth   f. 9v   happen / pertain to
    That clerkes p(ro)p(er)tes of old men calleth
    Thus men mowen se who so rede can   may, read
    What beþ þe condycio(u)ns of an olde man
670   And forther more rede we may
    Of the end of man at his deþ day.[1]
    Here bigynneþ þe ende of mannes lif.[2]
    The laste ende of a mannes lyf ys hard
    That is whan he draweþ to the deth ward   draws
675   Ffor whan he is sik in any manere wyse   sick, fashion
    And is so feble that he may nouȝt ryse   not rise
    Thanne beþ men in doute and[3] uncertayn
    Whethur he schal deye or keuere agayn   recover
    Ȝet conneth some men that ben slye   know, cunning
680   Y wyte wheþ(er) he schall lyue or deye
    Thorowh certayne tokenes in pows and breþ   pulse
    That byfalleth whan he is nyhe the deþ.   near
    Thanne bygynneth his front a donward falle
    And his browes bycometh heuy wyth alle
685   Also the lyfte yȝe of hym schul seme lasse   left eye
    And narwer than the tothur er he hen(n)es passe   narrower
    His nose at the poynt schal scharp bycome
    And his chyn schal a down bynome
    His pows schal by stylle wyth oute sterynge   pulse, moving
690   His fete schul wexe colde his wombe chonynge[4]   cleaving asunder, shriveling
    And ȝif a ȝong [deth][5] man nyȝ the deth be   near
    He is euere wakyng for slepe may nat he
    And ȝif an olde man be nyȝ the deth
    He schal fram slepyng hym kepe unneth   scarcely
695   Many man seiþ these tokenes eu(er)ychone
    Beþ of man whan he schal dye sone
    The while a man lyueth he is lyche to a man
    Ac whan he is ded and bycome wan   pale
    Thanne may a man his lyknes y se
700   Al chawnged as it hadde neuere be he   changed
    And whan his lif is broȝte to ende
    Than schal he in that wyse hennes wende   go
    Pore and naked ryght as he hidur come
    Whan he fram his modur wombe was nome   taken
705   Ffor he broughte wyth hym in thulke day   that

---

[1] This dotted *y* does not parallel the undotted *y* of its rhyme *(may)*. But the *y*'s in *agayn* (l.678), *slye* (l.679), and *deye* (l.680), just below are dotted. See folio 1v, footnote 5.

[2] Scribed with slightly larger letters in red ink.

[3] The last three words are scribed over an erasure, as has *man be myȝ* below (l. 693).

[4] Morris' Northern version reads *clinges* (l. 823), Hanna and Wood's reads *clynges*, and Morey's TEAMS edition reads *clyng* (l. 823) "withers or dries up."

[5] The word *deth* is underlined with dots, presumably to cancel it.

	No thyng and so he schal wende away	f. 10r
	But it be onlyche a wyndyng clothe[1]	
	That schal be lappyd aboute hym forsothe	draped
	Ffor whan the lyf passeth fram hym away	
710	Than is he but a lytyl erthe and clay	
	That torneth to more corrupcyon al aboute	
	Than any stynkyng careyne that lyth þer oute	carrion
	Ffor the corrupcyon of his body and in eche syde	
	ʒif it aboue the erþe lygge in eny tyde	time
715	Hit myght the eyr so corrupt make	air
	That men her deþ þerof schulde take	
	So stynkyng it is and so vyolent	
	As wytnesseþ þerof the grete clerk innocent.	
	Quid eni(m) fetidi(us) humano cadavare aut quid horribili(us) homine mortuo.[2]	
720	He saith what thyng may fouler be	
	Than mannes careyne ys for to se	
	And what ys more horrybyle in eny place	
	Than ys forto se a ded mannes face	
	And whan he is beryed and in erthe bywonde	buried, shrouded
725	Wormes wol hym gnawe in a lytil stownde	time
	Fforto al his flesch be clene away bete[3]	
	Ensample we fyndeth þ(er)eof in book y wrete	written
	Cum autem moriet(ur) homo hereditabit serpentes et vermes[4].	
	The bok saith that whan a man schal deye	
730	Hys herytage he schal take by alle weye	heritage
	To wormes and eddres that foule beth of syght	adders
	For whi to hem byfalleth man(n)es flesch by ryght.	because
	Therfore undyr erthe eche man schal slepe	
	Al among wormes that on hym schal crepe	
735	And gnawe and ete his stynkyng karkoys[5]	carcass
	And ther of to us holy wryt maketh his voys	
	Omnes enim in pulv(er)e dormient et vermes op(er)ient eos[6].	
	That is in powdyr schal slepe eu(er)y man	powder
	And wormes hym keuere fram too to the pan	cover, toe, head
740	Ffor in this world so wytty a man ys ther non	witty
	Ne so fayr ne so ʒong in flesch ne in bon	
	Emp(er)our kyng no knyght no non other cayser	kaiser
	Ne none other lord that in grete stat is her	estate
	Ryche ne pore ne bonde ne fre	

---

[1] *A wyndyng clothe* is a shroud in which to wrap the dead.
[2] "For what stinks more than the human corpse, or what is more dreadful than a dead man?" [*PL* 217, col. 737, in *Innocent III, De Miseria,* ed. Lewis, p. 207].
[3] The spaces beneath the last *e* of *bete* and above *wrete* have been erased and *e* has been written in it.
[4] "When man dies, he will inherit serpents and. worms" [*PL* 217. col. 735, in *Innocent III*, ed. Lewis, p. 205].
[5] The author grounds his somewhat gothic imagination in Biblical lore, but his images remain startling in their blatant and insistent presentation. He also concretizes, and exaggerates suggestive Biblical statements.
[6] "They shall all sleep together in the dust and worms shall cover them" [Job 21:26, Pseudo-Bernard *PL*184, col 490, in *Innocent III,* ed. Lewis, p. 204]. The scribe failed to underline this Latin quotation as he does the others.

Part II. The Instability of the World (745–782)

745	Lered ne lewed wheþur that he be	f. 10v	Learned, ignorant
	That he ne schal torne aftur his laste day		
	To pouder and to erthe and to foul clay		
	Wherfore in thought y haue muche wond(er)		
	Sucche that wormes schul us rende asond(er)		tear apart (with teeth)
750	That no man on erthe wol unnethe y se		
	What he was and ys and what he schal be		
	Ac who so wele yn his herte caste		
	What that he was and schal ben at the laste		
	And what he is whiles he lyueth here		
755	He scholde fynde wel lytyl matiere		reason / cause
	To make mery while he here dwelluþ		to laugh at
	As a wys versifio(ur) in his metre telluþ		poet, poetry / verse
	Si quis sentiret quo tendit et unde veniret		
	nu(m)q(ua)m gauderet sed in omni tempore fleret.[1]		
	He saith who so wele fele and y se		be aware
760	Whennes that he come and whid(ur) schal he		
	He scholde ioye eu(er) forsake		
	And eu(er)e wepe and euer sorowe make		
	Ffor who so of a man thanne hadde a syght		
	Whan wormes to drawe hym hauen outryght		
765	And gnawen his flesch to the harde bon		
	So grysly a syght syhe he neuer non		ugly, saw
	As he myght yse of hys karkoys y wys		carcass
	And so seint bernard seith in his metre y wys		
	Post homine(m) v(er)mis post v(er)mem fetor et horror		
	Et sic in non homine(m) vertit(ur) omnis homo.[2]		
770	He seith that aftyr deþ man ys vermyn bycome		
	And aftyr v(er)myn to stynche he ys ynome		taken
	And so eu(er)y man torned schal be		
	Fram man into noman as it were nat he.		
	Thus men may ise as it is ywryte before		
775	How man of his modur ys in wrecchidnesse ybore		mother, born
	Here bigynneþ þe secunde part þ(a)t telleþ of þe condyc(i)on and of þe unstable[-]		
	Al þis world as y may undurtake **nesse of this**		
	Our lord god made for mannys sake. **world.**[3]		
	And alle þynges þer ynne as clerkes proue		
780	He made also to mannes byhoue		profit
	That man scholde hym wurschipe and honoure		
	And loue and drede in euery houre.		

---

[1] "Whoever perceives where he is going or whence he has come, should never rejoice but always weep" [source unknown].
[2] "After man, worm; after worm, stench and horror; thus, every man is turned into no man" [from Pseudo-Bernard, *PL* 184, col. 490].
[3] Headings in the top margins, partially or fully chopped, record "Secunda pars" throughout this section.

	Ac ȝif man loue worldly thyng more by eny wey	f. 11r	
	Than he doth our lord that sytteth an hey		on high
785	Than ys thulke man to god unkynde		without reverence
	That so lytyl on hym setteth his mynde		
	Ffor god ys more wurthi loued for to be		
	Than any othur creat(ur)e that me(n) may ise		see
	Sutthe that he is the bygynnere of al man(er)e thyng		Since
790	And schal of alle creat(ur)es make the endyng.		
	Thus y seye by tho men that ȝyueth hem ofte		those, give
	To this worldys lykyng that semeþ so softe		desires
	And loueth alle thynge that ther to be falleth[1]		
	Suche man(er) men worldly men me calleth[2]		
795	Ffor here loue more in the world they setteth		their
	The whiche the loue of god outryght letteth		impedes
	And for loue of this worldlys vanyte		
	A man at the laste for barred may be		prevented / stopped
	Ffor the hie heuene there al the ioye ys		
800	Where a man schal be with outen ende y wys		indeed
	Ac a grete clerk saith that me(n) clepeth bartolmewe[3]		
	That ther beth twey worldys p(ri)ncipally for to schewe		
	Ac than o world is invysible and clene		one
	And that othur is bodyly and may be y sene.		physical
805	The gostly world that no man may se		spiritual
	Is heuene where god sitteth in trynite		
	And þidur schul we come and there leue ay		live always
	Ȝif we thidurward holde now the ryȝt way.		
	Nowe wol y no leng(er) here up on stonde		dwell upon this
810	For aftyrward schal come this matere more in honde		discussed
	Ac thulk world that men may ise		
	In two parties dyuyded may be		
	Ffor bothe the parties men mowe knowe		may
	Bot that on is hye and that othur lowe.		one, high
815	The hye recheþ fram the mone ryght euene		
	To the heyest place of the sterred heuene		starred
	And thulke world ys bryght and ful of fayrnesse		such
	For ther ys no corrypcyo(u)n ne no derknesse		
	Bot sterres and alle planetys schynynge		stars
820	Wher of any man may haue undyrstondynge		
	Ac the lowest world the which may be falle		
	Conteyneth soþly the elementys alle		truly

---

[1] Perhaps the sense at the end of this line is "thereto pertains, " or "to them happens ... that I call such manner of men 'worldly men'."

[2] The space beneath "me calleth" has been erased, as has that beneath "worldys" (l. 802), "The hye recheþ (l. 815), "fayrnesse" (l. 817), "derknesse (l. 818), and "soþly" (l.822), probably by the *Piers* rubicator.

[3] Bartholomaeus Anglicus, author of *De Proprietatibus Rurum*, the thirteenth century encyclopedia translated by John of Trevisa c. 1398 (*On the Properties of Things: John Trevisa's Translation of Bartholomaeus Anglicus De Proprietatibus Rerum*, ed. M. C. Seymour et al., Oxford, 1975-88).

44 Part II. The Instability of the World (823–862)

	That on ys erthe that þ(er) aboute stondes	f. 11v	one, is situated
	In the whiche men dwelleth of dyv(er)se londs		various
825	Ffor in this world is bothe wele and wo		
	And that ofte chaungeth now to and fro		
	Ac to sum(m)e the world is softe and to sum(m)e hard		easy, difficult
	As ȝe schul here sone telle aftirward.		
	Ac the world that passeth al man(er) þyng		
830	Was made for mannes endles wonyng		dwelling / habitation
	Ffor eu(er)y man schul haue there a place		
	To ben eu(er) in ioye þ(a)t on erþe haþ g(ra)ce		
	Thulke world was mad for our avauntage		
	For þere byfalleþ to be our ryȝt erytage		heritage
835	Ac that othur world that ys lower atwynne		divided
	Where that the sterres beþ and þe planets ynne		
	God ordeyned only for our bi houe		designed, profit
	By þis reso(u)n that y can þerof p(ro)ue		
	Ffor the eyr f(ro)m þen(n)ys and the hete of the son(n)e		air
840	Susteyneth the erthe whan thei beþ þ(er)to y won(n)e[1]		
	And norscheþ alle þyng þat fruyt ȝeueth		nurse
	To conforte man and beste þ(a)t on erþe lyueth		
	And tempreth our kynde and our complexion.		temper, nature
	And setteth þe tymes of þe ȝere in her ryȝt seso(u)n		
845	And ȝyueth us lyght that we mowe here dwelle		light, might
	For ell were this world as derk as any helle		otherwise
	And the lowest world was made for man.		
	By this skyle yleue as y ȝowe telle can		reason, I believe
	Ffor þat man schulde be þ(er)ynne wonynge		living
850	And travalye for his sustynaunce with trewe lyuynge[2]		work, sustinence
	Goddys comandementys and also his wylle		
	For to knowe and to kepe and to full fylle		
	And to p(ro)uyd herein goostly batayle		spiritual
	For many enemys þ(er) beþ þat often men asaile		
855	So þorowe gostly strenkþe and þorowe victorye		
	They mowe to hem wynne endeles glorye		might
	And to haue the crowne of ay endeles blys		always
	In þulke world þat is wyth oute any anguys		
	Two worldes to gyd(re) here mowe be falle		may happen
860	Þe whiche alle men mowen erþlyche calle.		
	On is þe dale that we beþ ynne dwellynge		
	And an othur is þe man that þ(er)ynne is wonynge		living

---

[1] "… succeed in reaching it."
[2] All but the first two words are written over an erasure by the *Piers* rubicator, and both rewritten *y's* in *lyuynge* are dotted. See folio 1v, footnote 5.

	This same dale where we wonyeth ynne	f. 12r
	That is ful of wrecchidnesse, sorwe and synne	
865	Of wyse clerkes in bokes y clepud ys	wise, is called
	The more world .¹ and man the lasse is ywys	
	Of the lasse world wol y nat ȝut speke²	
	For aftyrward y wol into þat mat(er) breke	yet
	Of the more world more y wol telle	I will
870	Er y passe f(ro)m my mat(er) where on y dwelle	Before
	Than wol y aftyrward schewe as by falleþ	it happens
	Good reso(u)n whi men a man³ þe world calleþ	
	The more world god wolde on erþe sette	will
	For it schulde to man eu(er) be sogette	obedient / subordinate
875	Man for to s(er)ve and man nat yt⁴	
	And so god it ordeynyd for man(n)es p(ro)fit	
	Ac nowe þis world that men lyueth ynne	
	Wexeth so lethur and is so full of synne	wicked
	That manye this world maketh her sou(er)ayn	lord
880	And alle here werkes torneth in to vayn⁵	
	And sum(m)e man ȝyueth hi(m) þ(er)to al þat he may	
	To s(er)ve thulk world bothe nyght and day	
	Ac þe world that ys here is no þyng elles	
	Bot the man(er)s of men þat þ(er)yn dwelles	customs
885	Ffor thes worldly men knowe mowe we noȝt⁶	may
	But by the condycio(u)n þat þey haueþ y wroȝt	created
	Ffor what myȝt men by þe world und(er)stonde	
	Ȝif none worldlyche men were lyuyng in londe	
	Ac thei that þe world s(er)veth and haueth it in loue	
890	S(er)veþ þe deuel and nouȝt our lord aboue	
	Ffor þe world is the deuels s(er)uaunt	
	While he doth hym s(er)uice aftyr his ha(u)nt	does his bidding
	Many aftyr the worldys wele lusteth	wealth desire
	Ac he is no thyng wys that ther on t(ru)steth	
895	Ffor þis world is fekyl and wel deseyvable	deceptive
	And in dede ful unsikur and ryght unstable.	uncertain, mutable / changing
	Therfore y holde thulk man no thyng wytty	such, wise
	That a boute the world makeþ hym to besy	
	Ffor a man may nat goddes s(er)uant be	
900	Bot he the man(er)s of the world wol fle	unless
	He ne may nat god loue but he the world despyse	
	For þe holy gospel techeþ us in this wyse	

---

[1] The scribe has used a period here, perhaps to ensure clarity of his idea, but has not capitalized the next word.
[2] Probably "and man the lasse [who] is ywys / Of the lasse world wol y nay ȝut speke." Note the continued diminution of mankind.
[3] The sense seems to be: later I will show "Good reso(u)n whi [God wolde on erþe sette] ... a man [in] þe world [which men] call / The greater world."
[4] In other words, the world should be subject to man, and man not subject to it. The *y* of *yt* is dotted. See folio 1v, footnote 5.
[5] "And all their works are done in vain."
[6] "Mowe we noȝt" likely means "we cannot know these worldly men."

Part II. The Instability of the World

Nemo potest duobus d(o)m(ini)s s(er)vire . aut   f.12v
    e(ni)m u(nu)m odio habebit et alt(er)um
      diliget . aut u(nu)m sustinebit et altern(um) contempnet.[1]

	He saith no man may s(er)ve rygthfuly[2]	
905	Ne two lordes to gydre that beþ cont(ra)ry	together
	Ffor he schal þ(at) on hate in his dede	one
	And þat othur loue aftyr his manhede	
	Or elles he schal that on manteyne outryght	one uphold
	And that othur despyse and sette by hym lygth	think little of him
910	The world ys goddes enemy and so me(n) may it calle	
	For it is contr(ar)ious to goddes workes alle	contrary
	And so beth alle they þ(a)t þe world loueth wel	
	As the euangelyst sayth in his gospel	

Qui vult esse amic(us) hui(us) mundi . inimic(us)
    dei constituit(ur).[3]

915	He saith whoso wole the worldys frend be	
	Goddes enemy for sothe than bycometh he	certain
	And for worldly men greueth god al day ywis	injure
	Therfore the apostel in his pystyl saith is:	epistle

Nolite diligere mu(n)du(m) . nec ea que in
    mu(n)do su(n)t[4].

920	Ne loueþ nat the world saith he	Neither
	Ne no thing that may in the world be	
	Ffor as thing in this world that any man telle can	
	Othur it is couetyse or lust of flesch of man	desire
	Othur couetyse of yen wher wyth we may loke	eyes
925	Or elles p(ri)de of lyf as it is wryte in boke	

Omne quod est in m(u)ndo aut est concupiscencia carnis
    Aut concupiscencia oculor(um) aut sup(er)bia vite[5]

	Couetyse of flesch is by hym selue othyng	one thing
	The wyche falleth to mannys lust and lykyng	desire, pleasure
	Couetyse of eyʒe as eche man may gesse	eyes
930	Ys rycchesse þat comeþ to man wyth bysynesse	wealth, industry / effort
	And pride of lyf that men kepeþ in her thought	
	Desireth into grete wurschipe forto ben y brought	honor
	To lust and to lykyng of our fleschly materye	substance
	Engendreþ the foule synne of lecherye.	
935	Ac god made the world as hym self is wytnesse	
	To s(e)rve man, nowt man to s(er)ve it in bux(o)mnesse	obedience
	Wher to is man s(er)va(u)nt to the world thanne	
	And maketh hym selue þe worldys bonde man(n)e	bondsman
	Whan that he may s(er)ve god and eu(er) more be fre	
940	And out of thraldom of the fals world be	slavery

---

[1] "No man can serve two masters, for either he will hate the one and love the other, or he will sustain the one and despise the other" [Matt. 6:24].
[2] The word "rygthfuly" has been written over an erasure by the *Piers* rubricator, as has been "to gydre that beþ contr(ar)y" (905), "þ(a)t on" (906), "by hym lygth" (909), "it" (911), "al day" (917), "with bysynesse" (930), and "it in bux(o)mnesse" (936).
[3] "Whoever therefore will be a friend of this world, becometh an enemy of God" [James 4:4].
[4] "Love not the world, nor the things which are in the world" [1 John 2:15].
[5] "For all that is in the world, is the concupiscence of the flesh and the concupiscence of the eyes, and the pride of life" [1 John 2:16]. The usual *punctus* at the end of a Latin quotation is missing here.

	Ac wolde a man knowe ryght wel ay	f. 13r	always
	What the world is and his falsnesse euery day		
	Him schulde nat luste as y undyrstonde		desire
	Aftyr this worldes lykyng any þing to fonde		try / experience
945	Ffor lo what sayþ bartholmewe þe grete clerk		
	That spekeþ of the world þ(a)t is in syn(n)e derk		
	Mundus nichil aliud est n(isi) quoddam exiliu(m) .		
	O(mn)i erupna . labore . dolore .¹ dolorum t(ri)sticia plenu(m).²		
	He saith that the world is nauȝt elles		
	Bote an hard exil that man yn dwelles		
950	Bothe derk and dym and a delful dale		dolcful
	The whiche is full of sorowe and of byt(er) bale		suffering
	And a stede full of meche wrecchidnesse		place
	Of t(ra)vayle and ang(uish) and all bysynesse		work, misery
	Of peyne of synne and al man(er) folye		
955	Of schendschipe and al bodyly vylanye		shame
	Of lettyng and of many a taryenge		hindrance, delay
	Of frowardnesse and muche sturinge		agitation
	Of alle felþede stynkyng corruptio(u)n		filth of
	Of grete violence and many man(er) oppressio(u)n		types of
960	And full of gyle and muche falshede		trickery
	Of tresou(n) and dyscord and contynuel drede		conflict
	So þat in the world is nought man to ava(u)nce		
	But wrechidnes and al man(er) meschaunce		ill fortune
	And pompe and p(ri)de and fowl couetyse		greed
965	Veyn glory, slewþe, and muche queyntyse		sloth, craftiness
	The world to hym draweþ &³ to his route		company
	And by clyppeth all men that þ(er)to wolleþ loute		embraces, bow
	And many it greueth and to fewe avayleþ		helps
	For his louyers he desceyueþ ofte and fayleþ		lets down
970	And alle that hym despiseþ he awayteþ faste		
	And thenkeþ hem sone in to myschef caste		suffering brought / thrown
	Ffor whan that hym lykeþ he wol soco(ur)e		help
	And make hym hyȝe(^st)⁴ wyth rycchesse hono(ur)e		
	Ac he faste wayteþ to begyle him at þe laste		deceive
975	And into gret pouert he wol hym caste.		poverty
	Therfore worldly wurschipe may be y tolde		accounted as
	An ydelnesse that bet(ra)yeth boþe ȝong and olde		
	And worldly rycches howh so þat it come to hep		increase / accumulate
	Y holde it nat elles bot as a metyng in a mannys slep⁵		dream

---

¹ The three periods here function like commas to slow down the reader, to emphasize and highlight the world's evil.
² "The world is nothing else but a kind of exile, full of every distress, hardship, grief, and sadness arising from pains," Bartholomew, *De Proprietatibus Rerum* Book 8, 1: 446, 308. See Morey, p. 228 for a fuller translation. Notice how much elaboration follows this relatively short Latin quotation; the poet has a gift for embellishment, often using it to shock and stimulate his audience by sensational images and language. He begins with the theme of exile, much used in major Old English poetry, both religious and secular, e.g., "The Wanderer" and "The Seafarer." No doubt the poet has plundered the Bible and the preachers' manuals to develop this theme.
³ The ampersand here has been written over an erasure, leaving some extra space.
⁴ The "st" is superscripted here by the scribe.
⁵ L. 979 is blurred due to an erasure.

48 Part II. The Instability of the World

980	The world haþ wyth vanite many man ysmyled	f. 13v	
	And wyth pompe and p(ri)de hym ofte bygyled.		tricked
	Therfore an holy man as ȝe mown here		must hear
	Spekeþ to þe world and saith on this manere:		
	O munde immunde utina(m) ita immundus e(ss)es		
	ut me non tang(er)es aut ita mundus e(ss)es		
	ut me non i(ni)quares.[1]		
985	That ys on englys thus forto mene		
	O thu world he saith þ(a)t eu(er) art unclene[2]		
	Whi ne myght thu eu(er) so unclene be		Would that you
	That thu ne myghtest neu(er) towche me		touch
	Or elles be so clene in þy wurkes alle		
990	That thu make me into no synne falle		cause
	How þe world may be ilikned to þe see.[3]		compared to
	The world þorow many grete encheso(u)n		occasions
	May to foure thynges by ylykened by reso(u)n		compared
	Fferst the world may be lykened y wys		
995	Most p(ro)p(er)ly to the see that long and brod ys		sea
	Ffor why the see aftyr his owne s(er)tayn tyde		certain
	Ebbeþ and floweþ and may nat stedefast abyde		remain
	And bygynneþ þorow stormes grete tempest d(ra)we		create
	And so than aftyr maketh many hard wawe.[4]		
1000	So casteþ the world w(i)t(h) his queynte favo(ur)		predetermines
	A man into rycchesse and into mechel hono(ur)		much
	And aftyr that he him casteþ y(s) fro clene a down		
	Into strong pouert and grete t(ri)bulacyo(u)n.		poverty, trial
	And they beþ the grete stormes and kene		sharp
1005	That bryngeþ a man in wo er he it wene		before, know
	How þe world may be likned to a wildernesse.		
	But may the world that is set so wyde		
	Be lykned to a wyldurnesse by eu(er)y syde		
	That is ful of bestes that beþ wond(er) wylde		amazingly
1010	As lyo(u)ns . lybardes and wolves unmylde		leopards, fierce
	The whiche wolleþ men strangle and destroye		
	And sle here bestes and sore hem anoye		severely, disturb
	So ys the world full of mysdoers aboute		
	And of tirauntes that bryngeþ men in gret doute		tirants
1015	That beþ eu(er)e besy bothe nyght and day		
	Men to greue wyth euel a fray		terror
	How þe world may be likned to a forest.		
	The world also may lykned be		

---

[1] The author is punning on the Latin words *mundus, mundi*, m. "world," and *mundus, a, um*, "clean"; the semantic connection is the latter's connotation of "a way of living in the world." Thus, "O unclean world, would that you be so unclean that you touch me not, or that you do not render me unfavorable" [derived from Augustine *PL* 40 col. 1290 playing on 1 John 2:15-17: "Love not the world, nor the things which are in the world. If any man love the world, the charity of the Father is not in him. For all that is in the world, is the concupiscence of the flesh, and the concupiscence of the eyes, and the pride of life, which is not of the Father, but of the world. And the world passeth away, and the concupiscence thereof: but he that does the will of God abideth forever."

[2] The direct address and personification of the world here and in the Latin are dramatic tactics to increase interest.

[3] The three headings on this folio and one on the next are scribed in red ink and are slightly larger than the text.

[4] "Many a severe / cruel wave."

	To a forest that stant in a wylde contre	f. 14r	stands
1020	That is ful of theues and wykked outlawes		
	Þat often tyme to suche forestes drawes		
	And haunteth there here pas and robbeþ and reueþ¹		tracks, plunders
	Bothe men and wemmen and no thing hem byleueþ		relinquish
	So ys this world wheron we most dwelle		
1025	Ful of strong theues that beth deueles of helle		
	The wyche us awayteth and beþ eu(er)e besy		watchful
	Us to robbe and to reue of our goodys gostly.		plunder, spiritual
	How þe world may be likned to a batayle in a felde.		
	ꝫet the world as y schal schewe here		
1030	May be thus lykned in þe ferþe manere		
	To a fayr felde ful of dyuerse batayles²		various
	Of strong enemys that eche day men assailes		
	Ffor here we beþ y broȝt in wel mychel dowte		
	And hard w(i)t(h) enemys by set al abowte		beset
1035	And specialy wyth enemys thre		
	Aȝenst the whiche us behoueþ wel armed be		profits
	That aren the fend, the world, and the flesch		
	Whiche doth assaile euere ylyke freisch.		test, anew
	Therfore us byhoueþ by dai and by nyght		profit
1040	Euere to be redy aȝenst hem forto fyght		
	The world as clerkes doþ us to undurstonde		
	Euere aȝenst us fyghteþ wyth double honde		
	Wyth þe ryght hond and wyth the lefte		
	That euer haþ be our fleschly fo.		enemy
1045	The ryght hond ys welthe as y may wel holde		believe
	The lyft hond ys hap of angres colde		chance, sorrows
	The ryght assaileþ sum(m)e men a while		attacks
	Wyth the worldes wele hem to be gyle		wealth, trick
	And þat ys welþe w(i)t(h) owte ang(ui)s(h) and dolo(ur)		pain, sorrow
1050	Of worldly rycchesse and grete tresour		
	And wyth þe lyft hond he assaileþ eft sone		
	And maketh men for sorowe ofte grone		
	And þat is w(i)t(h) anguish and grete trebulacyo(u)n		
	And wyþ pouerte and contynuel p(er)secucyo(u)n		
1055	Suche thinges clerkes the lyft hand calleþ		
	Þat in þe world often tymes falleþ		
	And wyþ þe world comeþ dame fortune³		
	And eythur hand chaungeþ in to a newe tune.⁴		

---

[1] "And stalk them there and rob and plunder."
[2] This line recalls the line in *Piers Plowman* (a text of which is also in HM 128), "the fair field full of folk."
[3] Note the poet's use of Dame Fortuna, a common medieval figure of a capricious old woman randomly turning the world's wheel of fortune for the unmerited benefit or demise of its inhabitants. Her roots are classical.
[4] The last six words are scribed over an erasure by the *Piers* rubricator.

Part II. The Instability of the World (1059–1096)

	For sche torneth aboute euere here wheele	f. 14v
1060	Sum(m)e tyme into wele and sum tyme into euele	fortune, into misfortune
	And whan sche makeþ the whel aboute go	
	Sche torneþ sum(m)e adown f(ro)m wele into wo	happiness, woe
	And eft sone f(ro)m woe into myche blys	often
	Þus torneþ sche her whel w(i)t(h) outen any lis	respite
1065	That ilk whel clerkes no thyng ell calleþ	same, else
	Bot hap othur cha(u)nce that sodeynly falleþ	
	Bot thulk hap y holde no þyng elles	this
	But wraþþe and hate that wyþ men dwelles.	wrath
	Therfore worldlyche wele ys euere in doute	happiness
1070	While þat dame fortune torneþ her whel aboute	
	Wherfore p(ro)fit men that her lyf aryght ledeþ	correctly
	Bothe þe welthe of the world and her flesch dredeth	
	Ffor welþe draweþ a man f(ro)m the ryght way	
	And ledeth hym fro god bothe nyght and day.	
1075	Thus eu(er)y man may drede welthe who so kan	knows
	For thus seyþ seynt ierom the good holy man[1]	
	The more he saith that we wexeþ upryght	are attracted by
	In welthe or in eny worldly myght	
	The more we schuld haue drede in our þouȝt	
1080	That we f(ro)m the hie ioye falle nought[2]:	
	Quanto magis in v(ir)tutibus crescimus: tanto plus timere	
	Debem(us). ne sublimi(tam) corriamus.[3]	
	To this acordeþ a clerk seneca the wyse	agrees
	That conseileþ thus the world to despise	
	Tunc tibi salubre conciliu(m) advoca:	
	Cum tibi alludu(n)t mundi p(ro)sp(er)a.[4]	
1085	Seneca saith and ȝyueþ good conceyl	
	Whan that this world makeþ his m(er)vail	performs its tricks
	Seke thu thy wyt and aftyr good conseil calle	
	That muche welthe þene make into peril falle	
	Ffor welþe nys bot a schadewe somdel derk	
1090	As therof spekeþ gregory the grete clerk	
	Si omnis fortuna timenda est: magis t(ame)n	
	p(ro)sp(er)a quam adv(er)sa.[5]	
	Seint gregory saith now in this man(er)e	
	That ȝif eu(er)y hap be to drede here	if, chance
	Ȝut is hap of welþe forto drede more	chance of wealth
1095	Than eu(er)y chaunce of ang(uish) þaw it sm(er)te sore	sorrow, stings
	Ffor ang(uish) mannes lif clanseþ and p(re)ueþ	cleanses, proves

---

[1] Saint Jerome is the referernt. Erasures mark this and the following line; the characteristic *w* of the *Piers* rubricator indicates his emendations.
[2] Thus, dread wealth because its loss means pain.
[3] "The more we grow in virtues, the more we should fear, lest we fall from the heights" [Jerome, *PL* 30, col 381].
[4] "When the riches of the world sport with you, then seek sound advice for yourself" [Marbodus, *PL* 171, col. 381)].
[5] "If all fortune is to be feared, yet good fortune is more to be feared than its opposite [Petrus Blesensis, adapted from Gregory the Great, *PL* 207, col. 989].

	And welthe his lyf sone into synne meueth[1]	f. 15r	moves
	So may man lyghtly his owne soule spylle		easily, kill
	Þorw welthe þat he haþ here at his owne wylle.		
1100	And so come aftyrward to endeles pyne		
	As witnesseþ the doctur Seynt Austyn[2]		
	Sanitas continua et rerum habundancia eterne dampnacio(n)is sunt indicia.[3]		
	He saith that continuel hele and worldly wele		material prosperity
	As contynuel rycches to many and fele		much
1105	Beþ tokenes as it in bok wryton ys		symbols
	Of the dampnacyo(u)n that is endeles y wys		
	And to thes wordes that som men myspayeth		displease
	Acordeþ seint gregory that thus sayeth:		agrees
	Continu(us) successus temporaliu(m) et(er)ne dampnac(iones) est indiciu(m).[4]		
1110	He saith that contynual hap comynge		chance
	Of worldly goodis it is a tokenynge		
	Of the dampnacio(u)n that schal at the laste be		
	Before god that schal be wyth oute pyte		
	Ac the world preyseþ no men but hem only		
1115	That to alle worldlyche welþis beth happy		riches
	And in worldly thynges setteth her herte		
	And fleth euere the symple stat of pouerte.		
	Suche men both besy and gadreth faste		gather
	And fareþ as here lyf scholde ay laste		act
1120	To hem the world is queynte and favo(ur)able		remarkable
	In al man(er) thyng that hem thinkeþ p(ro)fytable.		
	And þey conneþ so muche of worldly queyntyse		know, strategy
	Þat the world hem holdeþ good men and wyse		
	And to hem comeþ goodes manyfolde		
1125	Ac it is to her dampnacyo(u)n as y haue tolde		
	Ffor in heuene ther may no man haue an hom		
	Þat foloweþ the world and the worldys wysdom		
	The whiche wysdam as saith a man wytty		wise
	Byfore god is holde but a grete foly:		
1130	*Sapiencia*[5] *hui(us) mu(n)di stulticia est apud deu(m)*		
	Ac many men myche in þe world lusteþ[6]		desire
	But he is no thing wys that ther ynne trusteþ		deceit, wiles
	Ffor it ledeþ a man wyth wrenches and wyles		tricks
	And hym at the laste falsly bygylis		
1135	And he may be itold bothe wytty and wys		accounted

---

[1] The poet is consistently concerned with corruption—both bodily (at man's birth, as he ages, and in elde) and spiritual (as wealth here corrupts the soul). This theme permeates the poem until the advent of the heavenly experience.

[2] The poet uncharacteristically has capitalized a proper name here, perhaps for emphasis.

[3] "To lay up in store for themselves a good foundation against the time to come:" Continued good health and an abundance of wealth are signs of eternal damnation. [Source unknown, perhaps Augustine, *PL* 39, col. 1522 alluding to 1 Timothy 6:1819].

[4] "Continued success in the affairs of the world is an indication of eternal damnation" [Gregory, *PL 76,* col 368].

[5] "For the wisdom of this world is foolishness with God" [1 Corinthians. 3:19].

[6] The *Piers* rubricator has emended this and the following line as his backhanded slant and dotted, tailed *y* suggest. See folio 1v, footnote 5.

52   Part II. The Instability of the World   (1136–1174)

	Þat kan the world fle and sette at lityl p(ri)s	f. 15v
	And hateþ the maners þat þe world loueþ most	customs
	And thenkeþ at the laste to blis bryng his gost	spirit
	And on this worldly lyf ne tryst ryght nought	
1140	Ac euere in the tothur lyf setteth hys thouȝt	other
	Ffor no syker dwellynge schul we here yfynde	secure
	As the apostel saith þ(er)of as we haue in mynde.	
	Non habemus hic manente(m) civitate(m) sed	
	fut(ur)a inq(ui)rim(us)[1].	
	He saith no sykur wonyng here haue we	no certain dwelling / home
1145	Ac we seketh a nothur that eu(er)e schal be	
	And as gestys we heere owre dwellyng make[2]	guests
	A lytel while forto we schulleth hennys betake	go / make our way
	And that may falle sonner þan any ma(n) wold wene	think
	For we beþ here bot as it were an alyene	alien
1150	Fforto t(ra)vaile in the way here in alle tymes	
	To go our contre ryght as doþ pylgrymes.	
	Therfore the pr(o)phet saith to our lord thus	
	David in the sawt(er) therwyth to techen us:	
	Ne sileas qu(on)i(am) advena ego sum apud te.	
	Et p(er)eg(rin)u(s) sicut omnes patres mei.[3]	
1155	Ne be thu nat stylle[4] lord saith he	quiet
	For whi y am a comeling to be toward the	stranger
	And a pylg(ri)m y am as all my fadres were	
	Þus may euery man seye that leueþ in world here	
	That is to seye lord ne be þ(u) nat so stylle	quiet
1160	That thu ne make me here to knowe thi wylle	
	And suche confort to my soule þat thu kythe	show
	The whiche may here be boþe glad and blythe	
	And seie thus þerto: y am thi saluacyon	
	For thu art my pylgrym trewe wyth deuocyo(u)n.	
1165	**Of two weies that ben in this world.**[5]	ways
	Two weyes þer beþ in thys world wel ryue	worn
	That on is the wey of deþ, that othur is of lyue.	one
	This world is the wey and the passage	
	Þorow the whiche lyggeþ our pylg(ri)mage	lies
1170	By þis wey us behoueþ forto go .	profits
	And eu(er)y man mut byleue þat it is so	must
	In this world beþ two weyes by kynde	
	And whoso wel assaye the sothe he may fynde	will test, truth
	That on is the wey of deþ as er y ȝowe tolde	death, before

---

[1] "For we have not here a lasting city, but we seek one that is to come" [Hebrews 13:14].
[2] These four words and *betake* in the next line are corrected by the *Piers* rubricator.
[3] "Be not silent for I am a stranger with thee, and a sojourner as all of my fathers were" *(*Psalm 38:13*)*.
[4] This dotted *y* is by the scribe of this text, not an emender.
[5] Besides his creative imagery and allegory of life as pilgrimage, in the tradition of *Pelerinage de la vie humaine*, the author here (and elsewhere) turns to logical discourse to convince his audience.

1175	And that othur is the wey of lyf ywys as yholde.[1]	f. 16r	held
	Ac þe wey of deþ semeth large and esy		
	For þat may us lede euene and lyghtly		
	To þe gryslyche lond of al derknesse[2]		grisly
	Þere sorowe and peyne is and al wrecehidnesse		
1180	Ac þe wey of lif semeth narow and hard		
	The whiche ledeþ euene to our countreward		opposite way
	And that is þe kyngdom of heuene bryght		
	Where we schul eu(er) be in goddes syght		
	And as goddes sones ther ynne beþ y tolde		
1185	ȝif we holde the wey of lyf boþ ȝong and olde		
	Ffor the wey of þes world here is unstable		inconstant
	And our lif is ofte swythe chaungable		so
	As it is ysene alday in many man(er) wyse		
	By tymes and wedres that makeþ us ofte agryse		storms, tremble
1190	The world and the worldly lif yset yfere		together
	Cha(u)ngeþ ofte and torneþ in dyuerse manere		
	And her stat ne dwelleþ bot a schort while		
	Unnethe to the space of a lityl myle		scarcely
	And for that the world is so unstedefast		inconstant
1195	Al that men seþ ther yn(n)e is sone ou(er)cast.		passed/overturned
	Of the unstabulnesse of þis world.		instability
	God thus ordeyned as it was his wylle		
	Dyuerse varyac(i)ons the cesons to fulfulle		seasons
	And the tymes of the wedres and othur cesouns		storms
1200	Into tokne of the fals worldes condic(i)ons		
	That so unstable beþ to a man(nes) honde		inconstant
	That schort while mowe in her stat stonde		may, state /condition remain
	Ffor god wol that men thorow token(is) knowe		wishes
	How unstable þe world is in uche thorowe		each
1205	So that men schulde þ(er)on the lasse truste		
	And for no welþe þ(er)on to muche set her luste		
	The tymes chaungeth ofte and beþ nat in o stat		one condition
	As now is erly morowe and sone is eue lat		late
	And nowe it is day and now it is nyght		
1210	And now[3] it is derk and now it is lyght		
	And now it is cold and now is grete hete		heat
	And now it is druye and now it is wete		dry,
	And now is snow and hayl and reyn swythe strong		rain extremely
	And now is fayr wedur and somer schyny(n)ge among		

---

[1] These three words have been amended by the *Piers* rubricator.
[2] Derived from Matthew 7: 13-14. "Narrow is the gate that leads to heaven, wide is the way to hell." See James H. Morey, ed *Prick of Conscience*, 225 note to lines 453-64. A foreshadowing of his depiction of hell in section VI.
[3] It appears this and all subsequent "nows" were first scribed as "nowe" but the "e" of each has been deleted.

54   Part II. The Instability of the World   (1215–1254)

1215	And now is þe wedur clere and fayr wyth alle	f. 16v	weather
	And now it is derk whiles the reyn doþ falle		
	By al þese varya(u)nces mowe be undyrstonde		changes, must
	The tokenes of thys world þ(er)w(i)t(h) us to fonde		try
	Ʒut ther beth mo token(es) that we mowe lere		may learn
1220	Of the unstablenesse of the world here.		
	Ffor now is murthe and now is mornynge		
	And now is lawght(er) and now is wepynge		
	And now beth men wel and now beþ hem wo[1]		
	And now is a man frend and now is he fo		enemy
1225	And now is a man lyght and now he is heuy		
	And now is a man blythe &[2] now is he drery		happy
	And now haue we ioye & now haue we pyne		
	And now we good wynneþ & now it doþ away dwyne		goods, dwindle
	And now we beth ryche and now we beþ pore		
1230	And now haue we lyte and now haue we more		little
	And now haue we reste and now haue we t(ra)vaile		work
	And now we fonde our strenkþe what it may availe		proved
	And now be we bygge and nowe beþ we bare		built up
	And now be we hole and now we beth in care		healthy
1235	And now be we smart & nowe beþ we slowe		
	And now be we hie & sone aft(er) lowe		
	And now is loue, now hate, now pes, nowe st(ri)f[3]		conflict
	All these beþ the maners of eche mannys lyf.[4]		
	Þe whiche betokneþ meche unstedefastnes ywis		instability
1240	Of þis worldes welþe that ful chaungable is.		
	And as this lyf is euere more passynge		
	Ryght so is this world eu(er)y day peyr(s)ynge		perishing
	Ffor the world to the ende draweþ wel faste		quickly
	As clerkes by many thinges conne caste.		can, reckon
1245	Therfore þe world as clerkes me haueþ told		
	Is as muche to mene as the world old		
	Ffor two erþlyche worldes to this lyf byfalleþ		
	As it is byfore y tolde and as clerkes calleþ.		
	Ac the more world and also the lasse		macrocosm, microcosm
1250	Wel chaungable thei beth and doþ aweyward passe.		away
	The more world is the world long and brode		
	Ac the lasse is man him self to knowe in manhode.		
	How þe roundnesse of þis world is likned to a man.		
	And as the more world is round yset[5]		

---

[1] " … now men are happy, now they are distressed / miserable."
[2] An ampersand is used for this "and" and for those in l.1227, l.1228, l.1235, and l.1236.
[3] The author uses these comparisons as examples of worldly instability, another instance of his literary versatility. He is nothing if not exhaustive, perhaps to a fault.
[4] The space under *eche mannys* has been erased; all three final words of the line are scribed by the *Piers* rubricator using no dotted *y*'s.
[5] HM 128 is misbound at this point: the text jumps from 16v to 25r and then from 32v back to 17r. the bound sequence of the text continues in HM 128 on f.25r. This edition corrects that misbinding so that the text continues logically, as originally written and scribed on f.17r.

1255	So is the lasse as man ther to ys ymet[1]	f. 17r	measured / appraised
	Ffor in the brede of a man ys as God wolde sende		breadth
	All so muche space f(ro)m the longe fyngres ende		
	Of the ryght hond w(i)t(h) the armes out spredynge		
	To the fyngres ende of þe left hond out strecchynge		
1260	And fro þe heuyd aboue at the corowne		head, crown
	Istreyht so to the sole of þe fote þer downe		Outstretched, down to
	Than ȝif a man his armes out sprede		
	No more is the lenkþe of him than is the brede		breadth
	So a man may be ymete al w(i)t(h) oute		even
1265	Ryght as a compas is round al aboute.		
	Thus haþ that lasse world þat man is		
	The schap of the more world iwis.[2]		
	Ac thes worldes bothe the more and the lasse		
	Schul faile at the laste and away passe		
1270	Ffor ere þe more eelde that thei schull bere		before, the older
	The more thei apeyreth and bycomeþ feblere		decline
	As men may se who so takeþ to hem entent		attention
	As saith in his sawes the pope innocent		
	Senuit iam mundus uterque . et maior mundus . et		
	minor mundus . et quanto p(ro)lixius utriusque		
	senect(us) p(ro)ducit(ur): tanto det(er)i(us) ut(ri)usque		
	nat(ur)a p(ro)bat(ur).)[3]		
1275	He saith as it is in latyn itold		
	Eythur world wexeth now the ful old		Both world(s) become
	And the leng(or) þat her tyme ys here isowt		examined / investigated
	And the eelde of eythur world ys forthe browt		age, prolonged
	The more in gret wo and febulnesse y wys		
1280	Þe kynde of eythur of hem medlyd ys.		mixed
	Of þe condicions of þeose worldlyche men.		these worldly
	Of this worldes grete outrage we may se		
	Is pride and pompe and al man(er) vanyte		
	In selcouþe maide and dyuerse dygyse[4]		outlandishly made, disguise
1285	The whiche is now used in many man(er) wyse		
	In worldly hauyng and in hie berynge		high
	In ydel aparaile and ther of foul werynge		vain fashion
	The whiche takeþ ou(er) muche ydel costage		vain expense
	And torneþ at the laste in to gret outrage		
1290	Ffor suche degises and suche manere		
	Now ȝong men hauntȝ and now doth lere		frequent
	Ffor now is eu(er)y day continuely seyȝe		seen
	That before this tyme myght be by no weyȝe		way

---

[1] Consider Michaelangelo's famous imagery of man and the world deriving from Aby Warburg's vision; the English translation of Warburg occurs in *The Renewal of Pagan Mythology*. Los Angeles: Getty Research Institute for the History of Arts and Humanity, 1999, 563-92. See also Fritz Saxl "Beitrage zur einer Geschichet der Planetendarstalleingen im Orient und im Okzident zur einer Geschichet der Planetendarstalleingen im Orient und im Okzident," *Islam* 3 (1912), 151-77.

[2] Thus it happens that the small world that man is has the shape of the greater world [the imagery is Michaelangelo's vision of man and th world as noted.

[3] "Already each world grows older, both the greater world and smaller world, and the longer the old age of each is prolonged, the worse th nature of each is shown to be" [HSG consulting *Innocent III*, ed. Robert E. Lewis, p. 137, *PL* 217, col. 715]. Interestingly, *pope* has not been excised here as it has been and will be subsequently.

[4] "In outlandishly made and various newfangled fashions."

56 Part II. The Instability of the World (1294–1333)

	And that men wolde somtyme for curtesye calle	f. 17v
1295	For velany it is now holde almest among alle	practiced almost
	Ffor now makeþ men so ofte her chaungyng	
	Of many maners and dyuerse clothyng	various
	Ffor now wereth men schort clothes and now side	short, long
	And now thei useþ narewe and now þey useþ wyde	
1300	Somme haueth ther cloþes hangyng as stooles	stoles
	And sum(m)e goth ydagged[1] as it were fooles	ragged
	And sum(m)e gon wryckyng to and fro	flitting
	And sum(m)e gon tryppyng as doþ a do[2]	capering, doe
	And thus now useth men all the newe get	fashion
1305	And þ(er) w(i)t(h) the deuel hem caccheþ into his net	catch
	And thorow such uncomely pompe and pryde	
	Þey ne wyteþ whethur thei mow gon othur ryde	know, may
	Ffor so muche p(ri)de as now is ysene	
	Was neu(er) sey byfore as y wene.	think
1310	I drede that thei mowe wel token(es) be yseid	fear, may, called
	For suche gyses as cometh of suche men(nes) red	fashions, advice
	Of grete myschefs and hasty to undurstonde	
	That to the world cometh thorow goddes sonde	dispensation
	And ther to goddes wreche schal wyth hem mete	vengeance, meet
1315	As wytnesseth david the holy p(ro)phete	
	Et irritaverur(n)t deum in vanitatib(us) suis.[3]	
	And thei stured hym to wreche seyth he	stirred, vengeance
	In here newe fyndyngynges[4] of vanyte.	inventions
	This may be said as the bok preueth	
1320	By hem that such newe gyses contreueth	
	Ffor suche men wyth her gyses god greueþ	
	And therfore god his g(ra)ce f(ro)m hem bereueth.	deprives
	God wol at the laste to hem sodeynly sende	
	Hard vengaunce but thei þe rathur amende	
1325	God leteþ hem awhile here to haue her wylle	allows
	And in her folies so do dwelle stylle	
	And that may be knowe by many man(er) gyse	types of ways
	As david in the sawt(er) seiþ in this wyse	Psalter
	Et dimisi eos s(e)c(un)d(u)m desideria cordis eor(um)[5]	
1330	The prophet david here speketh thus	
	In goddes name as this vers scheweth us	verse
	I lefte hem he saith out of all couerte	secrecy
	Aftyr the lustes and lykynges of her herte.	desires, wishes

---

[1] *Ydagged:* with hems ornamented with slits. It has been emended by the *Piers* rubricator.

[2] These fantastic images of current fashions can only be thought humorous—not exactly comic relief, since they are not amidst or a foil to fearful or intimidating preaching, but comic nonetheless.

[3] "And they have angered God with their vanities" [Not David; Deut 32:21]. Note that neither David nor Deuteronomy says anything of newfangledness or extreme clothing here, but the author expounds with sensational images in his inimitable dashing style. This is the first page of the text to be defaced: a deep scratch begins at the second *a* of *vanitatibus* and ends at the first *s* of *gyses* (1.1321).

[4] The scribe meant to write *fyndynges*; this is a case of dittography.

[5] "So I let them go according to the desires of their heart" [Psalm 80:13].

	And in here newe fyndyngʒ þey schal go	f. 18r	discoveries
1335	Wel may this be said by suche and alle tho		
	That god sufferþ in folye and his wylle leueþ		allows, abandons
	And after her lustes newe fyndynges cheseþ		desires, choose
	The whiche to the world maketh hem gay		
	And her þouʒt torneþ bothe nyght and day		
1340	Ac þey schulleþ at the last henn(es) wende		
	In here syght to peynes wyþ outen ende.		
	Therfore i rede [ʒow]¹ that thei [he] al vanytes for sake		advise
	And in this world by tyme sone amendes make		
	ʒut hath the world that is so trech(er)ows		
1345	Mo othur man(er)s that beth contr(ar)ious		
	Ffor now is vertu torned into vice		
	And play and murthe into malice		
	And now is deuocio(u)n in many side		
	Ryght foule betorned into pomp and p(ri)de		
1350	Now is wit and wysdom holde folye		folly
	A mong² olde and ʒong and torned in to treccherye		
	And foly is iholde now for gret wysdom		
	And þerto torneth ryche, pore, swayn, and grom		
	And nowe is clene loue torned into lecherye		lechery
1355	And al ryghtfulnesse into strong tyrauntrye		tyranny
	And thus is the world torned up so down		upside down
	To many man(n)ys soule ful dampnacion		
	Ac suche men semeþ as thei were wode		
	Ffor thei holdeþ good thyng euel and euyl thyng goode.		
1360	Wo schal hem be therfore as clerkes telle		Sorrow
	For þi cryst hym self þus saith in his gospelle		
	Wo be to ʒow alle that seieþ wyth ʒour wille		
	That euel þyng is good and good þyng is ille		
	That is to seie hem schal be ful wo		woeful
1365	Þat in þis world norscheþ her lif so.		
	Thus is þis world and man(nes) lif ther ynne		
	Fulfulled wyth vanite, wrecchednesse and synne		
	Ac som(m)e men loueþ so muche þis lif		
	And this world that is so full of stryf		conflict
1370	That thei thenkeþ neu(er) dep(ar)te ther fro		leave
	But euere leue here ʒif it myʒt be so		live
	And thei loueþ so muche the worldes vanite		
	Þat thei wolde that neuer othur lyf schold be		

---

¹ The two bracketed words in this line are canceled by dotted lines under and through them.

² The scribe probably intended *Among*.

	Bote wolde a man wel hym undyrstonde	f. 18v	if a man would
1375	Why the world is so redy to mannes honde		accessible
	And what he schall haue þ(er)of at þe last ende		
	Whan he schal henn(es) out of þis world wende.		
	Than hym schulde luste bothe nyght and day		desire
	Murthes away caste and syng weilaway.		throw
1380	Therfore he moste suche werkes forsake		
	And to goddes mercy only his herte take		
	And lede his life in pena(u)nce and in pouerte		
	In fasting and in othur penances smerte		severe
	And wel knowe his conscience inward		
1385	To haue the blysse of heuene þer aft(ir)ward.		
	Thus scholde eche man hym selue be þenche		remember
	ʒif he wolde goddes grace to hym wrenche¹		grace turn to himself
	Now haue y schewed in dyuerse manere		
	The condicio(u)nes of man(nes) lyf and of þe world here		
1390	And now y wol in this bok passe forth(er) more		
	To schewe in the þrydde part som what of my lore		
	The which spekeþ spekeþ² specially as y schal rede		
	Of deþ and why deþ is for to drede.		fear
	Here bigynneþ the þridde part of þis book þ(a)t telleþ of deþ.³		third, death
1395	**D**eþ is þe most dredful þing that is		
	In all the world as þe bok w(i)tnesseþ ywys⁴		
	Ffor þ(er) nis no quyk þi(n)g on erþe lyuyng		living / animate
	Þat it nis aʒens þe deþ sore dredyng		is not, much
	And fleþ þe deþ as long as it may		
1400	But at the laste it moot be þe deþes p(re)y		prey
	And whan deþ comeþ and makeþ his debate		
	All thinges he setteþ in a nothur state		
	Ffor no man may aʒens hym stonde		
	Where that he cometh in eny man(er) londe		Wherever, land
1405	Ac by that name of deþ it may so be don		
	That me⁵ schal undirstonde mo deþes than on.		one
	Of the maneres of deþ.		
	As thes clerkes fyndeþ y wryte and redeth		
	Þre maners of deþ þer beþ that men dredeþ		types
1410	That on is bodyli deþ that aft(er) kynde doþ wende		one, nature, go
	Þe secunde is gostli deþ . the þridde wyth oute ende		spiritual
	Bodily deth that is kyndely y wrouʒt		
	Is whan the body and the soule beþ asonder brouʒt		separated

---

[1] These last four words are corrected in this scribe's hand, as are *man, may* (with dotted y), and *hym* in line 1403.
[2] The scribe rewrote *spekeþ* but failed to cancel it in any way.
[3] No doubt the headings once read *Tertia Pars*, but have been trimmed away; only the tail of the parif is visible, indicating blue for recto and red for verso.
[4] This last word *ywys* is corrected by the *Piers* rubricator.
[5] "Me" is a standard form for "men."

	Ac thulk deth is wel bytur and hard	f. 19r	This
1415	Of þe whiche i wole telle to yow aft(ir)ward.		
	Gostly deþ is departynge of synne		spiritual
	Bytwene god and mannes soule wyth ynne		
	Ffor ryght as the sowle is lyf of the body		
	Ryght so the lyf of the sowle is god almyghty[1]		
1420	And as the body is with owten eny dowte		
	Anon dede whan the soule is owte		
	Ryght so the soule is ded of man also		
	Whan that god departeþ ther fro		
	Ffor where that synne is there is the deuel of helle		
1425	And in place where syn(n)e is god wol not dwelle		
	Ffor dedly synne and the deuel and he		
	In o sted ne mowe nought to gidur be		one place might not
	And whan mannys soule is y bounde in synne		
	God passeth out and the deuel is ynne.		
1430	Than is the soule a fore god ded in dede		before
	While that synne and the deuel dwellen in that stede.		place
	How mannes soule is ded þorowh synne.		
	𝔄 s a mannes body may be islawe		slain
	Wyth sum(m)e wepne that is to him idrawe		
1435	So is the soule islawe thorow synne		
	Wherfore god and sche departeth atwynne.		have separated / come apart
	Than is gostly deth forto drede more		spiritual
	Than any bodily deth thaw it greue sore		though, much
	In al so muche as the soule namely		
1440	Is more wurthi than is a mannys body		
	Ffor al thei the soule thorow synne be ded		
	Fram our lord that is al myghty in godhed		
	Ȝut it most euere lyue and hard peynes fynde		
	Ac the body is anon[2] ded thorow flesches kynde		
1445	But of bodely deth is non aȝen tornyng		
	For of erthlyche lyf hit maketh here an ending		
	And the wey it is that we mote wende		must
	To ioye or to peyne that is wyth outen ende		
	Natheles ȝif the soule be slayn þorow synne be slayn[3]		
1450	Ȝut he may thorow g(ra)ce quyk bycome a gayn		alive
	Ffor god her dere a bought on the rode tre		cross
	In the blys of paradys euere to be		
	For alle gostly woundes that beth of synne		spiritual

---

[1] The last seven words have been emended, probably by the *Piers* rubricator.

[2] There is a space between *a* and *non* but the context clearly indicates *anon*.

[3] The first *be slayn* was probably meant to be deleted, and the second *be slayn* kept to rhyme with *gayn*.

	Mowen thorow pena(u)nces take helthe wyth ynne f. 19v		Must
1455	And thaw god be euere ryghtful and myghty		just
	ȝut he is ful of goodnes and mercy		
	And forto [loue][1] saue mannes soule more redy is he		
	Than any man is redy to his mercy fle		
	Ffor the lif of the soule paieþ hym more[2]		
1460	Þan doth the deth as hym self saiþ in his lore		
	Nolo mortem pecc(at)oris sed ut conv(er)tat(ur) et vivat.[3]		
	Y wol nat he saith the deth of the synful alyue		
	But that he be more torned[4] and do hym schryue		converted, confess
	Than may a synful man þat his soule hath islawe		
1465	Be iturned to g(ra)ce and f(ro)m dampnacion be idrawe		
	How endeles deth is in helle.[5]		
	Endeles deth is deth of helle		
	And þ(a)t is byt(ur) to hem þ(a)t þere schul dwelle		
	Ffor helle is yholde a wel dyspytous place		held, unpitying
1470	For ther is endeles wo w(i)t(h) outen eny g(ra)ce		any
	And peines and sorowes that neu(er) schulleth blyn(n)e		cease
	And ȝut ne may noȝt þe sowle deye that is ther ynne[6]		
	But ȝif sche myght die as the body doth here		
	Of all her peynes þanne delyuered[7] sche were		
1475	Ffor the deth of helle is deth euere leuynge		
	And it is a deth euere more lastynge.		
	Of thys maner of deth a man may rede and loke		
	Ynow in the sixte partye of thys boke		enough
	That speketh muche of the paynes of helle		
1480	Therfore y wol no leng(er) here on dwelle		
	What maner thyng ys deth.		
	Deþ is nought elles to telle soþly		truly
	But a departyng betwene þe[8] soule and body		
	And as y haue in partye before saide		
1485	Þis may be clepid a dethus braide		stroke
	And a p(ri)uey pryuacion of the lyf		depriving
	Whan it departeþ f(ro)m the body w(i)t(h) stryf		conflict / agony
	As ȝe may wel wyte in alle ȝour þought		know
	That derknes kyndly is to fele nought		feel
1490	But where that no maner of lyȝt yseyȝe		
	Þere is properly derknesse in eche weyȝe		way
	So that derknesse is pryuac(i)on of lyght		deprivation
	And so is deþ of lyf when man is away twyght		

---

[1] The word *love* has been cancelled by a brisk line through it.
[2] Corrections here and above were done by the scribe of the text.
[3] "I desire not the death of the wicked, but that the wicked turn from his way and live" [Ezechiel 33:11].
[4] This line and a half is a quite literal translation of the Latin.
[5] The treatise here is very organized and rational, using little striking imagery or narrative, but appealing to reason rather than emotion.
[6] The last six words have been corrected by the *Piers* rubricator.
[7] The words *þanne delyuered* are written over an erasure in a smaller hand than the rest of the line; probably the erased letters were fewer than these fourteen.
[8] The *e* is superscripted.

	Thus for deþ that alle men dredeþ most	f. 20r	
1495	Whan the lif fayleth he ʒeldeþ up the gost.		yields
	How men dreden deþ for foure skyles.		reasons
	Foure skyles y fynde as y in bok rede		
	Whi men specially don the deþ drede		
	That on is for deth is strong and felle		one, fierce
1500	And haþ more payne than any man kan telle.		
	The secunde is for syght that he schal se		
	Of fendes that aboute hym than schul be.		devils
	The þrydde is for acountes that he schal ʒelde		third
	Of alle his lyf þat he haþ do in ʒowþe and in elde.		old age
1505	The ferþ is for he is euer more uncertayn		
	Wheþ(er) he schal wende to ioye or to payn.		
	Thus drede of deþ bryngeþ a man in care		
	And hys ioye byreuyth and makeþ hym bare		deprives
	And so it semeth as saith the bok		
1510	Whanne cryst deyde i(n) manhede þat he tok		
	Ffor byfore he deyde up on þe rode		cross
	For drede of deth he swatt dropes of blode		sweated
	Ffor he wuste er he to the deþ made his pas[1]		
	What the peyne of bodyliche deþ was.		physical
1515	Than may we knowe þerby ryght wel		
	Þat the peine of deth is hard somdel		somewhat
	And of the deþ men may thenk wondur		
	For al þing it wol to bresten asondur		burst apart
	As it scheweþ by diuerse weies to us		ways
1520	Þerfore an holy man in his bok saiþ þus:		
	Mors omnis solvit.[2]		
	The deþ he saith loseþ al thyng		unbinds
	And of eche mannes lif makeþ endyng.		
	The furst skyle whi men dreduþ deþ.		reason
1525	Ferst a man moche dredeþ deþ in his herte		
	Þat is for the peynes of deþ beþ wel sm(er)te		sharp
	That is the laste schour and the ende		attack
	Whan the sowle schal fram the body wende		
	A deelful departyng it is for to telle		sorrowful
1530	For thei loueþ to gydre eu(er) for to dwelle[3]		live
	Non of hem wolde gladly othur for go		wishes
	So muche is the loue eu(er) bytwene hem two		
	And the saddur that two beþ to gidres in loue		

---

[1] "For he knew before he passed over to death …"
[2] "Death dissolves everything" [Justinian, *Codex of Canon Law*].
[3] This dualist presentation of body and soul which permeates the poem returns the text to a symbolic mode, comparing body and soul to husband and wife dreading separation.

	As man and his wyf by godes g(ra)ce aboue	f. 20v
1535	Wel the more sorowe and leng(er) mornyng	longer mourning
	Bytwene hem schal be at her departyng	
	Ac the body and the sowle wyth þe lif	
	Loueþ more to gydres þa(n) man and his wyf	
	And whether that þey go in good way or ille	
1540	Euere more to gydre þei wolde dwelle stylle	
	And þis is o skyle as me(n) may se[1]	one, reason
	Whi þei wolde euer in o company be	wish, one
	Ffor god thorow his g(ra)ce and hys wyt	
	[Þai][2] The body and soule ferst to gydur knyt.	originally, knit
1545	Anothur skele is for that on may no þyng do	reason
	But ȝif that othur wol helpe þer to.	unless
	The þrydde is this for þei schul to gydre come	third
	Byfore god in flesch and blod at the day of dome.	judgment
	The ferthe skyle is þis for whan þey comeþ þyder yfere	fourth reason
1550	Þei schulleþ be aft(er)ward in o company euery where	one
	Therfore the more her peyne is and her care	
	Whan that on schal fro that othur fare	
	This departyng may be iclepud deþ	called
	Þat[3] fleþ al aboute as doth the breth	flies
1555	Thorow al londys bothe fer and ner	
	And spareth no thing that he haþ ou(er) power[4]	
	Ffor prayer no for ȝift[5] that any man may ȝiue	
	Where that deþ cometh he suffreþ no man lyue	allows
	Ffor he ne spareþ ryche, pore, ne lowe	
1560	That he ne reueþ of hem þ(er)e lif in a lytyl þorowe	steals, time
	So deþ haþ no mercy of none kynnes whiȝt	any kind of creature
	As seint bernard seyth to us wel aryght	
	Non miseret(ur) inopie . non reveretur diviciis	
	Non sapiencie non moribus non etati(bus).[6]	
	He saith that deþ [is][7] of pou(er)te non m(er)cy haþ	
1565	Neythur to rycchesse no rewarde he naþ	neither ... nor
	Ne to wysdom that men conneþ [to] schewe	know
	Ne to the elde men for her daies beþ but fewe	
	Deþ wol haue no reuerence ne no man(es) favour	kind
	Ne no maner frendschipe of king ne emp(er)our	
1570	Ne of pope, ne buschop, ne no prelat	
	Ne of non oþer of gret astat.	
	Therfore seynt bernard thus seyth in hys wrytynge	

---

[1] Indecipherable erasure or lightly smeared inkblot follows.
[2] Canceled with one firm line. Other erasures on this page are by the *Piers* rubricator.
[3] The text reads *Þaf* but undoubtedly the word should be *Þat;* the following *f* of *fleþ* may have influenced the error in a case of prolepsis.
[4] "Power over."
[5] "Neither for / through prayer nor for gift."
[6] "It (i.e. death) has no compassion for the helpless, nor does it respect riches, or wisdom, or character or age"; (in other words, death does not pity helplessness, want, or need) [adapted from Bernard, *PL* 182, col 843].
[7] Cancelled with underscored dots; in l. 1566, *to* is cancelled with one firm line.

	For eu(er)y man scholde be war of deþes þretyng	f. 21r	threat
	Mortem esse commu(n)e(m) cunctis scito viventib(us).[1]		
1575	Know thow he saith þat deþ wol by the passe		come to you
	For it is com(m)une to all bothe more and lasse.		
	Thus schal deþ visite oueral eche man.		
	Ac ȝut what deþ is no man discerne[2] kan		
	Ȝut þe payne of deþ that eche lyf feleþ sore		
1580	A philisophre telleþ us in hys lore.[3]		philosopher
	How a philisophre discreueth deþ.		describes
	Here he lykneþ mannes lif to a tre		likens
	That were growynge ȝif it myȝt so be		
	Thorow a mannes herte and so schuld sprynge		
1585	Þat it myght at the laste lif þ(er)on brynge		
	And the croppe at the mowþe out come myghte		
	And to euery a joynt a rote schulde dyghte		be prepared
	And that ech a veine þat is in a mannes body		
	Hadde a rote fastned harde ther by		
1590	And to ech a toe and fyng(er) in hond also		
	Were a rote f(ro)m the tre growyng þ(er)to		
	And in eche leme þat is in any side		
	Þe rotes of the tre schulde faste[4] abide		remain
	And ȝif þulk tre were owhere ypullid abowte		anywhere
1595	Þat þe rotes most aryse and schewe hem wyþ oute		
	Than schulde the rotys þ(er)wyth sone aryse		
	And euery veyne and synew also in his wyse		
	Than a more peyne couthe no man caste		
	Þan þis were as long as it schulde laste.		
1600	Ȝut holde the peyne of deþ more strong		Yet, severe
	And hardur in his tyme ac it lasteþ not long.		although
	Therfore eche man as it is for said		aforementioned
	May gretly drede the harde deþes braid.		cruel stroke of death
	Ac the moste drede is than(n)e w(i)t(h)ynne		fear
1605	Ȝif a mannes soule be in dedly synne		if
	Therfore þe prophet seyth þus in his bok		
	And warneth us þat we þ(er)to haue a lok:		
	O mors quam amara memoria tua ho(min)i iniusto.[5]		
	O thow byttur deth and dredful saith he		
1610	Ful gresly it is for to thenk on the		terrifying
	And namely to thulk man þ(a)t is ful of synne		
	Wherfore his conscience ys greuyd with ynne		

---

[1] "Know that death is universal for all the living" [Pseudo-Bede *PL* 90, col. 1077, alluding to Scipio].

[2] In this case of metathesis of *er/re*, the manuscript text reads *discrene*.

[3] The last four words are emended by the *Piers* rubricator.

[4] Scribed over an erasure.

[5] "O death, how bitter is the remembrance of thee (to a man that hath peace in his possessions)." (Variant: "to an unjust man" [Ezechiel 3: 20]).

	Wherfore me þynkeþ þat he is nat sly	f. 21v	clever
	Þat me makeþ hym to þe deþ al redy		
1615	Ffor so sertayn on erþe is no man		
	Þat his endyng day [þat his]¹ for soþe telle kan		
	Ne þe tyme of deþ ne kan he heere loke		see
	Þerfore seint bernard seith þus in his boke		
	Quid in rebus humanis cercius est morte.		
	*Et quid incercius hora mortis invenit(ur).*²		
1620	He saith what is to man more certayn		
	Þan is deþ þat is eu(er)e sodayn		
	And what is more uncertayn þing		
	Þan is the tyme of deþes comyng		
	Therfore³ saiþ seint austyn⁴ þ(a)t good man		
1625	Seiþe⁵ þus as y heere to ȝow schewe [ ]⁶ kan		
	Nescis qua hora veniat mors . ideo semp(er) vigila ut cu(m) ven(er)it paratu(m)		
	*te inveniat . et tempus illius forte nescis . [sed] ut deo semp(er) e(st)is parat(us).*⁷		
	Man þu knowest nought seith he		
	What tyme deþes comyng schal be		
	Therfore wake as þu haddest ay knowyng		watch, always
1630	Of the t(i)ne and tyme of deþes comyng		moment
	That deþ finde þe whan he come schal		
	Euere in alle þinges as goddes owne þral		servant
	Ffor thu schuldest not p(er)chaunce knowe		
	The comynge of deþ to holde þe lowe		
1635	And in thi conscience to make þe ȝare		ready
	For in his comyng he wol not spare		
	Whan behoueþ us our lif for to kaste		profits, fashion
	As eu(er)y dai of our lyf [it] were þe laste		
	And eu(er)y day þ(er)to us aredy make		prepared
1640	Ryght as we schulde eche day the deþ take		
	And nat abide tyl deþ us visite		wait
	Therfore seint austyn in his bok doþ wryte		
	Latet nobis ultim(us) dies: ut b(e)n(e) obs(er)vent(ur) cet(er)i dies.		
	Sero eni(m) parant(ur) remedia: cu(m) mortis ven(er)int p(er)ic(u)la ⁸.		
	The last dai of man he saith is hud bi alle assaies		hid, trials
1645	For he schulde kepe wel alle his othur daies		
	Ffor men ordeineþ remedie al to late		
	Whan þe pereles of deþ beþ ate gate		dangers
	And in thulk stat that he is ynne yfounde		that

---

[1] One line cancels these two words.

[2] "What is more certain in human affairs than death and what is more uncertain is when the hour of death will come about" [Bernard, *PL* 182, col. 621, and Anselm, *Liber Meditationum,* Meditatio VII; consulting Sister Benedicta Ward's translation in *The Prayers and Meditations of Saint Anselm With The Proslogion* (London: Penguin Books, 1973)].

[3] The final *e* appears to have been added in a darker ink.

[4] The *a* of Austyn is not appreciably larger than the other letters in the name here, as it is in some other places.

[5] *Seiþe* is lightly crossed out here; *saiþ* occurs in the previous line.

[6] An erasure and a blank space occur here between *schewe* and *kan*.

[7] "You do not know at what hour death will come: therefore, always be watchful so that when it does come, it will find you ready. Perhaps you do not know its time, but you will always be prepared for God" [Augustine *PL* 37, col. 1606]. The word *sed* has been crossed out.

[8] "The last day is concealed from us so that the other days may be closely watched. For a remedy is prepared too late when the peril of death has come" [Augustine *PL* 38, col. 241, supplied by Chris Nighman, Department of History, Wilfred Laurier University, Waterloo, Ontario. Nighman reads *Paro* as *Sero* but the letter does not extend below the line line as would an "S." This quotation is attributed to *Augustinus in quandam epistola,* echoing Eccles. 5: 8-9 and I Tim. 6:19].

	He schal ben y demed in a lytyll stonde	f. 22r	judged, time
1650	Wherfore a man for drede of lettynge		impediment
	Schulde nat abide the deþes comynge		wait for
	Bot make hym redy ar he fele any hard		hardship
	And him self wel kepe aftyrward		
	Ffor whan deþ is to the ȝate ycome		gate
1655	Þan he haþ his warnynge al to late inome		
	Ffor deþ f(ro)m a man his mynde bereueþ		deprives
	And no kyndly wit w(i)t(h) hym be byleueþ		wisdom, is left / remains
	Ffor than he schal fynde suche peyne and drede		
	Þat he ne schal þanne thenk in no mysdede		sin
1660	But in his peyne and in no þing elles.		
	As seynt austyn þe grete clerk telles.		
	Timor mortis tota(m) an(im)am sibi vendicat . ut non de p(ec)c(a)tis libeat cogitare.[1]		
	Drede he saith of deþ whan it assaileþ a man		attacks
	Chalangeth the soule and makeþ þe bodi wan		claims, faint
1665	So that him lusteþ þan(n)e to haue no thouȝt		
	Of his synnes that he haþ here iwrouȝt.		committed
	Therfore y consaile ech a man to amende hym here		advise, repair
	Or deth come to hym or sende his messangere		Before
	And ȝif he byfore be so wel y ware		
1670	Þan schal deþ of sinnes fynde him al bare		naked
	His messag(er) for sothe may be clepid sikness		called
	Þat comeþ afore and bryngeþ a man in distresse		
	Ffor siknesse ofte tymes pyneþ a man so		
	Þat for gret siknesse his mynde passeþ hi(m) fro		
1675	Ffor in that tyme he may thenke o no thyng elles		
	But in that peyne that on hym dwelles		
	Ac whan to hym deþ comeþ sone afturward		
	Than schal he fele peynes more hard		
	Ffor than he schal be set in suche a drede		
1680	Þat he schal of hym self take but lytil hede		
	And that is skyle for that he nolde nouȝt		reason
	Whiles that he myght haue god in his þouȝt.		
	Therfore he schal thanne leose al his mynde		
	For thus wel we mowe in austynes wordes fynde		
1685	*Hac animav(er)sione p(er)cutit(ur) peccator ut moriens . Obliviscator sui . qui du(m) viveret oblitus est dei.*[2]		
	The synful man he saith as it is ywryte		
	W(i)t(h) the payne of deþ he schal be ysmyte.		struck

---

[1] "The fear of death claims the entire soul for itself, so that it does not willingly think about its sins" [Rupertus, *PL* 167, col. 1811].
[2] "The sinner, while he is dying, is stuck by this perception: unmindful of himself while he was living, he forgot God" [Pseudo-Augustine, *PL* 39, col. 2153].

Part III. Death

	That for the peyne that on hym schal falle	f. 22v
	Hym self he forȝeteþ and aftur non helpe can calle	forgets
1690	Or while he leued heere aft(ur) his own wille	
	He forȝat god and wolde nat his hestes fulfulle	promises
	Also synful men haueþ here not g(ra)ce	
	To haue of repentaunce noþ(ur) tyme ne space.	
	Thus schal he die and leose heuene blysse	
1695	And be iput in peyne þ(a)t is w(i)t(h)oute lysse	respite
	Ffor that þei be to god so uncorteis in dede	rude
	Wherfore in the saut(e)r david þus doþ grede	Psalter, cry out
	Vos autem sicut homines moriemini et	
	sicut unus de principib(us) cadetis.[1]	
	He saith that ȝe men [ȝe][2] schul die alle	
1700	And as on of þe p(ri)nces[3] ȝe schull do(u)n falle.	one
	That is þus to seie ȝe schal die in þat manere	
	As alle men dieþ in þis world here	
	And as þe gostes[4] felle f(ro)m heuene ado(u)n	
	And were into helle cast w(i)t(h) sturyng of asoun.	stirring / rushing, sound
1705	Therfore to eche man it were a gret wysdom	
	Him repente of his synnes ar þat deþ com[5]	before
	And haue god in mynde while a lyue he is	alive
	As the prophet comaundeþ þat to us saiþ þis	
	Memento creatoris tui an(te)q(ua)m veniat tempus	
	visitac(i)o(n)is sue[6].	
1710	Thenk man he saith and e(ve)re haue in þi þouȝt	
	Him that the made here ferst of nouȝt	
	While þu art aliue and er þy tyme schal be	before
	Whan god wyth deþ wol visite the	death
	Ffor deþ mannes mynde clene al to brekeþ	breaks to bits
1715	And therfore david þus to god spekeþ	
	Dom(i)ne non est in morte qui memor sit tui.[7]	
	Lord he saith þat man on lyue is nought	
	Þat in tyme of deþ in þe haþ his þouȝt	you
	Ac men mowe undyrstonde ther by	must
1720	Þe deþ of soule þorow synne namly	
	For the man that on god myndeles ys	forgetful
	Hit semeþ that in soule he is ded iwis	
	God visiteþ us ou(er) al by eu(er)y away	
	Where þe toknes of deþ fele me(n) may	symbols
1725	Ffor ȝif we cowthe us wel undurstonde	could
	Þe toknes of deþ eche day doþ us fond	

---

[1] "But you like men shall die, and shall fall like one of the princes" [Psalm 81:7]. The second Latin line is not underlined in red as are most others.

[2] Note the scribe's textual emendation in deleting the second ȝe here.

[3] Before their sin of pride, Lucifer and his band were called "princes" in Psalm 81:6-7. The irony is that God tells Lucifer that he will die like human beings and fall like one of the (human) princes.

[4] Again, referring to the Biblical fall of the angels after their sin against God.

[5] Various emendations on this line and on the rest of f. 22r appear to be auto-corrections; the erasures are visible, but not what was erased.

[6] "Remember thy Creator in the days of thy youth, before the time of his affliction come … " [Eccles. 12:1].

[7] "Lord, there is no one in death, that is mindful of thee" [Psalm 6:6].

	Wherfore me thinkeþ al that here semeth	f. 23r	
	In more deþ than lif for wyse man so demeþ		judge
	Ffor the bok¹ seith as it is y wryte byfore		
1730	Þan a man as sone as he is y bore		That
	He bygi(n)neþ toward the deþ forto drawe		
	And with dyuerse eueles ys oft ygnawe		gnawed
	As angurnesses and siknesses that falleþ al day		distress
	Þe whiche as dethes þrowes calle me(n) may		throes
1735	And in othur weies and p(er)elles many on		one
	Þat ofte greueþ men in flesch and bon		bone
	Than is our burthe heere abydynge		awaiting
	A bodely deþ whiche is our endynge		physical
	Ffor eu(er)e the more that a man wexeþ old		becomes
1740	The more may his lif deþ be itold		
	Than semeþ our lyf here no thing elles		
	Bote al as deþ so us the bok telles		
	And to that othur lyf ne wende we now3t		
	Tyl deþ to an ende þis lyf haþ brow3t		
1745	Ac whan deþ of our lyf haþ y made an ende		But
	Þan wite we neu(er) to sothe wedur we wende		know, truly, whither / when
	Wheþ(er) we schul be in wele or in wo		happiness
	Ac to þat on for certayn we schul nedes go		one
	And to good men deþ is the next way		
1750	To þe blysse of heuene þat schal lasten ay		always
	And to euel men that passeþ þat entre		entrance
	In the pyne of helle þei schulleþ eu(er) be		
	Therfore david that was an holy p(ro)phete		
	Þus spekeþ to god w(i)t(h) wordes fayr and swete		
1755	*Qui exaltas me de portis mortis ut annunciem*		
	*O(mn)es laudaciones tuas in portis filie syon.*²		
	Lord ihu cryst he seith thu art he		Jesus
	That fram the 3ates of deþ lefteþ me		
	That i may schewe ouer al thinges		reveal
	Þe grete mychulnesse of þy preysynges		magnitude
1760	In the gates of thi holy doughtur syon		
	Þulke gate as clerkes telleþ þat cunneþ þ(er)on³		This, know
	Is holy cherche þat god formest ches		first chose
	By the whiche men comeþ to the gate of pes		peace
	And by gates of deþ as men may se		
1765	The deþ of helle may undurstonded be		

---

¹ The *b* of *bok* is somewhat smeared with ink, filling in the lower lobe. *Þan* in the next line might be an error for *Þat*. Note that this page contains many lines beginning with a form of *þan*.
² "Thou that liftest me up from the gates of death, that I may declare all thy praises in the gates of the daughter of Sion" [Psalm. 91:15].
³ An emendation by the *Piers* rubricator marks the last two words of the line, as well as *men may* (l.1764) and *be* (l.1765). *Syon* (l.1760) appears to be autocorrected.

Part III. Death (1766–1803)

	Ffram the wyche god lufteþ us up both nygth[1] and day	f. 23v	lifts
	To schewe us his loue al that he may		
	Therfore we schulde serue hym and his wylle wurche		work
	In the good bileue of all holy churche		belief
1770	So þat we may þeraftyrward wende		go
	To þe cite of pes the whiche haþ non ende		peace
	Ac alle men that schulleþ to þat cite come		
	Schulleþ hennes passe w(i)t(h) deþ alle and some		
	Ac thulk deþ is to hem no thing ille		that
1775	Þat lyueþ on erþe aftur goddes wylle		according to
	And in suche lyf stedefastly dwelleþ		
	As seint austyn þer of thus telleþ		
	Mala mors illi putanda non est . quem		
	in vita boni actus precesseru(n)t.[2]		
	He saith me(n) schulde nat euel deþ to him wene		suppose
1780	Þat in good dedes wolde his lif mene		signify
	Ffor no thing makeþ a man so euel of bost		boasting / bragging
	As euell dedes that foloweþ deþ most		
	Ffor þei arn dedly in her dedes þat syn(n)e wolleþ do		are
	And therfore seint austyn seith more ther to		
1785	*Non potest male mori . qui bene vixerit .*		
	Et vix bene moritur . qui male vixerit.[3]		
	He saith he may nat euel deþ haue		
	Þat in godes lawe leueþ his soule to saue		lives
	Ac unneþe men mowen se by any reso(u)n		scarcely, might
	That he dieþ wel þat ledeþ his lyf in treso(u)n.		
1790	Ac he þat hateþ þis lyues lykynge		desires
	Ne dar neuer drede of deþes comynge		
	Ffor aftur his deþ no thyng schal hym greue[4]		
	As caton in ensample doþ us to bileue		
	Non metuit mortem . qui scit contempn(er)e vita(m).[5]		
1795	He saith he þat kan this lif despise		knows how to
	Schal neu(er) deþ drede in no wyse		fashion
	Ffor so dede þe martures[6] þ(a)t þe deþ souȝte		martyrs
	For aftur this world no þing þei ne wrouȝte		
	And oþur holy men coueytid to deþe be ditht		disposed
1800	To be w(i)t(h) god an hie in heuene bryght		
	As the bokes of her lyf scheweþ to us		
	For so dede an holy man that saith þus		
	Cupio dissolui et esse cum xpo.[7]		

---

[1] The last seven words have been emended by the *Piers* rubricator who has reversed *ht* to *th* here, perhaps a dialectical variation. The Latin quotations on this page and elsewhere are written in a larger hand.

[2] "Death cannot be considered evil which good acts have preceeded in this life" [Augustine, *PL* 41, col. 25].

[3] "One who has lived well cannot die badly. And one who has lived badly will scarcely die well" [Augustine, *PL* 40, col. 676].

[4] The last six words have been emended by the *Piers* rebricator.

[5] "One who knows how to despise life does not fear death" [*Distichs of* Cato, IV: *22*].

[6] This word should likely read "martures" although the text ambiguously appears to read either "martires" or "martures."

[7] "I desire to be dissolved and to be with with Christ" [adapted from Philippians 1:23]. The scribe has penned an abbreviation sign above the "xpo for ("christ"), but the final *o* in the ablative case ("christo") is correct without further abbreviating the ending.

	I coueyte he saith hennes forto wende	f. 24r	desired
1805	Fro this lif and to be wyth cryst w(i)t(h)outen ende		
	And for holi men þoughten that al þis lif		
	Was nought but angur, travayle, and strif		grief, work
	Therfore þei coueited þe ende of her lif day		desired
	As an holy man saith as me(n) heere rede may		
1810	*Melius est dies mortis qu(am) dies nativitatis.*[1]		
	He saith bet(ter) is the day of the deþ alone		
	Þanne the day of burþe þ(a)t is ful of wo and mone		complaint
	Ffor a good man dieþ forto wende to reste		go
	Where that lif is endeles and ioye at the beste		
1815	Whan the soule schal f(ro)m the body gon		
	As in the apokalypss saith seint iohon		Apocalypse
	Beati mortui qui in d(omi)no moriuntur.[2]		
	I blessid be thei alle in dede and in word		
	That dieth here in wurschipe of our lord		honor
1820	Ffor al þo þat doþ in god lyf ende		
	Þey dieþ in god and schulleþ to him wende		
	To the blisse of heuene that is so an hy		
	And wel is hym þ(a)t þorowh deþ may come so ny		near
	Ac naw3t for than þou3 holy men die wel		
1825	3ut the peynes of deþ þei schul fele somdel		somewhat
	Ac than thei schulleþ a newe lif wynne		
	Whan the bodi and þe soule beth departed atwynne.		are separated / come apart
	Therfore in party þei shulleþ haue drede		
	Þorow mannes kynde and þorow al manhede		nature
1830	Ffor suþþe that crist dred deþ in his passio(u)n		since
	Þorow kynde of his flesch as it was reso(u)n		nature
	Than owt a man bothe lasse and more		
	Of þe bit(ter) deþ to drede more sore		severely
	The secunde skile whi men dredeþ deþ.		
1835	ℭhe secunde skyle is as y in bok rede		council
	Whi that deþ so gretly to drede		
	Ffor þe gresly sight of many fendes		horrible
	Þat a man schal yse and fewe othur frendes		
	Whan that mannes lif draweþ to þe ende		
1840	Man wot neu(er) wodur he schal thanne wende[3]		whither
	Ffor whan the lif of a man heere is in dowte		
	Þan wolleþ deueles come hym faste abowte		
	To rauaische with hem the poore sowle away		

---

[1] "Better is the day of death than the day of of birth" [Eccles. 7:2]. The full text reads: "A good name is better than precious ointments and the day of death than the day of one's birth."

[2] "Blessed are the dead who die in the Lord" [Apocalypse. 14:13].

[3] The last four lines have been corrected by the *Piers* rubricator.

	To þe pyne of helle for þat is her pray	f. 24v	prey
1845	Ffor as wode lions thei schulleþ þan fare		wild
	And raunpe¹ on hym and grysly grenne and stare		rear up, injure, terrify
	And grymly on hem grone and her tonges blere²		wail, bellow
	And wyth hidoȝ lokynge hem sore afere		hideous stares, terrify
	And so thei wolleþ stonde stille at his endynge		silent
1850	Ȝif thei myght by any wey hym in wanhope brynge		despair
	Torow thre tynges that thei wolleþ þanne make		through
	And þorow the drede that thei schulleþ take		
	Ffor ful hidos siȝtes thei wolleþ to hem schewe		sights
	Of the company that stondeth in her rewe³		
1855	Wherfore þe holi p(ro)phete . Jeremye⁴		
	Telleth thes wordes in his p(ro)phecye		
	*Omnes inimici eiu(s) apprehenderu(n)t eu(m) int(er) angustias.*⁵		
	He saith that among his anguisches grete		
	His enemys schulleþ him take and nat lete.		release
1860	Than is it no wondur þaw the deueles come		
	To the synful man whan he is w(i)t(h) deth in(n)ome		taken
	As the fend cam to seint bernard at his laste day		
	Him for to bryng in to strong afray.		terrify
	How þe deuel apered to seynt bernard.		
1865	Thus it is founde in þe bok of seint bernard .		
	Whan that he drowhe faste to þe deþward .		drew
	That the fend so grysly for soþe as ytelle		horrid
	Þus him asked w(i)t(h) wordes swithe felle .		very terrible
	Thorow what skyle he askede þe kyngdom of heuene		
1870	So as he had ben gulty in þe dedly synnes seuene.		
	Than answered seint bernard to hym this		
	And saide þat y am a man unwurþi ywys		
	Thorowh myn own desert it forto haue		
	Whan y schal fram this lyf wende to my g(ra)ue		
1875	Ac my lord ihu crist that ful his⁶ of myght		Jesu(s)
	And al þing weldeþ þorow his owne ryght⁷		right
	And þorowe the right of his fadres eritage		heritage
	And also for cristen mann(es) avantage		advantage
	And þorow riht of his harde passio(u)n		justice
1880	Þe which he suffred for our saluacyon		salvation
	That ilke right freli he grauntyd me		
	And þat othur del to hym self schuld be		part
	Of whos riht y chalange heuene riche⁸		claim

---

¹ This word and several others on this page have been corrected by the *Piers* rubricator.
² This vivid depiction of the devil uses boldly effective sensory details: touch as he rears up upon the soul, hearing as he groans, taste and sight as his tongue protrudes, and he stares menacingly in this dualistic framework of body-soul/mind dichotomy. This characteristic of using sensational detail makes the poem compelling and memorable, and may in part account for its great popularity.
³ "… lines up with their group."
⁴ Uncharacteristically, the scribe seems to have capitalized "Jeremye."
⁵ "All her persecutors have taken her in the midst of straits." Lamentations 1:3 uses the feminine *eam* because it refers to a feminine gender noun, Juda, but the poet was writing of a male soul not a female soul, and so substitutes *eum* for *eam*.
⁶ A more logical reading is probably *is* rather than *his*, which error may have been prompted by the next line's "*his*;" it could also be a dialectical variation.
⁷ The word *right* refers to the deity's prerogative as creator and owner of all.
⁸ The textual misbinding ends here: the manuscript order, from f. 1-16v (p. 23–54), then from f. 25r-32v (p. 71–86), then from p. 55–70 to 24 v now continues properly here from 33-94v (p. 87–209).

	As his mercy weele that al þing is unliche	f. 25r	unequal
1885	Ac whan þe fend had iherd him þus speke		devil
	As ouercome he bygan anon away to breke		
	And the holy man whan al þis was don		
	Torned to his mynde there after anon		
	And ȝelde up his gost and deyde right þo		died
1890	And þo his soule into heuene gan go .		went
	Ac ȝut it is more wondur forto telle		amazing
	Whi god suffred the deuel of helle		allowed
	To apere to hym self that is of myghtes most		power
	Whan þat he dieȝed hym self and ȝaf up his gost		died
1895	Ffor gret doctors witnesseþ it		
	In her bokes that beþ of holy writ		
	Than semeþ it wel that he wolde þus		
	Suffre þe fend of helle apere to us		allow
	In þe tyme of deþ at our laste ende		
1900	Whan þat we schulleþ f(ro)m [hem]¹ hennes wende		
	Ac a strong peyne to us that schal be		
	Þe sight of hem that we schul þanne ise		
	Ffor þei beþ so grysly² as saith the boke		horrid
	And so blak and so hidouȝ on to loke		
1905	That alle men de³ þat may on erþe devise		
	Of þulke foul sight might sore agryse .		that, be horrified
	Ffor alle þe men that beþ on erþe aliue		
	So gresly a sight ne cowthe discryue		could describe
	Ne non so sly peynt(our)s on erþe aliue nas		clever painter
1910	No his slyþe neuere so muche was		cleverness
	That cowthe owht deuise for his horriblenesse⁴		could anything describe
	Oþur peinte a poynt of his liknesse		Or, detail
	Ffor that in þis lif may no man make		
	Ne se the forme that thei hauen take		perceive
1915	Ac ȝif thei hadde of god so large powere		Unless
	In such forme as thei beþ to schewen hem here.		
	Al out of witte þei schuld make men agast⁵		insane, terrified souls
	For þei beþ into so horrible sight icast.		
	And so hardi a man was ȝut neu(er) non		
1920	Þat leued in erþe in flesch and bon		
	That ȝif he siȝe a deuel in his fig(ure) aright		saw
	He schulde for drede of þat foule sight		
	Wel sone die or elles leose his wit		

---

¹ This is an auto-correct, crossed out with a single stroke.
² The first *y* has been written over an erasure, possibly by the *Piers* rubricator; neither is dotted.
³ The sense appears to be "se" although the scribe wrote "de." Morey's edition, ll. 2302–03, confirms the reading as "see."

⁴ The *Piers* rubricator has scribed the word "horriblenesse" over an erasure; the readers reminded of many of Dante's scenes of horror.
⁵ This is another instance of the poet's hyperbolic imagination, as terrified souls go mad or fall over dead from the sight of devils. He is very creative.

	As sone as he hadde biholde it	f. 25v
1925	Bot in that forme as i undirstonde can	
	Thei ne scheweþ hem here to no lyuynge man.	
	Bot only to hem to wham the deþ is nere	
	For god haþ so refreynyd hem her powere¹	restrained
	That þei mowe tempte no man no greue	may, injure
1930	No more forþur þan god hath 3oue hem leue	further, given
	Whan þat deþ wol a man assaile	test
	In his foulest fig(ur)e he wol be at his tayle.²	
	Therfore eche man dredyng schulde be	
	A3enst þe tyme that he schulde hem se	
1935	Ac iwole to 3ow schewe wysliche	
	Whi thei beþ so foule and so grysliche	horrible
	Ffor sum tyme whan thei were angels bryght	
	As þei beþ þat now beþ afore goddes sight	
	Ffram þulke place þorow synne þei felle	
1940	And anon bicome foule fendes of helle	
	And were horibly disfugured for synne	because of
	Where with þei were deffoulyd and iwrapped ynne³	dirtied
	Ffor 3if synne ne were þey hadden be stille	
	Bright angels as [as]⁴ þei were ferst þorow goddes wille	
1945	Ac now þei beþ foule and unsemliche	ugly
	And þat is þorow þe synne of p(ri)de onliche⁵	only
	That synne is more foul and more wlatsome	disgusting
	Þan any fend that out of helle may come	
	Ffor clerkes saith that beþ of gret connynge	
1950	Þat synne is so foul and so grysly a thynge	horrid
	That 3if a man myght so bifore him se hys synne	
	In þe same liknesse that he falleþ inne	
	He scholde than for drede it raþ(er) fle	run
	Þan any fende of helle that he myght se.	
1955	Than is þe soule of a synful man w(i)t(h)ynne	
	Fouler than a fend that goþ bounde w(i)t(h) synne.	Dirtier
	Therfore a man scholde where so þat he wendes	
	More drede synne than the sight of fendes.	
	The whiche schullen apere to hym at his deþ day	
1960	For his synne schal þan(n)e be at fowler aray	array
	Of þe whiche he wolde nat hym schryue	confess
	Ne repentaunce heere take in his lyue	
	Ffor us bihoueþ echone in godes owne sight	profits

---

[1] The phrase "refreynyd hem her powere" can be translated as "restrained them in their use of power."
[2] The phrase "at his tayle" suggests "following him or behind him," and "at the end of his life." This expression also implies an animal image, further debasing the lost soul. Similarly, this image further suggests these ideas in Chaucer's Prologue to the *Summoner's Tale*.
[3] The image of befouled devils all wrapped up in physical "sin" like a corn husk or a garbage bag is ingenious. John Milton's *Paradise Lost*, drawing upon Milton's patristic knowledge, deals in the same type of imagery when describing Lucifer (the Light Bearer) after his fall.
[4] Note scribal emendation to delete ... the repeated word *as*.
[5] The *Piers* rubricator has emended this word and several others on this page.

	Acowntes ȝelde of þe wrong . as wel as of þe right	f. 26r	give
1965	And of alle thinges that eu(er) here we wrought		did
	In werk in wille in word in thought		
	Here is þe þridde skile . why men dreden deþ.		
	The þridde skile is þis to our undurstondynge		third
	Whi eche lif dredeþ þe deþes comynge		
1970	Ffor al thyng schal ben schewed and sene		
	Boþe good and ille, foule and eke clene		also
	And be reherced as þe bok telleþ out right		revealed
	Bitwene foule fendes and angeles bright		devils
	Thei schulleþ þanne despute of al our lif		contend for
1975	Wyþ muche discord and also gret strif		conflict
	Ffor þanne al thyng schal ben ikyd		made known
	Bitwix hem þere and no thyng ben hid		secret
	Bot only synne that is iclansed here		purged
	And goode dedes that beth ido in right manere		done
1980	Than we schulleþ ihere and ise		
	Alle the pryue dedes that euer wroȝt we		performed
	Therfore crist saith in his gospelle		
	In this manere as iwol ȝowe telle		
	Nichil opertu(m) est . quod non reveletur.[1]		
1985	No þyng he saith here is so ihud		hidden
	That ne schal thanne be schewid and ikid		made known
	Than abide ther nedis moste we		wait, must
	For al our lyf clene examinid schal be		
	Therfore seint anselm as the boke telleþ us		
1990	Spekeþ scharpli to the soule[2] and saith þus		
	Wrecchid soule he saith what may thow wynne		
	Whan þat thow and þi bodi departen atwynne		are separated / come apart
	Than bihoueþ þe acountes to ȝelde		
	Of alle dedes þat þu hast do in ȝowþe and elde		
1995	Ffram the furst day þ(a)t þu haddest manes wit		reason
	Into þe laste day that þu schalt hennys flit.		escape
	Welaway[3] þan schal be þi song		
	For þu hast dispended þi wittes w(i)t(h) wrong.		dissipated
	Than schul þi synnes alle ben ischewed		avoided
2000	Wheþur thow be lered man oþ(er) lewed		
	Of the whiche þu schalt þanne more drede		fear
	Þan of the deueles that wollen þe awey[4] lede.		
	Thus schal eche man at his endynge		

---

[1] The Latin is correctly translated in the following lines: "Nothing is concealed that is not revealed." The author or scribe here and in HM 125 uses *nichil* instead of *nihil*; also HM 125 uses the future tense: *non revelabitur*–"will not be revealed."
[2] Another instance of the mind-body dualism as Anselm speaks to the deceased soul without its body.
[3] "Alas! Woe!" Morris, Hanna & Wood gloss this as "an exclamation of sorrow—'Well-away!' 'Well-away'" (under *walaway*, interj., l. 2434).
[4] This and other emendations on this page were made by the *Piers* rubricator.

	Ben yset to haue an harde rekenynge	f. 26v	accounting
2005	For þane schal no synne to hym be untold		
	Be it neuer so p(ri)ue ne be hit neuer so old		private
	And ifinde iwrite þre skiles whi		reasons
	Þat no man may trust sykurly[1]		surely
	In his goode dedes that he hath doon here		
2010	Þerefore þese skiles beþ good to lere		
	On is þawe alle þinges beþ for good itold		One
	Thei beþ of god ycome ther w(i)t(h) to make man bolde		
	So þat alle good dedes that ben iwrought		done
	Godes owne dedes þey beþ and our nought		ours
2015	Ac alle our synnes that men may iknow		But
	Comeþ of our seluen and thulke beþ our owe		own
	Ȝut anothur skile þat yknow also		
	Is for that we beþ redy euere mo		
	In hundred sithes rathur for to do synne		times
2020	Than ones a goode dede forto bigynne		once
	And so we may trewly rekene and rede		reckon / add up
	An hundred synnes aȝens o good dede.		
	The thridde skile is forto schewe among		third
	For our goode dedys ofte beþ don al with wrong		
2025	And nowȝt in right manere as þey schold be		not
	And p(er)chaunce þey beth don owt of charite		
	And þ(er)fore our goode dedys we schulde preyse nought		
	For saint austyn þ(at) aȝenst haþ þis reson wroȝt:[2]		
	Om(ne)s iusticie n(ost)re . quasi pannus menstruate[3]		
2030	He saith our goode dedes mowe ben isene		
	As a cloþ defouled with a thyng unclene.		defiled
	Therfore the sothe whot here man non[4]		knows
	How he schal fare whan he is hennes gon		
	Ac we schul bileue wiþ outen eny drede		
2035	That god wole us aquyte eche good dede		
	Ac ȝut we buþ not sikur þ(er) of in these daies		be, certain
	As witnesseþ an holy man that þus saies		
	Nescit homo utru(m) sit dign(us) per actibus suis amore v(e)l odio.[5]		
	He saith for certayn a man ne wot nowȝt		knows nothing
2040	Thaw he haue neu(er)e so muche good iwroȝt		done
	Wheþur he be wurþi after his dede		
	To haue loue of God othur hatrede		
	And isydre the[6] clerk as þe bok telluþ us		Isidore

---

[1] The last five words of this line and others on this page were emended by the *Piers* rubricator.
[2] "For Saint Augustine, who countering this argument, has composed...."
[3] "All our justices are as the rag of a menstrous woman" [Pseudo-Augustine, *PL* 39 col. 1943, adapted from Douay-Rheims].
[4] Man knows not the truth here.
[5] "And yet man knoweth not whether, by his acts, he be worthy of love or hatred" [adapted from Douay-Rheims: Eccles 9:1]. Morris's Northern version reads *"Nescit homo utrum dignus sit odio vel amore"* (2514-15 in Hanna and Wood's re-edition of Morris).
[6] The scribe seems to have written *that*, but then erases the *t* and modified the *a* to look like an *e*: an auto correct.

	Acordeþ ther to and spekeþ þus:	f. 27r
2045	*Servus dei du(m) bonu(m) agit . utru(m) sit*	
	ei ad bonu(m) incertus est[1].	
	He saith he that is eu(er)e godes s(er)uaunt	
	And to al goodnesse makeþ his haunt[2]	
	Ʒut is he nowt certayn in thouʒt	not
	Whethur it[3] be to hym good oþ(er) nowʒt	or not
2050	Wherfore our lyuyng here is hard	
	And so witnesseþ wel seint bernard	
	Quis hic p(otes)t vita(m) sua(m) duce(re) sine t(ri)bulac(i)one et dolore.[4]	
	He saith who may his lif here lede	
	With oute gret tribulacion and drede	
2055	And therfore seint bernard to us here	
	Spekeþ of his lif in this manere	
	Teret me tota vita mea . que diligent(er) discussa	
	Apparet michi aut p(e)c(cat)u(m) aut sterilitas	
	Aut res similata et imp(er)fecta.[5]	
	Thes beþ bernardes wordis that seith þus	
	Al my lif here sore me greueþ iwis	
2060	Ffor ʒif it wel and euene discussid be	justly
	It semeþ, no þing elles here to me	
	But synne that the soule most dereþ	injures
	Othur bareyn thing that no fruit bereþ	Or barren
	And ʒif any fruit myght þ(er)inne seme	
2065	It mithte thus ben iset by skile forto deme.	might, judge
	Oþur afeyned thing to schewen in sitht	pretended, sight
	Othur elles a thing that is nat don al w(i)t(h) ritht	right
	So that it may bi no way be forþ brouʒt	
	To paie þer with god that us make of noʒt	satisfy
2070	So that al a mannes life is wyth sorowe ilad	led
	Wherfore no wondur is þei we be selde glad	though, seldom
	What may a synful man seie ther to	
	Whan he that was so holy in leuynge euer mo	wholly, living
	No cowþe no fruit in his life ise	could see
2075	Than may a man ful dredful be	
	Of his lif þat is euere unclene	
	In the whiche ther may no fruit ben isene	
	The ferþe skile whi men dred deþ.	
	𝕿he ferþe skile and the laste [is][6] forto telle[7]	
2080	Whi men dreden deth þat is so wond(er) felle	marvelously cruel
	Is for a man wot nat whodur to wende	whither

---

[1] While the servant of God does a good work, yet is he uncertain whether it is for his good" [Isidore Hispalensis, *PL* 83, col. 694].

[2] "Practices all goodness."

[3] This *Piers* rubricator emendation leaves spaces around *it;* the original word may have been longer.

[4] "He who is able to lead his life here without sorrow and tribulation ..." [Bernard *PL* 183, col. 662-63 "kist some ... dolore"].

[5] "My entire life terrifies me; carefully analyzed, it appears to me either sinful or unfruitful, or something counterfeited or imperfect" [Anselm of Canterbury, Mediation I, trans. Sister M. Benedicta Ward. Also Pseudo-Bernard *PL* 184, col. 525].

[6] This deletion is crossed off by two light strokes.

[7] Three large ink dots forming a triangle near the right margin of l. 2079-l. 2080 may be accidental or purposeful.

Part III. Death

	To joye or to peyne after his liues ende	f. 27v
	Ffor so wys a man was þer neuer non	
	That wist whan þe deþ schulde to hym gon	knew
2085	Ne wyst whan he schuld hennes fare	hence, go
	Ne wheþur that he schulde to ioy or to care	
	Ffor whan þe deueles and þe angels bryȝt	
	Haueþ al our lyf discussid out right	openly
	Than our dom schuld we haue	judgment
2090	Whethur that god wele[1] us dampne or saue	damn
	And wheþur we schulleþ to ioye or to peyne	
	As seynt austyn putte us in certeyn	

Bene unus q(ui)sq(ue) de die novissi(m)o pensar(et) debet q(ui)a
    unu(m) q(ue)mque in eode(m) statu quo invenit novissim(us) dies.
    T(a)lis en(im) iudicabit do(minus) in die ulti(m)o,[2]

	Eche man he saith that hennes schal passe away	
2095	Scholde euere drede his laste endyng day	
	Ffor in what stat that he be þan ifounde	
	Such schal he be demed in a lityl stounde	judged, time
	Therfore the laste day þat schal us bifalle	happen
	Our day of dome we may wel calle	judgment
2100	Ac at the general day of dome whan god schal come	doom
	Wiþ[3] our bodies þan we schal be inome	called
	Byfore ihu cryst that is almighti kyng	Jesus
	That schal on that day deme al þing	
	Ffor the bodies schal wende into þulke place	
2105	There as þe soule is demed þorow Goddes g(ra)ce	
	And othur thei schulleþ ioye haue ifere	together
	Othur ful sorowe whan they beþ ibroȝt þere	either, brought
	And euere after they schul to gidur dwelle	
	Wheþur that they wende to heuene or to helle	
2110	Ac in þe erþe schul dwelle þe bodies alle	But, earth
	Tyl that dredful day of dom be falle.	judgment
	And thulke dom schal be most streit and hard	such judgment
	As þis boke wol telle ther of aftyrward[4]	
	Ac the synful soule goþ þane to helle	
2115	In peyne that is endeles eu(er)e forto dwelle	
	Ac the clene soule goþ þanne ful euene	justly
	W(i)t(h) outen any lettynge an hi into heuene	delay
	Bot many a soule that god wol saue	
	Ar it come to blisse it mot peyne haue	Before
2120	In purgatory place and dwelle þ(er)ynne	

---

[1] An auto-correct with space around the correction.
[2] "Well ought everyone think about the last day, and the last day ought to find everyone in the same condition [of the soul]. For such the lord will judge on the final day." The Latin of the Northern version differs significantly: *Bene unusquisque de die novissimo formidare debet, quia unumquenque in quo invenerit suus novissimus dies, cum de hoc seculo egreditur, talis in die novissimo iudicatur.* [Augustine, *PL* 33, col. 905].
[3] The scribe has written an *h* in *Whiþ*, but this is likely just a regional variant.
[4] Another narrative device of this author is to tie his treatise together by anticipating and noting future elaborations of his discussion.

	Fort sche be iclansid clene owt of synne	f. 28r	purified
	Ffor in heuene may no soule be seie		seen
	Tyl sche be iclansid by eu(er)y aweie		way
	Oþur heere þorowe penaunce as clerkes us kenneþ		Or, show
2125	Or elles in purgatory þorow fuyr that hote brenneth		
	And þat sowle that is iclansid wel		cleansed
	Of alle dedly synnes and eke of veniel		venial
	Thorowe penaunce don here and also almesdede		almsgiving
	Angels of heuene schulleth here sone lede		
2130	Whan þat sche passeþ f(ro)m the body away		
	An hy into heuene to blysse þat lasteþ ay.		always
	Therfore wo so wele folowe wysdome		
	He scholde ben war er þat deþ come		prudent
	And make hym redy and clanse hym clene		
2135	Of alle þe spices of synne þat myght on hym be sene		types
	So that deþ hym fynde clene out of synne		
	Whan body and soule schul departe atwynne		separate / come apart
	And euere þenke on his lyues ende		
	Whiles þat he leueþ forto he hennes wende		until
2140	And so he may hym kepe f(ro)m the deueles s(er)uise		
	For thus us techeth salamon the wyse		
	In omnib(u)s o(per)ibus tuis . memorare novissima		
	tua, et ineternu(m) non per cabis.[1]		
	He saith thenk man euere on thin endyng day		
	ʒif þu[2] thenkest god wel to queme and to pay		satisfy
2145	Euere whan thow schalt any werk bigynne		
	And than schalt þu falle in no synne		
	And þenke þat þu schalt die and wost neu(er) whanne		know
	Ne in what state þu myst be take thanne.		must
	Wherfore by the morowe whan þu seost liʒt		see
2150	Thenke þat thu mayst deye[3] long ar it be nyʒt		before
	And whan thow gost to slepe ʒif þu do as þe wyse		
	Thenk riʒt as thow scholdest þyn endyng day [day][4] divise		plan
	For seint austyn seith þus in his holy boke		
	Let euere þin herte on thi last ende loke		
2155	And whoso weel þenkeþ in þis manere		considers
	And of alle his synnes clanseþ him heere		
	Than may he the lightlior purgatory passe		liklier
	And his bytur peynes somdel make lasse		
	And come to the blysse of heuene so bryght		
2160	Where it is euere day and neu(er) more night.		always

---

[1] "In all thy works, remember thy last end, and thou shalt never sin" [Eccles. 7: 40]. Small tight, even script marks this Latin quotation, perhaps because the scribe wanted it to fit on one line.

[2] The *u* is superscripted here (l. 2144) and in ll. 2146 and 2151. Several dotted y's are used, as at 2136 "synne," and 2143 "day."

[3] *Mayst deye* and *at* are emended by the *Piers* rubricator; *deye* has a dotted *y*.

[4] The second *day* has been deleted with a line through it, but the ink looks fainter than that of the text, and so may have been corrected later.

Here biginneþ þe feorþ part of þis book þat telleþ of p(ur)gatorie.[1] f. 28v

    Many man spekeþ as he in boke redeþ   men
    Of the place of purgatory ac fewe it dredeþ   fear
    Ffor many men wote nere what it ys.   never know

2165   Þerfore þei dredeþ it wel the lasse iwys
And that is for some haueþ no knowynge   because
Of purgatory ne no good undurstondynge.
Therfore i wol telle what it ys in lyknesse   essentially
And where it is as the bok bereþ wytnesse

2170 And why soules þidur goþ and for what synne
And what maner peynes þei suffreþ þ(er)e w(i)t(h)ynne
And also what þy(n)g ys most in certayne
That myghte soules brynge owt of þat peyne.

Here he[2] **telleþ what purgatorie is.**

2175   Purgatorye soþly is now3t elles to telle   truly
    Bot a clansyng place where sowles schul dwelle   purifying
The whiche hauen don synne and take cont(ri)cion
And beþ in the wey of salvacyon
And þere þei schul soffre peyne wol towe   very severe

2180 Tyl þei ben clansed p(ar)fitly ynowe   enough
Of alle here synnes that they eu(er)e wro3te .   committed
In worde . in wil . in dede .[3] and in þo3te   will, deed or act and thought
Ffor so clene ipured neu(er) gold was   purified
As þei schullen be that passeþ that pas.   passage

2185 Wherfore þe peyne þat the soule þere hente   experiences
Ys more bit(ter) than was al the tormente
That alle martires suffred boþe 3ong and olde
Suþþe þat god for us was bou3t and solde   Since
Ffor þe leste peyne of hem that beþ þere

2190 Is more than the moste that euer was here .
As telluþ a gret clerk to us þus schortly   briefly
In a bok that spekeþ of peynes of purgatory
Minima purgatorii pena . est maior maxi(m)a pena mu(n)di.[4]
He saiþ the leste peine is wel more

2195 Of purgatory that sm(ar)teþ sore   hurts grievously
Than the moste payne that might be
In al þis world to fele or to se
Ffor the peine þere is more fers and felle   cruel
Þan herte may þenke or any tong telle

2200 Ffor bitwene the peyne of helle certeynly

---

[1] The page has been defaced by a sharp object running across its surface from top to bottom, and penetrating through the vellum. The text is still legible, so the act appears a symbolic gesture (a rejection of the concept of Purgatory?). The red ink of *p(ur)gatorie* is smeared, perhaps by water contact. Headings, usually with blue paraph for rectos and red for versos, are here modified: blue is used for this verso, (because of a preponderance of red on this page?). Manuscript trimming makes the words "Quarta pars" barely visible. See Jacques le Goff, *The Birth of Purgatory*, Chicago: University of Chacago Press (1986).

[2] An odd heading, since we don't know who "he" is if not the scribe or author himself.

[3] Periods functioning as commas seem to emphasize the constitutionary parts of the whole person involved in committing different kinds of sins. They are not *puncti elevati*. They are the faculties of the soul and considered analogues of the Trinity.

[4] "The least pain of purgatory is greater than the greatest pain on earth" [Augustine *PL* 41.728, echoed by the "gret clerk" Peter Abelard, *PL* 178, col. 672].

	And bitwene the peyne of purgatory[1]	f. 29r.	
	Is no maner difference bot for þat on		type of, except, one
	Haþ an ende and that othur neu(er) hath non		
	Ffor þe peynes of helle schul neu(er) cese		cease
2205	Ne the soules ther ynne neuer haue relece		release
	Ac in purgatory the soules dwelleþ stille		yet
	Til thei ben iclansed of synne that is ille		
	And as muche beþ were fourty daies tolde		
	As here fourty ȝere be a man neu(er) so olde		years
2210	So the peyne of o day there is to se		one, to be perceived
	As muche as here a ȝere may [be][2] itolde be		
	Ac euery day of penaunce idon here		done
	May stonde in stede of an hole ȝere there		replace
	As cryst saith openly swyþe wel		so
2215	By his holy prophete . eȝechiel[3]		
	Diem pro anno dedi tibi.[4]		
	That is on englysch forto seie now		
	For an hole ȝere yȝaf a day to ȝow		I gave
	Than s(er)veþ thulk peyne as the bok telluþ		this
2220	To clanse soules that ther ynne dwelleþ		
	Ac penaunce here don with a good wille		
	S(er)veþ for two thynges lawe to fulfulle.		
	O reso(u)n ther is to clanse þe soule wel		One
	Of alle dedly synnes and alle veniel.		Mortal, venial
2225	Anothur is to haue in heuene the more mede.		reward
	To these two thynges may penaunce us lede		
	The soule fro euery penaunce that he doþ here		
	Schal haue a special ioye in heuene wel clere		
	That with outen ende euere schal laste		
2230	ȝif sche[5] do penaunce w(i)t(h) herte stede faste.		constant
	Where and in what place purgatorie is.		
	The stede that purgatory is holde		place, believed
	Undur the erþe it is as clerkes me(n) tolde		
	Aboue þe place as som(m)e clerkes telleþ		
2235	There þ(a)t uncristned children dede dwelleþ		Where, unbaptized
	That fro the sight of godes face		
	Beth yput for eu(er)e w(i)t(h) owten eny g(ra)ce.		
	Thulke stede is euene aboue helle put		This place, pit
	Bitwene purgatory and helle ischut		
2240	Thus is thulke sted of purgatory set.		

---

[1] This page is simlarly defaced by a single line scratched through it, although the force of the line appears less heavy than that of the previous folio, and the surface of the vellum has not been punctured. While the brown ink color of the defacement is similar to that of the text, the date of the defacement cannot be determined.

[2] *Be* is underlined with dots to cancel it since it is redundant.

[3] The use of punctuation is gradually becoming more prevalent, as in this line.

[4] "A day for a year I have appointed to you" [derived from Ezechiel 4:6].

[5] Interestingly, the author alternates the gender of the soul, from masculine in line l. 2227 to feminine (here) in line l. 2230. The purpose is not obvious.

80   Part IV. Purgatory

	Ac aboue hem bothe oþur sowles beþ iset[1]	f. 29v	But
	What bihoueþ nedes þere peyne forto haue[2]		profits
	Bot ʒif thei haue grace that god wol hem saue		
	Ʒut aboue that ther is the ferþe place		
2245	That cryst after his deth visited þorowe his g(ra)ce		
	And alle that there were w(i)t(h) hym þo he toke		
	And lefte neuyron þere ynne as saith the boke		no one
	Ne f(ro)m that ilke tyme as clerkes can telle		same
	Com neuer no soule þer in forto dwelle		
2250	Ne neu(er) here aft(er) schal non ther ynne falle		
	For þat place hatte lymbʒ among clerkys alle		called, limbo
	The whiche is a fre prison as it in bok ys founde		
	Where þat our holy fadres in derknesse were ybounde.		
	Ac of these foure me(n) may oon helle make		one, call
2255	And alle as for helle þey mowe ben itake		may
	Wherfore holy churche þ(a)t for soules p(re)yeþ		
	Called purgatory helle and þus saieþ		
	D(omi)ne ihesu criste libera a(nim)as om(niu)m		Jesu
	fideliu(m) defunctor(um) de manu inferni.[3]		
	Lord delyuere þow owt of helle hond		
2260	Alle cristene soules þat beþ þere und(er) bond		bondage
	That is thus to seie out of p(ur)gatory into blys		
	For þere soules beþ clansed in gret anguysch		
	Ac f(ro)m the lowest helle w(i)t(h)owten eny doute		
	Ne may no soule be delyuered þ(er)oute		
2265	Ffor of mercy there is nothur help ne tryste		
	So sayth iob that the sothe wiste:		
	Q(ui)a in inferno nulla est redemp(ci)o[4].		
	He saith that in helle put that is so fer a do(u)n		pit
	Is neuer delyueraunce ne no ra(u)nsom		
2270	Wherfore masses and p(r)iere ne helpeþ nought		
	To the soules that beth thedur ibroght		
	Ffor no thing may abate her pyne[5]		
	As proueth the doctor seint austeyne:		
	Si scirem patrem meum aut matrem in inferno: pro		
	eis non orarem.[6]		
2275	He saith ʒif my fadur or my modur were		
	Down in helle put and iwist hem there		I knew
	I wolde neuere by nyght ne be daye		
	For hem to my god bydde no praye		ask nor pray
	Ne purgatorye so longe laste ne may		

---

[1] Light lines, both circular and straight crossing out, drawn through this folio indicate it was defaced. A brown ink smudge was transferred to the opposite folio, suggesting haste.
[2] "Why it is necessary to experience pain … ?".
[3] "Lord Jesus Christ, deliver from the hands of Hell all the souls of the faithful" [Berno Augiensis, *PL* 142, col. 1146].
[4] "Because in hell there is no redemption" Morey, p. 229, states Petrus Blesensis, *Compendium in Job* (*PL* 207: 823). [*Office of the Dead*. Response to Lectio Septima of Matins, Third Nocturn, *Job* 19: 20-27; Ps. Bede, *PL* 93, col, 950. Also in *Innocent III*, Lewis ed. Ps. 219 a from Breviary (111.9, p. 217); *Piers Plowman,* Passus 18; *Parliament of the Three Ages*.]
[5] A *Piers* rubricator emendation with a dotted *y*.
[6] "If I knew my father or mother were in hell: I would not pray for them."

2280	For it lasteþ no leng(er)e than domysday	f. 30r	
	Ffor after that day as clerkes conneþ se		
	Þe place of purgatory schal nowhere be		
	Thanne schal helle be ful of fendes w(i)t(h)ynne		
	The whiche schal eu(er)e last for vengaunce[1] of synne		
2285	Bot sum(m)e men haueth wondur and askeþ whi		doubt
	That god haþ ordeyned p(ur)gatory with mercy		ordered
	And helle withoute m(er)cy and the erþe so lowe		
	Þe skile whi by þis reso(u)n me(n) may knowe		cause for
	Ffor the synne that is on erthe iwroght		done
2290	Fram the erþe upward ne passeth noght		
	Than ypunysched moste by that synne		
	Othur aboue erthe or elles with ynne		Either
	That is to seie here where we most dwelle		must
	Oþ(ur) in purgatory or elles in helle		
2295	For þe foul synne is so heuy and hard		severe
	Þ(a)t it draweþ þe soule eu(er) adonward		
	And for to synne w(i)t(h) penaunce be away nome		always named
	Arst may þe soule neuere to heuene come		Any earlier
	Of two purgatories that beþ ordeyned bi god.		
2300	Ȝut seith þese clerkes more oponly		openly
	Þ(a)t þer beþ two purgatories namly		
	That on is with ynne þe erþe aboue hell		one
	That comeþ f(ro)m the erþe as wat(er) fro the welle		
	And that other is specially þorowe grace		
2305	Here on erþe in dyuerse place.		
	Ffor sum(m)e beþ nowȝt i(n) þe eo(rþ)e stede ipiȝt		place thrust
	Ac þey beþ punysched here oth(er) day or nyȝt		either
	In many diuerse stedes in here gost		places
	Where þat þei haue synne ido most		
2310	Ac that peine may be brought owt of drede		
	Þorow praiers of frendes and almesdede		
	To the whiche þei mowe gostliche apere		must spiritually
	Þorow grace in dyuerse stedes here.		various places
	Thulke peyne as iferst tolde sore greueþ		Such, greatly hurts
2315	Ac it is a warnynge to hem þ(a)t bihynde leueþ		
	And thus may men skylfully se		intelligently see
	Where that purgatory bifalleth to be.		
	Of þe peynes that beþ in purgatorie.		
	In purgatory as the bok witnesse bereþ		

---

[1] This [ȝ] is a voiced velar stop, regularly used in this manuscript.

2320	Beþ diuerse peynes that the soule dereþ[1]	**Quarta Pars** f. 30v	injures
	Many mo than y kan telle sothly		
	Ac ifinde ther of y write seuene sykurly		with certainty
	The whiche mowe ben clepud peynes wel		called
	And of hem I wol[2] ȝowe certefie somdel.		
2325	The ferst peyne of tho seuene iwis		
	As me(n) may knowe who so redeþ þis		
	Is the grete drede þat þe soule is ynne		fear
	Whan the body and sche departen atwynne		separate / come apart
	Ffor the soule seþ than aboute here stonde		sees, standing
2330	Many afoul fende to bryng here to schonde		destruction
	And that ilke sight . is peyne ryght greuous		serious
	For the fendes beþ so foule and so hidous		devils
	That so hardy a man was þer neuere non		strong
	On erþe lyuynge in flesch and in bon		
2335	Ȝif he siȝt the sight þat þe soule schal se		saw
	Owt of witte for drede anon he scholde be		fear
	A grete peyne thanne to him schal be that sight		
	Ac more ȝut to the soule þat þer w(i)t(h) schal fight.		
	The secunde peine that is nexst afturward		
2340	Is þe grete drede of deþ that is smart and hard		sharp
	That the soule schal haue wyth deol and care		misery
	Forto his dom be ȝiue how he schal fare		Until
	Ffor angels schulleþ alredy be þere		
	And fendes also wiþ a gryslich chere		fearful countenance
2345	Thanne schal the soule bitwene hem stonde		
	And the angels schulleþ be in here right hond		
	Ac the deueles schulleþ be in here left side		
	So the soule mot there in gret dred abide		
	Tyl that ilke strif be ibrought to ende		
2350	For arst sche ne wote nat whodur to wende		
	Whethur that god wole here dampne or saue		
	Þanne schal the soule gret drede haue		
	And be in perel and wote nat whydur to fle		danger, know
	Right as a man that is amyddes the se		sea
2355	Whan tempestes falleþ and stormes smerte		severe
	For thanne may he forsothe nowhare asterte		escape nowhere
	And as a man hath a bodyli drede		physical fear
	Whan he is apechid of a felonys dede		impeached
	By fore the kynges iustice and the contre		

---

[1] A light line runs through the length of this page.

[2] *Iwol* is a form of first-person sg. *I will*.

2360	That beþ ichard on þe book ȝif he gulty be[1]	f. 31r	accused, guilty
	Thanne wot he nat whethur he schal ben ispild		destroyed
	Othur be delyuered and the lawe fulfild		saved
	In gret doute of his lif may that man be		
	Ȝut hath the soule more drede þan suche þre.		fear
2365	Ffor ȝif he hath the dome of dampnac(i)on here		
	Þanne goþ it to helle to be the deueles fere		companion
	And ȝif the soule be dampnyd to that place		
	Than ys þer nethur mercy hope ne grace		
	What wondur is thanne þaw the soule haþ drede		
2370	Ffor to god aftur mercy ne dar sche nat grede.		cry out
	The þrydde peine is as it were an exile		
	Whan the soules here aȝenst here wyll[2]		
	Bethe exiled from the lif and in peine ibrougtht		
	For of aȝen tornynge ne knoweþ þey richt noght		returning
2375	Therefore thei schulleþ haue gret mornynge		
	Whan thei beþ departed f(ro)m her lykynge		desires
	And the mornyng that thei haue w(i)t(h) out lysse		respite
	Schal be to hem thanne a grete anguisse.		
	The fourthe is dyuerse siknesse		
2380	That the soules haueth þere in gret distresse .		
	Ffor thei schulleþ diuerse eueles ther ynne		shall [have]
	For diuerse dedes that beþ unclansyd of synne		unabsolved
	Somme for pride that they haue used ofte		customarily displayed
	Schul haue the cold feuer and that is no thing softe		easy
2385	Ffor that schal dere the soule more byturly		injure
	Þan euere dyde here any feu(er) mannes body		
	And sum(m)e schulleþ haue there for her coueytyse		greed
	The dropesie that thei schulleþ nat up ryse		dropsy
	And sum(m)e schul haue in here lemys abowte		limbs
2390	For slewthe a potagre and ther to a cold gowte .		gout of the feet
	And buyles and felonnes and a postem(us) ther two[3]		boils, sores, pustules
	The whiche beþ ofte into a mannes lemes ido		limbs attacking
	And sum(m)e for wratthe schul haue the palesie		wrath, palsy
	The whiche schal do the soule myche velanye		bring the soul great disgrace
2395	And sum(m)e for glotanye schul haue euere more		
	The streite squynesie that schal hem greue sore		painful quinsey
	And sum(m)e for the synne of lechery also		
	Schul haue the foule lepre where that thei go		leprosy
	Thus schal the soule that god will saue		

---

[1] A line runs through most of this page.

[2] An erasure under the word *wyll* makes the word unclear, with a final *e* possible, but not certain. Emendations at *l.* 2372 and elsewhere on this page were made by the *Piers* rubricator.

[3] The words *ther to* would be more logical here. James H. Morey's edition of *The Prik of Conscience*, based on New Haven, Beinecke Library, Osborn a. 13, reads "postumus," abcesses (p. 78).

2400	For dyuerese synnes dyuerse peynes haue	f.31v	
	That on erthe hadden veray repentaunce		true
	And hadde nauȝt fulfuld her repentaunce.		
	Now thenke we what peine þe bodies syffreþ here		
	Throw maladies that hem greueþ eu(er)y where		torture
2405	Thei it ne lasteþ but a lytil stounde		time
	Ȝut it bryngeþ sone a man to þe grounde		
	As as thulke maladye greueþ the body sore		illness hurts, bitterly
	Ȝut it greueth in the tyme þe soule myche more		injures
	So þat þe soule haþ the more penaunce		
2410	Þan haþ the body whan it haþ greuaunce		
	But now may a man segge here agayne		
	And aske how the soule may suffre payne		
	That aftur deþ is so sotyl as y in boke rede		ethereal
	For it may ocupye no maner of stede[1]		place
2415	To þis y may thus answer right wel		
	As y here ther of clerkes make here spel.		story
	The soule lyf is to the body for soþe		
	Of euery man more and lasse boþe		
	And with oute lif is no thyng lyuynge		
2420	For in no ded thing many be no felynge		
	Than is al the felynge of the lif oonly		
	In the soule and no thing in the body		
	Ffor whan the soule is passed away		
	Thanne is the body but erthe and clay		
2425	The whiche is a ded thing as in the ston		
	Þat feleþ no thing by hym self alon		only
	Ȝut may sum(m)e man þe soule that dwelleþ in wo		
	Be pyned with schuch maladie w(i)t(h) owte		such
	Þe whiche in dyuerse lemes is of þe body abowte		limbs
2430	So as it hath nothur body ne heued		neither head
	Ne non othur leme is ther on byleued		remaining
	To this may thus answere schortly		
	That the soule þaw it haue no body		
	Sche schal be ipeyned as in lemes þere		
2435	Wyth þe whiche sche haþ do most synne here		
	Ffor euery to othur schal seme thanne iwis		[it] seem
	As þaw it hadde the schap of body as a man ys		
	And in this manere eche man schall othur ise .		

---

[1] Can be translated as "cannot occupy any space."

	Ac non of hem may nat feled be[1]	f.32r	be felt
2440	Ne more þanne a mannys breth may[2]		
	Whan it[3] passeþ f(ro)m the mouthe away		
	By ensample of laȝar and of a riche man[4]		Lazarus
	This matere heere y menyd for soþe preue ycan .		story, truth, mentioned, prove
	The riche man wernede þe laȝar mete		denied the leper food
2445	Þat in abrah(a)ms bosom hadde mad hys sete		
	Ac the riche man was beried in helle		
	And as he siȝe laȝar in heuene dwelle		saw
	He cried to abrah(a)m and p(re)yed fayre w(i)t(h) alle		
	Þat o drope of wat(er) might adown falle		one
2450	On his tong f(ro)m his fyngres ende		tongue
	For he myght by noway from þat peyne wende		escape
	Ac þe ryche man þat spak þus to that othur		
	Hadde no leme ne tonge nothur		limb, either
	Ne laȝar as ȝe may wel undyrstonde		
2455	Hadde noþ(er) fyng(er) ne fot ne honde		neither
	Ffor þei were boþe spyrytis oonly		spirits
	Þat hadden no lemes ne verey body		true
	Ac þe riche mannes soule feled peyne in helle		felt
	As þawe it hadde be a body in flesch and in felle		skin
2460	And lazares soule semed to hym þanne		
	As þas it had y haad the lemes of manne		
	Ȝut haue y herd some clerkes mayntene		
	Suche maner opynyones many tyme ywene		
	That þe soule þat ys in þe peyne of purgatory		
2465	Or elles in helle haþ of þe eyr a body		air
	Ffor to suffre peyne in his lemes þere		
	After that he haþ ysynned on erþe here		
	Ac whethur the sowle haue body or non		
	Sche schal fele peyne as the body haþ don.		
2470	The fyfthe peyne thaw it be somdel late		fifth, though
	Hote fuyr is that no thyng may abate		fire, stop
	Bot almesdede, masses and prayere[5]		
	That frendes doth for the soule here		
	To abate that fuyr tho thre aren beste .		those
2475	For thei bryngeþ sone a mannes soule to reste		
	Ac thulke fuyr is hottyr and more kene		that, hotter
	Than al the fuyr that in this world may be sene		seen
	For al the watur that a man may thenche		think

---

[1] This page has been slightly defaced: light lines run through the top, and darker lines diagonally through the bottom from line 2461 *manne* on.
[2] Several dotted y's, including including the one in *may* are written on this page.
[3] This *it* has been emended, leaving a space around it.
[4] See Luke 16.
[5] The word appears to have been originally written as *praoere*, but another hand has written what looks like a *y* over the *o*.

86   Part IV. Purgatory   (2479–2518)

	A sparcle of that ne myght aquenche[1]	f. 32v	spark, quench
2480	Ffor a sparcul ther of is more brennynge		burning
	Than al the fuyr that is on erthe lyghttyngge		lightening
	And the soule is more tendre and nesche		soft
	Than is the body w(i)t(h) blod and flesch		
	Than the soule that is so tendre of kynde		nature
2485	Mot nedys her penaunce hardur fynde		learn that its penance is more difficult
	Than any body that euere alyue was		
	Þaw it þer þorow schuld make his pas		though [it], passage
	Ac no soule may f(ro)m thennes wende		there go
	Tyl of here penaunce be made an ende		
2490	But thulke fuyr wurcheþ nat þorow kynde ryght		such, works, nature
	In the soule that is to þulke penaunce dight		prepared
	As doth that ilke fuyr þ(a)t on erþe brenneþ here		same, burns
	Ar it wurcheþ in a nothur wondurful manere		
	As god haþ y ordeyned for whi it is so		ordained
2495	As a inst(ru)ment þ(a)t rightfully longeþ ther to		belongs
	Thorw þe whiche þe sow[ ]le yclansyd mot be[2]		cleansed must
	In p(ur)gatory that sche mowe clere god ise		may clearly, see
	Ffor whi al the fuyr that was þ(er)ynne		
	Is bot a maner fuyr to wasty synne		consume / burn up
2500	Ffor as fuyr[3] on this erthe may al thyng brenne		burn
	And metal melte that it schal aboute renne		run
	Ryght so the fuyr were þorow long hete		
	Wasteþ bothe smale synnes and grete		Consumes
	Ac there be nat fuyres lasse and more		
2505	But o maner fuyr that brenneþ swithe sore		one type of
	And as the hete of the synne may ou(er) al men passe		suffer
	And sum(m)e greueth more and sum(m)e men lasse		
	Right so the fuyr that is in purgatory ibrought		grieve, not
	Some soules greuyp more and some ryght nought		must
2510	Ffor al the soules mote nede dwelle ther ynne		
	After that her charge is gret of synne.		
	Ac sum(m)e soule schal þere be delyuered sone		freed
	That haþ on erthe fulfuld his penaunces echone		each one
	Ac somme soule schal dwelle there many aȝere		a year
2515	That haþ litel penaunce don with his body here		
	And haþ lyued longe in his synne also		lived
	Þerfore seint austyn seiþ þese wordes þ(er)to		
	Necesse est ut tantus sit dolor p(er) p(e)cc(at)is quantus .[4]		

---

[1] This page has been defaced by a light line running through it, ending in a loop through the bottom half.
[2] The entire line has been written over an erasure, and a 3-letter gap has been left between *sow* and *le*. The *e* of the first *þe* has been superscripted.
[3] Written over an erasure with a 2-letter gap following *fuyr*.
[4] "It is necessary that there be so much pain for so many sins" [based on Augustine, *De Civitate Dei* lib. 21: 26.4, *PL* 41, col. 745]. As noted, the manuscript text is out of order through misbinding of one quire; this quotation should be followed by f. 33r as this volume presents it, not by f. 25 r as HM 128 presents it.

Fuerit amor . tanto diucius anima torquet(ur)   f. 33r
   In penis quanto affectius mu(n)danis inherebat desiderys.[1]

	Seynt austyn saith that nedful it were	necessary
2520	That as muche sorowe were and heuy chere	
	Ffor eu(er)y synne and euery trespas	transgression
	As lust and lykynge in the synne was	sexual desire
	He seith also as y before haue rad	advised
	That the more lykynge that a man in his synne had	pleasure
2525	And ȝiueþ euere therto his lust and his wille	sexual consent
	His flesches lykynge in synne to fulfulle	
	The lengere it ys skile that his soule in peyne be	longer, reason[able]
	In the fuyr of purgatory the whiche he may nat fle	escape
	And ar the soules mowen se god in his face	must
2530	As þre thinges thei moten be brend in that place	burned
	That is to seie as wode and hey also[2]	say, wood, hay
	And stobel that sone w(i)t(h) þe fuyr wol away go	stubble, disintegrate
	Ffor the moste venial synnes schulleþ brenne longe	burn [as] long
	As the wode that haþ mores and branches stronge	roots
2535	Ac the smale synnes schullen sone brenne aweye	
	As doth the stobel whan fuyr comeþ hym neye	near
	Ac the mene synnes brenneþ nought so sone	moderate, intermediate
	Ffor thei bren(n)eþ slowly and haueþ more to done	
	Right as hey þat is with a lytil fuyr itende	hay, ignited
2540	And longe smokeþ or hit may be þorow brende	
	Thus schulleth thei ben ibrend and iwasted sore	burned. destroyed
	For her venial synnes bothe lasse and more	
	An[3] dedly synnes of the whiche thei beþ ischryue	absolved
	And the trespase there of god haþ clene forgiue	sin
2545	Ffor the which penaunces [ne][4] beþ nat fulfild here	
	Schulleth þere be ibrend in the same manere	
	And whan þei beþ so fyned and ymaad bright	refined / purified
	Þanne schul they be ibroȝt bifore goddes sight	
	In to paradyse that is so blissfull a place	
2550	Where ynne is euere ioye and reste and muche g(ra)ce.	
	The sixte peyne is forto telle	
	For the soules unclansed schullen dwelle	unabsolved
	In purgatory and there been ybounde faste[5]	
	Wiþ bondes of synne that makeþ hem sore agaste	fetters, very terrified
2555	And as many as beþ in that pryso(u)n	prison
	For no ȝyfte they mowe ne for no raunso(u)n	bribe, may, ransom

---

[1] "The greater its love was, the longer the soul will be tormented with punishments according to the degree that desires for worldly things clung more deeply" [Paraphrase of Augustine, *De Civ. Dei,* lib 21.26.4, *PL,* 41, col. 745; also adapted by Bonaventura, *Breviloquium,* trans. Dominic V. Monti, O.F.M., p. 271]. The Latin Vulgate offers *desideriis* rather than *desiderys.*

[2] A single diagonal line defaces this page—running from this spot at l. 2531 to the lower left corner.

[3] Middle English Dictionary includes *an* as a variant of *and.*

[4] This superfluous double negative is lightly crossed out with a single stroke.

[5] The last three words are written over an erasure by the *Piers* rubricator, as is ȝyfte in l. 2556.

	Out of thulke peyne hem self wynne[1]	f.33v
	Tyl þat fuyr haue brend[2] the bondes of synne	
	And thus they beþ ibounde boþe honde and fot	
2560	In brennynge lye the which is swithe hote.	
	Me thynketh thanne þat no peyne may be more	
	Þanne sowles suffreþ and that greueth hem sore	injures
	Ffor there may no thing hem begge no borowe	beg
	Forto abregge any thyng of her sorowe	abridge / compensate
2565	Ne to helpe hem that thei were hennes brought	
	For here owne p(ra)iere helpeþ ryght nought	
	But ȝif thei on erthe any good dede wrought	performed
	Othur here frendes for hem to god bysought	Or
	And wolden for hem do som almesdede	almsgiving
2570	Þat myght hem sone f(ro)m suche peynes lede	
	Ffor harde beþ the peynes that thei suffreþ there	
	Ȝif hope of mercy sone ther after ne were	
	Ac som tyme so muche peyne thei schul haue	
	That they takeþ no kepe that god wol hem saue	forget / do not remember
2575	Therfore we scholde þenke that on erþe lyueþ here	lives
	What peyne the soule suffreþ in such manere	
	Among foule fendes that þere haueþ leue	licence
	Somtyme þe soule to tormente and greue	
	As longe as they haueþ any spot of synne	
2580	For arst þei ne mowe fram the peine hem wynne	first, may, redeem
	Tyl thei ben iclansed and y made clene	purified
	Of all þe spottys of synne þ(a)t non be isene	
	Ac whan they beþ iclensid f(ro)m al encomberaunce	
	Þan thei schulleþ fele no more penaunce	experience
2585	Bote sone ther after þey schulleþ wende	
	To þe blysse of heuene þat is w(i)t(h) outen ende.	
	ℭhe seuenþ peyne is þus in liknesse	as if
	Þere þat soules be in wyldernesse	
	Where þat grete defaute is of al man(er) þyng	default
2590	Of the which a man myghte haue his likynge	desire
	Ffor her peyne is to hem hard wel many folde[3]	in various ways
	For now þei beþ in gret hete and now i(n) [strang] colde	
	And þulke penaunce is to hem swiþe long	
	As now w(i)t(h) hete and now chele among	chill
2595	And þei schulleþ suffre boþe hong(er) and þerste	hunger, thirst
	And euyr be in travayle with owte eny reste.	travail, out, any

---

[1] Very faint, sometimes illegible lines have been drawn through this page, although the loop at the bottom is more evident than the lines at the top.
[2] This and other emendations on this page appear to be auto-corrections.
[3] A brown smear on this and the facing folio blocks out parts of *many folde* here and *strang colde* on the next line. *Strang* is reclaimed from HM 125.

	And thei beþ þere ibete to make more her peyne	f. 34r	beaten
	With smarte stormes of wynde and of reyne		sharp
	And also wiþ hayl both scharpe and kene		
2600	For so smarte¹ stormes were neuer er sene		before seen
	As soules schulleþ there fele and yse²		feel, see
	And in dyuerse manere þerw(i)t(h) ipeyned be		hurt
	Ffor sum(m)e schulleþ many a ȝere for her synne		owed, year
	Þere be or thei may the siȝt of god wynne		before, sight
2605	Suche manere peynes þei schull haue eu(er) more		type of
	W(i)t(h) othur many mo that schal hem greue sore		more, injure
	Ac ouer al þyng ȝut schal þis a gret peyne be		
	The grete couetyse that³ thei haueþ to se		greed
	The swete face of our lord that is so bright		
2610	And the longe taryenge of that same sight.		delaying
	Ac to that cyte may þey neuere come⁴		city
	Tyl alle her synnes f(ro)m hem be clene ynome		called
	Here haue y tolde in party somdel to ȝow		somewhat
	Of the peynes of p(ur)gatory that beþ ful of wow.		sorrow
2615	**Of hem that schullen abide in purgatorie.⁵**		
	And whiche schullen nought abide.		
	The soules that to p(ur)gatory schul wende		
	Aftur þat deþ of her lyf haþ made an ende		
	Nedes bihoueþ to dwelle there ynne		
2620	Tyl þey ben clansid of al maner synne		
	Thorow bytur peynes that they schul þere ifynde		
	For eu(er)y synne schal be punnysched aft(er) his kynde		
	Aftur þat it is in dede more othur lasse		
	And aftyr her penaunce is ido or þey hennes passe		before
2625	Ac alle soules abideþ nouȝt in þat place		
	For some anon after her deþ haueþ g(ra)ce		
	And schulleþ sikurliche wende to blysse		securely
	As holy in(n)ocentes that neu(e)r dede amysse		committed sin
	And othur soules of gode men and parfite		perfect
2630	The whiche in non erþly þyng had delite		
	Bot only [in g(ra)ce]⁶ that hem dere abouȝte		redeemed at a high price
	And in her lyf grete [grete]⁷ penaunce wrouȝte.		performed
	Ac some that the deþ sodeynly doþe take		
	And beþ in dedly synne bounde as bere to a stake		bear
2635	Streight forþ into helle þey schullen wende		
	And there beþ ipult to peyne w(i)t(h) outen eny ende		thrust in

---

[1] The first three words of this line, written over an erasure, are scribed in tiny script (to fit them into this space?).

[2] This correction, *yse*, and *þey* on l. 2611 use dotted *y*'s.

[3] The space between *a* and *t* is filled with ink, appearing to be a blot or glob of extra ink.

[4] The words *cyte* and *þey* are scribed in small hand over erasures to fit into small spaces.

[5] The red-inked letters *urgato* of *purgatorie* are drawn through with two or three brown ink-lines, defacing but not obliterating the word. This is likely a later modification, perhaps a mark indicating disagreement with the concept of purgatory. It appears an intellectual, not emotional response, as the lines are not strong.

[6] Nearly obliterated by the blot noted on previous facing page; *in* is undecipherable.

[7] The second, repeated, *grete* is underlined, presumably to delete it.

	And therof no wondur ihaue in my mynde[1]	f. 34v	doubt
	For whi dedly synne is so heuy of kynde		serious by nature
	That it may w(i)t(h) ynne a lytyl stounde		time
2640	Brynge a mannes soule into helle grounde		
	Ac the soule þat is [þat is][2] of dedly synne schryue		absolved
	And his trespas here be clene forȝiue		sin
	And ȝif þe penaunce that on hym was leyd[3]		imposed
	Ne beþ nat fulfuld ar þe deþes breyd		before, braid / throes
2645	So þat the soule is nat clansed clene		purified
	Of oþur smale synnes that comeþ e(ue)re bytwene		
	Thanne þes soules schulleþ ben saue		
	Ac ȝut in p(ur)gatory hem bihoueþ to haue		they must have
	Hard peyne and byttur and þer ynne dwelle longe		
2650	Tyl the soules haue al clannesse yfonge		acquired
	As they were ferst . whan þey tok flesch and bon		bone
	And holy baptysme of the prest at the fontston		baptism font
	Ȝut seyþ thes clerkes on þis manere		
	That so clene out of synne lyueþ no man here		
2655	Ne so parfit is no man in cristen lawe		
	Ne the childe that is f(ro)m his modur wombe drawe		taken
	That aftur his deþ schall wende to heuene in eny manere		fashion
	Er than he passe thulke streite wey þ(a)t he schal fynde þere		Before, this straight
	And ar he haue seyȝe þe peynes there echone		seen, each one
2660	Ac þe ȝong children therof shul fele none		
	Ffor thei couthe neuere no synne wirche		commit
	But passeþ forþ in þe fey of holy chirche.		faith
	Therfore they schulleþ þorow purgatory fle		fly
	As the foul thorow the wynd as men may yse		bird
2665	Wiþ oute eny peyne that myght hem derie		injure
	And f(ro)m al euel sight me(n) schal hem werye		protect themselves
	Ac unneþe may any man quyt þ(er) þorow go		scarcely, freed / excused
	That ne schal of p(ur)gatory fele som wo		sorrow
	Ffor that fuyr wol fonde hem forto brenne		try
2670	Ȝif it may on hem any venyal synne kenne		perceive
	Ffor undurstondeth wel as y telle kan		can
	That þer is founde non so parfit man		
	That he somtyme thenkeþ an ydel thought		idle
	And leteþ it litelly passe and chargeþ it nought		lightly, consider
2675	Of the which he schal yclansed be		purified
	Er he may the bryght face of god yse		Before, see

---

[1] The words *i have* have been written together by the scribe. Light lines run down this page, circling at the bottom.

[2] These two repeated words are scratched out with a single line; they seem to mark but not obliterate the text.

[3] The last four words here and *breyd* in the next line have been emended by the *Piers* rubricator, using no dotted *y*'s, unlike the *Piers* rubricator's *yse* (2667) and the autocorrect of *yfonge* (2653) using dotted *y*'s.

	Ffor as gold that schineþ clere and bryght[1]	f.35r	
	Semeþ wel ipuryd to a mannes sight		purified
	And ȝut ȝif hit were iput into the fuyr eftsone		afterwards
2680	Hit scholde be more clere in hym self alone		
	Right so soules in the same manere		
	Of the parfit men that semeþ most clere		
	Of alle synnes and makeþ hym to god all ȝare		ready
	Ȝut þey schal in purgatory somdel fele of care		some degree
2685	Ffor alle there thorow þey most nedes passe		
	Alle ȝonge and olde boþe more and lasse		
	Ffor þat ilke fuyr that is there with ynne		
	Schal fynde in hem som scrypul of synne		scruple
	As light thoughtes the whiche ben in veyne		
2690	Wherfore thei schulleþ there suffre peyne		
	Ffor so wel yfyned neu(er) so gold[2] on erthe was		purified
	Thorow fuyr as þei beþ that goþ that ylke pas.		way
	Ffor þe which synnes þe soule goþ to helle[3]		
	Many maner synnes that the soule greueþ		types, suffers
2695	Regneþ among men that here on eorþe leueþ		reigns
	Some ther of beth dedly in thought and in dede		
	And sum(m)e beth venial as me(n) may in bokes rede		
	Ac tho synnes that me(n) may dedlyche calle		deadly
	Schulleþ nat in purgatory be ipurged alle		cleansed
2700	Ac thei beþ ipunysched euere more in helle		
	And whiche thei beþ sone ischal ȝow telle.		
	These be the hed synnes y ȝow certefie		chief, certify
	Ferst pryde . than wraþþe . and enuye .		
	Glotany and slouthe in goddes s(er)uise		sloth
2705	Þe foule lecherye and endeles couetyse		
	Manslauȝt(er) and fals hothes swerynge		oaths swearing
	Sacrilege and fals witnesse berynge		
	Thefte and to poremen to do raueyne.		plunder
	Thes synnes ledeþ a man to helle peyne		
2710	Ffor eche of these is a dedly synne		
	And letteþ mannes soule heuene to wynne.		prevents
	Hatrede also is a dedly synne amonge[4]		
	Ȝif it be in herte of man ihold longe		held
	And ȝut dronkenesse is dedly synne also		
2715	Ȝif hit be oft and contynuelly ido		
	Wherfor ho so telleþ hym gulty in any of this .		who

---

[1] Lines through this page are somewhat darker and more visible than those on the previous page.
[2] This small erasure is replaced by -ld, so perhaps the scribe penned *god* first insted of *gold*.
[3] One of the few times the scribe does not end his red-inked heading with a *punctus*.
[4] This line is written over a long erasure spanning the line.

	And þenkeþ his soule to brynge to blys	f. 35v	joy
	But he hem amende ar he hennes wende		changes
	He schal nat thei he wolde aftur his lyues ende		though
2720	Ne to purgatory schal he nat come		
	But al wiþ owte mercy to helle be inome		named
	And ȝif a man repente hym and wiþ good wille hym shryue		confess
	Of alle suche synnes clene by hys lyue		
	Ffram helle pyne than may he hym self saue		
2725	Ac ȝut penaunce in his body nedes he mot haue		must
	Than mot the soule gon as iwene		I think
	To p(ur)gatory fort sche of alle synne be clene		
	Ffor penaunce for synne yȝeue as[1] y seide ere		given
	Mot nedes be fulfuld here or elles where		Must
2730	**What þynges fordon veniall synnes . and whiche ben venyal**		
	Eche a venyal synne þe soule may dere	**synnes**[2]	harm
	Ac thei beþ nat wel heuy forto bere		
	As beþ dedly synnes for thei may be for do		blotted out
	In a light manere who so haþ wil þ(er) to		desire
2735	Ffor as y here clerkes ther of alegge		make allegations
	Eche man may lightly suche synnes abregge		reduce
	And þorow help of praiers suche g(ra)ce wynne		
	Þat it may for don eche venyal synne		destroy
	That is to seiȝe ȝif he right clene be		
2740	Out of dedly synne and wole it eu(er) fle		flee
	Ffor y fynde writen that ten thynkes alone[3]		things
	May for don venyal synnes echone.		
	I schal hem telle alle: takeþ hede irede.		I advise
	The furst is holy watur the second is almesdede		
2745	Ffastyng and hosel of goddes sacrement[4]		Eucharist
	Prayere of pater nost(er) . saide w(i)t(h) good entent		
	General schryfte that eche day may be made		
	And benyso(u)n of a buschep makeþ the soule glade		blessing
	And namely in the ende of an holy masse		
2750	For hit is a grete mede bothe to more and to lasse		
	And knokkenge of brest and kyssenge of þe grounde		
	And þe laste anoyntynge in þe deþes stounde.		The hour of death
	Thes ten . doþ venyal synnes away clene		
	As me(n) may here clerkes ther of mene		mention
2755	Nat for þan so many venyal synnes ifere		combined
	Mowen ben igadred and in suche manere		Must, gathered

---

[1] These two words are run together as *yȝeveas,* but a thin line has been inserted between them as a separator.

[2] The scribe penned the first half line; the *Piers* rubricator finished after the *punctus* with *and*; no final *punctus*.

[3] The author here continues his logical, organized approach to instruction: he includes details such as gestures indicating sincerity of intent, but without spectacular or sensational images used elsewhere in the treatise. The following comparison of the soul bearing its sins is likened to a horse carrying its burdens: although an individual grain of corn is a light load, many grains make it heavy. His image maintains interest but is not shocking.

[4] A wide mark going through *sacrament,* down four lines to *glade,* and recurring at the page bottom mars this page.

	That thei may weiʒe on the soule so sore[1]	f. 36r	weigh, heavily
	Þan o dedly synne doþ þat scholde greue more		one, injure
	Ffor it sleþ the soule and eu(er) god myspaieþ		slays, displeases
2760	And þerfore þe poete to us þus seieþ		
	De minimis granis . fit maxi(m)a sum(m)a caballi.[2]		
	Of many smale cornes gadred wel brode		gathered
	Me(n) may make to on hors a wel heuy lode		one
	Right so may venyal synnes gadred many folde		times
2765	Make an heuy synne þat may dedly be tolde		
	Ffor thei gadreþ to the soule in echa side wel þikke		numerous
	And cleueþ to gidre the soule sore to prykke[3]		cleve together
	Ac ʒif þey beþ away don sone w(i)t(h) repentaunce		
	And eu(er)e as þey comeþ þerfore do penaunce		
2770	Than schul they the soule bot alytyl greue[4]		a little suffer
	For þan þei haueþ no place where on to bleue		remain
	Ffor so parfit a man ys non unassailed		untested
	Of venial synnes and w(i)t(h) hem ofte travayled		assailed / burdened
	Ffor a man synneth eche day that here dwelleþ		each
2775	As the boke saith that on this maner telleþ:		
	Septies in die cadit iustus[5].		
	The rightful man into synne falle may		
	Seuene sythes at the leste in on day		times, one
	As in venyal synnes that sone wolleþ awey passe		
2780	Ac sum(m)e ther of beþ more and sum(m)e beþ lasse		
	And in so many synnes we may sone falle		
	Þat no man may telle ne rykne hem alle		calculate
	Ac for than somme of hem rykne ikan		I can
	As seint austyn telleþ, that good man		
2785	Ffor in a boke of his reherseþ some		discusses
	Þe whiche beþ most usyd by custome		customarily
	And to telle hem this he bygynnes		recalls
	And seyth that ther beþ many venial synnes		
	Fferst whan a man eteþ or drynkeþ more		eat
2790	In eny time wherby his wombe akeþ sore		stomach ached badly
	And þu myʒst any man avayle w(i)t(h) wyt and wille		might, help
	And no man wolt helpe bot holdest the stylle[6]		
	And whan thu spekest scharply to a pore man		
	That askeþ good at thi dore as symply as he can		goods
2795	And whan thu art hole in thi body and may wel laste		whole
	And thanne þow etest lustyly whan tyme is forto faste		heartily

---

[1] Defacement on this folio is primarily by a dark diagonal line across the bottom of the page which has been blotted against the previous facing page. Much finer, lighter lines, not interfering with the text, cross the top half of the folio.

[2] "From the smallest seeds [is made] the greatest load for a horse" [Alanus de Insulis, *PL* 210, col. 581].

[3] This is the first internal reference to the "Prykke of Conscience" which refers to its meaning, not simply mentioning the title: here the author conceptualizes the conglomerate of sins weighing on the soul as the prick piercing it.

[4] The poet suggests not allowing sins to accumulate, but repent and do penance immediately, as soon as committed.

[5] "For a just man may fall seven times a day" [Proverbs 24:16].

[6] "And no man will help unless he holds himself still, i.e. keeps quiet."

	And whan the lusteþ nat slepe and wiltnat aryse[1]	f. 36v	desire, will not
	Ac eu(er)e comest to late to here goddes s(er)vise		
	And makest for thi synnes no sykynge		sighing
2800	Whan thu art in good state and in lykynge		comfortable, desire
	Oþur whan thu p(re)yest and makest þyn oryson		
	And haste þer on but a lytyl deuocyon		hurry, devotion
	And whan a man haþ lust and lykynge of lyf		
	On his bed flescly to dele wyþ his wyf		deal
2805	Only his lust more to fulfulle		
	Þat to beʒete a child þorowe godes wylle.		Than
	Also whan me(n) visite men ou(er) late		
	Þ(a)t beþ syk and ibrought in to a feble state		
	Oþ(er) men that lyggeth in strong pryso(u)n		
2810	Or haueþ in body eny t(ri)bulacyon		sadness
	Or men þat beþ synful and sory		miserable
	For her frendes soulys þ(a)t are in p(ur)gatory		
	Hem to visite it were grete mede		reward
	Þorow good p(re)yers and almesdede		
2815	Also ʒif þu t(ra)vaylest nat aft(er) þyn astate[2]		take pains
	For to make hem acorde þ(at) beþ at debate[3]		
	And ʒif þu spekest to any man bot ʒif þu wyte why		know
	Ou(er) byturly wyth noyse or wyth gret cry		
	And whan thow pr(ay)sest any man more		praise
2820	More for flatryng þan for his good lore		flattery, learning
	And whan þow in cherche makest janglynge		chattering
	Or þenkest any idelnesse in any man(er) þynge		
	Be it w(i)t(h) oute þe cherche or w(i)t(h)ynne		
	It ys yne(m)pned for a venyal synne		called
2825	And whan þu art ou(er) liʒtly wroþe		angry
	And sweryst and myst nat holde þyn oþe		oath
	Also whan þu acorsest any man(er) man		curse
	In wham þu ne fyndest no cause to ban		
	And whan þu supposest any wikydnesse		
2830	Þorow suspecyo(u)n and trowest falsnesse		believe
	These beþ þynges as seynt austyn telleþ		
	Þorow þe whiche many a soule dwelleþ		
	In p(ur)gatory in ful gret wo.		sorrow
	And ʒut þer beþ othur ful many mo		more
2835	Of venyal synnes wel many ascore		twenty
	Ou(er) all thulke that y haue told bifore		these

---

[1] Defacement of this page consists of a full-page inked line forming a loop at the bottom half and doubling at the top half.

[2] "… according to your rank or status." The *u* of *þu* is superscripted here and in the following lines.

[3] "… bring them into agreement."

	Bot so wytty ys non erþlyche man[1]	f. 37r	prudent, earthly
	That alle þe venyal synnes wel telle can		
	Ffor ofte sythe in þe day eu(er)y man falleþ		times
2840	In synnes that clerkes venyal calleþ		
	And euery synne ys wurþy apeyne		worthy
	Þat is ido by word and þou3t in veyne		
	The whiche most clanlyche befor don		cleanly
	Or here or in p(ur)gatory eu(er)ychon.		Either, every one
2845	Therfore y rede eche man þat wol be wys		advise
	Þat he use þese ten þynges that beþ of grete prys		
	The whiche fordoþ anon þorow holy mannys lore		destroy, teaching
	Alle venyall synnes both lasse and more		
	And yif any man falle in a dedly synne		
2850	Lete hym þerfro aryse and nat longe abydeþ þ(er)ynne		
	And sone he take a prest hym for to schryue		absolve him
	And þanne do his penaunce on erþe by his lyue		
	And haue repentaunce eu(er) in his thought		
	For synnes þat he haþ here euel iwrought		wrought
2855	And so penaunce do w(i)t(h) alle his myght		
	And make his p(ra)iers bothe day and nyght		
	And go wulward[2] and ofte faste and wake		clothed in hairs
	And suffre muche hardnesse for godes sake		suffer, anguish
	Ffor no man may into heuene go		
2860	But 3if he soffre here boþe ang(uish) and wo		
	And whan god sendeþ a man ang(uish) in any wyse		fashion
	Þanne he schulde it suffre w(i)t(h)oute feyntyse		unflinchingly
	Be it siknesse or ought elles þ(a)t may greue		hurt
	Othur lost of catell that god hym wol bireue		Or, property, deprive
2865	Othur unkyndenesse, falshede or any treso(u)n		
	Oþur any grete a(n)uye that be a3en reso(u)n		injury
	Than suffre it mekeliche and þenke in þy þo3t		
	Þat w(i)t(h)oute cause ne comeþ it nought		reason
	Ac god wot wel þe cause whi that it ys		reason
2870	P(er)chaunce for som thyng that he haþ don amys		wrong
	To chastyse hym on suche manere		
	For his synnes the whiche he haþ don here[3]		
	Oþur it may be hym here to preue		Or, prove
	To the loue of god the more hym to meue		move
2875	Ffor ofte sythes whan god wele a man saue[4]		wills to
	He letyth hym tribulac(i)oun and many desesys haue		allows, diseases

---

[1] One quite dark long line beginning at the top of the page extends to the bottom and loops back to the middle.

[2] "With wool next to the skin; in penance; wearing a hair shirt."

[3] A large dot has been placed above the r of *here;* its purpose or meaning is unclear. The page contains several dotted y's (*wys, feyntyse, amys*) in the rhyme-position.

[4] Most of these last two lines have been emended by the *Piers* rubricator.

Part IV. Purgatory

	Oþur for his synnes is thulke schonde[1]	f. 37v	ignominy
	Þan schulde he god thanke of all his sonde		dispensation
	And take mekely al that god hym sendeþ		
2880	And fle al euel thing that he diffendeþ		forbids
	Ffor þorow myschef and angres grete		trouble, anguish
	He makeþ a man his p(ri)son that is for forlete		forfeited / left
	Penaunce to suffre for his owne folie		
	That he haþ wrought þorowh the deueles t(re)cherye		deception
2885	Ffor ȝif he hit suffreþ w(i)t(h) oute grucchynge		complaining
	It stondeþ hym in stede of penaunce alowynge[2]		
	And ther wiþ god wil do more ther to		
	Ȝiue hym grete mede and gr(ac)e also		reward
	And ful ioye in heuene he schal haue therfore		
2890	Ȝif he mekely suffre thaw it smerte sore		hurt excessively
	As þe good sone suffreþ mekely and[3] stille		
	Whan the fadur hym chastiseþ at his owne wille		chastise
	So schulde eche man suffre god be alle way[4]		
	And do al the good that he myght ay		always
2895	And specially almesdede is forto make		
	And cloth the naked . to the hongry mete take		food
	And othur werkes of mercy also forto werche		work
	As telleþ these good men of holy cherche		
	And kepe hym clene into his lyues ende		
2900	And aftur his deþ thanne schal his sowle wende		
	To blysse and all peynes lyghtly passe		
	Al clene f(ro)m purgatory bothe more and lasse.		
	Here hav y schewyd now to ȝowe alle[5]		showed
	Þe synnes that austyn venyal doþ calle		
2905	And nowe wol y schewe what helpeþ in certayn		
	To the soule that is in p(ur)gatories peyne		
	Of helpe of lyuynge frendes for þe dede.		
	The soules that to purgatory wendes		goes
	Beþ iholpe þorow help of leuynge frendes		living
2910	That for hem doþ almesdede fyn		beneficial
	For thus saiþ the doctor seynt austyn		
	Non est negandu(m) q(ui)d sp(iri)t(us) defunctoru(m) pietate . amicoru(m)		
	suoru(m) viventiu(m) possunt relevari ab omnibus penis eorum.[6]		
	He saith it is not to deny in non man(er)e		fashion
	Þat the soules of hem that beþ dede here		

---

[1] Some defacing occurs with an "X" drawn across the bottom of the page. The capital *T* (2901) is quite smudged.

[2] " ... it serves in place of allowing him penance."

[3] The scribe wrote *ad* for *and* here.

[4] Both *way* and *ay*, and *t(re)cherye* of l. 2884 are the *Piers* rubricator's corrections with dotted *y*'s.

[5] The question of audience is interesting, but unresolved. This authorial address to "ȝou alle" could be aimed at a listening or reading audience, possibly within a monastery. The assumed scrupulousness of conscience especially with regard to venial sin--over-eating or sleeping, suspicion, speaking harshly, etc.--would not be limited to a clerical audience, however, but was a shared, if not always achieved, expectation.

[6] "It cannot be denied that the souls of the dead, by the sense of duty of their living friends, can be freed from all their punishments" [Augustine *PL 40*, col. 158. Perhaps *pietate* retains its Roman sense of *pious duty* in Augustine's Latin, as in Virgil's *Pius Aenias*].

2915	Of peyne myghte sone relessed be	f. 38r	
	Thorow frendes on erþe þat on hem haueþ pite		
	Ffoure man(er) helpes me(n) may generally calle		kinds of assistance
	Þe whiche in purgatory avayleþ to the soules alle		helps
	That is to seye pater n(oste)r and fastynge		
2920	Almesdede in charyte and masses synkynge		charity, singing
	And in two maners as clerkes couþe ise		could see
	The soule f(ro)m peyne delyuered may be		
	That on is thorw grace of godes goodnesse		one
	And þat oþ(er) is wey of ryghtfullnesse		
2925	By wey of g(ra)ce in two manere		
	As it is iwrite in thys book here		written
	Fferst þorow p(re)iere to cryst þat ys our hede		
	Whan he is offred in þe forme of brede		
	Thorow the prestes hondes in good entent		
2930	Whan the bred is tornyd into sacrement		transformed
	Also þorow p(re)yere of goddes s(er)uauntes here		
	Þat eu(er) beþ besy in here prayere		
	Than may þe soule þat in p(ur)gatory is		
	By wey of gr(ac)e specially haue this		
2935	Alle delyueraunce of peyne that here greueþ		deliverane, hurts
	Þorow masses and praiers¹ þat here releueþ.		prayers, relieve
	By wey of rightfulnesse sche ys holpe also		righteousness
	In two maneres and that me(n) may schewe þ(er)to		
	Fferst þorow almesdede that men ȝiueþ to the pore		
2940	Þe soule is holpen out of peyne þat greueþ her sore		
	Onothur is of his penaunce a breggynge		reduction
	Þorowe penaunce of frendes and fastynge		
	Thus may the soule as þe boke is witnesse		
	Ben yholpe by the wey of ryghtfulnesse		
2945	That is to seie that thei may in that nede		
	Be ibrought f(ro)m peyne with almesdede		
	And þorow penaunce and pardoun		
	Tyl there be paied a certain raunsom		
	And þanne sche may be delyuered away		
2950	Þorow frendes that wolleþ it for hem pay		
	In these wyse may soules that wendes		
	To purgatory ben holpe w(i)t(h) frendes		helped
	Ac some frendes may helpe and som(m)e nought		
	The soules that to purgatory² beþ brought		

---

[1] The scribe wrote *braiers,* a scribal error for *praiers.*

[2] This folio is defaced on line 2957 where the word *purgatory* has been written through, with two light lines through and just above the letters.

98   Part IV. Purgatory

2955	Ac thorowe suche they mowe holpen be[1]	f. 38v	may
	That here lyueþ in parfyt charyte		
	Ffor þe helpe of hem þat charyte fayleþ		
	Þere to the soules no thyng avayleþ		benefits / helps
	Ffor thei beþ alle as lemes of o body		limbs, one
2960	Thei that þere beþ and thei in purgatory		
	And as we may ise p(ro)prely here		
	O body haue many lemes ifere		One, limbs, together
	And euery of hem boþe lasse and more		
	May helpe oþur 3if any þyng hem greueþ sore		afflicts greatly
2965	Ac 3if o lemys myght bygynneþ to faile		one [of the] limbs
	Þulke leme to þe oþ(er) may no thing availe		Such, help
	Right so it fareþ on the same wyse		
	By hym that in peyne lyþ and may nat aryse		
	Ac þey þat beþ in p(ur)gatory in penaunce		
2970	W(i)t(h)oute help of frendes haueþ non allegiaunce[2]		relief / forgiveness
	Ac who in dedly synne ys ybrought		
	And in herte charyte he haueþ nought		not
	He nys bot as ded in his soule w(i)t(h) ynne		
	As longe as he lieþ in dedly synne		
2975	And al his helpe is bot as in veyn		
	To the soules that dwelleþ in peyn		
	Ffor his helpe in hym self stondeþ in no stede[3]		it avails not / is of no advantage
	For it is nought that he haþ ibede		offered
	Ac neuer þe lattur thaw it so be		latter, though
2980	That he be in dedly synne and nat out of charyte		
	3ut may the soule ben iholpe þus		
	3if he to þe pore 3iue almes		charity
	That he for þe soule specyallyche do preye		particularly
	For þat helpeþ the soule þ(a)t in p(ur)gatory haþ leye		lain
2985	3ut may þe helpe and þe grete travayle		anguish
	Of þe synful man to the soule avayle		help
	3if it þorow good p(re)yere be ido		
	Of a frend that he in his lyf tresteþ to		
	Thulke help may avayle to hym wel sone		
2990	In soule þat ascheþ for hym suche a bone		asks, boon
	That in his herte hath charyte faste iknet		knit
	And for his sake wole don it		
	Ffor whi God wole do no3t for his sake		Therefore
	That wole nat in his herte charyte take		

---

[1] Several faint lines in the shape of a loop and an "X" are written over the text of this page. The usual half dozen erasures are overwritten with corrections.

[2] Several end-of-line corrections, as here (2970) and *haþ leye (leye* having a dotted *y* at l. 2984), were made by the *Piers* rubricator; *ys ybrought* (l 2971) are both emended and given dotted *y*'s.

[3] "… in itself does not serve, is of no avail."

2995	This case ofte falleþ as y haue undyrstonde[1]	f. 39r	situation, arises
	By twene a lord and his s(er)uaunt that is to hym bonde		bondman / a tenant or serf
	Where that the lord good and ryghtfull is		
	And þe s(er)uaunt of scherewdenesse bereþ the p(ri)s[2]		takes the prize
	Ac ȝif þe s(er)uaunt do any man(er) thyng		
3000	The whiche is good at þe lordes byddynge		command
	Ȝut it may avayle to som good p(ro)fit		
	They he in goodnesse haue no delit		Though
	Ac þat is by reso(u)n thorow the goodnesse iwis		
	Of hym of wham thulke byddynge ys		such request
3005	Ffor þey it be aȝenst the [ ][3] wylle		though
	Ȝut aȝens the byddere it stondeþ stylle		Yet, remains anyway
	Ac ȝif in charyte they were boþe		
	Þe more were þe help to þe dede for soþe.		truth
	Also þawe a prest in any time be		though
3010	Synful and out of parfit charyte		
	Ȝut he is goddes minister and holy churches		
	That the sacrament on the aut(er) werches		altar works
	The whiche is neu(er) the lasse of myght		power
	Al þaw the prest lyue nat aryght		morally
3015	Ffor þawe a prest that syngeþ a messe		
	Be neu(er) so full of wykkednesse		
	Ȝut þulke sacrament that is so holy		such
	May nat ben apeyryd by his foly		impaired
	Than may a masse soules f(ro)m peyne brynge		
3020	Al thawe a synful prest the masse synge		
	Ffor he syngeth the masse in godes name		
	And þ(er)fore to þe sacrament he may do no schame		
	But oþer prayers ymade w(i)t(h) good entent		
	Þe whiche ben iused be sides the sacrament		
3025	Of a good prest beth betre god to paye		satisfy
	Þan of an euel prest y dar sauely saie		safely
	Ac þe offrenge of goddes body that is so swete		
	Helpeþ to brynge soules f(ro)m her peynes grete.		
	Wherfore it semeþ that masses syngynge		
3030	May moste þe soules f(ro)m peynes brynge		
	That passeþ out of þis world in charyte		
	And in p(ur)gatorye clansed schul be		purified
	Ac to hem that beþ dampned for ay		damned forever
	No good dede helpe ne avayle may		

---

[1] A fairly light loop is drawn on the bottom half of this page.

[2] "... has the reputation (for)."

[3] Illegible erased word here, leaving a blank space of four or five lines, seeming to end in an *s*. Perhaps the word was *doers* since both Morey's and Hanna and Wood's versions have *doer* (*l.* 3678 in both). Thus, if *doer* and *bidder* were both more charitable, the dead would be more helped in truth.

3035	Noþur almesdede p(ra)yer ne masse[1]	f. 39v	neither
	For they beþ as the book bereþ witnesse		
	Departed f(ro)m cryst that was of mary bore		
	And þe soules of hem beþ for eu(er) ilore		lost
	Ffor as þe lemes that ben dede and ilayd in clay		limbs
3040	And beþ don clene f(ro)m the body away		
	Than no þyng may helpe in no man(er) kynde		
	Þulke lemes that beþ drie as þe wynde.		Those
	Right so al the help that any man kan telle		
	Right nauȝt avayleþ to hem that beþ in helle		
3045	Ac help of frendes ido in godes s(er)vise		done
	May þo soules avayleþ in som(m)e man(er) wyse		help
	Ffor suche s(er)vise may to god ben iwrought		done
	That soules schulleþ to þe lasse peyne be brought		
	Ffor þer to avayleþ almesdede, masse and bedes		help, (rosary) beads
3050	To þe soules þat beþ in alle þre stedes		three places
	Ffor it availeþ to þe soule that in p(ur)gatory is		profits
	For to delyuere hem out of peyne þe hasty lok(lier)[2] iwis.		deliver, more quickly
	Also it availeþ to hem þ(at) in heuene ben iset		ready
	For þey multiplieþ þ(er)fore eche day þe bet		multiply, better
3055	And þe mo þat comeþ to that holy place		more
	Þe more is her ioye afore goddes face		before
	Also it avayleþ to hem that beþ in helle		profits
	For the fewer comeþ þider þ(er)e forto dwelle		
	And þe fewer that þider comeþ for synne		
3060	Þe lasse peyne þey haueþ that dwelle þ(er)ynne		live there
	And þe mo that to þulke place wendeþ		that place
	Þe more is her peyne that neu(er) amendeþ		heals
	Thus may help of frendes availe by reso(u)n		reasonably help
	To the soules that beþ in any preso(u)n		prison
3065	And namely to hem that beþ in helle		
	And also to hem that schulleþ in p(ur)gatory dwelle		
	Bot it ne doþ þe soule f(ro)m peyne wende		
	Bot charyte be wyþ hym at eu(er)y ende		point
	Ffor in helle ne was ne ys neuere charyte		neither was nor is
3070	And in heuene no nede þer of may be		
	And as a man may here wyþ his bond		binding force
	Make a fele for a noþur that is undur hond		chasten / correct
	That is not of power hit forto make		
	Ac a noþur it makeþ for his sake.[3]		But another

---

[1] The expected line drawn through the text again makes a loop through the bottom of the folio. The line looks carelessly drawn, with force (of anger?) as seen in some previous defacement.

[2] This anomalous phrase seems to indicate the comparative of *hasty*; both Morey and Hanna and Wood have *mare hastily*.

[3] Thus a man in purgatory may chasen another not for power over him but for his sake.

3075	Ryght so may a man for þe dede do[1]	f. 40r	Similarly, dead
	For he haþ of help meche nede þerto		
	And þe soules þ(a)t beþ to paradys gon		brought
	Nede of help þey haueþ right non		
	Ac ȝif any good dede be for hem iwrought		done
3080	It may to the nedfull in help ben ibrought		
	Ffor al þe help that specially is don here		
	Avayleþ to the soules þ(a)t in p(ur)gatory beþ þere		Profits
	Ac for þan to som(m)e more and to som(m)e lesse		
	Aftur that þey beþ itold of wurþinesse		
3085	And aftur þat charyte is on hem clcr ynow		clearly enough
	Of hem þat lyueþ here amonges ȝow		
	The whiche moste be besy eu(er) wele to do		happiness
	As wel for hem self as for hem þat ben in wo[2]		sorrow
	Ffor whan a man schal f(ro)m hennys flytte		hence flies
3090	Þan kan no man telle bi al his witte		knowledge
	Wheþ(er) þat he schal to p(ur)gatory wende		
	Oþur to blis oþur to peyne w(i)t(h) outen ende		Either
	Ffor som(m)e semeþ good and parfit alone		
	Þat after þe deþ beþ dampned wel sone		damned
3095	Ffor p(er)chaunce þey beþ foul wiþ ynne		
	And passeþ awey in dedly synne		
	And som(m)e semeþ here leuynge amys		living wrong
	Þ(a)t beþ saued and broȝt sone into heuene blis		joy of heaven
	Ffor p(er)chaunce afore here deyȝynge		perhaps before, dying
3100	Þey beþ amendyd of here mys leuynge		sinful life
	Ac of þis may no man incerteyn be		
	For it bilongeþ to godes pryuuyte		divine mystery
	Naþeles we schul trowe and suppose ay		believe, always
	Þat alle þat dieþ wendeþ good way		go
3105	Whom we se[3] here good werkes wurche		perform
	And haueþ al þe sacrements of holy churche		
	Ac wheþ(er) it be so oþur nought so		or not so
	Alle þat is in us we schulleþ eu(er) do		
	And eu(er) p(re)ye boþ loude and stille		
3110	For alle crystene soules as it is godes wille.		
	Ȝut som(m)e mowe aske whi me(n) doþ masses synge		may
	For a ȝong child aftur his deyȝinge		dying
	That of p(re)yere ne masse haþ non nede		
	For it wrought neu(er) synfull dede		performed

---

[1] Defacement is almost exclusively limited to the bottom half of the folio, with its loop encompassing the final four lines and the lower marginal space. This first line is relatively heavy or emphatic.
[2] The last nine words have been emended by the *Piers* rubricator, as has *ynow* (l. 3085).
[3] The first three words are written over an erasure of greater size than these words require by the *Piers* rubricator.

3115	This may be þe ryght answere by reso(u)n	f.40v	
	Þat for the honour of god me(n) haþ encheso(u)n		occasion
	Masses to synge and p(re)ieres to make		
	Þat he to ʒonge and to olde is m(er)cy take.[1]		
	Also for þe good usage of holy cherche		
3120	And for hem þat beþ dede som good to wurche		perform
	Here ʒe haueþ iherd as þe bok is witnesse		
	How almesdede, penaunce, p(re)iers, and messe		almsgiving, masses
	That beþ idon þorow trewe frendes and c(er)teyne		
	May helpe þe soules þat liggeþ in peyne		lie
3125	And nowe wol ischewe more þerto		I show
	What p(ro)fit p(ar)don may to þe soule do		
	Þe whiche is p(ur)chased in right manere		earned
	And in clene lyf on erþe here		
	Of pardon what it availeþ to þe soule.[2]		
3130	**P**ardon hem helpeþ in many wayes		
	Þ(a)t haueþ it p(ur)chaced in her lyf daies		earned
	Ffor pardon of [pope]s[3] and buschopes hie		archbishops
	Þat is here g(rau)nted er a man diʒe		dies
	May avayle to þe soule þ(a)t in p(ur)gatory is		help
3135	Ʒif it be p(u)rchaced wurþiliche iwis		purchased justly / reverently
	And ʒif þey haueþ of her synnes cont(ri)tion		
	And beþ ischryue byfore þulke pardon		shriven
	Than pardon aftur deþ þorow godes sonde		grace
	In p(ur)gatory to hem may[4] grete stede stonde		stand them in great stead
3140	Ffor pardon þe whiche is rightful and c(er)teyn		
	May hem boþ relece of dette and of peyn		release, debt
	As ferforþ as þe pardon may areche		far, reach
	For þus hav y herd grete clerkes teche		
	Pardon p(ro)p(er)ly is nauʒt elles in liknesse		nothing
3145	Bot of peyne that is dette forʒiuenesse		debt
	And pardon may no man haue bot ʒif he wol werche		unless, work
	For it is þe tresour of al holy cherche		treasure
	The whiche is g(ra)nted for the mede pardo(u)n		reward
	Þorowe vertu of crystes holy passio(u)n		
3150	And of þe wurþynesse and of the dedes		
	Of his goode halwes and of her medes[5]		saints, rewards
	And it is gadred of many a maner good		
	Ferst of martyrs þat schadde her blood		First, shed
	The whiche were sad in crystes lay		established, law

---

[1] Middle English Distionary notes that *is* is a variant of *his*, and *take* also means *bestow / take*.
[2] A forceful brown-inked line is drawn under and through this red-inked heading; *pardon* is additionally marked out.
[3] The word *popes* has been almost fully obliterated, but the *s* remains; nothing has been scribed over the erasure, so it was certainly not done by the original scribe who would have replaced scribal errors with correction. The manuscript has clearly undergone revision by a Protestant.
[4] Written in very small letters over a small erasure; perhaps *may* is replacing *is*.
[5] The last four lines are heavily amended by the *Piers* rubricator, but are not cleanly erased and are thus unclear.

3155	And for hys loue hadde many gret afray	f. 41r	terror
	And of penaunce and t(ra)vayle of confessours		work
	Of the holy techinge of wyse doctours		
	And of þe chastite of virgynes holy and clene		
	That euere to god wolde her mone mene		complaint
3160	And also of holy cherche werkes		
	And of p(ra)yers of prestes and clerkes		
	Of al þis þat y haue here bifore told		
	Ys gadred this treso(ur) bothe newe and old		
	Of the whiche tresour the [pope bereþ þe keies][1]		bears keys
3165	Wherwiþ he openyþ and speryþ aftyr synnes weies[2]		closes, ways
	And that bifalleþ to hym of office to holde		
	For god on eorþe his vicarye hym make wolde		vicar
	Thulke keies beþ nought elles to undyrstonde		
	Bot playn power ʒiue to hym þorow godes sonde		grace
3170	Thorowe þe whiche he may boþe lowde and stille		
	Al thing lose and bynde at his owne wille		
	Ffor the same power hym bifalleþ to haue		
	Þat cryst ʒafe to petur soules to saue		gave
	Ffor cryst ʒaf to petur ful powere		
3175	And saide to hym in this manere		
	Quodcu(n)q(ue) ligaveris sup(er) terra(m)		
	erit ligatu(m) et in celis. et quodcu(n)que		
	solveris sup(er) terra(m) erit erit [sic]		
	solutu(m) et i(n) celis.[3]		
	Al þat þu byndest on erþe sayþ he		
	Schal in heuene euere bounde be		
	And þat þu losest in erþe aright		loose
3180	Schal ben ilosed in heuene bright		
	This power to alle [popes][4] ʒau our lord		
	Aftur petur to holde þulke word		this
	As scheweþ þ(er)of an exposicio(u)n		
	Of the holy gospel in a lesson		
3185	Than semeþ it wel by this reson		
	That eche [po]pe haþ a large iurisdict(i)oun		jurisdiction
	To assoile a man and hym clene forʒiue		absolve
	Al þe dettys of peyne wherto he schold be dryue		debts, compelled
	Ac ʒut mot a man ʒelde aʒen ʒif he be myghty þ(er)to		recompense
3190	Al þat he haþ wrongfully take othur ido		taken or done
	Ffor þe [pope] whan [whan] he doþ þulke g(ra)ce[5]		
	He byndeþ holy cherche in þulke [holy] place		binds
	Ffor hym to wham þulke g(ra)ce avayleþ		profits

---

[1] These four words have been heavily scratched out. Lines have also been drawn through the text on top and bottom of this folio.

[2] The pope can open or close the treasury of the Church. Note that "according to sin's ways" refers to church teaching that certain sins are reserved to the papacy for absolution. This line is written over an erasure. A line has been drawn through the last eight of the nine words in this line.

[3] "And whatsoever thou shalt bind upon earth, it shall be bound also in heaven: and whatsoever thou shalt loose on earth, it shall be loosed also in heaven" [Matt. 16:19].

[4] The word *popes* has been erased here, and pope partially erased in l. 3189.

[5] The word *pope* is erased and the redundant *whan* is crossed out (the first by a defacer, the second by an emendor?), as is *holy* on the next line, but with a firmer stroke.

	To fulfille all þynges that to hym fayleþ	f. 41v	is lacking
3195	Bot þe buschopes that beþ of lasse stat		estate
	Haueþ lasse power as clerkes knoweþ þat		
	Ffor why her dignyte is muche more lasse		therefore
	And þerfore they ne moweþ ou(er) her pou(er) passe		might not surpass
	Ac for þan they it ne be so suffisaunte		Although, sufficient
3200	As (þe [pope] is ȝut they may make ag(rau)nte		
	Of her pardon gret plente)¹		
	To here undyrlynges of eche degre		
	Ac ȝut it moste as y haue bifore sed		must
	Ben iȝiue of holy cherches tresour þorow good red		advice
3205	Ac for þan ther may no man pardon wynne		
	Bot he be clene of dedly synne		unless
	Ffor [ ]² he þat haþ þe kepinge of þulke treso(ur)		
	Þat is to mannes soule so precyous a flour		flower
	May nawȝt it dele to holy cherches foos		foes
3210	Laste he wynne þ(er)by to hym selue an euel loos		Lest, reputation
	Ffor suche men it beþ and non oþ(u)r iwys		
	Bot þey þat dwelleþ in synne and eu(er) doþ amys		wrong
	Ffor þey beþ out of holy cherche lawe		
	And þey mowe no pardon to hem drawe		may
3215	Ac þe frendes of holy cherche mowen [ ] craue³		desire
	Rightfully aftur pardon for þey schulleþ it haue		
	Ffor þey beþ suche þat eu(er) beþ fre		
	Out of dedly synne and in parfit charyte		
	To the whiche pardon schal neu(er) fayle		
3220	Ac in p(ur)gatory it schal hem avayle		profit
	To brynge out of peyne her soules clene		purity
	As fer⁴ forþ as it may areche oþur mene		reach, men
	The whiche as clerkes saieþ god wol sette		
	For the remenaunt of peynes þat beþ dette		remainder, debt
3225	That p(er)chaunce is left [ ] and undo here		
	As it may falle in dyuerse manere		
	As a partye of penance þat enioyned is⁵		
	And nat fulfuld for rechelnysse ywis		recklessness
	And in party for venyal synnes wroȝt		
3230	And in party for synnes þat beþ out of thouȝt		forgotten
	And in party for ouerlytel repentaunce		insufficient
	And in party for ouerlytyll penaunce		
	And in party for penaunce enioynyd and not do .		given, done

---

¹ Most of these two lines have a wavy line drawn through them; the word *pope* has been erased and a large, round, black ink mark has be made in the middle of the missing space. Morey's edition provides *popes* at l. 3875 and Hanna and Wood's edition *papes* at the same line

² A space is left here, perhaps an erasure of the word *pope* since the pope has the keys to the kingdome of heaven, "þulke treso(ur) Þat is mannes soule so precyous a flour; another space is found on l. 3215 saying the friends of the church want pardon (from the pope?) and a third on l. 3225 suggesting perchance the pope is left to undo purgatory's pains.

³ Morey's and Hanna and Wood's editions provide *wyn* here.

⁴ No doubt the scribe meant to write "fer" but the following word "forþ" confused him.

⁵ This line and the next are smeared and somewhat unclear.

	And p(er)chaunce wiþ lytyl deuocyo(u)n set þ(er)to	f. 42r	
3235	Alle these mowe ben yclepud þe remena(u)nt		remainder
	Of þe dette of peyne that is naw3t suffisa(u)nt		
	The whiche schold be fulfyllyd on erthe here		
	Or in p(ur)gatory to make the soules þe more clere		
	Ac all suche dette may sone þ(er)e bequyt		be requited
3240	Ho so to any such pardon haþ any delyt		to whomever
	In for3iuenesse of al man(er) trespas þ(a)t may be iwro3t		committed
	Whethur it be enioyned here oþur nowt		
	Ffor so myche pardon may a man purchace		acquire
	In his lyf here that he may þan haue g(ra)ce		
3245	In p(ur)gatory quyt to be f(ro)m alle dette		
	The whiche fro þe blysse of heuene mygth hym lette		be hindered
	Ffor so large ys holy cherches treso(ur)		
	That it may soules brynge f(ro)m alle dolo(ur)		sorrow
	And f(ro)m al the peyne of dette that may be		
3250	Of alle þe men that beþ in crystyente.		christianity
	Thus pardon in p(ur)gatory to soules may avayle		benefit
	Ac 3ut some clerkes doth us consayle		
	That we scholde it res(er)ue and hollyche spare		wholly
	Forto we to p(ur)gatory comen al bare		bereft / naked
3255	And here do penaunce whiles we may[1]		
	For a man schall thenke in p(ur)gatory o day		one
	Lengur than eu(er) hym þought on erþe here		Longer
	Þe spas for soþe of on halfe 3ere		space
	Than o day of pardon in for3iuenesse		one
3260	More is wurþy þan al þis worldes rycchesse		
	Ffor the soule hadde leu(er) that suche peyne schal dryue		rather
	O day of pardon than any þyng on lyue[2]		One
	Ffor al þis wyde world 3if it were his		
	He wolde it 3iue to haue reste iwys		
3265	Of þis mater wherof we makeþ mencio(u)n		
	That is of help of frendes and of pardon[3]		
	Avayleth to hem that beþ in p(ur)gatory set		Profits
	Wherof y haue myne marters for me here iset		martyrs
	Ffor þerof spekeþ innocent and seynt austyn		
3270	In bokes where these marters beþ set wel afyn		at the end
	And mayster raymond[4] spekeþ of þe same		
	In a boke that ys clepud aftur his name		called
	And thomas alquyn spekeþ also .		Aquinas

---

[1] The *Piers* rubricator has written over *may*, leaving about three letters' space before it. The right margin contains a pineapple-shaped indentation which extends into the lines; it may be a natural feature of the vellum and not a defacement. Other defacing lines are drawn at the top and bottom of the page.

[2] The text does not capitalize the letter *O* at the beginning of the line.

[3] A worm hole that does not fully penetrate the vellum occurs in the right margin here.

[4] Hanna and Wood identify him as Raymond of Penaforte, author of a standard treatise on penance; Morey identifies him as Raymond Llul, a Catalan theologian who died in 1315. I incline toward the former.

106 Part V. Ten Signs of Doomsday (3274–3313)

	Of this mater and of oþur mo	f. 42v	
3275	In a boke of right gret philosofye		
	The whiche is clepud veritas theologie.[1]		
	Heere to ȝowe y haue many maters red		advised
	And the furþe party of þis boke isped		accomplished
	In the whiche ȝe haueþ iherd me specifie		specify
3280	Alle condycyo(u)ns of purgatorye		
	And nowe iwole to þe fyfþe party wende		
	And þe mat(er)s þ(er)of telle unto þe ende		
	That[2] spekeþ holly of þe day of dome		wholly
	And of the toknes þat schal bifore come		
3285	Here us to warne þat we beþ eu(er) ȝare		ready
	Our soules f(ro)m synne eu(er) to spare		
	Here bigynneþ þe fifþe party of this book.[3]		
	In this party me(n) may of ten thynges rede		read
	The whiche towcheþ þe grete day of drede		pertain to
3290	And som(m)e schulleþ afore that day be		before
	And som(m)e at þat day as men may se[4]		
	Also bifore that day dyv(er)se toknes schul come		indicators
	Of þe whiche man may here fynde some		
	The whiche tokenes men schul þenke hard		
3295	As ȝe may ihere sone here afturward		
	And hoso wol hym right wel avyse[5]		whoso, consider
	He may eche day se in many awyse		ways
	Toknes where þorow he may haue und(yr)stondynge		
	Þat þe day of dome is faste comynge		
3300	Ffor wondres þat schul falle as y wene		miracles
	Aȝens þe worldes ende beþ now wel isene		
	Thorow þe wondres that god let sende		
	Men knoweþ þat þe world ys ny the ende		near
	Wherfore we scholde us eu(er) redy make		
3305	The laste daies comynge w(i)t(h)out drede take		
	Ccrystes[6] discyples that coueytyd to haue knowynge		desired
	Of some tokenes aȝenst his laste comynge		
	Thus spaken to cryst as ȝe may ihure heere		spoke, hear
	As þe gospel witnesseþ ryght in þis manere		fashion
3310	*Dic nobis signu(m) advent(us) tui et consumac(ion)is sec(u)li.*[7]		
	Sey now to us quaþ þey of thy comynge at þe laste		quote
	And how thu wolt an end of þe world caste		make
	Et r(espo)ndens dixit ihesus . eis vidite ne quis vos seducat.[8]		Jesus

---

[1] "... the truth of theology." The scribe omitted the second *o* normally in *theologie*. This refers to Hugo the Dominican friar, Hugo Ripelin of Strasbourg, *Compendium Theologiae Veritates*. Aquinas's version is a *Compendium Theologica*.

[2] This and the next three lines are erased and smeared above the large capital I, clouding the text.

[3] Stacy A. Waters has edited Book V of the *Pricke of Conscience* from H.M. 125. I am very grateful to him for providing his unpublished edition for comparison to this edition of H.M. 128. Significant comparisons are noted in footnotes below. For example, the capital beginning Part V is nine rather than six lines.

[4] H.M. 125 includes twenty lines enumerating ten tokens marking doomsday.

[5] A letter-size blue smudge occurs 3/4 of an inch to the right of this word, directly above the *on* of *und(ur)stondynge*.

[6] No other scribe has written two *C*'s at the beginning of this word.

[7] "Tell us what shall be the sign of thy coming, and of the consummation of the world?" [Matt. 24:3].

[8] "And Jesus answering, said to them: take heed that no man seduce you" [Matt. 24: 4].

Multi eni(m) venient in n(omin)e meo . dicentes,   f. 43r   Christ
Ego su(m) xpc . et multos Seducent. Surget gens contra gentem
Et regnum adv(er)s(us) regnu(m) et eru(n)t pestilencie et fames
Et t(er)re motus magni p(er) loca . terrores que de celo et signa
Magna erunt. Hec autem o(mn)ia inicia sunt dolorum.[1]

     Than answeryd cryst and seyde to hem þis
3315 Loke that no man desteyne[2] ȝow amys   See that, sully
     Ffor many schullen come in my name[3]
     And sey þus y am cryst, god and lord[4] of fame
     And wel many thei schullen bigyle   deceive
     Ac they schul regne bot alytyl while
3320 And kyngdom aȝenst kyngdom in þe same wyse
     And men agenst men schullen aryse
     Also pestilences and hongres schul be   famines
     And erþe myuynges in many contre   earthquakes
     Al þis schal be þe bygynnynge of hard   hardship / misfortune
3325 Of sorow and care that schal come afturward
     Thanne schal wykkednesse wexe many fold   increase
     And the charyte of many schal bicome cold.
     These toknes to his disciples tolde he
     Þe whiche agenst þe worldes ende[5] schal be
3330 Ac some of þese tokenes beþ to ende ibrought
     And some of hem ȝut schewed hem nought   appeared to
     Bot of þe tokenes that ȝut schulleþ come
     Ȝif ȝe wolleþ iwul telle ȝow some
     Ac ferst of antecryst now wul y speke
3335 The whiche afore domes day schal out breke
     Aftur þulke tyme þ(a)t distructyon schul be
     Of the empire of rome that ȝut[6] is fre
     Ffor some tyme al the londes of the world aboute
     Were suggettys to rome and most þ(er)to aloute   subject of, allowed
3340 And scholde ȝyue therto trew age[7]   tribute / truage
     As þe custome than was and the usage .
     That ylke custome most all the londes do   same, follow
     As seyn powle sayþ this matere ther to
     Nisi pri(m)us ven(er)it discenc(i)o ita ut o(mn)ia regna descendat a Roma-
         no imp(er)io que p(rim)us erant s(u)bdita non antea veniet antecristus[8].
3345 He sayþ that bot ȝif ferst discencyon come   unless if first dissensio
     Þat ys alle londes holde aȝenst rome   withstand
     So that it be iput to dystrucc(i)on   put

---

[1] "For many will come in my name saying, I am Christ, and they will seduce many. For nation shall arise against nation and kingdom against kingdo[m] and there shall be pestilences, and famine and earthquakes in places" [Matt 24:5-8], "and terrors from heaven; and there shall be great signs."[*Luke* 21:11]. H.M. 125 adds 1 ¼ lines here: *Et quoniam habundanit iniquitas refrigesset caritas multurum.*

[2] H.M. 125 uses *dosayue.*

[3] Although there is no erasure here, this line is written appreciably smaller than the one preceding it. The scribe has fit 40 lines on this page. which is more than on most.

[4] H.M. 125 reads to "crist and lord."

[5] H.M. 125 states "evil" on this and the following lines.

[6] H.M. 125 provides "us sette" here.

[7] H.M. 125 connects these words: "therto trewage," but H.M. 128 does not.

[8] "Antichrist will not come unless their first comes a revolt, so that every kingdom formerly subjected to the Roman empire falls away from it" [*nisi primus venerit discencio* is from II Thess. 2:3. The remainder appears to be the Northern poet's paraphrase and explanation of II Thess. verse 3].

Part V. Ten Signs of Doomsday (3348–3387)

	Of hem that were ferst in subiectyon	f. 43v	subjection
	Antecryst er that tyme schall nat come		
3350	No þo day of dome schall nat arst bynome		judgment, be taken
	That ylke destruccion holy writ seyþ schal be		
	Ac þe tyme þerof men schal nauȝt ȝut ise		
	Ffor in thulke tyme schal no lond in no syde		region
	In subieccion of Rome[1] no lengo(r) abyde		subjection, longer remain
3355	Ne schal no man bux(u)n ben ifounde		obedient
	Ne to the cherche of rome obedyent ben ibounde		
	Ac now me(n) may se the empyre that so myghti was		
	Ys destruyd and bare ymade in many a plas		
	Bot as y sayde er it schal be destruyd at þe laste		before
3360	And þe moste party of þe lond me(n) schal ou(ur) kaste		greatest portion, expel
	Ac þe dignyte that þ(er)to scholde falle		
	Schal nawt in that tyme be y mad þralle		not, slave
	Ffor it stonde schal and dwelle with oute doute		remain
	In al man(er) regions that stondeþ þ(er)aboute		
3365	Thus schal the ferst token at rome bigynne		
	Þat ys hed of crystendom to make her atwynne		head, joined, apart
	Ffor whan it is pult[2] to destructio(u)n		pulled
	Al holy cherehe schal be pult ado(u)n		
	As some clerkes seyeth that on schal come[3]		one
3370	To hold þe empire al and some		
	And holly it[4] haue and the corowne here		wholly, crown
	In ful pes that no lond schal hym dere		injure
	Ffor he schal be þe laste emp(er)o(ur) þ(a)t þere schal be		
	And most of all kynges and man of gret pouste		power
3375	The whiche schal wel manteyne his astat		
	And al his empire w(i)t(h)oute any debat		
	And it gou(er)ne thorow lawe and good reso(u)n		
	For no man scholde[5] do no treso(u)n		treachery
	Bote aftyrward at the laste ende		
3380	Forþ into ieru(sa)l(e)m he schal wende		
	Up on þe hie mount of olyuete		Mount of Olives
	There he schal the septre of Rome sete		
	And his corone he schal legge adown also		crown, lay
	And leue hem there and gon hem fro.		
3385	Thus schal the dignyte of Rome away be nome		always, taken away
	And sone afturward schal antecryst come		
	As clerkes seyeþ þat haueþ undyrstondynge		

---

[1] The use of capitalization – of "Rome" here and on *ll.* 3382 and 3385 below is comparatively rare.
[2] H.M. 125 uses "yputt."
[3] H.M. 125 writes " of rome shal be ynome."
[4] H.M. 125 uses "hure" for it.
[5] H.M. 125 adds "to hym" here.

	Of seynt poules and daniels seyȝynge	f. 44r
	Of the lyf of Anticrist.	
3390	Thanne schal antecristes tyme bigynne	
	Þat seynt poule calleþ the man of synne	
	Ffor they[1] he be man ȝut neu(er) the lesse	though, yet
	He schal be the welle of wikydnesse	
	And the deueles sone he schal be itold	
3395	Ac good kynde men schul nowȝt so hym hold	not hold him so
	Ac þorow his tornynge f(ro)m the good into ylle[2]	conversion
	For he schal euere the deuels wyl fulfulle	always
	And in al þe power of the deuel of helle	
	And al his wyt with hym schal dwelle	
3400	And in hym al maner treson and malyce	
	Schal ben ihud f(ro)m all other[3] vice	
	He schal to our lord cryst contr(ar)ious be	
	And to all his lymes that he may se	limbs
	And he schal make hym self hie þorow p(ri)de[4]	
3405	And ben as god in al this world wyde	
	And holde hym self most in all thinge	
	And the fals godes make his undurlynge	underling
	That is to seye jubyter and mercurye	Jupiter
	And the grete apolonye and erculye	Apollo, Hercules
3410	And nat only to ben aboue thes planetys[5] alle	planets
	Þe whiche þe paynemes her godes doþ calle	pagans
	But he schal hym sette in gret dignyte	
	And make hym to ben aboue the t(ri)nyte	
	Whom all creato(ur)s that euere weren in kynde	nature
3415	By skile scholden honoure and hym haue in mynde	
	Wel synful schal be his bigynnynge	
	Ac more wonderful schal be his endynge	amazing
	For to a ssodayn[6] ende he schal drawe	
	And þorow the myght of god he schal ben islawe	slain
3420	Ac in his tyme schal be so muchel tribulacyou(n)	
	And so muchel anguys and p(er)secucyou(n)	
	That unneþe schal any man ȝiue graunt	scarcely, admit
	That he is of crystes lore . or his s(er)uaunt	
	Ffor more p(er)secucio(u)n schal thanne be iwonne	gained
3425	Than eu(er) was suþþe þe world[7] was bigonne	since
	Ffor antecryst ys thus mychul forto segge	say
	As he that wole eu(er) aȝen goddes lawes alegge	argue

---

[1] H.M. 125 provides *al þei*.
[2] H.M 125 writes *þe gode into þe ille*.
[3] These two words *all othur* have been auto-corrected.
[4] H.M. 125 says "priute" followed by: "Ffor above god he wolde hym pute more worþe" for the next line.
[5] H.M. 125 uses *goddes* instead of *planetys* here.
[6] Occasionally this author or scribe uses a double first letter, as here in *ssodayn*, perhaps to indicate emphasis. The usual doubling occurs with the *Ff* or *ff* and sometimes indicates a capital letter.
[7] H.M. 125 lacks "world," seemingly an error.

Part V. Ten Signs of Doomsday

	[1]Than mowen al these antecrystes ben itold	f. 44v	may
	Þat aȝenst crystes lawes wurcheþ many fold		works
3430	Ac many suche men me(n)[2] may forþ drawe		
	That muchel wurcheþ [3]aȝenst Godes lawe.		work seriously
	Bot antecryst as the boke sayth this		
	Schal come at the laste that kam nat ȝut iwys		came
	As he that is most tyraunt w(i)t(h)oute pyte		tyrannous
3435	That eu(er) was or that eu(er) schal be		
	And ho so[4] wole alytyl while dwelle		
	Aparty of hym y wol openly telle[5]		a part
	Of[6] the maners of his bigynnynge		ways
	And of his lyf and of his fowle endynge.		
3440	He schal be byȝete as y well telle can		begotten
	By twixe a synful man and a womman		
	And aftyr the tyme that he conseyued be		conceived
	Þe fend schal euer thorow his pouste		power
	Wiþ ynne his moders wombe brede		mother's, grow
3445	For so seyn clerkes as y in bok rede		
	Thorow whos myght he schal be forþ brought		
	And wondres þorow hym schulleþ ben iwrought		miracles, enacted
	He schal ben iclepud the child forlore		called, lost
	And in[7] coroȝaym he schal be ibore		Corozain, born
3450	Of a womman of the kynrede of dan		lineage
	Bot of crystendom he[8] schal be wan		won
	And he schal be malicious[9] and ful of envye		
	For þus of hym spekeþ the holy[10] profecye:		
	FFiet dan coluber in via sedens . mordens ungulas equi . ut cadat		
	Ascensor . eius . hoc est antecrist(us) sicut serpens sedebit in via insidia(n)s		
	Eis ut eos qui p(er) semitas iusticie ambulant fereat.		
	Veneno sue malicie . et occidat . et cetera.[11]		
3455	The dan he saiþ schal þe adder be		
	Syttynge in the wey that man mowen se.		may
	He schal byte þe hors by the houe hard		horse, hoof
	And make þe upstyere falle bakward		rider
	And þat is þus mychel to seye in good fey		
3460	Þat anti xpe as an adder schal sytte bi þe wey		Christ
	And smyten hem boþe more and lasse		strike / sting
	Þat walken þe weies of rightfulnesse		
	And hem sle thorow wikked venym		slay, wicked venom
	Þorow þe malice that schal come of hym		

---

[1] H.M. 125 precedes this line with the following: Than may iche man þat doth any euyl thyng ille / Ne jclepyd antecryst for he doth aȝeyn gods wille (ll. 4141-42).

[2] The repetition of me(n) seems to be an uncorrected dittograph mistake also occurring in H.M. 125.

[3] H.M. 125 states "wolleþ meche do" here.

[4] Midddle English Dictionary indicates this is a variant of who so.

[5] The following lines occur parenthetically in H.M. 125: Wherefore jholde al þese mysdoers / As antecristes lamys and his forgoers.

[6] An indentation becoming brown extends from this Of (l. 3438) to womman (l. 3441).

[7] Space for about two letters occurs between these words.

[8] H.M. 125 says "she."

[9] ... unbaptized, lacking grace, hence malicious.

[10] The word holy is omitted in H.M. 125.

[11] "Lo Dan be a snake in the way ... that biteth the horse's heels that his rider may fall backward" [Gen 49:17. The gloss reads "That is, antichrist will sit in the way, lying in ambush to strike those who tried the paths of justice."]

3465	And ȝut he schal be icircu(m)cised	f. 45r	
	And also aft(er) þe olde lawe be dysgised		
	To make his malyce the more ihud		hid
	As he¹ seyþ godes sone iwol be cud.		I will be known
	Also to hym than schal assignyd be		
3470	A good angel the whiche he schal nat se		
	Aftur his burthe in his bygynnyge		
	The which of hym schal haue the kepynge		
	Ac for he [ ]² is aȝenst al goodnesse		since
	He schal be iharded in al wykydnesse		hardened
3475	His good angel schal f(ro)m hym wende		
	And bileue hym in þe kepynge of the fende		
	And he schal ben ilerned as the deueles s(er)uaunt³		
	And lengest dwelle ther ynne and be most cons(er)uaunt		longest, preserving
	In the cite of Bethsaida and there his m(er)þes make.⁴		
3480	An⁵ in capharnaum he schal his regne take		
	The whiche capharnaum and bethsaida þ(er)to		
	And coroȝaym god acursid w(i)t(h) othur mo		
	And god spak to þese citees thus		
	As here the gospel telleþ us:		
3485	Ve tibi Coroȝaym . Ve tibi Bethsaida . Ve tibi Capharnaum.⁶		
	He saith wo [^to]⁷ the coȝoȝaym⁸ mut come		sorrow
	And bethsaida and capharnaum be þ(er)to ynome		seized
	Ffor in the ferste he schal ben ibred and ibore		born
	And in that oþur be norsched for it is mad þ(er)fore		nursed
3490	And ⁹ in the þrydde he schal regne as a kynge		third
	Þerfore tho þre cites god acursid ou(er) al þynge		
	Than schal he grade¹⁰ to gydre wel many a man		gather together
	Þat any þing of the deueles craft can		knows
	As nygromauncers and fals enchantours		necromancers
3495	And also witches and tregettours		sorcerers
	The whiche the fendes schuylleþ hym kenne		devils, know
	And þerby many on he schal brynge to his denne		a one, den
	And aftyrward þorowe þe deueles ledynge		leadership
	To [ih]¹¹ ier(usa)l(e)m he schal make his wendynge.		Jerusalem, departure
3500	And þere bigynne to dwelle in thuke cite		that
	And amyddes þe temple he schal make his se		see
	And seie to all that þ(er)ynne schull wone		dwell
	Þat he is cryst of heuene¹² godes owne sone		own son
	And make þe folk to hym do honour		

---

¹ The second letter is ambiguous: if it were meant to be an o, the meaning might be who(ever). H.M. 125 reads who. He or ho/who both refer to the Antichrist.

² An erasure under this space has left a gap of about 4 or 5 letters. H.M .125 reads þat here.

³ H.M. 125 states "conuersant."

⁴ "... take his pleasures."

⁵ Middle English Dictionary indicates an is a variant of and. H.M. 125 reads Ande.

⁶ "Woe to thee, Corozaym, woe to thee Bethsaida, and thou Capharnaum" [Matt. 11:21, 23]. See also Luke 10:13, Luke 15.

⁷ The word to has been inserted with a caret.

⁸ Apparently the scribe wrote ȝ rather than r in Coroȝaym, creating a scribal error.

⁹ This erasure looks notably different, having a white substance under the current word. Probably an auto-erasure.

¹⁰ Although the scribe penned grade, he no doubt should have written gadre, a simple reversal of letters or metathesis, as H.M. 125 reads. He might have been confused by "to gadre."

¹¹ The ih is lightly crossed out; perhaps the scribe at first glance thought the word was Je(sus) instead of Jerusalem, and began that abbreviation.

¹² "Of hevene" is not in H.M. 125.

3505	And to hem seyȝe that he is her sauyour	f. 45v	say, savior
	And he schal seyȝe þat no crystene man		
	Right lyf bifore his tyme neu(er) bigan		Moral / true life
	Bot fals antecrystes he schal hem calle		
	And seye þat þey leueden in þe fals fey alle		lived, false faith
3510	That haueþ ibe f(ro)m the worldes bigynnynge		
	Into þulke tyme of his comynge		
	He schal also be lusty and lechours		desirous
	And þerto deceyvable and trechours.		deceptive, treacherous
	Fferst he schal as an holy man hym schewe		show
3515	And as an ypocryte and speke wordes fewe		hypocrite
	Fforto desceyue crystene men and trewe		
	As danyel us telleþ tydynges þ(er)of¹ newe		
	In ap(er)to eni(m) p(er) ipocrysim p(ri)mo		
	simulabit : ut facilius decip(er)e posset		
	*in deo credentes.*²		
	He saith he schal ap(er)ty to þe ye		openly, eye
3520	Feyne holynesse þorow ipocrysie		Pretend holiness, hypocrisy
	The lightlokur þat he mowe þe peple bigyle		likelier, may, trick
	Ac þulke tyme schal laste bot a lytyl while		
	And he schal kynges and p(ri)nces to hym drawe		
	And tornen hem holliche to his lawe		convert
3525	And þorow hym al þe peple schal be itorned		perverted
	And in no lond no þyng schal be hym ywerned		refused
	And in alle stedes he schal walke and make his pas		places, passage
	Where þat cryst walked whan he on eorþe was		
	And in suche a p(re)sempcion³ he schal falle		presumption / pride
3530	Þat he schal hym self holden ou(er) lordes alle.		maintain
	Thorow pride he schal aȝenst God aryse		Through
	And hym disclaundre and his lawes despise		slaunder
	And he schal hym force and wel busy make		
	His lawe to chaunge tyl it be forsake		given up
3535	And he schal the peple torne to his lawe		convert
	On foure maners . and hem to hym drawe.⁴		ways
	❰O❱ maner schal be þorow fals prechynge		One
	A nothur þorow false myracles schewȝynge		showing
	The þrydde is large ȝiftes to ȝiue on gret emp(ri)se.		third, gifts, enterprise
3540	Þe ferþe for drede of tormentes ido in many wise		tortures, ways
	Ffor þorow false p(re)chynge in eu(er)y contre		
	Many men to hym torned schull be		converted
	Ffor he schal sende þorow al the world wyde		through

---

¹ H.M. 125 writes *þerof tydynges*.
² "For at first he will openly feign, hypocritically, so he might more easily deceive those who believe in God" [Adso or Haymo of Halberstadt, *PL* 118, col. 641 based on Augustine, *De Civitate Dei*, Book 20, chapters 19-20. Not taken directly from *Daniel*, as the poet claims.].
³ The Middle English Dictionary offers no "presempcioun." There is no other record of this variant spelling. Morey's version from Osborn a. 13, reads "pryde" (p. 104, l. 260). Hanna and Wood's version reads "presumption" (p. 118, *l.* 4249)
⁴ The poet reveals his literary versatility by slipping from straight narrative instruction into the more dramatic, frightful theme of the dangerous Antichrist, and back to the empirical, enumerative details of how the Antichrist ensnares his prey. Thus his tract is compelling for his creative visions, but by reinforcing them with scripture and logical evidence, he makes them credible to his audience.

	His prechours forto preche in eu(er)y side	f. 46r	
3545	The whiche schulleþ undyr false colour		shall
	Seye þat crystes lawe nys bot error		mistaken
	And antecrystes lawe þey schulle comende		respect
	And aȝenst soþnesse faste it deffende		protect
	And forbede eu(er)y man that he ne holde		forbid, accept
3550	Of þe newe lawe where of cryst hem tolde		
	And his mynystres schulleþ be so full of wytt		ministers, knowledge
	That no man schall aȝenst hem expowne holy writ.[1]		expound
	That is to seye to haue[2] undyrstondynge		
	For þey schul segge þat it is bot a lesynge		say, lie
3555	And make þe peple to forsake godes m(er)cy		
	And seye þat þey schull nat be saued þ(er)by		therby
	Thus schull þey þe folk in an erro(ur) brynge		
	Þorow fals colour and þorow her p(re)chynge		rhetoric, preaching
	So that his lawes schull passe and her[3] power		might
3560	F(ro)m the est into the west . þorow þe world here		east, through
	And from the soughþ[4] into the norþe also		south
	His lawes and his power schul þ(er)ynne go .		
	And he schal do men Godes lay furȝete[5]		make, law forget
	Þorow fals myracles and wondres grete		
3565	Ffor he schal w(i)t(h) wondres hym seluen avaunce		advance
	Þorow enchauntement and nygromaunce		necromancy
	So gretly þat þe peple schal ise		
	That þorow the fendes power it[6] schal be		
	Of þe whiche wondres y not telle some		miracles
3570	For he schal do fuyr adown fro heuene come		make
	Ac þat schal be an euel spirit on of þe meste		one
	Þat out of þe eyr schal come at his heste		air, bidding
	Among his disciples he schall adown lighte		alight
	And with dyuerse tonges to hem speke outrighte		many languges, plainly
3575	As dede to þe apostles þe holy gost[7]		
	And in syght of þe peple þ(a)t schal be do[8] most		influenced
	And þey þat his disciples schul ben itolde		called
	Schullen þanne be avaunced many folde		advanced
	And bet(er)e of lyf hem holde and to god more dere		
3580	Þan eu(er)e weren on eorþe crystes disciples here		
	Also þorow the deueles craft and his myght		
	He schal hym feyne ded [and][9] to mannys syȝt		feign death
	And on þe furþe day thorow þe fendes red .		advise

---

[1] The last three words have been corrected by the *Piers* rubricator.
[2] H.M. 125 states "to knowe þe riȝt vnderstandyng" for "have [undyrstondynge]".
[3] H.M. 125 writes *hys* rather than *her*.
[4] H.M. 125 uses the form *souþ*.
[5] H.M. 125 uses *forlete* rather than *furȝete*.
[6] Again, the *Piers* rubricator has emended -s power it ....H.M. 125 writes simply *þe fend*.
[7] A reference to Pentecost when biblical tradition says tongues of fire/inspiration came down upon the apostles in the Upper Room forty days after the Resurrection, also re-enacted by the antichrist below.
[8] H.M. 125 deletes *do* making the phrasing more awkward.
[9] The word *and* is crossed out here.

Part V. Ten Signs of Doomsday (3584–3623)

	He schal him feyne to aryse from ded	f. 46v	pretend
3585	Ac deueles schulleþ hym bere aft(er) that euene		
	Into þe eyr as he scholde flie to heuene¹		air, fly
	Thus schal antecryst thanne conterfete		counterfeit
	The wondres of crist on eorþ grete		
	And mo wondres ȝut wurche schal he		perform
3590	Þ(a)t þe peple schal openly þanne ise		
	Ffor he schal do tres wexen and flouren in þat place		make trees, flower
	And an hy in þe eyr þe wynd aboute chace.		on high, air
	He schal do adown falle f(ro)m heuene reigne schourys²		rain
	And make watres renne aboute castelles and tourys		towers
3595	He schal troble þe see . at his owne wille		stir up
	And whan that hym lykeþ make it stonde stille³		desires
	He schal make ymagys def and dome⁴		statues
	To spek of þinges that ben to come.		
	He schal also dede men make up aryse		
3600	Þat schulleþ oþur men by gyle in many wyse.⁵		trick
	Ac þat schal be þorow þe deuelys queyntise be don		craft
	For wikkyd spiritys schulle entre into dede bodyes son⁶		
	And in that man(er) bereþ the deþes aboute		
	So þat many men schullen be in gret doute		
3605	Wheþ(er) he be god veray or nowȝt		truly, not
	And þus schullen⁷ in an erro(r) be brouȝt.		
	¶ On the⁸ þridde man(er)e ȝet he schal bigile		third
	Many man w(i)t(h) ȝeftes in a schort while		gifts
	And make hem to his fals lay be dryue		religion, driven
3610	Þorow large ȝiftes þe whiche he schal hem ȝiue		gifts
	Ffor than he schal þe olde tresour fynde		
	Þe whiche was and is ihud owt of mynde		hid
	Undur the eorþe or owher in any place elles		either, else
	Þat may nat now be iwist as⁹ some clerkes telles		known
3615	That wel more tresour undur þe eorthe ys hud		
	Þan aboue eorþe may be knowe and kud		understood
	Of þe whiche he schal hem ryche make .		
	That the lawe of cryst here wolleþ forsake.		
	Thus schal he þe worldes welþe forþ schewe		
3620	To desceyue hem that wollen gon in his rewe		deceive, follow him
	Also in þe furþe man(er) after than		fourth
	He schal torne to hym many a man		
	And make hem to folowen his t(ra)ces.		

---

¹ H.M. 125 offers *stye* instead of *flie* here. Four additional lines are insered into H.M. 125 after these lines.
² H.M. 125 writes *rayne shoures* and *castel toures* in the next line.
³ Two more lines in H.M. 125 are inserted here: "And he schal manie þinges chaunge in diuerse manere
    In-to oþer þinges as þei it were."
⁴ Here H.M. 125 reads: "He shal þe dowmbe and þe lede ymages make
    To speke of þynȝes that men mowen noȝt take."
⁵ This line concludes "by þe hond sayȝe" in H.M. 125.
⁶ "Ffor þai to þe dede bodyes doþ seruyse" is written in H.M. 125.
⁷ H.M. 125 adds *men* here which is necessary for the meaning.
⁸ A thin crease, occurring after scribing, begins here and extends through *rewe* (1. 3620).
⁹ H.M. 125 writes *for* rather than *as*.

	Þorowe grete tormentes and manaces	f 47r	
3625	And þorow drede of deþ þ(a)t may most greue		frighten
	For elles he wol no man on lyue leue		omit
	Wel grete tribulacions he schal þanne schewe		sorrows
	As cryst in þe gospel seiþ be¹ seint mathewe		
	Tanta erit tribulac(i)o ut in errorem inducant(ur)		
	si fieri posset eciam² et electi.³		
3630	He saith þat þer schal be so muche t(ri)bulacio(u)n		
	Among mankynde of eu(er)y nacion		
	Thorow þe world boþe fer and nere		through, far near
	Þat þo men þat god haþ chosen here		those
	Scholden be ibrought in an erro(ur) sone		
3635	Ȝif god ne wolde þat it were to done		Unless
	Ffor in the apocalips thus spekeþ seynt iohn		Apocalypse
	Of þing þat is derk [.....]⁴ to undurstonde of us echon:		hard
	*Pedes eius sunt similes auricalco.*⁵		
	He seiþ þat his feet beþ lik to laton bright		similar to brass
3640	Which is in a chymeny brennyng light		fireplace burning
	And þis was þat iohn saw in a vision		
	Of hym þat semed to be þe maiden(es) sone.		
	By his feet þat as laton were schynynge		shining
	Cristes lymes men may haue in undurstondynge		limbs, keep in memory
3645	The whiche schulleþ be p(ar)fit in charite		
	Ac aȝenst þe worldes ende martered schul be		martyred
	That is to seie in þe tyme of antecrystes maystrye		mastery / rule
	Þorow whom many soules schul be lore þorow t(ra)it(ery)e		lost, deception
	And the chymenye brennynge wiþ þe hete		
3650	Bitokeneþ tribulacions and angres grete		Signifies dismay, sorrows
	That schul be whan antecrist ys⁶ come		
	Þorow wham many to þe deþ schull be inome		taken
	Ffor antecrist schul be þe moste tiraunte		greatest tyrant
	That eu(er) whas for he schul besily hawnte		busily practice / adopt
3655	Alle man(er) gret torment and strong w(i)t(h) alle		types
	In the whiche any martres biforen hauen falle		martyrs
	Ffor in diuerse manere he schal hem tormente		plague
	Alle þat wollen nawt to his lawes assente		agree
	And putte hem to þe hard deþ at þe laste		
3660	That were in þe trewe wey⁷ stedefaste		constant
	Ac alle cristene men in þe contre aboute		
	Where cryst walkede . schul be in most doute.		greatest uncertainty

---

[1] Be is a variant of *by*.
[2] This Mediaeval Latin form of Classical Latin *etiam*, meaning *even or certainly*, is used throughout.
[3] "There will be great tribulation such that if possible, even the elect will be lead into error" [Matt. 24: 24].
[4] An erasure has been made here leaving a space of about two or three letters; *of* has been written over an erasure.
[5] "His feet like unto fine brass" [Apocalypse 1:15].
[6] H.M. 125 says *shal* here.
[7] H.M. 125 writes *fey* rather than *wey* here.

	As haymo¹ seyþe þat gret clerk was	f.47v	
	His tirauntrye þorow þe world schal make his pas		tyranny, passage
3665	Ffor þe fendes that beþ now ibounde so		
	Þat þey ne moweþ neyþ(ur) fle no go		might
	Ne no man greue so muchel as þey wolde		
	Schulleþ þan be lose and no thing hem holde		loosed
	And in þat ilke tyme . schal no man² preche		
3670	For þey schul ben ipult to al maner wreche		pushed, pain
	Ne no man schal w(i)t(h) hem bugge ne selle		buy
	Ne felawschipe hold ne with hem dwelle		
	Bot only wiþ hem þat han cryst forsake		
	And hauen þe marke of antecryst itake		
3675	That men mowen knowe and wel undurstonde		must
	Whiche beþ assentaunt³ to be at his honde		agreement
	Ffor all þe men schul bere his merkes		
	That forsaken to leue in cristes werkes		believe
	And schulle folowe antecristes lawe		
3680	And by þat merke men schul hem knawe		
	The whiche they schullen bere as clerkes telleþ me		
	Oþur in the front or in þe right hond it schall be		Either
	Ac þo that willeþ nat don aftur his red		advice
	Schullen þorow torment sone be ded⁴		
3685	And godes lawe schal sone be iput adown		laid aside
	As in þe apocalips iohn makeþ his sermon:		
	Cauda eius t(er)ciam partem stellaru(m) celi		
	*trahebat et misit eas in terram.*⁵		
	He saiþ wiþ his tayl he drow adown euene		tail, drew
	Þe þridde party of þe sterres of heuene		third part, stars
3690	And into þe eorþe sent hem adown right		
	Where þey myght not schine ne ȝiue⁶ no light		
	This was þe taile of þe foule dragon		
	Þat seynt iohn sawe in a vision.		
	By þulke dragon is undurstonde þe fende		
3695	And his tayle is antecryst p(a)t folweþ at þe ende⁷		
	And the þrydde party of þe sterres bright		
	Beþ crystene men to undurstonde be⁸ right		
	The whiche he schal from the trewe wey⁹ drawe		
	And make hem on eorþe to kepyn his lawe		
3700	And the worldlyche men that ben coueytouse		
	He schal torne to hym wiþ ȝiftes p(re)ciouse		

---

[1] Haimo of Auxere, *Commentary on the Book of Jonah*, translated by Deborah Everhart (1993).
[2] H.M. 125 states "no cristene man" here.
[3] H.M. 125 reads *assentaunt to be at hys sonde* here.
[4] These two lines follow this line: In þere foure maners as j have schewed
    He schal torn to hym both leryd and lewyd.
[5] "His tail drew the third part of the stars of heaven and cast them to earth" [Apocalypse 12:4].
[6] H.M. 125 lacks ȝive.
[7] H.M. 125 reads *at þat on ende* rather than *at þe ende*.
[8] H.M. 125 uses *by* rather than *be*.
[9] H.M. 125 reads *fay* rather than *wey*.

Part V. Ten Signs of Doomsday

	Ffor he schal ȝiue to hem þ(a)t wolleþ ben itorned	f. 48r	converted
	Gold ynow and no þing schal be to[1] hem werned		enough, denied
	Also many men [^of] symple connynge		understanding
3705	He schal torne þorow miracles and fals[2] p(re)chynge		
	And gode [^men] þat holden godes comanndements		keep
	He schal torne þorow manaces and torments		convince, threats
	And many that semen good and right wise		seem, upright
	Schulleþ on hym bileue and god despise		
3710	Ffor ferst in myldenesse antecrist schal come		mildness
	And aȝenst trewþ his p(re)chinge schal be nome[3]		
	And myracles schulleþ þorow hym be ywrought[4]		performed
	And þanne schulle iewys to hym ben ybrought		Jews, brought
	And be itorned to hym al þe hole flok[5]		converted
3715	Ac in þat tyme schulle come elie and ennok		Eli, Enoch
	And make her prechinge aȝenst hym wel hard		
	As ȝe may here wel sone afterward.		
	Than schal antecryst fellich bigyn(n)e		cruelly
	To p(ur)sue men to his lawe hem forto wynne		
3720	And gret persecucio(u)n þanne schall be wurche		enacted
	Aȝenst cristene men and holy[6] cherche.		
	Thanne schal he destruye cristene lawe		
	And gog and magog also to hym drawe		
	The which beþ iholde as men tellis		held
3725	Þe worst folk that in al þe world dwelles		
	Ac som(m)e seyȝen that they ben closed only[7]		say, enclosed
	Biȝende þe grete montaynes of caspy		Behind, Caspean mountains
	Ac þey ne beþ so closed aboute		
	Þ(a)t þei ne mowe lightly wynne hem self oute[8]		
3730	Ȝif a quene ne were [9] þat eu(er) holdeþ hem ynne		
	Þorow strenkþe þat þey mowen nat owt wynne		might, overcome
	The which is iclepud þe quene of amazone		Amazons
	Undur whos power þat folk dwellen echone		each one
	Bot[10] þey schulleþ out breke at þe laste		
3735	And destruy many londes and hem sore agaste		severely terrify
	Ffor þe iewes hauen suche a pprophecie[11]		
	And seyn amonges hem and ofte don it c(ri)e		
	That þis folk aȝenst þe worldes ende		
	Schulleþ out come and [^to] ier(usa)l(e)m wende		travel
3740	Wiþ her crist [ ][12] that wondres schal wirche		work
	And þan þey schulle destruye al holy cherche		

---

[1] H.M. 125 reads *fro* here.
[2] H.M. 125 lacks *fals*.
[3] "And contrary to truth / doctrine his preaching shall be received."
[4] Undecipherable scribal corrections have been made to this and the next line.
[5] H.M. 125 says "alle in on flok."
[6] H.M 125 says "alle holy churche."
[7] H.M. 125 reads "enclosed holly" here.
[8] "... might easily make their way out."
[9] "If it were not for a queen."
[10] H.M. 125 adds ȝette here.
[11] The double "pp" may be a scribal error, or used for emphasis, or triggered by the *ff* in *Ffor* in the that line.
[12] A space of two or three letters with a very neat erasure, barely visible with magnifying glass, follows "crist." H.M. 125 says *cristes* here.

Part V. Ten Signs of Doomsday (3742–3781)

	Ac some clerkes seyen as þe gospel[1] telles	f. 48v
	Þat gog and magog is no thing elles	
	Bot þe host of antecrist þat schal come	
3745	Sodeynly afore domesday as seyʒen some	
	And aʒen al holy cherche verament	against, truly
	For it destruyeþ out right he haþ yment.	completely, intended
	The glose of þe bok þus seyeþ also	
	Þat bi gog beþ undurstonden alle þo	
3750	Thorow þe whiche þe fend our most enemy[2]	greatest
	Alle cristene men schal pursue p(ri)ueyly	secretly
	And be magog may undurstonded be	be
	Alle þo þat wollen to his lore fle	will, flee
	Thorow þe whiche opene p(ur)sut schal be mad[3]	
3755	To all þat in cristes law wolleþ[4] be sad	constant
	Oþur þese beþ by hem to undurstonde	Or
	Þat in antecristes type wolleþ fonde	tempt
	Pryuely and after ward openly wurche	work
	Wikkednesse aʒenst al holy cherche.	
3760	¶ Gog is as muchel to seie as cou(er)te	secret
	And magog was muchel as[5] aperte.	open
	These two as clerkes seieþ some	
	Bifore elie and ennok schul come	
	Byfore þe tyme of the comyng pryue	secret coming
3765	Of antecrist whan he schal bore be	born
	Ffor þe tyme of his opene comynge	
	Schal ben iknow þorow his[6] prechinge	known
	And þorow opene dedes of p(er)secution	
	Þat he schal schewe þanne in div(er)se nacion	
3770	And bitwene þulke tyme the p(ro)phetes two	
	In dyuerse parties schullen preche so	various parts
	That þorow her p(re)chinge þey schulleþ drawe	
	And conv(er)te þe iewes to cristen lawe	
	For þus spekeþ þe p(ro)phet malachie	Malachi
3775	In a boke that is of his p(ro)phecie:	
	Conuertant corda patru(m) in filios[7]	
	He seyth thei schullen come þorow godes myght	be converted, power
	Þe fadres hertes into þe sones outright.	completely
	That is to seie þey schal torne þe iewerye	convert
3780	Into right cristendom f(ro)m alle trecherye	deception
	Ffor þanne schulle þe iewes þe same lawe holde	

---

[1] H.M. 125 says *glose* rather than *gospel*.
[2] H.M. 125 reads *enemy most*, precluding a rhyme with the next line.
[3] "Through which open pursuit shall be made / Against all who in Christ's law will be constant."
[4] H.M. 125 writes *firste fonde* here.
[5] H.M. 125 reads *noʒt elles but as aperte*.
[6] H.M. 125 reads *open prechyng*.
[7] Note the allegory: "They shall convert the fathers' [the Old Law / traditional / Hebrew] hearts / attitude / belief system] into the sons' [the New Law of Christianity]" … "That they might turn the hearts of the fathers unto the children" [adapted from Luke 1:17 which echoes Malachias 4:6]. The source, the Vulgate Luke, reads *convertat*, singular, but this manuscript reads *conuertant*, plural.

Part V. Ten Signs of Doomsday

	Right as þey haueþ þat cristene be scholde	f 49r	should
	And as cristene men doþ so schul thei do		
	As the glose saiþ that acordeþ þus þerto		gospel, connected
3785	*Percipient fidem quam ip(s)i habueru(n)t.*[1]		
	He seiþ the iewes schul take with hert(es) sadde		
	The trewe fey þat cristene men biforen hadde		faith
	And þulke two prophetes schull hem teche		
	For thei schulle to iewes and to cristene men preche.		
3790	And þanne schul þey þorow good entencion		
	Assente to crist as men that beþ of[2] religion		Accept
	And þei schulleþ preche as þe apocalips saies		
	A fol þousand and two[3] hundred daies		full
	And sixti as men schulle þere ise[4]		
3795	Ac as þe glose seiþe that is euene ȝeres þre		says
	And þei schulleþ as þe apocalips saiþ forsoþe		in truth
	Be cloþed[5] in heires and in sakcloþe		hair shirts, sackcloth
	That is to mene þei schulle penaunce preche		signify
	And þorow ensample oþur men teche.		
3800	Ac as sone as antecrist knoweþ bi any sawe		saying
	Þat þei torne þe iewes to cristene lawe[6]		convert
	Thorow ensample that thei scheweþ and good sarmon		
	Thanne schal he schewe to hem grete p(er)secucion		
	And he schal hem greuously tormente[7]		seriously
3805	Þat to his lawe wulleþ nat assente.[8]		accept
	Than schal antecrist and his desciples boþe		
	Lete take þe prophetes sone for soþe[9]		capture
	And into ier(usa)l(e)m hastly hem lede		Jerusalem
	And þere hem sle þorow þe fendes rede.		advice
3810	Thanne schulle her bodies so ligge stille		
	In the strete for bestes scholde hem spille		kill
	Thre daies ful and an half ther to		
	Þat no man berienge to hem do[10]		burying
	Ffor her drede thanne schal be so gret		Since, terror
3815	That unneþe me(n) schal fynde in any strete		scarcely
	Any man that dar[11] o word oute crake		dare, one, crack
	Suche hard þretynges he schal make		threats
	Ac whan Enuch and Ely[12] beþ to deþ ibrouȝt		
	Glad schal he þan ben of that he haþ iwrouȝt		done
3820	And whan þei beþ dede in suche a man(er) wise		
	Aftur þre daies and an half þei schulleþ up ryse.[13]		shall rise up

---

[1] "They will understand the faith which they themselves have held" [*Innocent III, PL* 217, col. 848].

[2] H.M. 125 adds *on* (one) to *religion*.

[3] The letters *wo* have been added over a longer erasure of a word beginning with *t* (possibly *three*).

[4] H.M. 125 ends this line *se þere* and the next line *þre ȝere*.

[5] H.M. 125 adds *harde* here.

[6] The following lines are missing in H.M. 128 but reclaimed from H.M. 125:
> As crist wole þat alle thing schalle
> To teche hem þe same lawe þat we mote have

[7] The poet again displays literary talents, evoking intense emotions at the torture of the faithful, persecution of Enoch and Eli, the attacking of their bodies by beasts in the streets, and the horrified reaction of on-lookers, intimidated into submission by the Antichrist.

[8] The following two lines are missing in H.M. 128 but reclaimed from H.M. 125:
> And bryng hem to harde deth at þe last
> If þei in þe trewe feye be stedfast

[9] H.M. 125 reads *fforto do take þe prophetes forsoþe*.

[10] H.M. 125 reads *þat non be so hardy buryyng to hem do*.

[11] A clean erasure of about one letter follows *dar*.

[12] These prophets Enoch and Elijah are uncharacteristically capitalized here and in l 3831 (f. 49 v).

[13] This Old Testament "resurrection" prefigures Christ's in the New Testament and recalls that of various other religious leaders such as Osiris, Baal, Asclepius, Odin, Dionysus, Krishna and others. They are Old Testament figures operating in New Testament time, and cannot be resurrected because they have not yet died.

Part V. Ten Signs of Doomsday (3822–3859)

	And here enemys schullen a vois ihere	
	Spekynge to hem as thorow a leme of fuyre	gleam
	And seye Enuch and Elie styeþ up anon boþe[1]	see, ascend
3825	For ȝe beþ ipassed al euel for soþe	finished with all evil
	And also sone as þey han herd this steuene	voice
	Wiþ a cloude they schulleþ up to heuene	must ascend
	That al þe peple schal se al aboute	see
	And for þe wondur be in grete doute.	miracle, confusion
3830	Ac anon after here deþ as þe bok saies	But then
	Antecrist schal regne bot fiftene daies	
	Than schal he torne to hym alle men[2] eu(er)iwhere	
	That were torned bi þe p(ro)phetys while þei on liue were	
	And alle tho that on hym bileuen nought	those
3835	Schulleþ thorow torment to deþe be ibrought	torture
	And antecrist schal thorow his tirauntrie	tyranny
	Þre ȝer and an half regne w(i)t(h) muche velanye	
	Therfore god schal his daies abregge	shorten
	So seynt mathew in his gospel doþ segge.	
3840	*Nisi abbreviati fuissent dies eius.*	
	Non salva erit omnis caro.[3]	
	Bot ȝif his daies be a breggeg[4] seith he	lessened
	Fewe men elles scholde isaued be	
	Ac his tyme schal be schorted þorow godes might	shortened
	So saiþ seynt grigory þese wordes outright	
3845	*Qu(on)i(am) inf(i)rmos nos respicit deus . dies malos quos*	
	Singularit(er) nobis intulit misericordit(er) abbreviab(i)t.[5]	
	He saith for þat god iseoþ right þis	since, sees
	Þat we be feble of myght iwis	weak
	The daies þat beþ euele and heuy to bere	difficult
	That beþ iput to men ther wiþ hem to dere	thrust, injure
3850	Thulke daies at þe laste abregged schal be	These, abridged
	Thorow his owne goodnesse and gret pite	
	And antecrist schal be wiþ oute pere	equal
	And liue here on eorþ two and þretty ȝere	
	And an half as some clerkes conneþ ise	can determine
3855	For of so many ȝeris schal his age be	
	Ffro þe tyme of his ferst bigynnynge	
	Into the tyme of his laste endynge[6]	
	And whan he haþ ileued so longe	lived
	No man schal of hym euel no more fonge .	endure

f. 49v

---

[1] A rehearsal of the biblical image of the prophets entering heaven; the celestial voice of direct address through the visual gleam of fire directing them upwards adds to this dramatic sensory vision, as does the amazement of the audience.

[2] Written with very small letters over an erasure.

[3] "Unless his [the Antichrist's] days be shortened, no flesh will be saved" [Matt 24: 22]. The Vulgate and Douay-Rheime read *illi* (*those* days), and *fuissent* (*would have been* and *should be*, respectively).

[4] The scribe may have intended to write *abregged* (as in line 3857) rather than *a breggeg*.

[5] "Because God is mindful that we are weak, He will mercifully shorten the evil days that he inflicts on us individually" [*Gregory* I, *PL* 76, col. 650].

[6] H.M. 125 prints these two lines here: And som clerkis seith þat he schal lyue in erth here
   As god lyued in mannes kynde here.

3860	He schal thanne fele godes veniaunce	f. 50r	feel, vengeance
	And die on euel deþ wiþ oute repentaunce		an
	Ffor sodeynliche he schal ben islawe		slain
	Ffor that he destruyed so godes lawe		Because
	Right upon þe mount of olyuet		Mount of Olives
3865	Where that crist sette his fet		
	Whan he fley into heuene bright[1]		flew
	And there ende his lif þorow godes might.		through, power
	Some clerkes seieþ it is no lesynge		say, falsehood
	That seynt myschel[2] schal hym to deþe brynge		
3870	Thorow goddes heste in þulke selue grounde		behest, this same
	In þe whiche he schal be ded yfounde[3]		found
	And antecrystes mynystres aftur he is ded		ministers
	Schulleþ gret ioye make and also take here red		their advice
	And lyve in delices boþe nyght and day		live, pleasures
3875	And wyves[4] to hem wedde eche to his pay		liking
	Ac as they thus lyueþ than thei schullen alle		
	Sodeynly to ded . sone adown falle[5]		fall down to death
	Thorow the myght of our almyghty lord		
	They schulleþ þus dyȝe . w(i)t(h) outen eny word.		die
3880	And whanne þey beþ alle thus for do		destroyed
	The grete dome schal not ȝut come þ(er)to		judgment
	So sone þere upon as men wolden wene		think
	For god wole g(ra)unte oþur daies bitwene		
	Ffor þe glose of daniel seyþ this writynge		gloss / gospel
3885	God ȝiueþ fyue and fourty daies of abidynge		waiting
	To alle that thanne schul desceyued be		deceived
	Thorow antecrist and oþ(er) that were of his degre		
	That thei haue tyme to ben amended of her synne		repented
	And to do some penaunce ar þe dome bigynne.		before
3890	And þan þe iewes þorow godes myght		
	Schulleþ into þe trewe fey stedefastly be pyȝt		be confirmed in the true faith
	And so schal god fulfulle in the laste daies		
	Þe word that hym self in þe gospel saies		
	Et fiet unu(m) ovile et unus pastor.[6]		
3895	He saith alle folk schull to on flok falle		one, become
	And on herde schall be to kepen hem alle		one shepherd
	That folk iewes and cristene beþ iholde		held together
	For undur on fey þey schulle be boþ ȝong and olde		faith
	And f(ro)m that tyme forward schal holy cherche be		

---

[1] H.M. 125 writes *stey* for *flew*. The fine irony of place here is interesting.
[2] An unusual spelling of *Michael/Michel/ Mychel;* a dotted *y* is used. H.M. 125 spells it *michel*.
[3] The (dotted) *y* of *yfounde* appears to have been squeezed in by the *Piers* rubricator after the line was written.
[4] The internal rhyme of *lyue* and *wyues* situated similarly in two consecutive lines provides beautiful phonetic resonance.
[5] The scribe has marked two caesuras at ll. 3883 and 3885 and later in this text, as done in the *Piers Plowman* bound in this manuscript. Shocking drama—followers of the Antichrist suddenly dropping dead in l. 3869—adds to the interest of the poem. This could also be personification of fall to Death. H.M. 125 prints:

    And sey þus þei he be dede þat was oure prince
    We have nowe pese and in oure welth wil wynce.

[6] "And there shall be one fold and one shepherd" [John 10:16].

122 Part V. Ten Signs of Doomsday   (3900–3937)

3900	In pes and in reste¹ wiþ oute adversite	f. 50v	
	Ffor þan schal the powere of the fend away wende		disappear
	Fro þat tyme into this worldes ende		
	So that he schall noþ(er) tempte ne greue		neither, injure
	Holy cherche ne no man that schal alyue leue.		remain alive
3905	Ac how muche spas schal be fro þan		space
	To þe day of dome telle can no man		
	Ffor alle the prophetes that any man can telle		
	And alle the halwes that in heuene dwelle		saints
	Ne myght neu(er) wite ne knowe þat pryuyte		understand, secret
3910	What tyme þe day of dome scholde be		
	Ffor god wole nat that any man it wyte		wishes, know
	Bot only² hym self as it ys in boke iwrite.		written
	Therefore³ to his disciples he seyde thus		
	As iohn in þe gospel scheweþ ys		shows
3915	*Non est v(est)ru(m) nosce tempora vel momenta*		
	*Que pater meus posuit in sua potestate.*⁴		
	He saith it bifalleþ nouȝt ȝow to knowe .		it is not fitting for
	Þe tymes þat comeþ in a lytel þorowe		while
	The whiche þe fadur haþ in his power set		established
	His wil ther of to don and to haue no let		do, hindrance
3920	Therfore scholde no man aske ne make assay		investigation
	Howe myche we haueþ into domys day⁵		
	Bot we scholde eu(er)e⁶ aredy make us alle		
	As þe day of dome scholde to morowe falle		as if
	And eu(er) þenke on thulke dredful dome		this fearful doom
3925	As þe⁷ dede the god man seynt Jerome		
	That eu(er) boþe nyght and day þ(er)e upon þoughte		
	And þerfore this sawe to us he brought		saying
	Sine comedam siue bibam . siue aliq(ui)d aliud		
	facia(m) . se(m)p(er) m(ich)i videtur Illa tuba		
	sonare in aurib(us) meis et dice(tur) . mortui		
	*venite ad iudicium).*⁸		
	He saith wheþ(er) þat i ete oþur that y drynke		eat or
3930	Or that i do owt elles eu(er) more i þenke		anything
	That the beem that schal blowe at domes day		trumpet
	Sowneþ in myn ere and seiþ to us ay.⁹		sounds, ear, always
	Aryse ȝe that beþ dede and comeþ anon		Rise up, now
	To the grete dome boþe in flesch and in bon¹⁰		
3935	**Of mo tokenes that schal come afore þe dome.**		more signs
	Many mo tokenes ȝut we mowen se		more, must see
	Þe whiche bifore þe dome schullen be		

---

[1] The scribe has not added a caesura here but has left a larger space where one would be placed.
[2] H.M. 125 omits *only* in this line.
[3] H.M. 125 specifies *criste* here.
[4] "It is not for you to know the time or moments which my Father hath put in power" [Acts 1:7]. H.M. 125 omits *meus*.
[5] These two lines follow in H.M. 125: Ne we scholde not couette hit to lere
           To wite wheþer hit were fer or nere."
[6] H.M. 125 lacks *euere* here.
[7] The word *þe* seems superfluous and is not in H.M. 125. Contrary to usual practice for proper nouns, *Jerome* is capitalized in this line.
[8] "Whether I am eating, whether I am drinking, whether I am doing anything else, it always seems to me that that trumpet sounds in my ears and 'Dead, come to judgment' is proclaimed" [Eusebius Hieronymus, aka St. Jerome, *PL* 30, col 417].
[9] The last three words have been scribed in spread-out fashion over a long erasure, probably by the *Piers* rubricator. H.M. 125 prints *as I here may* here.
[10] H.M. 125 offers four lines of conclusion of this time.

	Boþ in eorþe and also in heuene aboue	f. 51r	
	Þe whiche god wold schewe for our loue		
3940	For in þe gospel of mo tokenes he doþ us lere		symbols, teach
	The whiche schullen be and seyþ on this manere.		

*Erunt signa in sole et luna et stellis et in terris.
Pressura gentiu(m) . p(re) confusione sonit(us)
maris et fluc[-] tuu(m) arescentib(us) ho(min)ib(us)
pre timore . et exp(ec)tac(i)one que sup(er)venie(n)t
univ(er)so orbi . na(m) v(ir)tutes celoru(m) move[-]
bunt(ur) et tunc videbu(nt) filiu(m) ho(min)is venientem
In nubibus celi . cum potestate et magestate magna.*[1]

	He saiþ and ordeyneþ as hym þinkeþ to done.	orders
	Þat tokenes schulleþ be boþe in sonne and mone	symbols
3945	And in sterrys of heuene that men mowen se	may
	And in eorþe gret p(re)sure of men schal be	distress
	Ffor þe noyse of þe se and the dredful soun	sound
	And of the flodes that than schal come adown	
	And men schulle drie wexe and ryght þynne	dry become, gaunt
3950	For drede and long abydynge ther ynne	fear
	The whiche into al the world schal be ipreued	displayed
	And þanne þe myghtes of heuene schulleþ ben ymeued	powers, moved
	And they schulleþ se the mannes sone	
	In cloudes comynge adown aȝenst his wone	contrary to his custom
3955	Wiþ his grete myght and opene[2] mageste	majesty
	For in þat tyme schal þe grete dome be.	
	Thes tokens beþ told aftur þe lett(er) here	according to
	Þey may ben expounyd in a noþ(ur) manere	explicated, another
	As God þat alle thyngges knoweþ wel[3]	
3960	Þerfore þus [he][4] seiþ bi his p(ro)phet ioel	

*Dabo prodigia in celo sursu(m) et signa in t(er)ra
deorsu(m) sangu(in)e(m) . Ignem . et vaporemfumi .
Sol convertetur in tenebras et luna in sangu(in)e(m) .
antequ(a)m veniet . dies domini magnus et terribilis.*[5]

	He saith i schal ȝiue wondres many folde	give miracles
	Up in heuene to make men the more unbolde	
	And tokenes on eorþe adown þ(er)e on to loke	
3965	Fuyr and blood and grete breþ of smoke	stench
	The sonne schal torne in to derknesse	
	And the mone into blood and lese here brightnesse	
	Bifore ar the day of our lord schal falle	
	Þe whiche schal openly be schewed to us alle.	

---

[1] "And there shall be signs in the sun, and in the moon, and in the stars; and upon the earth distress of nations by reason of the confusion o the roaring of the sea and of the waves; men withering away for fear, and expectation of what shall come upon the whole world. For the powers of heaven shall be moved; and then they shall see the Son of man coming in a cloud, with great power and majesty" [Luke 21:25-27].

[2] H.M. 125 prints *vppon* rather than *opene* here.

[3] The last five words have been emended by the *Piers* rubricator.

[4] The "he" is crossed off with three lines instead of the usual single line, perhaps expressing impatience with the miscopying.

[5] "I shall show wonders in heaven [above]; and in earth [below], blood and fire, and vapor of smoke. The sun shall be turned into darknes: and the moon into blood; before the great and dreadful day of the Lord doth come" [adapted from Joel 2:30-31].

Part V. Ten Signs of Doomsday (3970–4009)

3970	Thulke day¹ of alle daies schal be þe laste	f. 51 v	this
	Aʒenst wham alle þese tokenes schull ben icaste		signs
	Than mowe men by suche tokenes iwite		may, know
	Þat it is þe moste day that may be undurʒete		realized
	And the streytest and the moste hard		
3975	As me(n) may ihere sone afturward²		hear
	Of viftene tokenes that schull come before þe dome.		signs
	Ʒut spekeþ þe good man seynt Jerom³		
	Of fiftene tokenes that comeþ afore the dom.		
	And afore cristes comynge as he sayes		
3980	The whiche schull falle in fiftene daies		
	Ac ʒif any othur dayes schulle be twene falle		whether, between
	Þese dayes . oþur they schulleþ alle		or
	Come contynuelly day aftur day		
	Seynt Jerom saiþ þat he kan nowʒt say		
3985	Ac ʒut for acertayn he approueþ nouʒt		certain
	Þat þe fiftene daies . schulleþ be owt sowht		sought out
	Bot he reh(er)ceþ þese tokenes fiftene		recounts
	And telleþ outright . what þey beþ to mene		directly
	As in some bokes of þe hebrues me(n) may fynde		Hebrews
3990	Þese fiftene iset to haue in mynde .		established
	As seynt Jerom scheweþ here naught elles		
	Bot as he fond iwryte ryght so he telles		found
	In þe hebrues bokes . right so as he hem fond		
	So he reherseþ hem as þey come to his hond		repeats
3995	Eche day aftur oþ(ur) as iwole here sette		I will
	Ʒe schulleþ hem knowe . wiþouten eny lette.		any impediment
	¶ Þe ferste of þese tokenes is to bigynne		
	Þe see schall aryse and many wat(er)es þ(er)to wynne⁴		increase
	So þat þe see schal be more hy		higher
4000	Þan any montayne that is þ(er)to hy⁵		mountain
	By fourty cubites and so an hi stonde		a high place
	As it were a drie hul that were on drie londe.		dry hill
	¶ In þe secu(n)de day þe see schal wexe so lowe		become
	Þat unneþe any man schal it knowe.		
4005	¶ The þrydde day þe see schal be playn		flat
	And euene stonde in his cours agayn		steady place
	As it stod first at his bigynnynge		
	Wiþ outen eny more arysynge.		
	¶ The feorþ day schal wondurfull be		

---

[1] The number of caesura marks and dotted y's have much increased, with at least twenty of the latter on this page.
[2] H.M. 125 writes "as me may yhure here afterward."
[3] Again, an unlikely capitalization of "Jerom" here and on ll. 3984 and 3991.
[4] The poet's descriptions of natural phenomenon gone awry is dramatically emphatic as is his following of a standard sequence of such signs; they are intended to arouse fear and thus coerce his audience into submission or obedient behavior. See William W. Heist, *The Fifteen Signs Before Doomsday.* East Lansing : Michigan State College University Press, 1952.
[5] H.M. 125 writes *mey* here.

4010	The moste wondurfull fisches of þe see	f. 52r	
	Schulleþ to gidur come and arorynge make		roaring
	Þat for drede þ(er)of many man schal quake		
	Ac what þat rorynge þanne schal signyfie		
	No man may iwite bot god þat sitteþ an hie.		know
4015	¶ The fifþe day all þe see schal brenne		burn
	And alle þe watres þat þ(er)to don renne		run
	And þat schal laste fro þe risynge of þe sonne		
	To þe tyme þat sche be down aȝen iwonne.		has set again
	¶ The sixte day schal sprynge a blody dewe		spread
4020	On gras and tres as it schal þ(er)on schewe		
	On þe seuenþe day howses schullen down falle		
	And castelles and toures swiþe fele w(i)t(h) alle.		towers so many
	¶ The eiȝtþe day grete rokkes and heuy stones		
	Schulleþ þanne fight to gidre all a tones		at once
4025	And eche of hem . oþur down caste		the other
	And eche aȝenst oþur hortly faste		exceedingly fast
	So þat eche ston in dyv(er)se man(er) wise		
	Schal oþur to breste[1] and in þre parties dyvyse.		
	¶ On þe nyþe day schal gret erþe dene be		ninth, earthquake
4030	Gen(er)ally in eu(er)y lond . and in eche acontre		every country
	Ac so grete eorþe quave as schal be þanne		quake, then
	Schal no man telle þe tyme ne whanne.		
	¶ On the tenþe day folowynge wel euene[2]		
	Wynd schal come adown f(ro)m heuene		
4035	The whiche hulles and dales schul torne clene		hills, completely
	Into a playn that non hull schal be sene.		plain
	¶ Of þe enleueþ day men schulleþ out route		rush
	Of caves and holes and so wende aboute		go
	As wood men that no witt ne conne		mad, wits, understanding
4040	And no speche to oþur schal be iwonne.		others, gained
	¶ On the twelþe day among mon alle		
	A signe f(ro)m heuene adown schal falle		
	¶ On þe þritteneþ day schull dede mennes bones		thirteenth
	Be iset to gidre and rise up atones		be, at once
4045	And upon her g(ra)ues þey schul so stonde		
	For þis schal falle in eche londe[3].		
	¶ On the fourteneþ day as i forsoþe telle can		
	Schal diȝe boþe womman and eke man.[4]		die, also
	¶ On þe fifteneþ day thus it schal betide[5]		happen

---

[1] "shall break / destroy the other."
[2] "...following quite precisely on the tenth day." *Folowynge* and *wel even* are both *Piers* rubricator emendations.
[3] H.M. 125 provides: "ande in þis maner hit shal byfalle in yche londe."
[4] H.M. 125 writes "child man and womman" here.
[5] H.M. 125 adds these lines: "Ffor þei schalle with hym aȝene aryse to lyue
        That weryn aforn dede and wyth hem stond belyue."

Part V. Ten Signs of Doomsday

4050	Þe world schal brenne on eu(er)y side	f. 52v
	And þe eorþe wheron now we doþ dwelle	
	Schal ben ibrend in to the laste ende of helle.[1]	
	Thus telleþ ierom þese tokenes fiftene	
	As þey beþ write in þe hebrues bokes clene	Hebrews', completely
4055	Ac for al þe toknes that men mowen se	may see
	Ȝut schal no man in certayn be	
	What tyme cryst to the dome schal come	judgment
	So sodaynly he schal therto be ynome	taken
	Ffor as it befel in lothes and noes dayes	Lot's, Noah's
4060	So schal he come as luk in þe gospel sayes:	Luke

Sicut f(a)c(tu)m est in dieb(us) . Noe . ita erit advent(us) filii
  ho(min)is nam edebant viri et bibebant et uxores eis dabantur
  ad nupcias usq(ue) in diem qua intravit noe in archam et subito
  venit diluviu(m) et p(er)didit om(ne)s. Si(mi)l(ite)r ut factu(m)
  est in dieb(us) loth . Edebant viri et bibebant . emebant
  [et emebant][2] vendebant . et uxores ducebant usque in diem
  qua exiit loth a sodomis . et subito venit ignis et sulphur de celo
  et perdidit omnes. S(e)c(un)d(u)m autem hec . erit advent(us) filii hominis.[3]

	These beþ þe wordys of the gospelle	
	Þe whiche beþ on englisch þus forto telle	
	As it was ido in þe day of noe	
4065	So mannys sone schall come saiþ he	
	Ffor men eeten and dronken and were swithe glade[4]	so happy
	And wedded wyues and brydales made	
	In to þe day namliche þat noe wente	that is to say
	Into þe schip and wyf and children w(i)t(h) hym hente	took
4070	Ac sodeynly come the flood in that ilke tyde	very time
	And fordede al þe world in eueriche aside.	destroyed, everywhere
	Also in þe dayes of loth it was so bifalle	happened
	Men eten and dronken and were m(er)y wiþ alle	
	And eche man wiþ oþ(er) boþe solde and bought	
4075	And planted and biggyd and houses wrought	cultivated, built / made
	In to þe day that loth ȝede owt of sodom p(er)chaunce	Lot went out
	Whan sodeynly [on] þ(er)on [ ][5] come godes vengeaunce[6]	
	Right so it schal falle as men schulleþ ise	
	Bi þe day of dome þat schewed schal be.	
4080	**Of þe fuyr that schall brenne al þe world.**	
	In þe ende of the world afore domys day	before doomsday
	Schal come a fuyr that neu(er) man such on say	such a one saw

---

[1] The signs begin by revealing acts of wonder and awe, but move progressively to more fearful, dangerous events, culminating in total annihilation of earth as it melds into hell. This "crescendo" mode of expression is very powerful.

[2] The scribe has deleted *et emebant* with a single stroke through these words.

[3] "And as it came to pass in the days of Noe, so shall it be also in the days of the Son of man. They did eat and drink, they married wives, and were given in marriage, until the day that Noe entered into the ark; and the flood came and destroyed them all. Likewise, it came to pass, in the days of Lot: They did eat and drink, they bought and sold ... [and they married wives until the day] that Lot went out of Sodom, [and suddenly] it rained fire and brimstone from heaven, and destroyed them all" [Luke: 17:26-29. Bracketed phrases are added or adapted by the poet].

[4] The last three words by the *Piers* rubricator are slightly smaller, written over an erasure, and somewhat backhand.

[5] The word *on* has been crossed out once here; a space of about two letters where a caesura would be remains after a long erasure under þ(er)on.

[6] H.M. 125 adds: Ffor it reyned from heuyn boþe fyre and brimstone
  And loste hem alle ande sparedde none.

	The whiche all þe world schal brenne	f. 53r	
	And no þyng spare þat it may ou(er) renne		overrun
4085	Ffor al þe eorþe schal brenne clene w(i)t(h)oute		completely
	And also þe elementes and þe eyr aboute		
	And al þi(n)g that god haþ on eorþe iwrought		created
	Schal þane be ibrend and wasted to nought		wiped out
	This fuyr that þorow þe world schal arise		
4090	Þanne schal come in dyuerse wise		fashions
	Ffor al þe fuyr that is in the spere aboue		sphere
	And undur eorþe schal be to gidre ischoue		pushed
	And alle at ones it schal to gidre mete		
	And brenne al þyng and no þyng lete		leave
4095	That on eorþe groweþ and haþ þ(er)onne reste		
	Til it be clansyd and mad fayr at þe beste		
	Ffram al corrupcion that men mowe sen		may see
	Þat in þe eir or in þe eorþe myght ben		
	Ac þis fuyr as þe boke saiþ doþ us kenne		do we know
4100	On four maners schal wurche and brenne.		By four ways, work
	It schal wurche as doþ þe fuyr of helle		
	To punysche hem that there don dwelle		
	It schal be as þe fuyr of purgatory[1] also		
	To clanse hem that haue venyal synnes ido		
4105	And it schal wurche as doþ þe fuyr on eorþ here		
	Þe whuche ouer al schall brenne boþe fer and nere		
	To waste al þing þat on eorþe sprynges		destroy, grows
	As gras and trees and alle oþur þynges		
	And also þe bodys of eueriche man		
4110	It schal brenne to askes as y telle can		ashes
	It schal wurche also as þe fuyr of þe spere		
	To make þe elementes boþe fayr and clere		
	So þat al þe eyr schal be mad bryght of hewe		color
	And thanne heuenes[2] schullyþ seme newe		
4115	Thour þis fuyr þat þus schal reyke aboute		through, spread
	Þe schap[3] of þe eorþe schal brenne wiþ oute		
	And þe schap of [^þe][4] world schal be fordo abrod		destroyed
	As it was ferst in þe tyme of Noes flod		
	And as þe flood passed þo . cubites fiftene		then, cubits
4120	And ou(er) þe heiȝest[5] montayne was wel sene		
	Right so as hy schal þe fuyr make his pas		passage
	And be as myghty as þe water was		

---

[1] Parts of *purgatory* and *have* (next line) have been erased, certainly a later objection to the concept of purgatory.
[2] The first eleven letters are written over an erasure; the first nine letters are written very small to fit in the space.
[3] H.M. 125 uses *face* here.
[4] The word *þe* is inserted above and between *of* and *world* in superscript.
[5] H.M. 125 writes *hexte* rather than *heiȝest*.

	And as god byfore his ferste comynge	f. 53v	
	Wolde here fordo wiþ oute eny lettynge		destroy unhindered
4125	Al the world þorow wat(er) of vengeaunce		retribution / punishment
	Aȝenst þe fuyr of lecchery þ(a)t is ful of enco(m)beraunce		temptation
	Right so bifore his comynge at þe laste		
	He schal of þe world an endyng caste		chart / prepare
	Thorow fuyr þat so schal brenny(n)g be		
4130	Aȝenst alle þe good dedys of charyte.		deeds
	The wurchyng of þis fuyr brenny(n)g so sore		working
	Schal contyne þeos þre times¹ eu(er)e more		contain
	That is to seyȝe bigynnyng, mydward, and ende		
	As me(n) may fynde wo so wole þ(er)to wende.²		
4135	Fferst þulke fuyr at þulke³ bygynnynge		
	Schal come bifore crystes comynge		
	The whiche schal þe good men clanse and fyne		cleanse, refine / purify
	And þe synful hard punysche and pyne		torture
	That here loueden synne and þought it swete		
4140	And þerfore thus seyþ davyd þe p(ro)phete		
	Ignis ante ip(su)m precedet et inflammabit		
	*in circuitu inimicos eius.*⁴		
	He saiþ fuyr bifore hym in dyuerse partyes		fire, various parts
	Schal gon aboute and brenne hys enemys⁵		
	Thus schal þat fuyr come al bifore		
4145	And destruye al þyng that ys on eorþe ibore⁶		born
	And whan þe world is ibrent as i erst tolde		first
	Than schul al men aryse boþe ȝonge and olde		arise
	Out of her g(ra)ues boþ soule and body ifere⁷		together
	And come to þe dome wiþ a rewful⁸ chere.		sorrowful
4150	Our lord schal come adown as y telle can		
	And sitte in dome as doþ a domys man		judge
	And deme al men boþe good and ille		
	As ȝe schullen here ȝif it be ȝour wille		hear
	But ȝut þulke selue fuyr in þat tyde		this same, time
4155	Schal brenne aboute hym in eu(er)y side		
	As david bereþ witnesse and saiþ þis		
	In þe saut(er) boke þere it wryten is		Psalter, where
	Ignis in conspectu eius exardescet et		
	*In circuitu eius tempestas valida.*⁹		
	He seyþ þe fuyr schal brenne in his sight		
4160	And aboute hym gret tempest schal be dight¹⁰		enacted / made

---

¹ The word *times* is no doubt correct, although the *i* looks like an *h*. H.M. 125 uses *termes*.
² "... whoso may investigate."
³ H.M. 125 omits the work *þulke*.
⁴ "A fire shall go before him, and shall burn his enemies round about" [Psalm 96, 3-4]. An indecipherable erasure follows.
⁵ H.M. 125 adds: " Þat fuir mannis bodies to askes schal brenne
    And al þing þat me mai in þe world kenne."
⁶ H.M. 125 replaces this line with: "Ar criste to þe dom come to save þat was forelore."
⁷ This line ends with *ysere* rather than *yfere* in H.M. 125.
⁸ H.M. 125 uses *dredful* rather than *rewful* here.
⁹ "Fire will burst out round him and the storm vehemently encircle him" [Psalm 49-53].
¹⁰ The *Piers* rubricator has emended the last three words in smaller script in an upward angle, as if hurriedly.

	And as long as þulke dome schall laste	f. 54r	
	Þat fuyr schal brenne in eu(er)y side faste		quickly
	And whan þe dome is brought to þe ende		
	Þey þat beþ idampned þanne schull wende		go
4165	Into helle put to dwelle þ(er)ynne		pit
	For non oþur g(ra)ce þan schull þey wynne		
	And þanne þat ilke fuyr schal be swope adoun¹		swept
	Forþ into helle wiþ all his corrupcion²		forth
	Ac whan þe fuyr haþ þus wasted al þing		
4170	Þan schal heuene cese of all mouyng.		stop moving

Of þe general arysyng of alle men to þe dome.

	Oure lord or he come adown f(ro)m his trone	before, throne
	To sitte in dome in his p(ro)pre persone	proper role
	He schal his angels bifore hym sende	
4175	On foure parties into þe worldes ende³	
	And make hem wiþ her beomes blowe	trumpets
	That alle men schulleþ ihere and knowe	hear
	And alle men they schullen up calle	
	And bydden hem come to þe dome alle	bid
4180	Thanne schul alle men aryse þat euer hadde lif⁴	
	Boþe man and wom(m)a(n) child mayden and wif	
	Boþe gode and [and]⁵ wikked⁶ in flesch and in felle	skin
	In body and in soule as clerkes conneþ telle	can
	And þat in as schort tyme as herte may þenke	
4185	Oþur a mannys ye doþe opene oþur wynke	eye, blink
	As sone as þey hereþ⁷ þulke dredfull sown	such, sound
	And þerfore þe apostel saiþ in his lesso(u)n:	
	*Om(ne)s eni(m) resurgent⁸ [ ] in momento in ictu oculi in novissima tuba.*⁹	
	He seyþ alle schullen rise in a lytil doynge	quickly
4190	As in þe spas of an ey3es wynkynge	eye's winking
	Whan þat þey hereþ þulke dredful blaste	such fearful
	Of þe beome that thanne schal blowe laste¹⁰	trumpet
	Thanne þey schulleþ arise in þe same elde	age
	Þat crist¹¹ hadde here þat al þyng may welde	rule
4195	Whan þat he arose þorow his myght	
	F(ro)m deþ to lyue as it falleþ hym bi right	rightly
	Ffor þanne was he of þritty 3er elde and two	thirty
	And 3ut þ(er)wiþ þre monþes also	besides
	In þat age they schullen arise echone .	each one

---

[1] The last four words are written over an erasure, and are somewhat cramped.
[2] H.M. 125 includes these lines here: Þus þorow al þe world þat fuir schal brenne
                                                          And hit clanse of alle fulþed and wenne.
[3] "... in four directions, to the end of the world."
[4] The last five words are carefully scribed over an erasure, and are the same size and slant as others in the line.
[5] The duplicated word has been forcefully crossed off once.
[6] H.M. 125 reads *ille* for *wikked*.
[7] These five words have been emended by the *Piers* rubricator.
[8] This is correct, although H.M. 125 writes *resurgemus*.
[9] "We shall all rise again: in a moment, in the twinkling of an eye at the last trumpet" [1 Corinth. 15-52], The letters *ur* seem to have been erased here (changing the verb *resurgent* from passive to active), leaving a space.
[10] Four lines in H.M. 125 summarize the rising of the dead here.
[11] H.M. 125 writes *god* here.

Part V. Ten Signs of Doomsday

4200	Whan that the beom makeþ his mone	f. 54v	trumpet, complaint
	Wiþ her bodyes wiþ outen eny more tale		further ado
	And [ ]¹ wiþ her lemys boþe grete and smale		limbs
	Ffor þey þe bodyes of eu(er)y man		
	Were al ibrent to askes þan		ashes
4205	And ȝut they þe askes of alle her bodyes		
	Were to scatered in dyuerse parties		scattered, places
	Thorow eche lond and echa contre		
	Ȝut þey schulleþ alle to gidre be		
	And eu(er)y body schal ryse wiþ his lemys alle		
4210	As þey scholde bi kynde to þe body falle		by nature
	And wiþ al þe here in body and in heued		hair, head
	So þat no þing schal f(ro)m hem be bi reued		taken away
	Ffor þer schal non here be ilore iwis		lost
	As seynt luk bereþ witnesse and seiþ þis		
4215	*Capillus de capite vestro non peribit.*²		
	He saiþ non her schal perysche no faile		perish
	Þat bilongeþ to þe heued and may it avayle		head, if, be of use
	And þe lemes of men that here beþ unsemeliche		ugly
	Þorow foul outrage of kynde nameliche³		nature namely
4220	God schal abate þat outrage þorow his myght		stop
	And make þe lemys more semely to sight		
	And ȝif any leme wantede þat schold bifalle		was missing
	To þe body aboute grete oþur smalle		or
	Thorow defaute of kynde þanne god of his wille		default
4225	Schal alle þe defautys of lemes fulfylle		rectify
	Thus schal he do p(ri)ncipally to alle þo		
	Þat schulleþ be isaued and to blis go		
	And here bodyes schulle be semly and bright		
	Wiþ alle þe lemes to eche mannys sight.		
4230	Ffor here bodyes schulleþ unsemely be [Ac he ne schal amende in no partyes		
	And foule in eu(er)y leme forto se þo defautes of lemys of synful bodyes.]⁴		
	Than alle þat beþ good and rightwise		
	Þat schulle ben isaued . þan schul arise		
	And into þe eyr be rauasched an hy		ravished
4235	For þanne is cristes comynge ny		near
	And þere þei schull hym kepe forto he come		wait until
	As þe hie iustice⁵ to deme alle and some		judge
	Ac þe moste parfit men schulleþ ferst crist kepe		perfect, notice
	And alle oþur aftur hem come in on hepe		all at once

---

¹ A two- or three-letter erasure here leaves a blank space.
² "But a hair of your head shall not perish" [Luke 21: 18].
³ The last three words are written over an erasure in the *Piers* rubricator's hand.
⁴ This section is an insert from the right margin of this folio, written in the *Piers* rubricator's hand, with much lighter ink and smaller script. A line is drawn to a spot between *sight* and *be* (ll. 4236 and 4237) to indicate the place of the couplet. H.M. 125 places these lines appropriately in the test.
⁵ H.M. 125 begins this line "As he þat ys domesman ..."

4240	And so be¹ wiþ hym eu(er)e in body and in soule f. 55r	
	As telleþ þe trewe apostel poule	
	Quoniam ipse d(omin)us in iussu et in voce archangeli et in tuba dei descen[-]	
	det de celo et mortui qui in xpo sunt resurgent primi .	
	Deinde nos qui vivim(us)qui relinquim(ur) si(mu)l	
	rapiemur . cu(m) illis in nubibus obvia(m) xpo in a[ ]²	
	*era et sic semper cu(m) d(omi)no eri(mus).*³	
	He seiþ our lord schal come adown f(ro)m heuene	
	In godys biddynge and archangels steuene	command
4245	And in þe form of crystes owne beome	trumpet
	Alle þe world to dome þorow his swete leome	gleam / radiance
	And all þat beþ dede in cristes name	
	Schulleþ ferst arise wiþ outen eny schame	
	And afturward in þulke selue manere	this same way
4250	Alle we þat 3et leuen and beþ ileft here	
	Than(n)e schulle wiþ hym in cloudys be irauesched	transported
	Into þe eir .⁴ and eu(er) aftur wiþ crist be inorsched	air, nourished
	Ac the synfull þat schullen arise in þulke tide	But this time
	Beneþe on þe eorþe schal crist abide	beneath, await
4255	And wepen and sorowen for her foule synne	
	For þei ne mowe nawhare þennys wynne⁵	might, then gain [heaven
	And hem schal leu(er)e þan(n)e to be in helle	rather
	Þanne to come bifore god her synnes to telle.⁶	
	Than schulle many men haue gret drede	fear
4260	To come biforen hym to sen his manhede	see, human nature
	And namely synful men þat beþ wiþ oute hope	
	Of godes mercy to haue [to haue] a litil drope	
	Therfore iob in his bok þeose wordes sette	Job
	Euery mannys inwit þ(er)wiþ to whette⁷	conscience, sharpen
4265	*Quis michi hoc tribuat ut in inferno p(ro)tegas me*	
	*et abscondas me donec p(er)t(ra)nseat furor tuus.*⁸	
	Lord ho may 3iue to me saiþ he	who
	Þat þow in helle woldest 3elde me	relent to me
	And keu(er)e me at þulke dredfull day	protect
	Tyl þat þy wreche were passid away	anger
4270	Than it is no wondur þei it greue sore	
	A synful man to haue drede muche more	
	That schal be dampned and for eu(er)e ilore	
	For his synnes þat he haþ don bifore	
	Ffor crist so wrechefull schal be in þat stounde	vengeful
4275	Þat noman wiþ oute drede schal ben ifounde .	found

---

¹ H.M. 125 contains a superfluous *we* here.
² The Latin Vulgate reads *aera*, which seems what the scribe's correction indicates.
³ "For the Lord himself shall come down from heaven with commandment, and with the voice of an archangel, and with the trumpet of God: and the dead who are in Christ shall rise first. Then we who are alive, who are left, shall be taken up together with them in the clouds to meet Christ, into the air, and so shall we be always with the Lord" [1Thess. 4: 16-18].
⁴ An uncharacteristic flourish and period above the space following it marks this passage.
⁵ H.M. 125 reads: "ffor þei ne shulleþ now heder þennes wynne."
⁶ These lines are inserted in H.M 125: They schulle ve-lyhm fle if þe might
   Outher be hid hem fro þe domesman syght
   Outher in þe erthe ouþer in som oþer place
   They ne roghte so þe com noght afore his face.
   [Twelve more lines are inserted following these.]
⁷ Nine more lines follow in H.M. 125.
⁸ "Who will grant me this, that those mayst protect me in hell, and hide me till thy wrath pass?" [Job 14:13].

132 Part V. Ten Signs of Doomsday (4276–4313)

Of Godes comynge to þe dome.   f.55v

    Our lord þorowe his grete myght
    Schal come adown f(ro)m heuene light
    And as domys man in dome forto sitte   judge
4280   And wiþ hym gret multitude ful of witt   knowledge
    And angels and archangels many on   a one
    And oþ(ur) halwes that schullen wiþ hym gon   saints
    Ffor þus telleþ þe boke us þ(er)wiþ to lere   teach
    Þat we of his comynge knewe[1] þe man(er)e.
4285   *Ecce d(omin)us veniet et om(ne)s s(anc)ti eius cu(m) eo[2].*
    Lo our lord he seyþ schal to þe dome come   judgment
    And all his alwene[3] schall wiþ hym be nome   saints, taken
    And so sodaynly he schal hym þer[4] schewe
    As seyþ þe gospel of seynt mathewe
4290   *Sicut fulgur exit ab oriente et paret in*
        Occidente . ita erit advent(us) filii ho(min)is.[5]
    As þe ligthtnynge[6] out goþ he seiþ in schort tyde   lightning, time
    Clene f(ro)m þe est . into þe west side
    Riȝt so þe comynge of mannys sone schal be   son
    Sodeyn bright and dredful in soþe forto se[7]
4295   He schal come wiþ oute eny lettyng adown
    Aȝenst þe mount of olyuete in his p(ro)pre p(er)son   Mount Olive
    Where þat he in his manhede fly into heuene[8]   flew
    F(ro)m his disciples to his fadur wel euene   very directly
    In suche a forme as he up stey[9]   ascended
4300   He schal aȝen come and deme þanne in good fey   faith
    Good and euel . boþe ȝong and olde
    As þe angels to his disciples tolde:
        Hic ihe[10] qui assu(m)pt(us) est a vobis in celu(m) .
        Sic veniet que(m) admodu(m) vidistis
        eu(m) eunte(m) in celu(m).[11]
    They seiden ihe that is here uptaken anon   Jesus, arisen now
4305   F(ro)m ȝow to heuene in flesch and bon   bone
    So schal he come at þe worldys ende   world's
    Right as ȝe siȝe hym into heuene wende   saw, go
    And so schal aȝen come in þe forme of man
    And al þyng at his wille deme as he wel can.
4310   **Of þe stede that Crist schull deme ynne**
    Whan crist is come adown for to deme
    In forme of man he schal þanne seme
    Yn a place he schal his dom holde

---

[1] H.M. 125 uses the present tense *knowe* here.
[2] "Behold, the Lord shall come, and all his saints with him" [Zachar. 14:5; *Ecce*, i.e. behold, is the poet's wording, not in the Vulgate].
[3] H.M. 125 writes *halwen*, "holy saints."
[4] H.M. 125 says *hym þeder shews*.
[5] "For as the lightning cometh out of the East, and appeareth even into the West: so shall also the coming of the Son of man be" [Matt. 24: 27].
[6] H.M. 125 writes *evenynge* here.
[7] The poet appears to be using fear and intimidation to coerce his audience into proper behavior throughout the doomsday discussion.
[8] A reference to the Ascension of Christ. H.M. 125 writes *stey* instead of *fly*.
[9] A dotted *y* is used in *stey*.
[10] H.M. 125 uses *iesus* here, and *iesu* below in l. 4309.
[11] "This Jesus who is taken up from you into heaven, shall so come, as you have seen him going into heaven" [Acts 1:11].

	Þat is þe vale of Josephat as hym self wolde	f. 56r	wishes
4315	Where þat alle men schulleþ to gidre mete		
	As crist telleþ by ioel his p(ro)phete		
	Congregabo gentes om(ne)s . et adduca(m) *eas in valle iosaphat.*[1]		
	He seyþ ischal alle men to gidre calle		I shall
	And in to þe vale of iosaphat lede hem alle		
4320	And ȝut more þ(er)to he seyþ þus		yet, tells
	As god bi þe p(ro)phete scheweþ to us		
	Consurgent et ascendent om(ne)s gentes in *valle iosaphat . quia ibi sedebo ut* *iudice(m) om(ne)s gentes.*[2]		
	He saiþ alle men schulleþ to þe dome aryse		
	And into þe vale of iosaphat come in alle wise		all manners
4325	Ffor þere i schal sitte in my p(ro)pre p(er)sone		proper role
	To deme[3] as þey be wurþy men eu(er)ichone.		judge
	Josaphat is þus muche forto saye		
	As þe stede of dome at þe laste daye		place
	But god schal nat thanne fully adoun come[4]		
4330	To þe erthe and þ(er)on sytte and holde hys dome		
	Ac up in þe eyr he schal sytte as a lord .		
	In a whit cloude as holy wryt seyþ þis word		writ
	Ecce apparebit d(omin)us sup(er) nubem candidam.[5]		
	Lo he seiþ our lord schal hym schewe		
4335	In a whit cloude wiþ alle his angels arewe		in a row
	Euene aboue that vale he schal ben houynge		hovering
	Where alle men schulle hym se in dome sittynge		
	Ac þe skile whi he schal sytte þere		reason
	Men may fynde by this sawe here		saying
4340	Ffor þe vale of iosaphat ys set in awey lete		crossroads
	Bitwene þe hye mount of olyuete		
	And ier(usa)l(e)m in that oþur side		
	Þe whiche stondeþ amyddys þe world wyde		in the middle of
	And also þere ys þe mount of calvarye		Calvary
4345	And þe sepulcre of cryst and of our lady marye		sepulcher
	And also in þat place stondeþ bethlem		Bethlehem
	Nat fer f(ro)m the syte of ier(usa)l(e)m		city
	Therfore god schal sytte on þat day þere		
	Þe grete dome to ȝiue in this manere		
4350	"Lo here is as [^ȝe][6] mowen now ise		may, see
	Þe vale of iosaphat þat ys nowe undur me		
	Where þat my modur beryed was marye		mother buried

---

[1] "I will gather together all nations, and will bring them down into the valley of Josaphat" [Joel 3:2].
[2] "All men should bestir themselves and arise into the valley of Josaphat where I will sit in order to judge all men" [Joel 3: 12 King James Version; Joel 4:12 Douay-Rheims]. H.M. 125 writes *congregent* repeating the verb from the Latin in l. 4322.
[3] *Dene* as written is a scribal error for *deme* here.
[4] This couplet has been emended by the *Piers* scribe. H.M. 125 uses *criste* instead of *god* here. The following line in H.M. 125 is: "ffor bifore he haþ þe kynde of erþe ynome."
[5] "Behold, the Lord will appear upon a white cloud" [apparently adapted from *Apocalypse* 14: 14:and behold a white cloud; and upon the one sitting like to the Son of man"] (JEJ).
[6] A small caret below the line and the inserted word ȝe superscripted just above the text are entered here; it is unclear whether this is in a later hand or not.

Part V. Ten Signs of Doomsday (4353–4392)

	Of wham y took flesch and blood wiþoute vilanye"	f. 56v	lust
	He may seye also here ʒe mowen se now		say, may
4355	Þe cite of bethlem where y was bore for ʒow		born
	And in cloutys cloþyd and ʒut honouryd lasse		rags clothed
	In a crybbe iwas leyd bitwixe an oxe and an asse.		
	He may seie also here ʒe may se stonde		say, stands
	The cite of ier(usa)l(e)m that is ny to ʒoure honde		near you
4360	Where y hadde for ʒow many a boffet		buffet
	And wiþ scharp scowrgys alle aboute biset		scourges, beset
	And suþþe the cros to me was ymad ful ʒare		since, cross, ready
	And þanne y leyd upon my schuldrys bare		shoulders
	He may seie also . lo here faste by		nearby
4365	Is as ʒe may se the mount of calvary		
	Where y[1] was anhangyd on hy upon þe rode		hanged on high, cross
	By twene two þeuys and schad for ʒow my blode		thieves, shed
	Where that for ʒow my peyne was most		
	And wher that y deyde and ʒaf up my gost.[2]		
4370	He may ʒut seye ryght thus also		
	Lo here ys þe sepulcre a lytyl þer fro,		sepulcher, little
	Here ynne iwas ileyd as for a man ded		laid
	Whan y was yberyed as þe p(ro)phet haþ sed.		buried
	He may seye also here was my sete		see / abode
4375	Whan y wente to my deþ f(ro)m the mount of olyuete		death
	Where angels hem schewyd in mannys liknesse		
	Whan i fley[3] into heuene where is euere blysse		flew, bliss
	And tolde to ʒow how my comynge scholde be		
	To the laste dome as ʒe mow nowe ise.		
4380	Now haue ʒe iherd wel the encheson		reason
	Whi he wolle sitte aboue that vale by reson		
	The whiche men the vale of iosaphat calleþ		
	For it in the mydward of the world falleþ		
	Also anoþur reson may be forþ brought		posited
4385	Whi he schal come adown þere and ell where nought		not elsewhere
	Ffor þere was his ferst comynge adown		
	Into this world for mannys salvacyon		
	Whan that he ferst [toke][4] "flesch and blood tok		
	Of the mayden marye" as tellyþ the book.[5]		
4390	**Of the forme of man þat crist schal deme ynne.**		
	Crist sterne of syght schal thanne be[6]		somber / strict
	Aʒenst synful[7] . that hym schal yse.		the sinful

---

[1] A dotted *y* replaces a longer word; perhaps the scribe was at first confused by first person narration.
[2] Editorial note: Placing the report of his sufferings directly in Christ's mouth for a first-person account is emotionally and literarily effective.
[3] H.M. 125 reads the less likely *stey* [climbed] for *fley*.
[4] The word *toke* is incompletely erased here, confirmed by H.M. 125, but deleted as repetitious.
[5] These are the direct words of Christ. I use quotation marks for clarity. H.M. 125 concludes with these lines: "And þus he schalle com downe and sitte þere / To deme alle þe worlde als j seyede ere."
[6] The words *be* here, *yse* in the next line, and some above are wearing away; the *y* of *yse* almost looks like an erasure.
[7] H.M. 125 writes *þe synful man* here.

	And dredful as it ys iwryte in boke	f. 57r	fearful
	He schal to hem be whan þey on hym schal loke		
4395	And lykyne and delytable he schal be in syght		pleasing, delightful
	To goode men that here han lyuyd aryght.		lived rightfully
	Ac alle p(er)sonys of the holy trynyte		persons
	Schulleþ nouȝt ben ischewyd in that pryuyte		shown, sacred mystery
	Ne the godhede schal not apere thanne		
4400	Bot ihu cryst alone in the form of manne		Jesus
	Ffor godys sone he is that schal deme us		
	And þerfore seynt luk in his bok sayþ thus:		
	Omne iudiciu(m). pat(er) dedit filio . ut		
	omnes honorificent filiu(m). sicut		
	honorificat(ur) p(at)rem.[1]		
	He seyth god haþ ȝoue to his sone al the dome		given
4405	Þat schal be ȝoue ar we come tyl ȝour[2] home		before
	Ffor that men scholde honoure the sone aryght		Therefore
	As they honouryþ the fadur that is ful of myght		
	The good men schulle hym ise in his manhode		
	Wiþ þe godhede as man in flesch and blood		
4410	The whiche he schal nat hide f(ro)m hem		
	Ac as god and man he schal apere to the goode men.[3]		
	Ac þe euel men in manhode hym schull ise		
	Only right as he heng on the rode tre		hung, cross
	Blewe . wan . and blody as he thanne was		blue, pale
4415	Whan that he deyed for our trespas		sins
	Ffor in the forme of man he schal than seme		
	And as iuge sytte all men to deme[4]		judge sits
	And god schal at his down comynge		
	The token of the croys wiþ hym brynge[5]		cross
4420	This tokene thanne schal ben ischewyd		
	As the bok seyþ bothe to leryd and lewyd		learned, ignorant
	Hoc signu(m) crucis erit in celo . cu(m)		
	d(omin)us ad iudicandu(m) ven(er)it.[6]		
	The tokene of the cros f(ro)m heuene schal bynome		be taken
	Whan that our lord to the dome schal come		
4425	Ac this tokene as iwene schal naught be		I think
	Thulke same crois ne the same tre		that
	On þe whiche cryst was naylyd fot and hond		
	Bot a tokene of the cros ther on to undurstond		symbol, thereby
	Ȝut some men seyþ and it may wel be soþ		
4430	That the tokene of þe spere[7] wiþ þe croys goþ		
	Wiþ the whiche . cryst was stong to the herte rote .		depths of his heart

---

[1] "The father hath given all judgment to the Son: that all men may honour the Son, as they honor the Father" [Not Luke, as the poet says, but John 5:22-23].

[2] H.M. 125 reads *oure* rather than *ȝour*.

[3] H.M. 125 adds: "Than schall þat be a blissedfull sight
   So fayre as he schalle schyne and so bright."

[4] H.M. 125 writes: "And riȝt so in hys manhede he schall him deme." Six additional lines are included after this line.

[5] Six more lines are here added in H.M. 125.

[6] "This sign of the cross will be in the sky when the Lord comes to judge" [*Breviarium Romanum*, I Vespers, in *Exaltatione Sanctae Crucis*].

[7] The reference is to the sword which pierced the side of Christ while on the cross.

	And wiþ naylys smyte . thorow hond and fote[1]	f. 57v	nails struck
	Alle þeos tokenes schulleþ thanne be schewyd		shown
	Bifore al men bothe lered and lewyd		
4435	Ac the synful that schulleþ idampnyd be		
	To her schenschipe schulleþ hem y se		shame / destruction
	Ffor cryst schal to hem schewe[2] his woundys wide		
	In heuyd, in hond, in foot and syde		head
	The whiche fresch and newe schulle seme		
4440	To the synful man that he schal there deme[3]		
	Ffor he schal thanne schewe to here confusio(u)n		
	Alle the tokenes of his harde passyo(u)n		
	And that schal be to here schendschipe eu(er)e mo		disgrace
	As seynt austyn p(re)veþ that it is so		proves
4445	*Ffortasse in corpore suo cicatrices vulneru(m) suoru(m) servavit d(omin)us.*		
	Ut in iudic(i)o hostes exprobraret . et convincens eos . dicat.		
	Ecce deus et homo cui credere noluistis ecce homo quem		
	crucifixistis . agnostite Lat(us) quod p(er)forastis quod		
	p(ro)pt(er) vos apertu(m) est et venir(us) ad me reunistis[4].		
	He saiþ our lord godes sone of heuene		
	Haþ ikept in his body as iseye wel euene		I say, equally
	The sores of his woundys swiþe clere		so plainly
	That he suffrede (^for) mannys synnes here		
4450	Hem to schewe to his enemys in that wise		
	Whan he schall sitte in dome as hie iustice		high
	He schal saie lo here the man in flesch and blood[5]		
	Þe whiche ȝe heengen an hy on the rood		hung, high, cross
	Biholdeþ þe woundes the whiche ȝe on me stikede		inflicted
4455	And þe side that a knyȝt wiþ his spere prykede		pierced
	Þe whiche for ȝow was open eu(er) more		
	Ac ȝe nolde no thyng take of my lore		would not take, learning
	A gret schendschipe . schall this be to hem alle		shame
	That haueþ cryst forsake and beþ in synne falle		
4460	And wroughten no thing to godys honour		wrought / performed
	Þat suffred for hem many an hard schour		attack
	What may thei thanne answere and saye		
	Þey haþ no thing hem to excuse . ne to forþ[6] laie		produce
	Ffor on that day bereþ[7] the boke witnesse		
4465	Schal no thing be schewed bot ryghtfulnese		shown
	And grete reddure to the sinful namely		severity
	Þat schulleþ be demed to peyne wurþily		condemned
	Ffor here defens is thanne to hem wel uncouþe		defense, unknown

---

[1] A barely visible period separates the two halves of this line and line 4463.
[2] The letter *w* has been overwritten in the same hand but in a darker ink.
[3] H.M. 125 lacks this line.
[4] "Perhaps the lord has preserved scars of his wounds in his body so at trial He might charge His enemies and convict them, and say 'Behold God and Man in whom you refused to believe, behold the Man whom you have crucified. Recognize the side which you have pierced, which for you is opened and you [have refused to] reunite [with one]'" Augustine, *De Symbolo ad catechumena*, ii. 8, as quoted by Aquinas, *Catena Aurea*, on John 20:27. The blocked translation is conjectural since the form *venir(us)* is not an attestable Latin word].
[5] H.M. 125 adds "is" here.
[6] H.M. 125 reads *forats* instead of *forþ*.
[7] No doubt the scribe intended to write *bereþ* as H.M. 125 says, instead of *beþeþ* as he did.

	As therof telleþ iohn wiþ þe gyldon mowthe.[1] f. 58r	golden
4470	*Non erit locus deffencionis . ubi videbu((n)t xpm exhibentem*	
	testimonia et signa que su(n)t sue passionis.[2]	
	He seyþ no place of defens schal be þanne founde	
	Whan cryst schal be seie in that stounde	seen, moment
	Schewynge witnesse and toknes enviro(u)n	round about
	Of his grete peynys and of his passiou(n)[3]	
4475	And that day þer schal be noþur angel no man	neither ... nor
	Þat þey ne schull tremble and for drede bycome wan	pale
	All þaw þey wite our lord wol hem saue	Although
	Ʒut they schulle ⌊naught⌋[4] on þat day gret drede haue	
	Ffor the grete austeryte and the grete afray	harshness, fear / dismay
4480	That god schal schewe on that ilke day	
	Aʒenst þe synful as y may rehercy	describe
	That schulleþ be dampnyd wiþ outen any mercy	
	Ac suþþe the rightful men that god wol saue	since
	And angels so muche drede schulle haue	
4485	Muche more dred the synful schull haue in that stounde	anxiety
	As an holy man seyþ and haþ in his book founde	
	Si colu(m)pne celi contremiscent et pavebunt adventu(m)	
	xpi et ang(e)li dei amare flebu(n)t peccatores	Christ
	aute(m) quid facient?[5]	
	He seiþ ʒif þe pilers of heuene bryght	pillars
	The whiche beþ holy men that lyueþ aryght	righteously
4490	Schulle drede crystys comynge in manhede	
	And the angels also schullen haue drede	
	And wel sore wepe and bitturly þ(er)to	harshly
	What schal the synful man than do	
	That schal be dampnyd wiþ outen eny g(ra)ce	
4495	Therfore that holy man seyþ thus in a noþ(ur) place:	another
	Si iustus vix salvabitur impius et p(ec)c(a)tor(es) ubi parebu(n)t?[6]	
	He seiþ ʒif þe rightful man þ(a)t is clene out of synne	
	Schal unneþe salvacyon to his soule wynne	
	The synful man and the wikked on that on ende	wicked, one
4500	Wheþur schulleþ þey thanne hem biwende[7]	Where, turn
	Ffor thanne schal our lord in his manhede sitte	
	Aboue the synfull men and hem ʒiue an hard ritte	severe sentence
	Ffor he schal be wroþ and sterne of chere	severe, face
	Hem forto deme that hauyþ mysleued here	lived wicked lives
4505	And helle that is byneþe wyde and depe	
	Thanne schal be opened hem forto kepe	

---

[1] The last four words written over an erasure by the *Piers* rubricator are darker and higher than others on the page. H.M. 125 ends "wiþ his mouþ;" "wiþ þe guld on mowthe" are in another hand in H.M. 128.
[2] "There will be no grounds for defense, when they see Christ showing the evidence and proofs of his passion." [Perhaps adapted from St. John Chrysostom, a Greek Father famed for his preaching, hence *chrys* / golden, *oston* / mouth.]
[3] H.M. 125 concludes: "And on þat day as y in bokes rede
         Schulleþ alle men be in gret drede."
[4] Crossed off with one bold line.
[5] "If the pillars of heaven tremble and quake at the coming of Christ and the angels of God will weep bitterly, yet what will sinners do" [adapted from Job 26:11].
[6] "If the just man shall scarcely be saved, where shall the ungodly and the sinner appear?" [1Peter 4:18].
[7] H.M. 125 adds "Rightfulle men as þe booke makethe mencioun
         Schulle be ysaued for her perfeccioun."

Part V. Ten Signs of Doomsday (4507–4546)

	And the eorþe that they on stonden schal quake f. 58v	
	And tremble for her synne and al to schake	
	So that unneþe it schal hem bere	
4510	So muche her synnys schull þe eorþ dere	injure
	And al þe world aboue hem schal be brennynge	
	And fendys on eu(er)y side of hem stondynge.	
	Thanne grete sorowe schal be hem among	
	For heuene schal hem smyte al a long	strike forever
4515	Wiþ þondur dentys and lyghtnynges ifere	thunder claps, together
	And they wolde it fle ac þey fyndeþ no place þere	
	Ffor þey schull so be biset by eu(er)y side	beset
	Þat þey moot[1] nedys all her myschef abyde.	must, accept
	Of þe acusors that schull acuse þe synful man at þe day of dome.	
4520	Many acuso(re)s schulleþ be thanne	
	To acuse þe synful afore þe domes man(n)e i)e	judge
	Ffor as ȝe schulleþ here fynde iwryte	
	Fyftene acusours þanne schullyþ nat be forȝete.	forgotten
	Conscyence is the ferst and þat is þe inwit of man	inner voice / understanding
4525	And his synnes the whiche wel rikne ykan	enumerate, can
	And godys creatours that we schulleþ þere iknowe	creatures
	And angels of heuene and deuelys þat beþ lowe	
	And martires that haueþ suffred tormentys many on	one
	And seyntys that haueþ had peynys in flesch and bon	
4530	And mennys children that wered[2] unchastised	undisciplined
	And pore men þat in euel aray weren disgysed	
	And suggettys and benefices þat beþ resceyued here	subjects, received
	And þe torment of crystis passion al ifere	
	And god hym self and þe holy trynyte	
4535	Aȝen the synful man thanne schulleþ be.	
	How mannes conscience schall hem accuse.	
	Ferst schal mannys owne conscyence	
	Acuse hym self in crystis presence	
	That al openly schal ben icud	known
4540	For no thing thanne schal be ihud	
	Alle thing schall ben ischewed þ(er)e to þe ye	eye
	As danyel seiþ in his prophecie:	
	Dedit iudiciu(m) et libri aperti sunt.[3]	
	He ȝaf dome he seiþ and the bokys beþ openyd wide	
4545	And tho bokys schulle ben iseye at that tide	seen, time
	These bokys be conscyence and nought ellys	conscience

---

[1] A thin straight line separates these two words which are written close together. This is unusual because this scribe often runs words together or separates parts of words unnecessarily; thus someone else may have drawn the line.

[2] This is a scribal error for *were*.

[3] "He gave judgment and the books were opened" [adapted from Daniel 7:10. Douay-Rheims translates *Judiceum sedit* as *the judgment sat*; Morris' Northern version reads *Sedit judicium*, which its poet or scribe translates as *þe dome satt*].

	And þer of þe glose on this manere tellis f. 59r	
	Consciencia omnib(us) revelabitur[1].	
	Concyence he saiþ of all man(er) þynge	
4550	Schal ben ischewyd to mannys knowynge.	
	How mennes synnes schull hem accuse	
	Here synnys also boþe more and lesse	
	Schullen hem acuse as the boke bereth wytnesse[2]	
	Ffor stolyn thing acuseþ a þefe þ(er)wiþ ifounde	thief
4555	Whan it is aboute his nekke faste ibounde	
	Right so her synnys schulle hem acuse þere	
	As a boute hur nekke ibounde that þey were	
	Thanne schulleþ her synnys seye thus:[3]	
	O þu synful man thu wrouʒtest us	committed
4560	And we beþ þyne wiþ outen eny doute	any
	For þu hast long tyme iboren us aboute.	carried
	Holy writt . how schall hem accuse.	
	Also acuse hem schal al holy writ	
	And namly hem þat knowiþ it	
4565	Oþur þe p(er)elys haueþ ilernyd þat bifalleþ þ(er)to	happens
	And wolde nat aftur þe holy writt do.	follow
	How godes creatures . schull hem accuse.	
	Ʒut schulleþ godys creatures þere	
	Acuse hem also . in dyv(er)se man(er)e	
4570	As þe sonne and þe mone and þe sterrys an hy	stars
	And þe firmament that is to us here ny	near
	And al þe world that þanne be ʒare	ready
	Hem to acuse and to bryng in care	
	Ffor alle maner creatures hem hate schal	
4575	Whan that he is wroþ þat is makere of al.	angry
	How þe fendes schull hem accuse.	
	Alle þe deuelys schullen hem acuse sore	
	Of alle her synnes boþe lasse and more	
	And of þe synnys that þey spared out to speke	refrained
4580	And hadde drede þerof þat god wolde be awreke	avenged
	Of alle þis þey schulle hem acuse þere al a brod	broadly
	As a þef doþ an noþur . þat in þefte wiþ hym abod	thief, theft, abides
	And acuse hym of þat same thyng	
	Þat he wiþ hym dede þorow his eggyng[4]	provoking
4585	The fendys han iwryte . al synnys in her þought	
	For þe whiche mannys soule may to peyne be brought	

---

[1] "Conscience will be revealed to all" [Walafridus Strabonis, *PL* 114, col 294 but Walafridus also sees it as "the conscience of all"].

[2] The last two words are written over an erasure, and at an inclining angle, perhaps indicating haste. H.M. 125 adds four lines here.

[3] The personification and speaking of man's sins is clever and effective.

[4] H.M. adds two lines here: "ffor to devils schulle be redy at the dome
That to tempte men euyr bethe j come."

	And alle the synnys eche of hem reherce kan	f. 59v	recount can
	And þerfore thus seyþ iob þat holy man		
	Scribis eni(m) cont(ra) me amaritudines et		
	*p(er)mittis cont(ra) me scribi p(e)cca(ta) mea*¹		
4590	He seiþ lord þu suffredust as it lykyde þe		you wished
	Myne bittur synnes to be wryton aȝenst me.		
	How þe aungels . schullen hem acuse.		
	Angels also ihere clerkys sugge		say
	Schullyþ grete resons aȝenst hem alegge		make allegations
4595	Ffor whi . god that her soulys to hem toke		
	Hem forto kepe as it is wryte in boke		
	Schal aske of hem at his down comynge		
	Acountys to ȝelde of her mys kepynge		poor stewardship
	Thanne schulleþ þe aungels answere there		
4600	And seye þat aftyr our conseyl þey nolden don here²		advice, would not
	Ac aȝenst our wille þey wolde her folyes use		follies follow
	Thus schulleþ þe angels þe synful acuse		
	How þe heþene men schull hem acuse.		heathen
	Also þe heþene men that were in uvel eu(er)e bold		evil, aggressive
4605	Ne crystendom ne trewe fey neu(er) take wolde		true faith
	As iewes and sarsens and paynems³ manyon		many a one
	Þat ne knoweþ nought how godes lawe scholde be don		
	Ȝut þey schulle hem acuse wiþ a stordy mood		fierce temper
	And seiȝe ȝe false crystene men þat neu(er) dede good		say
4610	Howe mowe ȝe excused be of ȝoure ipocrysye		may, hypocrisy
	Þat þoughten god to bygile wiþ ȝo(ur)e folye.		trick
	Ffor þe heþene men at thuke grete asise		assembly / inquest
	Schulleþ ben iholde as men ryght wise		held
	As to regarde of false crystene men		in comparison with
4615	Þat wolde nat kepe godys hestys ten.		commandments
	Wherefore thei schulleþ haue þe more peyne		
	For þey dispendyd hur wittys all in veyne		wasted, five senses
	In þe put of helle that more schal hem greue		pit
	Than the heþene men . that beþ of mysbileue		false religion
4620	**How þe halwes of heuene schull hem accuse.**		saints
	The halwes of heuene schulle hem acuse also		
	Þo that schulle be dampned and to helle go		
	And namly martyres . that beþ godys⁴ knyghtes		
	For þey schulle acuse alle synful wightes		creatures
4625	As wikede tirauntys that hem pyne and slowe		tormented, slew

---

¹ "For thou writest bitter things against me and allow any sins to be ascribed against me" [Job 13:26 and gloss].

² After God asks the angels why they did not protect the souls assigned to them, "Then shall the angels answer there / And say that the sinners would not follow our advice here."

³ Beside Christianity, Judiasm, Saracen, and Pagan beliefs probably represented all the then-known religious belief systems of the European medieval world.

⁴ H.M. 125 adds *owne* here.

	And alle oþur þat to [ ]¹ torment hem drowe	f. 60r	drew
	And eu(er)e of ven(n)iaunce þey schul to god crye		vengeance
	As the apoalips sayþ that wol nat lye:		Apocalypse
	*Usquequo d(omi)ne s(anc)t(u)s et verus . non vindicas sanguine(m) n(ost)r(u)m de hiis qui habita(n)t in terra.*²		
4630	That is to seie . holy lord and soþfaste good		true God
	Howe longe schal it be ar thu auenge our blood		before
	Of our enemys that ȝut on eorþe dwelleþ		
	On this manere þe apocalips us telleþ³.		
	Of hem that soffreþ wronges here.		
4635	Þey þat haueþ soffred here any wrong		
	Of hure enemys that beþ in euel strong		their
	On þat day þey schull be acused sone		
	Of hem that of suche wrong makeþ her mone.		complaint
	How þe children schull acuse þe fadres.		
4640	Ȝut schulleþ the childrene⁴ þat unchastiȝed were		undisciplined
	Acuse her fadres and here modres þere		
	Ffor þey were recheles and somdel slowe		heedless, somewhat
	To chastise hem and to holde hem lowe		admonish
	And wolde no þyng hem teche of good þewes		morals
4645	As þe wise man in his boke schewys		
	*De patre impio conquerentur filii Q(uo)ni(am) p(ro)pt(er) ip(su)m su(n)t in obprobriu(m).*⁵		
	The sones he seiþ schul playne . þ(a)t it is þe fadres gult		complain, fault
	Of þat þey haue mysdo . for þey were to no lore ipult		learning pushed
	Ffor þorowe defaute of hem þey beþ for lore		lack, lost
4650	For þey ne lernyd no good . suþþe þey were bore		since, born
	And for defaute of gode disciplyne		lack
	P(er)chaunce thei may be dampnyd into helle pyne⁶		
	And þe fadur also may be wiþ hem ispild		destroyed
	For he haþ nouȝt in hem godes heste fulfild.		command
4655	**How þe pore schull acuse þe riche.**		
	Ȝut þe pore men schulleþ playne by right		complain rightly
	Upon þe ryche men afore godys sight		before
	And þanne hem acuse and ofte rehercy		repeat
	Þat of hure nede nadde no mercy		had no
4660	To helpe hem f(ro)m myschefe þorow almysdede		almsgiving
	Ne þat þey wolde hem neyþ(ur) cloþe no fede		neither
	Ac in gold and seluer . was alle her triste		trust
	And alle þey wolde into her tresour þryste		would cram / thrust

---

¹ A small space of about two letters remains after an erasure.
² "How long, O Lord, holy and true, dost thou not judge and revenge our blood on them that dwell on earth?" [Apoc. 6:10].
³ Four lines follow in H.M. 125.
⁴ H.M. 125 calls the children "sones and douȝtres" here and elsewhere.
⁵ "Because of a reprobate father, the children will weep, who are in disgrace because of him" [Taken from Ecclesiasticus 41:10, derived from *De Abundantia Explorum*].
⁶ "… damned to the punishment of Hell".

	And þerof to þe pore wolde naught ȝiue	f. 60v
4665	Thow þey for myschef to deþ were idryue	hardship, driven
	Therfore þe lust of þulke foule monee	desire, money
	Thanne aȝen hem sone iwryte schal be	against, written
	And for þat mouȝtys han ibred¹ wel þykke	moths, bred
	In her cloþes it schall be to hem a wel sory p(ri)kke	very woeful time
4670	Alle þeos on þat day to witnesse schull be brought	
	For þat in myschefe þe pore þey holpe nought.	hardship, helped
	How þe suggettes schull accuse hure sou(er)aynes.	subjects, sovereigns
	They þat were suggettys to any mannys s(er)vise	
	Schulleþ here sou(er)eyns acuse in this wise	their
4675	That haueþ hem greuyd þorowe myght and maystrye	authority
	And ofte wiþ wrong wiþ hold² her salarye.	wrongly, payment
	Of þe benefices that god haþ ido to man.	helps
	The beneficys that god haþ do to man here	benefits
	Schulliþ hem acuse in dyuerse manere	
4680	Aȝen hem crist schal a legge wel sone	declare
	What he haþ for hem ido boþe in ȝifte and lone	gift, reward
	And reherce his benefices³ boþe more and lasse	enumerate
	To repreue hem of here unkyndenesse	reproach
	Of þe torment of crystes passion.	
4685	Also þe torment of cristys passyo(u)n	
	Þat he suffrede for mannys sa(l)uacio(u)n	
	Schal hem acuse at thulke grete dome	this
	For þus seiþ þe good man seynt jerome:	
	Crux testimoniu(m) cont(ra) te portabit . cicat(r)ices .	
	*dei cont(ra) te loqu(en)(ur) clavi de te conq(ue)ren(ur)*⁴	
4690	He seiþ [ ] þe crois on þe whiche he⁵ wolde⁶ deye for man	cross, would die
	Schal aȝenst þe synful sowles plete than.	plead then
	And god also wiþ his swete woundys wide	
	Schal harde aȝen hem alegge in þe same tide	make allegations
	And the tokens of his woundys schal make a speche	
4695	Aȝen hem and contynuellyche aske hem of wreche	vengeance
	And þe nailes þat in hond and foot⁷ were stonge	pierced
	Schul playne wiþ þe blood þ(a)t was on hem iclonge.	Complain, dried up
	How þe holy trynyte schull hem accuse.	
	At þe laste god hym selfe . þ(a)t is most of myght⁸	
4700	And þe holy trynyte . schull hem acuse outryght	
	Boþe fadur and þe sone and þe holy goste.	
	Þerfore þulke acusacion . schal be þe moste.	This

---

¹ H.M. 125 reads *red* for *ibred*.

² H.M. 125 reads *bynome* rather than *wiþ hold*.

³ H.M. 125 says *benefetes* rather than *benefices*.

⁴ "The cross will bear witness against you; the wounds of God will speak against you; the keys will complain against you" [Peter Comestor, alluded to by Thomas Aquinas, and by Jacobus de Benevento, *De praeambulis ad judicium*, on-line corpus Thomisticum, p. 15. Neither mentions Hieronymus / Jerome. Hanna and Wood attribute the quotation to Jerome in *De Abundantia Exemplorum*].

⁵ The next line and a half in H.M. 125 reads he " … for man deye / Shal þanne aȝaynes þe synful man preye."

⁶ This word *for* at this spot in the manuscript is an unnecessary repetition of *die for man*.

⁷ In H.M. 125, "hys wounds" replaces "hond and foot."

⁸ An interesting pattern of marked caesuras has been scribed here.

	For the secunde p(er)sone than all þyng schal deme f. 61r	
	Þat is goddys sone þ(a)t men there schal seme.	reconcile
4705	**Of þe streit acountes þ(a)t men schull ȝyue at þe dome.**	
	Alle þat comeþ bifore crist in þat day	
	Schulleþ acountys ȝelde er þey passe away	yield
	Of alle hur life that þey on eorþe ladde	followed
	Wheþ(ur) þey to good drow oþur to badde	drew
4710	And þat schal afore al þe world be schewyd	shown
	Þat alle men schulleþ knowe boþe lered and lewed	
	And bifore al þe wikkyd men also	
	Þat schulleþ be dampned to endeles wo	
	And alle men schulleþ be þere boþe good and ille	
4715	Forto deme and to be demed aftur godes wille[1]	judge
	Ffor þus in þe saut(er) it is iwryte	
	David bereþ witnesse as he haþ undurȝete	perceived
	Advocavit celu(m) desursu(m) et t(er)ra(m)	
	discern(er)e p(o)p(u)l(u)m su(um)[2]	
	He seiþ he schal do bifore hym calle	
4720	Þe heuenes aboue and the eorþe þ(a)t is down falle	
	Rightful dome on that day forto alegge	judgment, make allegations
	And so muche is þis vers forto segge	say
	He schal bifore hym calle heuenes schunyng[3] bryght	shining
	Þat beþ undurstonde holy men and parfit	perfect
4725	The whiche wiþ hym þanne in dome schull sitte	
	And wiþ hym deme by conseyl of here witte	counsel
	Ac þe eorþe is naught elles forto telle	
	Bot wikked men and foule fendys of helle[4]	filthy fiends
	How men schul ȝiue aco(u)ntes of all her tyme and of eu(er)y moment[5]	
4730	Thanne schalle eu(er)y man ȝiue rekenynge	accounting
	To telle of ech a tyme of alle his leuynge	life, lifetime
	Ffor þanne schulleþ men streyt acountys ȝelde	correct
	Of alle her tyme boþ ȝong and elde	
	And of alle þe tymes þat God haþ here isent	
4735	And specially of ech a tyme and moment	
	Ffor no moment schal þanne be untolde	
	As bernard witnesseþ þ(er)of many folde	many times
	Sicut non p(er)ibit capillus de capite . ita non erit momentu(m)	
	de t(ot)o no(n) habem(us) diem reddere racione(m).[6]	
	He saiþ as non her of alle our hed	hair
4740	Schal nouȝt p(er)eische ne þ(er) fro be reuyd[7]	perish, pulled / plucked
	Right so þ(er) schal be no moment	

---

[1] H.M. 125 adds these lines: "ffor criste þat is rightfulle domesman
                  Schalle iche man þer call þat þere lyfe wan."

[2] "He shall call heaven from above, and the earth, to judge his people" [*Psalm* 49:4].

[3] Possibly a spelling error or just an unusual form; the Middle English Dictionary and LALME: Linguistic Atlas of Late Mediaeval English include *shonyng* and *shonnen*.

[4] H.M. 125 inserts: The whiche he schal call after his own wille
                     Ffor to deporte oute the goode from þe ille.

[5] H.M. 125 includes   A moment of tyme in name oþer thynge
                      And a schorte tyme of ane eghes twynkelynge.

[6] "Just as a hair from your head will not perish, so there will be no moment at all for which we do not have to render an account" [Bernard, echoing *Luke* 21: 18, *PL* 184, col. 1198].

[7] Perhaps the scribe intended "reuvyd." H.M. 125 writes "þerfro be byreued."

Part V. Ten Signs of Doomsday (4742–4779)

    Of al þe tyme þat god haþ to us ilent   f. 61v

    Of þe whiche we mote ȝiue a rekenynge   *must*

    In tyme of þe laste daies comynge

4745   **How men schull ȝiue aco(u)ntes of eche an ydel word.**   *give accounts*

    Also þey schal ȝelde a countys in certeyn

    Of eu(er)e ydel word that is ispoke in veyn

    As holy wryt þ(er)of bereþ witnesse

    Þe raþur that we leue þe wordes of ydelnesse   *sooner, quicker*

4750   *De omni verbo ocioso reddenda est rac(i)o.*[1]

    The boke seiþ schortly on þis manere

    That of eu(er)y idel woord that is spoken here

    A reso(u)n schal be ȝolde þ(er)of wel aright   *given*

    At þe day of dome bifore godys sight[2]

4755   Ffor excuse hem mowe þey nowt   *may*

    Noþur of idel speche ne of idel þouȝt[3]

    Wherefore our lord that sitteþ on heuene hie

    Thus spekeþ bi his p(ro)fit isaye   *Isiah*

    Venio ut congregem cogitac(i)ones eoru(m)

        cu(m) gentib(us) . ad iudicandu(m) illas

        sicut dum indicabo gentes.[4]

4760   He seiþ y come to gadre wiþ men aboute

    Þe þouȝtis of men wiþ ynne and wiþ oute

    Fforto deme hem alle boþe more and lasse

    As y schal the men deme þorow rightfulnesse

    Sore ouȝt eu(er)y man to drede þerfore   *Greatly should, fear*

4765   Þat haþ iþought ful ydelly suþþe þat he was bore   *thought, since, born*

    Wherfore seynt gregory in his boke seiþ þis

    To make us be war to thenk ought amys:[5]   *anything*

    Sic deus vias uniuscuisque considerat ut nec cogitac(i)nes

        Que apud nos sunt in iudic(i)o indiscusse remaneant.[6]

    He saiþ god that al wisdom kan   *knows*

4770   So biholdeþ þe weyes of eu(er)y man

    That þe leste þought þat eu(er) þought we   *thought*

    At þe dome schal naught induscussed be   *undiscussed*

    And nauȝt only of eche an idel word and þought

    Bot of alle idel werkes . that man haþ wrought

4775   **How men schal ȝelde acountes nought only**

    Of þe dedes of elde . ac of þe dedes of ȝouþe.

    Ȝet þey schulleþ acountys ȝelde   *give*

    Nouȝt only of þe grete dedys of elde

    Bot also of al the dedys of ȝouþe   *youth*

---

[1] "For every idle word ... an account shall be rendered" [adapted from *Matt.* 12:36].

[2] H.M. 125 adds: "That noghte onely of jdal wordes spekyng / And of eche ane jdal þoght be which is aȝens godes pleding."

[3] H.M. 125 includes: "That þei spokyn or þoght sith þei had witte / Of theye were neuyr afore with itte."

[4] "I come that I may gather their thoughts together with ... the nations ... [to judge them, just as] I will the nations" [adapted from Isaias 66:18].

[5] " ... be careful not to think wrongly."

[6] "Thus God regards the ways of each of us so the thoughts that we have are not left unexamined at the judgment" [As Hanna and Wood note on p. 337, ultimately from Gregory *Moralia in Job* 1, *PL* 76, col. 194, but the poet has taken the quotation from *De Abundantia Exemplorum*].

4780	F(ro)m tyme þat þey any wit couþe	f. 62r	knowledge know
	That þey haueþ ido by nyght or be day		
	Wherfore ȝe may here salamon say:		
	Letare iuvenis in adolescencia tua, et in bonis actibus		
	Sit cor tuu(m) in dieb(us) iuventutis tue . et ambula		
	in viis cordis tui et in intuitu oculoru(m) tuoru(m).		
	Et scito q(uo)d pro hiis o(mn)ib(us) adducet te		
	d(eu)s in iud(ic)iu(m).[1]		
	He seiþ þow ȝong man be glad and blyþe		joyful
4785	In tyme of ȝouþe that passeþ swiþe		youth
	And þat þyn herte in goodnesse be set faste		steadfast
	Whiles þe dayes of ȝouþe mowe laste		may
	And in the weyes of þyn herte þat þu go		
	And in þy sight of þyn eyen two		eyes
4790	And wite þu wel for al þyn ȝonghede		know, youth
	Our lord þe schal to þe dome lede		judgment
	Where þat resons schulde be holde wel clere		
	And þ(er)fore seiþ iob on this manere:		
	Et consum(er)e me vis peccatis adolescencie mee .[2]		
4795	He seiþ lord þu wolt waste me al to nought		exhaust / use up
	Thorow þe synnys of ȝouþe that y haue wrought.		committed
	How men schull ȝelde aco(u)ntes of þat þei haue offended god þorow		
	They schulleþ ȝiue also acountys among	**heryng**	hearing
	Nat only of that they haue don wiþ wrong		
4800	Wytyngly þorow [þorow][3] her owne knowynge		Consciously, own
	Bot also that þey haueþ mysdo þorow herynge		sinned, hearing
	As idel talys and bagge bitynge þat þey hereþ alday		tales, backbiting
	And þ(er)to ȝiueþ good ere and seiþ nat onys nay		ear, once no
	Of þe whiche no man hym self excuse kan		can
4805	As in a book openly thus telleþ a wise man		
	Pro om(n)i errore adducetur homo in iudiciu(m).[4]		
	He seiþ for eu(er)y thyng that is into erro(ur) torned		sin turned
	Good or euel that may be g(ra)ntyd oþ(ur) werned		refused
	Man at þe laste day þ(er)fore schal be lad		led
4810	To þe dome that schal hym sore make adrad.		judgment, afraid
	And þ(er)fore david in þe saut(er) book telleþ us		Psalter
	How dredful he was whan he saide þus:		fearful
	Et ignorancias meas ne memin(er)is[5]		
	Lord he seiþ bithenke þe nought		consider
4815	Of myn euel unknowyng of þought.		thought
	How men schul ȝelde aco(u)ntes of euery euel p(ri)uy dede.		

---

[1] "Rejoice, therefore, O young man, in thy youth, and let thy heart be in that which is good in the days of thy youth, and walk in the ways of thy heart, and in the sight of thy eyes: and know that for all these God will bring thee unto judgment" [Ecclesiastes 11: 9].

[2] "... and thou wilt consume me for the sins of my youth" [Job 13:26]. The scribe has failed to underline this Latin quotation as he has the others.

[3] Duplicate word is crossed out here.

[4] "For every error, man will be brought into judgment" [adapted from Ecclesiastes 12:14].

[5] "Do not remember my ignorance" (... According to thy mercy remember thou me for thy goodness' sake") [Psalm 24:7].

Part V. Ten Signs of Doomsday (4817–4855)

    They schulleþ acounyys ȝelde as y in book rede   f. 62v   yield, read
    Nat only of eu(er)y open euel dede
    Ac of eu(er)y euel dede that is preue   secret
4820 That semed to her sight a good dede to be   seemed
    Ffor some dede his euel that semyþ good here
    And þerfore seynt gregory seiþ on this manere:
    Interdu(m) sordet f(a)ctu(m) oculo iudicis quod fulget
        oculo factoris[1]
    He seiþ sum dede is foul to þe domys mannys sight   judge's
4825 Þe whiche to þe doer þ(er)of schyneþ bright
    Bot þat at þe dome schal be discussed clene   fully
    As þe saut(er) book þ(er)of doþ us mene   Psalter
    Cu(m) accep(er)o temp(us) ego iusticias iudicabo.[2]
    He saiþ whan ischal take my tyme aright
4830 Þanne y shal deme rightfulnesse þorow myght.   power

How men schul ȝeld acco(u)ntes of þe seuene werkes of m(er)cy.[3]

    Ȝet bihoueþ eu(er)y man as wel as he kan   must
    Ȝiue good acountys bifore þe domys man
    Nat only of werkys that he hath ywrought   accomplished
4835 Ac also of þe dedes that he dude nought
    As of þe werkes of m(er)cy and almys dede also
    That he dude nought as þe book acordeþ þerto
    Esurivi et non dedistis michi manducare
        Sitivi et non dedistis michi bibere.[4]
    That is to seie y hongrid and ȝe nolde me fede
4840 Y ferstede[5] sore and no drynke ȝe wolde me bede.   thirsted, offer
    Thus god alle þe dedys þat beþ of m(er)cy
    To þe synful man wole þanne rehercy.   rehearse

How men schull ȝiue acountes of her soules.[6]

    Men schul also acountys ȝelde   yield
4845 Of her soules that þey han to welde
    Of þe whiche þey schullen answere ȝyuen   give
    Of all þe tyme that they on erþe leuen   live
    Ffor ȝif a kyng oþur a lord þat were riche[7]
    Hadde a dought(er) that were to hym lyche   daughter, similar
4850 Of fayrnesse and of face and of body semynge   bodily appearance
    Whom þat he loued specially ou(er) all thynge
    And þouȝt to make here a lady of wurschipe   honor
    And bitawȝt here a man to kepe   bestowed
    Thanne ȝif þat man kept here amys   poorly
4855 Me thynkeþ it were no wondur of þis

---

[1] "Sometimes the deed that shines in the eye of the perpetrator is contemptible in the eye of the judge" [Gregory I *PL* 75, col. 690].

[2] "When I shall take a time, I will judge justices" [Psalm 74:3].

[3] The heading of H.M. 125 reads "How man shulleþ ȝyue acountes atte day of dom of þe dedes of þe seuene werkes of mercy þat þai haveþ noȝt ydo in here lyf daies." The text of H.M. 128 is generally tighter than that of H.M. 125.

[4] "For I was hungry, and you gave me not to eat: I was thirsty, and you gave me not to drink" [Matt. 25: 42]. These two lines follow in H.M. 125: "þas to segge as ȝe schulle yhere afterward
    How god wole ȝive a sentence þer of swiþe hard."

[5] The form *ferstede* is an attested variant of *thirsted* in MED as found in *Book to a Mother* in MS Bodley 416.

[6] This heading of H.M. 125 adds: "Afore god atte dredful day of dome."

[7] This narrative vignette is an allegory by which the poet maintains interest, stirs emotion and instructs his audience.

	They¹ þe kyng wolde haue of hym rekenynge²	f.63r	Though, accounting
	And a resonable answere of þulke kepynge		
	And þe more wurce that sche were by ʒemed		graver, cared for
	þe more greuouslokur that man schold be demed		grievously
4860	Ffor it semyþ wel that he haþ encheso(u)n		occasion
	To putte hym [^to] p(re)soun for his treso(u)n		
	What schulde thanne þe kyng of heuyn do		heaven
	To men and wommen that doþ so		
	To wham he haþ by take forto kepe here		entrusted
4865	His dought(er) to hym boþe leue and dere		beloved
	That is mannys soule that his owne liknesse is		
	Al þe tyme that sche doþ nought amys		wrong
	The whiche he þought coroune to his quene		crown
	In heuene where schal no sorowe be sene		
4870	Ac he³ þat her kepeþ rechelsly and ille		carelessly
	He schal be aresound . al aʒenst his wille		called to account
	Of þat ilke kepyng that he of god toke		
	As seiþ þe wise man þus in his boke:		
	*Custodi solicite a(n)i(m)am tuam*⁴.		
4875	That is on this man(er)e to undurstonde		
	Kep þi soule wel þ(a)t no fend here bryng to schonde.		devil, destruction
	Ac⁵ he ys wel that⁶ thus seie may		
	In þe tyme of deþ at his endyng day		
	I ʒelde my soule at this deþes schour		yield, clamour / attack
4880	To þe my lord iesu þat art my savyour.		
	How men schal ʒelde aco(u)ntes as wel of her sowles but also of her bodye.		
	Men schullen also acountys ʒelde		give
	Nat only of þe soule that þey myght welde		be in possession of
	Ac of here bodyes also that beþ wiþ oute		
4885	That þey hadde to kepe and to bere aboute		
	Of þe whiche þey schullen ʒiue a good rekenynge		
	Suþþe þey haueþ ihad þ(er)of þe kepynge		since
	Ffor euery mannys body may wel be itold		
	A castel þat is y mad to ben astrong⁷ holde		castle, defense
4890	That is iʒoue to man of god forto kepe		given
	For his owne prophyt and godes wurschepe eke		honor also
	Ac envye assaileþ [ ]⁸ it wiþ sawtes swythe harde		assaults, so
	And þ(er)fore to us saiþ thus seynt bernarde:		
	*Bonu(m) castru(m) custodit qui corpus suum honeste custodit.*⁹		
4895	He seiþ a good castel and a strong kepeþ he		

---

¹ The translation begins "No wonder that / though the king would have accounting of them ..."
² "Though the king would demand from him ..."
³ A thin line is drawn between these two run-on words, *he þat*.
⁴ "Keep ... thy soul carefully" [adapted from Deut. 4:9].
⁵ The upper segment of the letter A is colored with red ink.
⁶ H.M. 125 adds *sikerly* here.
⁷ These two words *a strong* are run together in the text.
⁸ A small erasure occurs before *it*.
⁹ "He maintains a good fortress who guards his body honorably" [Bernardus, *PL.* 183, col. 418].

Part V. Ten Signs of Doomsday (4896–4935)

  Þat his owne body kepeþ eu(er)e in honeste.   f.63v

How men schul ȝelde acountes of her bodies and her soules togidre.[1]   yield

  Men schulleþ acountys ȝelde also
  At þat day of dome er þey hennys go

4900 That day schall be sodeyn for the none[2]   indeed
  Nouȝt only of her soulys by hem self alone
  Ne only of her bodyes that beþ þ(er)by .
  Bot of boþe to gidre boþe ioyntly[3]   together
  That is to seie . eche schall as he kan

4905 Ȝelde acountys hollich of a ful man   wholly, with both body and soul
  Ffor propurly men may nat a man calle   actually
  Bot ȝif þe body and þe soule to gidre falle   are joined
  Ffor þe soule by her self ys man non
  Ne þe body wiþ oute soule ys bot flesch and bon   flesch, bone

4910 Ffor þese clerkys þat konneþ muche of clergie   are very steeped in theology
  Calleþ an ynner man and an utter man in þis wise   outer
  The ynner man is þe soule soþ forto saye
  And þe utter man þe body þ(er)to forto laye .
  And þus þe body and þe soule right bitwene hem two

4915 Soþly þey makeþ o man and no mo.   Truly, one, more
  Therfore men schull . ȝelde acountys soþly   yield
  Of boþe to gidre þe soule and þe body.[4]

How men schull ȝelde acountes nat only of he(m)self ac of her ney3bo(r)s.

  Men schullen acountys ȝiue of her neyhȝebore   neighbors
4920 Þat he be nat for myschef lore   wickedness lost
  That is to seye . þat eu(er)y man aftur his myght   power
  Schall his neyȝebore helpe in alle right
  And þey þat mowe hem helpe . and wolleþ nought   might
  Schulleþ þanne to harde acountys be brought.

4925 **How fadres schul ȝelde acountes of her children.**

  Also fadres and modres at domes day
  Schulleþ ȝiue acountes wiþ oute nay
  Of her children that þey forþ brought
  For no chastisment on hem þey wrought

4930 Ac soffreþ hem to do at her owne wille   allow
  So longe tyll þey begonne to spylle.   began, perish

How lordes schull ȝelde acountes of her mayne.   household

  Also lordys þat haueþ s(er)uauntys hem aboute
  And soffreþ hem to become sterne and stoute[5]   allow, bold, brave
4935 And wole nat do on hem no iustificacyon[6]   will not punish / rectify them

---

[1] The heading of H.M. 125 is "How men schulleþ ȝere accountes noȝe only of þe soule by here self and of þe body by hit self but of boþe to-gadre enioyned."

[2] H.M. 125 reads "and sone" rather than "for the none."

[3] H.M. 125 reads "Bote of boþe to-gadre al ioynyngly."

[4] H.M. 125 adds a four-line summary here.

[5] H.M. 125 reads "proute" here.

[6] The word *iustificacyon* is written over a very neat erasure.

	Bifore god þey schull make þ(er)of a declaracyon.	f.64r	accounting
	How maistres schull ȝelde acountes of her desciples.		scholars
	And maystres of her disciples also		
	Schul ȝelde acountys for þey unchastised lete hem go		
4940	And chastised hem nouȝt forto lere		learn
	Þ(er)fore seiþ salomon on this manere.		
	Virga discipline fugabit stulticia(m) in corde pueri colligata(m).[1]		
	Þe ȝerde he seiþ of discipline smerte		rod, correction severe
	Schal driue folie f(ro)m þe childys herte		
4945	Wherfore maistres þat doþ wel[2] undurstonde		
	Schulde kepe her children eu(er) undur hond.		
	How p(re)lates schull ȝelde acountes of her suggettes.		subjects
	P(re)latys of hie ordre and dignyte		
	Schullen acountys ȝiue in dyuerse degre		
4950	Of hure suggettys that þey be kept out of strif		their
	And that he rewele hem in ensample of good lif		rule
	Ffor answere he schal for hem ȝif þey lyued not wel		lived
	As þ(er)of bereþ witnesse þe p(ro)phet eȝechiell		
	Ecce ego requira(m) gregem meu(m) de manu pastoris.[3]		
4955	God seiþ þus þorow þe holy p(ro)phetys mouþ		
	Lo y wol aske my flokk[4] þat is to me couþ		known
	Þe herde þat hem hadde undur honde		shepherd
	Þ(er)fore it were good þat prelotys wolde þis undurstonde.		prelates
	How men schull ȝeue acountes of the goodes þ(a)t god haþ to he(m).		
4960	Men schulleþ also to rekenynge be idryue	ilent	driven
	Of alle þe goodes þat god haþ to hem yȝiue[5]		
	Of þe whiche þey nolden in no wise bede		would in no way offer
	To þe pore that þerto hadde nede		
	Ffor alle we beþ on o body on eorþe here		one
4965	As þe apostel witnesseþ on þis manere		apostle [Paul]
	Omnes eni(m) unu(m) corpus habemus.[6]		
	He seiþ we beþ alle o body in þis lyue		one, life
	Þat haþ dyuerse lemes to make it to pryue		limbs, prove it
	And as þe lemes of a body beþ ȝare fer and nere		prepared far, near
4970	In al maner þyng aftur here powere		according to
	To s(er)ve þe oþur lemes boþe wiþ ynne and wiþ oute		limbs
	Of suche office as it bereþ hym aboute		as it is entrusted to him
	Riȝt so eche a man þat here on eorþe lyueþ		
	Of þat good þat god þorow his grace hem ȝiueþ		
4975	Oþur schulde helpe . [hem][7] and serue at nede		Or

---

[1] "Folly is bound up in the heart of the child, and the rod of correction shall drive it away" [Proverbs 22:15].

[2] H.M. 125 replaces "wel" with "doe not."

[3] "Behold ... I will require my flock at [the] hand [of the shepherd]" [adapted from Ezechiel 34:10; the text literally reads; "Behold, I myself come upon the shepherds, I will require my flock at their hand"].

[4] H.M. 125 adds "of shep" here.

[5] H.M. 125 adds twenty-two lines here descussing goods suchs as strength, beauty, discretion, love or contemplation, honor, and riches.

[6] "For we all have one body" [Loosely adapted from I Corinth. 12:12 which actually reads "all members of the body, whereas they are many, yet are one body."]

[7] The word *hem* is crossed out in the manuscript.

Part V. Ten Signs of Doomsday

	And wiþ oute askynge of hem þ(er)of bede.	f.64v	some of it
	Ac wel many men liueþ here in wo		
	And to hem wol riche men no good do		
	Thouȝ þat he be myghty and gret of hous hold		Though, household
4980	Þey soffreþ hem in mysese manyfold		allow, in distress
	Ffor þey [þey]¹ þenkeþ nought on þulke laste day		nothing
	Where þat þey schulleþ nat answery onys nay		once
	Of hure mysdedes þat þey haueþ wrouȝt		their sins
	Where þorow her neyȝebors beþ in care ibrought.		on account of which, neighbors
4985	Also men of lawe schulden do her travaile		work
	To helpe oþ(ur) in nede wiþ her good consaile		advice
	And leches þat beþ in fisik wise		physicians, medicine
	Schulleþ to þe seek men don her s(er)uise		sick
	Hem forto helpe wiþ alle her conning²		knowledge
4990	And þorowe goddes grace hem to hele brynge		health
	And þese clerkes þat beþ maistres of science		masters
	Schulde teche oþ(ur) that they mowe make defence .		might
	Aȝenst þeos eretikes that distruyen godes lawe		heretics, destroy
	And wolde wiþ her erro(ur) oþur to hem drawe		deviation / aberration
4995	And prechours that conneþ godes word preche .		know
	Scholden to oþur men þe wey of lif teche		
	Ffor þus is eu(er)y man holde wiþ good entente		bound
	Oþ(ur) to helpe þorow grace . that god hem sente		Other(s)
	Ffrely for godes loue and nouȝt elles		else
5000	For so seynt petre in his epistel telles		epistle
	Unusquisque sicut accepit gracia(m) illam		
	*ministrare debet.*³		
	He saiþ eche man that haþ grace fonde here		
	Þorow Godes sonde . in thulke same manere		grace
	He schal it mynistre and forþ bede		provide, offer
5005	To euery man that haþ þer to nede		
	And þus is eu(er)y man iholde forto do		bound
	As in the gospel crist seiþ þus þerto		
	*Gratis accepistis gratis date . et c(etera)*⁴		
	He seiþ as ȝe haueþ fonge grace frely of me		received freely
5010	As frely ȝiueþ it to eche a man in his degre		each man according to
	Thus schull þey ȝiue resons good and sad		
	Of all the grace þat þey on eorþ had.		
	Of eu(er)y day in all her lif dispended in veyn		dissipated
	And of ech a tyme and in eche a moment in certeyn		for certain
5015	And of eche an idel word and þought		

---

¹ The word *þey* is also crossed out in the text.
² A minim may be missing here, so the word appears to read *coming*, although the clear intent is *conning*.
³ "As every man hath received grace, he ought to minister it [to another]" [adapted from 1 Peter 4:10].
⁴ "Freely have you received, freely give" [Matt. 10:8]. This citation reads *date*, the second person singular imperative of *dare*.

	And of echa idel dede . that man haþ iwrought¹	f.65r	committed
	Oþur in his elde oþur in his ȝowþe		
	Oþur on eorþe go oþur spoke wiþ his mowþe²		earth, mouth
	Aftur þe tyme that he ferst couþe		could
5020	Knowe euel and good boþe þanne and nouþe		now
	Of all thes thinges they schull be asked þat day		
	To loke of all men . who hym excuse may		look upon
	Ffor þere schal no thing ben ihud		hid
	Ac þorow harde acountys it schul ben icud		made known
5025	Thanne wel is thulke man and wom(m)an		this
	That a good rekenynge þ(er)of ȝelde kan		account, yield can
	So þat he may at þat tyme passe quyt³ and fre		excused
	Of alle þyng that to hym may rekenyd be .		
	And to alle hem may right wel be tyde		happen
5030	Þat haueþ charite euere by here side		
	Ffor he þat haþ in charite here good endynge		
	Schal [ ]⁴ þere liȝtly passe þulke rekenynge.		this
	Of hem that schulleþ deme and of hem þat		judge
	Schulleþ nougȝt deme and of hem þ(a)t schull be		not
5035	**Idemed and of hem þ(a)t schulleþ nat be demed.**		
	At þe day of dome as ihaue bifore tolde		judgment
	Euery man schal be boþ ȝong and olde		
	And þidur come schull boþe goode and ille		thither
	Of here lyuynge to here [to here]⁵ godes wille.		
5040	How þey schull be demed after thei han wrought		done
	Ac som(m)e of hem schul deme and som(m)e nought⁶		
	And þey that schulleþ deme and demed be nought		
	Schulleþ parfit men be in dede and in þought.		Should perfect
	They that schull be demed . and deme none oþ(ur) creature		
5045	Schulleþ come to blysse . and þ(er)of be ful sure		joy
	Ac som(m)e schul be demed and to helle wende		go
	To soffre sorowe and care eu(er) wiþ outen eny ende.⁷		forever
	Ac alle tho that be leueþ nought as do we		those believe not
	Schulleþ noþur deme neyþur demed be		judge nor be judged
5050	And for þat þey nolde to our trewe fey come		will not, true faith
	Þ(er)fore wiþ oute dome thei schul to helle be nome.		taken
	Ac thei that wiþ god schull deme on that day		
	And nought be idemed ne brought in no afray		fear / dismay
	Schul be þey that here forsoke the worldes solas		
5055	And folowyd in al ryghtfulnesse cristes pas.		path

---

¹ A strip at the bottom of this folio has been cut out to within a half inch of the binding; the outer dimension of the excision is about 1 1/2 inches, and the inner dimension about 3/4 of an inch. It does not impede reading of the folio.
² The third and fourth lines of this folio are reversed in H.M. 125.
³ H.M. 125 writes *whit* for *quyt*.
⁴ A good-sized erasure of about four letters remains in this space.
⁵ The repetitive *to here* is crossed out several times, less neatly than other textual emendations of the scribe. Two lines are inserted into H.M. 125 here.
⁶ Six lines are inserted into H.M. 125 here.
⁷ H.M. 125 says "Where sorwe and care ys wiþ-outen ende."

152 Part V. Ten Signs of Doomsday (5056–5094)

	As holy apostles and oþur many mo	f.65v	other, more
	That for his loue heere suffred suche wo[1]		here suffered, sorrow
	They schul oþur deme for thei wiþ crist dwelleþ		judge, dwell
	As hym selue [telleþ][2] in þe gospell telleþ:		
5060	*Vos qui secuti estis me: sedebitis sup(er) sedes*		
	duodecim . iudicantes duodecim trib(us) Israel[3].		
	He seiþ ȝe that folowed me here in lyuynge		life
	Schulleþ sitte on twelf setys demynge		twelve seats judging
	The twelþe nacions of Israel wiþ oute strif		conflict
	Ac that ben thei that here in trewe fey ladde her lif.		those who, true faith
5065	But some schul nouȝt deme bot her dome take		judge, judgment
	For here charite schal hem rightful make[4]		justified
	And somme schull nought deme ac be idemed		condemed
	To the peyne of helle and fro crist be flemed		pain, put to flight
	As thulke that beþ fals cristene men		those, false
5070	That wolde nat kepe godes hestis ten		ten commandments
	And wolde nat by her lyue forsake her sinne		life give up
	Ac whiles thei leued eu(er)e dwelle þ(er)ynne.		lived
	And som(m)e schul nought be demed at that day		judged
	For thei schul to peyne go that lasteþ ay		always
5075	As paynymes and saraȝenes that holdeþ no lawe[5]		Pagans, Saracens
	And iewes that our lord haueþ islawe.		slain
	Therfore thei schulleþ to endeles peyne go		pain
	Wiþ oute dome for holy wryt telleþ so.		judgment
	Qui sine lege peccant . sine lege p(er)ibunt.[6]		
5080	He seiþ þo þ(a)t wiþoute lawe usen her synne .		commit
	Wiþ oute eny lawe . schul perisch þ(er)ynne[7]		any, perish
	Wel hard men schulleþ that day ise		see
	Whan alle thing schul thus discussid be		discussed
	And on that day schal no man thus be excused		
5085	Of thing that he haþ wiþ wrong iused		wrongly committed
	That sowneþ into euel in any maner dede		tends toward
	Of the whiche he hadde in his þought no dred		fear
	Ne þe synful man schal there no m(er)cy haue		
	For þer may no goodnesse hem saue.		
5090	Ffor whi he schal thanne no help wynne		Therefore, obtain
	Of servaunt no advoket that beþ quyut of synne		advocate, freed of
	Ne of non othur that kan for hym plede		can, plead
	Ne hym to consail wisse ne rede		counsel, guide, advise
	Ne none halwes schulleþ for hym p(re)ye		saints, pray

---

[1] H.M. 125 ends this line with "angres and wo" rather than "suche wo."
[2] The repetitive *telleþ* has been crossed out in the manuscript.
[3] "... you, who have followed me, ...you ... shall sit on twelve seats judging the twelve tribes of Israel" [Adapted from Matt. 19:28].
[4] H.M. 125 adds the following here: "ffor þat hui fulfillede þe werkes of merci
　　　　　And no dedlisinne þer after reherci" [deadly sin].
[5] Apparently a medieval misconception or belief.
[6] "For whosoever have sinned without the law, shall perish without the law" [Rom. 2:12].
[7] H.M. 125 includes:　"And þerefore at þat day of dome j-wis
　　　　　Alle man schal haue als he worthy is."

5095	That myght þe domes mannys wraþþe alaye	f.66r	judge's wrath allay
	Ffor as þe boke [seiþ]¹ þ(er)of bereþ witnesse		
	Þere schal no thing be shewyd bot ryghtfulnesse		shown, righteousness
	And grete reddure wiþ outen eny mercy		violence
	To þe synful that schulleþ thanne perischy.²		perish
5100	And to helle wende . wiþ grete affray		go, fear / dismay
	And þerfore men mowe wel clepe that day³		may, call
	The day of wraþþe and of wrecchidnesse		wrath, wrechedness
	Þe day of bale and bitturnesse .		sorrow
	Þe day of playnynge and of acusynge		complaint
5105	Þe day of answere &⁴ of streit rekenynge		straight accounting
	Þe day of iugement wiþouten eny lisse		leniency
	Þe day of angur and of anguisse		anguish
	Þe day of drede and of tremlynge		
	Þe day of wepynge and of weylynge⁵		wailing
5110	Þe day of cryenge and no thing to wynne		crying
	Þe day of sorowe that schal neu(er) blynne⁶		cease
	Þe day of mornynge and of grete affray		mourning, fright
	Þe day of departynge f(ro)m crist al away		completely
	Þe day of lourynge and of gret derknesse		looking sullen
5115	Þe day that is last and most of swartnesse .		deepest darkness
	Þe day that God schal make an ende of alle		
	Þus men may discreue þat day and calle.		describe, name
	Of þe fynall dome that god shal ȝyue.		
	Øwr lord crist that is full of witte		Our, wisdom
5120	At the laste day of dome schal sitte		
	As a kyng and rightful domes man		
	Al þe world to deme as he wel kan.⁷		can
	Ac how that he schal deme . y þenke . here⁸ . schewe		I think, here show
	As þe gospel telleþ . of seynt mathewe.		
5125	*Ang(e)li aute(m) domini . sep(ar)abu(n)t malos*		
	*A bonis sicut pastor segregat hedos ab agnis.*⁹		
	He seiþ his angels thanne after his wille		according to his desire
	Schulleþ departy þe good fram þe ille		separate
	As þe schepherde doþ þe schep fro þe gete		goats
	And bryngeþ hem in pasture that is no þyng wete.		wet
5130	By þe gete we mowen wel undurstonde		goats
	Wikked men that thanne goþ to schonde		destruction
	Ac þe good men schull be set on his right side		
	And the wikked on the left half . schulleþ abide		shall remain

---

¹ The word *seiþ* is lightly crossed out as redundant in the line.
² H.M. 125 adds four summary lines here.
³ H.M. 125 contains these lines here: "Þe grete day of fele delyueraunce
    Þe day of wreche and of veniaunce."
⁴ The only time the ampersand is used in this list is here.
⁵ H.M. 125 uses "foul goulynge"(howling) instead of "weylynge" here.
⁶ H.M. 125 writes "lynne" instead of "blynne."
⁷ H.M. 125 includes six extra lines here.
⁸ "But how He will judge I intend here to demonstrate/show/reveal, As the Gospel of St. Matthew tells it."
⁹ "However, the angels of the Lord will separate the evil from the good, as the sheperd separated the sheep from the goats" [adapted from Matt. 25:31-32]. This quotation appears to be the Southern Recension's poet's addition to the Main or Northern version and does not appear in Morey's or Hanna and Wood's editions, although a brief reference to angels is provided by them.

154 Part V. Ten Signs of Doomsday (5134–5172)

	¶ Thanne schal god seie wiþ a mylde steuen	f.66v	voice
5135	To hem that stondeþ on his right side of heuene:		
	Venite benedicti patris mei p(er)cipite vobis.		
	Regnu(m) . quod [est] paratu(m) est ab		
	origine mundi.[1]		
	He schal þanne seye comeþ now to me		
	My fadres blessed children now beþ ʒe		faher's
	And resceyueþ þe blysse that is to ʒow idight.		joy, prepared
5140	F(ro)m the begynnynge of the world . as ʒour owne ryght[2]		
	Ffor y hongred sore and ʒe me fedde at need .		hungered greatly, fed
	Y þristed sore and drynke ʒe wolde me bede		thirsted, drink bid
	Of herborowe as a pilgrym grete nede y hadde		lodging
	And gladly into ʒoure yn . ʒe me ladde.		inn, led
5145	Naked i was and hadde aboute me no cloþ		
	And ʒe me clothed warme forsoþ.		indeed, warmly
	Syk y was and brought into heuy[3] state		Sick, severe
	And ʒe me visitede boþe erly and late		
	And whan iwas ibounde in prison ful ille		bound, badly
5150	ʒe comen to me wiþ wel good wille.		
	¶ Thanne schulleþ the rightful men for hem alegge.		offer justifications
	And to our lord answere thus and segge		say
	Lord whan sie we þe hongry for any fast[4]		saw, hungry, abstinence
	And fram us was any mete to the ykast		food, given
5155	Whan myght we þe . þristy ise		thirsty see
	And we ʒoue þe drynke . wiþ herte fre		give, heart free
	Whan we sie the for nede herborow c(ra)ve .		shelter need
	And we herborwed þe thi body to saue		sheltered
	Whan we sie þe wiþ oute . cloþes and naked		saw
5160	Othur in prisone or in body sike imaked .		sick made
	Whan we visidede þe wiþ all our wille and myght .		
	And conforted the as it full be ryght .[5]		comforted by right
	¶ Thanne schal our lord answerie hem thus		
	And soþli seie as the gospel telleþ us .		
5165	*Quod uni ex minimis meis fecistis . michi fecistis.*[6]		
	Whan any thing he seiþ ʒe hauen iwrought		done
	In any tyme or ellys for my loue yʒeue ought.[7]		else, given anything
	To any of the leste that ʒe myght ise		least, see
	Of myne . breþerne than ʒe dude it to me .		brethren, did
5170	Thanne schal our lord lufte up his honde[8]		lift
	To hem that on his lift half schull stonde .		
	And seie to hem . wiþ a sterne chere .		strict demeanor

---

[1] "Come, ye blessed of my father, possess you the kingdom prepared for you from the foundation of the world" [Matt: 25:34].
[2] The word *ryght* seems to have been added later in the same hand: it is written in a lighter ink, at an upward slant. The following injunctions are a rendering of the Corporal Works of Mercy.
[3] H.M. 125 reads "wycked" here.
[4] The left margin, starting at this line, is marked with dark smudges two to three inches into the text.
[5] H.M. 125 says "byfel to vs by riʒte" rather than "full be ryght."
[6] "As long as you did it to one of these my least brethren, you did it to me" [a partial quotation from Matt. 25:40].
[7] H.M. 125 reads "also and ʒyueþ ouʒt" for "or ellys for my love yʒeve ought."
[8] H.M. 125 states "marke wiþ hys honde" rather than "lufte up his honde."

	Þese wordes that beþ iwryten here	f.67r
	Discedite a me . maladicti in ignem et(er)nu(m)	
	Qui preparatus est diabolo et angelis eius[1] .	
5175	Ȝe cursed gostes wendeþ out f(ro)m my sight	go
	To þe peyne endeles þat schal to ȝowe be dight	prepared
	That is ȝare to the fend and to his angeles echone	ready, each one
	And thanne he schal speke to hem þus eftsone:	afterward
	Esurivi et non dedistis in manducare . sitivi et non	
	dedistis in bibere. hospes fui et non coligistis me . nudus	
	et non coop(er)uistis me . infirm(us) fui. et non visitastis me.[2]	
5180	I hongred and had deffaute of mete .	lack, food
	And ȝe ȝaue me no thing therto ete	nothing, eat
	I þristed and hadde of drynke grate nede	thirsted
	Ac ȝe wolde non to me bede .	grant
	Me wantede herborow and þat y souȝte ofte .	I needed shelter, sought
5185	Ac ȝe me nolde in bed leie softe	lie gently
	Naked and wiþ oute cloþ i was .	clothes
	And so clothles ȝe lete me pas .	without clothing, pass
	Syk y was and bedrede y lay	bedridden, lay
	Ac ȝe me visited noþur nyght ne day.[3]	
5190	In prison i was as ȝe þe soþe wiste	truth know
	Ac out me to fette . y ne myghte to ȝow triste	fetch, trust
	¶ Thanne schul þei answere wiþ sory chere .	
	And seie to crist[4] on this manere	
	D(omi)ne quando vidim(us) te esuriente(m) .	
	aut siciente(m) aut hospitem . aut infirmu(m).	
	aut nudu(m) et non minist(rav)im(us) tibi.[5]	
5195	Lord whan sie we þe[6] hongre and þurste	hunger, thrust
	Oþur of herborow haue any grete luste .	shelter, desire
	Or naked or sike oþur elles in prison be	
	And we in no thing wolde s(er)ve þe [?][7]	serve
	Thanne schal our lord answere [ ][8] agayn	
5200	And to hem þeose wordes seie in certayn:	say certainly
	Quamdiu unii ex minimis meis non fecistis . n(ec) in michi fecistis[9]	
	Soþly iseie to ȝow as it by falleþ therto	I say, happens
	In al the tyme that ȝe wolde no thing do	
	To on of the leste . that is to me icud	least, made known
5205	So longe was ȝour almys f(ro)m me ihud	charity hidden
	¶ Thus schal our lord þere rehercy	
	To the rightfull men þe werkes of mercy	
	To make openly hem to be knowe	

---

[1] "Depart from me, you cursed, into everlasting fire, which was prepared for the devil and his angels" [Matt. 25:41.]

[2] "For I was hungry, and you gave me not to eat; I was thirsty, and you gave me not to drink; I was a stranger, and you took me not in; naked, and you covered me not; sick, and you did not visit me" [Matt. 25:42-43]. H.M. 125 reads *susceptis* instead of *coligistis*. Neither Morey's nor Hanna and Wood's editions include this quotation.

[3] Some smudges, as on the previous folio, are located in the center of this folio starting here, primarily in the margin.

[4] H.M. 125 reads "oure lord" here.

[5] "Lord, when did we see thee hungry [or] thirsty [or] homeless [or] a stranger, [or] naked, and [did not minister unto thee?]" [Adapted from Matt. 25:37-39].

[6] H.M. 125 adds "haue" in this line.

[7] The scribe has not provided a question mark for this question. Both Morey's and Hanna & Wood's editions use a quotation mark here.

[8] A space remains here following the auto-corrected *e*; the remainder of a *y*-tail may be in this space.

[9] "As long as you did it not to one of these least, neither did you do it to me" [Matt. 25:45]. *Nec* has a dot above the *n* and *michi* has a perpendicular stroke through the *m*. H.M. 125 reads the first three words as *Quam diu vni* rather than *Quamdiu unii*.

156 Part V. Ten Signs of Doomsday (5209–5248)

	To grete wurschipe of hem . boþe hie and lowe	f.67v	honor
5210	And to the synful he schal schewe here unkyndenesse		lack of regard
	For that þei nolde þo werkes do wiþ myldenesse.[1]		Since they would not
	Ac whan god haþ þus itold and mad an ende		
	Þe synful men schull wiþ þe deueles wende		go
	To þe fuyr of helle . that neu(er) schal slake		slacken
5215	Bot an hidous cry than schul thei make .		
	And seie alas that euere were we wroȝt		say, created
	Into mannys kynde and into lyue ibroȝt		life brought
	Whi ne hadde god mad us so in the bygynnyng[2]		
	Noþur of wele ne of wo to haue y had felyng		Neither, happiness, woe
5220	Now we schulleþ brenne . in the fuyr of helle		burn
	And euere wiþ outen ende . there forto dwelle.		
	Thanne schal helle hem swolowe and sore bite		swallow, lacerate / gnaw
	Wiþ oute any lengor abod or any respite.		hesitation, delay
	And þanne al þe fuyr that eu(er) was ifounde .		fire, found
5225	Wiþ alle corrupcion that is aboue þe gro(u)nde		corruption
	And alle þe felþe hedes[3] þat foule schulleþ stynke		excrement of, stink
	Out of þe world thanne schulleþ synke		
	Down wiþ hem right into helle put .		pit
	To agregge her sorowe þat þ(er)ynne schull be schut.		aggravate, shut
5230	Ac þe rightful men as þe boke bereþ witnesse		
	Schulleþ wende to ioye . that is ful of goodnesse		go
	Euere there to be wiþ godes angels echone		each one
	Bright(er) schinynge than doþ sonne or mone .		shining
	Here may a man rede that haþ þ(er)to good gome		pleasure
5235	A ful long processe of þe day of dome .		
	Þe whiche a long tyme aftur[4] þat y haue red .		
	Scholde conteyne bi reso(u)n er it were isped.		contain, finished
	Ac ȝe schulleþ undurstonde and þe soþe iwite .		know
	As men mowen se in holy bokes write .		see, writtem
5240	That þorow þe grete wisdom and holy v(er)tu		
	And þe mechilnesse of our lord ihu		magnitude, Jesus
	Alle manere processe that schal be on that day		types of processes
	Þat any clerk kan speke oþur contreue may .		can, or contrive
	Schal þanne so schortly be sped and ido		concluded
5245	That unneþe þ(er)e schal be a moment þ(er)to .		scarcely
	A moment is of a tyme bigynnynge .		
	As schort as an eiȝes wynkynge .		eye's winking
	Thanne may this for a grete wondur be icud .		known

---

[1] Here H.M. 125 includes: "And for þe werkes of mercy ne were to ham leue
They schalle be to hem þan wel grete repreue."
[2] H.M. 125 uses *bygyr aynge* rather than *bygynnyng* here.
[3] H.M. 125 links *felþe hedes* together presumably to indicate *filthiness*.
[4] A fine slanted line has been drawn following the word *aftur,* seemingly to separate the two halves of the line. This is an unusual punctuation mark for this scribe; he usually uses a caesura or punctus which functions as a comma, with spaces before it. This is seen in the large number of caesuras at the end of lines on this page which tend to appear in clusters.

	The whiche god haþ eu(er)e in his pryueite ihud	f.68r	secrecy hid
5250	That in so schort atyme of his comynge thanne		
	Schal deme þe dedes of eueryche manne		every
	Ac of this scholde carpe noþur lered ne lewed		dispute, learned, ignorant
	For many as grete wondres crist haþ y schewed .		miracles shown
	Ffor as gret wondur it was whan that he wrought		amazement created
5255	Al þe world wiþ o word and to his kynde it brought		one, nature
	As the prophet david witnesseþ of this		
	That saiþ þus as in the saut(er) wryten it is.		Psalter
	Quonia(m) ip(s)e dixit et facta sunt.[1]		
	He seiþ god spak and al was don aftur his bone		as he wished
5260	And he commanded[2] and al thing was mad sone		done
	Thus in a schort tyme al thyng made he		
	More wondur thanne this is myght non be .		amazing
	Thanne may he as schortly make the endynge		
	Of alle thing as he made the begynnynge		
5265	Ffor to witty and myghty is he euere mo		prudent, powerful
	That to hym no thing ympossible is to be do		
	Therfore the processe of that day as y bifore tolde .		
	Alle men leuynge boþe ȝong and olde .		living
	Schulleþ se and undurstonde it al		
5270	As schort a tyme as bifalle schal.		short, happen
	How men schul be safe[3] . þorow m(er)cy p(er)chaced here in her lyue.		
	Alle that here haueþ m(er)cy God wol saue		
	And alle that askeþ mercy schulleþ it haue		
	ȝif they it be secheþ . whiles thei ben on lyue		beeseech, alive
5275	And trusteþ in god that he is of mercy ryue		abundant
	And wolleþ hem to amende and her synnes forsake		wishes, give up
	Bifore the tyme er that deþ hem take		
	And heere do oþ(ur)e [do][4] mercy and charite.		
	Thanne schulleþ þey mercy wynne and isaued be[5]		
5280	Ffor þey a man do neu(er) so muche synne		though
	ȝif he wole hym amende he may mercy wynne		repent
	Ffor þe mercy of God is so muche in echa tide.		each time
	That it arecheþ boþe fer and nere by echa syde		reaches, far
	And all þe synnes that a man may do.		
5285	It may aslake and þe peyne that bilongeþ þ(er)to		diminish, pertains
	And therfore seint austyn here seiþ þus		
	A good woord that well may conforte us.		
	Sicut sintilla[6] ignis in medio maris.		

---

[1] "For he spoke, and they were made" [Part of Psalm 148:5].

[2] The scribe has written *comannded* instead of *commanded* here.

[3] H.M. 125 adds "atte day of dom" here.

[4] The redundant word *do* is here crossed out in the text. H.M. 125 uses *to* for the first *do*.

[5] H.M. 125 includes six summary lines here.

[6] The manuscript reads *sintilla* rather than the correct Latin *scintilla*. "Like a spark in the middle of the ocean, so is each ungodly deed of man [compared] to the mercy of God" [(Ennarationes, in Psalm 148.5), and attributed to Augustine in *Speculum Christi,* but also to Bernard *in Fasciculus Morum.*] This quotation continues on f. 68v.

Sic om(n)is impietas viri ad mi(sericord)iam dei. f. 68v

5290	As a lytle sparcle of fuyr seiþ he	fire
	Ys a myddes the gretness of the se	amidst, sea
	Right so litil is a mannys synne	
	Aȝenst the mercy of god who so may it wynne .	redeem

How mercy passeþ all mennes synne.

	Heere men mowen se what ys m(er)cy	may
5295	Þ(a)t fordoþ alle synnes and wol nat hem rehercy .	destroys, repeat
	Ffor whi ȝif a man hadde idon here	Therefore if
	Also muche synne and in as foul manere	
	As alle the men of þe world hauen iwrought	created
	Al may his mercy fordo . and bryng to nought	destroy, bring
5300	And ȝif it were possible as it may nought be so	
	That o man [may]¹ hadde as muche synne ido	one, done
	As alle men that eu(er)e were more oþ(er) lasse	
	Ȝut myght his mercy alle his synnes passe.	Yet, eliminate
	Thanne semeþ it wel as men may se .	
5305	That of his mercy is grete plenty	
	Ffor his mercy spredeþ in eu(er)y side	
	Þorow al þe world brod and wide .	
	And he scheweþ it by many weies and grete	shows, ways
	And therfore in the saut(er) thus seiþ þe p(ro)phete.	Psalter
5310	*Misericordia d(omi)ni plena est terra.*²	
	Þe eorþe he seiþ is ful of godes m(er)cy aboute .	
	Than dare no man þerof haue doute	doubt
	And he that haueþ m(er)cy . ar he hennes wende .	before, hence goes
	Than at þe day of dome god schal hym m(er)cy sende .	
5315	Where rightfulnesse schal only be haunted .	righteousness, practiced
	Ac no m(er)cy þ(er)e after schal be igranted .	

How þe world schall seme newe after þe dome.

	After þe dome al þe world þider ilad	conducted
	Schal seme as it were al newe mad.	
5320	Þe eorþe schal be euene and hol ouer al	level, whole
	And smoþe ynowe and clere as cristal	smooth enough, crystal
	And þe eyr aboue . schal shine swiþe bright	air, so
	For it schal be eu(er)e day and neu(er)e nyght .	
	And alle the elementys schal be fayr and clene³	
5325	That no corrupcion on hem schal be sene	
	Thanne schal the world . haue a fayr pris⁴	
	For it schal seme . as it were . paradys.⁵	

---

¹ The word *may* is excised in the text, and is probably another scribal error.
² "… the earth is full of the mercy of the Lord" [Psalm 32:5].
³ H.M. 125 reads "shuleþ alle be clene."
⁴ "Take the prize for beauty" .
⁵ As the scribe has progressed through this text, his errors have decreased until he is producing folios such as this one without any visible erasures, and only once does he cross off a repeated word.

	And þe planetys and þe sterres echone	f.69r	stars
	Schulleþ schine bryghtor than euere thei schone		
5330	And þe sunne schal be as many clerkys demeþ		clerks posit
	Seuene siþes briȝtor than it now semeþ		seven times
	Ffor it schal be as bright as it ferst was		
	Bifore that adam dude his trespas		committed his sin
	And þe mone schal be as bright and as clere		
5335	As the sonne is now that schineþ here .		
	And the sonne schal euene in the est stonde .		
	Wiþ outen eny meuynge ouer any londe		motion
	And þe mone schal be euene in þe west		
	No more t(ra)vayle ac eu(er)e be in rest .		work
5340	Right as þei weren set . at þe ferst bygynnynge		
	Whan that god hem made and alle oþ(ur) þynge .[1]		
	Ac þe mone and þe heuene goþ now aboute		
	And the sonne takeþ his cours al wiþoute		course
	And alle þe planetes meueþ echone		move, each one
5345	About in her cours as þey haueþ to done .		
	And alle the elementys kyndely doþ her myght		naturally
	Al thyng that is nedful to man forto dight .		prepare
	Thus god hem ordeyned forto s(er)ve mankynde		ordered
	Ac suche s(er)vise . me(n) schal nat þanne ifynde		find
5350	Ffor al manere of men after domesday anon		
	Schull be þere þey mut dwelle in flesch and in bon[2].		must, flesh, bone
	The good men schulleþ ben in reste and in pes		
	And the [world][3] wykked in peyne endeles		pain endless
	What nede were it þ(a)t þeose creat(ur)es scholde þanne		should
5355	Schewe eny suche seruyse to manne		show any, service
	Ffor no creature schal thanne be a lyue[4]		alive
	Þorow out al the world that men may discryue.		describe
	No thing schal thanne growe noþ(er) gras no tre		neither grass nor tree
	No scragges no roches þ(er)e schulleþ none be		outcroppings of barren rocks
5360	No dale, no hul, no montayne an hey		hill, mountain on high
	For al the eorþe schal be playn and euene wey		flat, even
	And be ymad as fayr and as clene		
	As any cristal is to a mannes eyȝe sene		eyes seen
	Ffor it schal be ipurged and ifyned wiþoute		refined
5365	As alle þe elementys beþ now aboute		elements
	And no more be travayled in no side		troubled, manner
	Ne no charge schal þer on abyde .[5]		burden

---

[1] H.M. 125 incluces: ffor þei were þan bryghter of ble
   Than þei beth nowe as iche man may se.
[2] H.M. 125 includes "as" here which clarifies the line; alternately, þere could be rendered there.
[3] The word world is crossed out in the text.
[4] In the left margin of this line is drawn a large X with a small circle in one quadrant, connected with a line to the word Ffor, perhaps to mark this passage.
[5] H.M. 125 offers 14 lines concluding the fifth part of this book, again warning of the pains of Hell.

Part VI. The Pains of Hell

Here bigynneþ þe sixte p(ar)ty of þis book þ(a)t spekeþ of þe peynes of helle.   f.69v

	Many man spekeþ and telleþ of helle	
5370	Ac the peynes þ(er)of fewe con telle	can describe
	Ac who so myght on eorþe iwete	be aware
	And wel knowe and þe soþe undurʒete	truth perceive
	What peynes þe synful schul fele þere	feel
	He myght þan heere haue grete fere .	fear
5375	Ffor men mowen be sore aferd to haue þ(er)on mynde	may, greviously afraid
	So bittur and so horrible þey beþ in her kynde	naturely
	Of þe whiche iwol ʒow telle right as ikan	I will, I can
	That beþ wiþ outen ende to þe synful man	
	As ferst iwol ʒow schewe . where is helle	
5380	As y haue iherd . clerkes þerof telle .	
	Somme clerkes seieþ as þey fyndeþ wryte ywis	find written
	That helle euene amyddes the eorþe is	in the middle of
	Ffor al the eorþe by reso(u)n y likned may be	earth, compared
	To a fayr round appul of a tre	
5385	The whiche in the myddel haþ a colke .	middle, core of fruit
	Ryght as amyddys þe ey is a ʒolke	Just, amidst, egg, yolk
	Ryʒt so his helle put as clerkes telleþ	pit
	Amyddes þe eorþe and nowher elles.	
	Ac ful muche and hidous is helle ikud	hideous, known
5390	For it is al wiþ ynne þe eorþe ihud	hidden
	And þidur schullen the synful be idryue	
	Al so sone as þe laste dome is iʒiue	
	Wiþ alle þe fendys þ(er)e eu(er) to dwelle	devils
	That now beþ in þe eyr, in eorþe and in helle	air
5395	Ac þere is so muche sorowe and bale	woe
	And so many peynes wiþ outen tale	number
	That thaw alle þe clerkes that eu(er)e hadden witte	knowledge
	And hadden al thing lerned . that is in holy wrytte	learned
	Kouþe ʒut nouʒt telle ne schewe þorow lore .	could, learning
5400	How many peynes þ(er)e[1] beþ eu(er) more.	
	Ac men mowen fynde wo so wol loke	may, whoso will
	Somme manere of peynes iwryten in boke	
	Ffro þe ferste byggynnynge into helle grounde	
	Among alle oþ(ur)e that beþ þer ynne ifounde	
5405	Ac þe man that in helle comeþ for certeyn	comes
	May nought so liʒtly þennes torne ageyn	lightly thence turn
	Ffor he schal there dwelle and neu(er) þennes come .	return

---

[1] The final *e* here has been inserted in a darker ink, perhaps as a correction.

	As þe boke of wisdom haþ þerof this sawe ynome	f.70r	saying received
	Non est agnitus qui reversus est ab inferis.[1]		
5410	That is to segge me(n) knoweþ none		say
	That comeþ fro helle the whiche is þider ygone		come back from
	Ffor alle that there beþ mowe dwelle for ay		must, forever
	For thennes they ne mowe be ibroȝt away .		thence, might, brought
	Bot ȝif hit were only þorow myracle oþur loue		unless
5415	And of the special grace of god that is aboue		
	Thorow wham some that in helle haueþ ibe .		been
	And the horrible peynes there myght ise		see
	Haueþ be out brouȝt fro al þulke strif		brought out, such
	And yturned aȝen fro deþ to þe lif		returned
5420	As laȝar that was maryes broþur magdaleine		Lazarus, Magdalene
	The whiche sie[2] þere many an hard peyne		saw
	Ffor his body in g(ra)ue lay foure daies .		
	After that he was ded as þe boke saies		says
	Ac at the laste god arered hym upright		But, raised
5425	F(ro)m deþ to lyue thorow his swete myght		
	Of that he þere sie he no thing forȝat.		saw, forgot
	Ac sone þer after whan he on lyue sat		alive
	Wiþ crist at þe mete in marthaes hows		food, house
	He tolde of peynes that beþ so hidous		
5430	Ac ȝut dorst he nouȝt telle þe peynes [of][3] alle .		But yet darest
	For drede of crist that sat in that halle		fear
	And he lyued þer after full fiftene ȝere		
	Ac he ne lowhe, neuer ne made good chere		laughed
	Ffor drede of deþ that he scholde efte sones die .		fear
5435	And for þe peynes that he saw he[4] . wiþ his yȝe		saw, eyes
	And two children that out come of symyones rote		Simeon's ancestry
	The whiche careyne and lentheryne . weren ihote		Caryn, Lentyn, called
	Whan that crist[5] diede on the rode		cross
	Thei arysen f(ro)m the deþ in flesch and in blod .[6]		
5440	And many oþur that weren dede þo		then
	Hauen be somtyme in þulke stede also		that place
	And iseye þere many an idous peyne .		saw, hideous
	And ȝet þorow myracle torned to lyue ageyne .		
	Bot among alle men that conneþ þ(er)of iwite		know of that knowledge
5445	I fynde only feftene peynes iwryte		
	The whiche mowen wel be told peynes of helle		may, called
	And whiche that thei ben iwole ȝow telle .		I will

---

[1] "No man hath been known to have returned from hell" [Wisdom 2:1].

[2] As seen here and various times above, *Sie / sye* are attested by LALME as forms of both sg. and pl. in Warwickshire.

[3] The word *of* is here crossed out.

[4] The sense of this sentence suggests that perhaps *he* should be cancelled.

[5] *Crist* has been emended by the *Piers* rubricator (*Piers* hand three), fitting it into a smaller space (perhaps where an abbreviation was previously written).

[6] Matt. 27: 52-53.

162   Part VI. The Pains of Hell

The ferst peyne is of þe fuyr of helle . and how hote it is.   f.70v

5450	The ferst peyne [^is] hote fuyr in his state	
	Þe whiche no man(er) thing may abate	kind of, lessen
	Where ynne the synful schul be peyned ay	always
	For god bi his prophete thus doþ to us say[1]:	
	Ignis succensus est in furore meo . et	
	ardebit usque ad inferni novissima.[2]	
	The fuyr is kyndled in my wraþþe saiþ he	wrath
5455	And schal brenne tyl an ende of helle schal be	burn
	Ac þat is eu(er)e more as god fowcheþ saue	vouchesafe
	For helle schal neu(er)e non ende haue.	
	That fuyr is so hot and euere brenneþ	
	That thei al the watur that stondeþ oþ(ur)e renneþ	though, runs
5460	In þe eorþe and in the seos wiþ oute	seas
	The whiche encloseþ þe eorþe al aboute	
	Scholde renne into thulke fuyr so hote	
	Ȝut myght it þerof nought quenche afote .	be quenched / extinguished
	Ffor as the fuyr that brenneþ here to our sight	
5465	Is hottere and haþ muche more myght	power
	Than a fuyr that is peynted on a wowe .	wall
	And is þeron peynted hie oþ(er) lowe .	high or low
	To mannys sight wiþ a rede colour	
	Þat no þyng brenneþ ne of fuyr . haþ odour	
5470	Right so the fuyr of helle is hatt(er) in his kynde	by nature
	Ac two fuyres thereof iwrite ifynde	written I find
	Qu(am) focus est mundi picto fervencior igne	
	tam focus inferni sup(er)at fervencia mu(n)di.[3]	
	He saiþ as þe worldyche[4] fuyr is hatt(er) yn his kynde	worldly / by nature
	Than is þe fuyr paynted that ȝiueþ no lyght bihinde	behind
5475	Right so þe fuyr of helle passeþ þorow myght of hete	surpasses, power
	Alle worldly fuyres boþe smale and grete .	
	Ac for that synful men brende in this wise	fashion
	Heore on eorþe in the synful couetyse	Here, greed
	It is ryght that he brenne and haue peynes sore	severe
5480	In thulke fuyr that lasteþ euere more	
	Of the grete cold that is in helle.	
	The secunde peyne is also gret colde	
	That synful schul fele boþe yong and olde	
	Thulke cold schal be so strong and so kene	fierce
5485	That they the moste roch that may owher bisene .	though, cliff, anywhere be seen

---

[1] Clearly *ay*, as the scribe wrote, should be *say*. The *s* of *us* may have confused the scribe. James H. Morey's edition of *The Prik of Conscience* from Osborn a.13, Beinecke Library, New Haven, specifies "Davyd" as the prophet here (p. 155, fol. 97v, 173). Morey notes the citation to Deuteronomy 33:22 is held to be by Moses, whereas David is associated with the Psalms.

[2] The poet's translation is quite literal here: "A fire is kindled in my wrath, and shall burn even to the lowest hell"[Deut 32:22, recurring in Jeremias 15:14 and Jeremias 17:41].

[3] "Just as the burning [fire] on earth is hotter than a painting of fire, so does the fire of hell surpass the burning fire of earth" [attributed to Augustine in *Fasciculus Morum, A Fourteenth Century Preacher's Handbook,* ed. Siegfried Wenzel, (University Park, PA: The Pennsylvania UP), p. 112; Augustine, perhaps an echo in *PL* 36, col. 569].

[4] Apparently the scribe omitted the second *l* in *worldlyche*.

	Oþur the moste montayn that is in any londe	f.71r	mountain
	Were al at ones turned into a fuyr bronde .		brand
	And a myddes thulke cold were set on		amidst
	Ȝut it scholde frese and torne into ys anon		turn, ice
5490	And fendes hem schullen f(ro)m that fuyr take .		fiends
	And caste hem into cold tyl thei bigynne to quake .		
	And þanne drawe hem from that colde place[1]		
	And eft caste hem into þe fuyr bifore þe fendes face .		
	Thus schul þey hem caste euere [caste][2] to and fro		
5495	And wiþ outen ende hem pyne so		hurt
	Of þis peyne þe holy man bereþ witnesse		
	Job that seiþ a good word of soþnesse .		truthfulness
	Ab aquis niviu(m) frigidis . t(ra)nsibu(n)t ad calorem nimium[3].		
	Owt of watres[4] cold he seiþ thei schullen wende .		go
5500	Into ouer muche hete that haþ non ende.		
	And seynt austyn seiþ on this manere		
	In a book as it is iwriten here .		
	Dicunt(ur) namq(ue) mali colore ignis candere		
	ext(er)ius . ut ferru(m) in fornace . et		
	int(er)ius frigere ut glacies in yeme .[5]		
	He seiþ þe wiked schul ben wiþute glowynge		glowing outside
5505	For hete as iren in the fuyr brennyngge		
	And wiþynne wiþ cold scharp and kene .		inside
	As it is in þe wyntres daies wel sene .		
	Of this word seynt Jerom witnesseþ to us		
	As it is here iwrite . and seiþ þus.		written
5510	*Inferni pene sunt hec . flamma . v(er)mis et*		
	tenebre . chorus demon(um) fetor frigus		
	fames sitis horror . flet(us) pudor morsus		
	s(er)pentu(m) mors et desperacionis.[6]		
	He seiþ þe peynes of helle[7] is cold and grete hete .		
	Wiþ oþur tormentes boþ scharpe and grete.		
	Of þe felþe and stynkþe that is in helle.		
	The þridde peyne that is in helle		
5515	Ys grete stynche as y here clerkes telle.		
	Of þis stynche seynt Jerom the good man		
	Seiþ þus in his book as y ȝow telle can:		other torments
	Ibi est ignis inextinguibilis . et fetor intollerabilis.[8]		
	There is fuyr he seiþ of so grete pouste		power
5520	That it may neuer aquenched be		
	And such felþe and stynke is in that hole		filth, stench
	That non eorþly[9] man may it þole		earthly, endure
	And ȝet þe fuyr þat schal hem brenne þere		

---

[1] The last four words have been auto-corrected; the erasure appears to extend beyond the line into the right margin.

[2] The repetitive word *cast* is crossed out here.

[3] "They will pass from icy waters to extreme heat." [*Job* 24:19, used in Innocent III's *De Miseria* ed. Lewis, III.7, p. 214 and *Fasciculus Morum,* ed. and trans. Wenzel, pp. 112-13].

[4] The texts reads *to cold* but the *to* is superfluous.

[5] "For the evil are said to glow on the outside with the hue of fire, like iron in the furnace, and on the inside, to freeze like ice in winter" [Honorius, *PL* 172, col. 1160]. Morey and Hanna & Wood provide "candere exterius calore" before the first causera.

[6] "The punishments of Hell are these: fire, the worm, and darkness, a chorus of demons, stench, cold, hunger, thirst, trembling [with dread], wailing, shame, bites of serpents, death and despair" [Honorius, *PL* 172, col. 1159].

[7] Although the Latin is clearly *sunt*, the scribe wrote "seynes of hell is ..." rather than *are*.

[8] "There the fire is unextinguishable, and the stench, intolerable" [Honorious, *PL* 172, col. 1159].

[9] It appears the scribe meant to write *eorþly* instead of *eorly* as appears in the text.

5525	Schal ȝiue a strong stynch among hem yfere .	f.71v	together
	Ffor it schal be full of pich . and of brymston .		pitch, brimstone
	And of oþur felþes þ(er)to many on		filths, one
	Ac for þe synful delited here al in folie		because, folly
	And in þe fulþede of foule lecherye		lechery
5530	Therfore it is right that thei euere among		
	Be in stench [ ]¹ þat is to hem no wrong		injustice
	Of the grete hongor that schal be in helle.		
	ℸhe feorþe peyne as iherde clerkes telle		
	Is strong hongour that eu(er) þere schal dwelle		
5535	The whiche synful men schull fele sore		feel extremely
	For eche day in helle² . it wexeþ more and more.		grows
	And þat hard hongor . schal hem so harde chace		
	Þat her owne flesch . þei schullen al to race .		scratch / claw
	And þei schul coueite for hongor it to ete .		covet, eat
5540	For þei schul þere to hem wynne non oþ(ur) mete		other food
	So þat for hungur þey schul bicome . as brayn wod		frenzied / mad
	For þe hard deþ schal be all her fod		food
	And þei schull ben fed wiþ þe hard deþes stounde .		hour of death
	Þerfore þus seiþ þe prophet . as y haue in boke ifounde		found
5545	*Mors depascet eos . et c(etera).*³		
	Þat is on engelisch þus forto rede		read
	Þat deþ hem schal deollfully fede		sorrowfully feed
	And he þat haþ here ⁴ no þing forto ete		
	Hym lusteþ þorow kynde most forto haue mete		desires naturally
5550	Right so⁵ the synful þat schulleþ dwelle		
	Schal more longy after deþ in helle		desire
	The whiche þey hateden and most dradden here		hated, dreaded
	Ac ȝut þey may nat die in no manere.		way
	Of þis word seynt Jon witnesseþ þis		
5555	As in þe apocalips it wryten is		apocalypse
	*Desiderabunt mori . et mors fugiet ab eis.*⁶		
	Þei schul willyn after deþ wiþ muche wo		sorrow
	And deþ schal euere fle hem fro		flee
	And þat is for þey nolde no mete ȝiue		because, would no food
5560	To þe pore that wiþ hongor were al to dryue		poor, pursued
	And hadden of hem noþur mercy ne reuþe		pity
	Bot lyued eu(er)e in glotanye and in untrewþe		gluttony, injustice
	Therfore it is ryght that þei haue þis penaunce.		
	Grete hongor in helle wiþ alle oþur meschaunce.		evils

---

¹ An erasure of about four letters was made here; the *h* of *stench* is unusual, flourishing to the right instead of the left.
² No doubt *elle* is an error for *helle*. No MED entry attests to the form *elle*, s.v. "helle," n.
³ "Death shall feed upon them" [based on Psalm 48:15, quoted in *Innocent III*, ed. Lewis, p. 215, a variant in *Fasciculus Morum*, ed. Wenzel, pp. 112-113].
⁴ An extra bit of space has been left here where a caesura mark might have gone; in fact, this and the previous are alliterating lines. Perhaps he is scribing the alliterative *Piers* text in this manuscript at the same time, or alternately.
⁵ The ink has smeared over the beginning of this line and the next.
⁶ "Men shall seek death … and death shall fly from them" [Adapted from Apocalypse 9:6, also quoted in *Fasc. Morum* ed. Wenzel, pp.112-113, and *Innocent III*, ed. Lewis, p. 215].

5565	**Of þe grete þurst þat schal be in helle.**	f.72r	
	The fiþe peyne þat to synful . schal bifalle		fifth
	Is grete þurst þat þey schal haue alle.		
	Ffor so muche in helle schal here þurst be .		
	Þat her heortes schulleþ ichined be .		hearts, burst open
5570	And þe flamme of fuyr þey schulleþ drynke .		
	Medled wiþ bremston that foule schal stynke .		mixed, brimstone
	And wiþ the smokes of fuyr and wyndes blaste		
	And wiþ oþur stormes that euere schal laste .		
	The whiche schulleþ þanne to gidre mete .		together meet
5575	As [ ] seiþ þerof þus . david þe p(ro)phete .		
	Ignis sulphur et spiritus p(ro)cellaru(m) pars calicis eoru(m).[1]		
	He saiþ þus as iwrite we mowen fynde		written, may
	Fuyr and brymston and stormes of þe wynde		fire, brimstone, storms
	A party schal be of hur drynke		part, their
5580	Y menged wiþ smoke þat foule schal stynke		mingled
	And ȝut þei schul drynke agenst her wille		
	Anoþur drynke that is more ille		disgusting
	Galle and venym sowr and no þyng[2] swete		Gall venom sour
	For þus it is iwryte by david þe p(ro)phete .		
5585	*Ffel draconu(m) vinu(m) eoru(m) et venenu(m) aspidu(m) insanabile*[3].		
	He seiþ galle of dragons her wyn schal be		wine
	And venym of addres þerwiþ seiþ he		venom, adders with it
	The whiche may be helud wiþ no leche		healed, physician
	So violent it is and so ful of wreche		wrechedness
5590	Thei schul þorow brennynge þirst to hem wynne		burning
	Þat her herte schal brenne as cole wiþ ynne .		
	Ffor no man(er) man [ ][4] þey schul fynde ne fele		perceive
	Þat may her þirst quenche and her hertes kele		cool
	And þis in holy wrytt eche man may fynde .		
5595	As iob telleþ whan it com to his mynde.		
	Capita aspidum suggent.[5]		
	He seiþ þey schulle for þirst þe heuedes sukke .		heads suck
	Of addres þat about hem schullen rukke		adders, lie coiled
	As a child þat sitteþ in his modur lappe		
5600	And lusteþ to sukke of her pappe .		
	But þat is for þey nolde wiþ good wille .		would not
	Ȝyue drynke to þe pore . bot for myschef let hem spille.		poor, die
	Þerfore it is ryȝtful þat þey in helle fele .		feel
	Brennynge þurst þat schal neuer akele .		cool

---

[1] "Fire and brimstone and storms of winds shall be the portion of their cup" [Psalm 10:7].
[2] A pitted spot touches the *g*, but does not penetrate the folio.
[3] "Their wine is the gall of dragons and the venom of asps, which is incurable" [Deut. 32:33 is the source; not David as the poet says].
[4] It appears the scribe wrote *man(er)* twice, and then erased the abbreviation sign, leaving *man* and a small space.
[5] "They shall suck the heads of asps" [Job 20:16]. The Vulgate Bible uses the singular forms *caput* and *suget*, but the scribe pluralizes them (*they* and *heads*). *Suggent* is an accepted variant for *sugent*].

Of þe gret derknesse that schul be in helle.

5605	The sixte peyn is ou(er) muche derknesse .	
	Þat in helle schal be and neu(er) mad lesse .	lessened
	Ffor so þikke it is þat men may it grope	
	Ac þe synful may it now3t away swope .	sweep
5610	Ffor no herte may þenke ne no tonge telle	
	Þe derknesse þat is eu(er)e in helle	
	Of þe whiche Job spekeþ and telleþ þis	
	And seiþ þe synful schul grope and fele iwis	grope, feel
	Eu(er)e a grete derknesse . and muche at mydday	
5615	As at mydnyght þe whiche lasteþ ay.	always
	Palpabunt teneb(ra)s in meridie ut[1] in media nocte.	
	Ffor in helle is neuer day ac eu(er)e nyght	
	And þere brenneþ fuyr ac it 3iueþ no li3t	light
	3ut þe synful schulleþ openly se .	see
5620	Alle þe care and sorowe þat þ(er)ynne schul be	anguish
	And echa peyne and eu(er)y maner torment	type of
	Þorow sparcles þat aboute schul ben ispreynt.	scattered
	Thus to eke her peynes þei schullen a sight haue	increase
	Wiþ outen any confort [2] þe wiche my3t hem saue	
5625	And for þat helle is euere li3tles ifounde .	lightless found
	It is clepud þe lond of derknesse into helle grounde	called
	Þe whiche is depe and derk and hidous wiþ alle.	
	Þerfore iob in his book þus doþ it calle.	
	Ut non rev(er)tar ad t(er)ram tenebrosam.[3]	
5630	He seiþ lord þat y torne now3t away .	turn not
	To þe derke lond . where sorow is ay .	always
	Ffor þe wonynge þere is hidous and ille	dwelling, horrible, bad
	As iob seiþ þis word more to fulfyfe.	
	Ubi nullus ordo s(e)d sempit(er)n(us) horror inhabita(n)s.[4]	
5635	Where þat non ordre is as seiþ he	
	Bot hidousnesse þat eu(er) more schal be	hideousness
	Ac for þe synful here in her lif	because
	Eu(er)e loued derknesse of synne and strif .	
	And nolde hem torne þ(er)fro while þei myght	would not, turn
5640	Ne neu(er) coueyted to come to godes sight .	
	Þerfore it is good ri3t þorow godes lore	teaching
	Þat þei dwelle in derknesse eu(er) more.	

Of þe hidous sight . of deueles þat is in helle

	The sefþe peyne of þe fourtene	seventh

---

[1] Hanna and Wood's version prints *sicut* instead of *ut*. The psalm reads: "They shall … grope … darkness at noonday as in the middle of the night." [Adapted from Job 5:14. Similar imagery occurs in *Innocent III*, ed. Robert Lewis, p. 215 which Lewis attributes to Job 10:20-22].

[2] An extra space is left where a caesura mark would have been made had this been an alliterative line.

[3] "… and I return no more, to a land that is dark …" [Adapted from Job, 10:21; *Innocent III* also quotes this; see Lewis, p. 215].

[4] "… where no order but everlasting horror dwelleth" [Adapted from Job 10:22; also quoted in *Innocent III*. ed. Lewis, p. 215; Douay-Rheims reads "A land of misery and darkness, where the shadow of death, and no order, but everlasting horror dwelleth." The Latin Vulgate states "terram miseriae et tenebrarum, ubi umbra mortis et nullus ordo, sed sempiternus horror inhabitat"].

5645	Is þe sight of fendys wherof ymene	f.73r	devils, together
	The synful schul hem ise that beþ in helle		
	In whos company þey schulleþ eu(er)e dwelle.		
	Þat sight schul be so foul and hidous to see		
	That all men that eu(er)e were in cristiente		Christianity
5650	Cowþe nought now þorow[1] wit ymagyne aright		could, reason imagine
	No descryue by no wey so hidous a sight		nor describe
	As þey schullen sen in helle eu(er)e more		
	Of fendes þat hem schul pyne sore		greviously
	Ffor þanne schul be in helle deueles mo		
5655	Than tonge may telle oþur rikne þerto		reckon
	And euerych of hem schal greflokur seme		more grevious seem
	Þan any man kan ymagine oþ(ur) deme .		consider
	Ffor so hardy is no man no so bold .		
	In þis world wide noþur ȝong non old .		
5660	That he myght aright conceyue in his mynde		
	How gretly a fend is in his kynde .		his by nature
	He ne dorste for alle þe good that eu(er)e was		dare
	Sen a fend here by hym make his pas .		see, passage
	Ffor no wit of man may þerto endure		mind
5665	To sen a fend in his p(ro)pre figure.		proper shape
	Ac þe synful schulleþ eu(er)e on hem loke		
	For þus we fynden wryte in boke.		
	In inferno videbu(n)t eos facie ad facie(m)		
	Quorum op(er)a in terris dilexerunt.[2]		
	Þey schullen se hem in helle face to face		
5670	Whos werkes þey loued and folowed her trace		track
	Whiles that they were heore on eorþe on lyue		
	For euere to do synne . þey hasted wel blyue.		hurried, quickly
	Þerfore þey schulleþ deolfully crie in gret sorowe		sorrowfully
	For seynt austyn seiþ that no þyng may hem borowe		preserve
5675	*Per sintillas ignis demones videbu(n)t et miserabile(m)*		
	Clamore(m) dampnatoru(m) audient.[3]		
	He seiþ þey schul se fendes many on		
	Þorow sparcles that out of þe fuyr schull gon		sparks
	And here þer wiþ in eu(er)y partye		
	The synful soules wepe and crye.		
5680	Ac þe sorowe and þe deol þat they schul make		anguish
	Schal neuer more cese no slake.		slacken
	Of þe horrible sight of v(er)myn that is in helle.		vermin

---

[1] A barely visible erasure occurs here, leaving a one-letter space.
[2] "In hell they will see face to face those whose deeds they loved on earth" [Perhaps parodic blending of 1 Cor. 13:12 and John 3:19 which read, taken together "We see now through a glass in a dark manner, but then *face to face* ... men loved *darkness* rather than the light for their works were evil"]. Italics highlight comparisons.
[3] "They will see demons through the sparks of fire and hear the wretched din of the damned" [similar to Honorius, *PL* 172, col. 1160].

Part VI. The Pains of Hell

	The eithþe peyne as þe boke telleþ us	f.73v	eighth
	Ys þe horrible sygth of v(er)myn venemous .		
5685	And of foule dragons and addres swiþe kene		adders so sharp
	And oþur foule bestes that beþ foul to mene		mention
	And alle oþur vermyn that is ful of venym[1] .		
	And wood bestes that beþ gresly and grym		mad
	Þe whiche wiþ her teþ schul hem byte.[2]		teeth, bite
5690	And alle her lemes wheron þey hadde delite		limbs
	Synful dedes to bigynne and worche		work
	Aȝenst þe lawe of God . and al holy cherche.		
	Ac for þey euere lyued . aȝenst Godes lawe .		But, ever lived
	Bestes and vermyn . þ(er)fore schul hem gnawe		
5695	Ffor her synne that to hem was so swete		
	Þerfore god seiþ þus by david þe prophete		
	Dentes bestiaru(m) immitta(m) in eos cu(m)		
	furore t(ra)henciu(m) sup(er) t(er)ra(m)		
	atq(ue) s(er)pentu(m)[3]		
	Y schal sende in the synful man seiþ he		
	Þe teþ of bestes that sterne schul be		teeth, strong
5700	Wiþ woodnesse drawynge into helle wel sone		madness
	And of addres harde gnawyng by þe bone.		
	This peyne þey schul soffre eu(er) mo		
	For that vermyn schal neuyr dye ne wend hem fro		
	And eu(er)e lyuynge wiþ hem dwelle		
5705	As our lord thus seiþ in his gospelle		
	Vermes eoru(m) non moriet(ur) . et ignis		
	eor(um) . non extinguet(ur).[4]		
	He seiþ that her v(er)myn schal neu(er) deye		
	No her fuyr schal aquenche by no weye		quench
	And to þis sawe þus seiþ seynt austyn		saying
5710	And spekeþ of þulke foule v(er)myn.		
	Vermis infernales su(n)t immortales . qui ut pisces		
	Vivu(n)t in aqua . ita ip(s)i vivunt in flamma.[5]		
	He seiþ the v(er)myn of helle schal eury lyue		ever
	The which is to þe synful man yȝiue		given
	The whiche schal lyue in þe leit of fuyre		light of fire
5715	As fisches in þe water mot nedes dure		must endure
	That vermyn schal eu(er)e on hem crepe		
	And on hem fasten here cloches wel depe.		claws
	Þe v(er)myn of helle schal be her cloþynge[6]		
	And wormes schul be her beddynge		
5720	Þey schul haue no cloþes forto gon ynne		clothes except vermin
	No bed bot the foule v(er)mynes skynne .		

---

[1] Several lines in this section display alliteration, although not necessarily in the "a . a . a . x" pattern.

[2] The poet's graphic descriptions are becoming even more grotesque and intriguing.

[3] "I will send the teeth of beasts upon them, with the fury of creatures that trail upon the ground, and of serpents" [not David, as the poet claims, but Deut. 32:24].

[4] "[Where] their worms dieth not, and their fire is not extinguished" (Mark 9: 46)

[5] One minim is omitted in *immortals*. "The worms of hell are immortal; just as fish live in water, so they live in fire" [Wernerus, *PL* 157, col. 922, Honorius, *PL* 172, col. 1160].

[6] They will have no clothing except the vermin.

	Wherefore ifynde iwrite as y haue red	f.74r	written, read
	How þe p(ro)phete descreueþ such a bed		describes
	To a kyng nabugodonoʒor was his name		Nebuchadnezzar
5725	Þe raþur þat he hym kepe out of blame		
	Subt(er) sternet te tinea . et v(er)mis		
	operimentu(m) tuu(m).[1]		
	He seiþ of wormes þi bed schal be		says, worms
	That schal ben istrewed þikke undur þe		strewn thick
	And þe couertour that þ(er)on schal be sene		coverlet
5730	Schal ben of v(er)myn swiþ scharp and kene.		so, bitter
	Thus schull þey be pyned for her synne		
	Wiþ oute wiþ fuyr and vermyn wiþ ynne		
	Ffor þus in holy writt we fynden iwrite		
	In þe boke of iudiþ wo so wol it wite:		Judith, who so
5735	*Dabit D(omin)us igne(m) et vermes in carnes eorum . ut*		
	Urant(ur) et puniant(ur) usque in sempit(er)nu(m).[2]		
	He seiþ fuyr and v(er)myn that eu(er)e schal lyue		
	Our lord to þe fleisch of synful schal ʒiue		
	So þat þis peyne is more to fele and to se		
	Þan alle þe peynes that on eorþ mowe be .		might
5740	Ac ʒut þ(er) aʒenst men may a reson fynde		in response to that
	For after þe laste dome men schull haue no mynde		judgment
	Of no wikked creature that any man telle can		
	Bote only of angel . deuel and man		
	Thanne how scholde in helle oþ(ur) owhere elles		anywhere else
5745	Any such v(er)myn [^ be][3] as men þerof telles		
	Oþur any oþur best that myght þe synful dere?[4]		injure
	Ac þ(er)to me(n) may ʒiue a good answere		
	On þis wise who so kan it speke		manner
	For þe vermyn that þanne schal out breke		break out
5750	It is nouʒt elles as y understonde		
	Bot deueles in vermynes lyknes men to fonde		torment
	That schulleþ bite þe synful sore		greviously
	To eke her peyne and to make it more		increase
	And for þe synful is full of trecherie		because
5755	Wraþþe and hatered, couetyse and envye.		
	Therfore it is reson þorow godes lawe		
	Þat þulke vermyn in helle eu(er)e on hem gnawe		such vermin
	How þe fendes schull þe synful bete.		beat
	𝕿he deueles schulleþ eu(er)e þe synfull bete		
5760	Wiþ glowynge ham(er)es huge and grete .		glowing

---

[1] "Under thee shall the moth be strewn, and worms shall be thy covering" [adapted from Isaiah 14:11].
[2] "The Lord will give fire and worms into their flesh that they may burn and may be punished forever" [adapted from Judith 16:21; *Innocent III*, ed. Lewis, p. 207. The Vulgate bible reads: "Urantur" and "sentient" for "veniantur" and "puniantur"].
[3] The word *be* is inserted in superscript in the text at this point.
[4] The scribe does not use question marks but this one has been added.

Part VI. The Pains of Hell

	Ffor as þe smyþes smyteþ on þe iren faste	f.74v	smiths hammer, iron
	So þat it brekeþ and bresteþ ate laste		bursts
	Right so schull þe fendes eu(er)e more dynge		strike
	Of þe synful soule wiþ out feyntynge.		fainting
5765	Ac so harde dentes 3af neu(er) non engyne		contraption / ingenuity
	As þey schulleþ 3iue as seiþ seynt austyn		

*Sicut machina bellica p(er)cuttit muros oppidi;
ita demones immo asp(er)ius et crudelius
corpora maloru(m) et animas flagellabu(n)t
post iudiciu(m).*[1]

	He saiþ as þe engyne is seie harde caste		seen
	And to þe walles of a castel strike faste		
5770	Wiþ huge stones heuy and grete		
	So schulleþ þe fendes þe synful bete		
	Ffor þey schulleþ eu(er)e haue power and leue .		permission gravely,
	Þe synful bodies sore forto greue		grieve
	As in a bok it is ischewed to us		
5775	That seynt austyn[2] made and seiþ þus		

*Parata sunt iudicia dei blasphematorib(us).
similiter Et p(er)cientibus cu(m) malleis
illoru(m) corpora.*[3]

	He seiþ þe domes schul eu(er)e be redy be wone		custom
	To the sclaundrers of crist godes sone .		slanders
	And þe deueles to hem schul be smytynge		
5780	Þe synfyl wiþ hameres sore bitynge.		hammers

Of the gnawyng of her conscience wiþ ynne.

	The tenþe peyne is gnawynge wiþ ynne		gnawing
	Of here conscience þat schul neu(er) blynne		cease
	Ffor hem wiþ ynne schall frete the worm of concience[4]		devour
5785	Þat þey mowe þ(er) a3enst make no deffence		may
	Ffor eu(er)e þey schul crye and grede weylawey		scream out
	And alas synge boþe nyght and day		sing
	What peyne and sorowe is to us dight		made
	For þe on crist bileued nought aright.		
5790	Thus schullen þei chide for her wikkednesse		
	And þus seie as þe bok bereþ witnesse:		

*Quid nobis p(ro)fuit sup(er)bia . quid divitiaru(m)
iactancai O(mn)ia velud umbra t(ra)nsieru(n)t .
et tanq(uam) nuncius p(er)curre(n)s et
Tanquam navis p(ro)cedens influente(m) aquam .
et tanquam avis Tr(an)svolans . cui(us)
itin(er)is. non est invenire vestigiu(m).*[5]

	What helpe us pride et[6] what may it avayle		benefit
	What bostyng of good et of cloþes riche ap(er)aile		boasting, apparel

---

[1] "As a battering ram strikes the walls of a city, so do demons, after judgment, whip the bodies and souls of the evil, but more harshly and cruelly" [source unknown].

[2] Clearly not capitalized. See note to line 5830.

[3] "The judgments of God are prepared for blasphemers, and likewise, blows with hammers for the bodies of fools." [Wernerus, *PL* 157, col. 923. N.B. Honorious, *PL* 172 col. 1160 seems clearer: "Sunt parata judicia blasphematoribus, et percutientes mallei stultorum corporibus: and blows of a hammer for the bodies of fools." A second reading might be: "… for blasphermers and likewise for those striking their (i.e., damned human) bodies with hammers"].

[4] The scribe has omitted the *s* from *conscience* here.

[5] "What hath pride profited us, or what advantage hath the boasting of riches [brought us]? All those things are passed away like a shadow, and like a messenger that runneth on, And as a ship that passeth through the waves, Or as when a bird flieth through [the air], of the passage of which no mark can be found" [Wisdom 5:8-11; also in Innocent III's *De Miseria Humanae Conditionis,* Lewis, p.207].

[6] The scribe has written *e(t)* on this and the next line.

5795	Alle þulke pride is nowe ibrouȝt ful lowe[1]	f.75r	such, brought
	And passeþ away as schadwe on þe wowe		wall
	And as a messag(e) þat is bifore goynge		messenger, preceeding
	And as a schip in full water seilynge		sailing
	And as a soule þat fleþ in þe eir by þe wynde		flies, air
5800	Of þe whiche men may no trace ifynde.		
	Thus schal her pomp aweiward make his pas		pomposity, away
	And eu(er)e be þer after as þyng þ(a)t neu(er) was.		
	Thanne schal hem þenke whan al þis is away		passed
	That al her lif nas bot as an hour of o day		one
5805	Thanne schul þei seie on this manere		
	Þouȝ þei neu(er) so longe hadden lyued here		
	Right nowe we were into þis world ibore		born
	And nowe we haueþ al our delites ilore.		delights lost
	Right nowe we died and gonne þenne passe		
5810	Ac nowe we beþ in helle boþe more and lasse.		
	Thanne schul þey knowe how þei ladde her lif .		
	Whan þat her concience hem bryngeþ in such strif		conflict
	Ac for that her concience stered hem nought		guided
	To forsake her folies that thei hadden wrought		give up, done
5815	Bot eu(er)e folowed her fleisches wille		
	Therfore it is reson that þei soffren ille .		reasonble
	And þat þe worm of concience hem gnawe and bite		
	For þat in alle vanytes þei hadden eu(er)e delite.		
	Of þe teres þat þe synful schul wepe in helle.		
5820	ℂhe synful schulleþ eu(er)e wepe as seiþ þe booke		
	What for sorowe and wraþþe for þiknesse of smoke		anger, density
	And þe teres of her yen schullen eu(er)e renne		eyes, run
	So sore þe smoke of þe fuyr schal hem brenne		severely
	And fram her yen so muche wat(er) schal falle		
5825	For þanne at ones wepe þei schull alle[2]		once
	And fro her yen it schal renne so stronge		eyes, profusely
	And her wepynge schal laste so longe		
	That in al þe world nowe as iwene		as I suppose
	Is nouȝt so much water isene.		
5830	Wherfore seynt austyn[3] in his book seiþ þus		
	Whose wordes beþ autentik to us		authentic
	In inferno pl(u)res effundent(ur) lac(ri)me . quam		
	gutte aque sunt in mari.[4]		
	In helle out sched schul ben seiþ he		poured
	Mo teres þan dropes of wat(er) beþ in þe se		More, sea

---

[1] This is an amazingly well-scribed page, with small, tight, even, accurate writing on which I can locate no erasures or emendations. A slice of parchment just over an inch wide has been taken out of the bottom of this folio.

[2] "For then at once, they all shall weep."

[3] It is unclear if the scribe intended to capitalize *Austyn*; the *a* is identical in shape but larger than the other *a*'s, but he does not use capitals for other proper names.

[4] "In hell, more tears will be shed than there are drops of water in the sea". [No exact source found but this is the antithesis of Hieronymus, *PL* 29, col. 438. Cf. Isidore Hispalensis, *PL* 83, col. 1298: "in inferno peccatorum lacrymae et stridor dentium:" "in hell, tears of sins and gnashing of teeth." Images of sea drops are also found in Rabanus Maurus, *PL* 109, col. 882. The Latin quotation also echoes images of Ecclesiasticus 18:8, in which drops are likened to days of this life].

5835	Ffor þe synful þere schulleþ eu(er) wepe	
	And her teres schul be of so grete hete[1]	
	That þe water þerof schal adown renne	run
	Fro her yen and hem scalde and brenne	eyes
	Ffor it schal be hattor þan eu(er)e was	hotter
5840	Any led molde or eny walled bras	lead mold, molten brass
	As i haue herde gret clerkes telle	
	That hauen descryued þe peynes of helle	
	And for þey hadden here eu(er)e lykynge	liking
	In here synnes and neu(er)e for þenkynge	renunciation / repentence
5845	Ne sorowe þ(er)fore ac þo3t it to hem eu(er) swete.	but thought
	Þerfore þei schullen in helle eu(er)e more wepe	
	And wiþ her teres be iscalded sore	scalded severely
	To eke her peyne and to make it more.	increase

Of þe schame that þe synfull haue in helle for her synnes.

5850	The twelþe peyne is schendschipe and schame	disgrace
	That þei schull haue in helle eu(er)y[2] bi his name	
	Ffor eu(er)y synne þat þei dude and was ihud .[3]	did, hidden
	Þere schal it openly be knowe and kud.	recognized
	Ac þat schame wiþ hem schal eu(er) laste	
5855	And þei ne mowe it away f(ro)m hem kaste.	may, throw
	Of all her synnes of þou3t and werk	
	As seynt austyn seiþ þe grete clerk:	
	O(mn)ia eorum [ ] p(ec)c(a)ta tunc	
	patebu(n)t(ur) . et se abscondere non valebu(n)t.[4]	
	Alle her synnes he seiþ schullen schewed be	
5860	And þey ne mowe hem hide ne nowher fle	
	And þey schull haue more schame for her synne	
	And more schendschipe þei schul to hem wynne	disgrace
	Thanne eu(er)e had here any man in his þou3t	
	For any dede that he on eorþe wrought	did
5865	Thanne may þei seie þat þ(er)e schul dwelle	
	As david in þe saut(er) here doþ telle	
	Tota die verecundia mea cont(ra) me est.	
	Et confusio faciei mee cooperuit me[5].	
	He saiþ my schame is al day a3enst me	
	And eu(er)e me pursueþ þat y encombred be	encumbered
5870	And þe schendschipe of my owne face	disgrace
	Eu(er)e me keuereþ in eu(er)y aplace.	covers
	Wherfore 3if þ(er) wer no peyne in helle	
	Bot only that schame wherof itelle	

---

[1] This *wepe / hete* couplet is an unusual rhyme pair: generally the poet's rhymes are more accurately matched.
[2] *Every* may mean *everyone*, or *ever*: "[shame] ... ever associated with his name."
[3] Occasional internal rhyme such as *dude* and *ihud* can be found throughout.
[4] "All their sins will be made manifest then, and they will be unable to conceal themselves" [Honorius, *PL* 172, col. 1160]. The space after *eorum* may represent an erasure. Honorius' diction here echoes that of Luke 8:17 and 12:2 and Apocalypse 6:16.
[5] "All the day long my shame is before me, and the confusion of my face hath covered me" [Psalm 43:16].

	It scholde þanne be to hem more peyne[1] f.76r	
5875	Þan any man on eorþe myght ordeyne	
	And for that thei here in her lyue	because of
	For schame of synne dorst hem neu(er) schryue	darest, confess
	Bot wiþ oute schame þ(er)of were bolde	disgrace
	Þ(er)fore it is right þ(a)t þey haue as y bifore tolde	
5880	Schame in helle for here synnes here ido	their
	Þe whiche þei wolde neu(er)e lete hem fro .	refrain
	Of þe bondes of fuyr wherwiþ þe synful schul be ibounde.	
	The þryteneþ peyne is wiþ oute bot	thirteenth, without remedy
	Þat is bondes of fuyr brennynge hote	fetters, burning
5885	Wiþ þe whiche þe synful schull ben ibounde	
	As in somme books iwrite it is ifounde	written, found
	Ac thulke bondes schulleþ neu(er) aslake	such bonds let up
	For þat þey nolde her synne here forsake	would not, give up
	Wiþ her synnes they God myspayed	displeased
5890	Wherfore in þe gospel þus he said	
	Ligate eis man(es) et pedes et mittite eos in teneb(ra)s ext(er)iores[2].	
	He saiþ byndeþ hem hand and fot faste	
	And into þe utter derknesse ȝe hem caste	throw
	Ac þat is into þe deppest put of helle	deepest pit
5895	Where more sorow is þan any tong may telle	
	Þus þei schulle be peyned in þis manere	
	Wiþ oþur peynes that sore hem schulleþ afere	greatly, frighten
	As a clerk seyþ to to us in opene heryngge	
	In a book that he made þorow his studyynge[3]	study
5900	That is cleped flos sciencie[4]	called Handbook of Knowledge
	And telleþ of dyuerse questions of dyvynite	
	And in þulke bok þus he bigynneþ to telle	
	Of þe peyne þat þe synful schull haue in helle	
	Capita eoru(m)[5] *adinvice(m) deorsu(m) versa et pedes sursu(m) sunt erecti et penis undique distenti*[6].	
5905	He saiþ in þe ground of hele dungeon	hell's dungeon
	Þe heuedes of þe synful schull be turned adown	heads, upside down
	And the feet upward iknyt swiþe faste	joined so tight
	And so into that put me [ ][7] schull hem caste	pit, throw
	Right þus in helle þei schul ben ibounde	
5910	And eu(er)e þ(er)e soffre many an hard stounde.	time
	The XIIII peyne is wanhope . þ(a)t þe synfull Schulleþ euere haue in helle.	despair

---

[1] A somewhat larger slice of parchment has been cut out of the bottom of this folio than the last.
[2] "Bind [their] hands and feet, and cast [them] into the exterior darkness" [adapted from Matt. 22:13].
[3] The dotted consecutive *y*'s are quite different from each other: the first is smaller; the second is dotted with a large tail. The dotted *y* is syllabic which acts as the main vowel of the word.
[4] Morris' Northern version glosses this phrase as "þe flour of knoyng" (l. 7206) or "flower of knowing."
[5] Smudged here and just below on the following line.
[6] "By turns, their heads are plunged downwards and their feet are raised upwards, and they are stretched out for punishments from all sides" [Honorius of Autun, *PL* 172, col. 1160; Wernerus, *PL* 157, col. 923].
[7] A small space of one or two letters remains after an erasure here. Perhaps he first wrote *men*.

Part VI. The Pains of Hell

	The fourteenþ peyne is wanhope .	f.76v	despair
	For of godes mercy þey tresteþ to haue no drope		
5915	With oute hope of mercy þey beþ for her s(er)uyse		during their (religious) service
	And þ(er)fore seiþ salomon in this wise:		
	Omnes qui descendunt in infernu(m). non		
	Rev(er)tentur nec app(re)hendant		
	semitas iusticie.[1]		
	He seiþ alle thei that to helle wendeþ		go
	Wanhope in her hertes the deuel sendeþ		Despair, sends
5920	And neuer þer after þey schul torne agayn		return
	Mercy to take oþur þe wey of lif certayn		
	Ffor whan thei beþ dampned þorow iugement		
	And with body and soule to helle beþ ihent		seized
	They schullen neu(er) þ(er)after wiþ oute doute		
5925	Haue hope no þou3t to be brou3t þ(er)oute		
	Than euere in wanhope þus to abide		despair, remain
	A strong peyne it is by eu(er)y side.		
	Ffor here haþ no man peyne so strong		
	That he ne haþ sum tyme hope among		never has some
5930	Of sum remedie that a man may caste		
	Oþur þat it ne schall euere laste		
	And elles scholde his herte for sorowe and care		otherwise
	Sone faile and of conseil be wel bare		fail, destitute
	Ffor in sorowe hope conforteþ at þe beste		comforts
5935	As me seiþ 3if hope ne were . herte scholde to breste		burst
	Ac in helle non hope may falle in þou3t		come to mind
	Ne hertes to breste mowen nought		burst may not
	Ffor þey ben yordeyned[2] eu(er)e þ(er)e to lyue		ordained, live
	And wiþ strong peynes eu(er)e to be vordryue .		driven about
5940	**Of þe peyne of wantyng of Godes sight.**		
	3ut is þ(er) anoþur peyne as general		
	Þat of alle oþ(er) is most p(ri)ncipal		primary
	And þat is þe wantyng eu(er)e of Godes sight		
	Of our lord god þat is ful of myght		
5945	Ffor the whiche sight þat þei haueþ ilore		lost
	Sorow f(ro)m hem may neu(er)e ben forbore		endured
	Ac þe sorow þat to hem þ(er)fore schall falle		
	Schal be þe moste peyne among hem alle		
	Ffor as þe sight of god in heuene is		
5950	Þe moste ioye of alle iwis		
	Right so þe faylyng of þat blysfull sight		

---

[1] The text reads: "for her house inclineth unto death and her paths to hell and paths of life;" the Proverb says: "None who descend to hell shall return again, neither shall they take hold of the paths of justice" [blending of Proverbs 2:8, 2:9, and 2:19]. Morris's Northern Version has only Proverbs. 2:19 verbatim]. The scribe wrote *iusticie* for *iusticiae*, first declension genitive case. Morey and Hanna & Wood end with *vite*.

[2] The scribe first penned *iordeyned* and then wrote a *y* over the *i*.

	Is þe moste peyne that to þe synfull is dight¹	f.77r	made
	Ffor alle þe peynes þat beþ in helle long and brod		
	Scholde nouȝt hem greue ȝif þei myght se god .		
5955	Ac ȝut þ(er) schal be peynes many mo		more
	As þe bok seiþ and sorowe more and wo		
	Than alle þe men alyue olde and ȝonge		
	Myght wiþ herte þenke oþ(er) telle wiþ tonge.		
	Wel hidous þyng it is forto telle		
5960	Of þe noyse that þanne schal be in helle		
	Ffor þanne wollen þe fendes hem to greue more		will, afflict
	In eu(er)y side of hem hidously crye and rore		roar
	Ffor so gret noyse [that]² þanne schall þey make .		
	As þey al þe world . schold to schake .		quake
5965	And euery synful man schal oþur aneye		harm / vex
	And in al that he may foule destruye		
	Right as þey were wood men on þis lyue .		mad, life
	So thei schullen fight and togidre stryue		contend / oppose
	And eu(er)y schal oþur cracche in þe face .		scratch
5970	And hure owne flesch to rende and to race		rip, claw /tear to pieces
	So that eche schal wilyn³ hym selues to sle		wish, slay
	For her grete sorowe ȝif it myght be		
	Ac þ(er)to þei schull haue no myght		but, power
	For þe deþ schal neu(er) on hem alight		
5975	Eu(er)y man schal gnawe her tonges asonder		apart
	And eu(er)y of oþ(er) schal haue muche wondur		amazement
	And þus þey schulleþ her playnt alegge		of their complaint proclaim
	And þer wiþ god disclaundre and segge		slander, say
	Wherto made god us after his liknesse		why
5980	And soffre us to dwelle in þis derknesse		allow / permit
	As it semeþ wel þ(at) he made us in veyne		
	Seþþe þat we beþ ipult to endles peyne?⁴		Since, dragged
	Thus þei schullen disclaundre god hem among		slander
	So harde her peyne schal be and strong		
5985	They schullen eche on oþ(er) stare and grenne		snarl / scoff
	And seie alas how long schull we brenne		burn
	Thus þei schull soffre peynes many on		a one
	Anon after þat þei beþ to helle agon.		gone
	Therfore þenkeþ eu(er)e boþe ȝong and olde		
5990	Of þeose peynes that i bifore tolde		
	Howe hidous thei beþ forto descryue		

---

[1] This is the third consecutive folio in which a slice of parchment has been removed.
[2] The word *that* has been deleted by the scribe.
[3] It appears the scribe has first written *wilun* and overwrote the *u* with a *y*.
[4] Again, I have inserted a question mark where needed.

176 Part VII. The Joys of Heaven (5992–6031)

	And makeþ ȝowe clene in ȝowr lyue¹	f.77v
	Of alle felþedes of folye and synne	filth
	And makeþ ȝow redy heuene blys to wynne	
5995	Ffor alle þey þat wolleþ her synne forsake	give up
	Whiles þat þey lyueþ ar deþ to hem take²	takes possession
	And torneþ to god and leueþ her synne	turn, leave
	And askeþ his mercy and trusteþ þ(er)ynne	
	And be lonynge³ to hym and buxu(m) bicome	are longing for, obedient
6000	[And]⁴ Þanne to þeose peynes schal he be neu(er) nome	taken
	Bote euene to þe blys of heuene wende	go
	And þere to wone wiþouten ende.	dwell
	Here haue ispoke of þe peynes of helle	
	As ȝe hauen iherd me openly telle	
6005	Of the sixte partye of þis book now an ende y make.	sixth part
	And to þe seuenþ part my mater itake.	matter I take
	Here bigynneþ þe seuenþ party of þis book	
	Þat telleþ openly of þe ioyes of heuene.	
	Many men coueyten the blys of heuene	desire
6010	Ac fewe þe right wey þeder draweþ euene.	
	Ffor somme þorow synne beþ so blynde	
	Þe right way þeder þey mowe nouȝt fynde	
	And somme wolden be þ(er)e wiþ outen eny doute	any
	Bot no þyng þey wolleþ t(ra)vaile þ(er) aboute	strive
6015	Ac to þe kyngdom of heuene may no man come	
	Bot ȝif he þe right wey of wisdom haue y nome	Unless, taken
	And þat wey of wysdom is hollich meknesse	complete
	Wiþ oþ(ur) vertues many more and lesse	
	And þat is iclepud þe gostly wey	called, spiritual
6020	By þe whiche men schold t(ra)vaile boþe nyght and day	
	Ffor by non oþur way may no man þider tee	thither proceed
	Bot he in alle his werkes boþe meke and mylde bee .	Unless, works, meek
	Ac no man may gesse so long a space .	how
	As is f(ro)m hennes to þulke hie place .	hence, this high
6025	Dyuerse heuenes god ordeyned for dyv(er)se þynges	Various, ordered
	Ac þe hiest he made for our wonyenges .	dwellings
	Thre heuenes þ(er) beþ abouen us wel hie	
	As þeose clerkes seieþ þat beþ wise slie.	say, wisely ingenious
	On ys that we þe sterred heuene schul calle	One, starred
6030	Where þat þo planetys beþ and þo sterrys alle.	planets, stars
	Anoþ(er) is þat clerkys calleþ þe heuene cristalle .	

---

¹ The poet engages in some sermonizing and instructing here as he concludes this part of his treatise. Here his methodology is to use reason, not fear, shock, dramatic exaggeration or entertainment as he has used above.

² This means "before death takes possession of them."

³ *Be lonynge* is not attested to by the MED but the word obviously means "are longing for."

⁴ After several lines beginning "And," the scribe mistakenly began this line the same way, but corrected his error with a single stroke.

	Þe whiche in his kynde schyneþ ou(er) alle	f.78r	nature shines
	Ac somme clerkes it calleþ on þis man(er)e		
	Þe watry heuene for it is wondur clere		amazingly
6035	That houeþ¹ þere as cristal eu(er)y w(er)e aboue		hovers, everywhere
	Whan wat(er) þorow frost to gidre is ischone.		together, illuminated / made manifest
	Theose two heuenes aboute goþ ay		rotate always
	And schulleþ neu(er) cese forto domes day		
	Ac of her meuynge haue we no wondur		motion / moving
6040	For it norischeþ all þyng that is þ(er) undur		nourishes
	Alle þyng that lyueþ boþe gras and tre		
	And alle oþur þyng þat on eorþ may be		
	Ffor ȝif þey stode neu(er) so schort atyme stille		motionlessly
	All þat is on eorþ scholde p(er)ische and spille		die
6045	Thus telleþ þese clerkes of clergie		
	Þat haueþ ilernyd astronomye		
	Ac þe þrydde heuene is so fer fro þe ye .		third, far, eye
	Þat no þyng may be aboue þat iseie		seen
	¶ Ȝut clerkes of mo heuenes makeþ her speche		speak
6050	And of seuene oþur heuenes conneþ teche		can teach
	As þe seuene planetes þ(a)t beþ aboute us		planets
	Þe ferst is þe mone and þanne m(er)curie and venus		
	And also þe sonne and mars and jubit(er)²		Jupiter
	And þanne saturnus þat is aboue hem fer		far
6055	Eche of hem her cours aboute heuene makeþ		orbit
	In her sercles as god an ordynaunce hem takeþ.		spheres, makes a decree / plan (for them)
	Thei stikeþ not faste as small sterres doþ		are not firmly fixed
	Ac eche wiþ his cours þorow out oþ(er) goþ		other goes
	As eu(er)y planet falleþ to be in his kynde		moves to be in its proper place
6060	Somme more heier to be þan me(n) schal anoþ(er) fynde.		
	And abouen us beþ planetes seuene		
	And echa sercle of hem is clepped an heuene		sphere, called
	The whiche beþ wondurly fayr and bright		miraculously
	And s(er)veþ to mannes bihoue boþe day and nyght.		profit
6065	¶ Ȝut þ(er) is an noþ(er) heuene þat me(n) may þe eir calle		air
	Þe whiche is next a man bifore þ(a)t oþ(er) alle		
	Ac it is nouȝt so cler no to sight so clene		nor
	As þese oþer heuenes beþ no so wel sene		
	And f(ro)m þe eorþe to þe sercle of þe mone is .		
6070	The space of . v . ³hundred ȝer and no lesse iwis .		
	So seiþ a philisofre . of wham telle ikan .		

---

¹ Although usually following the scribe's use of *u* for *v*, here I have chosen to transcribe *houeþ* as *hoveþ* since it more closely resembles its meaning of "hovers."
² A smudge mars the first two letters of this word "jubiter." An autocorrection of the last four words occurs here.
³ The scribe has positioned his Roman numeral between two *puncti elevati* (raised dots or periods), perhaps for added emphasis. This folio is remarkably accurate, with no erasures or deletions.

178 Part VII. The Joys of Heaven (6072–6111)

	That hat raby moyses[1] a wondur wise man	f.78v	Rabbi Moses
	And f(ro)m þe poynt of þe eorþe to sat(ur)nus		Saturn
	Þe whiche is þe heiȝest planet as clerkes telleþ us		
6075	Is þe wey of seuene þousand ȝere outright		years
	And iii. hundred as it is wryte to our sight.		
	And echa sercle þat is to us here isene		orbit
	Of eu(er)y planet may conteyne wiþ oute wene.		contain, undoubtedly
	Also muche space as me(n) may fynde here		
6080	As a man myght go in þre hundred ȝere		
	Ffor raby moyses in his bokes seiþ þis .		
	And þese wordes beþ no[^u]ȝt[2] myne bot his		nought
	Bot wheþur al þis be soþ oþur nowȝt		true or not
	God wot best þat al þyng haþ wrought		knows
6085	Ffor hym self upward haþ mete þe way		measured
	Whan he fly tyl heuene on holy þorsday.		to
	Ac in þe heyȝest place of þe sterred heuene		starry
	Aboue alle þe oþ(er) places seuene .		spaces
	Stondeþ so many sterres lytel and smale		Stands, stars little
6090	Þat no man may hem telle bi tale		count in order / by number
	The whiche faste stonden as þe bok preueþ		remains fixed, proves
	And beþ ilad aboute wiþ þe heuene þ(a)t meueþ		led, moves
	As nayles þat beþ in a whel wiþ oute		nails, outside
	And euere wiþ þe whel torneþ aboute		
6095	The sterren semeþ smale as we demeþ		judge from our perspective
	Ac þey beþ nought so smale as þey semeþ		
	Ffor þe leste sterre þat we may on loke		smallest
	Is more þan al þe eorþe as we redeþ in boke		
	Ffor clerkes seien þaw al þe world a fuyr were		say though. fire
6100	And it possible were . þat a man myght be þ(er)e		
	Hym schold þenk þaw al þe eorþ brend bright		though, burned
	Lasse þan þe leste sterre þat schyneþ by nyght.		Smallest, was reflected
	Ac to þe hie heuene cowþe no clerk by non art		could
	Þe space gesse by a þousand part		
6105	Hit is so [so][3] hie as sidrak[4] seiþ in his menynge		high, interpretation
	Þat[5] ȝif a ston were þere at a peys beyȝinge		stone, weight being
	That were of an hundred mennes liftynge		as many as a hundred men could lift
	Ȝut it scholde be in þe down fallynge		
	A þousand ȝere and nowt on lasse		
6110	Er it myȝt all þe heuenes passe		Before
	This heuene is heiȝest of heuenes alle .		

---

[1] Moses Maimonides (1135-1204) is the well-known astronomer to whom he refers.
[2] The scribe has inserted the *u* in superscript here.
[3] This unnecessary repetition of the word *so* has been crossed off with three diagonal lines.
[4] Sidrak is the Chaldee name of the Hebrew Hananiah, one of Daniel's three companions in Babylon during the reign of King Nebuchadnezzar. The three miraculously survived the King's attempt to burn them to death. Sidrak was a wise man who foretold the birth of Christ and God's covenant with man among other prophecies. See Daniel 1.7 ff. (JEJ)
[5] The ink has smeared this word, almost looking as if the scribe crossed it out.

	For hior is no þyng þat may bifalle	f.79r	higher
	Right as helle is þe lowest þyng þat me(n) may fynde		
	So is heuene hiest that me(n) may haue in mynde		highest
6115	This heuene is clepud the heuene empyre		called, empyrean
	That is to seie þe heuene that is full of fuyre		
	Ffor it semeþ al as fuyr of grete myght		
	Þat brenneþ nought bot schyneþ bright.		
	Þis heuene bifalleþ noȝt aboute to go		happens, to circle about
6120	Ne it meueþ nat as doþ þe oþ(ur) two .		
	Ac stondeþ eu(er)e stille for it is þe beste		But stands, still
	And most worþi place of pes and of reste.		worthy, peace
	This heuene is clepud goddes owne se		called, seat
	For þ(er)ynne sitteþ þe holy trynyte		therein
6125	And alle the angels as þe book telleþ .		
	And alle holy seyntes þ(er)ynne dwelleþ .		saints therein

Of þe blysse that is in heuene.

	Thanne schal be in heuene more ioye and blysse		bliss
	Þan herte may þenke whan it is in lisse		rest
6130	Ffor þat ioye passeþ alle a mannys witte		passes, understanding
	As it is iwrite þus in holy writte .		
	Quod oculus non vidit . nec auris audivit nec		
	in cor. Ho(min)is ascendit . que p(re)paravit		
	deus diligentib(us) se.[1]		
	That is to seie ere myght neu(er) here		
	Ne into mannes herte come no tonge þ(er)to dure		endure
6135	To telle þe ioyes that he haþ þ(er)to dight		prepared
	To alle þat loueþ hym aright		rightly
	Ffor so wyse a man was non biȝete		begotten
	Ne non so sly . ne sotel . þat myght iwete		clever, subtle, know
	Hadde he neu(er) so muche undurstondynge		
6140	Bot crist only that knoweþ all þyng		
	To telle o poynt þorowe engynne[2]		one point, ingenuity
	Of the ioyes that a man schal haue þ(er)yn		
	Ffor þere is eu(er)e lif wiþoute any deþ		
	And alle ioyes beþ þere ispoke wiþ abreþ		breath
6145	And þere is eu(er)e ȝouþe wiþouten any elde		
	And þere is alle welþe þat me(n) may awelde		rule / control
	And þere is eu(er)e reste wiþ out any t(ra)vayle		work
	And þere is alle man(er) good þat neu(er) schal faile		
	And þere is eu(er)e pes wiþ out any strif		conflict
6150	And þere is alle man(er) lykynge of lif.		enjoyment

---

[1] "That eye hath not seen, nor ear heard, neither hath it entered into the heart of man, what things God hath prepared for them that love him" [I Corinthians 2:9].

[2] *Engynne* has been auto-corrected over an erasure using a dotted *y*.

180 Part VII. The Joys of Heaven   (6151–6190)

	And þere is eu(er)e day and neu(er) nyght	f.79v
	And þere ynne is neu(er) faylynge of light	
	And þere is eu(er)e som(er) bright forto se	
	For þer comeþ no wynt(ur) in þat contre	
6155	And þere is al maner of drewry and ricchesse	love tokens [of God]
	And þere is more nobleie þan any man may gesse	splendor / magnificence
	And þere is eu(er)e wurschipe and more honour	respect / praise
	Þan eu(er)e hadde here kyng or emp(er)our	
	And þere is al man(er) power and myght	
6160	And þere wol God our wonyeng dight	dwelling prepare
	And þere is al maner ese and gret delit	ease
	And þere is siker pes wiþ out any edwit	lasting sure, reproach
	And þere is ioye and blysse eu(er)e lastynge	
	And þere is eu(er)e m(er)þe and eu(er)e likynge	mirth, delight
6165	And þere is parfit ioye þe whiche is endles	
	And þere is gret blysfulhede of pes	happiness, peace
	And þere is eu(er)e swetnesse þat is in certayn	secure
	And þere is adwellynge wiþ oute tornyng agayn	returning
	And þere is gret melodie and angels song	
6170	And þere is eu(er)e preysynge and þonkyng among	praising, thanking everywhere
	And þere is all man(er) frendschipe þat may be	
	And þere is eu(er)e p(ar)fit loue and charite	
	And þere is eu(er)e good acord and onhede	unity
	And þere is ȝeldyng of mede for eu(er)y good dede	reward
6175	And þere is aloutyng wiþ great reu(er)ence	bowing
	And þere is eu(er)e buxumnesse and obedience	meekness / humility
	And þere beþ alle vertues . wiþouten any vices	
	And þere is alle plente of deynte and delices	elegance, delights
	And þere is alle þyng þat is good at wille	as desired
6180	And þere is no þyng þat may be ille	
	And þere is alle wisdom wiþ out folye	nonsense
	And þere is alle honeste wiþ oute vilanye	uprightness
	And þere is alle brightnesse and beaute	
	And þere is alle godnesse þat eu(er)e may be.	goodness / piety
6185	Here haue y schewed in a gen(er)al manere	shown
	Þe ioyes of heuene as it is iwriten here.	
	And now y wol openly telle more	
	Seuene ioyes þe whiche beþ þorow godes ore	mercy
	The whiche þey schulleþ in heuene haue	
6190	In body and soule þat god wol saue.	will save

	And of seuene peynes . that beþ in helle also .	f.80r	
	The whiche in alle þing beþ contr(ar)ie þ(er)to .¹		are contrary
	That to the synful schulleþ falle		befall
	To encres her peyne in gret care² wiþ alle .		increase, sorrow
6195	Of seuene blisses þe whiche þe body schal haue þat god wol		
	Saue . and of seuene peynes . þ(a)t þe dampned bodies schal haue.³		
	Seynt anselm seiþ þat good man		
	As y to ȝow openly telle kan		
	That among alle þe ioyes of heuene		
6200	Schull ben iseiȝen blyssus seuene		seen blisses
	That beþ ap(ro)pred to þe bodies s(er)vice		appropriate
	Of þulke men that on eorþ were right wise		such
	And hereþ now . for y þenke to telle		intend
	The ioyes that on hem schal dwelle .		in them
6205	**Of the blisse of brightnesse.**		
	The ferste blysse . is brightnesse ihold		considered [to be]
	Þat þe saued bodies . haue scholde		
	Ffor be her bodies neuere so dymme here		dim
	In heuene they schul be fayr and clere		
6210	And more schynynge and more light		shining
	Þan eu(er)e þey were here to mannes sight		
	And so fayr a sight . was neu(er)e iseie		
	As þan schal be ne so cler to mannes ye		eye
	Whan þat eu(er)y body that saued schal be .		
6215	So muche brightnesse on hym self schal ise .		appear
	Ffor ȝif a man hadde so bright yen in his heued		eyes, head
	And ȝif as muche sight . myȝt on hem be bileued		
	As haueþ alle creat(ur)es that lyueþ in londe		land
	Ȝut myght he not as y undurstonde		
6220	Aȝeyns so muche brightnesse ones to loke		once
	As a body schal haue þere . for so saiþ þe boke		
	Of þe contrarie of þat blisse.		opposite
	Bot þe dampned bodies þ(er) agayn		in control
	Schullen be foul and stynke in certayn		stink for certain
6225	And derk and dymme þey schulleþ eu(er)e be		
	And hidous and wlatsom forto se		disgusting
	Ffor so foul a sight sye neu(er) man		saw
	As þey schullen be . and in flesch bicome wan		pale
	The whiche schullen be in helle putt		pit
6230	And þ(er)ynne for eu(er)e . þey schullen be ischutt.		shut

---

[1] A magnifying glass reveals the presence of a small, light punctus, but it is very faint.
[2] This word is written over an erasure.
[3] One of the two *y*'s are dotted in this heading, which is the approximate percentage of dotted *y*'s in the text. The scribe did not write the word *Save* on the first line to create a rhyme with *have*, but an internal rhyme still occurs. The dotted *y*'s here indicate they are the syllabic vowel.

Of þe blisse of swiftnesse.*[1]   f.80v

The secunde blysse . is swiftnesse of gret p(ri)s — agility, esteem, worth
Þat eu(er)y body schal haue þat is right wys — righteous
Ffor in lasse while þan a man may wynke[2] — time, wink
6235 They schol fle whodur that þey wol þynke . — fly wherever, think
Wiþ body and soule to gidre in fliȝte — together, flight
F(ro)m heuene to þe eorþ and aȝen anon right
And f(ro)m þat o side of þis world so wyde — one
Ȝif þey wolleþ þey may fle into þat oþ(ur) side — will, fly
6240 And whodur that þey wol her þought sette — wherever, set their mind
No þing schal hem wiþstonde no lette. — Nothing, nor prevent
This þey mowen do wiþ out any t(ra)vayle
And þis swiftnesse shall hem neu(er) fayle
Ffor as þe light of þe sonne þorow strenkþe — potency
6245 May schyne f(ro)m þe est into þe west in lenkþe — distance
Right so þey mowen whodur that thei wol fle — may wherever, fly
In as lytyl awhile as wynkyng of an ye may be . — in as short a time, winking, eye
Ffor þey schul be so swift as y telle kan
As any þought þat is in herte of man.

Of þe contrarie of that blisse.*[3]
6250
Ac þe synful bodies schulleþ eu(er)e more
In an noþur man(er)e ben y pyned sore — punished, severely
Ffor þey schull so heuy be chargid wiþ synne — loaded
Boþe wiþ oute þe body and also wiþ ynne — outside, inside
6255 That þey schull haue no myght forto stonde
Ne forto renne neiþ(er) fot ne honde — move
Ne no leme of al þe body þ(er)to — Nor, limb
So heuy her synne schall aboute hem go . — encircle them

Of þe blisse of strenkþe.*[4]
6260
The þridde blysse is strenkþe and myght
Þat blyssed bodies schull haue bi right
Ffor þey on eorþ feble and weik were
Ȝut so muche myght þei schullen haue þ(er)e — power
And so muche strenkþe þorow godes sonde — grace
6265 Þat no þyng schal aȝenst hem stonde
So þat þey schul renne at her owne wille — run according to
Euery montayn and euery hille
That in þe world eu(er)e was y sene
And make it al playn and fayr and clene — flat /level
6270 Wiþouten any maner wiþstondynge[5] — opposition

---

[1] A kind of red-inked flourish consisting of a long horizontal line crossed vertically three times at the end, a second shorter line crossed twice at the end, and a third even shorter line crossed once at the end fills the rest of this line. This is the first of 19 such flourishes; the remainder, interspersed between here and folio 89v, are also marked with an asterisk. Why the scribe chose to adorn some and not other headings is unclear.

[2] This last word is written over an erasure.

[3] A small red flourish consisting of a line crossed thrice and a shorter line following ends this line.

[4] A third flourish—a horizontal line crossed thrice, and a second line with circular crossings—completes this line.

[5] This last word is written over an erasure.

	Of any þyng that myght make letttynge	f.81r	cause delay
	And in þat dede no more forto swynke		deed, work
	Þan a man doþ forto ete or drynke		does
	Of þe cont(ra)rie of that[1] blisse		
6275	Ac þe synful þat beþ dampned to pyne[2]		punishment
	Schullen be feble and for sorowe whyne		whine
	Ffor þey schal haue no myght to stonde on fote		power
	Ne to take wiþ her hond to hem any bote		remedy
	Ne fro her yȝen þe teres away caste		eyes, tears
6280	And þat feblenesse . schal eu(er)e wiþ hem laste.		weakness
	Of þe blysse of fredome.		
	The feorþe ioye is fredom in body and soule boþe		
	þe whiche þe saued bodies schullen haue for soþe		truth
	In heuene where all ioye is in dyuerse manere		various ways
6285	To don what þey wolleþ wiþ oute daungere		reservation
	Ffor whi þey schulleþ neu(er) fele no þyng		Therefore
	Bot all þat schal be at her lykyng		
	And no þyng schall hem werne no lette		hinder nor prevent
	To don her will wheron þey woll it sette		on which they're determined
6290	Ffor alle þyng schall to hem bowe low[3]		
	And no þyng to hem schall ben unknowe		concealed
	That may her wyl lette oþ(er) p(er)pos		allow, (their) intention
	To ou(er)come fendes þat weren her foos		devils, foes
	Ffor þ(er) is no þyng þat schal be so fre		
6295	On eorþe lyuynge þat y nepned[4] schall be		spoken of
	Ffor þey schull passe whidur þat it is her wille .		go wherever they want
	And all her lykynge þanne fulfylle[5]		desires
	This fayre fredom and þis fraunchise		priviledge
	Schal to þe saued bodies do seruise		
6300	Wiþ þe soules of hem þat god woll chese		choose
	And þis fredom þey schulleþ neuer lese.		lose
	Of þe contrarie of that blisse.		
	Ac in þe contrarye man(er)e of þat blysse		opposite
	Þe dampnede bodies schull fredom mysse		lack
6305	Ffor þey schullen in helle eu(er)e be mad þralle		be enslaved
	And al þyng þat may greue hem shal afore hem falle[6] .		in their presence, befall / happen to
	And þey schull ben charged euyr agens here skille .		burdened, judgment
	To all manere of þyng þat may hem lyken ille		
	Thus þey schull in helle in gret þraldom be		servitude
6310	F(ro)m þe whiche þey ne mowe neuer fle.		

---

[1] The red ink of *at* in *that* is somewhat smeared, perhaps from an excess of ink on the quill.
[2] This word is written over an erasure, probably an auto-correct.
[3] Internal rhyme here evinces the writer's poetic flair for language and sound.
[4] Here *ynepned* is not abbreviated as is at in f. 36v, l. 2824.
[5] The (undotted) *y* in *fulfylle* is written over an erasure in another hand, perhaps that of the *Piers* rubricator.
[6] This word is emended by the *Piers* rubricator, written over an erasure.

Of þe blysse of helthe.*¹   f.81v

The fifþe blysse as clerkes telleþ is hele
That þe saued bodies schulleþ eu(er)e fele
Wiþ outen any siknesse or any greuaunce
6315 Or of any angor of peyne or of penaunce   distress, agony
Ffor no peyne to hem may be iȝyue   given
Ac in alle lykynge þey schul eu(er)e lyue   pleasure
Wiþ ioye in heuene in eu(er)y side   everywhere
And euer more þ(er)ynne þey schul abide.   therein, remain
6320 **Of þe contr(ar)ie of that blysse.***²
Ac þe dampned bodies in an noþ(ur) wise   way
Schulleþ for siknesse sore agryse   be frightened
As þe soules haueþ þat in p(ur)gatorye dwelleþ
For a certayn tyme as þe book telleþ
6325 Ac so longe lasteþ no siknesse þat greueþ sore   so much
As it doþ in helle for it lasteþ eu(er)e more   forever
For in purgatorye som g(ra)ce god doþ sende
Ac in helle alle peynes beþ wiþ outen ende.
Of þe blysse of delites.*³
6330 The sixte blysse is gret delite   delight / pleasure (spiritual)
Þat þe bodies schulleþ haue þat beþ parfite   perfect
Ffor no man alyue in his þouȝt kenne may   may know
Ne so muche desire by nyght ne be day
Ffor here þey myght neuer so wel fare
6335 Wiþ so muche delit as þ(er) is eu(er)e ȝare .   prepared
Ne by alle her wittes so muche ioye haue   Nor, understanding
As þey schulle haue that god wele saue*⁴   choses to save
Ffor þey schull haue so muche ioye þore   there
That non of hem schall desire more
6340 Ffor as þe yren is in the fuyr hot glowynge
Þorow strenkþe of þe fuyr faste brennynge   power
Semeþ wel betre to be fuyr bright
Þan yren bifore any mannes sight
Right so þey þat beþ to heuene ywonne   have gained / arrived at
6345 Schulleþ schyne bright(er) þan þe sonne
And euere more be fulfuld in þat place
Of þe loue of god and of his grace
And of alle delites of ioye and blysse
Of þe wyche ioye þey mowe neu(er)e mysse .   fail to obtain
6350 **Of þe cont(ra)rie of that blysse.***⁵

---

[1] The same embellishments or flourishes noted above in note 1 on folio 80v. complete the heading lines on this and the next folio.
[2] Similar embellishments or flourishes complete this line.
[3] Similar embellishments or flourishes complete this line as well.
[4] The last five words are written over an erasure as is *þore* in the next line. Similar embellishments or flourishes complete this line.
[5] Similar embellishments or flourishes complete this line.

	Ac þe dampned bodies aȝenward*¹	f.82r	on the other hand
	Schull in helle fele strong peyne and hard .		
	Ffor þey schull brenne in fuyr echone		each one
	That schall ben medled wiþ brymstone		mixed
6355	And wiþ hot brymston and stynkynge pich		stinking pitch
	And wiþ oþ(ur) þyng þat is þ(er)to comelych .²		appropriate / fitting
	That is vermyn that schal hem sore bite		vermin, grievously / painfully bite
	And fendes þat schullen hem harde smyte		fiends, beat
	And wiþ oþ(ur) peynes strong and felle		fierce
6360	Mo þan herte may þenke oþ(ur) tong telle.		More
	Of þe blysse of endeles life.		
	The seuenþe blysse is endles lif .		
	Þat þey schull haue wiþ outen strif		conflict
	Euer more in heuene þat is so hie		
6365	For þey schall eu(er)e lyue and neu(er) die.		
	Ac ȝif a man myght so long leue here		
	Tyl he a þousand ȝere old were .		
	Ȝut scholde his lif ben ibrought to þe ende		
	And fro þis world he moste nedes wende		go
6370	Thanne scholde he þenke ȝif he took kepe		
	Þat þis lif nys bot a drem in slepe		was not but
	And þanne þe lenkþe of alle his lyue dayes .³		all his life
	Semeþ bote on day as þe p(ro)phet saies		one
	Q(uo)ni(am) mille anni an(te) oculos tuos tanq(uam)		
	*dies hest(er)na que p(re)t(er)iit.*⁴		
6375	He seiþ þus o my lord a þousand ȝere⁵		
	Bifore þyn yȝen that all þyng sest here		eyes, [you] see
	Is nougȝt elles bot as ȝusturday		else but as yesterday
	Þat was awhile and is ipassid away.		a time, passed
	Thus whan þis lif is to ende ibrought		brought
6380	All þe tyme þere of semeþ as þing of nought		a worthless thing
	Thanne is o day in heuene more clere		one, glorious / excellent
	Þan beþ here many a þousand ȝere		
	Ffor þ(er)e is eu(er)e day and neu(er) night		
	As david þe p(ro)phet seiþ to us aright		rightly
6385	*Melior est dies una in atriis tuis sup(er) milia.*⁶		
	He seiþ Lord, bet(er)e is in þyn halle o day		your hall one
	Þan a þousand ȝeres þat passeþ sone away		soon
	Ffor in o day . in heuene þat god schall sende		one
	Is all þe tyme þat neu(er)e schall haue ende		
6390	Bot i se wel now how schort a day is here		

---

¹ The same embellishments or flourishes noted above (Note 1, folio 80v.) complete the heading line here.
² Morey's edition (l. 8088) offers the more expected *wycke* ("wicked"). The brimstone and pitch of Hell are fitting in the mix of punishments he describes.
³ The upper lobe of the A has been filled in with red ink, as has the Q of Q(uo)ni(am) in l. 6376, the only such coloring in this text. A few in brown ink appear to be accidental.
⁴ "For a thousand years in thy sight are as yesterday, which is past" [Psalm 89:4].
⁵ The use of direct address from the Psalm here adds literary interest, and makes the poem more engaging.
⁶ "For one day in thy courts is better than thousands" [elsewhere]. [A close rendition of Psalm 83:11 "I would rather serve one day in the house of the Lord than dwell in the tents of the wicked."]

	To regard of tyme of þousand ȝere	f.82v	in comparison to
	Ac ȝet þer beþ a þousand . þere les		less
	To regard of tyme þat is endles		
	Ffor seynt austyn telleþ in his sermon		
6395	Þat o day here may be a porcyon		one, a fraction
	Of an hundred ȝere as men may se		years
	Al þouȝ a porcion a lytil þyng be .		although, little thing
	Ac þe spas of an hundred ȝere iwis		period [of time], years
	No more porcion of endles blysse is		
6400	Ffor ȝif a þousand ȝere þat is more here		if, years
	Of endlesnesse any porcion were		
	After o þousand ȝer mo þousandes to caste		one, add to
	Þan scholde endlesnesse cesse at þe last		cease
	And ȝif endlesnese myght any ende holde		come to an end
6405	þanne unp(ro)prely endlesnesse telle me(n) scholde		incorrectly, count /judge
	And þanne semeþ it wel as i seid er		before
	Þat þulke lif shal be euer more þer		
	The whiche lif is siker and so is not þis		secure
	And þat lif is full of ioye and blys		
6410	The whiche to þe saued bodies schal ap(ro)pred be .		reserved
	And euere in heuene þey schulleþ god ise.		see
	Of the contrarye of that blisse.		opposite
	ᴛhe dampned bodies þat schulleþ to helle wende		damned, go
	þey schulleþ haue deþ þat is wiþ outen ende		
6415	And þat deþ schall hem newe eu(er)e greue		continually
	For þat deþ schall hem neuer leue[1]		leave, always / again, again / afresh
	Ac eu(er)e þ(er)wiþ be turmented among		tormented continually
	Wiþ many an noþ(ur) peyne þat is bitter and strong.		
	Ffor þey schull seme wheþ(ur) þey ligge or stonde		lie
6420	As men passyng toward þe deþes bonde		fetter / constraint
	They schullen eu(er)e dyȝynge lyue and lyuynge dyȝe		dying live
	And þe peyne of deþ eu(er)e before her ye.		eye
	Here haue itold in esy man(er)e and euene[2]		restrained / calm
	Þe seuene speciall ioyes that beþ in heuene		
6425	That þe saued bodies schulleþ haue þorow right		by
	And eu(er)e in heuene dwelle þorow Godes myght.		power
	And now will ischewe to ȝow all		
	Seuene man(er) ioyes that schulleþ falle		kinds of, come
	To þe soules wiþ þe bodies in s(er)vyse		
6430	Of alle þat beþ right good and wise.		

---

[1] The Northern edition of James Morey, *The Prik of Conscience* reads "and that deth shal ay him greeve / In which deth they shul ay leeve [live]" [p. 189, VII, 599-600]. This is just one interesting instance of many in which the Northern version and Southern recension differ.

[2] The self-conscious poet makes his voice heard here in his direct address.

Of þe blysse of wisdom þat þe soule schall haue.[1] f.83r

	The ferst blysse that þe soule schall haue	
	Of a rightful man that god woll saue	righteous, will
	Is wisdom . for þey schull knowe and ise	
6435	Alle þyng þat euer was and is and euer schal be.	
	They schullen haue ful knowynge of god	knowledge
	And also of þe fadres myghthod .	might
	They schulleþ knowe all þyng and iwite	understand
	Þat god haþ idon and may ben undurʒete	what, perceived
6440	And þey schulleþ haue so muche g(ra)ce	
	Whan þat þey seoþ god in his face	see
	That no þyng þat þorow god was ikud	known
	Ne schall f(ro)m hem þanne be ihud	hid
	Ffor seynt austyn that muche cowþe on clergie	knows about
6445	Seiþ þus in a sarmon wheron he wolde nought lie	sermon
	That in the sight of god þe whiche þey schulleþ ise	
	Þre man(er)e of knowynge to hem schal be	ways
	Ffor þey schull knowe hym boþe god and man	
	And also hem self and how he hem wan	won
6450	Right so as þe mowe þre þynges sen here	may, see
	In a myrrour of glas þat is fayr and cler.	mirror
	On ys þe myrour þat bifore us ys	one
	A noþur is þe liknesse of oure face iwis.	
	The þridde we mowen se þ(er)ynne ʒet	
6455	Al þyng þat is þ(er) aʒenst iset	set
	Right so þey schulle se god in his liknesse	
	In þe myrour of his gret brightnesse	
	They schulleþ sen also hem self in hym so bright	see
	And þat peple to gidre at on sight	one
6460	They schull sen alle creatures boþe in heuene and in helle	see
	And alle þe men at ones þat þere schulleþ dwelle	
	They schulleþ knowe also how god invisible is[2]	
	Unchangable and endles iwis	I know
	And how þat god was euere bifore all þyng	
6465	And also wiþ oute any bigynnynge	
	And how and whi that god schall be	
	Wiþouten ende þey schull þanne ise	
	And all þyng þat is now f(ro)m hem ihud	hid
	Schall þanne to hem be knowe and kud	understood
6470	And why þat on is uptake into a kyngdome	one taken up

---

[1] The word *þat* has been written over an erasure in a straighter, almost backhand slant. Large scrawly letters in later hand mar the right edge of this folio: first three letters, a space, then four or five letters, a dot, and the number 78 comprises the graffiti.

[2] The *Piers* rubricator has emended the last five words, but the originals are not visible; this is a possible doctrinal issue, although not one seemingly controversial.

	And whi somme beþ iput into alle manere þraldom	f.83v	servitude
	And why somme children beþ dede and ilore		lost
	In here modur wombe er þey were ibore.		born
	They schullen knowe also wiþ outen any drede		fear
6475	Why þat somme deyn in her childhede		
	And þey schullen wite as y telle can		know
	Whi þat som beþ ybore¹ in fayr schap of man		handsome appearance
	And somme in an uncomely stature		unattractive
	And whi þat somme doþ in pouerte dure		remain
6480	And whi þat som(m)e beþ biȝete in ful hordom		begotten, fornication
	And beþ ibaptiȝed . and haueþ cristendom		baptized, Christianity
	And whi somme beþ in wedlok bore		born
	And ar þey be cristned þey beþ forlore		before, christened, lost
	And whi somme bigynneþ to be stedfast		constant
6485	And bileueþ wel ac endeþ at þe last		believe
	And whi somme beþ of euel bygynnynge²		
	Ac ȝut at þe laste makeþ a good endynge		death
	Of þese þynges and oþur many mo		more
	Þe skiles whi to hem schull ben undo		causes revealed
6490	In þe book of lif þat wel opene schal be		
	And þat is þe sight of þe holy t(ry)nyte.		
	And þere schal eche man as wel knowe oþ(ur)		
	As on eorþe doþ suster or broþ(er)		sister
	And also knowe of whiche contre þey were		
6495	And who hem begat and who hem bere		bore
	And eu(er)y man schall knowe oþ(ur)es þouȝt		
	And alle þe dedes þat þey hauen wroȝt.		done
	Thus wise þey schulleþ be þat into heuene come		who
	Aft(er) þe dome whan þey beþ þider ynome		taken
6500	And alle be itold as godes of myght³		regarded
	As david in þe saut(er) seiþ to us outright		Psalter
	*Ego dixi dii estis et filii excelsi omnes.*⁴		
	He saiþ y seide ȝe be godes alle		says, said
	And as godes sones me(n) shal ȝow calle.		sons
6505	Thus ful of wit þey schull be eu(er)more		wisdom
	And as godes sones be undur his lore,		teaching
	Of þe contr(ar)ie of that blysse.*⁵		
	The soules þat wiþ þe bodies schull synke		sink
	Into helle put schulleþ [and]⁶ no good þynke		hell's pit, think / expect
6510	Ne haue no witte to wite ne to knowe .		brains to understand

---

[1] This has been emended over an erasure; the *y* is dotted.
[2] The poet's penchant for lists and categorization is here evidenced, enhanced by the inscrutability of Fortune.
[3] The somewhat heretical reading "and all be seen as gods of might" is also endorsed by the Northern reading: "And be alle als Godes of grete myght" *(Morris* 8287), and "and eke as goddes of great myght" *(Morey* 8288). Hanna & Wood's version reads "And be all als godes of gret myght" (8284).
[4] "I have said: you are gods and all of you the sons of the most high" [Psalm 81:6]. The Latin *dii* is a Vulgate plural form of *deus*.
[5] The same embellishments or flourishes noted above (See note1 folio 80v.) complete the heading here.
[6] The word *and* is crossed out in the text.

	No good dede þat eu(er)e was don in any þorowe	f.84r	occasion
	Bot in her peynes schal ben all her þou3t[1]		
	And in her foule synnes þat þey hauen[2] wrou3t		committed
	Ffor þey schulleþ of no þyng haue menynge		knowledge
6515	Bot only of her wikked lyuynge		behavior
	And of her sorow that is wiþ owten ende		
	And of her wrecchednesse that schall hem schende		destroy
	The whiche þey schull eu(er)e bifore ise		
	And þat sight schall to hem a schenschipe be		disgrace / humiliation
6520	**Of þe blysse of frendschipe and p(ar)fit loue.**		
	The seconde blysse þat þe soule schall haue		
	Wiþ þe bodies that god woll saue		
	Schall be gret frendschipe and p(ar)fit loue		
	That ys more allowed in þe blysse aboue		
6525	Than any dede þat any man may werche		do, perform
	Þat likeþ wel god and holy cherche		
	Ffor eu(er)y creature schall more loue þan he can		knows
	Oþ(ur) þan he loued on eorþ eu(er)e any man(er)e man		Or
	And þat loue schall be fastned so faste		confined, firmly
6530	That it schall neu(er) faile bot eu(er)e more faste[3]		
	And as ucha lyme þat is on a man bodiliche		each member, bodily
	Loueþ alle þe oþur lymes kyndeliche		limbs naturally
	And desireþ kyndely here hele		naturally their health
	Right so p(ar)fit loue me(n) schall on hem fele		feel
6535	Ffor þey alle schull ben ate on assent		of one accord
	And of one wille and of one entent		
	Ffor þey schull be as o body all in on		one body all together
	And o soule in dyuerse lemes in flesch and bon		one, limbs
	And god þat is her heued þorow his mercy and his ore		head, grace
6540	Þan schall hem loue[4] as muche oþ(ur) more		or
	As þe heued of man loueþ at þe beste[5]		head, best
	Alle þe lemes kyndely þat in þe body doþ reste		limbs naturally, reside
	So þat þulke cleor loue and þulke alliaunce		such, bond association
	Schall neuer faile for no defiaunce.		rejection
6545	**Of þe contrarie of that blysse.**		
	Ac þe contrarie men schull euene ise		fully see
	Among þe soules þat dampned schull be.		
	Ffor þey schull be fol of violentnesse		full, violence
	Of wraþþe of hatered and envyousnesse		wrath, hatred, envy
6550	So þat eche schall desire . wiþ oþ(ur) to fyghte[6] .		

---

[1] The *all* is either crossed (as if the *ll*'s were *tt*'s) or crossed out; the last two words look heavier and darker.

[2] The *a* in *haven* is slightly smeared, and the word is written somewhat unclearly.

[3] The sense might suggest *last*, but the word appears to be written as *fast*. The meanings are similar: *fast* could mean *stick* or *be fast*. Osborn a. 13 New Haven writes "That hitte shal ever hoolde and last" (p. 194. fol. 124r, l. 821).

[4] This word is written over an erasure, and a space of about two letters remains.

[5] Both Morey's and Hanna and Wood's editions posit loving the head of man as the body rather than *at the best*.

[6] The last two words are written over an unclean erasure by the *Piers* rubricator; the *y* is not dotted.

Part VII. The Joys of Heaven (6551–6590)

	And to astrangle eche oþ(er) ȝif þat þey myghte[1]	f.84v	strangle
	Thus þey schulleþ wille to stryuen echone		each one
	For pes amonges hem þer schall be none		peace among
	Ne reste ne ese ne no manner wurschipe		ease, honor
6555	Bot t(ra)vaile in peyne and all man(er) of schendschipe		torment
	And god þat is in heuene and alle hisse		his [subjects]
	Þat wiþ hym schull dwelle in þat blysse		
	Schulleþ hem in peyne and sorow ise		
	And of hem haue noþ(er) mercy no pite		
6560	Bote þanne hem calle godes enemys		
	And þat hatered schal be þanne right wis		lawful, just
	Ffor þat man þat god wol þanne saue		
	Of his owne sone no pite schal haue		
	That schal be idampned into helle pyne		
6565	Ne þe sone for þe fadre ones schal whyne		once, whine
	Ne for his fadre he schal haue no rewþe		pity
	Þow god haue hym dampned þorow trewþe		truth
	Ne þe modur on þe same manere		
	Of þe dought(er) þat sche loued wel here		
6570	Ne the dought(er) of þe modur neu(er)e þe more		
	Ne þe broþ(er) of þe soster schall nat greue sore		
	Ne the sister of her leuest broþer		
	Ne none of hem schall haue rewþe of oþer		pity
	Ne ȝet non oþ(er) þat any þyng of riȝtfulnesse kan		knows
6575	Schal no pite haue of a dampned man		
	Ac whan þe rightfull schulleþ þe dampned ise		
	Ipeyned in helle þanne glad þey schull be		
	And for two skiles þey beþ fayn:		reasons, joyful
	Þat on is for þey beþ ascaped peyn		one
6580	And an noþur for þat godes veniaunce		vengeance
	Is rightfully idon in al his ordynaunce		ordinance
	Ffor þis preueþ david þat seiþ þus		proves
	In þe saut(er) book and scheweþ it to us		Psalter
	Letabitur iustus cu(m) viderit vind(i)c(t)am.[2]		
6585	He seiþ þat eu(er)y rightful man		
	Glad and blyþe schal be þan .		
	Whan godes veniaunce he schal yse		
	On þe synful that dampned schul be.		
	Of þe blysse of onhede and of acord[3]		unity
6590	The þridde blysse as men mowe in book rede .		third, may

---

[1] In the upper right quadrant margin are three long indentation marks marring the vellum, but not affecting the text.
[2] "The just shall rejoice when he shall see the revenge" [Psalm 57:11].
[3] Uncharacteristically, this heading does not end with a *punctus*.

	Is þe good acorde and þe onhede	f.85r	cooperation, unity
	That þe soules schulleþ haue in heuene		
	Wiþ þe bodies þat þider come wel euene		very equal
	Ffor eche of hem schall folwe oþ(ur)es wille		follow other's
6595	And eche of hem schall oþ(ur)es likyng fulfylle		desires fulfill
	Ffor as þyn[1] on ye foloweþ euene right		one eye follows straight
	Þyn oþ(ur) ye þere þu settist þy sight		other eye, sets
	And non may torne hider no þider		none, turn
	Bot ȝif þey torne boþe her sight to gidre		unless
6600	Right so schall god acorde wiþ all his		be reconciled, his [subjects]
	And eche of hem wiþ oþ(ur) in þat blys		
	And to what þyng þe soule haþ talent		inclination / desire
	Þ(er)to þe body schall euere ȝyue his assent		give
	And what þyng god wole þat be to done		wills
6605	Þ(er)to þey schulleþ assent anon echone		each one
	And what þyng that þey haueþ in wille		desire
	God schall þat anon to hem full fylle.		
	This acord and onhede schall be endles		unity
	And eu(er)e more be in good reste and pes.		
6610	**Of the contrarie of that blysse.**		
	Ac þe dampned men schullen be in strif		
	Euere wiþ oþ(er) for her wikked lif		
	Ffor eu(er)y of hem schall oþ(ur) hate þanne		each
	And eche of hem schall oþ(ur) curse and banne.		blame / condemn
6615	The body schall hate þe soule by reso(u)n		rightly
	Þouȝ þe soul to synne were non encheso(u)n		Though, cause
	And þe soule schal hate þe body		
	For þe body wrought eu(er)e þe foly		
	Ac for þe soule first synne þoughte		but
6620	And þe body aftirward it wroȝte.		wrought
	Therfore boþe to gidre þey schull dwelle		
	Wiþ outen end in þe peynes of helle.		
	Of þe blisse of power and of strenkþe.		
	The feorþe blysse among þe oþ(ur) alle		
6625	Þat to þe sauede soules schall falle		
	Is so muche power and of all þyng þe maystrye		control
	And lordschipe ou(er) hem þat beþ idryue to vilanye.		domination, driven
	And what þyng þey þenkeþ in her þouȝt		
	All schall at her wille sone ben iwrouȝt		performed
6630	Ffor alle þyng schall bowe to her honde		bow

---

[1] This *þyn* and that on the next line have been written over erasures; only the first uses a dotted *y*. This is nearly a model page: logical, well and clearly written, with few emendations on an aesthetically clean folio.

	And no þing schal aȝenst her wyl stonde .	
	Thus þey schulleþ haue þ(er)e gret powere .	
	And hyȝnesse for her lownesse here .	arrrogance
	That þey hadde in her lyue dayes	
6635	And þerfore god þus in þe gospel saies:	
	Omnis qui se humiliat exaltabitur.[1]	
	He seiþ who so loweþ hym here aright	humbles, rightly
	He schal be hiȝed þ(er)fore in heuene bright .	raised
	Of þe contrairie of that blisse.	
6640	Ac þe dampned for al her travayle	travail
	Of suche power eu(er)e schul fayle	
	And þ(er)wiþ hem schal faile all oþur þynge	
	Wherof þey myght haue any lykynge	desire
	They schull no þyng haue after her wille	that they wish
6645	Bot al þyng þat schal hem lyke full ill	dislike totally
	Thanne gret sorowe schal hem betide	
	For her hiȝenesse and her muchil p(ri)de	arrrogance, excess
	As þe bok þ(er)of witnesseþ þis	
	And in þe fore said gospel writen it is	aforementioned
6650	*Qui se exaltat humiliabitur.*[2]	
	That is who so wol hym here hie bere	high bear
	He schall ben ilowed and put in daungere	lowered, subject to control of
	And þat is in þe dang(er) of þe fende	power, devil
	In þe peyne of helle þat haþ non ende.	
6655	**Of þe blisse of worschipe.***[3]	honor
	The rightfull schulle haue dyv(er)se hono(ur)es	
	And ben coroned as kynges and emp(er)oures	crowned
	And sitten in setes schynynge bright	thrones
	Wiþ alle maner nobleye þat me(n) may to hem dight	dignity, praise
6660	And þey schul ben honoured as godes frendes dere	
	And þerfore seiþ david on þis manere	
	Omnis honorati sunt amici tui deus.[4]	
	He seiþ lord þey þat on eorþe honoured þe	
	Beþ muche honoured and eu(er)e schull be .	
6665	**Of þe contrarie of þat blisse.***[5]	
	Ac þ(er)aȝen þe dampned schull be reuyled	opposed to this, reviled / denounced
	And foule be ischend and eu(er)e be despised	destroyed
	And peyned wiþ grett(or) peynes and stronge	
	Þan any man myght in þis world fonge	endured
6670	And þey schulleþ all soffre þat schendschipe is .	suffer, shame

f.85v

---

[1] "He that humbleth himself, shall be exalted" [Luke 14:11 and 18:14].
[2] "Everyone who exalts himself, shall be humbled" [Luke 14:11].
[3] The same embellishments or flourishes noted above in note 1, folio 80v. complete this heading also.
[4] "Thy friends, O God, are honoured" [adapted from Psalm 138:17]. The Vulgate Bible actually reads "*honorificati sunt amici tui Deus*"—"Your friends, O God, are made exceedingly honourable." Notice how differently the author translated this Latin line.
[5] The same embellishments or flourishes noted above complete this heading also.

	Wiþ peyne and sorowe þat haþ non ende iwis.	f.86r	
	Of þe blisse of sykernesse.*¹		security
	ℭhe sixte blysse of heuene sikernesse is		
	Where þe rightfull schulleþ be in gret ioye iwis		
6675	Ffor þey schulleþ eu(er)e be siker and certeyn²		secure
	To haue endles ioye and neuer peyn		
	Euer þer to dwelle wiþ outen any drede		fear
	And of no þyng þey schulleþ haue nede		
	Ac eu(er)y man þat here fareþ wel		
6680	Haþ drede to falle in daung(er) somdel		fear, peril, somewhat
	Ffor in þis world boþe kyng and emp(er)o(ur)		
	Hauen drede to lese here her honour		fear, lose
	And eu(er)y riche man haþ drede also		anxiety
	His goodes and his ricchesse to fur go.		forego
6685	Ac þey þat schulleþ come into heuene blys		
	Schulleþ haue no drede þat ioye to mys		lack fail to obtain
	Ffor þey schullen be þere siker ynow		secure enough
	Þat her ioye schall laste euere³ wiþ oute wow.		woe
	Of the contrairie of that blisse.*⁴		
6690	𝔄c þe peynes of þe synfull schull agregged be		increased
	And to hem be mad more greuous to se .		
	And fendes schulleþ eu(er)e gon hem among		
	To and fro . ou(er)þwoȝt and euenlong		athwart, across, head-to-tale
	And eu(er)more þey casten and ymagyne		deliberate / consider
6695	How þat þey mowen þe synfull pyne		might, punish
	And þe more peyne þat þey to þe synful seken		seek
	So muche more þer owne peyne þey eken.		increase
	Ac þow þey do so it is no wondur		though
	For þey beþ smyten wiþ sorow as it were aþondur		beaten, sorrow, thunderstorm
6700	And þe fendes schulleþ eu(er)e wiþ gret envie		
	Treden hem undur her feet and don hem vilanye		bring them disgrace
	And þresten hem down into fuyr and smoke		thrust
	And in helle leuen hem faste biloke		leave securely locked up
	As iob seiþ þus in a boke þat he made		
6705	Us wiþ to fere wiþ fendes þat beþ so fade⁵		hostile, fierce
	*Ibunt demones et redibu(n)t sup(er) filios inobediencie*⁶		
	He seiþ greslyche fendes schull gon and come		ugly devils
	Upon þe synful þat were to god unbuxome.		disobedient
	Thus in peyne þey schullen þere ben alle		
6710	And all maner sorowe me(n) schall afore hem calle.		before

---

¹ The same embellishments or flourishes noted above in note1, folio 80v. complete this heading also.
² The last three letters are written over a smudged erasure; a dotted *y* is used.
³ *Euere* is written over a smudged erasure spot that is too small for the word; hence it is crowded into the space.
⁴ The same embellishments or flourishes noted above complete this heading also.
⁵ The sense appears to be: "Fiends that he made to frighten us with, that are so fierce / hostile;" the extra *wiþ* seems superfluous.
⁶ "Demons will march out and descend upon the children of disobedience" [the source is untraced, but *filios inobediencie* appears to echo *filios superbial* of Job 41:25].

	And þey schull ben in certeyn eu(er)e to dwelle[1]	f.86v	certain
	And þat þey schull neu(er) come out of helle.		
	Of þe blisse of parfit loue.		
	The seuenþe blysse is ioye parfite		
6715	That þe soules schullen haue wiþ gret delite		
	Ffor þey schulleþ alle in that tyde		time
	In body and soule gloriously abide		reside
	And haue ful ioye and blys wiþ seyntes alle		
	Wiþ all maner m(er)þes that mowen bifalle		mirths, may happen
6720	For more blysse myght neu(er) non be		joy
	Þan eu(er)y of hem schal þanne on oþ(er)e ise		each / one and all
	Of þe whiche sight þey schulleþ more ioye haue		
	Þan any man may desire oþ(er)e craue		or
	And eu(er)y of hem schal be so wel apaied		satisfied
6725	For his ioye þat he haþ þere asaied		experienced
	The whiche he schal haue þorow godes ore		grace
	Þat he schal desire to haue no more.		
	Thanne schull eu(er)y man haue more ioye in heuene		
	Þan herte may þenke or tong speke wiþ steuene		voice
6730	Ffor þey schulleþ haue ioye wiþ ynne and wiþ oute		
	Boþe aboue and byneþe and all aboute		beneath
	Abouen hem þei schulleþ haue ioye upright		directly
	Of our lord all myghti þe fulle sight		
	And byneþe hem of sterres and planet(es) clere		
6735	And of þe world þat shall be bright eu(er)ywhere		
	Abouten hem[2] of heuene þat þey schullen ise		
	And of alle creatures þat faire schull be		fair
	Wiþ ynne hem of þe glorifienge of man		
	Of body and soule þat god þider wan		won
6740	Wiþ outen hem . of þat blysful companye		
	Of angels þat afore god makeþ melodye.		
	Of þe ioie þat þey schull haue in her . v . wittes		five senses
	And þe ferst is þe sight of þe t(ri)nyte.		
	Ferst þei schullen se wiþ her yȝen bright		see, eyes
6745	Many full fayre and blysfull sight		
	And þei schulleþ þere also ise		
	Alle þo þre p(er)sones þat beþ in t(ry)nyte		
	The fadur and sone and þe soþfast holy gost		faithful
	And þat schall be all here ioye most .		
6750	Thorowe þe whiche sight þey schull knowe		

---

[1] This entire page (86v) and the facing one (87r), on two folios, are scribed and emended by the *Piers* rubricator. It is a smaller, thinner hand, with a greater secretarial rather than artistic hand.

[2] The text reads "Abouten hem of hem of heuene, but the "of hem" appears redundant. Morey's edition reads "abouen hem of heven that they shul se" (p. 199, l. 1041). Joy of *hem* refers to the saved souls as a source of glory / light shining upon each other.

	Alle þyng þat is boþe hie and lowe	f.87r	high
	Alle þyng [þat]¹ they schullen þorow myght and g(ra)ce		
	Se in þe brightnesse of godes face		See
	Ac in þis lif men seoþ hym nouȝt		
6755	Bote in forme of bred þorow trewe fey in þouȝt²		bread, faith
	As it were þorow a myrour . a liknesse iwis		mirror
	Ac in heuene me(n) schall hym se right as he is		
	And þis ioye þey schulleþ alle þere haue		
	Wiþ outen ende þat our lord wol saue.		
6760	**Of the ioie of sight of our lady.**³		
	They schulleþ also y se sitte full hiȝe		see
	His blessed modur and mayden marie		
	That next god sitteþ in heuene bright		
	Abouen alle angels as it is right		proper
6765	For god ches here to be his modur dere		chose her
	And of her took flesch and blood here		
	And to sukke⁴ of here brest it was his wille		suck
	Þ(er)fore next hym sche schal sitte stille		always
	And sche is so fayre þere as sche sittes		there
6770	Þat her fayrnesse passeþ all mennys wyttes⁵		beauty surpasses, senses
	Than is it a gret ioye as y bifore tolde		
	Eu(er)e her fayrnesse so to biholde.		
	Of þe ioyfull sight of þe ordre of angels.		
	They schulleþ þ(er) ise as holy bokes telleþ		
6775	Þe nyne ordres of angels þ(a)t þ(er)ynne dwelleþ		
	That so delytable beþ onne to loke		delightful to look on
	And so fayr of chere as me(n) may reden in boke		countenance, read
	That all þe fayrnesse in þe world here		beauty
	Oþ(ur) euere was ifere in mannes chere		borne, countenance
6780	Oþur any man might ordeyne wiþ oute defaute		decree, fault
	Were nat apoynt þ(er)to to make any asaute⁶		properly to make an attack
	Ffor eu(er)y an ordre in his owne degree		rank
	Schal do all þyng þat most lykynge may be		desirable
	Boþe to god and to man well aright		
6785	A gret ioye schal be þanne of þat sight		
	And so fayre a sight as þat schal seme		seem
	Cowþe neu(er)e man ymagyne no deme		could, nor suppose
	Of þe ioyfull sight of þe halwes of heuene.		saints
	They schullen in heuene ise also		
6790	Patriarches, prophetis, and oþur mo .		

---

¹ The word is scratched off by the scribe.
² This refers to the transubstantiation of the mass, in which bread and wine are believed to be transformed into the body and blood of Christ.
³ A small flourish follows here.
⁴ These three words are scribed a bit high in the space on the "line" over an erasure by the *Piers* rubricator.
⁵ The last two words are written over an erasure at a slightly upward angle (in haste by a standing emender?).
⁶ Morey's edition reads "And were not bot oon paynt of her feyrnes" (p. 200 *l.* 8700).

	And holy apostles and euangelistes[1]	f.87v
	Þat folowed non oþ(ur) lawes bot cristes	
	And martures and confessourys many on	martyrs, confessors
	And doctours and heremytes þat wolde bare foot gon	hermits, barefoot go
6795	Also þey schulleþ ise holy v(ir)gynes þere	see
	Þat loueden god wel on eorþe here	
	And kepten hem chast for our lordes sake	chaste
	And for his loue deþ wolde take.	
	Thanne afayr siȝt is þis forto se	sight, see
6800	Alle þe fayre peple þat þ(er)e schall be	
	That bright(er) schull schyne þan eu(er)e sonne schon	sun shone
	And þis sight schall be among hem echone	each one
	Of þe ioyful sight of þe cite of heuene.	
	They schull heuene ise so long and wide	
6805	And fayr and rownd by eu(er)y side	
	Brightor schynynge þan doþ þe sonne.	
	Ac wel is hym þat þulke blysse haþ wonne	But, won / gained
	That þulke cite is so fayr on forto loke	same, lovely
	And so bright and so brod as seiþ þe boke	
6810	That all þis world þat we woneþ ynne	live in
	Were nought þ(er)e to bote as a poynt of a pynne[2]	as a defense, pin
	To regard of þat cite þat is so brod	in comparison to
	Þe whiche for us haþ maked our[3] god	made
	Ffor þulke lond is iclepud sou(er)eynlyche	this, called
6815	Þe kyngdom of heuene þat for man namlyche	especially
	Is ymad and þat is godes owne se	own abode / throne
	For many awonynge stede þ(er) ynne schal be	a dwelling place
	And þ(er)e alle holy men schulleþ dwelle.	
	Þ(er)fore god þus seiþ in þe gospelle	
6820	*In domo patris mei mansiones multe su(n)t.*[4]	
	He seiþ þer beþ wonyenges manye and fele	dwellings, various
	In my fadres hous þat is full of wele	prosperity / joy
	The whiche hous is a cite fayr and bright	beautiful
	Strong of werk and mychel of myght	work, much, power
6825	And seynt ion godes derlyng dere	John, darling dear
	Seiþ in þe apocalips on þis manere	Apocalypse
	Vidi civitatem s(anc)tam i(e)r(usa)l(e)m	
	nova(m) descendente(m) de celo	
	[nuptam] . a deo parata(m) tanq(uam)	
	sponsa(m) ornata(m) viro suo.[5]	
	I sawe he seiþ þat noble and holy cite	
	Of ier(usa)l(e)m all newe forto se	Jerusalem, see

---

[1] The primary scribal hand (as opposed to that of the *Piers* rubricator) has now continued.
[2] Morey's edition, Osborn a.13, New Haven Beinecke Library reads "Were nought bot as a myddyng pitte" (p. 201, fol 129r, l. 1162). This suggests the insignificance of earth compared to heaven as a habitation, the same statement that H. M. 128 suggests.
[3] This word *our* is written over an erasure.
[4] "In my Father's house there are many mansions" [John 14:2].
[5] "And I ... saw the holy city, the new Jerusalem, coming down out of heaven from God, prepared as a bride adorned for her husband" [Apocalypse 21:2]. The word *nuptam,* related to nuptials, marriage, wedding, (from L. *nuptus*) is crossed out (but visible) in the text.

6830	Comynge adown f(ro)m heuene bright	f.88r	
	Of god almyghty richely idight		appareled
	As a bride is¹ fayr mad to her spouse		lovely maid
	Þese wordes of ion be wel speciouse.		John, beautiful / fitting
	This cite is þus forto undurstonde		
6835	Holy cherche þat eu(er)e mot styfly sonde²		must valiantly stand / resist
	Aȝenst þe fend and his power to fight		
	For he it assaileþ by day and by nyght		assails
	Ac þat fight schal nouȝt eu(er)e laste³		not last forever
	For after þe dome god woll hym ou(er)caste.		judgement, will overthrow
6840	Thanne schal holy cherche of fightyng reste		
	And be wiþ god in loue and pes at þe beste		peace
	And eu(er)e to gidre wonye in heuene blysse		together live
	And wiþ alle her children þere be iwisse .⁴		indeed
	That to god haueþ ben bux(o)n and trewe		obedient, true
6845	And þat bitokneþ þe cite þat is so newe.		signifies
	Ac ȝut holy cherche þe whiche is godes bride		
	Bihoueþ to be fightynge and here to abide		is necessary, await
	The comynge of crist þat is her bridgome⁵		
	That is euere myghty his enemy to ou(er)come		
6850	Ffor holy cherche fighteþ eu(er)e for godes right		
	And god is ouercomer þorow his grete myght.		victor
	In two maneres may holy cherche be itake		understood
	Ac at þe laste me(n) schall of hem boþe on make		one [understanding] make
	As clerkes seiȝeþ and witnesseþ iwis		say
6855	That holy cherche in double man(er)e iclepud is		called
	Ecclesia militans . ecc(lesi)a triumphans.⁶		
	In o man(er)e is holy cherche clepud fightynge		one, called fighting
	And in an noþ(ur) manere sche is clepud ou(er)coming		victorious / triumphant
	Ac holy cherche þat eu(er)e is here fightynge		
6860	As clerkes þ(er)of bereþ witnessynge		bear witness
	Is nought elles bote agadrynge aboute		gathering
	Of cristene men⁷ wel lyuynge wiþ oute .		
	Holy cherche ou(er)comynge is also		
	God wiþ all þe company of þo		those
6865	That dwelleþ wiþ hym an hy in his blysse		
	Undur holy cherche þat fighteþ wiþ oute lysse.		respite
	Ac þat beþ alle men wiþouten les		truly
	That lyueþ in charite and loueþ reste and pes.		
	Here y haue told many afayr sight .		

---

¹ An erasure was made in this area, and auto-corrected.
² This military diction and alliteration sets up the expectation for *stonde*; it may be a scribal error or intentional. Another equally viable reading is *fonde,* or "try."
³ A blue ink smudge of about two letters width and one space high follows this word in the margin.
⁴ Notice the diminution of *punctus* use; this is one of a very few in the final pages of the poem.
⁵ A thin line has been inserted between *brid* and *gome*. *Bridgome* means a young man about to be married. In theology, it signifies Christ as spouse in mystical union with his Church members.
⁶ "The church fighting [Church Militant--on earth] and the church triumphing [Church Triumphant--in heaven]" [Rudulfus Ardens, *PL* 155, col. 1540; see also Peter Lombard, *PL* 191, col. 621, commentary on Psalm 67:14]. This quotation is not found in Morey's Northern version.
⁷ An erasure spot of about two letters separates these words.

198 Part VII. The Joys of Heaven (6870–6909)

6870	Þe whiche beþ ymade þorow godes myght	f.88v	
	And now wole itelle what peyne and wo		sorrow
	To the synful men schull ben ido		
	And of þe ioies þat þe gode schullen haue		
	In her . v . wittes that¹ god woll saue		five senses, save
6875	**Of þe peynes of sight þ(a)t þe synful w(i)þ oþ(er) peynes schul haue.**		
	Ferst þey schulleþ in helle abouten hem ise		
	More sorowe þan in al þis world may be²		
	And wiþ ynne helle þei schull ben loke		locked / shut
	That is ful of fuyr and stynkynge smoke		
6880	And þat schal be gresly and dym and derke		
	And hem to peyne schal be þe fendes werke		hurt, devils' work
	Ac ȝet all þowh³ in helle þer faile light		those, are lacking
	Ȝut of her peynes þei schulleþ haue sight		
	Thorow sparckles of fuyr as seiþ seynt austyn		
6885	Nouȝt to her confort . ⁴ bot to here pyne.		For their pain
	Of þe blisse of herynge.⁵*		
	The soule that is good schal haue to his heryng		
	Gret ioye in heuene and gret likynge		pleasure / delight
	Ffor þey schull here þere angels song		hear
6890	And wiþ hem þei schull synge eu(er)e among		sing
	Wiþ delitable vois and swiþe⁶ clere		delightful voice, so
	And also wiþ þat þei schulleþ haue þere		
	Alle oþ(er) manere of dyuerse melodie		various melodies
	Of wel likynge noyse . and of menstralsie		minstralcy
6895	And of alle man(er) tones of murye mysike		tones, merry music
	That to mannes herte wel myght lyke		please / give pleasure
	Wiþouten any man(er)e of t(ra)vaile		work
	And þat schal neu(er) cese ne fayle.		
	Ac þat noyse schal be so schil and so swete		sonorous, sweet
6900	And so delitable to smale and to grete		
	That all þe melodie of þis world here		
	That eu(er)y was iherd fer oþur nere		
	Were bot sorowe þ(er)to and care		sadness
	To þat swete blysse þat is in heuene ȝare⁷		[compared] to, prepared
6905	**Of the contrarie of þat blisse.**		
	Wel gret sorow schal þe synful be tide		happen to / befall
	For þey schull here on eu(er)y side		
	Fful gret noyse þat þe fendes wolleþ make		
	As þowh all þe world scholde to schake		break open

---

[1] The word *that* covers a smudged erasure.
[2] An ink blot is situated between *be* and *ise* (of the previous line).
[3] The word *þowh* is written over an erasure.
[4] This could be *a punctus,* or the remains of an erasure, conveniently falling at the caesura mark.
[5] This heading and the following have flourishes at the end of their line, but the next folio has none. See note 1, folio 80v.
[6] *Swiþe* and *schelleþ* (in the next line) are marred by a brown ink or erasure smudge.
[7] This word is written over an erasure by the scribe.

6910	Ffor alle men lyuynge þat myght it here	f.89r	hear
	Schulle her wite lese and no leng(er) lyue here		lose, longer
	Thanne þey schullen for sorowe her hondes wrynge		mind / hands wring
	And eu(er)e weylawey þey schull be cryenge		crying
	Of þe ioye of smellynge.		
6915	Among hem also schal be good sauo(ur)		flavor
	So swete come neu(er) of herbe ne flour		flower
	Ne of spicery myght neu(er) sprynge		spice
	So swete a finel . no of non oþur þynge		fennel, nor
	Ffor no herte may þenke no tonge telle		nor
6920	So swete eche of oþ(ur) þanne schal smelle		
	Thanne schall þat savo(ur) þat is so swete[1]		savor
	Be blyssfull ioye to hem and grete.		
	Of þe contrarie of that blisse.		opposite
	Ac þe synfull schull smelle more stench		
6925	Þan tonge may telle or heorte þynch		envision
	Of brennynge brymston and stynkyng piche		
	And oþur þynges þat þ(er)to beþ iliche		alike
	That schal be to hem a peyne strong		
	Whan þey schullen eu(er)e gon þ(er) among.		go
6930	**Of þe ioye of syngynge.**		
	The gode men schull preise god in her song		
	And þonke hym of his mercy ofte among		continually
	And eu(er)y man of þat blyssfull companye		
	Schall to oþ(er) speke wiþ gret curtasye		
6935	And fayr chere and glad semblaunt		countenance
	And þonke god þat þere to dwelle ȝaf hem g(ra)unt[2]		permission
	And haþ to hem her synnes furȝyuen here		forgiven
	Wherfore þey schull syng on þis manere .		sing this way
	Misericordias d(om)in(i) in et(er)nu(m) cantabo[3] .		
6940	That is y schal eu(er)e þe m(er)cy synge		
	Of our lord wiþ outen any cesynge		ceasing
	And for þey soffred anguisses in her lif dayes		suffered torments / pains
	Þei schulleþ synge as david saies		
	Letati sum(us) p(ro) diebus quib(us) nos humiliasti		
	humiliasti . annis qui(bus) vidim(us) mala.[4]		
6945	Fful glad he seiþ for þo dayes be we		says, those
	In þe whiche þu madest us lowe to be		humble
	In þulke ȝeres[5] where ynne we sawen much ille		
	For we hadde þo nought al our wille.		desire
	Of þe contrarie of that blisse .		

---

[1] The last five or six words have been written over an erasure.
[2] The last four words are written over an erasure, and ȝaf has been squeezed into place.
[3] "The mercies of the Lord I will sing forever" [Psalm 88:2].
[4] "We have rejoiced for the days in which thou hast humbled us: for the years in which we have seen evils" [Psalm 89:15].
[5] Some letters are wearing away on this and the next line.

6950	The synfull þrotes schull be yfouled among	f.89v	throats, fouled, also
	Wiþ [all]¹ þyng þat may be bitt(er) and strong		
	And schal be wiþ² smoke and fuyr y medled		mixed
	And of pich and brymston to gidre iwellyd		melting / boiling
	And also wiþ lede and bras y molte wiþal .		molten together
6955	And of oþ(ur) muche wellynge metal .		boiling
	This peyne schal wiþ hem eu(er)e laste		
	And mo oþ(ur) peynes me(n) schal þ(er)to caste.		more, calculate

Of the ioye of felynge.*³

	The good men schulleþ haue wurschipes grete		honor
6960	And eche of hem schall be iset in a riche sete		set, seat
	And as kynges be coroned þere faire		crowned, splendily
	Idight wiþ riche p(er)re and so set in a chaire		Prepared, jewelry
	And with stones of v(er)tu . and p(re)cious of chois .		power, choice
	As david seiþ to god wiþ a mylte vois .		merciful
6965	*Posuisti d(omi)ne sup(er) caput eius . corona(m) de lapide p(re)cioso.*⁴		
	Lord he seiþ on his hed þu settist wel aright .		says, head, set
	A corone of p(re)cious stones richely dight		crown, prepared
	Ac so fayr a corone was neu(er) non isene		fair, crown, seen
	In þis world on kynges heued non on queen .		head
6970	Ffor this corowne is þe corowne of blys		
	And þe ston is ioye wherof þey schull neuer mys .		lack
	They schull þere be fed and cloþed in cloþ .		
	Wiþ þe sight of þat is to hem no þyng loþ		not at all displeasing
	And þei schull þere worchen in non oþ(er) þyng		work
6975	Bote eu(er)e preyse God . wiþ outen endynge.		
	A versifiour seiþ in a vers þ(er)by .		poet, verse, about that
	That is mad in metre þus schortly		made, meter
	*Visio sit vict(us) . opus est laus lumen amict(us)*⁵.		
	That is wiþ þe sight of god þei schull ben ifed		fed
6980	And wiþ brightnesse of light be clanly icled .		entirely clothed / clad
	And hure werk schal be of god⁶ preisying		their work, praise
	In þe whiche þei schull haue gret lykynge.		delign / pleasure

Of the cont(ra)rie of þat blysse.*

	The synfull schulleþ as y haue bifore told .		
6985	Fele to muche hete and after to muche cold .		feel
	Ffor now þey schulleþ frese and now brenne		
	And so be y peyned þat now schal oþur kenne		reached by pain, discover
	And also be ibite wiþ dragons felle and kene		bitten, fierce / cruel, savage
	That schullen hem destruye outrightes clene .		utterly destroy / kill, completely

---

¹ The word *all* is crossed off with one single bold stroke, perhaps for better rhythm in the line.
² The word *wiþ* is written over an erasure.
³ The same embellishments or flourishes noted above in note 1, folio 80v. complete this heading and the other on this page also.
⁴ "… thou hast set on his head a crown of precious stones" [Psalm 20:4].
⁵ "Let the vision be [your] food; there is need for praise, clothed in light" [Pseudo-Ambrose, *PL* 17, col. 540; Pseudo-Augustinus, *PL* 42, col. 1203, 1206, commenting on Psalm 103:2; Pseudo-Augustinus, *PL 26,* col. 1131, commenting on Psalm 103; Paulus Winfridus, *PL,* 95, col. 1492; Gregorius I, *PL 76,* col. 628].
⁶ "A space of about two or three letters remains where an erasure has been made.

6990	And wiþ oþ(ur) vermyn and bestes felle[1]	f.90r	fierce
	That beþ nought elles bote fendes of helle		fiends / devils
	Thus þey schulleþ ben ipyned harde and sore		punished
	In alle hure . v . wittes durynge eu(er)more		their five senses lasting forever
	Ff(ro)m þe whiche pyne crist us schilde		shield
6995	Þorow þe prayer of his modur mylde		
	And to þe right wey of lyf god us eu(er)e wisse		guide
	Where þorow [ ][2] we mowe come to his blysse.		whereby, must
	How he likneþ heuene to a bodily þyng w(i)t(h) a gostly undurstondyng.[3]		likens, spiritual
	The cite of heuene that is so wide and brod		
7000	No man wote p(ro)prely by no wyt of manhod		properly, no human understanding
	How it is y made in eu(er)y place wiþ ynne		
	Bot he þe knowynge þerof þorow grace myght wynne		gain
	Ne no man þorow myght can telle in his þought		might, thought
	Of what man(er) mater it is iwrought.		type matter, created
7005	It is nauʒt ymaked of lym ne of ston		not, lime, stone
	Ne of tre for of such mater is it[4] non		wood
	For no þyng bifalleþ to be in þat cite		happens
	That britull oþ(ur) faylynge eu(er)e may be		mutable, transient
	Bot mater þerof as y suppose and trowe		matter / material, believe
7010	Ys made of alle þyng that is meke and lowe.		humble
	This cite was neuer made wiþ mann(es) hond		hand
	Bot þorow the myght of wit and godes sond		gift / dispensation
	And we findeþ iwrite that it is fayr and bright		
	Ac no man kan descryue it aright		
7015	Ffor so wis a clerk was neu(er) non alyue		
	That þe fayrnesse þerof couþe descryue		could describe
	And þaw y conne nought p(ro)p(re)ly desc(ry)ue that place		I can not properly
	ʒut y wole in my witt þorow godes grace		mind / understanding
	ʒyue there uppon som(m)e man(er) descripcion		type of description
7020	For y haue þerto a swiþe gret affeccion		so great
	And gret confort and solas it is to me[5]		encouragement
	To þynkyn and to speke of that fayr cite		
	And that t(ra)vayle may me greue no þyng		not at all
	For y haue þerynne so gret lykynge		therein, desire
7025	The cite of heuene is large and eu(er)e glad		
	Of þe whiche no compariso(u)n may be mad .		
	Ac ʒut as y ymagyne in my þought		
	Y likne it to a cite that were newe iwrought		I liken, newly created
	Of gold and p(re)ciouse stones eu(er)ywhere.		

---

[1] A parchment strip has been cut from the bottom of this folio.
[2] The space here seems motivated by the sense of the line, a pause for reflection, not an erasure or emendation.
[3] The page has been trimmed here; the only authority for a period is the scribe's consistent use of one after headings.
[4] Written over an erasure. This and several other minor emendations are auto-corrections. Perhaps the inversion of words confused the scribe, accounting for the erasure.
[5] This is one of the most personal statements of the poet, offering his emotional response to this part of the poem.

Part VII. The Joys of Heaven (7030–7069)

7030	And set upon a montayn of berel clere	f.90v	beryl
	Wiþ walles and wardes and hie t(ur)rettes		strongholds / battlements, turrets
	And entre of gates wiþ strong garettes		entrance
	And alle þe walles weren mad of þat cite		
	Of p(re)cious stones and riche p(er)re		jewels
7035	And alle þe t(ur)rettes of cristall schene		crystal shining
	And þe warde ou(er)gult and anamayled clene		ramparts completely gilded, enammeled
	And to þe gates scholde charbocles bifalle		carbuncles
	And alle þe garetes were rubies and coralle		garrets
	And þat cite hadde lanes and stretes wide		
7040	And ful fayre chambres on eu(er)y side		rooms
	As schynynge as gold that is fayr and bright		
	And wiþ all . man(er) ricchesse were idight		types, prepared
	And þat alle the stretes of þat riche house		noble, splendid
	Weren euere ipaued wiþ stones p(re)ciouse		
7045	And þat þe brede and þe lenkþe of þat riche cyte		breadth
	Were more than is here any contre		greater
	And þat þere were all manere of melodye		types
	That is of musik or of menstralsie		
	That myght be isewed wiþ hand or wiþ mowþ		performed, mouth
7050	And myryor sownynge þan any man telle cowþ		merrier, could
	And eu(er)y day it scholde so[ ]¹ bifalle		happen
	That non scholde be wery amonges hem alle		
	And þat eu(er)y lane and eu(er)y strete		
	Of þat cite were full of sauo(ur)es swete		aromas
7055	As of spicery and alle oþur þyng		spices
	Wherof any good savo(ur) myght out spryng		
	And þere were plente of mete and drynke		food
	And alle oþer delites that man may þynke		delicious foods
	And þat to eche man that scholde þ(er)e lyue		
7060	Also muche beaute were þanne iȝiue		
	As absolon hadde þat so fayr a creat(ur)e was		
	For so muche fayrnesse neu(er)e þ(er) nas		beauty
	In no maner man that was erþlich ibore		type of man, born
	Ne so clene of body was neu(er)e non yoore		comely / fair, of old
7065	And þ(er)wiþ hadde as muche strenkþe among		as well / also
	As hadde sampson that was so strong		
	And eu(er)y² where as swifte to make his pas		make his way
	And to renne on fote as asael³ was		run, Asahel
	That so swift was to renne and go		run and walk

---

[1] A space of three or four letters remains from an erasure at this point.
[2] The scribe intersperses y's and dotted y's, using about 21 of the former and 12 of the latter on this page. The dotted y seems to occur most often in words such as *fayre*, a diphthong.
[3] Asahel, youngest son of Zeruiah, David's sister, and Jesse's daughter, was known for his swiftness of foot, "like a gizelle in an open field" (2 Samuel 2:18). While commanding David's forces, Asahel pursued and caught Abner who then put the blunt end of a spear through Asahel's stomach, killing him (2 Samuel 2:23). His brothers killed Abner in revenge.

7070	That he myght torne boþe bok and ro	f.91r	circle both buck, roe
	And that eche of hem hadde as contynuely hele		continually good health
	As hadde moyses that neu(er) of siknesse myght fele		
	And also þ(er)wiþ ȝif it possible were		
	That eche of hem myght as long lyuen there[1]		
7075	As matusale that was here on lyue		Methusalah, alive
	A þousand ȝere er deþ wolde wiþ hem stryue		contend
	And þat eche of hem myght as wise be		each
	As Salomon[2] for þer was neuer non so wise as he		Solomon
	That þorow his witte hadde opene knowynge		senses, manifest
7080	Of alle maner þyng and undurstondyngc		kinds of
	And þat eu(er)y loued oþ(ur) as wel oþur more		everyone, or
	And as good frendes were eu(er)e more		
	As david and ionathas were on eorþe ifound		Jonathan
	For eche of hem tyl oþ(ur) in trewe loue was bounde		to other, true
7085	And þat eche of hem honoured were[3]		
	Of alle oþur men that beþ on lyue here		
	As iosep was of þe egipciens wel aright		Joseph, Egyptians
	Wham þey honoured as man of gret myght		whom, power
	And that eche of hem were as myghty in all þyng		things
7090	As eu(er)e was alisaunder that noble kyng		Alexander
	That conquered alle the landes about		
	And mowen as undurlynges to hym loute		might, subjects, bow
	And þat eche of hem therto as siker were		certain
	Of her dwellynge as longe to abide þ(er)e		remain
7095	As ennok and elie[4] beþ in þe same wise		Enoch, Elijah
	Syker of her dwellynge in ioyfull paradyse		sure / certain, home
	Ffor þe tyme that they were up ynome		taken
	And þere schulleþ be tyl antecrist come		until the antilchrist
	And he that hadde all þese v(er)tues iwis		powers
7100	As in þis boke it iwryten is		
	He hadde more ioye than any man cowþe telle		would have
	Þow in þis world he myght eu(er)e dwelle		
	Ac alle þese blisses wherof y tolde		
	As to þe ioye of heuene beþ nat iholde		compared
7105	Ffor as muche difference or more schold be		
	By twene heuene and such a riche cite		
	As bitwexe a kynges paleis y mad at denys[5]		palace, St. Denys
	And a swynes sty that is of lytil p(ry)s.		pigsty, value
	Thus y may likne and caste by all man(er) aray[6]		compare, arrange, appearance

---

[1] This one-word correction of *there* may have been done in another hand.

[2] This is one of the few times the author has capitalized a proper name

[3] A two-word correction of *honoured were* that appears to be done in another hand, with quite a different scribing of the letter *h*, compared to the *h* in the previous word *hem*. A high percentage of emendations occur at the end of lines and the end of pages, perhaps suggesting the scribe's attention waned at the end of a line or page.

[4] See p. 97, f. 49r, note 12, for prior explanation of these prophets.

[5] The Church of St. Denys, located outside of Paris, is noted for its great splendor.

[6] A smaller number of abbreviations occur on this page than most, especially earlier pages.

Part VII. The Joys of Heaven (7110–7149)

7110	Þe cite of heuene that is so hy of aray.	f.91v	exalted, magnificent
	¶ This cite is set on an hie hille		
	That no synfull man may come þ(er) tille		
	And that y likne to berel clene		compared, beryl
	Ac so fayr berel may non be sene		But such beautiful
7115	That hille is noȝt elles to undurstondynge		
	Bote holy þowȝtes and desir brennynge		
	That holy men hadde here to þat place		
	Whiles they hadden on eorþe her lyues space		lifetimes
	And y likne as y may ymagyne in my þought		compare
7120	Þe walles of heuene to walles þat were wrought		created
	Of alle maner p(re)cious stones iset ifere		stones set together
	And symented wiþ[1] gold . bright and clere		cemented
	Bot so bright gold no non so clene		not any at all, none
	Was in þis world neu(er) asene		seen
7125	Ne non so riche stones . ne non so p(re)cious .		
	As aboute heuene beþ no so vertuous .		powerful
	Ac þulke p(re)cious stones gostly mowe be .[2]		those, spiritual, must
	Good werkes ido . the gold is charyte		
	The wardes of the cite of heuene bright		battlements
7130	Y likne to wardes that were wel dight		I compare, prepared
	And clanly wrought and so tally entayled .		elegantly carved
	And on burned gold clanly anamailed[3] .		entirely, enamneled
	Bot the wardes of the cite of heuene aboue		battlements
	Beþ more craftyly yset[4] and hardore in loue		set, hardier
7135	Ac þe wardes of heuene that beþ so idight		prepared
	Mowen be itold power, strenkþe and myght		Can be considered / signified
	That soules in heuene schull haue		
	Of the good men that god wol saue.		
	The turettes of heuene grete and smale		turrets
7140	Y likne to þe turettes of clene cristale		clear crystal
	Ac þe t(ur)ettes of heuene beþ more schynynge		summits
	Than any crystal stones weren in her bigynnynge		
	Thulke t(ur)retes gostly . p(re)ue hono(ur) mowe be .		spiritual, secret / mysterious, may
	That good men schull fele and se.		experience and see
7145	The gates of heuene y likne all at ones		I compare, once
	To gates that weren maked of charabocle stones		carbuncle
	Ac þo gates gostly to speke beþ mekenesse		speaking metaphorically / spiritually
	And fredom of aright fey and buxumnesse .		faith, obedience
	They entre ȝiueþ tyl hem that schull be ynome .		entrance / gate

---

[1] The words *symented wiþ* are auto-corrected over an unclean erasure.
[2] Like most other end-line punctuation, the *punctus* is not near the word, but removed a bit to the right margin. The poet is here moving from concrete to symbolic imagery after luring his audience into the grandeur which he will lavishly describe.
[3] The first *a* of *anamailed* has been written over an erasure and does not quite line up with the *a* near it. Perhaps the scribe first wrote an *e*, smaller than an *a*, since a smaller space remained for the emendation.
[4] This word is emended by the *Piers* rubricator.

7150	Into þe cite of heuene to god forto come	f.92r	
	And þe garetes of heuene mowe be		may signify
	Hie states and lordschipes wyþ dignyte		estates
	The whiche alle that dwelleþ in þat cete		
	Schulleþ haue and wiþ god be preue		be private / secret with God
7155	And þe wonynge stedes that in heuene beþ aboue		dwelling places
	Y woll it likne to þe stedfaste loue		compare it to
	That eu(er)y man scholde to oþur haue		
	ʒif that he willeþ his soule to saue		
	The which schull schyne wiþ ynne and wiþ oute		
7160	On¹ eu(er)y side that þ(er) is aboute		waiting nearby
	Where alle rightfull schull wone		dwell
	In full ioye wiþ þe sight of godes sone		son
	And þerfore holy cherche thus p(re)ieþ		prays
	For soules in purgatory . and þus saieþ .		says
7165	*Tuam deus dep(re)cam(ur) clemencia(m) . ut eis*		
	*t(ri)buere digneris lucidas et quietas mansiones*² .		
	That is to seie god we askeþ þe m(er)cy and pite		thee / you familiar
	That thu fouche safe that we p(re)y to þe		vouchsafe
	To ʒiue to hem wonynge stedes bright		
	And full reste þat nede haueþ to þi light.		rest / peace, in your light
7170	Ac no bodyliche myght neu(er) ise³		
	A poynt of þe brightnesse þat þ(er)e schull be⁴		
	Ffor eu(er)y lane þat þer is and eu(er)y strete		
	Most nedes schyne for þ(er)e schulleþ mete		
	Boþe angels and men brightor schynynge		
7175	Þan doþ þe sonne in any mornynge		
	Ffor þe body of eche man schall so bright schyne		
	Þat all a contre myght þ(er)to drawe by lyne		entire, straight / evenly
	And eche an here þat is on a mannes heued		hair, head
	And eche here þat is on his body⁵ bileued .		left
7180	Alle schull schyne as bright as þe sonne		shine, sun
	Whan sche her strengest hete haþ most iwonne		for the most part, most intense reached
	Ffull bright schynyng abouen us		
	Wherfor þe book of autorites seiþ þus:		authorities
	*Ffulgebu(n)t iusti sicut sol.*⁶		
7185	He seiþ þe rightfull schul schyne as þe sonne iwis		righteous
	In heuene and þere wone⁷ eu(er) more in blys		live
	Ac ʒet þat ylke⁸ grete brightnesse		same
	That thei haueþ schall be lesse		less

---

¹ A space from an erasure precedes this word *On;* the o is smaller than other letters beginning a line.
² "We pray for your clemency, Lord, that you will deign to bestow on us your bright and peaceful dwellings" [From the *Liber Antiphonarius* attributed to Gregory I, *PL* 78, col. *722,* Gerhohus Reicherspergensis, *PL* 193, col. 1542].
³ "Nothing corporal can ever be behold."
⁴ A note in modern hand at this line reads "The other MS. ends here," but there is no indication which manuscript that might be.
⁵ A long tail and a space here may suggest a (logical) pause in the scribe's thought.
⁶ "Then shall the just shine as the sun" [Matt. 13:43].
⁷ A small space remains here, possibly from a clean erasure since the *e* appears to be added. A logical pause exists here as well.
⁸ The word *ylke* (with a dotted *y*) has been written over a larger erasure in an upward slant, probably by the main scribe.

206 Part VII. The Joys of Heaven (7189–7228)

	Than the brightnesse of god almyghty[1]	f.92v	
7190	For he schall þanne be seie full sighty		seen, visible
	Right as þe sterres haueþ her light iwonne		stars, gained
	And semeþ in brightnesse as doþ þe sonne		
	Ac ȝet þey beþ nouȝt so bright no so clere		
	As the sonne that schyneþ in her man(er)e		
7195	Right so schull we þere as þe sterres schyne		stars shine
	Ac god schall be brightnesse in þe sonnes lyne		But, sun's line of descent
¶	Eu(er)y lane and stret that in heuene may be		
	Is lengur than is here any oþ(ur) contre		longer
	Ac[2] þe lanes and þe stretes gostly to telle		to speak in a spiritual sense
7200	Beþ alle holy men þat þ(er)ynne schull dwelle		
	In that [that][3] cite schall be more ricchesse		wealth
	Than alle þe men of þe world mowe gesse		can
	Ac that ricchesse gostly to undurstonde		spiritually
	Beþ þe grete blisses thorow godes sonde		joys, messages
7205	The whiche alle that schull to heuene wende		go
	Schull fele and se wiþouten ende.		
¶	The pauement of heuene may ilikned be		compared
	To a pauement of precious stones and p(er)re		jewels
	Ac that pauement schall schyne more clere		brightly
7210	Than eu(er)e inde gold or precious stones here.		India
	The pauement of heuene is iset so faste		firmly
	That it ne may faile ac eu(er)e more laste		
	In þe whiche schull none creuers ben sene		crevices
	For it is all hole and euene and eu(er)more clene		completely / undivided, smooth
7215	This pauement of heuene þus craftly ymad .		skillfully
	Gostly to undurstonde is eu(er)e more blyþe and glad		shining
	Ffor it haþ parfit loue and endles lif .		has
	With pes and reste eu(er)e with out strif .		
¶	Thus may a man that haþ any discrecio(u)n		judgment
7220	All the cite of heuene likne by reso(u)n		reasonably
	To a bodyly thyng that is fayr and bright		
	And most delitable eu(er)e to mannes sight		delightful
	As to[4] p(re)cious stones that beth of gret v(er)tu .		
	And to golde and selv(er) that is of muche valu		
7225	Ac alle þe ricchesse that eu(er)e in þe world was		
	To þe ioye of heuene is nought an as[5] .		
	Ffor þ(er)e is all þyng that any man can craue		desire
	Or elles desireþ in thouȝt forto haue.		

---

[1] "Right so shall we shine there as the stars shine / But god shall be brightness in the lineage of the sun."
[2] The lower lobe of the *A* of *Ac* and the lower section of *whiche* (l. 7271) are filled in by ink, perhaps an unintentional blotting.
[3] The second *that* is lightly crossed off in paler ink than the text, either by the scribe or a later hand.
[4] These two words are auto-corrected over an unclean erasure.
[5] All the world's riches is as nothing—like rolling an ace in a dice game—compared to the joys of heaven.

	ꝑow is the laste part of þis boke y mad	f. 93r	finished / concluded
7230	And alle maters þ(er)of beþ to ȝow yrad		advised
	And nowe y haue as y ferst undurtoke		declared / promised
	Fulfuld þe seuene parties of þis boke[1]		
	That of dyuerse bokes y haue out drawe[2]		derived
	That the lewed peple may it þe bett(er) knawe		unlettered, know
7235	How they scholde god loue[3] and drede		fear
	Ȝif þei of this book wol take good hede		heed
	And who so wele loued god in right man(er)e		
	He haþ grete drede to wraþþe hym here		fear, anger
	¶ The prykke of conscience is this book ihote		called
7240	And that is undurstondynge of her soules bote		remedy
	Ffor who so this tretys to herte wele take[4]		
	He may his conscience the more tendur make		attentive
	And into þe right wey of lif hym brynge blyue		happily
	And his heorte to drede and mekenesse dryue		to fear [i.e. God], move / urge
7245	And þe undurstodynge of þese materes seuene		
	That men mowen se in this book wel euene		may see, quite precisely
	May make a man to knowe and to haue in mynde		
	Which he is here of his owne kynde		What, nature
	And what he schall be ȝif he woll þ(er)on loke		
7250	And whedur he schal he may wite by þis boke		where he must go, know
	Wheþur that he schall to ioye or to peyne		punishment / suffering
	This boke may hym make to be in certeyne.		certain
	Thus may this tretes wiþ þe sentence[5]		meaning
	To the good sturie a mannes conscience		guide / move
7255	And also a man may conceyue ther by		understand
	To do good deeds and fle foly		
	And to be siker of heuene blysse		sure
	Ȝif he hym amende of þat he haþ don mysse		change himself / make amends
	And drede any thyng to do aȝenst godes wille		fear
7260	And his commaundementes eu(er)e fulfylle.		
	¶ Of alle þis y haue dyv(er)se materes sowȝt		diverse materials
	And into seuene parties . y . haue hem brouȝt		
	And they beþ conteyned in þis tretys		contained, treatise
	That y haue maked after my dyvys		according to my design
7265	After that y hadde on hem undurstondynge		understood them
	All þowhe y be of symple connyngge[6] .		Although, knowledge
	Ac y praye ȝow alle pur[7] seynt charite		But, through
	That this tretys wolleþ rede or ise.		Who will read, see

---

[1] The formal closure here emphasizes the rhetorical dimension throughout, so well noted by Howell Chickering (see bibliography).
[2] The *w* has been written over an unclean erasure.
[3] *Love* is written over an erasure (and a small space remains after the word), as is *wel* (1. 7246).
[4] The last three words have been emended by the *Piers* rubricator.
[5] The last two letters, *ce,* are written over an erasure.
[6] Several erasures underlie words at the end of this folio, such as *connynge, ȝow* (1.7268), and *tretys* (1.7269).
[7] The scribe used a variant spelling in *pur* here; Morey's Osborn a.13 reads "per charité" (p. 218, fol. 139r. l. 1902). Interestingly, about a dozen errors mar this page; fewer errors occur when the scribe is translating or elaborating on Latin aphorisms.

	That ȝe haue me excused at þis tyme[1]		hold
7270	Þowh ȝe fynde any defaute in þis ryme	f.93v	though, default
	Ffor y ne rekke þouȝ þe rym be somdel brod		care if, rhyme, somewhat free
	So that the mater þerof be good		As long as the matter
	And ȝif any man that is[2] a clerk		cleric (literate or educated)
	Kan fynde any errour in þis holy werk		
7275	I p(re)y hem that they do me that favour		
	That þey wold amende thulke errour		correct / rectify, that
	Ffor ȝif me(n) may þ(er)on any erro(ur) ise		see
	Or any defaute in this treys be		defect, treatise
	I make here openly a protestacio(u)n		declare
7280	That y well stonde to alle good correctio(u)n		submit to
	Of euery rightfull and ilerned man		
	That my defaute heron amende kan.		error
	This tretis specially is mad in redynesse		made, eagerness
	Forto sturie lewed men the more to mekenesse		lead ignorant
7285	And to make hem good to loue[3] [ ] and drede		revere
	For who so woll this book y here or rede		desires
	I hope he schall be istered þerby .		stirred
	Of god for his synnes to haue mercy		
	And þat it doþ ihere oþ(ur) yse		whoever
7290	And may to goodnesse nat stured be		moved
	It semeþ that he is witles or out of g(ra)ce		irrational / insane
	Or elles so wikked in eu(er)y place		everywhere
	And is ou(er)muche combred wiþ synne		exceedingly
	That he may of þis non undurstondyng wynne.		no understanding gain
7295	Ac alle þat it redeþ lowde oþ(er) stille		aloud or silently
	Oþ(ur) it ihereþ wiþ any good wille		
	God graunt hem grace that þey mowe[4] alwey		may, always
	Be stered þerby in conscience to rightful wey		path of righteousness
	That is to seie to þe wey of right lyuynge		say, upright way of life
7300	And at þe laste be broght to good endynge.		a good death
	¶ Nowe ȝe that haueþ iherd þis tretis mad		
	And is in ȝour conscience openly sprad[5]		laid out
	Ffor þe loue of our lord ihu crist nowe		Jesus
	Prayeþ specially for hym þat it out drowe		composed
7305	And for hym also þat haþ iwriten it here[6]		
	Wheþur þat þei beþ fer oþ(er) nere.		far or near
	As for þe moste synfull man that lyueþ by bred .		lives
	That god forȝiue hym his synnes er he be ded .[7]		before he dies

---

[1] Although this is the standard humility trope / topos, the author achieves a personal tone through this direct address.

[2] Written over an erasure in the same hand.

[3] The last two letters are written over an erasure, and a blank space remains after the word, interestingly just as on the previous page. Perhaps the same longer erased word occurred at both spots, and was replaced by love in both places.

[4] The text reads "mowe be alwey / Be ..." so I have deleted the first redundancy of *be*.

[5] Another intriguing image: this treatise spread out inside the conscience(s) of the audience.

[6] He asks blessings for both author and scribe, quite a typical topos.

[7] Clearly a *punctus* ends this folio, but it is somewhat smeared and blurry.

	And ȝif þat god hem boþe saue f(ro)m wikkednesse	f.94r	
7310	And manteyne her lif in alle goodeness		preserve
	And ȝif þei ben dede as it falleþ by kynde .		die, naturally
	That god of her soules eu(er)e haue mynde		remember
	And brynge hem boþe to that blissfull place		
	Where endles ioye is in sight of godes face		
7315	To þe whiche he us brynge		
	That for our loue maked all þynge. Amen:		for love of us

Here endet þe prikke of conscience.[1]

ends

---

[1] This conclusion is bordered in red ink in larger script and is followed by a small drawing about one inch across.

Select Glossary
by Hoyt Greeson

Preface to the Glossary

The glossary to this edition of the *Pricke of Conscience*, based on Huntington Manuscript 128, includes, of course, words no longer current in modern English, as well as forms, i.e., spellings, apparently modern but whose meanings have undergone change in the years since the poem was written.

The headword for each entry is normally selected on the basis of its wider distribution in the text of the poem: that is, it occurs with greater frequency than its variant forms. If most of the variant forms are relatively similar, a dissimilar form may be selected as headword: e.g., **sey(e)**, not **say(e)**, will appear as the head word. When possible, two headwords are combined to save space. For example, **sey(e)** represents two forms, **sey** and **seye**. Graphic variants are also presented as two forms of the same headword. Thus, **anamailed, anamayled** co-occur because, as noted below, <i> and <y> are graphic equivalents. One further note: two-part forms such as **ther after** or **there after** are treated as one word, e.g., **therafter** or **thereafter**.

Forms apparently unrelated to a headword are cross-listed, e.g., **am** *see* **be**. Line references are provided for the first occurrence of each form and variant; they are also provided for subsequent forms whose meanings differ or which occur in idiomatic constructions.

Nearly every entry has been checked for variant meanings and idiomatic phrases by consulting *Middle English Dictionary*, ed. Hans Kurath, et al. The entries offer possible shades of meaning for the poem as a whole. But no attempt has been made to assign a particular meaning to any given occurrence of a word.

The alphabetic order of words follows, for the most part, current custom, with the following exceptions:

Vocalic <y> and <i> represent the same letter and occur initially with words in <i->; medially, they are listed after words beginning with <h->.

Consonantal <y> is treated as <y>, and occurs after words in <w->. Initial consonantal <i-> alternates with <j->, depending on the individual scribe's practice, and is listed with <j-> words.

The graphs <u> and <w> are equivalents in forms such as **couthe** and **cowþe**; word-initially, <u-> occurs before <w->. <u> also alternates with <v>. Representing a vowel, it occurs in words as <u>; when consonantal, it is represented by <v>.

The graphs <th> and <þ> are equivalents, but word-initially, <th-> words are to be found in alphabetical order with words in <t->; word-initially <þ-> follows the <t-> words, in alphabetical order.

Words with initial <sch-> are of wide distribution in the dialect of HM 128, so forms with initial <sh-> will normally be found as variant spellings of words in <sch->.

The graph <ȝ> can be an equivalent of <gh>, which it will follow, alphabetically, in the <g-> words. Initially, it may be the equivalent of <i/y>, and is found with words in <i->. <ȝ> can also represent <z> in this manuscript, as in **Corozaym**, Corozaim.

The following abbreviations are used in the glossary:

acc(usative)	*dat*(ive)	*obj*(ective)	*pl*(ural)	*refl*(exive)
adj(ective)	*imper*(ative)	*ord*(inal)	*poss*(essive)	*sg* = singular
adv(erb)	*impers*(onal)	*part*(iciple)	*prep*(osition)	*subj*(unctive)
aux(iliary)	*interj*(ection)	*ppl* = past participle	*pr*(esent tense)	*superl*(ative)
conj(unction)	*n*(oun)	*pa*(st tense)	*pron*(oun)	*v*(erb)
comp(arative)	*num*(eral)	*pers*(onal)	*rel*(ative)	*vbl* = verbal

211

Select Glossary (by Hoyt Greeson)

abate *v.* reduce, lessen, diminish; alleviate; end 585

abide, abyde *v.* wait (for); dwell, live; remain; endure 1641, 221; **faste** ~ remain fixed 1593; **abideþ** *pr3pl.* 2625

abidynge *vbl.n.* waiting, expectation; remaining; delay 3885

abod *n.* waiting; **wiþ oute any lengor** ~ without any further delay 5223

a bought *v.* redeemed *pa.3sg.* 1451; **abouȝte: dere** ~ redeemed at a high price 2631

abowte *adv.* around, throughout, round about 1034; **aboute: alle** ~ on all sides 4361; ~ **to go** to revolve 6119; **þer is aboute** is around it 7159

about(e) *prep.* around, including; throughout 5597, 708; ~ **chace** rush about 3592

abouten *prep.* about 6735

above *adv.* above; **evene** ~ just above 2238; **no þyng may be** ~ **þat iseie** nothing above that can be seen 6047

abregge *v.* shorten, reduce, 2564; curtail 2736; **abregged** *ppl.* 3850

a breggynge *vbl.n.* reduction 2941

abreþ *n.* life, spirit; breath 6143

abrod *adv.* across its breadth 4117

ac *conj.* but 38

accord(e) *v.* agree; correspond 6590, 2816; **acordeþ** *pr3sg.* 1082; **accordeþ** 272

acord(e) *n.* agreement, harmony, concord, good will 6172; **make ...** ~ reconcile 2816

acursid *v.* cursed *pa.3sg.* 3482

acusynge *vbl.n.* accusation 5104

adder *n.* snake 3455; **eddres** *pl.* 731 **addres** *poss.pl.* 5587

adonward *adv.* hanging, i.e., downward 649

adoun, adown, a down *adv.* down 1703, 1062, 613; **a-down bynome** droop downwards 688; **clene a down** completely down 1002; ~ **come** descend 4329; ~ **lighte** descend 3573; ~ **right** straight down 3690

adrad *ppl.adj.* afraid 4810

advoket *n.* advocate; champion 5091

adwellynge *n.* an abode 6167

afeyned *ppl.adj.* concealed 2066

aferd *ppl.adj.* afraid 5375

a fere, afere *v.* frighten, terrify 584, 1848

affeccion *n.* inclination, will, affection 7019

afore *prep.* before, in front of 1430; ~ **hem** in their presence 6306; *adv.* before, beforehand 1672

afray, affray *n.* fear, fright, terror; dismay, consternation; assault; **him to bring into ...** ~ to terrify him severely 1863; 5100; **a fray** 1016

after *prep.* after 430; ~ **than** after that, according to 1337; ~ **that y** according to how I; **aftur** 477; ~ **that** to the degree that 3084; ~ **þe letter** literally 3957; **aftyr** 36

afuyr, *adj.n.* on fire 4082

afyn *adv.* fully; **well** ~ completely, perfectly 3270

agast(e) *v.* frightened, terrified *ppl.* 1917, 2554

agayn *adv.* again, back 678; **answere** ~ reply 5199; **ageyn(e)** 5406, 5443

agregge *v.* aggravate 5229; **agregged** *ppl.* intensified, increased 6689

agrevyd *v.* distressed, annoyed *ppl.* 259

agryse *v.*: **makeþ us ...** ~ makes us frightened, tremble, be horrified *ppl.* 1189; **sore** ~ be deeply horrified 1906

aȝen *adv.* back, again 95; ~ **turne** return 367; ~ **bought** redeemed 94; **agayn** 678; ~ **torne** 5919; **ageyn(e): torne** ~ return from 5406; 5443

aȝenst *prep.* against; towards; compared to; in the presence of 1036; **is ...** ~ **me** is before me 5867; **agens** 6306; **agenst** 3320; **aȝen** 261; **aȝens** 144; **aȝeyns** 6219

aȝen tornyng(e) *vbl.n.* turning back, returning 1445; 2374, 6167

aȝenward *adv.* backward; conversely 6350

ay *adv.* always, eternally; forever 233

akele *v.* cool off 5603

alaye *v.* subdue, overcome; confute 5095

alday *adv.* always, constantly 1188

alegge *v.* plead; proclaim, declare, make a claim (in a court of law); **a legge** 4681; **aȝen ...** ~ infringe upon 3427; **resons aȝenst hem** ~ make allegations against them 4594; **dome ... forto** ~ produce proof 4721; **for hem** ~ offer justification 5151; **her playnt** ~ plead their case (in court) 5976

alyene *n.* foreigner, alien 1149

alight *v.* alight; descend: **on hem** ~ descend upon them 5973

alyve, alive *adj.* alive, living 1462, 1712; **on live, on lyve** 3835, 1717; ~ **leve** be alive 3904

allegiaunce *n.* relief; forgiveness 2970

alle þyng *pron.* everything 6040; **all þyng(e)** 6039, 7315; **alle thing** 5083; **al thing, al thing** 3171, 1522; **al þing, al þyng** 1518, 317

all þaw *conj.* although 4477; **all þowh(e)** 6881, 7265; **al thawe** 3020; **al thei** 1441; **al þaw** 3014; **al þouȝ** 6396

almesdede *n.* almes giving, charity 2128; **almysdede** 4660

alon(e) *adj.* alone 2426, 24

a long *adv.* forever, a long time 4514

alowynge *vbl.n* approving, accepting 2886

aloute *v.* bow (in deference, obeisance to) 3339

alle and some *see* **som(e)**

all so *conj.* also; as 69; **also** 189

almes *n.pl.* charity 2982; **almys dede** acts of charity 4836

aloutyng *vbl.n.* bowing 6174

al thei *see* **all þaw**

alwey *adv.* always 7296

alwene *adj.* own 4287; **own(e)** 1690, 144

am *see* **be**

amazone *n.* country of the Amazons 3732

amende *v.* improve, heals, put right, make amends for; change 1667; ~ **hym** reform himself 1667; **amendeþ** *pr3sg.* 3062; **amende** *pr.subj.3sg.* 339; **hym** ~ **of** make them amends for 7257; **but he hem** ~ unless he changes himself 2718; *pr.subj.3pl.* 1324; **amended** *ppl.*: **ben** ~ make amends for 3888; **amendyd: beþ** ~ **of** turn away from 3100

amendes *n.pl.* amends, compensation 1343

amyddes, a myddes *prep.* in the middle of, amidst 2354, 5290; **gretnes** ~ expanse, immensity; **amyddys** among 5388; *adv.* 4343

amys *adv.* wrong(ly); sinfully 90; **doþ** ~ live sinfully 3212; **amysse** 2628; **thenk ought** ~ think anything sinful 4767

among *adv.* as well 2594

among(e) *prep.* among; in addition; together 734, 2712; 1214, 6889; **hem** ~ amongst themselves 4514; **gon hem** ~ walk among them 6691

amonges *prep.* amongst 3086

an *prep.* on 784; *indef.art.* a, an 142

anamailed, anamayled *v.* ornamented, enameled *ppl.* 7131, 7035

aneye *v.* offend; annoy, harass; harm 5964; **anoye** 1012

angor *n.* distress, grief, agony; affliction; tribulation 6314; **angur** 5107; **angres** *n.pl.* 584; ~ **colde** baleful griefs 1046

anguish *n.* distress, (mental) anguish; hardship 1053; **anguisse** 2378; **anguys** 91; **anguysch** 2262; **anguisches** *n.pl.* 1858; **anguisses** 6941

angurnesses *n.pl.* afflictions 1733

anhangyd *v.* hanged *ppl.* 4366

anoyntynge *n.* **last** ~ Extreme Unction, the Last Rites for the dying 2752

an othur, an oþur *pron.* another 862, *adj.* 4583; **a nothur, a noþur** *pron.* 1145, 3072; **anoþer** *pron.* 6030; **another** *adj.* 647; **an noþur** *adj.* 6251; **onothur** 2941

anon *adv.* at once, immediately 646

answere *v.* answer, reply; explanation 2432; ~ **again** reply 5199; **answerie** 5163; **answer** 4983; **answered** *pa.3sg.* 1871; **answeryd** 3314

answere *n.* answer, reply 3115; ~ **ȝyven** give an explanation 4846

anvye *see* **envye**

apaied *v.* pleased, satisfied *ppl.* 6723

aparaile *n.* clothes 1287; **aperaile** 5793

aparty *adv.* especially, in particular; something about 3437

a pechid *v.* accused, charged *ppl.* 2358

apere *v.* appear 1893; **apered** *pa.3sg.* 1864

aperte *adj.* open, manifest 3761

aperty *adv.* clearly, plainly 3519

apeyne *v.* to be punished 2841

apeyreth *v. intr.* grow worse, decline; diminish *pr3pl.* 1271; **apeyryd** *tr. in*jured; diminished *ppl.* 3018

aplace *adv. phrase* place: **every** ~ everywhere 5870

apoynt *adv.* to the point, properly 6780

appul *n.* apple 5384

apropred *v.* reserved; **to...** ~ **be** be an attribute to *ppl.* 6200

aquenche *v. tr.* extinguish, put out 2479; **aquenched** *ppl.* 5520; *intr.* go out, be extinguished 5707

aquyte *v.* repay, requite 2035

ar *adv.* before 10; *conj.* 1652; ~ **þat** before 1706; **byfore** ~ before 10

aray *n.* condition, state; splendor; appearance; clothing 454; **array: hy of** ~ magnificent 7109; **of cold** ~ in baleful condition, in skimpy clothing 454; **in evel** ~ in bad condition, shabby garb 4531

areche *v.* reach, extend; be sufficient 3142; **arecheþ** *pr3sg.* 5283

aredy *adj.* ready, prepared: **us** ~ **make** make ourselves read 1639

aren *see* **be**

arered *v.* raised *pa3sg.* 5424

aresound *v.* called to account *ppl.* 4871

arewe *adv.* in a row; altogeter 4335

aright, aryght *adv.* properly, righteously;

Select Glossary (by Hoyt Greeson) 213

truly, exactly 1921, 465; **wel ~** quite truly 1562; **well ~** quite properly 6783; **nat ~** immorally 3014; **aryth** 386; **aryʒt** 103; **aright** *adj.* **~ fey** true faith 7147
arise, aryse *v.* rise, arise; appear 4089, 1595; **up ~** rise up 3599; **arisen** *pr3pl.* 5439; **aʒenst ... aryse** rise up, rebel against 3531
arysyng(e) *n.* resurrection; rising 4171, 4008
arn, art *see* **be**
arorynge *vbl.n.* roaring, howling: **make ~** let out a roar 4011
arst *see* **er(e)**
art *n.* knowledge, craft; **by non ~** by any knowledge 6102
as *n.* ace, the worst loosing number in dice; **nought an ~** not worth an ace 7225
asaied *v.* experienced *ppl.* 6724 *see* **assay** *v.*
asaute *n.* assault, attack 6780
ascaped *v.* escaped *ppl.* 6578
ascheþ *see* **aske**
ascore *n.* a score, i.e., twenty: **wel many ~** a very large number 2835
asene *v.* seen, caught sight of *ppl.* 7123
asise *n.* assize; **grete ~** the Last Judgment 4612
aske *v.* ask 2412; **ascheþ** *pr3sg.* 2990; **askeþ** 2794; *pr3pl.* 2285; **asked(e)** *pa3sg.* 1867, 1868; **asked** *ppl.* 5021; **askynge** *vbl.* 4976
askys, askes *n.pl.* ashes 366
aslake *v.* diminish; slaken, loosen; alleviate 5285
asonder *adv.* apart, asunder 749;
asoun *n.* a sound 1704. Cf. **soun** 3947
assay(e) *v.* try, test, experience, make trial 313, 1173; **who wele ~** whoever wants to make the effort 313; **asaied** *ppl.* of proven character 6724
assay *n.* attempt; trial; **make ~** try to investigate 3920; **at al ~** under any circumstances 110; **assaies** *pl.*: **bi alle ~** anyway (literally, by all trials) 1644
assaile *v.* attack 1038; **asaile** 854; **assaileþ** *pr3sg.* 1047
assent(e) *v.* agree, assent, consent; submit 6604, 3658
assent *n.* consent 6602; **ate on ~** of one accord, in complete agreement 6534
assentaunt *v.* assenting, agreeing *ppl.* 3676
assignyd *v.* assigned, appointed *ppl.* 3469
assoile *v.* absolve (of sin) 3187
astat(e) *n.* rank, position, status 1571, 2815; **gret ~** high position OR rank 1571
asterte *v.* escape 2356
astrangle *v.* strangle 6550
ate *prep.* at the 1647; **at** 8
aþondur *n.* a thunder storm 6698
atones *adv.* at once; together 4024; **at ones** 4093
atwynne *adv.* apart, separated 3366; **is ...~** is separated 835; **beth departed ~** have come apart, separated 1827, 1992, 2137, 2328, etc.
aungels *n.pl.* angels 4592
austeryte *n.* harshness 4479
austyn *prop.n.* St. Augustine of Hippo (born in Thagaste, Numidia, 354, d. 430); 1101; **Austeyne** 2273; **Austynes** *poss.sg.* 1684
autentik *adj.* trustworthy, reliable 5830
auter *n.* altar 3012
autorites *n.pl.* authorities i.e., Scripture 7182
avantage *n.* advantage 1878; **avauntage** 833

avaunce *v.* advance; promote, further 962; **avaunced** *ppl.* 3578
avayle, availe *v. impers.* help, avail; benefit, be of use 2791, 1232; **may no thing ~** cannot at all benefit i.e., can be of no use 2966; **avayleþ, availeþ** *pr3sg.* 968, 3049; **right nauʒt ~** is of no use at all 3044; **avayleth** 3267
avyse *v.* take thought, consider 3296
awayteþ *v.* wait; **~ faste** lies eagerly in wait *pr3sg.* 970
awey lete *n.* crossroads 4340
awey(e) *adv.* away; gone, passed 191, 2535; **away** 445; **al ~** completely away 595; **~ ... thorowe** cast off 289; **~ caste** lose 1379; **~ don** removed 2768; **~ go** disappear 2532; **~ nome** taken away 2297; **~ ... kaste** rid themselves of it 5854
aweiward, aweyward *adv.* away 5800, 1250
awelde *v.* rule, have control of 6145
awhile *n.* a time, while 1325; **in as lytyl ~ as wynkyng of an ye** quick as a wink of the eye 6246
awreke *v.* avenged *ppl.* 4580
badde *adj.* bad, evil 4709
bagge bitynge *n.* backbiting 4802
bak *n.* back 655
bale *n.* suffering, misery 951
ban *v.* condemn, ban 2828; **banne** 6613
bare *adj.* bare, naked 396; devoid; defenceless 438; **~ ymade** laid waste 3358; **of ... ~** devoid of 5932
bareyn *adj.* barren 2063
batayle *n.* battle 853; **batayles** *n.pl.* 1031
bawm *n.* balm 554
be *v.* be 19; **ben** 624; **bee** 6021; **been** 2553; **beth** *pr3sg.* 44; **ben** *pr.pl.* 679; **beth** 57; **bethe** 2373; **buþ** 2036; **be** *pres.subj.3sg.* 78; **bee** 6021; **ybe, y be** *ppl.* 113, 154; **ben** 1870; **ibe** 3510
beaute *n.* beauty 6182
become, bicome *v.* become 4934, 3327; **become** *pa.pl.* 1940
bede *v.* offer 4840; **nolden in no wise ~** would not offer at all 5183; **þerof ~** offer some of it 4976; **forþ ~** offer, share ... continually 5004
bedes *n.pl.* beads, rosary 3049
bedrede *adj.* bed-ridden 5188
beem *n.* trumpet 3931; **beom(e)** 4200, 4192; **beomes** *pl.* 4176
begge *v.* beg 2563
begyle *v.* beguile, deceive 974; **bigile** 3607; **bigyle** 3318; **bygile** 4611; **by gyle** 3600; **be gyle** 1048; **bygylis** *pr3sg.* 1134; **bygyled** *pa.3sg.* 981
beʒete *v.* beget 2806; **bigat** *past.3pl.* 6494; **biʒete** *ppl.* begotten, brought forth 6136; **byʒete** 381
behoveþ *see* **bihoveþ**
beyʒinge *vbl.adj.* being; **at a peys ~** being at rest 6105; **beyʒyng** 17
benefices *n.pl.* kindnesses, benefits 97; **beneficys** 4678
benysoun *n.* a blessing 2748
bequyt *v.* be repaid, settled; requited *ppl.* 3239
bere *v.* bear, endure; support; wear; carry 626; **hym ... hie ~** vaunt himself 6650; **bereth** *pr3sg.* 209; **bereþ** 2063; **~ þe keies** has the keys, i.e., has the power 3164;

bereþ *pr.3pl.* 617; **berynge** *pres.ppl.* 2707; **iboren** *ppl.* 4561
berel *n.* beryl 7029
beried *v.* buried, engulfed *ppl.* 2446; **beryed** 724; **yberyed** 4373
berienge *vbl.n.* burial 3813
berynge *vbl.n.* bearing, behavior: **hie ~** haughty behavior 1286
be secheþ *v.* beg, beseech; pray *pr3pl.* 5274; **bysought** *past.3pl.* 2568
be sides *prep.* in addition to 3024
besy *adj.* busy, solicitous, anxious 159; **busy** 3533
besily *adv.* intently, eagerly 3654; **bysyliche** 533
beste *n.* beast, animal 142; **best** 497; **bestes** *pl.* 68
beste *superl.adj.*: **at þe ~** most effectively 5933
be stered *v.* stirred up *ppl.* 7297
bet *comp.adv.* better; **þe ~** the better 3054
betake *v.* make one's way, go; **hennys ~** make (our) way hence 1147
bete *v.* beat, whip, flog 5757; **bete** *ppl.* 726; **ibete** 2597
betere *comp.adj.* better 3579; **better** 1811
betide, be tide *v.* befall, happen 4049, 6905; **be tyde: may right wel ~** may justice fully befall 5029
betokneþ *v.* indicates, signifies *pr3sg.* 1239; **bitokeneþ** 3650; **bitokneþ** 6844
betrayeth *v.* deceives, misleads *pr3sg.* 977
betre *adv.* better; **þe ~** the better 189; **better** 7233
betorned *v.* turned about *ppl.* 1349
be þenche *v.* remember, keep in mind; **hym selve ~** deliberate 1386; **bithenke** *imper.sg.*: **~ þe** remember 4814
bi, by *prep.* by; by means of 1644; **be** 139
by clyppeth *v.* embraces *pr3sg.* 967
bydde(n) *v.* ask; command; pray, plead 2278
byddere *n.* one who asks or commands 3006
biddynge *vbl.n.* command 4245; **byddynge** 3000
bifalle *v.* happen, come about; be fitting, appropriate; pertain 2098; **schal us ~** will happen, befall us 2098; **be falle** 821; **bifalleth** *pr3sg.* 2317; **bifalleþ** 3166; **~ noʒt** doesn't happen (to revolve) 6118; **hym ~** *impers.* it falls to his lot 3172; **it ~ nouʒt ʒow** it is not fitting for you 3916; **befalleth, byfalleth** 793, 732; **~ to be** happens to be, i.e., where it befits purgatory to be located 2317; **to hem ~ ... by right** belongs to them by right 732; **byfalleþ** 166; **by falleþ** is fitting 871; **as it ~ therto** as it pertains to this 5202; **byfalleth** *pr3pl.* 682; **befalle** *pr3subj.* 2111; **befel** *pa3sg.* 4059; **bifall** *ppl.*; **it was so ~** it so happened 4072
bifore *adv.* before, previously 2836; **befor** 2843; **before** 774; **biforen** 3656; **byfore** 10
bifore *prep.* before, in front of 1951; **before** 1113; **biforen** 4260; **byfore** 1129
bygge *ppl.adj.* wealthy, powerful, cultivated 1233
biggyd *v.* cultivated *pa3sg.* 4075
bigile *v.* deceive 3607; **by gyle** 3600
bigynne, bygynne *v.* begin, start, undertake 2020, 174; **bigynneþ** *pr3sg.* 314; **bygynneth** 664; **bygynneþ** 1; **byginneþ** 1731; **bygynnes** 2787; **bigan** *pa3sg.* 3507; **bygan**

214 Select Glossary (by Hoyt Greeson)

38; **gan:** followed by *infinitive*, forms past tense of the *inf.* 1890; **begonne** *pa3pl.* 4932; **gonne** 5809; **bigonne** *ppl.* 3425
bygynnere *n.* causer, beginner 789
bigynnynge *vbl.n.* beginning, start; basis; conception; creation 25; **beþ of evel ~** have an evil start 6486; **bygynnyge** [Sic!] 3471; **bygynnyng** 8; **the ferste ~** the very beginning 478; **bigynnyng** 4135; **begynnynge** 5140; **bygynnynge** 3324; **ferst ~** Creation 5340; **byggynnynge** 5403
by ȝemed *v.* looked after *ppl.* 4858
biȝende *prep.* beyond 3727
bihinde *adv.* from behinde 5474
biholde *v.* look at, see; consider 534; **be holde** 500; **biholdeþ** *pr3sg.*; **biholdeþ** *imper.pl.* 4454; **behold** 547; **biholde** *ppl.* 1924
bi hove, byhove *n.* profit 837, 780
bihoveþ *v.impers.* it is necessary: **us ~ echone** each one of us must *pr3sg.* 1963; **~ þe** you must 1993; **behoveþ: us ~** we must (be) 1036; **be hoveth** 124; **byhoveþ** 1039; **What ~ nedes** why is it necessary 2242; **nedes ~** most of necessity 2619; **hem ~ to have** they need to have 2648
bileve *v.* believe 1793; **byleve** 1171; **bileveþ** *pr3pl.* 6484; **byleveþ** 260; **bileven** 3834; **by leven** 269; **bileved** *pa1pl.* 5788; **bileved** *ppl.* 6216
bileve *v.tr.* leave, leave behind 3476; **bileved** *ppl.* 7178
bileve *n.* belief, faith 1769
byleveþ *v.* leave (them nothing) *pr3pl.* 1023; **bileved** *ppl.* remains, (what is) left 7179; **byleved is on ... ~** is left on it 2431; **byleveþ: be ~** is left 1657
biloke *v.* locked: **faste ~** securely locked up *ppl.* 6702
bilongeþ, bylongeþ, bylongeth *v.* belongs, pertains *pr3sg.* 5285, 569, 170; **it ~ to** it has to do with, pertains to it 3102
bynde *v.* bind, chain; imprison; subject to 3171; **byndest** *pr2sg.* 3177; **byndeþ** *pr3sg.* 3192; **byndeþ** *imper.pl.* 5891; **bounde** *ppl.*fettered, enmeshed 1956; **ibounde, ybounde** 2559, 2253; **faste ~** firmly fastened 4555; **y bounde** 1428
byneþe *adv.* beneath, below 528; **beneþe** 4254
byneþe *prep.* under, below 6730
bynome *v.* be taken, despoiled *ppl.* 3350; **from ... ~** be taken from (i.e., from heaven) 4423; be paralysed 688
bireve *v.* seize, deprive; take away; **by revyth** *v. pr3sg.* 214; **byrevyth: hys ioye ~ ... hym** deprives him of his joy 1508; **by reveþ** 265; **bereveth** 1322; **bereveþ** 1656; **hym ... ~** deprive him of 2864; **bi reved** *ppl.* 4212
bisene *v.* be seen, gazed at 5485
biset *v.* surrounded *ppl.* 4517; **byset** 1034; **alle aboute ~** afflicted on all sides 4361
by sett *v.* employ, use; **hem well ~** use them well 105
bysyliche *see* **besily**
bysynesse *n.* endeavor, industry 930; anxiety 953
by take *v.* committed, entrusted *ppl.* 4864
bitawȝt *v.* entrusted *pa3sg.* 4853
byte, bite *v.* bite, burn; hit 3457, 5222; **bitynge** *pr.ppl.* 57790; **bete** *ppl.* 726

bytur *adj.* bitter 1414; **byttur** 1609; **bittur** 4592; **byter** 951; **bytter** 303; **bitter** 1833
byturly *adv.* bitterly 2385; **bitterly** 4492
bitturnesse *n.* bitterness 5104
bitwene, bytwene *adv.* between; at times 2345, 2646; **be twene** 3981
bitwene *prep.* between 1973; **bytwene** 1417; **between** 1483
bitwix(e) *prep.* between 1977, 4357; **by twixe** 3441
biwende *v.* go; **hem ~** turn, go 4500
bywonde *v.* wrapped (in a shroud) *ppl.* 724
blak *adj.* black 1904
blaste *n.* a gust (of wind): **awey may a windes ~** a gust of wind can (blow it) away 580
blere *v.* wail, bellow, roar 1847
bleve *v.* remain 2771
blewe *adj.* blue i.e., black and blue from beating 4414
blynne *v.* cease 1471
blysfulhede *n.* beatitude, joy 6165
blysse, blisse *n.* joy, (heavenly) bliss 1385, 1822; **blys** 79; **blis** 1138; **corowne of ~** crown of beatitude 6969; **hevene ~** the joy of Heaven 3098; **blisses** *pl.* 6194; **blissus** 7102; **blyssus** 6199
blyssed *ppl.adj.* blessed 6260; **blessed** 5138; **iblessid** 1818
blyssfull *adj.* happy, blessed, blissful; glorious 6921; **blissfull** 2549; **blysfull** 5950; **blysful** 6739
blythe *adj.* happy, glad; joyous 1162; **blyþe** 4784
blyve *adv.* quickly 5671
blowe *v.* sound, blow (a horn) 3931; **bloweth** *pr3sg.* snorts (through the nose) 653
bodye *n.* body 4881; **body** 527; **~ abowte** (various limbs) of the surrounding body 4230; **in þe ~ doþ reste** are found in the body 6541; **bodi** 1664; **bodyes** *pl.* 3602; **bodies** 2101; **~ in servyse** bodies at their command, i.e., souls control their bodies 6428; **bodys** 4109
bodyly *adj.* bodily, physical, carnal, in the flesh 804; **bodily** 1412; **~ þyng** physical object 6998; **bodyli** 1410; **bodely** 1445; **bodyliche** 1514; **no ~** nothing physical 7169
bodiliche *adv.* in the flesh, bodily, physically 6530
boffet *n.* buffet, a blow 4360
bok(e) *n.* book 518, 46; **book(e)** 245, 598; **bokes** *pl.* 31; **bokys** 4544; **books** 5885
bold *adj.* brazen; shameless
bon *n.* bone 522; **bone** 5700; **bones** *pl.* 4043
bond *n.* constraint, binding force, fetter: **under ~** in fetters 2260; **bonde** 6419; **bondes** *pl.* 2553
bonde *adj.* enslaved; obligated 744
bonde manne *n.* serf, bondsman 938
bone *n.* request, prayer 2990; **aftur his ~** as he wished 5259
bore *v.* born *ppl.* 403; **ibore,** 3449; **ys on eorþe ~** was born on earth 4145; **ybore** 414; **y bore** 398
borowe *v.* save, preserve 5673
bosom *n.* **in Abrahams ~** abode of the righteous Old Testament dead 2445
bost *n.* boast, bragging: **makeþ a man so evel of ~** makes a man boast so wickedly 1781

bot *n.* remedy, escape 5882; **to ~** as a defence 6810
bot *conj.* but, unless, except 353; **~ ȝif** unless 2243; **~ as** but as 3992; **bote** 106; **but** 24
boþe, bothe *adv.* too, as well 2418, 591; **boþ** 3141
boþe, bothe *adj.* both 4917, 2241
boþe, bothe *conj.* both 977, 34; **both** 39; **boþ** 1185
bought *v.* bought *pa3sg.* 4074; **aȝen ~** redeemed, bought back 94; **bouȝt** *ppl.* 2188
bounde *see* **bynde**
bowe *v.* bow 6289; **~ to** submit to 6629
bowes *n.pl.* boughs, branches 560
braid *n.* stroke, attack, sundering (of body and soul by death) 1603; **braide** 1485; **breyd** 2644
braiers *n.pl.* prayers (scribal misspelling?) 2936
braynwod *adj.* mad, insane 5540
bred(e) *n.* bread 2930, 2928
brede *v.* breed, grow; gestate 3444; **brede** *ppl.* 3444; **ibred** 3488
brede *n.* breadth 1256
breke *v.* break 1886; **into þat matere ~** turn to that subject 868; **out ~** escape (prison), break out 3335; **breketh** *pr3sg.*; **wiþ þe wynd ~** scatters with the wind 356; **brekeþ** 5761; **y broke** *ppl.* 602
brenne *v.* burn; sting; irritate 2500; **brenneþ** *pr3sg.* 2492; **brenneth** 2125; **brenneþ** *pr3pl.* 2537; **brend** *pa3sg.* 6100; **brende** 5477; **brenne** *pr.subj.sg.* 5479; **brennynge** *pr.ppl.* 3649; **brennyng** 3640; **brenyngge** 5505; **brend** *ppl.* 2530; **brende** 2540; **ibrend** 2541; **ibrent** 4146
brennynge *vbl.adj.* burning, fiery 2560; **brennyng** 4131
brest *n.* breast, chest 574; **brestes** *pl.* **sle her ~** strike their chests 1012
bresteþ *v.intr.* bursts, shatters *pr3sg.* 5761
breth *n.*breath; odor, stench 653; **breþ** 559
brydales *n.pl.* wedding feasts 4067
bridgome *n.* bridegroom 6847
bryght *adj.* bright; gleaming, shining 334; **bryȝt** 2087; **bright** 1944
brightnesse *n.* radiance, brightness 3967
briȝtor *adj.comp.* brighter 5331; **brightor** 6805; **bryghtor** 5329
brymston(e) *n.* brimstone, sulphur 5525, 6353; **bremston** 5570
bring(e) *v.* bring, take; lead 196, 243; **bryngest** *pr2sg.* 552; **bryngeþ** *pr3sg.* 448; **bryngeth** 117; **bring** *pr.subj.3sg.* 9; **brynge: he us ~** may He bring us 7314; **brought** *pa3sg.* 3927; **broughte** 705; **brouȝt** *ppl.* 1413; **into sevene parties ... ~** arranged into seven parts 7261; **brouwȝt** 513; **~ in grete wurschipe** held in great honour 513; **browȝt** 1744; **broȝt(e)** 3098, 701; **browt: forthe ~** prolonged 1278; **broght** 7299; **brought** 91; **ibrought** 2349; **to ende ~** fulfilled 3330; **~ into lyve** restored to life 5217; **ibrouȝt, ybrouȝt** 3818, 520; **y broȝt** 1033; **y brought** 396
britull *n.* mutable, transient, changeable; fragile 7007

Select Glossary (by Hoyt Greeson) 215

brod(e) *adj.* broad, wide; abundant; free 64, 1251; **wel ~** very abundant 2762

bronde *n.* brand, torch 5487

broþer *n.* brother 6492; **broþur: Maryes ~ Magdaleine** the brother of Mary Magdalen 5420; **breþerne** *pl.* 5169

browe *n.* brow, forehead 654; **browes** *pl.* eyebrows 684

bugge *v.* buy; **with hem ~ ne selle** trade with them 3671

buyles *n.pl.* boils (i.e., on the skin) 2391

burned *ppl.adj.* burnished, shining 7131

burthe *n.* birth 1737; **burþ(e)** 430, 1812

buschep *n.* bishop 2748; **buschop** 1570; **buschopes** *pl.* 3132

but *conj.* unless; except 24, **buþ** *see* **be**

buxome *adj.* obedient; submissive 342; **buxon** 3355; **buxoun** 45; **buxun** 3355

buxomnesse *n.* humility, obedience 936; **buxumnesse** 6175

caccheþ *v.* catches *pr3sg.* 1305

cayser *n.* emperor 742

caytyfite *n.* captivity; misery 456; **caytyfte** 391

can *v. pr1–3sg/pl.* know, be able to 351; **kan: no good ne ~** doesn't know what is good 138; **~ nat** does not know 280; **conne** 1244; **ikan, ykan** *pr1sg.* I can 2783, 4525; **ycan** 2443; **y conne** 7016; **conneth** *pr3pl.* 45; **conneþ** 264; **~ se** have said 2281; **~ þerof iwite** are able to understand it 5444; **con** 5370; **cunneþ** 1761; **konneth reson ne wyt ~ non** cannot reason or understand 523; **konneþ** 4910; **couthe** *pa1–3sg/pl.* 1598; **couþe** 275; **cowþ(e)** 7049, 2074; **cowthe** 1725; **kouþe** 5399; **couþ** *ppl.* **to me ~** known to me 4956; **cud** 3468; **kud** 3616; **icud** 4539; **ikud** 5389; **þorow god was ~** was revealed by God 6441

care *n.* grief, pain, sorrow; care 397; **bryng in ~** lead into grief 4573

careyne *n.* dead carcass, corpse 493

carpe *v.* talk, dispute 5252

cas *n.* a matter 609; **case: ~ ofte falleþ** a situation often arises 2995

caspy *prop.n.* Caspia (lands around the Caspian Sea) 3727

caste *v.* throw; calculate; predetermine, foreordain; arrange; **how thu wolt an ende of þe world ~** how you will arrange OR calculate an end of the world 3312; **seie harde caste** seen violently throwing 5767; *v.refl.* deliberate, consider; decide; direct; plan, arrange; favour 752; **kaste** 1637; **over ~** overthrow 3360; **casteþ** *pr3sg.* 1000; **casten** *pr3pl.* 6694; **caste** *pa3sg.* 187; **cast(e)** *ppl.* 1704, 971; **icast(e)** 370, 3972; **ykast: mete to the ~** food bought to you 5154

catell *n.* property, goods 2864

cause *n.* cause 2828; **þe ~ whi** the reason 2869

certayn *adj.* sure, certain, assured, unfailing; set, fixed 1620; **in ~** certainly, in fact 2905; **certayne** 681; **certeyn(e)** 2092, 3123; **putte us in ~** assured us 2092; **certain** 2948; **sertayn ~ tyde** fixed or regular (ocean) tide 996; **in ~ be** feel confident, be assured 3101

certefie *v.* assure, affirm; inform 2324

certeyn *n.* confidence; certainty, truth 6711; **moment in ~** specified moment 5015

certeynly *adv.* certainy, assuredly 2200

cese *v.* cease 2204; **cesse** 6403

cesons *n.pl.* seasons 1198; **cesouns** 1199

cesynge *vbl.n.* stopping, ceasing 6941

chace *v.* pursue, afflict 5537; **aboute ~** rush about 3592; **harde ~** severely afflict 5537

chalange *v.* claim 1883; **chalangeth** *pr3sg.* 1664

charabocle *n.* carbuncle 7146; **charbocles** *pl.* 7037

charge *n.* burden, weight 5368

chargeþ *v.*: load; charge; **~ it nought** attaches no importance to it *imper.pl.* 2674; **chargid** *ppl.* loaded, burdened 6252; **charged** 6306

charite *n.* (Christian) love 2026; **Seinte ~** holy love 7266; **charyte** 2920

chast *adj.* chaste, (sexually) pure 6796

chastise *v.* discipline, chastise (verbally or physically) 4643

chaunce *n.* circumstance; event; occurrence; 1066

chaunge *v.tr.* change, alter 3534; **change** 587; *intr.* **chaungeth** *pr3sg.* 826; **chaungeþ: ~ in to a newe tune** changes her tune (metaphor befitting Fortune's fickleness) 1058; **chaungeþ** *pr.3pl.* 1207; **chawnged** *ppl.* changed 700

chaungyng *vbl.n.* change: **makeþ men so ofte ... her chaungyng** men ... change their customs so frequently 1296

chele *n.* cold, chill 2594

cherche *n.* church 1762; **chirche** 2662; **churche** 1769; **churches** *poss.sg.* 3011

chere *n.* face, countenance; expression 583; **setteþ ... his ~** set his heart on 158; **hevy ~** sadness 2520; **made good ~** was cheerful 5433; **fayr ~** friendly countenance 6934

chese *v.* choose; elect i.e., the Elect 72; **cheseth** *pr3sg.* 83; **cheseþ** 1337; **ches** *pa3sg.* 1762; **chosen** *ppl.* 3633

chide *v.* complain 5789

chymeny(e) *n.* fireplace 3640, 3649

chonynge *v.* cleaving asunder *pr.ppl.* 690

cite *n.* city 3500; **~ of pes** City of Peace, i.e., the New, Heavenly Jerusalem 1771; **cete** 7152; **cyte** 2611; **citees** *pl.* 3483; **cites** 3491

clanly *adv.* completely; clearly 6989; **clanlyche: ~ befor don** clearly committed before 2843

clannesse *n.* innocence, purity 175; **~ yfonde** have been purified 2650

clanse *v.* cleanse, purify (like gold) 2134; **clanseþ** *pr3sg.* 1096; **clansed** *ppl.* 305; **clansid** 2620; **clansyd** 409689; **iclansed** 1978; **iclansid** 2121; **iclensid** 2583; **yclansed: schal ~ be** must be purified 2675; **yclansyd** 2496

clansyng *vbl.adj.* purifying, cleansing 2176

clene *adv.* completely 12; **~ examinid** thoroughly scrutinized 1988; **~ out of synne** completely free of sin 2136; **don ~ from** completely removed 3040

clene *adj.* pure, clean 803

clepe *v.* call, summon; name 290; **clepeth** *pr3pl.* 801; **clepud** *ppl.* 2323; **cleped** 5989; **clepid** 1485; **clepped** 6061; **iclepud** 1553; **y clepud** 865

cler(e) *adv.* clearly, plainly, distinctly, openly; brightly 3085, 2497; **swiþe ~** quite distinctly 4448

cler(e) *adj.* bright, shining; clear; pure; fine, beautiful; pleasing 6066, 294; **soules ... most ~** soules ... most free (of sin) 2682; **cleor** 6542

clergie *n.* doctrine 4911; **muche cowþe on ~** was well-versed in theology 6443

clerk(e) *n.* scholar, clergyman 422, 354; **clerkes** *pl.* 463; **~ of clergie** learned scholars 6044; **clerkys** 2251

cleveþ *v.* cleve, adhere *pr3pl.*; **~ togidre** stick together 2767

cloches *n.pl.* claws: **fasten here ~** fasten their claws (on them) 5716

closed *v.* surrounded *ppl.* 3726

cloþ(e) *n.* cloth, clothing 2031; **clothe** 707; **cloþes** *pl.* clothes 4669; **clothes** 1298

cloþe *v.* clothe, dress 4661; **clothi** 2896; **clothed** *pa2sg.* 5146; **cloþed** *ppl.* 3797; **cloþyd** 4356; **icled** 6979

cloþynge *n.* clothes, dress 5717; **clothyng** 1297

clothles *adj.* without clothes, naked 5187

cloutys *n.pl.* rags 4356

cold(e) *n.* cold 5481, 2592

cold(e) *adj.* cold; hostile; phlegmatic 1211, 645; **of ~ aray** in skimpy clothing 454; **hap of angres ~** the lot of evil anger 1046; **~ fever** chills, the ague 2384

cole *n.* charcoal 5590

colke *n.* core, e.g. of an apple 5384

colour *n.* colour, complexion 587; **undyr false ~** by deceptive means 3558

com(e) *v.* come, approach 450, 121; **~ ...more in honde** be dealt with further 810; **~ ... faste abowte** will quickly surround 1842; **comest** *pr2sg.* 2798; **comeþ** *pr3sg.* 534; **cometh** 559; **comeþ** *pr.pl.*: **~ fro** return from 5412; **com** *pa.sg.* 2249; **cam** 443; **comen** *pa.pl.* 3254; **comeþ** 425; **cometh** 1313; **ycome** *ppl.* 1654

combred *v.* encumbered *ppl.* 7293; **~ wiþ** overwhelmed by 7293

comelych *adj.* fair, beautiful; appropriate, befitting 6356; **comely** 583

comeling *n.* stranger, newcomer 1156

comende *v.* approve, commend 3547

coming(e) *vbl.n.* approach, coming; arrival 447; 1628; **comynge** 447; **down ~** descent (from the cross) 4419; Second Coming (of Christ) 4598; **ferst ~ adown** (Christ's) Advent 4387

commune *adj.* common, shared 1576

companye *n.* host (i.e., of saints); group, company 6740; **company: wolde ever in o ~ be** would (wish) to be in one host (i.e., of saints) 1542

compass *n.* circle 1265

complexion *n.* condition, temperament 628; **complexioun** 646

conceyl *n.* counsel, advice

conceyve *v.* understand, perceive 5660; **conceyved** *ppl.* conceived 390; **conceyvyd** 383; **conseyved** 3442

conscience, concience *n.* conscience 5780; **the worm of ~** the gnawing pang of conscience 5783

condycioun *n.* nature, character, condition 647; **condycyon** 56; **condycion** 776; **condyciouns** *pl.* circumstances 669; **condycyouns** 3280; **condiciouns** 1389; **condicions** 1200

confessours *n.pl.* those who profess the

Christian faith despite threat of persecution, but are not martyred 3156; **confessourys** 6793
confort *n.* encouragement, support 294; **to her ~** for their relief 6885
conforte *v.* comfort, succor; encourage 842; **conforteþ** *pr3sg.* 5934; **conforted** *pa.pl.* 5163
confusioun *n.* ruin, shame 4442
conn— *see* **can**
connynge *vbl.n.* knowledge, understanding; skill 1949; **beth nauȝt wel ~** does not understand well 287; **connyngge: symple ~** modest competence 7266; **conning** 4990
connynge *vbl.adj.* skillful 287
consayle *v.* counsel, advise 3252; **consaile** 1667; **conseileþ** *pr3sg.* 1083
consail(e) *n.* counsel, advice 5094, 4987; **conseil** 277; **conseyl** 4601
conservaunt *adj.* preserving 3478
conteyne *v.* include, contain 5237; **contyne** 4132; **conteyneth** *pr3sg.* 378; **conteyned** *ppl.* 7262
conterfete *v.* counterfeit; imitate, simulate 3587
contynuellyche *adv.* continually, one after the other, consecutively 4695; **contynuelly** 535; **contynuely** 7070
contrairie *n.* opposite 6638; **contrarie** 6221; **contrary(e)** 338, 6302
contrarie *adj.* opposed 6545
contrarious *adj.* adverse, opposed, hostile 911
contre *n.* country, land 1019; **all a ~** everybody 7176
contreve *v.* devise, compose 5243; **contreveth** *pr.pl.* 1320
contricion *n.* contrition, i.e., sorrow for sin and the resolve not to sin again; **take ~** have contrition 2177
coralle *n.* coral 7037
cornes *n.pl.* grains 2762
corone *n.* crown 3383, 6966; **coroune** 4868; **corowne** top of the head 1260; **crowne** 857
coroned *v.* crowned *ppl.* 6657
Coroȝaym *prop.n.* Corozain 3449; **coȝoȝaym**: scribal error for Coroȝaym 3486
correctioun *n.* **stonde to ... ~** submit to correction 7280
corrupcion *n.* corruption, (moral) decay; contamination 4097; **corrupcyon** 711; **corruptioun** 958; **corrypcyoun** 818; **corypcyon** 393
costage *n.* expense, cost 1288
countreward *n.*: **to our ~** to/toward our country 1181
cours *n.* orbit, path; flow; ocean bed 4006
coveite *v.* covet; desire, yearn for 5538; **coveyte** *pr1sg.* 1804; **coveyten** *pr3pl.* 6008; **coveyted** *pa3pl.* 5639; **coveited** 1808; **coveytid** 1799; **coveytyd** 3306
covert *n.* concealment: **out of all ~** quite openly 1332
covert *adj.* concealed, covert, i.e., the meaning of the name *Magog* 3760
covertour *n.* coverlet, quilt 5728
covetyse *n.* covetousness, craving, greed, avarice; lust 923; **coveytyse** 2387; **couetyse** 923
covetous *adj.* greedy, covetous 660; **coveytous(e)** 660, 3700

cracche *v.* scratch 5968
craft *n.* art, guile 3493
craftly *adv.* skillfully, ingeneously 7214; **craftyly** 7133
crake *v.* crack, croak 3816
crave *v.* desire; long for; beg for 126
creature *n.* creature, i.e., a created thing 57; **creatures** *pl.* 29; **creatours** 3414; **creaturs** 44; **creaturys** 37
crepe *v.* creep 401
crevers *n.* crevice, crack 7212
cry *n.* shout, cry, outcry 412
crybbe *n.* manger 4357
crie *v.* shout, wail; proclaim: **don it ~** have it proclaimed 3737; **crye** 409; **cryeþ** *pr3sg.* 411; **cried** *pa3sg.* 2448
cryenge *vbl.n.* lamentation, wailing 5110; *vbl.adj.* 6912
crist *prop.n.* Christ 1830; **Cryst** 15; **Cristes** *poss.sg.* 3644; **Cristys** 4685; **Crystes** 3149; **Crystis** 4533; **Crystys** 4490
cristal(e) *n.* crystal 5321, 7139; **cristall(e)** 7034, 6030: **hevene ~** crystalline heaven; **crystal** 7141
cristendom, crystendom *n.* Christian belief, Christianity 3780, 3366
cristen(e) *adj.* Christian 1878, 167; **crystene** 3110
cristiente *n.* Christianity 5648; **crystyente** 3250
crois, croys *n.* cross 4426, 4419; **cros** 4362
croketh *v.* curves, bends *pr3sg.* 655
crop *n.* top 563; **croppe** 1586
cubites *n.pl.* a measurement of length: about eighteen inches 4003
cursed *v.* accursed *ppl.* 5175
curtasye *n.* courtesy, civility 6933; **curtesye** 1294
custome *n.* (traditional) practice, custom 2784
dai, day *n.* day 1039, 102; **daye** 2277; **daies** *pl.* 624; **dayes** 457; **lyve ~** lifetime 6371; **in her lif ~** in their lifetime 6941
dale *n.* valley 861; **dales** *pl.* 4035
dame *n.* Dame, Lady 1057
dampnacion *n.* damnation 1357; **dampnacion** 1355; **dampnacyoun** 1106
dampne *v.* damn, condemn 2090; **dampned** *ppl.* 309; **dampnede** 6303; **dampnyd** 2367; **idampned** 4164; **idampnyd** 4435
dampned *vbl.adj.* condemned, damned 6574
dan *prop.n.* Dan, the tribe of Israel mentioned in *Genesis* 49:17 3455
danyel *prop.n.* the Prophet Daniel 3517; **daniels** *poss.sg.* 3388
davyd *prop.n.* David 388
dar *v.* dare *pr.sg.* 1791; **dare** 5312; **dorst(e)** *pa.sg./pl.*: **he ne ~** he wouldn't dare 5661; **~ he nouȝt** he was unable 5430
daunger *n.* peril, difficulty; power 6679; **daungere: wiþ oute ~** without reservation 6284; **danger: in ~** under domination 6651; **in þe ~ of** in the power of 6652
debat *n.* disagreement, controversy; resistance 3376; **debate: makeþ his ~** makes a legal claim, brings suit i.e., kills 1401; **beþ at ~** are quarreling 2816
deceyvable *adj.* deceitful 3513; **deseyvable** 895
declaracyon *n.* inventory (of sins); declaration 4936
ded *n.* death 3582

ded(e) *adj.* dead 698, 488
dede *n.* deed, reality 896; **in his ~** for his deeds 906; **in any maner ~** for any kind of act 5086; **in ~** in fact, indeed 1430; **dedes** *pl.* 275; **dedys** 2024
dede *see also* **don**
dedly *adj.* deadly, mortal 1426; **~ synne** mortal sin (as opposed to venial) 1426; **dedlyche** 2698
deelful *adj.* doleful, sorrowful 1529; **delful** 950
def *adj.* deaf 3597; **deve** 656
defaute *n.* lack; fault, flaw, defect; absence 253; **for ~ of** through lack of 240; **deffaute** 5180; **~ of** need of 5180; **defautys** *pl.* 4225
defens *n.* defence 4468; **defence: they mowe make ~** they can defend themselves 4992; **deffence: mowe ... make no ~** cannot defend (against) 5784; **defence** 5784
deffende *v.* defend (verbally); prohibit 3548; **diffendeþ** *pr3sg.* 2880
deffoulyd *v.* defiled, polluted (by sin) *ppl.* 1942; **defouled** 2031; **defowled** 336
defiaunce *n.* challenge, resistance 6543
degises *see* **dygyse**
degre *n.* rank, position 3202; **in his ~** according to his rank 5011
deye *v.* die; **diȝe, dyȝe** 4049, 3879; **die, dye** 1473, 696; **dieþ** *pr3sg.* 1789; **deyn** *pr.pl.* 6474; **dieth** 1819; **deiþ** 1702; **diȝe** *pr.subj.sg.* 3133; **die** *pr.subj.pl.* 1824; **deyde** *pa.sg.* 1510; **diede** 5438; **dieȝed** 1894; **deyed** 4416; **died** *pa.pl.* 5809; **dyȝynge** *pr.ppl.* 6420
deyȝinge, deyȝynge *vbl.n.* death, dying 3112, 3099
deynte *n.* pleasure 6177
del *n.* part 1882
dele *v.* give, share 3209; **~ wyþ his wyf** have intercourse with his wife 2804
delful *adj.* doleful, sorrowful 950
delices *n.pl.* (fleshly) delights 3874
delit, delyt *n.* delight, pleasure; delicacy 62, 3240; **delite** 2630; **delites, delytes** *pl.* 5807, 232
delitable, delytable *adj.* delightful, pleasing 6890, 4395
delited *v.* took pleasure *pa3pl.* 5527
delyueraunce *n.* release, deliverance 2269
delyuere *v.* release, deliver (from prison) 3052; *imper.sg.* 2259; **delyuered** *ppl.* 1474
deme *v.* judge; consider, think; condemn; suppose 2103; **forto ~** to be judged 2065; **demeþ** *pr3sg.* 490; *pr.pl.* 5330; **demynge** *pr.ppl.* 5062; **demed** *ppl.* 2097; **idemed** 5035; **y demed** 1649
dene *n.* noise, din; **erþe ~** earthquake 4029
denne *n.* cave, den 3497
dentes *n.pl.* blows, dints 5764; **dentys: þondur ~** thunder claps 4515
deol *n.* misery, grief 2341
deolfully *adv.* painfully 5672; **deollfully** 5546
departe *v.tr.* separate 1370; **~ atwynne** separate 2137; **departy** 5127; **departen** *pr3pl.* 1992; **departeth** 1436; **departed** *ppl.* 1827; *v.intr.* **departe** depart, leave 1370; **departeþ** *pr3sg.* 1423
departyng(e) *vbl.n.* separation; departure 1483, 1416
depe *adv.* deep, far down 5716
depe *adj.* deep 4505; **deppest** *superl.* 5893

Select Glossary (by Hoyt Greeson) 217

dere *v.* harm, injure, wound, afflict 627; set loose upon; **derie** (in Purgatory, non-physical harm) 2665; **dereþ** *pr3sg.* 2062
dere *adv.* dearly, i.e., at a high price 1451
dere *adj.* excellent, noble; dear 122; ~ **and dere** beloved and dear 4866
derk *adj.* dark, obscure 392; **derke** 5630
derknes *n.* darkness 1489; **derknesse** 164; **torne in to** ~ become darkened 3966
derlyng *n.* favorite; beloved, darling 6824
desceyve *v.* deceive 3516; **desceyveþ** *pr3sg.* 969; **desceyved** *ppl.* 3886
desciples *n.pl.* disciples; students 3806; **disciples** 3328
descripcion *n.* description 7018
descryve *v.* describe 5651; **discreve** 5118; **discryve** 1908; **descreveþ** *pr3sg.* 5722; **discreveth: philisophre** ~ a philosopher defines 1581; **descryved** *ppl.* 5841
desert *n.* what is deserved: **thorowh myn owne** ~ because of my own merit 1873
desesys *n.pl.* misfortunes, anxieties 2876
desir *n.* desire 7115
despise *v.* renounce, disregard; disdain, revile 1083; **despyse** 340; **despiseþ** *pr3pl.* 970; **despised** *ppl.* 6666
despyt *n.* scorn, contempt; **in** ~ in order to spite 321
despute *v.* engage in controversy; ~ **of** argue hotly about 1974
desteyne *v.* sully, dishonour 3315
destruye *v.* devastate, ravage; overthrow; kill 3722; **foule** ~ severely harass 5965; **destruy** 3735; **destroye** 1011; **destruyeþ** *pr3sg.* 3747; **distruyen** *pr3pl.* 4993; **destruyed** *pa.sg.* 3863; **destruyd** *ppl.* 3358
deth see **don**
deþ(e) *n.* death 671, 1799; **deth** 37; ~ ... **take** suffer death 92; **hym to** ~ **brynge** kill him (i.e., Antichrist) 3871; **ded(e)** 3582, 2041; **deþes** *poss.sg.* 1400; ~ **bonde** fetters of death 6420; **dethes** 1734; **dethus** 1485; **deþes** *pl.* 1406
deth ward *prep.* **draweþ to the** ~ approaches death, is dying 674; **deþward** 1866
dette *n.* obligation, debt 3141; **dettys** *pl.* 3188
devel *n.* devil, Satan 890; **deuel** 1892; **develes** *poss.sg.* 2140; **devels** 891; **develys** 3601; **develes** *pl.* 1025; **develys** 4527
devise *v.* describe; think about 1905; **divise** 2152
deuocyoun *n.* religious fervor, devotion 1164; **devocioun** 1348; **devocyon** 2802
dight *v.* prepare, make, form; arrange, array; put 5347; **dyghte** 1587; **dight** *ppl.* 2491; **ditht** 1799; **idight** 5139; **y dyght** 385
dygyse *n.* strange dress, outlandish new style 1284; **degises** *pl.* newfangledness, ostentatious new fashions 1290
dignyte *n.* rank, high position; worth; reputation 84
diʒe see **deye**
dym *adj.* faint, dim 654; **derk and** ~ dark and dull 950; **dymme** 6207
dynge *v.* scourge, beat 5762
discencyon *n.* dissention, conflict 3345
discerne *v.* understand 1578
discipline *n.* chastisement; discipline 4652
disciplyne, see discipline.
disclaundre *v.* slander 3532
discord *n.* discord, disagreement 961

discrene, see discerne.
discrecioun *n.* moral discernment, discernment 7218
discussid *v.* decided *ppl.* 2060; **discussed** 4826
disfugured *v.* deformed *ppl.* 1941
disgysed *v.* strangely dressed, disguised *ppl.* 4531; **dysgised** 3466
dispendyd *v.* squandered *pa3pl.* 4617; **dispended** 1998; ~ **in veyn** pointlessly wasted 5013
dyscord, see discord.
dyspytous *adj.* cruel: **helle is yholde a ...** ~ **place** hell is considered a cruel place1469
distructyon *n.* ruin, devastation 3336; **destruccion** 3351; **dystruccion** 3347
dyuerse *adj.* various, different 285; **in** ~ **manere** in various ways 1191; **in** ~ **wise** in various ways 4041; ~ **þynges** diverse purposes 6024; **diuerse** 1519
dyuyded *v.* divided, separated *ppl.* 297; **in two parties** ~ divided into two parts 812
dyuynite *n.* theology 5900
dyuys *n.* scheme; **after my** ~ according to my design or plan 7263
dyuyse *v.* divide 4028
do *n.* doe 1303
doctor *n.* a doctor of the Church 2273; **doctur** 1101; **doctours** *pl.* 3157; **doctors** 1895
doer *n.* agent, doer, performer, perpetrator 4825
doynge *vbl.n.* **in a lytil** ~ quickly 4189
dolour *n.* sorrow, dolor 1049
dom(e) *n.* judgment 2089, 227; **domes** *poss.sg.*: ~ **Day** Judgment Day, Doomsday 3335; **þe** ~ **manne** the judge 4521; **domys** 3921
dombe *adj.* mute, dumb 44
domesday *n.* Judgment Day 3745; **domysday** 2280
don(e) *v.* do; carry out, complete; accomplish; commit; administer 251, 130; **lette to** ~ **her will** stop (them) from doing what they want 6287; **to do** doing 7258; **wele to** ~ to live virtuously 3087; **most ...** ~ had to carry on, i.e., the same custom 3342; **doþ** *pr3sg.* 516; ~ **his kynde** acts according to its nature 405; **doþe** 2633; **doth** 108; **deth** 93; **dede** *pa3sg.*1802; **dude** 4835; **dyde** 2386; **don(e)** *ppl.* 90, 276; **do: not** ~ not completed 3233; **be** ~ **most** be performed mostly [in sight of the people] 3576; **ido** 1979; **idon** 2212; **y do** 101
dongeon *n.* underground prison cell, dungeon 397; **hele** ~ underground prison of hell 5904; **dungeon** 392
donward *n.* downward 683; **downward** 563
dore *n.* door 2794
dorst, dorste see **dar**.
double *adj.* **wyth** ~ **honde** with both hands 1042; **in** ~ **manere** in two ways 6854
doughter *n.* daughter 4849; **doughtur** 1760
doun, down *adv.* down 1700, 568; **downe** 1261; ~ **comynge** descent 4418; ~ **fallynge** descent 6107
doute, dowte *n.* doubt, perplexity; fear; peril 678, 501; **in gret** ~ **of** in great fear for 2363; **with oute** ~ certainly 3363
drawe *v.tr.* draw, drag, pull; lead; bring on; take 966, 998; **wormes ...** ~ **hym** worms pull him apart 764; **no pardon to hem** ~ produce no pardon for themselves 3214; **forþ** ~ entice 3430; **oþur to hem** ~ attract others to them 4995; **draweþ** *pr3sg.* 1073; **drow(e)** *pa.* 3688, 4626; **out** ~ composed, wrote 7303; **drowhe:** ~ **faste to þe deþward** was swiftly approaching death 1866; **drawe** *ppl.* 2656; **yn Englyssh** ~ written in English 284; **out** ~ extracted, excerpted 7232; **idrawe: wepne ... to him** ~ weapon ... drawn against him 1434; **drawe** *vb.intr.* move, go 1731; **draweþ** *pr3sg.* 674; **drawes** *pr3pl.* 1021; **draweþ:** ~ **evene** reach ... directly 6009; **drow** *pa.* 4709; **drawynge** *pr.ppl.* 5699
dred(e) *n.* (reverential) fear, reverence; dread; anxiety, doubt; danger 2348, 119; **ryght** ~ proper reverence 290; **have no** ~ **... to mys** do not worry about failing to find ... 6685; **haven** ~ fear 6681; **haþ grete** ~ will be greatly concerned about 7237
drede *v.* fear (reverentially), revere; dread 134; **ys to** ~ is to be feared 303; **forto** ~ to be dreaded 1094; **dredeþ** *pr3sg.* 1525; **dreduþ** *pr3pl.* 1524; **dred** 2078; **dreden** 1496; **dredeth** 1072; **drdeþ** 1409
dredful *adj.* frightening, dreadful; apprehensive 188; **dredfull** 4268
dredyng *vbl.adj.* fearing, dreading 1398; ~ **schulde be** should fear 1933
drem *n.* dream 6370
drery *adj.* sad 1226
drewry *n.* treasure; tokens (of God's love) 6154
drie *adj.* dry; emaciated 3042; **druye** 1212
dryue *v.* drive, lead to, bring; subject, compel 3261; **wherto he schold be** ~ to which he must be subjected 3188; **dryue** *ppl.* 633; **idryue, ydryve** 4666, 37; **beþ** ~ **to vilanye** are moved to sin 6626
dronken *v.* drank *pa.pl.* 4063
dropesie *n.* dropsy 2388; **droposy** 593
droppeth *v.* runs, drips *pr3sg.* 653
dure *v.* endure, abide, continue, live, remain 5714; **duere** 657; **durynge** *pr.ppl.* 6992
dwelle *v.* exist, live; remain, endure, continue, last 35; **with hem** ~ keep company with them 3673; **dwelleþ** *pr3sg.* 392; **dwelles** 949; **dwelleth** 604; **dwelluþ** 756; **dwellen** *pr3pl.* 1431; **dwelles** 884; **dwelleth** 824; **dwelleþ** 2206
dwellynge *n.* home, dwelling 1141; **dwellyng: owre** ~ **make** make our residence 1146
dwellynge *vbl.adj.* living 861
dwyne *v.* wither; **away** ~ waste away 1228
ebbeþ *v.* ebbs, flows back *pr3sg.* 997
ech a, echa *adj.* each, every 1590, 2766; ~~ **tyme** every moment 4732; **that** ~ the same 1588; **eche** 105; ~ **of oþur** each alone 6920; **eche a** 380; **eche an** 4746; ~~ **here** every hair 7178; **ucha** 6531; **uche** 98
echon(e) *pron.* every one 3637, 1963; **of us** ~ for each of us 3637; **among hem** ~ among every one of them 6801
eddres see **adder**
edwyt *v.* reproach 322
edwit *n.* scorn 6161
eft *adv.* afterwards 5493
eft sone *adv.* immediately, soon after 1051; **efte sones** 5434; **eftsone** 2679
eggyng *vbl.n.* urging, tempting 4584

egipciens *n.pl.* Egyptians 7086
ey *n.* egg 5386
eyȝe *n.* eye 929; **ye** 4185; **bifore her ~** in their mind 6421; **yȝe** 685; **eyȝes** *poss.sg.* 4190; **eiȝes** *pl.* 5247; **eyen** 496; **yen** 924; **yȝen** 6278
eithþe *ord.* eighth 5683; **eiȝtþe** 4022
eke *v.* increase 5622; **eken** *pr3pl.* 6696
eke *adv.* also 513
elde *n.* age, old age 1504; **eelde** 1270
elde *adj.* old 1567
elementes *n.pl.* elements, i.e., air, earth, water, fire 4086; **elementys** 822
elle *see* **hell**
elles *adv.* otherwise, else 125; **ell** 846; **ellys** 5167
elles *adj.* else 353; **ell** 1065; **ellys** 462
ells where *adv.* elsewhere 2729; **ell where: ~ nought** nowhere else 4385
empyre *n.* empire 3357; **empire** 3337
emprise *n.* undertaking, enterprise; **on gret ~** of great intent 3539
enchantours *n.pl.* sorcerers 3494
enchauntement *n.* (magic) spell 3566
enchesoun *n.* cause(s), reason; pretext 992; **encheson** 4380
encloseþ *v.* surrounds *pr3sg.* 5462
encomberaunce *n.* hindrance, temptation 2583
encombred *v.* perplexed, beset *ppl.* 5868
encres *v.* increase 6193
end(e) *n.* end, conclusion 671, 30; **wyth outen ~** eternal 198; **wiþ outen eny ~** eternally 2636; **laste ~** the final part 673; **the laste ~** the farthest reach 4052; **on ~** finally 4499; **fyngres ~** fingertip 1257; **last ~** point of death 1376; **at the ~** at the end of the world 3379; **mad an ~** concluded 5212; **ibought to þe ~** brought to completion 6367
endeles *adj.* eternal 29; **endles** 830
endet *v.* ends *pr3sg.* 7316; **endeþ** 6484; **endyd** *ppl.* 643
endyng(e) *vbl.n.* conclusion, end; death 25, 187; **laste ~** end of life 479; **good ~** happy death, i.e., dying in the state of grace 9; **make the ~** bring about the end, i.e., the destruction 33; **~ day** dying day 1616; **endying** 1446
endlesnesse *n.* eternity, endlessness 6401; **endlesnese** 6404
endure *v.* suffer, put up with; **þerto ~** stand up to that 5663
engelisch *n.* English (language) 5545; **englisch** 4063; **englys** 985; **englysch** 2217; **englyssh** 284
engyne *n.* battering ram; ingenuity 5764; **engynne** 6140
engendreþ *v.* beget, bring about *pr3sg.* 934
eny *adj.* any 255; **any** 10
enioyned *v.* imposed *ppl.* 3227
enleueþ *ord.* eleventh 4037
ensample *n.* example 727; **in ~** a model 597; a parallel case 1793
entayled *v.* carved; **tally ~** elegantly decorated *ppl.* 7130
entencion *n.* intention 3790
entent(e) *n.* will, mind 2746; intention 2929; **takeþ to hem ~** pays attention to them 1272
entre *v.* enter 348
entre *n.* entrance, access 1751

enuye, envie *n.* envy, malice 2703, 6699; **anuye** harm, injury 2866
envyousnesse *n.* envy 6548
enviroun *adv.* round about 4473
eorþ(e) *n.* earth 3588, 2306; **eorthe** 3615; **erthe** 64; **erþe** 714
eorþly *adj.* mortal; worldly, earthly 5522; **erthlyche** 1446; **erþlich** 7062; **erþly** 2630; **erþlyche** 601
eorþ quave *n.* earthquake 4031
eoþly, see eorþly.
er(e) *adv.* before 1174, 2728; **arst** *superl.* first 2298; **~ bynome** first take place (?) 3350; **erst** 4146; **er** *conj.* before 686; **~ that** before 123; **~ than** before 2658; **ere** 1270; **ar: byfore ~** before 10; **~ þat** 1706; **or** 1668
erculye *prop.n.* Hercules 3409
ere *n.* ear 281; **eren** *pl.* 656
eretikes *n.pl.* heretics 4993
eritage, erytage *n.* inheritance 1877, 834; **herytage** 730
erlyche *adv.* early 611; **erly** 1208
errour *n.* heresy; sin, mistake 3557; **into ~ torned** converted into sin 4807; **error** 3546
erþe dene *n.* earthquake 4029
ese *n.* comfort, prosperity, pleasure 512
esy *adj.* easy, effortless; suitable 1176, 6423
est *n.* east 3560
ete *v.* eat 735; **etest** *pr2sg.* 2796; **eteþ** *pr3sg.* 2789; **ete** *pr.subj.sg.* 3929; **eten** *pa3pl.* 4073; **eeten** 4066
euangelyst *n.* one of the four Gospels writers 913; **euangelistes** *pl.* 6790
eue *n.* evening 613; **euene** 3585; **folowynge wel ~** just after twilight 4033
euel(e) *n.* evil 73, 1060; **euyl** 83; **uvel** 4605; **eueles** *pl.* 1732; **euels** 584; **euelys** 591; **euel** *adj.* 1016; **evele** 3850; **euell** 1782; **euyl** 1359
euel *adv.* wickedly 2854
evene, euene *adv.* smoothly; calmly; exactly 815, 1177; **ryght ~** directly 815; **ful ~** quite directly 2116; **wel ~** directly 4298; **~ right** quite exactly, exactly indeed 6595
euene *adj.* even, level; equally matched 5320
euenenesse *n.* equality; **by ~** equally 297;
euenlong *adj.* lengthwise: **overþwoȝt and ~** crosswise and lengthwise, i.e., completely 6692
euer(e), ever(e) *adv.* ever, always 1981; 23, 18, 7; **~ ylyke** constantly 1038; **~ among** continually 6169; always together, in a group 6889; **eury** 5711; **euyr** 2596
euere lastynge *adj.* eternal 6162
euery *pron.* each, each one; everyone; **~ to othur schal seme** they shall seem to each other 2436; **~ of hem** each of them 6612
euery *adj.* every 77, 130,165; **~ an eche** 6781; **~ aweie** every means 2123; **in ~ side** in every direction 3544; **in ~ side of hem** all around them 5961
euerych *pron.* everyone 5655
eueriche *adj.* every 4071; **~ aside** everywhere 4071; **eueryche: ~ side** everywhere 336; **euery** 77; **by ~ side** on every side 5926
euerichone *pron.* every one, each 4326; **euerychon(e)** 2844, 434
eueriwhere *adv.* everywhere 3832; **euery where** 1550; **euerywhere** 553
euer more *adv.* always, eternally, perpetually 6318; **euere more** 1241; **euer mo** 405; **euer more** 113

examinid *v.* investigated *ppl.* 1988
excuse *v.* absolve, justify; excuse, exempt 4463; **excuseth** *pr3sg.* 145; **excused** *ppl.* 4610; **have me ~** excuse me 7268
exil(e) *n.* exile 949, 2371
exiled *v.* banished, exiled *ppl.* 2373
exposicioun *n.* interpretation 3183
expowne *v.* explain, interpret 3352; **expounyd** *ppl.* 3958
Eȝechiel(l) *prop.n.* (the prophet) Ezechiel 2215, 4953
face *n.* face, countenance 650, 720, 2235; **mowen se god in his ~** may see God face to face 2529
fade *v.* wither 588; **faduth** *pr3sg.* 614; **fadyn** *pr3pl.* **stormes ~** storms abate 590
fade *adj.* hostile, fierce 6705
fadur *n.* father 2; **fadre** 6565; **fadres** *pl.* 1157; **fadres** *poss.sg.* 1877.
faile, fayle *v.tr.* lack, fail 6242; **hem schal ~** they shall lack 6640; *v.intr.* loose strength, be lacking, be missing 1269, 3219; **fayleth** *pr3sg.* 1495; **fayleþ** 969; **fayleþ** *pr3pl.*: **that to hym ~** that he is lacking 3194; **faile** *pr.subj.sg.*: **all þowh ... þer ~ light** although light be lacking there 6881
faylyng *vbl.n.* lack, failure 5950; **faylynge** *vbl.adj.* lacking; transient 7007
fayn *adj.* happy, joyful 6577
fayre, faire *adv.* well; fittingly 2448, 6960
fayr, fair *adj.* fair, beautiful; beautiful; good; bright, shining 587, 328; **have a ~ pris** take the prize for beauty 5326; **~ mad to** made beautiful for (her spouse) 6831; **fayre** 489; **faire** 6736
fayrnesse, fairnesse *n.* beauty; good looks 212, 585
falle *v.* happen; befall; fall, descend; sag; pertain (to); belong (together); be located 192; **þerto scholde ~** should pertain to it 3361; **sodeynly to ded ... adown ~** suddenly to fall down dead 3877; **to on flok ~** to gather into one flock 3895; **Haþ drede to ~** worries about falling 6679; **falleþ** *pr3sg.* 477; **that he ~ inne** i.e., visualize seeing himself commiting the sin that he yields to 1952; **every planet ~ to** it pertains to every planet 6058; **falleth: ~ to** pertains to 928; **falleþ** *pr3pl.* 1733; **it ~ hym** as befits Him 4196; **fel** *pa3sg.* 323; **full: as it ~ be ryght** as it rightfully happened 5162; **felle** *pa3pl.* 328; **fellen** 324; **fallee: be ~** come to pass, happen; come abut 859; **yfalle** *ppl.* **men beth ~** is alloted to men 637
falle *n.* fall; **donward ~** a precpitous fall 683
fals *adj.* false, spurious, untrue; treacherous 940; **~ enchantours** deceitful sorcerers 3494; **false** 3538; **~ colour** false pretense 3545
falshede *n.* deceitfulness 960
falsly *adv.* treacherously 1134
falsnesse *n.* deceitfulness 942
fame *n.* renown, reputation: **of ~** of renown, renowned 3317
fare *v.* go, depart; fare, act, do 439; **fareth, fareþ** *pr3sg.* 516, 6806; **it ~** it turns out 2967; **so wel ~** prosper so well i.e., do so well 6333; **fareth, fareþ** *pr3pl.* 233, 1119
fast *n.* abstinence from food, fast 5153
faste *adv.* firmly, tightly; swiftly; closely; eagerly; stoutly, vigorously 1842, 178; **~**

Select Glossary (by Hoyt Greeson) 219

by nearby 4364; ~ **stonden** remain fixed 6090
faste *v.* abstain from food, fast 2796
fasten *v.* attach, fasten 5716; **fastned** *ppl.* 1589; **love ... ~ so faste** love ... pledged so firmly 6528
fastynge *vbl.n.* fast(ing), abstinance from food 2919; **fasting** 1383; **Ffastyng** 2745
favour *n.* good will, favor 1000; **do me that ~** show me that good will 7274; **favor** 212
favourable *adj.* well-disposed 1120
feble *adj.* weak, feeble 586; **feblere** *comp.adj.* 629
feblenesse *n.* weakness 6279; **febulnesse** 437
fede *v.* feed, nourish 4661; **fedde** *pa2pl.* 5141; **fed** *ppl.* 5542; **ifed** 6978
feftene *num.* fifteen 5445; **fiftene, fyftene** 3831, 4523
fey *n.* faith; religious doctrine 170; **seye in good ~** tell the truth 3459; **skyle and ~** reason and faith 54
feyne *v.* pretend, dissemble 3520; **hym ~ ded** pretend he is dead 3582
feyntynge *vbl.n.* weakening; **wiþout ~** unflaggingly 5764
feyntyse *n.* faintheartedness; **with out ~** unflinchingly 2862
fekyl *adj.* false, fickle, inconstant 895
fel *adj.* treacherous; terrible 109; **felle** 1499; **wonder ~** extremely terrible 2080
felawschipe *n.* band of associates; **~ holde** keep company 3672
felde *n.* field, plain 1028
fele *v.* feel, sense, perceive, experience; understand 759; **of ... myght ~** might experience ... 7071; **to ~ nought** to perceive nothing 1489; **more to ~ and to se** longer to be experienced and to see 5737; **feleþ** 1579; **feled** *pa3sg.* 2458; **fele** *pr3subj.* 1652; **feled** *ppl.* 2439
fele *n.* file i.e., a rasp; **make a ~** make a file, i.e., a hardship that chastens or corrects 3072
fele *adj.* many; much 1127; **swiþe ~** very many 4024
felyng(e) *vbl.n.* feeling, sensation; experience, perception, knowledge 5219, 2420; **to have y had ~** to have had experience (of neither happiness nor sadness) 5219
felle *n.* skin, hide 75
fellich *adv.* treacherously 3718
felonys *n.pl.* traitors, criminals 2358
felonnes *n.pl.* sores 2391
felþe *n.* corruption, filth 5513; **felþes** *pl.* 5526
felthede *n.* uncleanness, filthiness 529; **felþede** 958; **felþedes** *pl.* 5992; **felþe hedes** 5226; **fulthede, fulþede** 395, 5528
fen *n.* dung, excrement; mud, i.e., *saccus stercorum* (bag of feces, dung) 486
fend(e) *n.* Satan, the Enemy; fiend, devil 1037, 35; **fendes** *poss.sg.* 5493; **fendys** 470; **fendes** *pl.* 1940; **fendys** 4512; **fendes** *poss.pl.* 1502; **fendys** 5644
feorthe *num.* a fourth; **the ~ partye** the fourth part, a quarter 304; **feorþ(e)** 2161, 5532; **ferthe** 1549; **ferþ(e)** 1505, 2078; **fourthe** 2379; **furþe** 3278
fer *adv.* far, distant 1555
fere *v.* frighten 6704
fere *n.* companion 2366
fere *n.* fear, fright 5374

ferforþ *adv.* far; **as ~ as** as far as 3142; **ferþ forþ** (scribal error?) 3222
fers *adj.* fierce, cruel 109
ferst *adv.* first, in the beginning 1,175; **Fferst** 994; **first** 6618
ferst *adj.* first 27; **ferste** 32; **furst** 1524
ferstede *v.* thirsted *pa1sg.* 4840
fet, fete *see* **fot**
fette *v.*: **out me to ~** to seek me out 5191
fifteneþ *ord.* fifteenth 4049
fifþe, fyfþe *ord.* fifth 3287, 3281; **vifte** 306; **fyfthe** 2470; **fiþe** 5565
fyght *n.* battle, fight 582
fyght(e) *v.* fight, do battle 1040, 6549; **~ to gidre** fight against each other 4024; **fyghteþ** *pr3sg.* 1042
fightynge *adj.* militant (Latin, *militans*) 6856
figure *n.* shape, appearance 5664
fyn *adj.* excellent, fine; beneficial 2910
fynall *adj.* final, ultimate 5118
finde, fynde *v.* find, discover; encounter; reveal; learn 1631, 31; **yfynde** 1141; **fynde** *pr1sg.* 205; **fyndest** *pr2sg.* 2828; **fyndeth** *pr1pl.* 727; **fyndeþ** 7142; **fynden** 5667; **fyndeþ** *pr3pl.* 1408; **fond** *pa3sg.* 3992; **founde** *ppl.* 1865; **ifounde, yfounde** 2096, 1648
fyndynges *vbl.n.pl.* discoveries, inventions, contrivances 1337; **fyndyngȝ** 1334; **fyndyngynges** [scribal error] 1318
fyne *v.* purify, refine 4136; **fyned** *ppl.* 2547; **ifyned, yfyned** 5364, 2691
finel *n.* fennel 6917
fynger *n.* finger 1590; **fyngres** *poss.sg.*: **~ ende** fingertip 1257; **fingres** *pl.* 578
firmament *n.* sky, heavens 564
fisches *n.pl.* fish 4010
fisik *n.* medicine 4987
fyve *num.* five 3885
flamme *n.* flame 5569
flatryng *vbl.n.* insincere praise 2820
fle *v.intr.* flee, escape, avoid; hurry, move quickly 156; **fleth** *pr3sg.* 1117; **fleþ** 1399
flemed *v.* banished *ppl.* 5068
flesch *n.* flesh 75; **lust of ~** carnal desires 923; **fleisch** 5736; **flesches** *poss.sg.*: **thorow ~ kynde** by the nature of flesh 1444; **his ~ lykynge** his carnal desire 2526; **fleisches** *poss.pl.* **~ wille** carnal desires 5814
fleschly *adj.* carnal; physical 933
flescly *adv.* carnally; **~ to deal with** to have intercourse with 2804
flie *v.* fly; ascend 3586; **fleþ** *pr3sg.* 1399, 1554; **fley** *pa.sg.* 3868; **fly** 4298
fliȝte *n.* flight, escape 6235; **flyght** 466
flit *v.* escape; depart 1996; **flytte** 3089
flod *n.* flood 4118; **flood** 4070; **flodes** *pl.* 3948
flok *n.* flock; group 3714; **flokk** 4955
flour *n.* flower 589; **floures** *pl.* 550
flouren *v.* bloom, flower 3591; **floureþ** *pr3sg.* 612
floweþ *v.* flow, run *pr3sg.* 997
fo *n.* foe 1044; **foos** *pl.* 3209
fod *n.* food, sustenance 5542; **fode** 394
fol *see* **full**
folie, folye *n.* folly, imprudence; sin, sinfulness 2883, 192; **foly** 283 1352; **folies** *pl.* 1326; **folyes** 237
folk *n.* people 212
folwe *v.* follow; obey 6593; **folowe** 2132; **folowen** 3623; **foloweþ** *pr3sg.* 517; **foloweþ**

3695; **foloweþ** *pr3pl.* 49; **folowed** *pa.* 5061; **~ her trace** followed their example 5669; **folowyd** 5055; **folowynge** *pr.ppl.* 572
folowynge *vbl.adj.* coming after, following 4033
fonde *v.* try, test; experience; tempt 944; **fonde** *pr1pl.* 1232
fondyng *vbl.n.* temptation 270
fonge *v.* receive, acquire; endure 3859; **fonge** *ppl.* 5009; **yfonge** 2650
fontston *n.* baptismal font 2652
for *conj.* because 15
for barred *v.* stopped, blocked *ppl.* 798
forbede *v.* forbid; **~ that ... ne holde** forbid ... from accepting 3549
forbore *v.* endured *ppl.* 5945
force *v.* compel; **hym ~** exert himself 3533
fordo *v.* overcome; destroy, blot out; devastate 4124; **for don** 2738; **fordoþ** *pr3sg.* 2847; **fordon** *pr3pl.* 2730; **fordede** *pa.sg.* 4071; **fordo** *ppl.* 4117
fore said *ppl.adj.* aforesaid, said before 6648; **for said** 1602; **forsayd** 126
forest *n.* wilderness, forest 1017; **forestes** *pl.* 1021
forgive *see* **forȝive**
for go *v.* give up, forgo; lose: **non ... wolde ... othur ~** neither would ... desert the other 1531; **fur go** 6683
forȝeteth *v.* forget, forget about *pr.3sg.*; **~ hym self** lacks self-awareness 217; **forȝeteþ** 1689; **forȝat** *pa3sg.* 1691; **for ȝete** *ppl.* 276; **forȝete** 4523
forȝiue *v.* forgive, pardon 3187; **forȝiue** *pr3subj.* 7307; **forȝiue** *ppl.* 2642; **forgiue** 2544; **furȝyuen** 6936
forȝiuenesse *n.* remission (of sin) 3145
forlete *v.* abandoned *ppl.* 2882
forlore *v.* lost, abandoned *ppl.* 411; **for lore** 4649
form(e) *n.* shape, appearance 4245, 1914
formest *adv.* first, foremost 1762
forsake *v.* abandon; forsake; renounce 761; **forsaken** *pr3pl.* 3678; **for sake** *pr3subj.* 1342; **forsoke** *pa3pl.* 5054; **forsake** *ppl.* 3534
forsetteth *v.* stop *pr3pl.*; **hym self they ~** they impede themselves 208
forsothe, for soþe *adv.* in truth, truly 708, 1616; **forsoþ** 5146
fort *conj.* until 2121
forth *adv.* forth; away 4168; **lyveth ~** lives on 142; **forthe** 450; **forþ** 549; **~ brouȝt** produced 2068
for than *conj.* because 2783; **~ þouȝ** because 1824; **Ffor than** 1658; **Ffor thanne** 408; **for þan** 2755
for that *conj.* because, since 1194; **Ffor that** 177; **for þat** 1844, 4669
forther *adv.* further; **~ passe** proceed, continue 379; **forþur** 1930
forther more *adv.* moreover 670
forto *infinitive marker* to 134; **Ffor to** 1150; **forto** *conj.* until 471; **Fforto** *adv.* until 726
Ffor þey *adv.* although; consequently 4204; **for þi** 1361; **for þei** 5540
for þenkynge *vbl.n.* repentance 5844
forward *adv.* forwards; **from that tyme ~** from that time on 3901
for whi, for why *conj.* because 732, 598; **FFor whi, Ffor why** 2498, 996

Select Glossary (by Hoyt Greeson)

fot(e) *n.* foot 2455, 401; **stonde on** ~ stand on their feet 6276; **foot** 4438; **fet** *pl.* 3865; **fete** 690; **feet** 576
fowcheþ save *v.* grants, permits, vouchesafes *pr3sg.* 5456; **fouche safe** *pr.subj.2sg.* 7166
foul *n.* bird 2664; **fowle** 466; **foules** *pl.* 2601
fowle *adv.* shamefully, badly, vilely, foul 556
foul(e) *adj.* bad, sinful, wicked, vile; severe; ugly 382, 731; **fowl(e)** 332, 191; **fouler** *compar.* 720; **fowler** 537; **more** ~ uglier 651; **Ffowler** 493; **foulest** *superl.* 318
foure *num.* four 205; ~ **score** eighty 637; **four** 4100; **Ffoure** 2917
fourtene *num.* fourteen 5644
fourteneþ *ord.* fourteenth 4039; **fourteenþ** 5912
fourty *num.* forty 2208
fram *prep.* from 323; **from** 528; **Ffram** 1766; **Ffrom** 6993
framward *adj.* stubborn, willful 658; **fraward:** ~ **to** disobedient to 219; **froward** 262
fraunchise *n.* right, privilege 6298
fre *adj.* free, unrestrained 85; **bond ne** ~ enslaved nor free(man) 744; ~ **prison** non-punitive custody 2252; **quyt and** ~ clear and free 5028
fredom(e) *n.* liberty, freedom 6281, 6280; **freedom** 7277
freisch *adv.* anew, suddenly 1038
frely, freli *adv.* freely, willingly 5010, 1881; **Ffrely** 4999
frend *n.* friend 915; **frendes** *pl.* 1838; **frendes** *poss.pl.* 2311
frendschipe *n.* friendship 1569
fresch *adj.* recent, fresh 4439
frese *v.* freeze 5489
frete *v.* gnaw, eat 5783
fro *adv.:* **to and** ~ back and forth 826
fro *prep.* from, away 219; **Ffro** 3856
front *n.* forehead; countenance 683
frowardnesse *n.* obstinacy 957
fruyt, fruit *n.* fruit; offspring 540, 551
fuyr(e) *n.* fire 2125, 3823; **do** ~ **adown fro hevene** cause fire to come down from the sky 3570; **fuyres** *pl.* 2504
ful *adv.* fully, very 896; **Fful** 6907
ful *adj.* full 13; **full** 21; **fulle** 6732; ~ **knowyng** complete knowledge 121; ~ **water** deep sea 5797; **hem lyke** ~ **ille** utterly displease them 6644; **fol** 3793
fulfille, fulfulle *v.* carry out; accomplish, complete; satisfy, gratify; fill 3194, 1198; **fulfylle** 4225; **full fylle** 852; **to hem** ~ accomplish for them 6606; **fulfylle** *pr.subj.3sg.* 7259; **fulfild** *ppl.* 2362; **fulfuld** 2402; ~ **Of** filled with 6346; **fulfulled** 1367; **fulfyllyd** 3237
fullyche *adv.* fully, completely 410; **fully** 4329
fulthede, fulþede *see* **felthede**
furȝete *v.* forget 3563; **forȝeteth** *pr3sg.* 217; **for ȝeteþ** 1689; **forȝat** *pa3sg.* 1691; **for ȝete** *ppl.* 276
gadre *v.* gather, collect, amass 3492; NB: a proleptic metathesis resulting in the erroneous form **grade**, conditioned by the following word, **gydre**; **gadreth** *pr3sg.* 1118; **gadreþ** 2766; **gadred** *ppl.* 2762; **igadred** 2756
gadrynge *pr.ppl.n.:* **a** ~ **about** an assembly 6860

gay *adj.* elegant; carefree 1338
galle *n.* bile; poison 5582
gan *see* **bigynne**
garetes *n.pl.* turrets 7037; **garettes** 7031
garnament *n.* garment 450
gate *n.* gate; way 1761; **ate** ~ at the gate, i.e., about to die 1647; **ȝate** 1654; **gates** *pl.* 1760; **ȝates** 1757
general *adj.* universal; absolute 2100; **in a** ~ **manere** in a comprehensive way 6184
generally *adv.* universally 2917
gentyll *adj.* noble (in rank or birth) 640
gesse *v.* guess, estimate; imagine, suppose 929; **mowe** ~ can imagine 7201
gestys *n.pl.* guests, travellers 1146
get *n.* mode, fashion 1304
gete *n.pl.* goats 5128
gyldon *adj.* golden; **John** ...~**mowthe** John Chrysostom 4469
gyle *n.* guile, deceit 960
gynnyng *vbl.n.* creation 615
gyse *n.* way, manner: **by many maner** ~ in various ways 1327; **gyses** *pl.* fashions 1311
give *see* **ȝive**
glad(e) *adj.* happy, glad, joyful, cheerful 1162, 2748; ~ **and blythe** happy and pleased 1162; **swithe** ~ very cheerful 4066
gladly *adv.* willingly 1531
glas *n.* glass; **myrrour of** ~ looking glass 6450
glet *n.* slime, phlegm 395
glorye *n.* (heavenly) glory 856
glorifienge *vbl.n.:* **alle creatures þat faire schull be Wiþ ynne hem of þe** ~ **of man** all creatures that shall be beautiful within themselves from the exaltation of man's body and soul (i.e., by investing them with radiance) 6736-37
gloriously *adv.* in a glorified state 6716
glose *n.* explanation, gloss 3748
glotany *n.* gluttony (one of the seven Deadly Sins); **glotanye** 2395
glowynge *vbl.n.* glow 5504
god(e) *adj.* good; good deeds 281, 2629; **good(e)** 9, 283
gode *n.* goodness; right, prudent; good persons 6872; **good(e)** 70, 231; ~ **kan** knows what is right OR prudent 440
godhed(e) *n.* divinity, nature of God 1442, 13
godnesse *n.* goodness; good deeds 6183; **goodnes** 1456; **goodnesse** 4
gog *prop.n.* Gog, followers of Antichrist 3723
goyng(e) *vbl.n.* wandering; departure 164, 5796; **goynge** *vbl.adj.* **is bifore** ~ precedes 5796
gome *n.* pleasure: **haþ** ... **good** ~ takes good pleasure in it 3324
gon *v.* go; walk 1307; **whethur thei mowe** ~ **othur ryde** i.e., whether they're coming or going 1307; ~ **hem fro** leave them 3384; **go** 400; **aboute hem** ~ encircle them 6257; **gost** *pr2sg.* 2151; **goþ** *pr3sg.* 1956; **aboute** ~ revolve 6036; **gothe** 655; **goþ** *pr3pl.* 2170; **goth** 1301; **gon** 163; **wente** *pa3sg.* 4068; **ȝede** 4076; **gon** *ppl.* 2033; **beþ to paradys** ~ have gone to heaven 3077; **ygone** 5411
gonne, gan *see* **bigynne**
good *n.* blessings; benefits; spiritual wealth, abundance 1123; **goodes** *pl.* possessions 6683; **goodis** 1111; **goodys:** ~ **gostly** spiritual wealth 1027
gost *n.* spirit, soul 622; **Holy** ~ the third Person of the Trinity 4; **in here** ~ in their souls 2308; **Goste** 16; **gostes** *pl.* 1703
gostly *adv.:* ~ **preve** prove spiritually 7142; ~ **to speke**, ~**to telle** speaking figuratively, spiritually 7146, 7198; ~ **to undurstonde** to interpret spiritually 7202; **gostly** *adj.* spiritual 805; **gostli:** ~ **deþ** death of the soul 1411; **gostliche** 2312; **goostly** 853
gowte, goute *n.* gout 2390, 594; **cold** ~ phlegmatic gout 2390
grace *n.* grace, gift (of God); favour 471; **out of** ~ in disfavor (i.e., with God) 7290
gracyous *adj.* merciful 111
gras *n.* grass 610
graunt *n.* permission 6935; **ȝive** ~ admit, confess 3422
graunte *v.* allow, grant 3885; **grauntyd** *pa3sg.* 1881; **graunt** *pr.sub.3sg.* 7296; **graunted** *ppl.* 3133; **granted** 3148; **igranted** 5316; **grantyd** 4808
grede *v.* cry out 1697
greflokur *comp.adj.* more hard to endure 5655
grenne *v.* grimmace; jeer 5984
gresly *adj.* horrible, hideous, grisly 1610; **greslyche** 6706; **gryslich** 2344; **grysliche** 1936; **grysly** 766; **gryslyche** 1178
gret(e) *adj.* great 91, 62; **grettor** *comp.adj.* 6667
gretly *adv.* greatly; strongly 262
gretness *n.* immensity, expanse; great size 5290
greuaunce *n.* misery; injury, pain 633
greue *v.* injure, afflict; distress; offend, bother; enrage; be painful 1016; **greuue** 1846; **greueth** *pr3sg.* 968; **greveþ: my lif** ... **sore me** ~ my life ... sorely vexes me 2059; **greueyth** 108; **greueth** *pr3pl.* 917; **greueþ** 1321; **greuys** 2509; **greue** *pr.subj.3sg.* 1438; **greuyd** *ppl.* 1612
grevous *adj.* painful 2331
grevously *adv.* seriously, severely 3804; **grevouslokur** *comp.adv.* 4859
grigory *prop.n.* Pope Gregory I 3844; **gregory** 1090
grym *adj.* ferocious 5687
grymly *adv.* ferociously 1847
grom *n.* servant, boy; retainer 1353
grond *n.* basis, foundation; depth; soil 177; **ground:** ~ **of helle** depth of hell 5904; **grounde: bryngeþ** ... **to þe** ~ strikes ... to the ground i.e., overpowers 2406
grone *v.* groan, moan 664
grope *v.* touch, feel 5612
gruccheþ *v.* grumble, complain *pr3pl.* 255; **grucchede** *pa.pl.* 259
grucchynge *vbl.n.* complaining 2885
gult *n.* guilt; sin 4647
gulty *adj.* guilty 1870
ȝare *adv.* ready, prepared; accessible, at hand 1635; **ful** ~ quite ready 4362
ȝater, ȝates *see* **gate**
ȝe *pron.2pl.nom.* you, ye 60
ȝede *see* **gon**
ȝeld(e) *v.* yield, give; pay, render 4831, 105; ~ **aȝen** make requital 3189; **ȝeldeþ** *pr1sg.* 4879; **ȝeldeþ** *pr3sg.* 1495; **ȝelde** *pa3sg.* 1889; **ȝolde** 4753
ȝeldyng *vbl.n.* paying, payment 6173
ȝeme *v.* **the** ~ take heed *imper2sg.* 549
ȝerde *n.* rod, stick 4943

ȝere *n.* year 844; ȝer(e) *pl.* 637, 616; ȝeres 3795; ȝeris 3855
ȝet *see* ȝut
ȝif *conj.* if 78; ~ god ne wolde unless God willed 3635 yif 2849
ȝift(e) *n.* gift; payment; bribe 1557, 4681; ȝyfte 2556; ȝiftes *pl.* 3539; ȝeftes 3608; ȝyftes 3
ȝiue, ȝyue *v.* give, grant; render, yield (i.e., fruit); emit 1557, 3340; ~ a strong stynch emit a strong stench 5524; ~ his assent give its consent 6602; ȝeue 4959; ȝyuen 4846; ȝiueþ *pr3sg.* 2524; ȝyueþ 1085; ȝeueth 540; ȝiueþ *pr3pl.* 2939; ȝyueþ 234; ȝiue *pr.subj.sg.* 2982; yȝaf *pa1sg.* 2218; ȝaf *pa3sg.* 69; ȝau 96; ȝaue *pa2sg.* 5181; ȝoue *pa.pl.* 5156; ȝoue *ppl.* 1930; ȝeue 615; ȝiue 2342; yȝeue 2728; iȝiue, yȝiue 3204, 4961; iȝoue 4890; iȝyue 6315
ȝolke *n.* yolk 5386
ȝong(e) *adj.* young 182, 2686; yong 5483; ȝonghede *n.* youth 406
ȝow(e) *pron.2pl.* you 354, 848; yow 354
ȝour(e) *poss.adj.* your 1362, 4359; ȝowr 5991
ȝouþe, ȝowþe *n.* youth 4776, 477; ȝowthe 213
ȝusturday *n.* yesterday 6376
ȝut *adv.* yet; also; besides; nevertheless 128; ȝet 679; ȝit 584
hayl *n.* hail, ice pellets 1213
half(e) *n.* half; side 3812, 3258; on the left ~ on the left side 5133; lift ~ left side 5171
halle *n.* hall; dwelling 54312
halwes *n.pl.* saints 3151
hameres *n. poss.sg.* hammer's 5779; hameres *pl.* 5760
hangeȝ *v.intr.* hangs *pr3sg.* 579; hongeþ 570; heng *pa3sg.* 4413; heengen *pa.pl.* 44534; hangyng *pr.ppl.* 1300
hap *n.* fate, (good) fortune, chance, lot; omen; accident 1046; ~ othur chaunce fortune or chance 1066
hard *n.* hardship, affliction; bygynnynge of ~ beginning of sorrows (i.e., Latin *dolorum*) 3324
hard *adv.* firmly; close; severely: wel ~ holdynge very close-fisted 660; ~ ...by set cruelly ... surrounded 1034; harde: fastned ~ securely attached 1589; ~ ... alegge vigorously ...make claims 4693
hard(e) *adj.* hard, enduring; cruel, painful; severe; difficult; strict 263, 81; thynkeþ hem ~ seems severe to them 263; ~ peyne severe punishment 2649; wel ~ very severe 3716; swythe ~ very severe 4892; hardur *comp.* 1601; hardore 7133
hardi *adj.* brave 1919; hardy 2333
hardnesse *n.* cruelty, austerity 2858
hasted *v.* hastened, hurried *pa.pl.* 5671
hasty *adj.* quick 1312
hasty loklier *advwwwp.* the more quickly 3052
hastly *adv.* speedily 3808
hate *n.* hatred 905, 1068
hateden *v.* hated *pa.pl.* 5551
hatered *n.* hatred 5754; hatrede 2042
hatte *v.* is called, is named 2251; ihote *ppl.* 5437
hatter, hattor *see* hote
haunt *n.* habit; makeþ his ~ makes a practice of (doing good deeds) 2047; aftyr his ~ according to his custom 892

hautayn *adj.* haughty, arrogant 218
hawnte *v.* frequent; practice; adopt; engage in 3654; haunteth *pr3pl.* ~ ... here pas track them down 1022; hauntȝ 1291; haunted *ppl.* 5315
haunt *n.* practice, custom; aftyr his ~ according to his custom 892; goodnesse makeþ his ~ makes a practice of (doing) good deeds 2047
haue, have *v.* have; possess, hold; exemplify 87; hav *pr1sg.* 2903; haue 748; haueth 154; ihaue 2637; hast *pr2sg.* 1994; haste 2802; haþ *pr3sg.* 364; hath 48; haue *pr.pl.* 68; hauen 1914; han 3673; haueth, haueþ, 201, 51; hauyþ 4505; hadde *pa.sg.* 62; hadd(e) 2630, 62; had 317; haddest *pa2sg.* 1629; hadde *pa.pl.* 131; ~ lif were alive 4180; hadden 276; had 5012; had *ppl.* 4529; ihad, y had 4887, 5219; y haad 2461
hauyng *vbl.n.* possessions 1286
haymo *prop.n.* Haymo of Halberstadt, 9th century abbot and author 3663
hebrues *n.poss.pl.* Hebrews' 3989
hed *see* heued
hed *adj.* chief, capital 2702
hede *n.* heed; takeþ ~ take notice, pay attention 420; take good ~ pay close attention 7235
heere *v.* hear; listen 291; here 6132; ihere, y here 1980, 7285; ihure: ~ heere hear here 3308; y here *pr1sg.* 2416; heere *pr.pl.* 291; ihereþ 7295; iherde *pa.1sg.* 5532; hereþ *imper.pl.* 6203; iherd *ppl.* 1885
heere *adv.* here 121; here 1, 184
hey *n.* hay 2531
hele *n.* health; salvation 1103
helle *n.* hell 34; hele 5904; ~ put the pit of hell 2238; may oon ~ make can make one hell (out of four...) 2254; ~ grounde the depths of hell 2640; elle 5535
help(e) *n.* help, support 2737; in ~ of as a portion of 555; helpes *pl.* 2917
helpe *v.* help, aid, support 1546; helpeþ *pr3sg.* 2566; What ~ us pride how does pride help us 5792; helpeȝ *pr3pl.* 160; helpeþ 2270; holpe *pa.pl.* 4671; holpe *ppl.* 2952; holpen 2940; iholpe, yholpe 2909, 2944
helthe *n.* health; cure 1454
helud *v.* healed, cured *ppl.* 5587
hem self *pron.sg.* himself 203; him self 1252; him selue 506; hem self *pl.* 203
hennes *adv.* hence, away, from here 702; he ~ wende he dies 2139; hennys 439
hente *v.* takes, seizes; experiences *pr3sg.* 4069; hente *pa3sg.* 2185; ihent *ppl.* 5922
heore *adv.* here 5478
hep *n.* heap; come to ~ is accumulated 978; hepe: in on ~ all at once 4239
herborwed *v.* gave shelter *pa.pl.* 5158
herburgh *n.* lodging 385; herborow(e) 5157, 5143
herde *n.* shepherd 3896
here *see* also heere
here *n.* hair 570; heires *pl.* 3797
heryng(e) *vbl.n.* hearing; a saying 4797, 4801; to his ~ in his presence 6886; heryngge: opene ~ a familiar text, well-known words 5897
herytage *n.* inheritance 730
herte *n.* heart; courage 148; to goddes mercy only his ~ take take courage in God's

mercy alone 1381; in ~ ... ihold kept in mind 2713; we ȝoue ... wiþ ~ fre we gave ... with kind heart, i.e., generously 5156; wiþ ~ þenke conceive, think of, with the heart 5957; heorte 6924; hertes *pl.* 3778; heortes 5568
heste *n.* command, commandment 3572; hestes *pl.* 77; hestis, hestys 5070,80
hete *n.* heat 839
heþene *adj.* heathen 4603
heued *n.* head 572; heuyd 1260; hed 570; ~ synnes capital, chief sins 2702; heuedes *pl.* 5596
heuene, hevene *n.* heaven 2225, 2; loye In ~ wel clere joy in heaven very bright 2228; heuyn 4863; heuenes *pl.* 4114
heuy *adj.* heavy; serious, severe; sad, dejected; grievous 648
hewe *n.* colour, shade 4113
hide *v.* hide, keep secret, conceal 4410; hid *ppl.* 1977; ihud 1985; hud 1644
hider *adv.* hither, here 438; ~ no þider here or there 6597; hidur 703
hidous *adj.* hideous (to behold); frightful: foule and so ~ vile and so hideous 2332; wel ~ quite frightful 5958; hidos 1853; hidouȝ 1904; hidoȝ 1848; idous 5442
hidously *adv.* fiercely, horribly 5961
hidousnesse *n.* horror 5635
hie *adv.* high; highly; have so ~ extol 231; hym here ~ bere vaunt himself 6650; hiȝe 6760
hie, hye *adj.* high; lofty; exalted; haughty 231, 814; an ~ aloft, on high 1800; hey 2531; hi, hy: an ~ aloft 2117, 2131; hior *compar.* 6112; heier 6059; heiȝest *superl.* 4120; heyest 816; heyȝest 6086; hiest 6025; hyȝest 973
hiȝed *v.* exalted *ppl.* 6637
hiȝenesse *n.* arrogance, presumption; exaltation 6646; hynesse 6632
hille *n.* hill 6266; hul 4002; hull 4036; hulles *pl.* 4035
hym selue *emphatic pron.* himself, itself 927; hym self 107; hym selfe 180; hym seluen 3565
his *pr.sg.* is 602. *see* be
hisse *poss.pron.* his 6555; hys 3
hit *pron.* it 715; yt 875
ho *see* who
hold(e) *v.* hold, keep, contain; consider (to be), believe, maintain, regard; urge; observe, have 3370, 72; holden: hym self ~ over consider himself above 3530; ~ hem lowe keep them humble 4643; holden 3530; holde *pr1sg.* 897; yholde 1175; holdest *pr2sg.* 2792; holdeth, holdeþ *pr3sg.* 662, 1123; holden *pr3pl.* 3530, 3706; holdeþ 1359; holde *pr.subj.3sg.* 506; holde *pr.subj. 3pl.*: ~ aȝenst oppose 3346; holde *pr.subj. 1pl.* 808; holde *ppl.* 1129; ihold(e) 2713, 1352; beþ nat ~ are of no avail 7103; y holde 82; is ~ for is regarded as 1352
holdynge *ppl.adj.* grasping 660
hole *n.* hole 5521; holes *pl.* clefts, pits 4038
hole *adj.* entire, whole; healthy; intact 1234; hol 5320
holi, holy *adj.* holy, pious 1806, 4
holynesse *n.* virtue, devotion 3520
hollich(e) *adv.* wholly, entirely; solely 4905, 3524; holly 3283; hollyche 3253

222 Select Glossary (by Hoyt Greeson)

hom(e) *n.* home, abode 1126, 4405
hond(e) *n.* hand 1043, 401; **hand** 1055; **helle** ~ the hand of hell, i.e., *manu inferni*, the control of hell 2259; þey come to his ~ as he acquired them 3994; **wiþ mannes** ~ by the hand of man 7010; **come ... more in** ~ be dealt with further 810; **wyth double** ~ with both hands 1042; **redy to mannes** ~ accessible to man's control 1375; **her** ~ their control 6629; **ben at his** ~ be in his control 3676; **ny to ȝoure** ~ close by you 4359; **undur** ~ close by 3072; under control 4946; **hondes** *pl.* 575
hondred *adj.* hundred 616; **hundred** 625
honeste *n.* honour; uprightness; chastity, purity 4896
hongor *n.* hunger 5531; **honger** 2595; **hongour** 5533; **hungur** 5540; **hongres** *pl.* famines 3322
hongre *v.* hunger 5195; **hongred** *pa.sg.* 5141; **hongrid** 4839
hongry *n.* the hungry 2896
honour(e) *v.* honour, venerate 55, 76; **honoureth** *pr3pl.* 50; **honouryþ** 4407; **honoured** *ppl.* 6659; **honouryd** 4356
honour(e) *n.* honour; respect; fame 1001, 973; **to hym do** ~ show him respect 3504; **honoures** *pl.* signs of respect 6655
hordom *n.* fornication, whoredom 6479
horibly *adv.* repulsively 1941
horrybyle *adj.* hideous, repulsive 722; **horrible** 1918
horriblenesse *n.* repusiveness 1911
hors *n.* horse 2763
hortly *adv.* very, exceedingly 4026
hosel *n.* the Eucharist, Holy Communion 2745
ho so *see* **who so**
host *n.* army, host 3744
hot(e) *adj.* hot 5458, 2125; **hatter** *comp.* 5470; **hattor** 5838; **hottere** 5465; **hottyr** 2476
hothes *see* **oþe**
hour *n.* hour 5803; **houre: in euery** ~ at all times 77
hous(e) *n.* home, house 6821, 7042; **hows** 5428; **houses** *pl.* 4075; **howses** 4021
hous hold *n.* household; **gret of** ~ (own) a magnificent home 4979
hove *n.* hoof 3457
houeþ *v.* hovers *pr3sg.* 6034
hovynge *vbl.adj.* hovering, motionless 4336
howh so *adv.* however 978
hud *see* **hide**
hul, hull *see* **hill**
hur *poss.pron.pl.* their 4558; **hure** 4636; **her** 232
I *pron.1sg.* I; *see* also **Y**
ibaptiȝed *v.* baptized *ppl.* 6480
ibe *see* **be**
ibede *v.* offered *ppl.* 2978
ibite *v.* bitten *ppl.* 6987
iboren *v.* carried *ppl.* 4561
ibounde *v.* bound, restrained, held; fettered *ppl.* 2559
ichard *v.* charged, accused at law *ppl.* 2360
icircumcised *v.* circumcized *ppl.* 3465
ichined *ppl.* burst, be split open, cracked 5568
icled *see* **cloþe**
iclonge *v.* congealed; dried up, withered *ppl.* 4697
icud *see* **can**

ydagged *v.* with hems ornamented with slits *ppl.* 1301
idel, ydel *adj.* empty; pointless 4752, 1287
ydelly *adv.* in vain 4765
idelnesse, ydelnesse *n.* vain thoughts, a vanity 2822, 158
idemed *see* **deme**
ido *v.* done, committed; put 1979 *ppl*; **idon** 2212
idous *adj.* frightful 5442
idrawe *v.* drawn *ppl.* 1434
ifere, yfere *adv.* together, combined 2106, 1190; **among hem** ~ among them collectively 5524
iferst *pron.* I + *adv.* I first (told) 2314
ifinde, ifynde *pron.* I + *pr1sg.* I finde 2007, 2621
ifyned *see* **fyne**
ifound(e) *pron.* I + *pa.1sg.* I found 7082, 2096
ygnawe *v.* gnawed *ppl.* 1732
iȝive, iȝove, iȝyve *see* **ȝive**
iharded *v.* hardened, fixed *ppl.* 3474
ihave *see* **have**
ihote *see* **hatte**
ihud *see* **hide**
iii *num.* roman numeral 3 6075
ikan *see* **can**
ikast *see* **cast**
ikid *v.* made known *ppl.* 1986; **ikud** 5389; **ikyd** 1976
ilent *v.* loaned, granted *ppl.* 4742
y lyche *adv.* alike, similarly, equally 237; **ylyke** 1038
iliche *adj.* similar, alike 6926
ilke *pron.* similar, alike; **that** ~ the very same 1881; **ilk(e)** as *adj.* **that** ~ 1065; **ylke** 412
ille, ylle *n.* the bad, evil 5127, 70
ille *adv.* badly; **hem lyken** ~ they may dislike 6307
ille, ylle *adj.* bad, evil, miserable; harmful 1363
ilore *see* **lese**
ilowed *v.* brought low, humbled *ppl.* 6651
ymagine, ymagyne *v.* visualize, imagine; conceive 5656, 5649; **ymagyne** *pr1sg.* 7026; **ymagyne** *pr3pl.* 6693
ymagys *n.pl.* statues, carvings 3597
y menged *v.* mingled *ppl.* 5579
y molte *v.* melted *ppl.* 6953
ympossible *adj.* impossible 5266
yn *n.* home; inn 5144
incerteyn *adj.* uncertain 3101; **uncertayn** 677
inde *adj.* (East) Indian, from India 7209
in dede *adv.* in fact, indeed 896
induscussed *v.* undiscussed, without notice *ppl.* 4772
inne, ynne *adv.* in, inside 1952, 452; **ynne** 3478; **yn** 949
ynner *adj.* inner, hidden 4911
innocent *prop.n.* Innocent III (Pope, 1198–1216) 432
innocentes *n.pl.* the innocent 2628
ynempned *v.* called, spoken of *ppl.* 2824; **y nepned** 6294
ynow(e) *adv.* enough, sufficiently 111, 2180
ynow *adj.* enough 3703
insyght, ynsyght *n.* perception 495, 216
in stede *prep.* in place of, instead of 2213, 2886

instrument *n.* a means 2495
inward *adv.* internally, privately 1384
inwit *n.* conscience; mind 4264
ipaued *v.* paved *ppl.* 7043
ipiȝt *v.* thrust, pitched; placed *ppl.* 2306
ipocrysie *n.* hypocrisy, trickery 3520; **ipocrysye** 4610
ypocryte *n.* hypocrite 3515
iprey *see* **prey**
ipured *v.* refined, purified *ppl.*; **clene** ~ completely purified 2183; **ipuryd** 2678
ipurged *v.* purged, purified *ppl.* 2699
irede *see* **rede**
iren, yren *n.* iron 5506, 6339
ys *poss.pron.* his 155
isaye *prop.n.* Isaias (the Old Testament Prophet) 4758; **ise** 620
ischal *see* **schal**
ischoue *v.* driven *ppl.*: **to gidre** ~ thrust together 4092
ischryve *v.* has confessed *ppl.* 3137; **beþ** ~ are absolved 2543
ise *see* **se**
iseoþ *see* **se**
iseye *see* **se** or **seye**
ysene *ppl. see* **se**; *adj. see* **isene**
isene, ysene *ppl.adj.* visible; manifest 3301, 1188
isent *v.* ordained; sent *ppl.* 4734
isewed *v.* undertaken *ppl.* 7048
islawe *see* **sle**
ysmyled *v.* smiled upon *ppl.* 980
isped *v.* I concluded, finished *pa1sg.* 3278. *see* also **sped** *pp.*
ispreynt *v.* scattered *ppl.* 5621
yssues *n.pl.* bodily orifices 536
istreyht *v.* outstretched *ppl.* 1261
istrewed *v.* strewn *ppl.* 5727
Isydre *prop.n.* Isidore (Bishop of Seville; ca. 560–636) 2043
itende *v.* kindled *ppl.* 2539
y ware *adj.* aware 1669
iwas *see* **be**
iwellyd *v.* boiled, seethed *ppl.* 6952
iwis, ywis *adv.* certainly, indeed 1267, 378; **y wis, y wys** 223, 135; **iwisse** 6842; **iwys, ywys** 2167, 46
iwite *see* **wite**
iwol *see* **willyn**
iwonne *see* **wynne**
iwrapped *v.* enveloped, wrapped, covered *ppl.* 1942; **y wrappyd** 452
iwrought *see* **werche**
iwul *see* **willyn**
janglynge *n.* chattering: **whan þow ... makest** ~ when you chatter.... 2821
iawndyse *n.* jaundice 593
Jeremye *prop.n.* Jeremias (Old Testament prophet) 1855
iewerye *n.* the Jews 3779
iob *prop.n.* Job 357: **Job** 5497, 5611
ioy(e), joye *n.* happiness 761, 2082; **all here** ~ **most** their greatest joy of all 6748; **ioie** 6741, 6759; **ioy** 2086; **ioyes** *pl.* 294
ioyntly *adv.* united, in union 4904
iohn *prop.n.* John the Apostle 3686; **iohn** 3636; **iohon** 1816; **Jon** 5553
ionathas *prop.n.* Jonathan 7082
iosaphat *prop.n.* Josaphat, Jehosaphat 4319; **Josaphat** 4327; **iosephat** 4314
jubiter, jubyter *prop.n.* Jupiter 6052, 3408

Select Glossary (by Hoyt Greeson) 223

iuge *n.* judge 4417
iugement *n.* judicial trial 5106
iurisdiccioun *n.* jurisdiction 3186
iustificacyon *n.* correction; **do on hem no ~** (will not) punish them) 4935
iustice *see* **justice**
iustice *n.* judge, justice 4237: **kynges ~** presiding judge of the king's court 2359
kam *see* **come**
karkoys *n.* corpse, carcass 735
kaste *see* **caste**
keies *n.pl.* keys 3164
kene *adj.* fierce; painful; sharp, cutting 1004
kenne *v.* reveal, discover; know; perceive 2670; **schuylleþ hym ~** will reveal to him 3496; **doþ us ~** causes us to know (that) 4099; **kenneþ** *pr3pl.* **us ~** show us 2124
kepe *v.* observe, mark; keep; preserve, guard 77; **kepen** 3896; **kepyn** 3699; **kepeþ** *pr3sg.* 4870; **kepeþ** *pr3pl.* 931; **kept** *pa3sg.* 4854; **kepten** *pa3pl.* 6796; **kep** *imp.2sg.* 4876; **kept** *ppl.* 4950; **ikept** 4447
kepe *n.* care, notice; **tok ~** took notice 326
kepynge *vbl.n.* protection, custody; guarding 3472; **mys ~** bad stewardship 4598; **kepinge** 3207; **kepyng** 4872
kevere *v.* protect; cover 678; **kevereþ** *pr3sg.* **me ~** envelops me 5870 [OF root]
kynde *n.* nature; type, kind; instinct 299; **by ~** by nature, properly 215; **of ~** by nature; naturally 2484; **wurcheþ nat þorow ~ ryght** works not according to natural law 2490; **mannes ~** man's nature 1829; **aft(er) his ~** according to its nature 2622; **to his ~** to its essential nature 5255; **in his ~** by its nature 6031; **kyndes** *pl.* 43
kynde *adj.* natural, kind 3395
kyndely *adv.* naturally, by nature 106; **kyndly** 1489; **kyndeliche** 6531
kyndly *adj.* natural 1657
kynnes *n.poss.* **none ~ whiʒt** any kind of creature 1561
kynrede *n.* tribe; family, kindred 3450
kyssenge *vbl.n.* kissing 2751
kythe *v.* show *pr.subj2sg.* 1161
knyt *v.* joined, knit *pa3sg.*1544; **iknet** *ppl.* **faste ~** firmly fixed 2991; **iknyt: ~ swiþe** tied very securely 5906
knokkenge *vbl.n.* beating 2751
knowe *v.* know, recognize; understand 70; **knowen** 184; **iknow(e)** 2015, 4526; **knawe** 3680; **yknow** *pr1sg.* 2017; **knowest** *pr2sg.* 1627; **knoweth** *pr3sg.* 141; **knoweþ** 515; **knowiþ** *pr.pl.* 4565; **knoweþ** 3196; **knowe** 238; **knewe** *pa.pl.* 4285; **know** *imper.sg.* 1575; **knowe** *pr.subj.sg.* 106; **knowe** *ppl.* 381; **iknow** 2015, 3767
knowyng(e) *vbl.n.* knowledge 121; **~ wynne** gain knowledge 123; **þre manere of ~ to hem schal be** They will have three kinds of knowledge 6446; **opene ~** manifest knowledge i.e., he was known for his knowledge 7078
lay *n.* faith, religion 132 [OF *lei*]
laie *v.* say, speak, allege; **forþ ~** put forth i.e., reply 4463; **laye** 4913
lane *n.* passageway, alley 7052; **lanes** *pl.* 7038
lappe *n.* **modur ~** mother's lap 5598
lappyd *ppl.* wrapped 708
large *adj.* broad, ample; liberal 1176
lasse, lesse *comp.adj.* less; smaller 402, 4552;
mad ~ lessened, reduced 5606; **les** 6391; **more and ~** greater and smaller 58; one and all 2418; the great and the humble 5809; **the ~ world** the microcosm 867
lasse *comp.adv.*: **the ~** the less 2165; **leste** *superl.* Least, smallest 403, 515
laste *v.* last, stay alive 2795; **ne schall euere ~** will not last forever 5930
laton *n.* brass 3639
lattur *comp.adj.* later; **neuer þe ~** none the later 2979
law(e) *n.* law; faith, religion 3755; **lawes** *pl.* 3427 [OE *lagu*, cf. OF *lei*]
laʒar *prop.n.* Lazarus; a leper 2442; **lazares** *poss.sg.* 2460
leche *n.* physician 5587; **leches** *pl.* 4987
lechery(e) *n.* fornication, adultery 2397, 934
lechours *adj.* lecherous, lascivious 3512
led *n.* lead 5839
lede *v.* lead, conduct; govern, control 132; **schulleth here sone ~** will quickly conduct her, i.e., the soul, Latin, anima, fem. gender; **ledeth** *pr3sg.* 116; **ledeþ** 1133; **ledeþ** *pr3pl.* 1071; **lad(d)** *pa3g.* 4809, 236; **ilad** *ppl.* 2070; **al þe world þider ~** all the world brought about there 5318
ledynge *vbl.n.* control; guidance 3498
lef *n.* leaf 579
legge *v.* lay, imposed 3383; **leyd** *ppl.* 2643; **ilayd** 3039; **ileyd, y leyd** 4372, 4363; **y leid** 488
legges *n.pl.* legs 576
leyd *see* **legge**
leit *n.* flash, flame 5713
leme *n.* limb; member, organ 1592; **lyme** 6530; **lemes** *pl.* 2392; **lemys** 2389; **lymes** 3403
leme *n.* flame, gleam; radiance 3823; **leome** 4246
lenger(e) *advwwwp.* longer 809, 2527; **euere the ~** the longer 632; **lengor** 1277; **lengur** 3257; **lengest** *adv.superl.* 3478
lenger *adjwwwp.* longer 1535; **lengor** 5223; **lengur** 7197
lenkþe *n.* length; distance; duration 1263
lepre *n.* leprosy 2398
lere *v.* learn; teach 183; **forto ~** in order to teach 4940; **lered** *ppl.adj.* learned; **~ and lewyd** learned and ignorant, i.e., clerical or laity 98; **leryd** 4421
lerne *v.* learn; teach; study 131; **lernyd** *pa3pl.* 4650; **lerned** *ppl.* 5398; **ilerned** 3477; **ilernyd** 4565
lernynge *vbl.n.* learning, knowledge 146
les *see* **lasse**
les *n.* lying; **wiþouten ~** truly 6866
lese *v.* lose 3967; **her wite ~** lose their minds 6910; **leose** 1683; **leseth** *pr3pl.* 590; **ilore, y lore** *ppl.* 3038, 470; **lore** 3648
lesynge *vbl.n.* lie 3554
lesse *see* **lasse** *adj.*
lesson *n.* a Scripture reading 3184; **lessoun** 4187
lete *v.* let, allow; leave, release 1859; **~ awey** give up 191; **~ take þe prophetes** have the prophets seized 3807; **it schall ... no þyng ~** it will ... leave nothing 4094; **~ hem fro** give up, caste from themselves 5880; **leteþ** *pr3sg.* 1325; **letyth** 2876; **lete** *ppl.* 5187; **let** 5601; **~ sende** has sent 3302; **let** *imper.sg.* 2154; **lete** *ppl.* unobstructed 4340
lethur *adj.* wicked, sinful 878
lette *v.* hinder, obstruct; delay; prevent: **fro ... hym ~** keep him from ... 3246; **her wyl ~ oþer perpos** (That may) obstruct their desire or intention (to overcome...) 6291; **letteth** *pr3sg.* 207; **letteþ: ~ ... to wynne** hinders ... from gaining 2711; **letteth** *pr3pl.* 224; **lettyth** 216
lette *n.* hindrance 3996; **let** 3919
letter *n.* (alphabetic) letter 416; **aftur þe ~** literally 3957; **letters** *pl.* 426
lettyng(e) *vbl.n.* hindrance, obstacle; prevention, opposition 956, 201; **wiþ out eny ~** unhindered 4124; **make ~** cause delay, hinder 6270
leue *see* also **lyue(n)**
leue *v.* believe: **men ... that forsaken to ~** men who give up believing 3678; **yleue** *pr1sg.* 848; **leueden** *pa.pl.* 3509
leue *n.* permission, leave; **ʒoue hem ~** gave them permission 1930
leue *adj.* dear, beloved 4865; **leuer(e)** *compar.* **hem schal ~** they would rather 4257; **had ~** would prefer 3261; **leuest** *superl.* 6571
leue(n) *v.* leave; abandon, forsake; omit, refrain (from); allow 3384, 6702; **he wol no man on lyue ~** he will spare no one alive OR leave no one alive 3626; **leueth** *pr3sg.* 83; **leueþ** 1336; **leueþ** *pr3pl.* 5996; **lefte** *pa.sg.* 1332; **leue** *pr.subj.sg.* 80; **leue** *pr.subj.pl.* 4749; **left(e)** *ppl.* 3225, 403; **ileft** 4250
lewed *adj.* ignorant; unlettered, simple 745; **lewyd** 98
lybardes *n.pl.* leopards 1010
lyche *adj.* similar, like 697; **to hym ~** similar to him 4849; **lik to** similar to 3639
lye *v.* lie, prevaricate 4628; **lie** 6444
lye *n.* lye 2560
lif(e) *n.* life 233, 1382; **~ day** life 1808; **lyf(e)** 36, 192; **~ daies** lifetime 3131; **lyue** 1167; **by hys ~** during his life 2723; **his ~ dayes** days of his life 6372; **on ~** alive 3262; **liues, lyues** *poss.sg.* 2082, 1790
lyft(e) *adj.* left 1046, 685; **left(e)** 1259, 1043
liftynge *vbl.n.* lifting; **of an hundred mennes ~** as much as a hundred men could lift 6106
ligge, lygge *v.* lie; lie down 3810, 409; **leie: me ... in bed ~** put me in bed 5185; **lyggeþ** *pr3sg.* 1169; **lieþ** 2974; **lyth, lyþ** 712, 2968; **liggeþ, lyggeth** *pr2pl.* 3124, 2809; **lay** *pa.sg.* 453; **lygge** *pr.subj.sg.* 714; **ligge** *pr.subj.pl.* 6418; **leye** *ppl.* 2984
light, liʒt *n.* light, illumination 3691, 2149; **lyght** 845; **lyʒt(e)** 1490, 165
light *adv.* brightly 3640; **lygth: sette by hym ~** hold him in low regard 909
light, lyght *adj.* easy; frivolous, foolish; bright 2689, 398 **lyghtnesse** *n.* levity 265
ligthtnynge *n.* lightning 429; **lyghttyngge: fuyr that is ... ~** fire that is ... burning 2481; **lyghtnynges** *pl.* 4515
liʒtles *adj.* dark, without light 5624
liʒtly *adv.* quickly; easily 5032; **over ~** too quickly 2825; **lightly, lyghtly** 2736, 658; **lightlior** *comp.* **the ~** the more easily 2157; **lightlokur** 3521; **litelly** 2674
lyke(n) *v. impers.* please + *dative of person*: **schal hem ~ full ill** will totally displease them 6644; **may hem ~ ille** may displease

224 Select Glossary (by Hoyt Greeson)

them 6307; **to ... wel myght** ~ that might well please 6895; **lyketh** *pr3sg.* **hym** ~ he prefers 663; it pleases him 3596; **þat** ~ **wel God** Who well pleases God 6525; **lykeþ** 972; **lykyde** *pa3sg.* **as it** ~ **þe** as it pleased you 4590

lykyne *adj.* pleasant, beautiful 4395

likyng(e) *vbl.n.* pleasure; desire, wish; happiness 157, 2590; **lykyng(e)** 6286, 1790; **her** ~ **... fulfylle** carry out their wish 6296; **in** ~ content 2800; **aȝen her** ~ against their will 261; **flesches** ~ sexual pleasure 2526; **lykynges** *pl.* inclinations; pleasures 252

likynge *pres.ppl.adj.* pleasing 6887

likne *v.* compare, liken 7108; **likne** *pr1sg.* 7027; **likyn** 7144; **likneþ, lykneþ** *pr3sg.* 6997, 1582; **likned, lykned** *ppl.* 1006, 522; **likned, lykened** 1253, 994; **ilikned, y likned** 991, 5383; **ylykened** 993

liknesse, lyknesse *n.* appearance; likeness; image 1912, 66; **in** ~ basically, essentially 2168; **lyknes** 699

lym *n.* lime, mortar 7004

lymbȝ *n.* Limbo 2251

lyne *n.* line; **by** ~ straight line 7176

lyne *n.* lineage, descent; **þe sonnes** ~ the sun's line of descent 7195

linx *n.* lynx 497

lyouns *n.pl.* lions 1010; **lions** 1845

lysse, lisse *n.* respite, relief; peace, rest 1695, 5106; **holy cherche ... fighteþ wiþ oute** ~ holy church fights ceaselessly 6865; **lis** 1064; **in** ~ at rest 6128

lyte *n.* little 1230

lytyl *n.* little 786; **a** ~ **þer fro** a short distance from it 4371; **lytul** 149

lytyl, lityl *adj.* little; short 346, 1136; **lytil, litil** 725, 4262; **lytel, litel** 1147, 2515; **lytyll** 1649; **lytle** 5289

lyue(n) *v.* live 36, 624; **leue** 457; **by her** ~ while they were alive 5071; **liue** 3853; **lyueth** *pr3sg.* 89; **lyueþ** 2654; **leueþ** 461; **bihynde** ~ live afterwards 2314 **leuen** *pr1pl.* 4250; **lyueþ** *pr3pl.* 1775; **lyueth** 842; **leueþ** 252; **lieuþ** 4977; **lyued** *pa3sg.* 5432; **leued** 1690; **leued** *pa3pl.* 5072; **lyu2d** 4953; **lyue** *pr.subj.sg.* 541; **lyuyng(e)** *pres.ppl.* 1397, 2334; **leuynge** ~ **amys** living sinfully 3097; **lyued** *ppl.* 2516; **lyuyd** 439; **ileued** 3858

lyue *see* **lif(e)**

lyuyng(e) *vbl.n.* living, life 2050, 850; **her wikked** ~ their wicked lives 6514; **leuynge** 195; **so holy in** ~ of so holy a life 2073; **right** ~ upright way of life 7298

lyuyng(e) *vbl.adj.* living 888, 1926; **is no thyng** ~ not alive at all 2419

lode *n.* load 2763

lok(e) *n.* look 1607; **to** ~ **of all men** in the sight of all men 5022

loke *v.* look, see; consider; contemplate 173; **Aȝeyns ...** ~ look directly at 6219; **onne to** ~ to look upon 6775; **loketh** *pr3sg.* 654; **loke** *imper.sg.*: ~ **that** make sure that 3315

loke *v.* locked, shut *ppl.*: **wiþ ynne helle þei schull ben** ~ they will be locked within hell 6877

lokynge *vbl.n.* staring 1848

lond *n.* land, country; soil 1178, 888; **in** ~ on the earth 6217; **londes** *pl.* 3338; **londs** 824; **londys** 1555; **landes** 7090

lone *n.* reward 4681

long(e) *adv.* long 1399, 657; **never so** ~ no matter how long 5805; ~ **tyme** for a long time 4561; **so** ~ **tyll** until 4931; **lenger** *comp.* 2279

long(e) *adj.* long, long-lasting; large 541, 1257; ~ **and brod** spacious 995

longeþ *v.* suits, befits *pr3sg.* 2495

longy *v.* long, yearn; ~ **after** long after 5550; **lonynge** *pr.ppl.* 5998 [scribal error]: **be** ~ **to** are longing for 5998

loos *n.* reputation 3210

lordschipe *n.* authority, power 6626; **lord-schipes** *pl.* powers; dignities 7151

lore *see also* **lese**

lore *n.* doctrine, teaching; knowledge 150; **undur his** ~ under his tutelage 6505

lose *v.* free; unbind 3171; **losest** *pr2sg.* 3179; **loseþ** *pr3sg.* 1522; **lose** *ppl.* 3668; **ilosed** 3180

lost *n.* loss 2864

loth *prop.n.* Lot 4076; **lothes** *poss.sg.* 4059

lothe *adj.* hateful: **ful** ~ quite hateful, 592; **loþ: no þyng** ~ not at all displeasing 6972

loude *adv.* loudly 4911

lowde, loude *adj.* loud; aloud 171, 3109

lourynge *vbl.n.* gloominess; scowling 5114; *vbl.adj.* sullen 661

loute *v.* bow 967

loue *v.* love 46; **loueth** *pr3sg.* 230; **loueþ** 1137; **loueth** *pr3pl.* 53; **loued** *pa3sg.* 4851; **loued** *pa3pl.* 5637; **loueden** 4139; **loueþ** *imper.pl.* 920; **loued** *ppl.* 787

loue *n.* love 795; **loue** 93; **for my/our** ~ for love of me/us 5167, 3939

louyers *n.pl.* flatterers 969

low(e) *adv.* low, humbly 6289, 655

lowe *adj.* humble, lowly: **his herte ... make** ~ humble his heart 148; **make hem** ~ humble themselves 204; **holde þe** ~ keep yourself humble 1634; **lower** *comp.* 835; **lowest** *superl.* 821

loweþ *v.* humbles *pr3sg.* 6636; **ilowed** 6651

lowhe *v.* laughed *pa3sg.* 5433

lownesse *n.* humble status; humility 6632

lufte *v.* lift, raise 5170; **lefteþ** *pr3sg.* 1757; **lufteþ** 1766

luys *n.pl.* lice 553

lust(e) *n.* peasure, desire; appetite, lust; inclination 2522, 2525; ~ **of flesch** sexual desire 923; ~ **and lykyng** appetite and desire, sensual pleasure 928; **to muche set her** ~ covet too much (the wealth of the mutable earth) 1206; **his** ~ **more to fulfulle** more to gratify his lust 2803; **lustes** *pl.* 191

luste *v.impers.* please; **him schulde nat** ~ it should not please him 943; **hym schulde** ~ it should please him 1378; **lusteþ** *pr3sg.* **him** ~ it peases him 1665; **the** ~ **nat** you do not wish 2797; **hym** ~ **þorow kynde** he naturally wants 5548; **lusteþ** *pr3pl.* 1131; **lusteth** *pr3pl.tr.* 893

lusty *adj.* lecherous 3512

lustyly *adv.* heartily 2796

maad, mad *see* **make**

mageste *n.* majesty; **opene** ~ manifest majesty, rulership 3955

mayden *n.* girl, young woman, virgin 4180; ~ **marye** the Virgin Mary 4389; **maidenes** *poss.sg.* 3642

mayne *n.* servants, household 4932

mayster *n.* master, scholar 3271; **maistres** *pl.* 4937; **maystres** 4938

maystrye *n.* authority; control, dominance, upper hand 3647

make *v.* make, cause; do; create; write, compose 33; ~ **hym self hie** exalt himself 3404; **on** ~ unite 6852; **makest** *pr2sg.* 2799; **maketh, makeþ** *pr3sg.* 109, 210; **maketh** *pr3pl.* 550; **makeþ** 1189; **made** *pa.sg.* 38; **maked** 7145; **makyng** *pr.ppl.* 435; **mad(e)** *ppl.* 317, 335; **newe** ~ newly created 5319; **maad** 465; **ymad: þis boke ... is** ~ **of** this book ... is written about 316; **y mad: now ... the laste part (is)** ~ now the last part is done 7228; **y made** 466; **maked** 311; **imaked, ymaked** 5160, 7004

maker(e) *n.* creator 32, 27

maladie, maladye *n.* illness, malady 2428, 2407; **maladies, maladyes** *pl.* 2404, 594

malice, malice *n.* wickedness, malice 3400, 3462

manaces *n.pl.* threats 3624

maner(e) *n.* custom, way, fashion; kind 105, 47; **al** ~ **wey** all kinds of ways 55; **by no** ~ **wey** by no means 348; **in his** ~ after his fashion 422; **no** ~ **thing** nothing at all 5450; **in no** ~ in any way 5552; **manner** 828; **maners** 884; **mo othur** ~ many other customs 1345; **y wol ... telle ... the** ~ I will speak of the particulars ... 3437; **telle** ~ **of ... mannys lyf** conditions of ...man's life 1238; **maneres** 225

manhede *n.* human nature: **aftyr his** ~ according to his human nature 907; **to sen his** ~ to see Him in the flesh 4260; **in** ~ in human form 4490; **manhod(e): 4408; **him self to knowe in** ~ looking upon himself in human form 1252; **wyt of** ~ human understanding 6999; 1252

many fold(e) *adv.* in various ways 3326; **wel** ~ many times over 2591

many folde *adj.* numerous, abundant 3962; **manyfolde** 1124

mankynde *n.* mankind, the human race; the human condition, human nature 101; **take** ~ assume human nature 92; **mannyskynde** 62

manne *n.* man 2461; **man** 35; **no manner** ~ no man whatever 7062; **mannes** *poss.sg.* 370; ~ **wit** human reason 1995; **mannys** 63; **men** *pl.* 31; **mennes** *poss.pl.* 639; **mennys** 111; **mennynes** [scribal error?] 206; **mon** 4041

many(e) *adj.* many 97, 879; **to** ~ **and fele** too many and (too) much 1104; ~ **on** many a 1735; **manyon** many a 4606; **othur** ~ **mo** many others 2606

manyfold(e), many folde *adj.* various, numerous; abundant 4980, 1124; **many folde** *adv.* in various ways 2591; in large numbers 2764

manslauȝter *n.* manslaughter; murder 2706

manteyne *v.* support, uphold; preserve; keep 908; **mayntene** 2462; **manteyne** *pr.subj.* 7309

marke *n.* imprint, mark 3674

martires *n. pl.* martyrs 1797

martures *n.pl.* martyrs 6792; **marters:** (in books where) ~ **beþ set wel afyn** martys are perfectly described 3270; **martres** 3655; **martyres** 4623; **martyrs** 3153

masse *n.* Mass 2749; **messe** 3015; **masses** *pl.* 2270; **doþ** ~ **synge** have masses sung 3111

Select Glossary (by Hoyt Greeson) 225

mater(e) *n.* subject; question; matter, material; substance 205; **maner** ~ kind of material 7003; **matiere** 755; **maters** *pl.* 3277; **materes** 7244; **materys** 313
materye *n.* substance 933
matusale *prop.n.* Methuselah 7074
meche(l) *adj.* much; great, large 201, 1001; **much(e)** 5823, 748; **ful** ~ in all its details 5389; **muchel** 3420; **muchil** 6646; **myche(l)** 212, 456; **wel** ~ very great 1033
mechilnesse *n.* magnitude; greatness 5241; **mychulnesse** 1759
mede *n.* reward, benefit 2225; **for the** ~ **pardoun** pardon as a reward 3148; **medes** *pl.* 3151
medled *v.* mixed, blended, mingled; confused *ppl.* 5570; **medlyd** 1280; **y medled** 6951
meke *adj.* humble, meek, pliant; modest 330; ~ **and mylde** humble and virtuous 347
mekeliche *adv.* humbly, meekly 2867; **mekely** 2879
mekenesse *n.* humility 118; **meknesse** 6016
melodie *n.* music, melody 6168; **melodye** 6740
mencioun *n.* mention; **makeþ** ~ report, write 3265
mene *v.* mean, signify; imply; intend; mention, say 985; **thus forto** ~ that is to say 985; **as muche to** ~ **as** as much as to say 1246; **what þey beþ to** ~ what they mean, intend to convey 3988; **beþ foul to** ~ are vile to mention 5685; **doþ us** ~ what does advise us 4827; **ymene** *pr1sg.* I mention 5644; **yment** *ppl.* 3747; **y menyd** 2443
mene *v.* complain; **her mone** ~ make their complaint 3159
mene *adj.* moderate, intermediate 2537
menynge *vbl.n.* meaning; interpretation 6104; purpose; knowledge **haue** ~ knowledge; remember 6513
menstralsie *n.* (instrumental) music, minstrelsy 6893, 7047
mery *adj.* merry 4073; **to make** ~ to laugh about 756; **murye** 6894; **myryor** *compar.* 7049
merke *n.* imprint 3680; **merkes** *pl.* 3677
merþe *n.* joy 6163; **murthe** 1221; **merþes** *pl.* **his** ~ **make** take his pleasures 3479; **murthes** 1379
mervail *n.* marvel, wonder; **makeþ his** ~ plays its tricks 1086
meschaunce *n.* affliction; misfortune 963
message *n.* messenger 5796
messager *n.* messenger 1671; **messangere** 1668
meste *adj.superl.* greatest; especially 3571; **most(e)** 5, 183, 363
mete *v.* meet; confront 1314; **to gidre** ~ collide 4093; assemble 4315; **ymet(e)** *ppl.* 1255
mete *v.* measure; go, traverse; **mete** *ppl.* 6084; **ymete**: translate: Thus a man can be measured on the outside/Just as a circle.... 1264
mete *n.* food 2444; **at þe** ~ at dinner 5428
me thinkeþ *v.* it seems to me *impers.3sg.* 454; **me þynkeþ** 1613
metyng *n.* dream 979
metre *n.* (a line of) verse, poetry 757
meue *v.* move; urge 2874; **meueth** *pr3sg.* 1097; **meueþ** 5344; **ymeued** *ppl.* 3952

meuynge *vbl.n.* motion, moving 5337; **mouyng** 4170; **myvynges** *pl.*: **erþe** ~ earthquakes 3323
mydward *n.* middle 373
myght *n.* power, might; ability: **doþ her** ~ do their utmost 5346; **passeþ þorow** ~ **of hete** surpasses by intensity of its heat 5475; **haue no** ~ have no permission or warrant 5972; **mychel of** ~ of great power 6823; **myghtes** *poss.sg.* ~ **moste** greatest of powers 363; **godes of** ~ mighty gods 6499; **þorow** ~ **and grace** by virtue and grace 6751; **might** 3843; **myghtes** *pl.* 363; **myȝhtes** 122; **myȝtes** 5; **myghtes** *poss.pl.* 1893
myghte *v. see* **mowe(n)**
myghthod *n.* power, might; abundance 6436
myghty *adj.* powerful, mighty, strong; able 1442; **myghti** 3356
myghtynesse *n.* power 637
mylde *adj.* humble; merciful; benign, kind 347; **mylte** 6963
myldenesse *n.* humility 3710
myle *n.* mile 1193
myn(e) *poss.adj.* my [occurs before a word beginning with a vowel or h— 1873, 3268
mynde *n.* mind, memory 69; **haueþ hym in** ~ remember him 51; **to haue þeron** ~ to remember it 5375; **haue no** ~ **Of** do not remember 5740–41; **haue in** ~ think of 6113; **iset to haue in** ~ added to keep in mind 3990; **haue** ~ **of** remember 194; **on hym setteth his** ~ fixes his will on him 786; **leose al his** ~ lose his consciousness 1683; **torned to his** ~ regained his senses 1888; **ihud owt of** ~ hidden, i.e., forgotten, out of memory 3612; **com to his** ~ occurred to him 5594; **conceyue in his** ~ understand in his mind 5659
myndeles *adj.* unmindful 1721
minister *n.* servant, minister 3011; **mynystres** *pl.* 3551
mynistre *v.* impart, dispense 5004
myrour *n.* mirror, image, reflection 6451; **myrrour:** ~ **... þat is fayr** mirror ... that is shining 6450
mysbileue *n.* false religion 4619
myschef(e) *n.* affliction, poverty, hardship; wickedness 971; **for** ~ because of hardship 5601; **myschefes** *pl.* ailments 591; **myschefs** 1312
myschel *prop.n.* variant of the name *Michael* 3869
mysdede *n.* sin; offence 1659; **mysdedes** *pl.* 4983
mysdo *v.* done amiss, wrong; sinned *ppl.* 4648; **haþ don mysse** has done amiss 7257
mysdoers *n.pl.* wrong-doers, sinners 1013
mysese *n.* suffering; **soffreþ hem in** ~ let them remain in distress 4980
mysike *n.* music 6894; **musik** 7047
mys kepynge *vbl.n.* bad stewardship 4598
mysleued *v.* led wicked lives *ppl.* 4504
mys leuynge *vbl.n.* evil life, sinful life 3100
myspaieþ *v.* displeases *pr3sg.* 2759; **myspayeth** *pr3pl.* 1107; **myspayed** *pa3pl.* 5888
mysse *v.* fail to find, obtain; lack 6348; **mys** 6970
mysse *see* **mysdo**
mo *adv.* more 405; **þe** ~ the more 3055
mo *adj., pron.* more 594, 2321; **oþur** ~ others in addition 3274

modur *n.* mother 390; **modur** *poss.sg.* 384; **moders** 3444; **modres** *pl.* 4641
moyses *prop.n.* Moses Maimonides (1135–1204), Jewish philosopher quoted by Aquinas et al. 6071
molde *n.* molde i.e., for molten metal 5839
mone *n.* complaint, moan, moaning (of a woman in childbirth) 435; **her** ~ **mene** utter their complaint, complain 3159
mone *n.* moon 815
monee *n.* wealth, money 4665
montayn(e) *n.* mountain 5487, 4000; **montaynes** *pl.* 3727
monþes *n.pl.* months 4198
mood *n.* mind, mood; **wiþ a stordy** ~ with intense emotion 4608
more *adj.* greater, larger; longer 58; **wel** ~ far greater 2194; **neuere þe** ~ never again 6569
mornyng(e) *vbl.n.* mourning, lament 1535, 1221
mornynge *n.* morning 7174
morowe *n.* morning 1208; **by the** ~ in the morning 2149
most *see* **meste, mot**
mot *v. pret.pr.* must; has to **mot** *pr1–3sg.* 630; ~ **nedys/nedes** must of necessity, must necessarily 2485, 2729; **moot** 1400; **mut** 1171; **mote** *pr1–3pl.* 1447; **moot** 4518; **moten** 2530; **mut** 5351; **most(e)** *pa.sg./pl.* 1024, 183 (NB: singular in sense)
mouȝtys *n.pl.* moths 4668
mowthe *n.* mouth; **gyldon** ~ Chryostom 4470; **mowþ(e)** 7048, 5018; **mouthe** 2441; **mouþ** 4955
mowe(n) *v. pret.pr.* can, be able; may **mayst** *pr2sg.* 2150; **myst** 2148; **myght: Whi ne** ~ **thu** why are you never able to 987; **may** *pr3sg.* 41; **in al that he** ~ as much as he can 5965; **mowe** 2497; **may** *pr3pl.* 31; **mow(e)** 1307, 202; **mowen** 668; **moweþ** 3198; **might, myght(e)** 1906, 19, 1586; **mithte** 2065; **myȝt** 130; **myghtest** *pa2sg.* 988; **myȝst** 2791; **myst** 2148
much(e) *adv.* greatly, much 1372, 1206; ~ **wellynge metal** constantly boiling metal 6954; **moche** 1525; **muchel** 3431; **myche(l)** 2408, 3459; **mychul** 3426
much(e) *adj.* much; great, as great 5828, 748; **over** ~ excessive 1288; **muchel** 3420; **muchil** 6646
multiplieþ *v.* increase, multiply, grow in number *pr3pl.* 3054
nabugodonoȝor *prop.n.* Nebuchadnezzar 5723
nacion *n.* country, nation 3631; **nacions** *pl.* 5063
nay *adv.* no; **seiþ ...** ~ say "No" 4803; **wiþ out** ~ undeniably 4929
nayles, nailes *n.pl.* nails 6092, 4696; **naylys** 4432
naylyd *v.* nailed *ppl.* 4427
nam *v.* took, seized; chosen; received *pa3sg.* 444; **nome** *ppl.* 120; **inome, ynome, y nome** 1655, 471, 79; **he is wyth wrecchidnesse** ~ he is seized by misery 526; **resoun ...** ~ an explanation he has received 481; **clene** ~ completely removed 2612; **boke of wisdom haþ ... this sawe** ~ the Book of Wisdom has chosen this saying 5408; **inome** 1861
namely *adv.* especially; indeed; in particular;

at least, that is 147; **namly** 1720; **nameliche** 4219; **namliche** 4068; **namlyche** 6814
narewe *adj.* narrow; stern, harsh 1299; **narow** 1180; **narwer** *compar.* 686
nas *v.* was not *pa3sg.* 1909; **ner** *pa.subj.sg.* 5871
naþ *v.* has not *pr3sg.* 1565; **nadde** *pa3pl.* had not 4659
natheles *adv.* none the less 1449; **naþeles** 3103
nawhare *adv.* nowhere; **þei ne mowe ~ þennys wynne** they cannot manage to go anywhere from there, i.e., they can't escape from hell 4256; **nowhare** 2356; **nowher(e)** 5388, 2282
ne ... ne *coord.conj.* neither ... nor 408
nede *n.* need; **hadde ~** needed 131; **at ~ in a** crisis, time of need 4975; **in that ~** in that time of need 2945; **for ~** out of necessity 5157; **need** 7
nede *adv.* necessarily 2510
nedes *adv.* of necessity, necessarily 1748; **nedis, nedys** 1987, 2485; **nedes: what bihoveþ ~** why is it necessary 2242; **~ bihoveþ** is required 2619
nedful *adj.* necessary 161; **nedfull** *n.* the needy, poor 3080
neye *see* **ny**
neyhȝebore *n.* neighbour 4919; **neyȝebores** *pl.* 4984; **neiȝbors** 4918
neythur *conj.* neither + negative particle **no** or **ne: ~ ... no** neither ... nor 400; **neyþur** 3666; **nethur** 2368; **neþur** 401; **nothir** 143; **nothur** 228; **noþur** 408; **noþer** 2455
nekke *n.* neck 572
ner(e) *adv.* near 1555, 1927
ner *v.* were no *pa.subj.sg.* 5871
nesche *adj.* soft, pliant 2482
neuer(e) *adv.* never 582, 700, 493, 19; **neuyr** 5702; **nere** 2164; **~ so** no matter how 2006; **~ so muche** no matter how much 5280
nevyron *pron.* no one, not one 2247
newe *adj.* new 1337, 1058; **~ fyndyngȝ** new inventions 1334; **~ get** new fashion 1304; **~ lawe** New Testament teachings 3550
newe *adv.* newly, recently, afresh 5319
nexst *adj.* next (in sequential order) 2339
next *adj.superl.* most direct, shortest: **~ way** the shortest way 1749
next *prep.* nearest to 571
ny *adv.* at hand, near 1823
ny *prep.* near 3303; **nyȝ** 691; **nyhe** 682; **neye** 2536
nygromauncers *n.pl.* sorcerers, necromancers 3494
nygromaunce *n.* sorcery, necromancy 3566
nyȝt *n.* night 102; **night, nyght** 2160, 882
nyne *num.* nine 498
nis, nys *v.* is not, is no *pr3sg.* 1398, 451
nytes *n.pl.* lice eggs 553
nyþe *adj.* ninth 4029
no, non(e) *adj.* 45, 394, 509
noble *adj.* splendid; noble 6827
nobleie *n.* splendor, nobility 6155; **nobleye** 6658
noe *prop.n.* Noah 4068; **noes** *poss.sg.* 4059
noyse *n.* noise; tumult, commotion; sound 2818; **wel likynge ~** fully pleasing sounds 6893
nolde *v.* would not; refused *pa3sg.* 1681; **~ ...**

do would not perform 5211; **nolden** *pa3pl.* 4600
noman *n.* nobody 773
nome *see* **nam**
non(e) *pron.* none 493, 19
none *interj.*: **for the ~** indeed! 4900
norscheþ *v.* nourishes, promotes the growth of; comforts; sustains, maintains *pr3sg.* 220; **norsched** *ppl.* raised, brought up 3489; **inorsched** 4252
no thing *adv.* not at all 1023; **no thyng** 894; **no þyng** 5129
not *v.* not know (contraction of **ne wot**) *pr3sg.* 407
nought, nouȝt *pron.* nothing, nothingness 317, 1711; **~ elles bot as** nothing other than 6376; **~ þere to** nothing compared to it 6810; **mowe ~** cannot 6011, 1427; **as þing of ~** like nothing 6379; **naught, nauȝt** 3991, 948; **nawht** 362; **nowht: ~ here** hear nothing 244; **noght, noȝt** 2374, 2069; **nouȝt** 6376; **nowȝt** 2039
nought, nouȝt *adv.* not 49, 108; **naught, nauȝt** 4425, 287; **nouȝst** 5034; **nowȝt** 1743; **~ elles to telle** Bot nothing else to say but 2175; **nawȝt** 1824; **noght, noȝt** 2290, 885; **nowt, nawt** 936, 3362
nouþe *adv.* now 5020; **now(e)** 618, 7
noway *adv.* by no means 2451
nowhare *adv.* nowhere 2356; **nowher(e)** 5388, 2282
o *interj.* Oh! 986
o, on, oon *adj.* one 803, 14, 2254; **wone** 16
o *prep.* of 1675; **of** 1
ocupye *v.* occupy 2414
odour *n.* odor, smell 5469
office *n.* duty, office; function (of the body) 4972; **of ~** by virtue of his position 3166
offred *v.* offered, sacrificed *ppl.* 2928
offrenge *vbl.n.* offering 3027
oft(e) *adv.* often 1732, 208; **~ tymes** many times 1673; **~ sythes** many times 2875
often tyme, often tymes *adv.* frequently, often 1021, 1056
oyle *n.* oil 555
olyuet(e) *prop.n.* Olivet, Mount of Olives, mentioned in *Matthew* 21:1 3864, 3381
on *pron.* one 107
on *adj.* one 14
ones *adv.* once 2020; **at ~** at the same time 4093; instantaneously 5487; **all at ~** all together 7144; **onys** 4804
onhede *n.* unity 14; **in ~ clene** in complete unity 12
only *adv.* only; apart 837
only *adj.* only, alone 1114; **oonly** 2421; **onliche, onlyche** 1944, 707
on liue, on lyue *adj.* alive 3833, 1717; **aliue, alyue** 1712, 1462
onne *prep.* on; **~ to loke** to look on 6775
onresonable *adj.* lacking reason 516
onuthur *see* **annoþur**
open(e) *adj.* manifest, open 4456, 3754
openly *adv.* plainly; distinctly, clearly 492; **oponly** 2300; **opynly** 458
opynyones *n.pl.* opinions 2463
oppressioun *n.* tyranny, oppression 959
or *conj.* before 1668
ordynaunce *n.* decree, plan 6055; **an ~ hem takeþ** imposes order on them 6055; **in al his ~** all according to his decree 6580

ordeyne *v.* devise; decree; allot; establish, prepare, create 5874; **ordeyneþ** *pr3sg.* 3943; **ordeineþ** *pr3pl.* 1646; **ordeyned** *pa.sg.* 42; **ordeynyd** 74; **ordeyned** *ppl.* 2286; **y ordeyned** 2494
ordre *n.* rank (in a hierarchy); order; natural course 4948; **ordres** *pl.* 6774
ore *n.* mercy 6187
oryson *n.* prayer 2801
oþe *n.* oath; **holde þyn ~** keep your oath 2826; **hothes** *pl.* **fals ~ sweryinge** committing perjury 2706
othyng *n.* one matter 927
othur, oþur *pron.* other, another; second 804, 3211; **oþur** others 4986; **mo ~** many more, others 6956; **oþer(e)** 1571, 6720; **of ~** on the other 6573; **othir** 59; **oþures** *poss.sg.* 6495; **oþure** *pl.* 5404
othur, oþur *adj.* other, another 329, 394; **non ~ þynge** anything else 6918; **oþer, other** 2809, 742; **othir, oþir** 37, 65
othur, oþur *conj.* or 500, 428; **~ ... or** either ... or 923; **oþer(e)** 2000, 6722; **other: ~ ... or** either ... or 2307; **othir** 73
ought *pron.* anything, ought 11; **outh** 652; **owt** 248; **owht** 1911
ouȝt *v.* ought 4764 *pr3sg.*; **owte** 41
owr(e) *adj.* our 5119, 6; **our(e)** 6, 6452; **~ nought** not ours 2014
our seluen *pron.pl.* ourselves 2016
owt(e) *adv.* out; openly 396, 1421; **oute** 3816
outrage *n.* excess; violence 1282; **foul ~** severe wantoness 4219
out right *adv.* directly, outright, openly, plainly 1972; **outrighte** 3574; **outryght, out ryȝt** 764, 217; **owtryght** 531; **outrightes: destruye ~ clene** utterly ravage/destroy 6988
ouer *adv.* over; overly, too 2818; **~ late** too late 2807; **~ liȝtly wroþe** too easily angry 2825; **~ muche** too much 5500
ouer *prep.* over, above, beyond 1758; **~ power** power over 1556; **~ al þyng** above all else 2607
ouer al *adv.* everywhere 1723; **ouer al, overal** 4107, 1577
ouercaste *v.* pass; overturn, overthrow; **ouercast** *ppl.* 1195; **ouercaste** 6838
ouercome *v.* conquer, overcome 1195, 6293; **ouercome** *ppl.* 1886
ouercomer *n.* victor, conqueror 6851
ouercoming, ouercomynge *vbl.n.* triumphant, conquering (Latin: **triumphans**) 6857, 6862
ouergult *v.* gilded *ppl.* 7035
ouerlytel *adj.* insufficient 3231; **ouerlytyll** 3232
ouermuche *adv.* very greatly 7292
ouer muche *adj.* too much, very great 1288
ouer renne *v.* sweep across 4084
ouerþwoȝt *adv.* across, crosswise 6692
ouur kaste *v.* expel 3360
owe *adj.* own 2016; **own(e)** 1690, 144
owher(e) *adv.* anywhere 3613, 1594; **~ ... elles** anywhere else 3613
pay *n.* reward; satisfaction 1844; **to all mennys ~** to the satisfaction of all 111; **to his ~** to his liking 3934
pay(e) *v.* please, satisfy 2144, 3025; **paie** 2069; **paieþ, payeþ** *pr3sg.* 1459, 244; **paied** *ppl.* 2948

Select Glossary (by Hoyt Greeson) 227

paynemes *n.pl.* pagans 3411; **paynems** 4606; **paynymes** 5075
paynted *ppl.adj.* feigned; painted 5474; **peynted** 5466
paleis *n.* palace 7106
palesie *n.* paralysis 2393
pan *n.* head, skull; **fram too to the ~** from head to toe 739
pappe *n.* breast 5599
parfit(e) *adj.* perfect, blameless 2655, 2629; **parfyt** 2956
parfitly *adv.* perfectly, completely 2180
part *n.* part; division 87
party(e) *n.* part; region; a (military) detachment 302; **þe moste ~ of** the greatest portion of 3360; **in ~** partially 1484; **parties, partyes** *pl.*374, 311; **schal his angels bifore hym sende ... On foure ~** he will send before him his angels in four detachments 4175. (i.e., metaphorically, a military engagement.)
pas *n.* step; track; **goþ that ylke ~** walk that same path 2692; **make his ~** make its way 2487; **by hym make his ~** walk by him 5662
pas(se) *v.* pass, go by, pass through; move; walk; leave; exceed, surpass; die 5187, 59; **away ~** cease to exist 1269; **~ further more** proceed, continue 1390; **by the ~** pass by you, i.e., come your way 1575; **purgatory ~** get through purgatory 2157; **gonne ... ~** have passed away, died 5808; **passeth, passeþ** *pr3sg.* 709, 49; **~ ther fro** departs from it 270; **~ out** leaves 1429; **passeþ** *pr3pl.* 6386; **~ that pas** make that journey 2184; **passe** *pr.subj.sg.;* **hennes ~** pass away, die 1773, 2624; **passed** *pa.sg.;* **~ þo cubites** exceeded those cubits 4120; **passed** *ppl.* 2423; **passid** 4269; **ipassed** 3825; **ipassid** 6377
passyng(e) *ppl.adj.* passing, fleeting; transitory 605, 1241
passioun, passyoun *n.* suffering, passion 1830, 4442; **passion** 4533
pater noster *n.* the Our Father, i.e., the Lord's Prayer 2746
Patriarches *prop.n.pl.* the Old Testament Patriarchs 6790
pauement *n.* street 7206
peine, peyne *n.* pain, suffering; torture, punishment; torment 1516, 954; **wende to ...~** pass on to punishment, torment 1448; **~ strong** severe punishment 6927; **payn(e)** 1506, 1500; **peyn** 5605; **pyne** 1100; **helle ~** the punishment of hell 2709; **peynes, peines** *pl.* 81, 1471; **paynes** 1479; **peynys** 4474
peyned *v.* punished *ppl.* 5451; **ipeyned, y peyned** 2434, 6986
peinte *v.* describe, portray 1912
peyntours *n.pl.* artists, painters 1909
peyrsynge *ppl.adj.* perishing 1242
peys *n.* weight 6105
penaunce *n.* satisfaction for sin, penance; repentance 1382; **penance** 3227; **penaunces** *pl.* 1454; **penances** 1383
peple *n.* people 3521
perchaced *v.* acquired, obtained *ppl.* 5271
perchaunce *adv.* perhaps, perchance, doubtless 1633
pere *n.* equal; **wiþ oute ~** peerless, unequalled 3852

pereische *v.* perish 4740; **perisch(e)** 5081, 6043; **perischy** 5099; **perysche** 4216
perel(l) *n.* peril, danger 2353, 137; **peril** 1088; **perels** *pl.* 229; **perelles** 1735; **perelys** 4565
perpos *n.* intention, purpose 6291
perre *n.* jewelry 6961
persecucioun, persecucyoun *n.* persecution 3720,1054; **persecution** 3768
person(e) *n.* person 4296, 4173; **in his propre ~** himself 4173; **in my propre ~** myself 4325; **persones** *pl.* 14; **personys** 43975
pes *n.* peace 1237
pich(e) *n.* pitch, tar 5525, 6925
pyȝt *v.* thrust *ppl.;* **into þe trewe fey ... be ~** be confirmed in the true faith 3891
pilers *n.pl.* columns, pillars 4488
pylgrim, pylgrym *n.* pilgrim, traveller 1157, 1164; **pylgrymes** *pl.* 1151
pylgrimage *n.* pilgrimage, foreign journey 1169
pyne *v.* torture, punish, torment 4138; **pyneþ** reduces, emaciates *pr3sg.* 1673; **pyne** *pr.3pl.* 4625; **pyned** *ppl.* 2428; **ipyned, y pyned** 6991, 6251
pyne *n.* pain, torment (arising from punishment, torture) 1100
pynne *n.* pin 6810
pystyl *n.* epistle, letter 918
pite, pyte *n.* pity, compassion 2916, 1113
place *n.* place; location; mansion 328; **in purgatory ~** in the mansion of purgatory 2120; **in every ~** everywhere 7000; **plas** 384; **places** *pl.* 6087
playn *n.* level area, a plain 4036
playn *adj.* level; clear 5361
playn *adj.* full 3169
playne *v.* complain 4647; **playneth** *pr3sg.* **~ sone** is quick to complain 665
playnynge *vbl.n.* complaint 5104
playnt *n.* complaint 5976
plede *v.* plead (a law case) 5092; **plete** 4691
pleyȝynge *vbl.n.* love play, amorous dalliance 511
plente *n.* abundance 3201
poynt *n.* tip, point; bit, part, detail; position, location 687; **a ~ of a pynne** a pin-point 6810
pomp(e) *n.* ostentation; vainglory 5800, 964; **~ and pride** ostentation and display 190
porcion, porcyon *n.* share, part; fraction 6398, 6396
pore *adj.* poor, humble 703; **poore** 1843
postemus *n.pl.* pustules? 2391. MED includes *pustule* but not *postemus.*
potagre *n.* gout (afflicting the feet) 2390
pouder *n.* dust, powder 747; **poudre** 356; **poudur** 362; **powdyr** 738
pouer *n.* power, ability: **ne moweþ her ~ passe** cannot exceed their authority 3198; **power(e)** 1, 1915
poule, powle *prop.n.* St. Paul the Apostle 3391, 3343; **poules** *poss.sg.* 3388
pows *n.* pulse 681
pouste *n.* power, authority 3374
pouert(e) *n.* poverty, want, lack 975, 1054
pray, prey *n.* prey, spoils 1844, 1400
praiere, prayere *n.* prayer 2565, 2472; **preyere** 2987; **prayer** 1557; **priere** 2270; **praiers, prayers** *pl.* 2311, 2814; **preieres** 3117

preche *v.* preach 3544
prechinge, prechynge *vbl.n.* preaching; prophecy 3716, 3537
prechours *n.pl.* preachers 3544
precious(e) *adj.* costly, precious 6962, 3701; **~ stones** jewels, gems 6966; **precyous: so ~ a flour** so rare a flower 3208
preye *v.* pray 2983; **praye** 2278; **praye** *pr1sg.* 7266; **prey** 7274; **preyest** *pr2sg.* 2801; **preieþ, preyeþ** *pr3sg.* 7162, 2256; **preyed** *pa3sg.* 2448; **prey** *pr.subj.pl.* 7166; **prayeþ** *imper.pl.* 7303
preise, preyse *v.* praise 6930, 2027; **praysest** *pr2sg.* 2819; **prayseth** *pr3sg.* 662; **preyseþ** 1114; **preysed** *pa3pl.* 275
preisying *vbl.n.* praise 6980; **preysynge** 6169; **preysynges** *pl.* 1759
prelat *n.* high-ranking churchman, e.g. a bishop 1570; **prelates** *pl.* 4947; **prelatys** 4948; **prelotys** 4958
presempcion *n.* presumption, arrogance 3529
presoun *n.* prison 3064; **prison(e)** 2252, 5160; **prysoun** 2555
prest *n.* priest 2652; **prestes** *poss.sg.* 2929
presure *n.* distress, suffering 3946
preue *v.* prove, establish, explain; test; demonstrate; discover 2443; **proue** 838; **preueth, preueþ** *pr3sg.* 1319, 1096; **proueth** 343; **proue** *pr3pl.* 779; **preve** *ppl.* 4819; **wiþ god be ~** be approved by God 7153; **ipreved: schal be ~** shall be made manifest 3951
prykke *v.* pierce, prick; incite, goad 2767; **prykede** *pa3sg.* 4455
prikke, prykke *n.* goad, stimulus; a state, condition 1, 7238; **wel sory ~** very woeful time 4669
principal *adj.* important, principal 59
principally, pryncypally *adv.* primarily 802, 118; **princypaly** 371
pris, prys *n.* worth, value; benefit 506, 2846; **bereþ the ~** has the reputation 2998; **haue a fayr ~** take the prize for beauty 5326
pryuacion *n.* deprivation, loss 1486
priue *adj.* private, secret; personal 2006; **in a ~ plas** in the genitalia 384; **priuey** 1486; **priuy** 4816; **pryue** 1981; **to make it to ~** to offer proof of this 4966
priueyly *adv.* covertly, secretly 3751; **pryuely** 3758
pryueite *n.* secrecy, mystery: **in his ~** in His mysteries 5249; **pryuyte: neuer wite ne knowe þat ~** never understand nor experience that mystery 3909; **pryuuyte: Godes ~** divine mystery 3102
processe *n.* an account, narrative; course of action, sequences of events 199
profit *n.* benefit, profit 63; **prophyt** 4891
profit *n.* prophet 256; **prophet(e)** 606, 258; **prophetes** *pl.* 3770; **prophetis, prophetys** 6789, 3833
profytable *adj.* expedient; profitable 1121
prologe *n.* prologue 1
properly *adv.* appropriately, properly; strictly; actually 995
propertes *n.pl.* characteristics, properties 667
prophecie, prophecye *n.* prophecy (of future events) 4541, 1856; **profecye** 3453; **pprophecie** 3736
propre *adj.* own, proper; actual 5664; **in his ~ persone** himself 4173

proprely *adv.* actually, truly; strictly (speaking) 2961; **propurly** 4906; **propurlyche** 184
protestacioun *n.* declaration; **I make ... a ~** I declare 7278
prowd, proud *adj.* proud 509, 218
prowdnesse *n.* pride 338
prouyd *v.* plan for 853
pult *v.* pulled; dragged, forced; plucked *ppl.* 3367; **~ adoun** destroyed 3368; **ipult** 2636; **þey were to no lore ~** they were not compelled to learn 4648; **ypullid** 1594
punysche *v.* punish 4102; **punysched** *ppl.* 2307; **punnysched** 2622; **ipunysched** 2700; **ypunysched: than ~ moste** then had to be punished 2291
pur *prep.*(French): pur Seynt Charite, i.e., by St. Charity/Holy Love 7266
purchace *v.* gain, acquire, obtain; purchase (with money) 3243; **purchaced** *ppl.* 3131; **purchased** 3127
purgatorie *n.* Purgatory, where saved souls expiate their sins 2174; **purgatory** 2120; **purgatorye** 304; **purgatories** *poss.sg.* 2906; *pl.* 2299
pursut *n.* pursuit: **opene ~** open assault 3754
put *n.* pit; **helle ~** the pit of hell 2238
putte *v.* put, place; send 3659; **putte** *pa3sg.*: **~ us in blame** put us at fault 417; **~ us in certeyn** made us certain, assured us 2092; **put** *ppl.* **~ in daungere** subjected to control of 6651; **iput, yput** 1695, 2237; **~ adown** rejected 3685
quake *v.* tremble, shiver; quake 4012
quaþ *v.* (they) say *pr3pl.* 3311
queynte *adj.* pleasing 1000
queyntise *n.* guile, cunning, strategem 3601; **queyntyse** 965
queme *v.* please, gratify 2144
quenche *v. tr.* slake, quench 5463
quene *n.* queen 3730
questions *n.pl.* problems, topics; **~ of dyvynite** problems of theology 5900
quyk *adj.* living, alive; animate 1397
quyt *v.* freed; excused; repaid *ppl.* 2667; **quyut** 5091; **bequyt:** scribal quirk for **be quyt** be repaid 3239
raby *n.* master, rabbi 6071
rad *see* **rede**
raymond *prop.n.* Raymond of Pennafort (1175–1275), Dominican theologian and canon lawyer 3271
rathur, raþur *adv.* sooner, at once, the more readily 1324, 4749; **þe ~** the more easily 4749; **raþer** 1953
raunpe *v.* rear up (on the hind legs) 1846
raunsom *n.* ransom 2269; **raunsoun** 2556
rauaische *v.* carry away; steal 1843; **rauasched** *ppl.*: **be ~ on hy** be transported on high 4234; **irauesched** 4251
raueyne *n.* rapine, greed; **do ~** rob 2708
recheles *adj.* heedless 4642
rechelnysse *n.* recklessness; negligence 3228
rechelsly *adv.* carelessly 4870
recheþ *v.* reaches *pr3sg.* 815
red *n.* counsel, advice; instigation, urging 1311; **don aftur his ~** follow his advice 3683
reddure *n.* severity 4466
rede *v.* advise, counsel; **wisse ne ~** direct nor advise 5093; **rede** *pr1sg.* 2845; **irede** 1342; **yrad** *ppl.* 7229

rede *v.* read; explain, teach, interpret 264; **to ~ to** be read 302; **reden** 6776; **rede** *pr1sg.* 1497; **redeþ** *pr3sg.* 2162; **redeþ** *pr3pl.* 6097; **redeth** 1408; **red** *ppl.* 3277; **rad** 2523
rede *adj.* red 5468
redy *adj.* ready, prepared 1040; **~ to** prepared for 1375; **make hym ~** get ready 1652
redynesse *n.* eagerness 7282
refreynyd *v.* restrained (in the use of) *ppl.* 1928
regard(e) *n.* **to ~ of** in comparison to 6390; **as to ~ of** in relation to 4614
regne *v.* reign; prevail, dominate 3319; **regneþ** *pr3pl.* 2695
regne *n.* reign 3480
reherce *v.* list, summarize; recount; discuss; teach, explain; relate, point out 4586; **rehercy** 4481; **rehercceþ** *pr3sg.* 3987; **reherseþ** 2785; **reherced** *ppl.* 1972
reigne *n.* rain 3593; **reyn(e)** 1213, 2598
reyke *v.* spread 4115
reyme *n.* placenta 449
rekene *v.* add up, reckon, calculate; consider, take into account; relate 2021; **rikne** 4525; **rekenyd** *ppl.* 5028; **to hym may ~ be** may be imputed or charged against him 5028. *see also* **rikne**
rekenynge *vbl.n.* account, accounting 2004
rekke *v.* care *pr1sg.* 7270
relece *v.* grant remission; release 3141; **relessed** *ppl.* 2915
relece *n.* release, relief 2205
releueþ *v.* relieve *pr3pl.* 2936
remedie *n.* remedy, relief 1646
remenaunt *n.* remainder, the rest 3224
rende *v.* mangle, rend; **~ asonder** tear apart 749
renne *v.* run; move 2501; **~ aboute** flow around 3594; **renneþ** *pr3sg.* 5459; **rennynge** *pr.ppl.* 529
repente *v.* repent *pr.subj.3.*; **him ~** is sorry 1706
repreue *v.* reproach 4684; **~ ... of** censure ... for 4683
resceyueþ *v.* receive *imper2sg.* 5139; **resceyued** *ppl.* 4532
reserue *v.* keep (for future use); set aside 3253
reson *n.* reason (i.e., the intellectual faculty); explantion; statement 69; **resoun** 52; **~ kan** has (the power of) reason 168; **him wanteþ ~** he is without reason 510; **by ~** reasonably, rightly, by rights 577; **by þis ~** by this explanation 2288; **by ~** because 3003; **haþ þis ~ wroȝt** made this reply 2028; **o ~ ... is** one reason is 2223; **aȝen ~** senseless 2866; **as it was ~** as was reasonable 1831; **it is ~** it is reasonable 5755; **resons** *pl.* accounts; motives; facts 4792; **~ ... alegge** make allegations (a legal term) 4594
resonable *adj.* reasonable, sensible 4857
respite *n.* reprieve; delay 5223
rest(e) *n.* repose, tranquility, rest; place of rest 5340, 141; **good ~** fortunate tranquility 6609
reste *v.* rest, repose; **haþ þeronne ~** has a place on it 4095; **in þe body doþ ~** are found in the body 6541; **of fightyng ~** cease fighting 6839; **ȝiue ... hem ...full ~ þat nede haueþ to þi light** to give them

complete repose who have need of your light 7168
rewe *n.* row; order 1854; **gon in his ~** walk in his company 3620
rewele *v.* rule *pr.subj.3sg.* 4951
rewful *adj.* sad 4149
rewlyche *adj.* pitiful 435
rewþe, reuþe *n.* pity 6565, 5560
reue *v.* plunder; pull; remove, pluck 1027; **reueþ** *pr3sg.* 1560; **reueþ** *pr3pl.* 1022; **reuyd** *ppl.* 4741
reuerence *n.* respect, honour 1568
reuyled *v.* reviled, denounced *ppl.* 6665
ricchesse *n.* riches, wealth; opulence 6154; **rycchesse** 213; **to ~ no rewarde he naþ** [neither] does he have any reward for the rich 1565; **rycches** 978
riche *n.* kingdom; **heuene ~** the kingdom of Heaven 1883
riche *adj.* rich; powerful; expensive, precious; splendid 2442; **ryche** 744
richely *adv.* splendidly 6830
ryde *v.* ride; **gon othur ~** walk or ride (a horse) 1307
riȝt *n.* a just claim, entitlement; right; the good; decree; justice 5640; **right** 1889; **ritht** 1883; **with ~** justly 2067; **ritte: an hard ~** a severe verdict 4502; **ryght, right** 732, 1877; **bi ~** by entitlement 4196; **in alle ~** in all justice 4922; **þorow ~** deservedly 6424
right, ryght *adv.* very, just; precisely 521; **~ so** just so 2508; **richt, rycht** (?) 2374, 344; **~ noght** absolutely nothing 2374; **riȝt, ryȝt** 2152, 129; **good ~** clearly just, fitting 5640
ryght, ryȝt *adj.* right, upright; fitting, just; straight, direct 200, 116
rightful(l) *adj.* upright, just, righteous, virtuous 2777, 5207; **~ wey** the path of righteousness 7297; **~ domes man** impartial judge 5121; **ryghtful(l)** 1455, 2997; **ryȝtful** 112
rightfully *adv.* justly, in good faith 2495; **rygthfuly** 904
rightfulnesse, ryghtfulnesse *n.* justice; righteousness 2937, 1355; **ryghtfullnesse** 2924; **riȝtfulnesse** 6573
right wis(e) *adj.* righteous, virtuous; legitimate 6560, 3708; **right wys** 6232; **ryght wise** 4613
rikne, rykne *v.* list, enumerate 4526, 2782; **telle oþur ~** count or number 5655. *see also* **rekene**, above.
rym(e) *n.* rhyme; verse 7270, 7269
ryncleþ *v.* wrinkles *pr3sg.* 650
ryse, rise *v.* rise 676, 4044
ryue *ppl.adj.* worn (i.e., a path well worn down by travellers) 1166
ryue *ppl.adj.* abundant; **of mercy ~** abundant in mercy 5275
ro *n.* the roe deer 7069
robbe *v.* rob 1027; **robbeþ** *pr3pl.* 1022
roch *n.* rock; cliff; **the moste ~** the largest cliff 5485; **roches** *pl.* 5359; **rokkes** 4023
rode *n.* the cross 1451; **rood** 4453; **~ tre** the cross 4413
rore *v.* roar 5961
rote *n.* root; source; lineage 564; **herte ~** depths of his heart 4431; **rotes** *pl.* 1593; **rotys** 1596
round, rownd *adj.* round, circular 1265, 6804; **is ~ yset** is created round 1254

Select Glossary (by Hoyt Greeson) 229

route *v.* rush 4037
route *n.* company, throng 966
rukke *v.* lie coiled 5597
sad *adj.* serious; constant; fixed, set; firm, unwavering 3154; **sadd(e)** 237, 3786; **saddur** *compar.* 1533
sak *n.* sack, bag 486
sakcloþe *n.* sackcloth, coarse cloth worn for mourning or penance 3797
salarye *n.* payment 4676
saluacyon *n.* salvation 1163; **savacioun** 4686
saraȝenes *prop.n.* Saracens, Moslems 5075; **sarsens** 4606
sarmon *n.* sermon; discourse, discussion 3802; **sermon: makeþ his ~** gives his account 3686
sauter, sawter *n.* psalter 272, 245
saue *v.* save, spare, preserve 334; **wele ~** wills to save 6336; **saued(e)** *ppl.* 3098, 6624; **saue** 2647; **isaued** 3842
sauely *adv.* certainly; safely 3026
sauyour *n.* savior 3505
sauour *n.* smell, scene, savor, aroma; perfume 6915; **sovour** 558; **sauoures** *pl.* 7053
sawe *n.* a saying, teaching; statement; rumor 139; **sawes** *pl.* 1273
sawtes *n.pl.* assaults 4892
scalde *v.* scald 5837; **iscalded** *ppl.* 5846
schad *v.* shed, poured *pa3sg.* 4367; **schadde** *pa3pl.* 3153; **sched** *ppl.*: **out ~** poured, shed 5832
schadewe *n.* shadow 1089; **schadwe** 5795; **schawdewe** 603
schal(l) *v.aux.* must, is to, have to; as auxiliary to indicate futurity: shall, will + verb; *1–3sg.* 188, 39; **ischal** *pr1sg.* 2701; **shal(l)** 4830, 33; **schul(l)** 685, 231; **schalt** 186; **schulleth** 154; **schalt** *pr2sg.* 367; **schall** *pr3sg.* 79; **Wheþur that he ~ to** whether he is to go to 7250; **schulleþ, schulleth** *pr1–3pl.* 28, 1147; **schul(l)** 12, 231; **schulle(n)** 255, 81; **schulliþ, schullyþ** 4679, 4114; **schulleþ** 6731; **schuylleþ** 3496; **schol** 6234; **shul** 2660; **schold(e)** *pa1–3sg.* 1373, 368; **schuld(e)** 340; **scholdest, schuldest** *pa2sg.* 2152, 1633; **riȝt as thow ~** just as if you had to ... 2152; **scholden, schulden** *pa.pl.* 3415, 325; **schuld(e)** 1079, 132
schame *n.* shame, disgrace 4248; **do no ~** bring no disgrace on 3022
schap *n.* form, fabric; shape; appearance 567; **comely of ~** good looking 583; **fayr ~** attractive appearance 6476
scharp(e) *adj.* keen, sharp; hard; intense 495; **~ and kene** sharp and painful 2599; **tormentes boþ ~ and grete** tortures both intense and numerous 5512
scharpli, sharply *adv.* forcefully; severely 1990, 2793
sche *pron.* she 504
schende *v.* afflict, destroy; damn 596; **ischend** *ppl.* disgraced; dishonoured 6666
schendschipe *n.* ruin, misfortune; disgrace, shame, humiliation 325; **schenschipe** 4436
schene *adj.* bright, shining 7034
schep *n.* sheep 5128
scheperde *n.* shepherd 5128
scherewdenesse *n.* wickedness 2998
schewe *v.* show, display; appear; reveal, relate, make known make manifest; teach 380; **men may ~ þerto** can lead men to it 2938; **forþ ~** display openly 3619; **persecution þat ... schal ~** persecution that he will cause 3768–69; **conneþ [to] ~** are able to display 1566; **~ hem** appear 1595; **~ suche servyse** perform such service 5355; **schewen** 1916; **ischewe: wol ~** I will show 3125; **scheweth, scheweþ** *pr3sg.* 1331, 1519; **schewys** 4645; **scheweth, scheweþ** *pr3pl.* 491, 1801; **~ hem** appear 1926; **schewyd** *pa3sg.* 99; **schewed** *pa.3pl.* appeared 3331; **hem ~** revealed themselves 4376; **schewynge** *pr.ppl.*: **~ witnesse** bearing witness 4473; **schewȝynge: false myracles ~** performing false miracles 3538; **schewed** *ppl.* 1388; **schewid, schewyd** 1986, 2903; **ischewed** 1999; **ischewyd** 4398; **y schewed** 5253
schewȝynge *vbl.n.* performing (a false miracle) 3538
schil *adj.* melodious 6898
schilde *pr.subj3sg.*: **crist us ~** may Christ protect us 6993
schine, schyne *v.* shine 3691, 6244; **schineþ, schyneþ** *pr3sg.* 2677, 4825; **schon** *pa3sg.* 6800; **schone** *pa3pl.* 5329; **schinynge** *pr.ppl.* 5233; **schunyng** 4723; **schynyng(e)** 7181, 819; **ischone** *ppl.* made manifest 6035
schynynge *vbl.adj.* bright, shining; brilliant, radiant: **somer ~ among** accompanied by bright summer 1214
schip *n.* ship 4069
schonde *n.* disgrace; ruin, destruction; damnation 243; **goþ to ~** are ruined 5131; **bryng to ~** bring to disgrace 243
schort *adj.* short, brief 461; **~ dayes** brief days 642; **hys mynde ys ~** he is short of memory 652; **schorter** *compar.* 630; **~ beth ... dayes** days are fewer 639; **schortest** *superl.*: **al þer ~** shortest of all 631
schorted *v.* shortened *ppl.* 3843
schortly *adv.* briefly, concisely; quickly 2191
schortnesse *n.* brevity; **is drawe into ~** is reaching its end 618
schour *n.* attack, onslaught; shower (of arrows?) 1527; **deþes ~** onset, attack of death 4879 **schourys** *pl.* 3593
schryfte *n.* sacramental confession of sins 2747
schryue, shryue *v.* confess, hear confession; **hym for to ~** to give him absolution 2851; *refl.* **hym ~** make his confession 1463, 2722; **schryue** *ppl.*: **is ...** is absolved 2641; **ischryve** 2543
schut *v.* shut; enclosed *ppl.* 5229; **ischut(t)** 2239, 4207
science *n.* knowledge, learning: **maistres of ~** masters of theology 4991
sciencie *n.* Latin. **flos ~** The Flower of Knowledge, a handbook of theological excerpts "picked" from the Fathers and others, like flowers from a "garden" i.e., a florilegium 5899
sclaundres *n.pl.* slanders 5777
score *n.* twenty; **foure ~** eighty 637
scowrgys *n.pl.* whips, scourges 4361
scragges *n.pl.* skrags, outcroppings of barren rocks 5359
scrypul *n.* a trace, small amount; scruple, a moral misgiving, a doubt 2688

se *v.* see, look at; behold; perceive; discover; foresee 179; **forto ~** to behold 723; **~ al aboute** look all around 3828; **sen** 4097; **see** 153; **seye** 3824; **ise, yse** 774, 533; **bifore ~** foresee 6517; **seost** *pr2sg.* 2149; **seþ** *pr3sg.* 331; **iseoþ** 3846; **seth, seþ** *pr3pl.* 45, 1195; **seoþ** 6440; **siȝe** *pr.subj.3sg.* 1921; **se** *pr.subj.pl.* 254; **saw(e)** *pa1–3sg.* 3641, 3693; **say: that never man such on ~** such as no one had ever beheld 4082; **siȝe** 1921; **sye** 503; **syhe** 766; **sawen** *pa.pl.* 6946; **siȝe** 4308; **sie** 5153; **seie, sey(e)** *ppl.* 2122, 1309, 223; **iseie, iseye** 6047, 4547; **seyȝe** 1292; **sene** 1970; **wel ~** fully visible 4120; **yseyȝe** 1490; **isene, y sene** 2030, 804
se *n.* seat, throne; the Papal *see* (from Latin *sedes*, chair) 3501
se *n.* sea 5833; **see** 995; **seos** *pl.* 5460
second(e) *num., adj.* second 2744, 6520; **secunde** 300
sede *v.* bear seed 550
sede *n.* seed 382
seek *see* also **sik**
sefþe *see* **seventh**
segge *see* **sey(e)**
sey(e) *v.* say, speak, tell 347, 1158; **seiȝe, seyȝe** 2739, 3506; **segge** 2411; **so muche ... forto ~** as much as to say 4722; **sugge** 4593; **say(e), saie** 3984, 4327, 3026; **seie** 1364; **(i)seye** *pr1sg.* 4447, 135; **saieþ, sayeth** *pr3sg.* 2257, 1108; **saith, sayþ, saiþ** 465, 210, 6220; **saiþe** 565; **seieþ, seyeþ** 2760, 3748; **saies, sayes** 2037, 458; **seith, seyth** 609, 415; **seiþ, seyþ** 695, 425; **seiþe, seyþe** 1625, 3663; **as me ~** as the saying goes 5934; **seien, seyen** *pr.pl.* 6098, 3742; **sey** 428; **seyeth** 3369; **seith** 2300; **seieþ, seyeþ** 1362, 3387; **seiȝeþ** 6853; **seyȝen** 3726; **seie** *imper.sg.* 1163; **sey** 3311; **seyȝe** 3506; **said(e), sayde** *pa.sg.* 5889, 344, 3359; **seid** 6406; **seide, seyde** 2728, 3314; **seiden** *pa.pl.* 4305; **said(e)** 1319, 1484 *ppl.* **sayd** 249; **sed** 3203; **seyȝe** 1292; **yseid** 1310
seyȝynge *vbl.n.* account, comment 3388
seilynge *vbl.n.* sailing 5797
seint, seynt *n.* saint 357, 209; **seyn** 3343; **seyntes** *pl.* 6125; **seyntys** 4529
seketh *v.* seeks, seek out; investigate *pr3pl.* 1145; **seken: to þe synful ~** cause, contrive for the sinful 6695; **seke** *imper.2sg.* **~ thu thu wyt** rack your brains 1087; **souȝte** *pa.sg.* 5184; **souȝte** *pa.3sg.* 1797; **sowht** *ppl.* **owt ~** inquired into 3986; **sowȝt** 7260; **isowt** 1277
sekurly *see* **sikurliche**
selcouþe *adv.* wonderously; **~ maide** outlandishly made 1284
selde *adv.* seldom 223
selue *adj.* self, self-same 3870
seluer *n.* silver 4662
semblaunt *n.* mien, (facial) expression; countenance; **glad ~** happy expression 6934
seme *v.* appear; seem 685; **semeth** *pr3sg.* 1176; **semeþ** 403; **lenkþe ~ bote on day** the length seems but one day 6371–72; **semyþ** 4821; **semeth** *pr3pl.* 489; **semeþ** 1358; **semen** 3708; **semed** *pa3sg.* 2460
semely *adj.* pleasing, seemly, comely 66; **semly** 4228
semynge *vbl.n.* appearance 4850
sende *v.* bestow, grant; send, dispatch 1256;

let ~ allowed to be sent 3302; **sendeþ** *pr3sg.* 2861; **sent(e)** *pa3sg.* 3690, 4998
sene *vbl.adj.* visible, observed, seen; plain 1970
sentence *n.* meaning, sense 7252
septre *n.* scepter 3382
sepulcre *n.* tomb, sepulcher 4345
sercle *n.* sphere, circle 6061; **sercles** *pl.* 6055
sertayn *see* **certayne**
seruaunt *n.* servant 891; **seruant** 899; **seruauntes** *pl.* 2931; **seruauntys** 4933
serue *v.* serve, attend; honour; provide for (the poor) 102; **serueþ** *pr3sg.* 2219; **serueth, serueþ** *pr3pl.* 889, 890
seruise, seruyse *n.* service; religious service 104, 5354; **for her** ~ for their conformity (to God's will) 5914; **from the deueles** ~ from servitude to the devil 2140; **don her** ~ be of assistance 4988; **do** ~ be of help 6298; **seruice: doth hym** ~ does his bidding 892
sesoun *n.* (proper) time 844
sete *n.* abode, dwelling; seat, throne 2445; **setes** *pl.* 6657; **setys** 5062
sette *v.* set, place; make; set down (in writing); select; appoint; establish, seat 873; **wheron þey woll it** ~ i.e., on which they've made up their minds 6288; **set(e)** 1206, 3382; ~ **by hym lygth** think little of him 909; ~ **at lityl pris** regard as of little value 1136; **settist** *pr2sg.* ~ **þy sight** i.e., focus your sight 6596; **setteth, setteþ** *pr3sg.* 786, 158; **setteth, setteþ** *pr3pl.* 795, 232; **set** *ppl.* 178; **wiþ lytyl deuocyoun** ~ **þerto** accompanied by little devotion 3234; ~ **faste** firmly fixed 4786; **iset, yset** 2065, 573; **bones** (shall) **be** ~ **to gidre** bones shall be joined 4044; **þer aȝenst** ~ placed in front of it 6454; **be** ~ **in a riche sete** be seated on a precious throne 6959; **stones** ~ **ifere** stones laid together (like bricks) 7120; **world is round** ~ the world is ordained to be spherical 1254
setthe *conj.* since, after; because 52; **seþþe:** ~ **þat** ever after 5981; **suþþe** 3425; ~ **that** after, since 1830; **sutthe** 84
seuene *cardinal number adj.* seven 3
seuenþ(e) *adj.* seventh 6005, 4021; **seueth** 310; **sefþe** 5643
side, syde *n.* side; part 1348, 336; **in many** ~ everywhere 1348; **in echa** ~ on every side 2766; **in euery** ~ in every direction 3544; **in no** ~ in any direction 3353; **rownd by euery** ~ circular on every side 6804
side *adj.* long; hanging down 1298
sight, syght, syȝt, siȝt *n.* view; a look, a glance; gaze; vision 1837, 490, 3582, 2335; ~ **of God** the Beatific Vision 2604; **to our** ~ as it seems to us i.e., from our perspective 5464; **at on** ~ at one glance 6458; **of** ~ in appearance 4391; **siȝt: afayr** ~ a beautiful sight 6798; **to his** ~ in appearance 504; **a** ~ **have** have a look 5622; **to mannys** ~ in full view of all 3582; **afore godys** ~ in the sight of God 4657; **bifore any mannes** ~ in anyone's opinion 6342
sighty *adj.* visible 7189
signyfie *v.* mean; symbolize 4013
sik(e), syk *adj.* sick, ill 675, 5160, 664; **seek** 4988
siker, syker *adj.* sure, certain; stable; safe, secure; lasting 6161, 1141; ~ **pes** lasting peace 6161; ~ **of** confident about 7095; **sikur, sykur** 2036, 1144
sikernesse, sykernesse *n.* security; certainty, stability 6672, 6671
sykynge *vbl.n.* sighing; groaning; **makest ... no** ~ show no repentance (for sins) 2799
siknesse *n.* sickness 1673; **siknesses** *pl.* 1733
sikurliche *adv.* surely; securely, safely; with certainty 2627; **sekurly** 282; **sykurly** 2008
symented *v.* cemented *ppl.* 7121
symple *adj.* simple, innocent 1117
symply *adv.* simply 2794
sympulnesse *n.* simplicity 119
synew *n.* sinew 1597
synful(l) *adj.* sinful 1462, 230; **sinful** 4466; **synfyl** 5779
synfully *adv.* sinfully, in sin 383
syng(e) *v.* sing; cry out 6937, 3117; ~ **weilaway** cry with pain "Alas!" 1379; **syngeth, syngeþ** *pr3sg.* 3021, 3015; **synge** *pr.subj.3sg.* 3020
syngynge *vbl.n.* singing, song 3029; **synkynge** 2920
synke *v.* go down, sink 5227
synne *n.* sin 80; **ȝif** ~ **ne were** if it were not for sin 1943; **couthe neuere no** ~ **wirche** never knew how to commit any sin 2661; **synnys** *pl.* 4510
synneth *v.* (man) sins *pr3sg.* 2774; **ysynned** *ppl.* 2467
syte *n.* city 4347
syxte *num.ord.* sixth 306
sith *n.* sight; vision 654; **sight, syght** 1837, 530; **to** ~ in appearance 490; **to his** ~ to his eyes 504; **sitht: schewen in** ~ reveal to sight 2064; **sytht** 601; **siȝt, syȝt** 2604, 3582; **siȝtes** *pl.* 1853
siȝt *see* **sight**
sithes, sythes, siþes *n.pl.* (numeral) + times 2019, 2778, 5331; **ofte** ~ often, many times 2875; **sythe: ofte** ~ often
sitte, sytte *v.* sit 4151, 3460; **sitten** 6657; **sitteth, sitteþ** *pr3sg.* 806, 4014; **sytteth** 784; **sittes** 6768; **sytt** 22; **sat** *pa3sg.* 5431
sittynge, syttynge *vbl.adj.* sitting 4337, 3456; ~ **in the wey** lying in the path 3456
sixte, syxte *ordinal number adj.* sixth 1478, 306
sixti *num.* sixty 3794
skile, skyle *n.* reason, judgment; cause; fitting 1834, 54; **ben iset by** ~ be reasonably regarded 2066; **þe** ~ **whi** the reason why 2288; **skele** 1545; **skille: agens ...** ~ improperly 6306; **skiles, skyles** *pl.* 2007, 319
skylfully *adv.* intelligently 2316
skyn(ne) *n.* skin 451, 5720
slake *v.* end; go out; diminish 5214
sle *v.* kill, slay 1012; **sleþ** *pr3sg.* 2759; **slowe** *pa3pl.* 4625; **slayn** *ppl.* 1449; **islawe** 1433
slepe *v.* sleep 692
slep(e) *n.* sleep 979, 6370
slepyng *vbl.n.* sleep 694
slewthe, slewþe *n.* sloth, laziness 2390, 965; **slouthe** 2704
slie *adj.* sly; clever; skillful; wise 6027; **wise** ~ slyly (prudently?) wise 6027; **sly(e)** 1613, 679
slyþe *n.* cleverness, ingenuity 1910
slowe *adj.* slow i.e., intellectually challenged; sluggish; **wol** ~ excessively slow (i.e., to learn) 162
smale *adj.* small, little 2503; **small(e)** 6056, 4223
smart *adj.* alert, quick; painful, severe; stinging 1235; ~ **and hard** severe and painful 2340; **smarte:** ~ **stormes** turbulent storms, tempests 2598; **smerte** 1383; **wel** ~ very severe 1526
smarteþ *v.* hurts, causes pain; burns *v.pr3sg.* 2195; **smerte** *pr.subj.3sg.* 1095; ~ **sore** causes severe distress 2890
smellynge *vbl.n.* sense of smell 6913
smyte(n) *v.* smite, strike; pierce; whip, flog 4514, 3461; **smyteþ** *pr3pl.* 5760; **smyte(n)** *ppl.* 4432, 6698; **ysmyte** 1687
smytynge *vbl.adj.* striking 5779
smyþes *n.pl.* blacksmiths 5760
smoþe *adj.* smooth 5321
snel *adj.* quick 247
so *adv.* so 31; such 69; **so as** as if 1870; ~ **... as** as ... as 6104
socoure *v.* aid, help 972
sodayn *adj.* sudden, unforseen 1621; **sodeyn** 4900
sodeyn *adv.* suddenly, unexpectedly 4294
sodeynly *adv.* suddenly 1066; **sodaynly** 4058; **sodeynliche** 3862
soffre *v.* suffer, endure; allow, permit; submit to 2179; ~ **peyne wol towe** endure very severe punishment 2179; **suffre** 1898; **sufferþ** *pr3sg.* 1336; **suffreþ** 1558; **soffreþ** *pr3pl.* 4634; **suffreþ** 2171; **soffren** 5815; **soffre** *pr.subj.3sg.*: ~ **us** allow us 5979; **suffre** 2890; **suffred(e)** *pa3sg.* 1880, 4450; **soffred** *pa3pl.* 6941; **suffred** 2187; **suffredust** *pa2sg.* 4590; **soffred** *ppl.* 4635; **suffred** 4528
softe *adv.* comfortably; gently 5185
softe *adj.* easy 792; **no thing** ~ not at all easy-going 2384
sogette *adj.* subject to, obedient 874
solas *n.* solace, consolation; pleasure; **worldes** ~ worldly pleasure 5054
som(e) *indef.pron.* some, one 6476, 269; **somme** 1300; **summe** 264
som(e) *adj.* some, certain 339, 679; **alle and** ~ one and all 1773; **somme** 1368; **sum(me)** 4824, 127
somdel *n.* a part 2613
somdel *adv.* partly; somewhat 1516; **some del** 275
somdel *adj.* somewhat, some degree 562
somer *n.* summer 1214; **somers** *poss.sg.* 603
somtyme *adv.* sometimes 1294; **som tyme** 2573
som what *pron.* a part 1391
son(e) *adv.* soon, quickly, 60; **sonner** *compar.* 1148
sond *n.* dispensation; gift, grace; a command 7011; **sonde: of all his** ~ for all He has sent 2878; **þorow goddes** ~ by God's grace 1313
sone *n.* son 3; **the mannes** ~ the Son of Man, i.e., Christ 3953; **sones** *poss.sg.* 3778; **sones** *pl.* 1184
sone *adv.* soon; immediately, at once, quickly 275; **wel** ~ very quickly 1923; **mad** ~ created instantaneously 5260; **al so** ~ **as** as soon as 644
sonne *n.* sun 839; **sunne** 5330; **sonnes** *poss.sg.* 7195
sore *adv.* sorely, painfully; intensely; grievously, bitterly; heavily 584

sores *n.pl.* sores, wounds; pains 4448
sory *adj.* sad, woful; sorry 2811; **wiþ ~ chere** with sad countenance 5192
sorow(e) *n.* sorrow, grief 3325, 326; **sorwe** 864; **makyng ~** grieving 435; **~ make** lament 762; **sorowes** *pl.* 1471
sorowen *v.* grieve 4255
soster, suster *n.* sister 6571, 6492; **sister** 6571
sotel *adj.* cunning; thin, ethereal 6137; **sotyl: so ~ as** as ethereal as 2413
soþ *adj.* true 4429
sothe, soþ(e) *n.* truth 349, 4913, 2417; **þe ~ to sey** to tell the truth 349; **for ~** indeed, in truth 428; **to ~** truly 1746
soþfast(e) *adj.* true, faithful 112, 4630
soþly *adv.* truly 822; **sothly** 2321
soþnesse *n.* truth; **in ~** in reality 315
soughþ *n.* south 3561
sowle *n.* soul 1418; **soule** 137; **sowles** *pl.* 2176; **soules** 305; **soulys** 2812
soun *n.* sound 3947; **sown** 4186
sowneþ *v.* sounds *pr3sg.*3932; **sownynge** *pr.ppl.* 7049
sowneþ *v.* tends towards *pr3sg.* 5086
sowr *adj.* sour, bitter 5582; **sour** 559
souerayn *n.* lord, sovereign 219; **soueraynes** *pl.* 4672; **souereyns** 4674
souereynlyche *adv.* royally, above all 6813
sowe *v.* sown *ppl.* 382
space *n.* space, distance; time span, duration, interval (of time) 1257; **~ of ... myle** time (to walk) a mile 1193; **tyme ne ~** time nor opportunity 1693; **lyves ~** life, were alive 7118; **spas** 3258; **spaces** *pl.* 374
sparcle *n.* spark 2479; **sparcul** 2480; **sparcles** *pl.* 5621; **sparckles** 6883
spare *v.* spare, refrain (from), hesitate to 1636; **hollyche ~** keep (it) entirely out of use 3253; **spareth, spareþ** *pr3sg.* 1556, 1559; **spared** *pa3pl.* 4579
spattyng *vbl.n.* spitting 557
speche *n.* language; speaking; speech 287; **makeþ her ~** talk 6047
special *adj.* distinctive, particular; special 2228; **speciall** 6424
specially, specyally *adv.* especially; in particular 1392, 8; **~ over all thynge** above all else 4852; **specialy** 1035; **specyallyche** 2983
specifie *v.* mention; identify 3279
speciouse *adj.* beautiful; fitting 6832
sped *v.* finished, concluded *ppl.* 5244; **isped** 5237
speed *n.* helper; aid 6
spek(e) *v.* speak, talk 3598, 867; **spekest** *pr2sg.* 2793; **speketh, spekeþ** *pr3sg.* 357, 946; **spak** *pa3sg.* 2452; **spoke** 5018; **spaken** *pa3pl.* 3308; **spekynge** *pr.ppl.* 3823; **spoken** *ppl.* 4752; **ispoke** 4747; **have ~ of** have I spoken of 6002
spel *n.* story: **make here ~** tell their story 2416
spenden *v.* use 104
spere *n.* sphere 4091
spere *n.* spear 4430
spare *v.* spare, leave (closed) 1636; **speryþ** *pr3sg.* leaves (closed) 3165; **spareth** 1556; **spareþ** 1559; **spared** *pa3pl.* 4580
spicery *n.* spices 6917
spices *n.pl.* kinds, types 2135
spille *v.tr.* kill; damn 3813; **spylle** 1098; **spille** *v.intr.* die, perish; be damned 5601; **spylle** 4931; **ispild** *ppl.* 2361
spirit *n.* demon; spirit 3571; **spiritys** *pl.* 3602; **spyrytis** 2456
spot *n.* blemish, defect 2579; **spottys** *pl.* 2582
sprawle *v.* toss about, sprawl 409
sprede *v.* extend, spread 551; **spredeþ** *pr3sg.* 5306; **sprede** *pr3subj.* 1262; **spredynge** *pr.ppl.:* **out ~** extending 1258; **sprad** *ppl.:* **openly ~** widely disseminated, spread 7301
spryng(e) *v.* spread; spring, grow, sprout, bloom; rise, appear 6916, 548; **out ~** originate; **spryngeth** *pr3sg.* 554; **sprynges** 4107
squynesie *n.* quinsy, i.e., tonsillitis 2396; **streite ~** painful, severe quinsy 2396
stalwurthe *adj.* stalwart, powerful 582
stat(e) *n.* condition, state; position, rank 604, 586; **tymes ... beþ nat in o stat** i.e., time is in a state of flux, not static 1207; **mowe in her ~ stonde** can remain in its condition 1202; **lasse ~** lower rank 3195; **states** *pl.* 7151
stature *n.* build, shape, stature; physical appearance 66
sted(e) *n.* place 1427, 393; **in þe eorþe ~** on earth 2306; **stedes** *pl.* 2308; **wonynge ~** dwelling places 7154
stedefast *n.* unchanging, unwavering; faithful; resolute, steadfast 997; **stedfast(e)** 6484, 7156; **stede faste** 2230
stedefastly *adv.* firmly, steadfastly, faithfully 1776
stere *v.* stir, move, prompt; guide, steer 130; **sture** 292; **sturie** 7253; **steryþ** *pr3sg.* 431; **stered** *pa3sg.* 5812; **stured** *pa3sg.:* **~ hym to wreche** moved him to vengeance 1317; **stured** *ppl.* 7289; **istered** 7286
sterynge *vbl.n.* motion, movement; agitation, provocation; rush (of sound) 689; **sturinge** 957; **sturyng** 1704
sterne *adj.* somber; bold, fierce 4391
sterre *n.* star 6096; **sterres** *pl.* 819; **sterrys** 3945; **sterren** 6094
sterred *adj.* starry 816
steven(e) *n.* voice 5134, 3828
styeþ *v.* ascend *pr3pl.* 3824; **stey** *pa3sg.* **up ~** rose up 4299
styfly *adv.* staunchly 6834
stikeþ *v.intr.* stick *pr3pl.* 6056; **thei ~ not faste** they are not firmly fixed 6056; **stikede** *v.tr.:* **ȝe on me ~** you inflicted on me *pa2pl.* 4454
stille, stylle *adv.* still, unmoved, motionless, quietly; motionlessly; continually, always 1849, 43
stille, stylle *adj.* silent, still 3109, 171; **stonde ~** become calm 3596; **it stondeþ ~** it remains unchanged 3006
stynch(e) *n.* stench, foul odor 5524, 542; **to ~ he ys ynome** he is turned to stench 771; **stynkþe** 5513
stynke *v.* stink 556; **stynketh** *pr3sg.* 653
stynke *n.* stink, stench 5521
stynkyng(e) *vbl.adj.* stinking; disgusting 486, 6354
stynkþe *see* **stynch(e)**
stobel *n.* stubble 2532
stok *n.* (tree) trunk 571
stolyn *v.* stolen *ppl.* 4554
ston(e) *n.* stone, rock 2425, 498; **stones** *pl.* 4023

stonde *v.* stand; remain; exist 43; **here up on ~** dwell on this 809; **aboute here ~** standing around her 2329; **to hem may grete stede ~** voice be of great advantage to them 3139; **se ~** see standing 4358; **~ to** endure, submit to 7279; **aȝenst hem ~** withstand them 6264; **stondes** *pr2sg.* 576; **stondeþ** *pr3sg.* 3006; **regions that ~ þeraboute** regions that remain around it (i.e., Rome) 3364; **watur that ~** water that stands motionless, i.e., is not running 5459; **~ ... stille** remains fixed, unmoved 6120; **stant** 1019; **~ somdel hard** stands rather firmly 562; **~ in stede of** function in place of (i.e., one day of penance on earth is worth 365 days in purgatory) 2213; **~ in no stede** avails not, is of no advantage 2977; **stondeth** *pr3pl.:* **~ in her rewe** line up with their group 1854; **stonden** 4507; **faste ~** remain fixed 6090; **stondes: þeraboute ~** that is situated around there 823; **stod** *pa3sg.* 4007; **stode** *pa3pl.:* **~ ... stille** stood ... motionlessly 6042
stondynge *vbl.adj.* standing 4512
stong(e) *v.* pierced; driven (into) *ppl.* 4431, 4696
stooles *n.pl.* stoles (ecclesiastical garment worn around the neck) 1300
stordy *adj.* **wiþ a ~ mood** with intense emotion, fierce temper 4608
stounde, stownde *n.* time, while, i.e., a little while 2097, 725; **in a lityl ~** in an instant 2097; **a lytil ~** a short while 2405; **hard ~** severe trial 5909; **stonde** 1649; **in þe deþes ~** at the hour of death 2752; **in þat ~** at that time 4274
stowpyng *vbl.adj.* stooped, bent 655
stoute *adj.* strong; cruel, overbearing; **sterne and ~** bold and brave 4934
strangle *v.* kill; choke to death 1011
strecchynge *v.* extending *pr.ppl.* 1259
streight *adv.* straight; directly; **~ forþ** all the way 2635
streit(e) *adj.* strict, exacting; painful 2112, 2396; **streyt** 4732; **streytest** *superl.* 3974
strenkþ(e) *n.* strength; intensity 585, 399; **þorow ~** forceably 3731
stret(e) *n.* road 7196, 3812; **stretes** *pl.* 7038
strif, stryf *n.* contention, dissention (over matters of doctrine), strife; affliction, travail 1237, 1369; **with ~** with agony 1487; **wiþ oute ~** peacefully 5063; **be in ~** quarrel 6610
strike *v.* strike; **~ faste** hurl swiftly 5768
stryue(n) *v.* contend, strive 5967, 6551; **togidre ~** contend against each other 5967
strong(e) *adj.* powerful, strong; severe; steadfast 542, 2534; **strang** 2592; **strengest** *superl.* **whan sche** (i.e., the sun) **her ~ hete haþ most iwonne** when she has, for the most part, reached her most intense heat 7180
studyynge *vbl.n.* study 5898
subieccion *n.* subjection; **in ~ of** in subjection to 3354; **subiectyon** 3348
substaunce *n.* in medieval theology, the self-subsistent being and absolute goodness of the Trinity 17
sucche *pron.* such; **~ that** so great that 749; **such(e)** 560, 26
such(e) *adj.* such 1306, 131; **schuch** 2428
suffisaunt(e) *adj.* sufficient 3236, 3199

suffre see **soffre**
suggettys see **sugette**
sukke *v.* suck 5596
sum see **som**
summe tyme *adv.* sometimes; at once 1060; **sum tyme** 1060; **haþ ~ hope among** have hope sometimes, now and then 5928
sunne see **sonne**
suppose *v.* believe, imagine, suppose 3103; **supposest** *pr2sg.* 2829
suspecyoun *n.* suspicion 2830
suster see **soster**
susteyneth *v.* support, sustain *pr3pl.* 840
sustynaunce *n.* sustenance; livelihood 850
suþþe *adv.* afterwards 4362
swayn *n.* servant 1353
swartnesse *n.* darkness; **most of ~** of deepest darknessness 5115
swatt *v.* sweated *pa3sg.* 1512
swerynge *vbl.n.* swearing; **fals hothes ~** swearing false oathes 2706
sweryst *v.* swear *pr2sg.* 2826
swete *adj.* sweet; fragrant; dear; pleasant, delightful 558
swetnesse *n.* delight, bliss 6166
swift(e) *adj.* in medieval theology: agile; swift 6247, 7066; **so ~ as ... þought** as swift as thought 6247–48
swiftnesse *n.* in theology, agility, i.e., movement of a spiritual body, quick as a blink 6230
swynes *n. poss.sg.* of a swine, pig 7107
swynke *v.* work, toil, labour; expend effort 6271
swithe, swythe *adv.* very 659, 219; **swyþe** 451; **swiþe** quickly 4785
swolowe *v.* swallow 5222
swope *v.* sweep 5608; **swope** *ppl.* 4167
tayl(e) *n.* tail 3688, 3695; **taile** 3692; **be at his ~** behind him, following him 1932
take *v.* take, take up; obtain; seize, grasp; accept, receive; select; partake; understand; consider 92; **to ~ wiþ her hond to hem any bote** to grab hold of anything to defend themselves 6277; **~ but litil hede** pay scant attention 1680; **itake** *pr1sg.*: **my mater ~** I commence my subject matter 6005; **taketh** *pr3sg.*: **~ he no kepe** he is not concerned about 514; **~ to hem entente** pays attention to them 1272; **~ his cours al wiþoute** (the sun) pursues its course on the outside (in Ptolemaic terms) 5343; **takeþ** *pr3pl.*: **~ hede** pays attention 420; **they ~ no kepe** they do not remember 2574; **take** *pr.subj.3sg.*: **is mercy ~** bestow his mercy to 3118; **ar deþ to hem ~** before death carry them off 5995; **take** *imper.pl.* 2743; **tok(e)** *pa3sg.* 1510, 2246; **alle ... with hym ... he ~** he led all who were with him 2246; **took** 4353; **manhede that he ~** human nature which he assumed 1510; **to hem ~** bestowed upon them 4596; **tok** *pa3pl.* 326; **~ flesch and bon** i.e., were born 2651; **take** *ppl.* 1914; **itake** 2255
tale *n.* tale; **wiþouten eny more ~** without further ado 4201; **talys** *pl.* 4802
tale *n.* count, tally; number 5396; **telle: bi ~** count (them) in order 6089
talent *n.* inclination, desire 6601
tally *adv.* elegantly; **~ entayled** finely carved 7130

taryenge *vbl.n.* delay 956
teche(n) *v.* teach 3143, 1153; **techeth** *pr3sg.* 2141; **techeþ** 902
techinge *vbl.n.* teaching 3157
tee *v.* go, proceed, draw near: **may no man þider ~** no one may draw near that place 6020
telle *v.* tell, speak of, mention, relate; proclaim; disclose, reveal; say; consider, count (as); describe; explain 828; **~ unto þe ende** speak fully of 3282; **ytelle** *pr1sg.* 1867; **itelle** 5872; **telleth, telleþ** *pr3sg.* 605, 1; **teleþ** 5900; **telluth, telluþ** 343, 757; **tellyþ** 4389; **telles** 544; **telles** 4547; **tellys** 463; **telleth, telleþ** *pr3sg.* 261, 263; **telles** 3614; **tellis, tellys** 3724, 463; **tolde** *pa1–3sg.* 1174; **tolde** *pa.pl.* 2233; **told(e)** *ppl.* 181, 1125; **erst ~** said before 4146; **itold(e)** 1135, 2211; **mowen be ~** can be considered 7135; **haþ ... ~** had spoken 5212; **y tolde** 374; **as goddes sones ... beþ ~** be considered as sons of god 1184; **fourty daies ~** altold, forty days 2208
tempest *n.* force; blast; storm 998; **tempestes** *pl.* 2355
tempreth *v.* (he) tempers, moderates *pr3sg.* 843
tempte *v.* tempt, incite 1929
tendre *adj.* soft, tender; careful 2482; **tendur: his conscience the more ~ make** make his conscience more careful 7241
tenþe *adj.* tenth 4033
tere *n.* tear(s): **tryvaile and ~** suffering and tears 463; **teres** *pl.* 5818
teþ *n.pl.* teeth 5689
than(ne) *adv.* then 54, 408; **þan(ne)** 120, 1974; **þann(e)** 57; **þene** 1088; **þenne** 5809; **tho, þo** 96, 66;
than *conj.* than 318; **thanne** 5262; **þan(ne)** 1948, 57; **þenne** 89
that *conj.* so that 107; **so unclene be ~ thu ... never towche me** be so unclean in such a way that you never involve me 987–988
thaw, þaw(e) *conj.* though, even if, if 1439, 1095, 2011; **thow, þow** 163, 6697; **thouȝ, þouȝ** 4980, 1824; **thei,** 2405; **they** 3002; **þowh** 6908
the, þe *pron.2sg.* you, thee 549, 1631
thedur see **þider**
thei, þei *pron.3pl.* those 51, 427; **they, þey** 53, 238
thei *conj.* see **thaw, þaw(e)**
thenk(e), þenk(e) *v.* think; conceive; imagine; intend; know 192, 351, 359, 2138; **~ on** remember 99; **~ in** think about 1659; **thenken** 525; **may ~** can imagine 4184; **thenche** 2478; **þynch** 6924; **þynke** 6234; **þynkyn** 7021; **thenkest, þenkest** *pr2sg.* 2144, 2822; **thenketh, þenketh** *pr1–3sg.* 652, 440; **thenkeþ, þenkeþ** 331, 2155; **~ in his thought** intend in his mind 331; **thenkeþ, þenkeþ** *pr3pl.* 1370, 4981; **þey ~ nought** they do not think 4981; **~ in her þouȝt** intend in their minds 6627; **thenke** *pr.subj.pl.* 2403; **thenk, þenk(e)** *imper.* 366, 359, 2867; **þynke: no good ~** expect no good 6508; **schal hem ~** it will seem to them 5802; **hym schold ~** it would seem to him 6100; **thought, þought(e)** *pa.sg.* 277, 4868, 3926; **the whiche he ~ to coroune to his quene**: whom he intended to crown as his queen 4868; **þouȝt** 4852; **þoȝt: ~ it to hem** it seemed to them 5844; **þoughten** *pa3pl.* 1806; **iþought: ~ ful ydelly** had only empty thoughts 4765
thennes *adv.* from there, thence 5413; **from ~** from there 2488; **þennes, þennys** 5406, 839
ther(e), þer(e) *adv.* there; where; then 341, 385, 5909, 1468; **þore** 6337
ther after, þer after *adv.* after that 2572, 5432; **ther aftyr** 93; **þerafter** 472; **there after, þere after** 1888, 5316
ther by *adv.* nearby 1589; *rel.* by this 1719; **þerby** 1515
there as, þere as *adv.* where 2105, 6034
there thorow *adv.* through it; throughout 2685; **þer þorow** 2487
there uppon *adv.* about it, on it 7018; **þere upon** 3884
therfore, ther fore *rel.* because of this, whereas 183, 163; **therfor** 245; **therefore** 2375; **þerfore** 432
ther fro *adv.* from there 270; **þerfro, þer fro** 2850, 4740
ther ynne, þer ynne *adv.* in it 1132, 779; **there ynne, þere ynne** 2619, 2247; **ther yinne** 3478; **þer in** 2249; **þerinne** 2064; **þerynne** 7024; **þeryn** 884
ther on *adv.* in it, on it; at it; about that 894; **þeron** 561; **þere on** 3964; **þeronne** 4095
ther to, therto *adv.* to it, for it; nearby; compared to (it); in addition 71, 102; **ther two** 2391; **þerto** 569; **þereto, þere to** 881, 2958
ther with, ther wiþ etc. see **þerwith** etc.
thi, þi *poss.adj. 2sg.* your 536, 1710; **thy, þy** 1087, 989; **þin, þyn(e)** [used when following word begins with a vowel] 2154, 2152, 4560
thidurward *adv.* in that direction 808
þikke *adj.* thick, dense; in throngs **wel ~** quite densely 2766
thilk(e) *adj.demons.* the same; this; that 293, 123; **thulk(e), þulk(e)** 811, 23, 1594, 858
thing(e), thyng(e) *n.* thing, object; matter; event 264, 3406, 10, 260; **~ ryȝt none** exactly nothing 129; **alle ~** everything 27; **no ~** nothing 41; **thynk, þynke** 241, 6234; **þing, þyng(e)** 1395, 1358, 2822; **ded ~** corpse 2420; **thinges, þinges** *pl.* 1055, 1632; **thynges, þynges** 129, 779; **thyngges** 3959; **thyngs** 666; **thyngys** 128; **thynkes** 2741
thinkeþ *v. impers.pr3sg. + dat. subj.* seems: **hem ~** it seems to them 1121; **þinkeþ: as hym ~ to do** as seems right for him to do 3943; **thynketh, thynkeþ** 2561, 263; **þought** *pa3sg.*: **hym ~** it seemed to him 3257; **hym ~** it seemed to them 5845
thys, this, þis *dem.adj.* this 193, 36, 115; **þes** 1186; **thes(e), þes(e)** *pl.* these 220, 216, 2647, 371; **theose, þeos(e)** 6036, 4132, 1281; **~ wyse** these ways 2951
tho see **þo**
þorow *adv.* completely 2502
thorowe *v.* throw 289
thorow(e), þorow(e) *prep.* through, throughout; by means of, because of 282, 471, 535, 855; **~ good red** in accordance with sound advice 3204; **~ godes sonde** by God's grace 7203; **thorowh, þorowh** 151, 208; **~ vertu** through the power 337; **thorw, þorw** 2496, 1099; **thour** 4116; **torow** 1851

Select Glossary (by Hoyt Greeson) 233

thow, þow *conj.* though, even if 163, 6566; **þowh** 6908; **þouȝ: for than ~** because 1824; **thouȝ** 4116

thouȝt, þouȝt *n.* thought, mind; will 1140, 1079; **setteth hys ~** focusses his attention on 1140; **out of ~** forgotten 3230; **no ~ to be** no exectation of being 5924; **in ... schal ben ... her ~** ...will be on their minds 6511; **in ~** in his mind, inwardly 7227; **haþ his ~** remembers 1718; **haue ... in our ~** be conscious of 1079; **had ... in his ~** was mindful of 5862; **thought, þought** 159, 1488; **in her ~** in their minds 4585; **in his ~ kenne may** can know in his mind 6331; **her ~ sette** focus their attention 6239; **thowth: ~ caste** direct his mind 187; **þoȝt(e)** 2867, 2182; **haue no ~** not to be reminded 1665; **falle in ~** come to mind 5935; **thoughtes** *pl.* 2689; **þouȝtis** 4761; **þowȝtes** 7115

thre, þre *num.* three 14, 1409; **suche ~** three times over, i.e., a triple share (of dread) 2364

thretynges *see* **þretyng**

thridde, þridde, thrydde, þrydde *adj.* third 2023, 1394, 302, 1391

thorowe, þorowe *n.* time, occasion: **in uche ~** at all times, always 1204; **a lytel ~** a little while 3917; **in any ~** at any time 6510

thu, þu *pron.2sg.* you, thou 366, 576; **thow, þow** 359, 2259

tide, tyde *n.* time, occasion; a while 4254, 324; **in schort ~** i.e as quick as a flash 4291; **in echa ~** at all times 5282

tydynges *n.pl.* news 3517

til, tyl *conj.* until 2207, 269; **tyll** 4931

tyl *prep.* to 6085

tyme, time *n.* time, occasion 269, 2790; **tyl a ~** for a time 269; **~ of deth** hour of death 226; **by ~** in time 1343; **what ~** when 1628; **take my ~** seize my opportunity 4830; **tymes** *pl.* seasons, times 12; **by ~ and wedres** by seasons and storms 1189

tine *n.* an instant 1630

tiraunte *n.* tyrant, despot 3653; **tyraunt: moste ~** greatest tyrant 3434; **tirauntes** *pl.* 1014; **tirauntys** 4625

tirauntrie, tirauntrye *n.* tyranny, despotism 3836, 3664

tisik *n.* phthisik, i.e., asthma or tuberculosis 594

to *adv.* too 898; **to** *adv.* too, excessive 5499; *prep.* to; for; **~ þe ioye of heuene** compared to the joy of heaven 7225

to brekeþ *v. tr. pr3sg.* shatters 1714

to breste(n) *v.intr.* shatter, burste 5936; *v.tr.* break apart 1518

to dryue *v.* pursued, driven about *ppl.* 5559

to gidre, to gydre *adv.* together; united 2767, 905; **to gidur, to gydur** 1427, 1544; **to gidres, to gydres** 1533, 1538; **to gadre** 4760

token(e) *n.* token, sign, symbol 3365, 4420; **~ of the croys** sign of the cross 4419; **tokne** 1203; **tokenes** *pl.* 307; translates Latin *indicia* in the preceding quotation 1105; **tokens** 1213; **toknes** 1724

tokenynge vbl.n. sign, portent 1111

tones *n.pl.* sounds, (musical) notes 6894

tong(e) *n.* tongue; word; power of speech 2199, 657; **telle wiþ ~** i.e., speak 5957; **tonges** *pl.* 1847

too *n.* toe 739; **toe** 1590; **toes** *pl.* 578

to race *v.* lacertate, mutilate 5537

to rende *v.* rip, mangle 5969

torment(e) *n.* torment, torture 3655, 2186; **tormentes** *pl.* 3624; **torments** 3707; **tormentys** 4528; **tormenties** 3540

tormente *v.* torment, torture 2578; **turmented** *ppl.* 6416

torne(n) *v.tr.* turn; convert; change 746, 3524; **~ to** convert to (his religion) 3535; **~ to hym** convert to himself 3622; **torneth, torneþ** *pr3sg.* 1059, 1062; **torne** *pr.subj. 3pl.* 3801; **torned** *ppl.* 772; **tornyd ~ into sacrement** transmuted i.e., transubstantiated into the Eucharist 2930; **turned** 5906; **turnyd** 563; **itorned** 3525; **iturned** 1465; **be more ~** be more transformed 1463; **torne(n)** *v.intr.* turn, return 367, 445; **~ away** return 445; **torneth** *pr3sg.* 647; **~ in to vayn** are brought about in vain 880; **torneþ** 1289; **~ aboute** revolve 6093; **her þouȝt ~** their mind changes 1339; **torneth** *pr3pl.* 647; **torneþ** 1191; **torned** *pa3sg.*: **~ to his myde** regained his senses 1888

tornyng(e) *vbl.n.* retreat; turning 1445, 2374; **aȝen ~** return 1445

to scatered *v.* dispersed, scattered *ppl.* 4206

to schake *v.* quake; shake apart, shake to pieces 5963

tothur *pron.* other 686; *adj.* 1140

towche *v.* involve; pertain to: **that thu ... never ~ me** in such a way that you ... never involve me 988; **towcheþ** *pr3sg.* 235; **~ þe grete day of drede** pertains to the great day of terror, i.e., Doomsday 3289

towe *adj.* tough; **wol ~** very severe 2179

toures *n.pl.* towers 4022; **tourys** 3594

toward *prep.* near; to, toward: **~ the** approaching, near you (NB translates the Latin *advena*, l. 1154) 1156

trace *n.* example; trace, track 5669; **traces** *pl.* 3623

traiterye *n.* treachery; rebellion 3648

travail(e) *n.* work, labour, effort; difficulty; suffering 468, 1231; **travayle** 638; **tryvaile: ~ and tere** suffering and tears 463

travayle *v.* work 465; **travalye** 850; **travaile** 1150; **do her ~** make an effort 4985; **travaylest** *pr2sg.*: **~ after** strive for 2815; **travayled** *ppl.* burdened; assailed 2773

tre(e) *n.* tree; wood 567, 573, 562; **the rode ~** the cross 1451; **nauȝt ymaked of ... ~** not made of wood 7006; **trees** *pl.* 551; **tres** 548

treccherye *n.* treachery, duplicity 1351; **trecherie, trecherye** 5753, 2884

trecherows *adj.* treacherous; traitorous 1344

trechours *n.pl.* traitors 3513

treden *v.* tread; stamp;: **~ hem undur her feet** destroy them 6700

tregettours *n.pl.* illusionists; sorcerers 3495

tremlynge *vbl.n.* trembling, quaking 5108

treson *n.* treason, betrayal; disloyalty, faithlessness 3400; **tresoun** 961

tresour *n.* wealth, treasure; vault, hoard 1050

trespas(e) *n.* offence, crime, transgression; sin 2521, 2544

tretys, tretis *n.* treatise, document 281, 7282; **tretes** 7252

trew age *n.* payment, tribute 3340

trew(e) *adj.* true; real; faithful 3340, 253

trewly *adv.* truly, honestly 2021

trewþ(e) *n.* truth; faith 3711; **þorow ~** by His righteousness 6566

tribulacioun, tribulacyoun *n.* suffering, affliction, tribulation; trouble; spiritual distress 2876, 1003; **tribulacion, tribulacyon** 2054, 2810; **trebulacyoun** 1053; **tribulacions** *pl.* 3627

tryfles *n.pl.* triffling matters, triffling tales 157

tryppyng *vbl.adj.* prancing, capering 1303

triste, tryste *n.* trust, faith 4662, 2265

troble *v.* trouble, disturb;: **~ þe see** stir up the sea 3595

trone *n.* throne 4172; **in his ~ sytt** sits enthroned 22

trowe *v.* believe, imagine 3103; **trowe** *pr1sg.* 7008; **trowest** *pr2sg.*: **þu ... ~ falsness** you suspect duplicity 2830

trust(e) *v.* trust, rely on 2008, 1205; **triste: to ȝow ~** have confidence in you 5192; **tryst** 1139; **trusteth, trusteþ** *pr3sg.* 894, 1132; **tresteþ: he ~ to** he relies on 2988; **trusteþ** *pr3pl.* 5275; **tresteþ: þey ~ to haue no** they despair of having any 5913

turettes *n.pl.* towers 7138; **turretes** 7142

turmented *see* **torment(e)**

twey *num.* two 802; **two** 319

twelf *num.* twelve 5062

twelþe *adj.* twelfth 4043

twyght *v.* plucked, snatched *ppl.* 1493

þat *rel.pron.* that, the one who 6704

þef(e) *n.* thief 4582, 4554

þefte, thefte *n.* theft 4582, 2708

þer, ther(e) *pleonastic* there 854, 802, 2265

þer about(e) *adv.* about, around it 6013, 823

þer aftirward *adv.* after that; afterwards 1385; **þeraftyrward** 1770

þer agayn *adv.* in contrast to that; opposed to this, in opposition to that 6222; **þeraȝen** 6665

þer aȝenst *adv.* in reply to that 5739

þer among *adv.* among them 6928

þer downe *adv.* down (to) 1261

þere *adv.* where, there 5351

þeron *adv.* on it 5467; **ther on** 894

þer oute, þeroute *adv.* outside, without 712, 2264

þerste *n.* thirst 2595; **þirst** 5589; **þurst(e)** 5564, 5195

þer tille *adv.* there, to it 7111

þer under *adv.* beneath it 6039

þerwith, þerwiþ, þer wiþ, þer with *adv.* wherby, by this 1218, 4198, 5977, 1305; **þerwyth** 1596; **þere wyth**, 272; **ther with** 2012; **ther wiþ** 2887; **ther wyth** 322

þer wiþin *adv.* within it, inside it 5677

þevys *n.pl.* thieves 4367; **theves** 1020

þewes *n.pl.* personal habits; morals 4644

þider, þyder *adv.* there, to that place 3058, 1549; **þeder** 6009; **þidur** 807; **thedur** 2271

þikke, þykke *adv.* in throngs; densely 2766; (mothes have bred) **wel ~** mothes have bred in multitudes 4668

þikke *adj.* thick, dense 5607

þiknesse *n.* thickness, density 5820

þynch, þynke, þynkyn, þenketh *see* **thenk(e)**

þyne *pron.* your 4560

þynge *n.* thing: **alle oþur ~** everything else 5341; **all maner ~** everything 4549; **þyng: what ~** whatever 6601

þynne *adj.* thin 451

þo, tho *adv.* then 66, 96
þo, tho *dem.pron.pl.* those 1820, 1335
þo, tho *dem.adj.pl.* those 3046, 791
þole *v.* suffer, endure 5522
þondur *n.* thunder 4515
þonke *v.* thank; ~ ... **of** thank for 6931; **thanke** 2878
þonkyng *vbl.n.* thanking; praise 6169
þorowe *n.* a space of time, occasion 6510; **in a lytyl ~** in a brief instant 1560
þorow out *adv.* throughout 5357
þorsday *n.* Thursday 6085
þouȝt *see* **thouȝt**
þousand *num.* thousand 3793; **by a ~ part** a thousandth as much 6103; **þousandes** *pl.* 6401
þral *n.* servant; slave 1632; **þralle: y mad ~** subjugated 3362; **be mad ~** be enslaved 6304
þraldom, thraldom *n.* servitude; slavery, bondage; imprisonment 6308, 940
þresten *v.* caste; thrust, push, cram 6701; **þryste** 4463
þretyng *vbl.n.* menace, threat 1573; **þretynges, thretynges** *pl.* 3817, 1851
þretty, þritty *num.* thirty 3853, 4197
þrist *see* **þerst**
þristy *adj.* thirsty 5155
þritteneþ *num.* thirteenth 4043; **þryteneþ** 5882
þrotes *n.pl.* throats 6949
þrowes *n.pl.* torments; **dethes ~** agonies of death 1734
þurste *v.* thirst 5195; **þristed** *pa.sg.* 5142
ucha, uche *see* **ech a, eche**
unassailed *v.* untested *ppl.* 2772
unbolde *adj.* timid 3963
unbuxome *adj.* disobedient, defiant 6707
unchangable *adj.* immutable 6462
unchastised, unchastiȝed *v.* undisiplined *ppl.* 4530, 4640
unclansed *v.* unabsolved *ppl.* 2552; **unclansyd** 2382
unclene *adj.* sinful; unclean 986
uncomely *adj.* unseemly; unattractive 1306
uncorteis *adj.* rude, discourteous; inconsiderate 1696
uncouþe *adj. adj.* unknown 4468
uncristned *v.* unbaptized *ppl.* 2235
undo *v.* remitted; revealed *ppl.* 3225
undur *prep.* under, beneath 2233; **~ holy cherche** i.e., Below, on earth, holy church (still fights) 6865; **under** 2260; **undyr** 654
undurȝete *v.* perceive, realize; understand 5372; **undurȝete** 277; **undurȝete** *ppl.* 3973
undurlynge *n.* an inferior, a subject 3407; **undurlynges** *pl.* 7091; **undyrlynges** 3202
undurstond(e) *v.* understand 4428, 1041; **us wel ~ recognize** 1725; **is ... forto ~** to be understood, to signify 6833; **understonde** 887; **undirstonde** 1925; **undyrstonde** 171; **that me schal ~** that I must believe 1406; **wel hym ~** recognize him 1374; **undurstonde** *pr1sg.* 6218; **understonde** 5749; **undyrstonde** 943; **undyrstonde** *pr.subj.3sg.* 171; **undurstondeth** *imper.pl.* 2671; **undurstonde** *ppl.* 3694; **undurstonded** 1765; **undurstonden** 3749; **undyrstonde** 1217
undurstondyng(e) *vbl.n.* awareness; knowledge; interpretation 7293, 1968; **haue in ~** keep in memory 3644; **Hadde he neuer so**

muche ~ No matter how much understanding he had 6138; **to ~ in meaning,** i.e., that hill means nothing else but ... 7114; **undyrstondyng(e)** 165, 127; **hadde on hem ~** how I interpreted them 7264; **gostly ~** spiritual awareness 6997; **have in ~** keep in memory 3644
undurtake *v.* agree; admit; declare 777; **undurtoke** *pa1sg.*: **as y ferst ~** as I first promised 7230
unkynde *adj.* without reverence 785
unkyndenesse *n.* enmity; ingratitude 2865; **schewe here ~** reveal their lack of regard (i.e., for others) 5210
unknowe *v.* concealed *ppl.* 6290
unknowyng(e) *vbl.n.* ignorance: **the ~ of hem self** lack of self-knowledge 207; **for defaulte of ~** through the fault of ignorance 240; **~ of þought** failure of thought, i.e., mental lapses 4815
unknowynge *adj.* ignorant, lacking knowledge, uninformed 128
unkonynge *vbl.n.* ignorance 145
unkonnyng *adj.* ignorant 151
unliche *adj.* unequal 1884
unmylde *adj.* fierce 1010
unneþe *adv.* with difficulty, scarcely 410; **unnethe(e)** 694, 750
unproprely *adv.* incorrectly 6404
unsemeliche *adj.* ugly, unattractive 4218; **unsemliche** 1945; **unsemely** 4230
unsikur *adj.* uncertain; unstable; **ful ~** very insecure, unsafe 896
unskylfull *adj.* irrational 142
unstable *adj.* mutable, changing 896; **~ ... to a mannes honde** uncontrollable by the hand of man 1201
unstablenesse *n.* transience, mutability; vacillation 776–777; **unstabulnesse** 301
unstedefaste *adj.* inconstant; mutable 278
unstedefastnes *n.* instability, vacillation 1239
unto *prep.* until 3282
untold(e) *v.* omitted; unconfessed; uncounted for *ppl.* 2005, 4736
untrewþe *n.* sin; infidelity, perfidy 5561
unwurþi *adj.* contemptible, unworthy 1872
up *adv.* up 568; **schulleþ ~** must ascend 3827; **~ stey** ascended, arose 4299
upright, upryght *adv.* up, erect(ly); steadfast; oriented toward 5424, 1077
up ryse *v.* stand up 2388
up so down *adv.* upside down 1356
upstyere *n.* rider 3458
uptake(n) *v.* taken up; received *ppl.* 6469, 4304
uryn *n.* urine 557
usage *n.* custom, practice 3119
useth *v.* he uses, practices, follows (i.e., a trend); wears *pr3sg.* 146; **useth, useþ** *pr3pl.* 1304, 1299; **usen** 5080; **þey ~ wyde** they wear wide (cut garments) 1299; **use** *pr.subj.3sg.* 2846; **(i)used** *ppl.* 3024; **dygyse ... now ~** outlandish fashions now displayed, worn 1285; **usyd: ~ by custome** engaged in by habit 2786
utter *adj.* outer 4911
uvel *n.* evil 4604. *see also* **evel(e)**
v *roman num.* five 6069
vayn *adj.* fruitless: **torneth in ~** are brought about in vain 880; **veyn(e)** 2975; **in ~** to no purpose, meaningless 2689

vale *n.* valley, vale 4314
valu *n.* value 7223
vanite, vanyte *n.* folly 980, 225; **vanytes** *pl.* vain things, frivolities, follies 289
varyacions *n.pl.* variations 1198
varyaunces *n.pl.* changes, variations 1217
veyne *n.* vein, blood vessel 1597
veyn glory *n.* vainglory, empty pride 965
venemous *adj.* venomous, poisonous 5683
vengaunce *n.* revenge; punishment; retribution 1324; **vengeaunce** 4077; **veniaunce** 3860
venial(l), venyal(l) *adj.* venial, forgiveable 2533, 2730, 2731, 2848; **veniel** 2127
venym *n.* venom, poison 3463
veray *adj.* true 2401; **God ~** true God 3605; **verey** 2457
verament *adv.* truly 3746
veryly *adv.* truly, profoundly 186
veritas theolgie *n. The Truth of Theology*, a theological handbook 3276
vermyn *n.* worm, vermin 553; **vermynes** *poss.sg.* 5750
vers *n.* verse, a line of poetry 423
versifiour *n.* a poet 757
vertu *n.* power; quality; virtue; **þorowe ~ of** by the power of 3149; **vertues** *pl.* 177
vertuous *adj.* powerful; virtuous 7125
vicarye *n.* vicar, a representative, e.g. Pope as vicar of Christ 3167
vice *n.* vice; defect; fault 1346; **vices** *pl.* 6176
victorye *n.* victory 855
vifte *adj.* fifth 306
vilanye, vylanye *n.* dishonour; churlishness; lust, sin, wickedness; injury, (physical) ruin 4353, 955; **don hem ~** bring them disgrace 6700; **velany(e): do the soule mych ~** bring great disgrace to the soul 2394
vyolent, violent *adj.* violent 717, 5587
violentnesse *n.* violence 6547
visite *v.* come to, visit; **hem to ~** come to (comfort) them 1577; **visiteþ** *pr3sg.* 1723; **visite** *pr.subj.3sg.* 1641; **visited(e)** *past.sg.* 2245, 5148; **visited** *pa.pl.* 5189
vois, voys *n.* voice, (vocal) sound 3822; **maketh his ~** speaks 736
vordryue *v.* driven about, beaten *ppl.* 5938
wa *interj.* waa, i.e., a baby's cry 414
wayteþ *v.* waits *pr3sg.*; **faste ~** waits eagerly 974
wake *v.* watch, keep watch *imper2sg.* 1629
wakyng *vbl.adj.* awake 692
walled *v.* molten *ppl.* 5839
walles *see* **wowe**
wan *see* **wynne**
wan *adj.* pale 461; faint
wanhope *n.* despair, i.e., insufficient faith in God's mercy 1850
wanteþ *v.* **him ~** he lacks *pr3sg. + dat.* 510; **wantede** *pa3sg.* was missing 4222; **me ~** I lacked 5184
wantyng *vbl.n.* lack, absence 5939
war *adj.* prudent 2133
warde *n.* rampart 7035; **wardes** *pl.* 7030
warme *adv.* warmly 5146
warne *v.* forewarn 3285; **warneth** *pr3sg.* 1607
was *v.* was *pa.sg.* 10; **iwas** *pa1sg.* 4357; **wasse** *pa3sg.* 380; **whas** 335; **wast** [MS Sic!] 67; **were(n)** *pa.pl.* 259; **were** *pa.subj.sg.* 161; **that as muche sorowe ~** that there be as much sorrow 2520

Select Glossary (by Hoyt Greeson)   235

waste *v.* destroy; consume (by fire) 4107; **wasty** 2499; **wasteþ** *pr3sg.* 2503; **wasted** *ppl.*: ~ **to nought** reduced to nothing 4088; **iwasted** 2541
watry *adj.* watery, full of moisture 6033
watur *n.* water 2744; **water** 2303; **wateres** *n.pl.* bodies of water 3998; **watres: make ~ renne** cause the waters to flow, run 3594
wawe *n.* wave; **many hard ~** many a cruel wave 999
wedlok *n.* wedlock; **in ~ bore** born in (lawful) wedlock, legitimate 6481
wedur *n.* weather 1214; **wedres** *pl.* storms 1189
weele *see* **wilyn**
wey(e) *n.* way, path, road, route; means 55; **by alle ~** by all means 730; **euene ~** level 5361; **by no maner ~** by no means 348; **way** 120; **be alle ~** in every way 2893; **good ~** the path of God 3104; **weyȝe** 1293; **eche ~** every way 1491; **weies, weyes** *pl.* 1165, 1166; **aftyr synnes ~** according to the ways of sin OR, reading **weies** as *weights*, according to the gravity of the sin 3165; **wayes** 3130
weiȝe *v.* weigh 2757
weik *adj.* weak 6261
weilaway *interj.* alas! 1379; **weylawey** 5785; **welaway** 1997
wel *adj.* blessed, fortunate, happy; appropriate 1223; **~ is hym** fortunate are they 1823; **semeþ it ~ as I seid er** it seems appropriate, as I said before 6406
wel(e) *adv.* well, fully 108, 7237; **ȝif þey lyved not ~** if they had not lived virtuously 4953; **well** 105; **weel** 2155; **wol** 162
welde *v.* rule, possess, be in possession of; preside over 4194; **weldeþ** *pr3sg.* 1876
wele *see* **willyn**
wele *n.* prosperity, joy, weal; eternal bliss 825
welkes *v.* droops, withers *pr3sg.* 614
welle *n.* well, spring 2303
wellynge *vbl.adj.* boiling, melting 6954
welth(e), welþe *n.* abundance, wealth 512, 1045, 1049; **welþis** *pl.*: **worldlyche ~** worldly riches 1115
wend(e) *v.* go, pass; depart, pass on, i.e., die; travel, wander; turn 5702, 197; **~ aboute** wander around 4038; **~ hem fro** depart from them 5702; **moste nedes ~** must of necessity pass on 6368; **away ~** leave 595; **~ away** depart 706; **wole þerto ~** will travel there 4134; **wendes** *pr3sg.* 1957; **wendeþ** *pr3pl.* 3061; **wende** *pr.subj.3sg.* 80
wendynge *vbl.n.* departure, journey 3499
wene *v.* suppose, expect 1148; **to him ~** expect for themselves 1779; **iwene, ywene** *pr1sg.* 2726, 2463; **hem ~** they suppose 580; **wene** *pr.subj.3sg.* 1005
wene *n.* speculation; **wiþ oute ~** undoubtedly 6077
wepe(n) *v.* weep, cry 409, 4255; **wepe** *pr3pl.* 5678
wepyng(e) *vbl.n.* weeping 430, 1222
wepne *n.* weapon 1434
werche *see* **wurche**
wereth *v.* wears *pr3pl.* 1298
wery *adj.* weary 7051
werye *v.* defend; **hem ~** protect themselves 2666
werynge *vbl.n.* fashion (of clothing): **foul ~** shameful style 1287

werk(e) *n.* work, deed; duty, service; building, construction 1966, 6881; **strong of ~** durable in its foundation 6823; **werkes** *pl.* 76; **werkys** 4834; **workes** 911; **wurkes** 989
werne *v.* hinder; refuse 6288; **wernede** *pa3sg.* 2444; **werned** *ppl.* 3703; **ywerned** 3526
wete *adj.* wet, damp 1212
wexe(n) *v.* grow, increase; become 690, 3591; **see schal ~so lowe ~** sea shall get so low 4003; **wexeth, wexeþ** *pr3sg.* **~ olde** grows old 644, 1077; **He ... wexeþ ~ al framward** becomes utterly stubborn 658; **wexeþ** *pr1pl.*; **the more ... we ~ upryght in welth** the more we incline toward wealth 1077; **wexeþ, wexeth** *pr3pl.*: **men ... ~ all froward** become very obstinant 261–262; **His eren ~ deve** his ears grow deaf 656
wham *see* **who**
what *pron.* what, whatever 222
whan(ne) *conj.* when 90, 1510; **~ þat** when 403; **when** 1493
whedur *adv.* where, whither 407; **~ he schal** where he is to go 7249
whel *n.* wheel 1061; **wheele** 1059
whennes *adverb.* whence 760; **whennys** 328
wher *adv., conj.*: **~ that** where 4369
wher by *adv.* by which 340
where ynne *adv.* in which 2550; **wherynne** 394
where so *adv.* wherever 1957
where that *adv.* where; when 305
where so *adv.* wherever 1425
where with, where wyþ *adv.* with which 1942, 452; **wherwiþ** 3165; **wher wyth** 924
wherfor(e) *adv.* wherefore, therefore; for which reason; what? 2716, 44; **wherefore** 4617
wher of, wherof *adv.* of which 820, 3265; **where of** 3550
wheron *adv.* on which 1024; **where on** 870
wher to *adv.* why; to which 937; **wherto** 3188
where þorow *adv.* by way of which 4984
whette *v.* sharpen 4264
whethur, wheþur *conj.* whether 413, 2000; **~ that** whether 541; **whethir** 73; **wheþer** 680; **whedur** 7249
whi, why *inter.adv.* why 303, 1375; **~ that** why 1836; **for ~** for what reason 598; **þe cause ~** the reason why 2869
which *adj.* which 120; **the ~** which 2545; **þe wyche** 6349
which(e) *rel.pron.* which; who 282, 172; **the ~, þe ~** which 190, 1880; **of þe ~** from which 1961; **whyche** 572; **þe whuche** 4106; **þe wich** 5623; **þe wyche** 36
whiȝt *n.* creature, man; **none kynnes ~** any sort of person 1561; **wightes** *pl.* 4624
while *n.* while, a period of time 1047; **wyle** 541; **the ~ the time** 697; **alytyl ~** a brief time 3319
while *conj.* while 756; **~ þat** while 1070
whiles *conj.* while 754; **~ that** as long as 1682
whyne *v.* whine, whimper 6275
whit(e) *adj.* white 4332, 491
whiþ *prep.* with 2101; **with, wyth** 204, 3; **wiþ** 356
who *pron.* who, whoever 313; **ho** 4266; **whos(e)** *gen.sg.* 1883, 5830; **whom** *obj.* 3105; **wham** 563
whodur *adv.* whither, where 2081; **~ that þey**

wol þynke wherever they want to imagine 6234; **whydur** 2353; **whidur** 6295; **whedur, wheþur** 407, 4500; **wedur** 1746; **wodur** 1840
who so, whoso *indef.pron.* whoever; anyone 280, 915; **wo so, ho so** 2132, 492; **wo so wole** whoever wants to 4134
whot *see* **wite**
wyde, wide *adj.* wide 1299, 4438; **set so ~** created so vast, i.e., spacious, large 1007
wyf, wif *n.* (mature) woman; wife 1534, 4181; **wyves** *pl.* **~ to hem wedde** get married to women (that please them) 3875
wikked, wykked *adj.* wicked, evil, harmful 3463, 1020; **wikkyd** 3602; **wiked(e)** 5504, 4625
wikkednesse, wykkednesse *n.* evil, iniquity, wickedness 3759, 3016; **wikydnesse, wykydnesse** 2829, 3474
wyl *see* **while,** *n.*
wylde *adj.* wild; fierce 1009
wyldernesse, wildernesse *n.* wilderness, desert; (a state of) desolation 2588, 1006; **wyldurnesse** 1008
wyles *n.pl.* cunning 1133
wylle *n.* will (in scholastic terms, the rational appetite for the good); desire 42; **wyl, wil** 247, 2182; **ȝaf hym wytt at ~** empowered them with reason 71; **will(e): to don her ~** (from) doing what they desire 6288, 1966; **haveþ in ~** have a desire for 6605; **at her owne ~** freely 3171; **wyth ȝour will** intentionally 1362; **aftur his own ~** according to his own pleasure 1690; **after his ~** according to his, i.e., Christ's, will 5126; **whidur þat it is her wille** wherever they want 6295; **after her ~** as they wish 6643; **nought al our ~** not all that we desired 6947; **at his owne ~** at his disposal 1099; **with a good ~** with good intention 2221; **willyn** *v.* will, intend; wish, want 5556; **wilyn** 5971; **wille** 6551; **iwol(e)** *pr1sg.* 1983, 1935; **iwul** 3333; **wul** 3334; **wylt** *pr2sg.* 533; **wilt** 2797; **wol(e)** *pr3sg.* 173, 915; **woll(e)** 6299, 4381; **wolt** 2792; **wil, wyl** 2887, 139; **will** 2399; **weele** 1884; **wele** 281; **willeþ** 7157; **wolleþ** *pr.pl.* 967; **wollen** 2002; **woll** 242; **wele** 281; **willeþ** 3683; **wulleþ** 3805; **wole** *pr.subj.sg.* 915; **wold(e)** *pa1–3sg.* 1148, 73; **woldest** *pa2sg.* 4267; **wolt** 4795; **wold(e)** *pa.pl.* 7275, 1294; **wolden** 2569
wyn *n.* wine 555
wynd(e) *n.* wind 356, 2598; **wyndes** *poss.sg.* 580
wyndyng *vbl.adj.* winding; **~ clothe** cerement, burial wrapping 707
wynke *v.* close, shut (i.e., eye), wink, blink 4185; **a man may ~** (the time) it takes a man to blink (an eye) 6233
wynkyng(e) *vbl.n.* blinking, winking; **eiȝes ~** blink of an eye 4190; **in as lyty awhile as ~ of an ye** i.e., quick as the blink of an eye 6246
wynne *v.* gain, win; redeem; suffer, incurr 123; **no thing to ~** not at all to gain 5110; **~ hem self oute** make their way out 3729; **mowen nat owt ~** might not escape 3731; **to hem ~** gain for themselves 856; **hem self ~** bring themselves 2557; **fram the peine hem ~** rescue themselves from the punishment 2580; **wynneþ** *pr3pl.* 1228;

wan *pa3sg.* 6448; **to hym ~** gained for them (i.e., mankind) 97; **god ... ~** God redeemed 6738 **wynne** *pr.subj.3sg.* 3210; **wan** *ppl.* **of ... ~** be won over from (Christianity) 3451; **wonne: blysse haþ ~** (eternal) joy have gained 6806; **iwonne: persecucioun schall ... be ~** persecution will be ... suffered 3424; **sche be down aȝen** she ~ has set again (i.e., the sun, Latin *sol*, fem.) 4018; **no speche ... schal be ~** no words will be uttered 4040; **ywonne: beþ to hevene ~** have reached heaven 6343; **y wonne: beþ þerto ~** succeed in reaching it 840
wynt(ur) *n.* winter 6153; **wyntres** *poss.sg.* 5508
wis(e), wys(e) *adj.* wise, prudent 7014, 4645, 21, 441; **~ slie** wisely ingenious 6028; **no thyng ~** not at all wise 894; **wysur** *compar.* 181
wysdom(e), wisdom *n.* wisdom, prudence 1127, 2132, 4769; **wysdam** 120
wise, wyse *n.* manner, way 4027, 105; **in any manere ~** no matter what (the illness) 675; **every veyne ... in his ~** every vein ... in its way 1597; **in no ~** in any way 1796; **whan god sendiþ ... anguish in any ~** when God sends grief in any form 2861; **a maner ~** in such a way 3820; **thus ~** in this manner 6497; **wise, wyse** *pl.* 4090, 2951; **alle ~** (by) all ways 4324; **in many ~** in many ways 3540; **in dyverse maner ~** in diverse ways 4027
wysliche *adv.* plainly, clearly 1935
wisse *v.* guide, direct 5093; **wisse** *subj.pr.3sg.* 6995
wysur *see* **wis(e)**
wit *see* **witt(e)**
wite, wyte *v.* know, understand 3909, 1488; **iwite** 3972; **iwete** 5371; **y wyte: conneth some men ... ~** some men can tell ... 680; **wot(e)** *pr1–3sg.* 1840, 2350; **whot** 2032; **wost** *pr2sg.* 2147; **wite** *pr.pl.* 1746; **wyteþ** 1307; **wote: ~ nere** never know 2164; **wyte** *pr.subj.sg.* 2817; **wite** *pr.subj.pl.* 4477; **wite** *imper.* 4790; **wist(e)** *pa1–3sg.* 2084, 2266; **iwist: ~ hem there** I knew them (to be) there 2276; **wuste** 1513; **wyst** 2085; **iwist** *ppl.* 3614
wyþ, wiþ *prep.* with 1054, 356; **with, wyth** 204, 3; **whiþ** 2101
with alle, wyth alle *adv.* altogether; moreover, also 638, 684; **fayre ~** courteously indeed 2448; **wiþal** 6953; **wiþ alle** 4073
wiþ hold *v.* withheld *ppl.* 4676
with ynne *adv.* within, inside 1612; **wiþ ynne,** 3095; **whith yn** 492; **wyth ynne** 124
without, with out *prep.* without; (from) the outside 2377, 7217; **withoute, with oute** 2287, 2054; **withouten, with outen** 18, 800; **with owte(n)** 2596, 1420; **wiþ out(e)** 6147, 2665; **wiþ outen** 2034; **~ hem. of þat blysful companye...** excepting them of that blessed company of angels ... 6739–40; **wiþ owte** 2721; **wyth oute(n)** 30, 198; **wyþ outen** 1341
with oute, wyth oute *adv.* out, outside, on the outside 1264, 502; **wiþ oute, wyþ oute** 4116, 1595; **wiþ outen: withoute** 4085
wiþstonde *v.* oppose 6240
wiþstondynge *vbl.n.* resistance, opposition 6269

wytyngly *adv.* willfully; knowingly 4800
witles *adj.* irrational, without understanding 7290
witnesse *n.* testimony 2707; **wytnesse** 209; **~ bereþ** corroborates, testifies 2319; **fals ~ berynge** giving false testimony 2707; **to ~ ... be brought** be called on as a witness 4670
witnesseþ *v.* testifies *pr3sg.* 1101; **~ it** testify to it 1895; **wetnessyt** 386; **wytnesseth, wytnesseþ** 46, 718; **witnesseþ** *pr.pl.* 1895
witnessynge *vbl.n.* testimony: **bereþ ~ give** 6859
witt(e), wytt *n.* mind; understanding; reason; intellect, intelligence; wisdom; learning; memory 4281, 1917; **wytt: the ~ of ȝowthe** the disposition, spirit, of youth 213; **in my ~ to my knowledge** 7018; **wit(e)** 168, 6910; **~ couþe** had any understanding 4780; **kyndly ~** natural mind 1657; **wyt(t)** 3, 71; **~ and wille** intelligence and desire 2791; **no ~ ne conne** have lost their minds 4039; **out of ~** out of their minds 1917; **full of ~** full of wisdom, understanding 5119; **wittes, wyttes** *pl.* intelligence; senses 1998, 104; **wittys** 4617; **her v. ~** their five senses 6741
witty, wytty *adj.* prudent, wise 5265, 740
wyturly *adv.* plainly 534
wlatsom(e) *adj.* disgusting, repulsive 449, 1947; **wlatsum** 395
wlatsomnesse *n.* repulsiveness 543
wo(e) *n.* woe, misery, affliction, adversity, sorrow 1005, 1063; **wow** 2614; **wele and ~** good times and bad 825; **wele into ~** fortune to misfortune 1062; **beþ hem ~** they are distressed, grieved 1223; **~ schal hem be** they will be woeful 1360; **hem schal be ful ~** they will be very woeful 1364
wode *n.* wood 2531
wode *adj.* mad, deranged; wild 1358; **wood** 82; **~ men** mad men 4039
wombe *n.* womb; stomach 384
womman *n.* woman 413; **woman** 500; **wommanes** *poss.sg.*: **of ~ kynde** of the female gender 418; **wommen** *pl.* 4863; **wemmen** 489
wondur *n.* wonder, marvel; amazement, surprize 1860; **more ~** greater marvel 5262; **haveth ~** are amazed 2285; **wonder** 748; **wondur: thenk ~** think ... remarkable 1517; **is it no ~** it is no surprise 1860; **wondres** *pl.* miracles (of God and Christ); marvels (of Antichrist etc); marvels (of nature) 3300; **~ þorow hym schulleþ ben iwrought** marvels will be performed by him 3447
wondur *adv.* very, extremely; wonderfully, marvelously 6071
wondurful(l) *adj.* marvelous, miraculous 2493, 4010
wondurly *adv.* marvelously 6062
wone *v.* dwell, live 3502; **wonye** 6841; **woneþ** *pr1pl.* 6810; **wonyeth** 863; **wonynge** *pr.ppl.* 849
wone *n.* habit, custom 5776; **aȝenst his ~** contrary to his custom 3954
wone *num.* one; **by ~** in one 16
wonyng(e) *vbl.n.* dwelling; existence 830, 5631; **~ þere is ... ille** existence there is ... miserable 5631; **wonyeng** 6159; **wonyenges** *pl.* 6025; **~ stedes** *adj.* dwelling places 7154
wonne *see* **wynne**

wood *see* **wode**
woodnesse *n.* madness 5699
woord *n.* word 4752; **word(e)** 1818, 2182; **wordes** *pl.* 249; **wordis, wordys** 2058, 4062; **wurdes** 274
world *n.* the universe, cosmos 64; the physical world, the earth 189; **more ~** the greater world, i.e., the macrocosm 866; **the lasse ~** the microcosm, i.e., the human body 867; **to the ~** with regard to the world, i.e., in the world's eye 1338
worldlyche *adj.* secular, worldly; temporal; earthly, on earth 888; **worldly** 783; **~ wele** worldly prosperity, i.e., in this world 1103
worm *n.* snake; worm; **the ~ of conscience** the pang of conscience, remorse 5783; **wormes** *pl.* 725 **wormes** *poss.pl.* 487
wowe *n.* wall 5466; **walles** *pl.* 498
wraþþe *n.* wrath, anger 1068; **drede to ~ hym** concern about angering Him 7237; **wraþe** 659; **wratthe** 2393
wrecchednesse *n.* misery; wrongdoing, sinfulness 456; **wrecchidnesse** 235; **wrechidnes** 963; **wrecchidnessys** *pl.* 378
wrecchid *adj.* miserable; sinful 525
wreche *n.* vengeance, retribution, destruction; anger 1314; **so ful of ~** so full of destruction 5588
wrechefull *adj.* vengeful 4274
wrenche *v.* turn, divert 1387
wrenches *n.pl.* tricks, wiles 1133
wryckyng *vbl.adj.* twisting, flitting 1302
wrynge *v.* wring hands 6911
writ, wryt *n.* writing, book; **holy ~** the Bible 1896, 736; **writt(e)** 4562, 6130; **wrytt(e)** 5593, 5398
wryte *v.* write; take note of; record 1642; **(i)wryte, (i)write** *ppl.* 3992, 174, 2007, 4054; **seieþ as þey fyndeþ ~** say what they've found written 5381; **y write, y wryte** 2322, 1408; **ywryte** 774; **ywrete** 727; **(i)wryten, (i)writen** 5173, 4157, 5502, 2741; **wryton** 1105
wrytyng(e) *vbl.n.* text, document, (written) work, writing 210, 1572; **writynge** 3884
wrong *n.* a wrong, injury; injustice; sin 1964; **with ~** wrongfully, sinfully 2024; **wronges** *pl.* injustices 4634
wrongfully *adv.* wrongfully, sinfully 3190
wroþ(e) *adj.* angry, irate 4503, 2825; **wroth; lyghtly ~** easily angered 658
wrought *see* **wurche**
wulward *adj.* in hairshirt, i.e., dressed with wool next to the skin as a form of penance 2857
wurce *comp.adj.* worse 56; **worst** 3725
wurche *v.* work, fashion; build, construct; bring about, create, compose; celebrate (the Eucharist); perform (i.e., wonders, penance), do; commit; suffer (anguish) 1768; **openly ~ Wikkednesse aȝenst** openly stir up evil 3758–59; **on four maners schal ~** shall operate in four ways 4100; **werche** 2897; **wirche** 2661; **her crist ... wondres schal ~** their christ, i.e., Antichrist, shall work marvels (n.b. not miracles) 3740; **worche(n)** 5690; **~ in** engage in 6973; **wurcheþ** *pr3sg.* 2490; **muchel ~** accomplishes much 3431; **werches** 3012; **wurcheþ** *pr3pl.* 3429; **wrought** *pa.1–3sg.* 1965; **wroȝt(e)** 1981, 6619; **wrouȝtest** *pa.2sg.*

Select Glossary (by Hoyt Greeson)

synful man thu ~ us sinful man, you committed us, i.e., Sins accusing the sinner of commiting sins 4559; **wroughten** *pa.pl.*: **That haveþ ... ~ no thing ...** who have ... done nothing 4460; **wrouȝte** 1798; **wroȝt(e)** 1981; 2181; **wrought** 1965; **(i)wrought, ywrought** *ppl.* 2013, 10, 3712; **(i)wrouȝt, y wrouȝt** 1666, 4983, 1412; **(i)wroȝt, y wroȝt** 2040, 2028, 886; **iwroght** 2289; **after thei han ~** according to their deeds 5040
wurchyng *vbl.n.* operation, action 4131

wurschipe *v.* worship, honour 781
wurschipe *n.* worship, honour, renown 513; **wurschepe** 4891; **worschipe** 6654; **wurschipes** *pl.* 6958
wurthi *adj.* worthy, deserving 67; **wurþi, wurþy** 2041, 2841; **more is ~ þan** is worth more than 3260 **worþi** 6121
wurþily *adv.* deservedly; fittingly 4468; **wurþiliche: purchased ~** bought at just value 3135
wurþinesse *n.* worthiness; **itold of ~** tested for (spiritual) worth 3084; **wurþynesse** 3150

Y *pron.1sg.* *see* also **I**
ydel *see* **idel**
ye, yen *see* **eyȝe**
yere *see* **ȝere**
yinne, ynne, yn *see* **inne**
yoore *adv.* long ago, of old 7063
yordeyned *see* **ordeyne**
ys *see* **be**
yȝe, yȝen *see* **eyȝe**

Select Bibliography: Content of HM 128

Abbreviations used in the bibliography

DAI: Dissertation Abstracts International
MLN: Modern Language Notes
MLR: Modern Language Review
N and Q: Notes and Queries
NM: Neuphilologische Mitteilungen
PMLA: Publications of the Modern Language Association
SEL: Studies in English Literature
SN: Studia Neophilologica

Alford, John. "Richard Rolle and Related Works." *Middle English Prose: A Guide to Major Authors and Genres*. ed. A.S.G. Edwards. New Brunswick: Rutgers University Press, 1984, 35–60.

Allen, Hope Emily. "The Authorship of the Pricke of Conscience." Radcliffe Monograph 15. Boston: Ginn and Co., 1910, pp. 115–70.

_____. "The Speculum Vitae: Addendum." *PMLA* 32 (1917), 133–62.

_____. "Two Middle English Translations from the Anglo-Norman." *MP* 13 (1916), 744–45.

_____. *Writings Ascribed to Richard Rolle Hermit of Hampole and Materials for His Biography*. New York: D. C. Heath and Co., 1927.

Andreae, Percy. *Die Handschriften des Pricke of Conscience von Richard Rolle de Hampole in Britischen Museum*. Berlin: G. Bernstein, 1888.

Aston, Margaret. "Lollardy and Literacy." *History* 62 (1977), 347–71, esp. pp. 362, 362 n71, 364–65, 364 n83.

Barr, Helen. *Signes and Sothe: Language in the Piers Plowman Tradition*. Cambridge: D.S. Brewer, 1994, quoting Marie-Louise Uhart, Ph.D. Dissertation, University of Leicester, 84.

Baugh, Nita Scudder. *A Worcestershire Miscellany*. Compiled by John Northwood, c. 1400. Edited from British Museum M.S. Add. 37,787. Philadelphia: privately printed, 1956.

Benskin, Michael, and Margaret Laing. "Translations and Mischsprachen in Middle English Manuscripts," in *So Meny People Longages and Tonges: Philological Essays on Scots and Mediaeval English Presented to Angus McIntosh*, ed. Michael Benskin and M. L. Samuels. Edinburgh: Benskin and Samuels, 1981, 55–106.

Biblia Sacra Juxta Vulgatam Clementinam. Rome: Typis Societatis S. Johannis Evangelistis. Desclee et Scoii, Edit. Pont, 1947.

Booke of the Pylgremage of the Sowle—from Guillaume de Guileville's French text, perhaps translated by Lydgate and printed by Caxton in 1483. Katherine Isabella Cust, ed. London: Basil Montague Pickering, 1859.

Britton, Derek. "The Sources of Lines 3562–3939 of the Prick of Conscience." *Anglia* 109 (1991): 87–93.

_____. "Unnoticed Fragments of the Prick of Conscience." *NM* 79 (1980), 327–34.

Bulbring, Karl D. "On Twenty-five Manuscripts of Richard Rolle's 'Pricke of Conscience,' Dublin, the Corser Manuscript, and Two in Lichfield Cathedral Library." *Transactions of the Philological Society, 1888–90* (1891), 261–83.

_____. "Zu Den Handschriften von Richard Rolle's Pricke of Conscience." *Englische Studien* 23 (1897), 1–30.

Burrow, J.A. *Medieval Writers and Their Works: Middle English Literature and Its Background 1100–1500*. Oxford: Oxford University Press, 1982.

Campbell, Killis. "A Neglected Manuscript of the Pricke of Conscience." *MLN* 20 (1905), 210–11.

Cappelli, A. *Dizionario di Abbreviature latine ed italiane*. Rozzano/Milano: Ulrico Hoepli, Editore, 1990, 1994.

Chickering, Howell. "Rhetorical Stimulus in the *Pricke of Conscience*" in *Medieval Paradigms: Essays in Honor of Jeremy Duquesnay Adams* Vol. I, ed. Stephanie Hayes-Healey. New York: Palgrave-Macmillan, 2005, 191–230.

Dareau, Margaret Grace, and Angus McIntosh. "A Dialect Word in Some West Midland Manuscripts of the Prick of Conscience," in *Edinburgh Studies in English and Scots*, A.J. Aiken, A. McIntosh, and H. Palsson, eds. London: Longmans, 1971, 20–26.

D'Evelyn, Charlotte. "An East Midland Recension of The Pricke of Conscience." *PMLA* 45 (1930), 180–200.

DiRicci, Seymour. *A Handlist of a Collection of Books and Manuscripts Belonging to Lord Amhurst of Hackey*. Cambridge: Cambridge University Press, 1906.

_____. *A Handlist of Manuscripts in The Library of the Earl of Leicester at Holkam Hall. Bibliographio Society*. Oxford: Oxford University Press, 1932.

DiRicci, Seymour, with the assistance of W.H. Wilson. *Census of Medieval and Renaissance Manuscripts in the U.S. and Canada*. New York: N.p., 1935–37; index 1944.

Doyle, A.I. "The Shaping of the Vernon and Simeon Manuscripts," in *Chaucer and Middle English Studies in Honor of Rossell Hope Robbins,* ed. Beryl Rowland. Kent, OH: The Kent State University Press, 1974, 328–41.

_____. "A Survey of the Origins and Circulation of Theological Writings in English in the 14th, 15th, and Early 16th Centuries with Special Consideration of the Part of the Clergy Therein" (2 vols.) (unpublished Ph.D. thesis, Cambridge University, 1953).

Dutschke, Consuelo, and Richard Rouse. *Medieval and Renaissance Manuscripts in the Claremont Libraries*. Berkeley: University of California Press, 1987.

Fowler, J.T. "The Fifteen Last Days of the World in Medieval Art and Literature." *The Yorkshire Archaeological Journal* 23 (1915), Plate II.

Gee, E.A. "The Painted Glass of All Saints' Church, North Street, York." *Archaeologie* 102 (1969), 151–202, esp 158–61.

Gillespie, Vincent. "Vernacular Books of Religion." *Book Production in England: 1375–1475*. Cambridge: Cambridge University Press, 1989, 317–44.

Grigsby, Bryon Lee. *Pestilence in Medieval and Early Modern English Literature*. Volume 23, Medieval History and Culture. New York: Routledge, 2004, ch. 3.

Hahn, Arnold. "Quellenuntersuchungen zu Richard Rolles englischen Schriften." Dissertation, Halle a/S., 1900, pp. 16–40.

Hanna, Ralph, and Sarah Wood. *Richard Morris's Prick of Conscience: A Corrected and Amplified Reading Text*. Early English Text

Societ, o.s. 342. Oxford: Oxford University Press, 2013.

Haselton, R.B., and H.C. Schultz. "Note on the Inscription in *H.M. 128*." *Huntington Library Bulletin* 8 (1935), 26–27.

Heist, William. *The Fifteen Signs Before Doomsday*. East Lansing: Michigan State College Press, 1952, pp. 131–22.

Holy Bible, Translated from the Latin Vulgate. New York: P.J. Kennedy & Sons, 1914.

Humphreys, K.W., and J. Lightbown. "Two Manuscripts of the Pricke of Conscience in the Brotherton Collection, University of Leeds." *Leeds Studies in English and Kindred Languages* 7–8 (1952), 29–38.

Innes-Parker, Catherine Ann. "Virgin, Bride and Lover: A Study of the Relationship between Sexuality and Spirituality in Anchoritic Literature." *DAI* 54 (1994): 3420A.

Jacobus de Benevento. *De Praeambulis ad judicium*. On-line corpus: *Thomisticum*.

Kohler, Reinhold. "Quellennachweise zu Richard Rolle's von Hampole Gedicht 'The Pricke of Conscience.'" *Jahrbuch fur romanische und englische Literatur* 6 (1865), 196–212.

Langfors, Arthur. "A Propos des explicit des manuscrits de la bibliotheque de Bruges." *NM* 37 (1936): 1–15.

Lewis, Robert E., ed. *De miseria condicionis humane/Lotario Dei Segni (Pope Innocent III)*. Athens: University of Georgia Press, 1978.

_____. "Editorial Technique in the *Index of Middle English Prose*," in *Middle English Prose: Essays on Bibliographical Problems*, ed. A.S.G. Edwards and Derek Pearsall. New York: Garland Publishing, 1981, 43–64.

_____. "Medieval Popularity: Modern Neglect: The Case of the *Pricke of Conscience*." *Fourteenth-Century English Mystics Newsletter* 2 (1976): 3–8.

_____. "The Relationship of the Vernon and Simeon Texts of the *Pricke of Conscience*." *So Many People, Longages and Tonges: Philological Essays in Scots and Mediaeval English Presented to Angus McIntosh*, ed. Michael Benskin and M. L. Samuels. Aberdeen: Aberdeen University Press/Mercat Press, 1986, 251–64.

Mabillon, "Operum Tomus Aliena et Supposititia" in "*Meditationes piissimae de cognitione humane conditionis*." *Patriologia Latina* 184 col.485A–508B.

McIntosh, Angus. "Scribal Profiles from Middle English Texts." *NM* 76 (1975), 231.

_____. "Two Unnoticed Interpolations in four Manuscripts of the *Prick of Conscience*." *NM* 77 (1976), 63–78.

McIntosh, Angus, and Robert E. Lewis. *A Descriptive Guide to the Manuscripts of the Prick of Conscience*. Medium Aevum Monographs. Society for the Study of Mediaeval Languages and Literature: Oxford, 1982.

Moorman, Charles. *How to Edit a Medieval Manuscript*. Jackson: University of Mississippi Press, 1975.

Morey, James H., ed. *The Prik of Conscience*. TEAMS: Middle English Texts Series. Kalamazoo: Medieval Institute Publications, Western Michigan University, 2012.

_____. *Book and Verse A Guide to Middle English Biblical Literature*. Urbana: University of Illinois Press, 2000.

Morris, Richard, ed. *The Prick of Conscience (Stimulus Conscientiae): A Northumbrian Poem by Richard Rolle de Hampole*. Berlin: A. Asher and Co., 1863; rpt. New York: AMS Press, 1973.

Peterson, Kate O. "The Sources of the Parson's Tale." Radcliffe College Monographs No. 12. Boston: Ginn and Co., 1901, esp. 212–14, 30.

Presson, Robert K. "Two Types of Dreams in the Elizabethan Drama, and Their Heritage: Somnium Animale and the Pricke of Conscience." *SEL* 7 (1967), 239–256.

Preston, Jean. "The Pricke of Conscience (Parts I–III) and its First Appearance in Print." *Library: Transactions of the Bibliographic Society* s6-VII (1985), 303–314.

R.M. "Hampole's Works." *Notes and Queries*, 3rd Series 2 (1962), 386a.

Ripelin, Hugh (of Strassborg). *Compendium theologiae veritatis*. In Albertus Magnus, *Opera omnia*, SCA Borgnet, ed. Paris. *Vives* 34 (1899), 1–261.

Riehle, Wolfgang. "The Authorship of the *Prick of Conscience* Reconsidered." *Anglia* 111 (1993), 1–18.

Ripelin, Hugh (of Strassborg). *Compendium theologiae veritatis*. In Albertus Magnus, *Opera omnia*, SCA Borgnet, ed. Paris. *Vives* 34 (1899), 1–261.

Robinson, Christine M. "A Machine-Readable Edition of the Text of the Speculum Vitae as Attested in BL MS Additional 33995 and Investigation of Claims for the Common Authorship of the 'Speculum Vitae' and 'The Prick of Conscience.'" *DAI* 49 (1989): 2206A.

Russell, G.H. "Some Early Responses to the C Version of *Piers Plowman*." *Viator* 15 (1984), 6–91; here 9.

Sajavaara, Kari. "The Relationship of the Vernon and Simeon Manuscripts." *NM* 68 (1967), 428–40.

Scase, Wendy. *The Making of the Vernon Manuscripts*. Turnhauts: Brepohls, 2013.

Schultz, H.C. "A Middle English Manuscript Used as Printer's Copy." *The Huntington Library Quarterly* 29 (1966), 325–36.

_____. "Manuscript Printer's Copy for a Lost Early English Book." *The Library*, 4th Series 22 (1942), 138–44.

Serjeantson, Mary S. "The Index of the Vernon Manuscript." *MLR* 32 (1937), 222–61.

Taavitsainen, Irma. "The Index of Middle English Prose, Handlist X: Manuscripts in Scandinavian Collections—Shorter Notices—Middle English." *Medium Aevum* 64.1 (1995), 178.

Ullman, J. "Studien zu Richard Rolle de Hampole I." *Englische Studien* 7(1884), 415–72, esp. 419–22, 468–70.

Waters, S.A. "A History of Pricke of Conscience Studies." *SN* 54 (1983), 147–51.

_____, ed. "The Pricke of Conscience: The Southern Recension, Book V." Unpublished Ph.D. thesis, University of Edinburgh, 1976.

Wenzel, Siegfried. *Fasciculus Morum: A Fourteenth-Century Preacher's Handbook*. University Park: The Pennsylvania State University Press, 19.

Wilson, Edward. "Langland's 'Book of Conscience': Two Middle English Analogues and Another Possible Latin Source." *N & Q* 228 (1983), 387–89.

Wilson, R.M. *The Lost Literature of Medieval England*, 2nd ed. London: Methuen & Co., 1970, 147.

Wogan-Browne, Jocelyn, Nicholas Watson, and Ruth Evans, eds. *The Idea of the Vernacular: An Anthology of Middle English Literary Theory*. University Park: Pennsylvania State University Press, 1999, pp. 240–44.

Woodforde, Christopher. *English Stained and Painted Glass*. Oxford: Clarendon Press, 1954, plate 34.

Yates, Joseph Brooks. "An Account of an Unprinted English Poem, Written in the Early Part of the Fourteenth Century, by Richard de Hampole, and Entitled 'Stimulus Conscience.'" *Archaeologia* 19 (1821), 314–35.

Select Bibliography: Dialect, Sources, and Definitions

by Hoyt Greeson

Bennett, J. A.W., and G.V. Smithers. *Early Middle English Verse and Prose,* 2nd ed. Oxford: Clarendon Press, 1968.

Benskin, Michael. "The 'fit'–Technique Explained." *Regionalism in Late Medieval Manuscripts and Texts,* ed. Felicity Riddy. Cambridge: D.S. Brewer, 1991, 9–26.

———."Descriptions of Dialect and Areal Distributions." *Speaking in Our Tongues: Proceedings of a Colloquium on Medieval Dialectology and Related Disciplines*, eds. Margaret Laind & Keith Williamson. Rochester, NY: University of Rochester Press, 1994, 169–187.

Benskin, Michael, and M.L. Samuels. *So many people longages and tonges.* Edinburgh: Middle English Dialect Project, 1981.

Blake, Norman. *The Cambridge History of the English Language*: *Volume II, 1066–1476.* Cambridge: Cambridge University Press, 1992.

Burchfield, Robert, Ed. *The Compact Edition of the Oxford English Dictionary,* 2 vols. Oxford: Oxford University Press, 1971.

Cappelli, Adriano. *Dizionario di abbreviature Latine et Italiane.* Sesta edizione. Milano: Editore Ulrico Hoepli, 1961.

Davis, Norman. *A Chaucer Glossary.* Oxford: Clarendon Press, 1979.

Denholm-Young, N. *Handwriting in England and Wales.* Cardiff: University of Wales Press, 1964.

Hector, L. C. *The Handwriting of English Documents,* 2nd ed. London: Edward Arnold (Publishers), Ltd., 1966.

Kristensson, Gillis. *A Survey of Middle English Dialects 1290–1350*: *The Six Northern Counties and Lincolnshire.* Lund Studies in English 35. Lund: C.W.K. Gleerup, 1967.

———. "OE ēo in the West Midlands in Late Middle English." *Historical & Editorial Studies in Medieval and Early Modern English,* ed. Mary-Jo Arn and H. Witjer, 1985, 97–112.

———. "A Middle English Dialect Boundary." *Linguistics Across Historical and Geographical Boundaries,* ed. Dieter Kastovsky & Aleksander Szuedek. Berlin: Mouton de Gruyter, 1987,443–457.

———. *A Survey of Middle English Dialects 1290–1350*: *The West Midland Counties.* Publications of the New Society of Letters at Lund 78. Lund: Lund University Press, 1987.

———. *A Survey of Middle English Dialects 1290–1350*: *The East Midlands Counties.* Publications of the New Society of Letters at Lund 88. Lund: Lund University Press, 1995.

Laing, Margaret. 1991. "Anchor Texts and Literary Manuscripts in Early Middle English." *Regionalism in Late Medieval Manuscripts and Texts,* ed. Felicity Riddy. Cambridge: D. S. Brewer, 1991, 27–49.

McIntosh, Angus, M. L. Samuels, and Michael Benskin. *A Linguistic Atlas of Late Mediaeval English.* 4 vols. Aberdeen: Aberdeen University Press, 1986.

McSparran, Frances, Chief Editor, Associate Professor of English, University of Michigan *Middle English Dictionary.* on-line: http://quod.lib.umich.edu/m/med/lookup.html.

Menner, R.J. "*Sir Gawain and the Green Knight* and the West Midland." *PMLA* 37: (1922), 503–526.

Mossé, Fernand. *A Handbook of Middle English,* trans. James A. Walker. Baltimore: The Johns Hopkins University Press, 1952.

Preston, Jean F., and Laetitia Yeandle. *English Handwriting 1400–1650.* Asheville, NC: Pegasus Press, 1999.

Robert Manning of Brunne. *The Chronicle,* ed. Iselle Sullens. Medieval & Renaissance Texts & Studies Vol. 153. Binghamton, NY: Medieval & Renaissance Texts & Studies, 1996.

Serjeantson, Mary S. "The Dialects of the West Midlands in Middle English." R.E.S. 3 (1927), 54–67, 186–303, 319–331.

Sisam, Kenneth. *Fourteenth Century Verse & Prose.* Oxford: At the Clarendon Press, 1921.

Smith, Jeremy J. "Tradition and Innovation in South-West Midland Middle English. *Regionalism in Late Medieval Manuscripts and Texts,* ed. Felicity Riddy. Cambridge, England: Derek Brewer, 1991, 53–65.

Sullens, Idelle, ed. *Robert Mannyng of Brunne, The Chronicle.* Medieval &Renaissance Texts & Studies, vol. 153. Binghamton: Binghamton University Press, 1996.

Tolkien, J.R.R. *A Middle English Vocabulary* in Kenneth Sisam, ed. *Fourteenth Century Verse & Prose.* Oxford: Clarendon Press, 1937.

University of Michigan on-line *Middle English Dictionary*: http://quod.lib.umich.edu/m/med/

Wyld, H.C. *A Short History of English*, 3rd ed., revised & enlarged. London: John Murray, Albermarle Street, W., 1927.

Index

Abelard, Peter 78n4
Abner 202n3
abode 196
Abraham's bosom 85
Absalom 202
accord 181, 189
accounts, accounting 143, 147, 151
accusers 138
Acts of the Apostles 122 n4, 131n11
Adam 25, 33, 159
adders 110, 165, 168
admonish 141
Adso 112n2
advise(d) 116, 119, 152, 207
afraid 145
agony 60
agreement 116
air 44, 85, 113, 114, 127, 130, 131, 133, 160, 177
Alanus de Insulis 93n2
Alexander 202
alien 52
alive 120, 122, 157, 159, 161, 167
allegations 140, 142
allegory 146
alms deeds 81, 85, 88, 92, 94, 96, 97, 100, 102, 146
almsgiving 141
amazement 175
Amazons 117
Ambrose, pseudo–Ambrose 200n5
amend 157
amiss 209
ancestry 161
angel(s) 66n4, 76, 77, 82, 111, 132, 134, 137, 140, 153, 155, 169, 179, 180, 184, 195, 198, 205
anger 139, 153, 184
anguish 49, 83, 96, 98, 109, 167
Anselm of Canterbury 64n2, 75n5, 93n2, 181
answer 153
antichrist(s) 107, 198, 109, 110, 112, 113, 114, 115, 116, 117, 118, 119, 120, 121, 203
anxiety 193
apocalypse 69n3, 115n5, 116n5, 119, 133n5, 141n2, 164n6
Apollo 109
Apostle(s) 113, 129, 149, 152, 196
apparel 55, 197
appearance 203
apple 160
Aquinas see Thomas Aquinas
archangels 131–32
archbishops 102
arise, arisen, arising 114, 129, 131, 161

Aristotle 37n2
arms 49
Asall 202n3
ashes 32, 127, 130
assails 197
assaults 147
assent 119, 191
association 189
astronomy 177
athwart 193
attack 136
Augustine, pseudo–Augustine/Austin 48n1, 51, 55, 64n4, 64n7, 64n8, 65n1, 65n2, 68n2, 68n3, 74n3, 76, 77n2, 78n4, 80n6, 86n4, 87n1, 93n6, 94, 96n6, 105, 112n2, 136n4. 157n6, 162n3, 162n4, 163n5, 167n3, 168, 170n3, 186
austerity 137
authority 142, 205
authorship 10
avenge(d) 139, 141

Baal 119n1
backbiting 145
baptism 34, 79, 90, 110n9, 188
barefoot 196
Bartholomew 43n3
battle 49; battlements 20
bear 89; bore 188
bear(s) witness 144, 153
beast(s) 48, 119, 169
beaten 193
beauty 180, 195, 202
bed 168, 169; bedding 169
begat 188
beginning 128, 159, 160, 187, 188, 204
begotten 188
beguile 11, 114
behavior 189
behest 113, 121
believe 29, 117, 120, 151, 188
beloved 147
benefices 138
Benedicta Ward, Sister M. 75n5
Benevento, Jacobus de 142n4
Bernard 28, 35n1, 36n3, 43n2, 62n6, 64n2, 75n4, 143n6, 147n9, 157n6; pseudo–Bernard 75n4
beryl 202, 204
Bethlehem 133, 134
Bethsaida 111
Bible 47n2, 120
bibliographies 17, 240
birth 42, 67, 111
bishop(s) 62, 92, 104
bite 169, 200

bitterness 153, 160, 186
blame 33
blast 144
bless 151, 154
blind 176
bliss 44, 96, 130, 176, 179, 180, 181, 182, 183, 186, 187, 189, 190, 191, 194, 196, 197, 199, 201, 203, 205, 206
blithe 206
blood 62, 86, 112, 134, 141, 142; bloody spread 125
blows 170
body, bodies 36 59, 60, 82, 84, 85, 86, 93, 97, 100, 114, 119, 127, 128, 129, 130, 131, 147, 148, 85, 86, 161, 174, 180, 181, 182, 183, 184, 185, 186, 188, 189, 191, 194; blessed bodies 182
boiling metal 200
boils, sores, pustules 83
bold 167
Bonaventure 87
bondman 46
bonds 173
bone(s) 125, 168
book/gospel 120, 127, 167
Book of Wisdom 161n1
Book to a Mother 146n5
born 141, 188
bound 173
bow 191
bowing 180
brains 188
brass 115, 200
bread 97, 195
breath 85, 179
brethren 154
Breviarum Romanum 135
Breviloquium 87n1
bride 197; bridegroom 197
brightness 177, 178, 181, 187, 191, 194, 195–197, 200, 205–206
brimstone 164, 165, 185, 199, 200
brother 186, 190
buck and roe 203
buffet 134
burden 159
burn, burning, burned 125, 127, 128, 130, 156, 165, 168, 184, 185, 175, 178, 199, 200, 204
burst 165
burying, buried 119, 134
buy 116
by number 178

Canon Law 61n2
Cantor, Petrus 35
Capharnaum 111

carbuncles 202, 204
care 151, 198
carrion 35, 41
Caryb 161
Caspian Mountains 117
castle(s) 114, 125, 147, 170
Cato see Distichs of Cato
cause 191
caves 125
challenge 195
charity 48, 97, 98, 99, 100, 101, 104, 115, 128, 151, 152, 155, 157, 180, 197, 204; Saint Charity 207
chastisement 148
chastity 103, 196
cheerful demeanor 199
Chickering, Howell 207n1
chide 170
children 31, 33, 90, 94, 101, 110, 129, 141, 148, 149, 154, 161, 165, 188, 197
chimney 115
Christ 57, 67n7, 69, 70, 73, 76, 79, 80, 99, 97, 100, 102–03, 106, 107, 109, 111, 113, 114, 115, 116, 117, 118, 121, 124, 128, 129, 130, 131, 133, 135, 136, 143, 150 n4, 152, 161, 170, 179, 196, 197, 201
Christianity 27, 70, 90, 105, 112, 114, 116, 117, 118, 119, 152, 167, 197; Christendom 110, 118, 140, 188
Christ's coming 112, 128
Christ's law 110
Christ's passion 102, 142, 69
church 94, 96, 99; see also holy church
circle 177, 178
circumcision 111
city 196, 206
city of heaven 201, 204, 205
clay 31, 32, 41, 81, 84, 100
clergy 187
clerk(s)/clerics 77, 79, 84, 91, 102, 103, 105, 108, 116, 118, 120, 121, 129, 137, 140, 148, 156, 159, 160, 163, 172, 173, 176, 177, 184, 197, 201, 208
cliff 162
clothing 56, 96, 141–142, 168, 200
cloud(s) 120, 123, 131, 133
Codex of Canon Law see Canon Law
cold 162–63
cold fever 83
Comestor, Peter 142n4

241

Index

comfort and solas 201
command 141
commandment(s) 24, 44, 117, 140, 152, 207
committed 139
companion 83
company 194, 197, 199
complaint 141, 153, 175
composed 208
conceived 110
concupiscence 48
condemn 136, 191
confess 92, 172; confessors 103, 196
conflict 171
confusion 136
conscience 30, 58, 63, 64, 131, 138, 170, 171, 207
consciously 145
consider 167, 193
constant 188
consummation 106*n*7
contrary, contraries 181, 198, 199
contrition 102
control 191
convert(ed) 169, 117, 118
cooperation 190, 191
corals 202
core 160
Corinth 129*n*9, 149*n*6
Corinthians 51*n*5, 167*n*2, 179*n*1
Corozain 110
corporal 205
Corporal Works of Mercy 154*n*2
corpse 41
corruption 41, 127, 158
counsel 105, 140, 143, 152, 174
countenance 195, 199
country 188, 206
courtesy 199
covetousness 89, 116, 169
craft 113
crave 194, 206
creation 24, 30, 181, 182, 183, 184, 186, 188, 189, 191, 192, 193, 204; *see also* newly created
creator(s) 66*n*6, 109
creature(s) 43, 139, 140, 159
crib 124
cross 59, 61, 134, 135; rode tree 61, 142, 161
crown 108, 200; crown of bliss 200; crown of head 55
crying 117, 153, 156, 167, 170 175, 196, 199
crystal 158, 159, 176, 177, 202, 204
cultivated 126
curse 191
customs 52, 54, 123; custom and usage 107

dale 159
Dame Fortuna 49
damnation 51, 60, 83, 101, 129, 136, 137, 140, 141, 143, 167, 181, 183, 184, 185, 186, 190, 191, 192
danger 192, 193
Daniel 109, 110, 121, 138*n*3, 178*n*4
darkness 53, 60, 166, 173, 175, 181, 198
dating of the manuscript 10
daughter 146–47

David 29, 32, 36, 52, 56*n*3, *n*5, 66*n*7, 67, 110, 112*n*2, 128, 143*n*2, 145*n*5, 162*n*1, 165*n*1, 168*n*1, 172*n*5, 185*n*6, 188*n*4, 190*n*2, 192*n*4, 199*n*4, 200*n*4
day 121, 125, 145, 170, 180, 184, 185, 197
De Abundantia Exemplorum 144*n*6
De Anima 37*n*2
De Miseria Conditiones Humanae 37*n*2
De Proprietatibus Rerum 43*n*3
deafness 114
death 25, 28, 30, 35, 38, 39, 40, 41, 52, 58–59, 89, 96, 98–99, 101, 102, 113–116, 119–122, 129, 131, 134, 142, 147, 161, 175, 179, 186, 196, 208
debt(s) 102, 105
deception 96, 114–115, 118
declaration 207
decree 177, 195
deed(s) 101, 171, 188
default 141
defense 147
deities 171
deliberate 193
delight(s) 135, 180, 194–195, 202, 206
demeanor 154
demons 167
den 111
derived 207
design 207
desire(s) 57, 142, 165, 184, 191, 192, 176, 199, 206; desired 180
despair 174
despise 117
destroy 175, 200
destruction 29, 107, 136
Deuteronomy 56*n*3, 147*n*4, 161*n*2, 168*n*3
devil(s) 45, 56, 59, 69, 76, 77, 96, 109, 111, 113, 114, 138, 139, 167, 169, 171, 174
devotion 94, 105, 153
die 121, 125, 156, 165, 168, 177, 185, 186, 188
dignity 108, 109, 149, 295
dim 181, 198
Dionysius 119*n*11
disciples 106, 113, 119, 122, 149
discipline 141, 149
diseases 95
disgrace 136, 172
disguised 56, 111
disgusting 181
disobedience 193
dispensation 56
displeased 173
Distichs of Cato 68*n*5
divine mystery 101
divinity 173
doctors 103, 196
domination 192
doom 106
doomsday 30, 81, 106, 107, 108, 118, 122, 123, 129, 150, 177
Douay-Rheims translation of the Bible 29*n*1, 36*n*1
doubt 84, 114
dragon(s) 116, 165, 168, 200
dread 30, 123, 131, 193
dream 185
drink 146, 154, 165, 202

dropsy 83
drunkenness 91
dumb 54, 114, 181
dwelling(s) 176, 180, 187, 191, 193, 194, 196, 203, 205, 206
dying 101, 102, 186

eagerness 208
ear 122, 145
earth 31, 32, 41, 79, 85, 86, 88, 91, 95, 103, 105, 112, 113, 114, 116, 120, 123, 126, 127, 128, 131, 133, 138, 141, 143, 146, 149, 158, 160, 162, 167*n*2, 172, 173, 177, 181 182, 189, 196, 203
earthquake 125
ease 180, 189, 190
east 132, 159, 182
eat 164
Ecclesia militans 197*n*6
Ecclesia triumphans 197*n*6
Ecclesiastes 64*n*8, 66*n*6, 69*n*1, 77*n*1, 145*n*1
Ecclesiasticus 171*n*4
education 143
egg 160
Egyptians 203
elde 61, 62, 144, 151
elegance 180
elements 43, 127, 159
Eli and Enoch *see* Enoch and Eli
emperor 62, 108, 180, 193
empire 108
empyrean heaven 179
enamel 202
enchantment 111, 113
encumbered 208
end 128, 185
ending 188
endlessness 186–187; endless life 185, 206
endured 174
enemy, enemies 48, 118, 120, 128, 128*n*4, 136, 141, 190, 197
Ennarationes 157*n*6
Enoch and Eli 117, 118, 119, 120, 203
entrance 202
enumerate 138
envy 91, 110, 147, 169, 189, 193
epistle 46, 150*n*3
equal 191
error 114, 115, 145, 208
estate(s) 102, 205
Eucharist 92, 97
Eusebius Hieronymus *see* Hieronymus
evangelist(s) 46, 196
Eve 33*n*3
evil(s) 57, 67, 83, 96, 107, 120, 121, 138, 140, 141, 145, 149
example 149
excuse 136
exile 47, 83
experience 194
eye(s) 46, 48, 159, 145, 156, 161, 171, 177, 181, 182, 183 185, 191
Ezekiel 69, 63*n*5, 74*n*4, 149*n*3

face 172, 175, 187, 195; face-to-face 167
facsimile of manuscript f.1r 21
failure 174, 192
fair 159, 161, 177, 181, 187, 196, 197

faith 27, 29, 90, 112, 119, 132, 140, 151, 152, 204; good faith 110, 195
faithful 194
false 110, 111, 112, 113, 140, 152; falsehood 95
false witness 91
famines 107
Fasciculus Morum 157*n*6
fashion 56
fasting 58, 92, 97
father(s) 96, 122, 135, 141, 142, 148, 154, 187, 190
father's house 196
fault 195
fear 137, 139, 160, 161, 188; fearful 135; fear God 209
feebleness 182, 183
feed 44
feel 78, 89; feeling 200
feign 113, 114
fellowship 116
felony 82
fennel 199
fetters 173, 186
fever 83
fiend(s) 49, 69, 70, 71, 81, 82, 88, 110, 111, 113, 116, 118, 119, 122, 138, 139, 143, 155, 160, 163, 167, 170, 175, 185, 192, 193, 197, 198, 201, 203
fierce 140, 193, 200
Fifteen Signs Before Doomsday 124*n*4
fighting 189, 197
filth 36, 47, 156, 176
finger(s) 55, 65
fire 84–86, 88, 90, 91, 113, 123, 126, 127, 128, 129, 130, 156, 158, 165, 166, 167, 168, 169, 173, 184, 185, 193, 198, 200
firebrand 163
fish(es) 125, 168
flame 165
flavor 199
flee 172
flesh 38, 42, 49, 62, 86, 87, 129, 169, 175, 181
flesh and blood 195
flesh and bone 36, 90, 122, 133, 138, 148, 159, 189
flesh's will 171
flight 182
flock 117
floods 123, 126, 127
flower(s) 114, 199
foe 54, 104
folly, follies 30, 47, 51, 56, 57, 140, 149, 171, 176, 180, 191, 207
food 96, 154, 202
foot 142, 173, 183; feet 115, 121
forest 48, 49
forever 151, 161, 176, 181
forget 113, 161; forgotten 138
forgive(n) 199, 208; forgiveness 102, 105
fornication 188
forsake 114, 152, 173, 176
foul(er) 36, 143, 165, 167; foul ending 110
franchise 183
freedom 151, 154, 183
freeze 163, 200
Friedman, John 37*n*2

Index 243

friendship 54, 62, 88, 96, 97, 98, 100, 102, 104, 180, 189, 192
fright 153, 173
frost 176
fruit 36, 37, 44

gall 165
garrets 202
gates 202
Genesis 32n1, 38n5, 110n11
Gerhohus Reicherspergensis 205n2
Ghost/spirit 134; ghostly 4; *see also* Holy Ghost
gift(s) 112, 114, 142, 201
glass 187
glory 44; glorifying 194
gloss 119, 137
glowing 163, 169, 184
gluttony 91, 164
gnaw 169, 175
goats 153
God 77, 81, 82, 83, 86, 87, 88, 89, 90, 91, 93, 94, 96, 97, 99, 100, 101, 102, 104, 107, 109, 111, 113, 115, 116, 120n3, 121, 122, 123, 125, 126, 127, 128, 130, 131; 133, 137, 138, 139, 140, 141 142, 143, 144, 145, 146, 147, 149, 156, 158, 162, 168, 170, 173, 175, 176, 181, 183, 184, 185, 187, 189, 190, 191, 192, 194, 196, 197, 198, 199, 200, 205, 207, 208, 209; Almighty 197, 206; Godhead 59, 135; gods 188; God's bride 197; God's face 100, 209; God's law 109, 110; God's messages 206; God's own sea 179; God's power 23; God's son 205; God's vengeance 56; God's will 29, 44, 48, 56, 59, 94, 151
Gog and Magog 117, 118
gold 78, 83, 91, 117, 141, 201, 204, 206; gold and silver 206
Golden Mouth of St. John 137
good deed 101, 189, 207
good faith 110
good men 199
good will 92
goodness 60, 99, 111, 145, 152
gore/slime 32
gospel 29, 31, 44, 45, 46, 57, 111, 115, 118, 19, 120n3, 121, 123, 126, 132, 136, 150n4, 152, 153n8–9, 168, 173, 192, 196
gout of the feet 83
grace 44, 56, 59, 60, 62, 76, 79, 80, 81, 83, 87, 89, 92, 96, 97, 102, 103, 105, 129, 137, 149, 150, 159, 183, 184, 187, 189, 194, 195, 201, 208
grass 125, 127, 177
grave(s) 125, 128, 161
greed 47, 83, 89
Gregory the Great 50n5, 51n3, 51n4, 120n5, 144n5, 146n1, 205n2; Gregorius 200n5
grievance 184; grieve(s) 175, 184, 190; grievous 167, 193
grope 166
guess 176, 206
guests 52
guide 201, 207
guilt 141

Haimo of Auxerra 116
hair 130, 143n6, 205
hair shirt(s) 95n2, 119
hammers 169, 170
hand(s) 85, 136, 142, 154, 173, 191, 199
handsome 188
happily 207
harbored 154
hardship 142
hate 46, 54, 139, 189, 191; hatred 91, 169, 189, 190
hay 89
Haymo of Halberstadt 112n2
head 55, 84, 130, 136, 146n6, 181, 205; heads 173
health 51, 60, 150, 184, 189
hear 48, 106, 120, 124, 151, 198, 199; hearing 145, 198
heart(s) 26, 31, 42, 61, 63, 91, 98, 119, 129, 145, 165, 166, 174, 179, 185, 194, 198, 199
heat 115; heat and cold 200, 205
heathen 140
heaven 66, 67, 69, 70, 71, 76, 77, 78, 79, 85, 88, 90, 100, 103, 111, 113, 114, 116, 120, 121, 122, 123, 131, 132, 134, 137, 138, 143, 144, 147, 159, 174, 176, 179, 181, 182, 184, 185, 186, 187, 188, 190, 191, 92, 193, 195, 196, 197, 201, 205, 206; heavens 127; heaven's bliss 207; *see also* city of heaven
Hebrews 52n1, 124, 126
Heist, William W. 124n4
hell 25, 26, 30, 31, 43, 44, 51, 58, 66, 72, 76, 85, 89, 91, 92, 97, 109, 127, 129, 130, 131, 137, 140, 141, 151, 153, 156, 160, 165, 166, 167, 168, 172, 179, 184, 185, 187, 190, 194, 198, 201
hell pit 181, 188
help 101
herb 199
Hercules 109
help 47, 101
herd 149, 207
heretics 150
heritage 44
hermits 196
hidden 187
hideous 160, 175, 198
Hieronymus 122n8, 171n4
high 195; higher 179
hill(s) 124, 125, 159, 204
holes 125
holy 176, 196
Holy Church 67, 90, 102, 117, 118, 121 122, 168, 189, 197; *see also* Church
Holy Ghost 32, 113, 142, 194
Holy Gospel 102, 103, 104, 106, 108
holy man 163
Holy Thursday 178
Holy Trinity 138, 142, 179, 188
holy water 92
Holy Writ 41, 71, 108, 113, 133, 138, 144, 152, 166, 167, 169, 179
honesty 46, 180
honor 102, 109, 111, 136, 146, 147, 156, 180, 190, 193, 200; honored 203

Honorius of Autun 163n5, 8, 167n3, 168n5, 170n3, 173n6
hope 83, 131, 174
horrible, horror 167
horse 93, 110
host 118
hot 162; hotter 173
hour 170; hour of stealth 92
house(s) 125, 161; household 148
Hugo Rupelon of Strassburg 106n1
human understanding 201
humility 180, 192, 199
hundred 186
hunger 88, 164; hungered 146; hungry 96, 154
hurt 89
hypocrisy 140; hypocrite 112

ice 163
ideal 151
idle fashion, expense 55; idleness 26, 47, 94
idle word, thoughts, works 144; idleness 28
ill 180
imagine 201, 204
inclination 191
inconstant 29
increased 193
ingenuity 179
injure 95, 138
injustice 164
Innocent III 31n3, 32n8, 33n3, 34n5, 36n1, 36n3, 38n1, 39n2, 39n4, 41n2, 41n4, 55n3, 105, 119n1, 163n3, 164n3, 166n1, 169n2
instability 30, 53, 54
intention 119
invisible 43, 187
iron 184
irrational 208
Isaiah 169n1
Isaias 144n4
Isidore Hispalensis 74, 75n1, 171n4
Islam 55n1
Israel 152

James 46n3
Jeremias 162n2; Jeremy 70
Jerome 50n1, 50n3, 122n8, 124n3, 126, 142n4, 142n5, 163n6, 163n8
Jerusalem 108, 111, 117, 119, 133, 134, 196
Jesus 132, 135, 147, 156, 208
jewelry 200
Jewery 118
Jews 117, 119, 121, 140, 152
Job 31, 33n5, 34, 38n1, 39n3, 41n6, 80n4, 131n8, 137n5, 140n1, 145n2, 163n3, 165n5, 166n1.3, 193n6
Joel 123n5, 133n1, 133n2
John 115n5, 46n4, 46n5, 48n1, 69n2, 116n5, 121n6, 122n4, 135n1, 135n4, 136n1, 164n6, 167n2, 196n4
John Chrysostom 137
Jonathan 203
Joseph 203
Josephat 133–34
joy 42, 43, 54, 55, 59, 61, 69, 76, 87, 96, 100, 156, 186, 193, 194, 195, 199, 200, 203, 205, 209;

joyful 190, 201; joys 180, 181, 184, 198
judge 129, 130, 132, 134, 135, 136, 138, 145, 146, 151, 152, 153
judgment 28, 62, 76, 82, 83, 121, 122, 124, 126, 128, 129, 130, 131, 132, 133, 134, 135, 136, 138, 142, 146, 148, 151, 152, 156, 158, 160, 170, 188, 197, 206
judgment day 158, 159; *see also* doomsday
Judith 169n2
Jupiter 109, 177
just 156; justice 82, 110n11, 130, 136, 186
Justinian 61n2

keys 103, 142n4
kill 60, 81
king 62, 76, 111, 146, 153, 180, 193, 200, 203; kings 108
kingdom 107, 176, 187, 196; kingdom of heaven 31
knights 140
know 187, 188; knowing 187; known 187
knowledge 145, 150, 160, 161, 167, 201
Krishna 119n11

Lamentations 70n5
land 58, 107, 108, 181; lands 62, 117
land of darkness
lanes and struts 202
language of the manuscript 10
last days 121
Latin usage 16, 24, 28, 30, 55
Latin Vulgate 166n4, 169n
laughed at 159, 161; laughter 54
law 102, 104, 108, 113, 114, 115, 116, 117, 118, 121, 140, 150, 152, 168; laws 111, 112, 196
Lazarus 85, 161
lead 200, 208
learn 27; learning 94, 142, 160, 188
leave their sin 176
lecherous 112, lechery 46, 57, 83, 128
left 153
le Goff, Jacques 78n1
leniency 153
lent 161
leopards 48
leprosy 83
Lewis, Robert E. 32n8, 36n1, 36n4, 37n3, 41n2, 41n4, 55n3, 163n3, 166n1, 170n5
Liber Antiphonarius 205n2
Liber Meditationum 64n2
lie 113, 141, 187, 188
life 52, 57, 59, 60, 67, 84, 95, 96, 105, 109, 110, 112, 113, 121, 129, 156, 161, 171, 185, 188, 201; lifetime 143
light 44, 60, 77, 162, 166, 173, 174, 175, 176, 179, 189, 190, 191, 200; lightless 166
lightning 86, 138
likeness 169, 187
liking 184
limbo 80

limb(s) 85, 130, 149, 168, 182, 189
lime 201
lineage 110
lions 48, 70
live 101, 120, 121, 131, 150, 169, 184, 185, 186, 197; lived 149, 161; living 102, 187, 198, 199
locked up 193
look 167
Lord 32, 41, 43, 45, 99, 121, 131, 133, 141, 145, 146, 147, 148, 166, 185; dear lord 199; lady 146; lords 46; lordship 191, 205
lost 115, 171, 188
Lot 126
love 25, 42, 43, 46, 54, 57, 61, 68, 102, 123, 150, 152, 154, 161, 174, 189, 194, 196, 97, 205, 207; love tokens 180; loved 190, 203; sinful love 28, 45
low 195
Lucifer 31n2, 66n3
Luke 29n4, 84, 107n1, 118n7, 123n1, 126n3, 130n2; 131n1, 143n6, 192n1, 192n2
lust(s) 27, 46, 53, 56, 87, 94, 164; lusty 112
lye 88, 89, 92

mad 164, 168
Magog see Gog and Magog
maid 197; maiden 129; see also Mary; Our Lady
Malachi 118n7
maladies 38, 84
malice 109; malicious 110
man 187; man's hand 201
manhood 131, 132, 137
mankind 45, 159
manner 177
manslaughter 91
Marbodus 50n4
Mark 168n4
Mars 161, 177
Martha 161
martyred 115; martyrs 78, 102, 105, 138, 140, 196
Mary 133; maiden Mary 134, 195; see also Our Lady
Mary Magdalen 161
mass(es) 85, 92, 97, 99–102
matter 201, 208
Matthew 31n5, 46n1, 53n2, 103n3, 106n7, 106n8, 111n6, 115n3, 120n3, 132n3, 132n5, 144n1, 146n4, 150n4, 153n8, 153n9, 154n1, 154n6, 155n1, 155n2, 155n5, 155n9, 173n2, 205n3
meaning 207
medicine 150
meek 31n5, 46n1, 53n2, 176, 201; meekness 25, 26, 27, 28, 31, 176, 180, 204, 208
melody, melodies 180, 194, 198, 202
men 129; men of law 150
menaces 115
Mercury 109, 177
mercy 60, 81, 83, 88, 92, 102, 112, 113, 131, 137, 152, 153, 158, 164, 174, 176, 180, 189, 190, 199, 205, 208; merciful 200
messages see God's messages
messenger 171

metal 86
Methuselah 203
Michael 121
Michelangelo 55n1, 55n3
midday 166
middle 128
midnight 166
might 120, 121, 123, 130, 146, 154, 187, 195
mighty 127, 194, 197
mild 176; mildness 156
mind 43, 160, 167
ministers 113, 121
minstrelsy 202
miracle(s) 110, 112, 113, 114, 116, 117, 120, 123, 161
mirror 187, 195
mirth(s) 180, 194
misbelief 140, 141
misfortune 107
miss 193
money 142
Monti, Dominic V., O.F.M. 87n1
moon 123, 156, 159, 177
Moorman, Charles 24
morals 141
Morey, James 53n2
Morris, Richard (re-edited by Hanna and Wood) 166n1, 174n1
Moses 161n1, 203
moth(s) 142, 169
mother(s) 42, 110, 141, 148, 188, 190, 195; mother mild 201
motion 159, 177; motionless 177
Mount of Olives 108, 121, 132–34
mountain 124, 127, 159, 163
mourning 62, 83, 153
mouth 36, 151, 202
music 198, 202
mutable 201
mystery 135

nails 136, 142, 178
naked 40, 96
natural places 177
naturally 159, 167, 189
nature 26, 27, 28, 36, 44, 69, 86, 130, 177, 207
Nebuchadnezzar 169
neck 138
necromancers 111, 113
neighbors 148
newly created 201
Nighman, Chris 64n8
night 121, 145, 180, 184, 185
Noah 126, 127
noble 196
noise 175, 198
north 113
nose 36
nourishes 177

oath(s) 91, 94
obedience 46, 180, 204; obedient 24, 108, 176, 197
Odin 119n11
odor 162
old 27, 32, 39, 40, 55, 57, 121; old and young 91, 102, 175
Old Testament 31n7, 119n11
open 118; openly 138
ordain(ed) 173, 174, 176; ordains 123
order 149, 166, 167; orders of angels 195

ordinance 190
Osiris 120n11
Our Lady 133, 195; see also Mary
Our Lord 29, 42, 45, 89, 103, 109, 129, 131, 132, 133, 136, 138, 137, 145, 152, 154, 155, 168, 169, 174, 194, 195, 196, 208, 209
outlaws 49
overcoming 197
overthrow 197

pagan(s) 109, 132, 140
pain(s) 59, 62, 65, 76, 78, 82, 88, 89, 90, 91, 92, 96, 97, 99, 100, 102, 103, 104, 105, 116, 128, 134, 137, 139, 141, 155, 157, 159, 160, 161, 162, 166, 168, 170, 173, 176, 181, 182, 184, 185, 186, 190, 192, 193, 198, 200; pained 162, 173, 200
palace 203
pale 137
palsy 83
paradise 59, 87, 158, 203
paraphs 78n1
pardon 97, 102, 104, 105
passion of Christ 135, 137, 138
pasture 153
path 151; path of righteousness 208
Paul 31n7, 107n8, 9 130–31
Paulus Winfridus 200n5
pavement 206
peace 54, 67, 68, 108, 122, 159, 179, 180, 190, 191, 197, 207
penance(s) 58, 60, 79, 84, 86, 88, 94, 95, 96, 98, 102, 104, 121, 164
penitence 89, 93, 184
Pentecost 104, 113n7
perceived 187
perfect 150, 184, 189, 194; perfect love 206
performance, performed 202
perils 139
perish 143, 148, 152, 53
permission 170, 199
persecution 49, 109, 117, 119
personification of sins 118, 121n5, 139
persons 194
pestilences 107
Peter 103, 137n6, 150n3
Peter Lombard 197
Petrus Blesensis 50n5
Philippians 68
philosopher 63, 177; philosophy 106
physical 201
physician(s) 150, 165
pierced 142
piety 180
pigsty 203
pilgrim(s) 52, 154
pilgrimage 52; of the Life of Man 31n7
pit of hell 173
pitch 164, 185, 199, 200
pity 97, 110, 164, 190, 205
planets 43, 44, 109, 120, 159, 176, 177, 194
planted 126
pleasing 135

pleasure(s) 22, 121
plunder 91
poem, poet 200
Poetics 37
point 196
poor 40, 62, 64, 93, 97, 141, 142, 149, 164; poorly 146
pope(s) 33n4, 36, 55n3, 62, 102n3, 103n1, 103n2, 103n3, 103n4, 103n5, 104n1
potency 182
poverty 47, 48, 49, 51, 58, 188
power(s) 103, 109, 110, 113, 122, 123, 132, 135, 142, 146, 149, 175, 179, 180, 182, 184, 186, 188, 191, 192, 196, 197, 198, 200, 201, 202, 203; powerful 150, 204
praise 199, 200; praising 180, 200
pray 94, 205, prayer(s) 62, 81, 85, 92, 94, 95, 97, 98, 99, 100, 102, 103, 201
preach 116, 118
preachers 113, 150; preaching 112, 118
precious 116; precious stones 201, 202, 206
prelate(s) 62, 149
price 158
pride, proud 28, 31, 35, 46, 47, 48, 55, 56, 70, 72, 83, 91, 109, 112, 171, 192
priest(s) 95, 97, 99, 103
princes 66n3, 112
prison 87, 94, 96, 147, 154; prisoner 100
privy 145
prize 99
profit 177
promises 66
property 193
prophecy 117; prophecies 118
prophet(s) 118, 119, 123, 128, 158n3, 162, 164n3, 165, 170n3, 185n4
proud see pride
provenance of the manuscript 10
proverb(s) 93n3, 149n1, 174n1
prudent 95
Prykke of Conscientie 23; Prykke of Conscience 93n3, 209
Psalm(s) 32n8, 36n1, 38n3, 52, 55n3, 56, 66n1, 66n3, 67n3, 128n4, 128n9, 143n2, 145n5, 146n2, 158n2, 162n1, 164n3, 165n1, 166n1, 172n5, 185n4, 185n6, 188n4, 192n4, 200n4
Psalter 29, 36, 38, 39n2, 52n3, 56n5, 66n1, 143n2, 145n5, 157, 158n2, 190n2, 199n3
Pseudo-Bede 63n1
punish 128, 193; punished 201; punishment 148, 207
purgatory 30, 76 77, 78, 81, 86, 87, 89, 90, 91, 92, 94, 96, 97, 98, 100, 101, 102, 104, 105, 127, 184, 205
pursue 118

quake 138
queen 117, 200

Rabanus Maurus 171n4
Rabbi Moses 178; see also Moses
rags 134

Index 245

raised 161
ramparts 202
ransom 87, 97
Raymond Llull 105*n4*
Raymond of Penaforte 105*n4*
read 146
reason(s) 27, 28, 35, 36, 37, 44, 45, 48, 73, 79, 81, 95, 99, 102 101, 102, 103, 108, 143, 144, 188, 190; reasonable 171; reasonably 206
received 117*n3*
reckoning 153
refined 159
reign 111, 114
religion 114
remain 188
remainder 105
remedy 174
remember 209
repent 92, 157; repentance 93, 95, 172
reproach 142, 180
repulsiveness 36
respite 197
rest 159, 174, 190, 191, 197, 206
resurrection 113*n7*
revere 208; reverence 180
reward(s) 79, 96, 102, 180
Rheims 29*n1*, 36*n1*
rich jewels 202
rich(es) 62, 64, 105, 114, 141, 146, 150, 193, 194, 206
right 154*n2*, 186; rightful 208
righteous 182; righteousness 97, 136, 153, 158, 190
rise, rise up 119, 130
roar 175; roaring 125
rocks 125, 159
Romans 152*n6*
Rome 107, 108
rosary 100
round 196
rubies 202
Rudolfus Ardens 197*n6*
rule 115, 129, 149, 179
run on foot 202
Rupertus 65*n1*

sackcloth 119
sacrament(s) 92, 97, 99, 100
sacred mystery *see* mystery
sacrilege 91
St. Denys Church 203*n5*
saints 102, 122, 138, 140, 152, 194, 195
salvation 52, 78, 134, 137, 142, 180
Sampson 202
Samuel 202*n3*
Saracens 140, 152
satisfied 194
Saturn 177
savage 200
save 80, 137, 166, 195, 198, 204, 205; saved 113, 130, 186, 187, 188, 189, 190, 191
savior 112, 147
savor 199
Saxl, Fritz 55*n1*
say 154, 197; says 129
scald(ed) 172
scholars 149
science 150, 173
Scipio 63*n1*

scoff 175
scourges 134
scratch 175
scream 190
sea(s) 48, 82, 123, 124, 158, 162
season(s) 44, 53
secret 118, 122, 146; secrecy 56, 157
secure 186, 193; security 193
seek 193
see(s) 36, 78, 89, 101, 120, 126, 131, 166, 186, 187, 188, 190, 193, 194, 195, 196, 198; seen 204, 206; saw 126, 196
senses 39, 198, 201, 203
sentence, judgment 137
sepulcher 133, 134
seriously 206
sermon 116, 119, 186, 187
serpents 41*n4*
servant(s) 64, 99, 109, 148, 152; servitude 188
service 159, 174, 186
severity 136
Seymour, M.C. 43*n3*
shadow 170
shake 175, 198
shame 31, 34, 136, 172
shelter 154
shepherd(s) 121, 153
shine 116, 196, 206; shining 181, 204, 205
ship 171
shone 131, 136, 196
shoulders 134
showers 114
sick 40, 154; sickness 95, 184
Sidrak 178*n4*
sight(s) 38, 41, 42, 57, 61, 70, 91, 113, 130, 144, 146, 166, 167, 168, 181, 187, 189, 191, 194, 195, 196, 200, 206; sight of God 174
silver 140, 206
Simeon 161
sing 58, 99, 102, 190, 199; singing 199
sin(s) 15, 25, 30, 32, 47, 48, 51, 59, 63, 72, 77, 81, 83, 84, 86, 87, 88, 89, 91, 92, 95, 96, 104, 106, 121, 128, 138, 139, 140, 145, 150, 158, 167, 189, 208; sinful 110, 128, 131, 134, 136, 137, 140, 152, 156, 160, 162, 165, 166, 197, 168, 170, 172, 175, 76, 181, 182, 183, 184
Sion 67*n2*, 67*n3*
sister 188, 190
sits 195
slain 121
slander(s) 170, 175
slavery 46
slay 175
sleep 185
sloth 47, 91
smart 54
smell, smelling 199
smiths 170
smoke 171, 193, 198, 200; smokes 165
snarl 175
Sodom 126
solace 151
Solomon 77*n1*, 145*n1*, 174*n1*
son 96, 142, 167, 170, 182, 184;

son of heaven 136; *see also* God's son
song(s) 73, 180, 198, 199
sonorous 195
sorrow(s) 31, 33, 34, 36, 39*n2*, 42, 45, 47, 48, 49, 53, 55, 62, 89, 94, 95, 105, 111, 115, 138, 143, 151, 152, 153, 156, 167, 170, 173, 174, 189, 190, 192, 193, 198
soul(s) 26, 51, 59, 60, 77, 78, 79, 80, 82, 84, 86, 87, 88, 89, 90, 91, 92, 93, 96, 97, 98, 99, 104, 106, 115, 128, 131, 139, 140, 146, 147, 170, 171, 100, 101, 174, 180, 183, 186 187, 188, 191, 194, 205; soul's remedy 206
sounds 122, 129
sour 165
south 113
sovereigns 142; sovereignty 196
space 66, 122, 177
spark 86; sparkles 158, 166
Speculum Christi 157*n6*
speech 125
sphere(s) 127, 177
spice(s) 199, 202
spirit(s) 85, 114, 155
spiritual 176, 201, 204; spirituality 206
splendor 180
spoke 151
spouse 197
stars 43, 44, 116, 123, 159, 178, 194, 206; starred 176
statues 114
stature 188
stench 163, 164, 199
stern 137
stink 165, 182; stinking 199
stirred 208
stones 125, 170, 200, 201; precious stones 204
storms 48, 165
straight 191
strength 44, 117, 185, 191, 202
strife 54, 149, 191, 206
strong 186, 196, 199; strongholds 202
study 173
subjects 138, 142, 149
suffer 171; suffered 96, 199; suffering 47, 207
summer 53, 180
summits 204
sun 44, 123, 159, 177, 196, 205, 206
swearing 91
sweet 198, 199; sweet aromas 202; sweetness 189
swift, swiftness 182

tail 116
teach 119, 150; teaching 95
tear to pieces 175
tears 171, 183
teeth 168
tempest 48
temple 111
tempt 118, 122; temptation 29
terrify 70; terrified 87
thank 199
theft(s) 91, 139
theology 148
Thessalonians 107*n8*, 131*n3*
thief 139; thieves 49, 134

thinking 180
thirst 88, 165; thirsted 146; thirsty 154
Thomas Aquinas 105
though 188
thought 95, 174, 182; thoughts 204
thousand(s) 185, 186; thousand years of life (like Methuselah) 203
thrall 183
threat(s) 63, 117, 200
throne 129
thrust 193
thunder claps 138
thunderstorm 193
time 64, 65, 66, 121, 144, 186
Timothy 51*n3*, 64*n8*
tired 202
tokens 123, 137; tokens of the cross 135, 136
tongue(s) 78, 85, 113, 167, 175, 179, 185, 199
torment(s) 112, 113, 114, 115, 120, 138, 141, 166, 167, 190, 194, 199; tormented 166
towers 114, 125
transgression 87
transient 201
travail 88, 102, 150, 159, 179, 182, 192, 201
treacherous 112; treachery 57, 108, 169
tread 193
treason 95, 147
treasure 102, 103, 104, 105, 114, 141
treasury of the Church 103*n2*
treatise 207
tree(s) 36, 37, 63, 114, 125, 127, 159, 160, 177, 178, 201
tremble 137
trespass 105
tribulation(s) 49, 95, 115
tribute 107
trickery 47; tricks 51
Trinity 23, 78*n3*, 109, 194
trouble 96, 114
true 195, 197; true love 203; truth 52, 113, 160, 163, 190
trumpets 122, 129, 130, 131
trust 141, 165, 174, 176
turrets 202
tyranny 115; tyrannies 110; tyrant(s) 48, 110, 115, 140

unattractive 188
unbaptized *see* baptized
unchangeable 187
unclean 48
understand 187; understanding 179, 184, 201, 207; understood 187
undisciplined 138, 141
uneducated 143
unity 180, 190, 191
unkindness 95, 156
unlettered 207
upper room 113
urine 36*n4*, 37

vainglory 47
valiantly 197
value 206
vanity 28, 48, 55, 56
vengeance 56, 121, 126, 141, 190; vengeful 131

venial sins 77, 79, 87, 90, 91, 92, 93, 104, 127
venom 110, 165, 168, 169; venomous 168
Venus 177
Veritas Theologie 106n1
vermin 37, 167, 168, 185, 201
vernacular 24
versions of text 8
vicar 103
vices 189
victor 197
villainy 56, 120, 180, 191, 193
violence 47, 153, 189; violent 165
virgins 196, 103
virtue(s) 176, 180, 203, 206
visible 206
vision 115
visited 154
voice 120, 154, 198, 194
Vulgate version Luke 118n7

Walafridus Strabonis 139n1
wanhope 173, 174
Warburg, Aby 55n1

watch 84, 85
water 162, 168, 171, 177; waters 114, 124; watery 177
Waters, Stacy A. 106n3
weak 182
wealth 35, 49, 51, 54, 114, 179
weather 54
wed 121; wedlock 188
weep 137, 172; weeping 54
well 114
Wenzel, Siegfried 162n3, 163n3, 164n3
Wernerus 168n5, 170n3, 173n6
west 113, 159, 182
wheel 178; Wheel of Fortune 49
whine 183
wicked 45, 114, 143, 159, 163, 191, 208; wickedness 109, 111, 118, 148, 170, 199
wife 62, 194; wives 121, 128
wilderness 48
will 24, 25, 26, 57, 93, 118, 128, 140, 143, 147, 183, 189, 191; will of God 48, 94; *see also* God's will
win/redeem 158

wind 125; winds 165
winking 126
winter 180
wise 45, 67, 141, 147, 179, 181, 186, 188; wisdom 25, 26, 51, 57, 62, 66, 77, 144, 156, 161, 170n5, 176, 180, 187, 188
wit 62, 93, 109, 113
witches 111
witness 137, 138, 191, 197
woe 160, 175, 193
wolves 48
woman 129
womb 32, 37, 40, 90, 110, 188
won 184, 187, 196
wonder 177
wood 86
word 198; idle word 144
work(s) 116, 150
Works of Mercy 96, 146, 155
world 42, 45, 50, 54, 59, 99, 106, 113, 114, 115, 123, 126, 127, 129, 138, 139, 151, 158, 171, 182, 185, 194, 196; old world 55; shaping of the world 55; worldly men 55

world's end/day of dread *see* doomsday
worms 41, 42, 168, 170, 171
worship 180, 192
worth 182; worthiness 101
wounds 142; wound of Christ 136
wrath 91, 94, 153, 162, 169, 189
wretchedness 45, 47, 53, 153; man's wretchedness 28, 30, 32, 33, 34
written 167
wrong 152, 199
wrought 191

year(s) 185, 186, 187, 199
yesterday 185
yolk 160
young 27, 32, 35, 37, 40, 41, 57, 73, 121; young and old 78, 91, 102, 143, 151, 159, 162; young nor old 167
youth 28, 33, 61, 144; youth without eld 179

Zacharias 132n2